EDITED BY

John J. Macionis
Kenyon College

Nijole V. Benokraitis
University of Baltimore

Peter Urmetzer
University of British Columbia Okanagan

Bruce Ravelli
Mount Royal College

W9-BXX-526

seeing ourselves

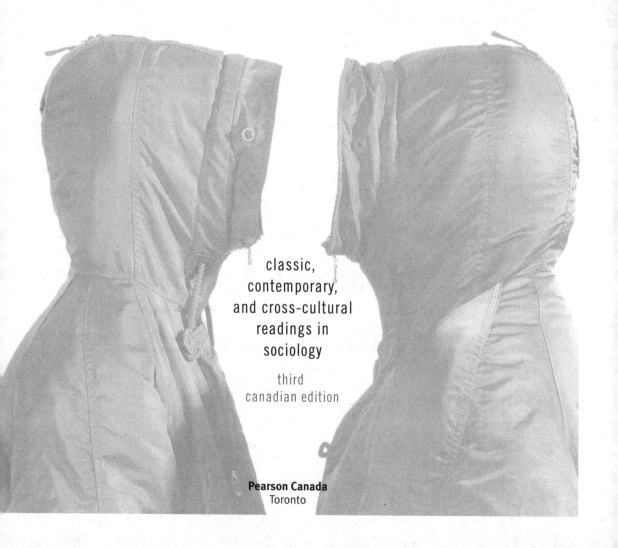

classic,
contemporary,
and cross-cultural
readings in
sociology

third
canadian edition

Pearson Canada
Toronto

Library and Archives Canada Cataloguing in Publication

Seeing ourselves : classic, contemporary, and cross-cultural readings in sociology / edited by John J. Macionis . . . [et al.].—3rd Canadian ed.

ISBN 978-0-13-714867-7

1. Sociology—Textbooks. 2. Sociology—Cross-cultural studies. 3. Canada—Social conditions—Textbooks. I. Macionis, John J.

HM586.S44 2010   301   C2008-906265-5

Copyright © 2010, 2007, 2004 Pearson Education Canada, a division of Pearson Canada Inc., Toronto, Ontario.

Pearson Prentice Hall. All rights reserved. This publication is protected by copyright and permission should be obtained from the publisher prior to any prohibited reproduction, storage in a retrieval system, or transmission in any form or by any means, electronic, mechanical, photocopying, recording, or likewise. For information regarding permission, write to the Permissions Department.

Original edition published by Pearson Education, Inc., Upper Saddle River, New Jersey, USA. Copyright © 2007 Pearson Education, Inc. This edition is authorized for sale only in Canada.

ISBN-13: 978-0-13-714867-7
ISBN-10: 0-13-714867-4

Vice-President, Editorial Director: Gary Bennett
Editor-in-Chief: Ky Pruesse
Senior Acquisitions Editor: Laura Forbes
Marketing Manager: Arthur Gee
Developmental Editor: Victoria Naik
Production Editor: Melissa Hajek
Copy Editor: John Firth
Proofreaders: Kelli Howey, Colleen Ste. Marie
Production Coordinator: Janis Raisen
Composition: Macmillan Publishing Solutions
Permissions Research: The Editing Company
Art Director: Julia Hall
Cover Design: Miriam Blier
Cover Image: Masterfile

For permission to reproduce copyrighted material, the publisher gratefully acknowledges the copyright holders listed on page xiii, which is considered an extension of this copyright page.

Statistics Canada information is used with the permission of Statistics Canada. Users are forbidden to copy the data and redisseminate them, in an original or modified form, for commercial purposes, without permission from Statistics Canada. Information on the availability of the wide range of data from Statistics Canada can be obtained from Statistics Canada's Regional Offices, its World Wide Web site at http://www.statcan.ca, and its toll-free access number 1-800-263-1136.

1 2 3 4 5   13 12 11 10 09

Printed and bound in the United States of America.

Annotated Table of Contents

 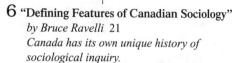

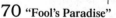

Preface

Two of the many advantages that sociology offers are its variety and its overlap with other disciplines. As an undergraduate student, I decided to study sociology partly because of this variety. Think of any topic and sociologists will likely have studied it. Suicide, sexual behaviour, food, health care, language, music, and organized crime are just a few examples. These topics can also be studied from a variety of perspectives, from the motives of the individual to the architecture of global systems such as the economy. This variety is reflected in the readings of this book. The sociological studies featured in this volume examine the behaviour of suicide bombers, the organization of work in strip clubs, drug takers, bike gangs, the economic elite, skate boarders, as well as many other topics. In terms of inter-disciplinarity, the topics covered overlap with, among others, demographics, economics, political science, anthropology, political economy, and women's studies.

One does not necessarily have to be a sociologist, or for that matter even an academic, to make sociological observations. Thus, several readings in this text are written by people who are not professional sociologists. This includes a pollster (Adams), a public intellectual (Wright), a journalist (Condon), and a health economist (Deber). These pieces summarize significant sociological issues (e.g., health care; aging population) in a way that is both informative and easy to understand for introductory students. These articles also suggest that students need not rely exclusively on academic journals to read sociological analysis, but that good sociology can be found in a variety of sources. For this reason, I suggest that students read widely and supplement their academic readings with newspapers and magazines in order to keep abreast of what is going on in the world. In the twenty-first century, this of course includes an almost infinite variety of sources on the Internet. Sociological theory can serve as a guide to put current events into

perspective. For example, the next time you read or hear something about the health care debate in Canada, try to analyze it through the perspective of Deber's article on health care funding.

This reader provides excellent material for use in a wide range of courses. *Seeing Ourselves*, Third Canadian Edition, is most widely used in introductory sociology, but it is also well suited for courses in social problems, cultural anthropology, social theory, social stratification, Canadian society, women's studies, and marriage and the family. The third Canadian edition offers seventy-seven readings that represent the widest range of material found in any similar text.

THE THREE C'S: CLASSIC, CONTEMPORARY, AND CROSS-CULTURAL

Seeing Ourselves, Third Canadian Edition, is the only reader that systematically weaves together three types of selections. For each general topic typically covered in a sociology course, three types of articles are included: classic, contemporary, and cross-cultural.

Classic articles—25 in all—are sociological statements of recognized importance and lasting significance. Included here are the ideas of sociology's founders and shakers—including Emile Durkheim, Karl Marx, Max Weber, Georg Simmel, as well as Margaret Mead, W. E. B. Du Bois, George Herbert Mead, Thomas Robert Malthus, and Charles Horton Cooley. There are also many more recent contributions by Alfred Kinsey, John Porter, Jessie Bernard, Erving Goffman, Peter Berger, C. Wright Mills, Leslie White, and Jo Freeman.

We realize that not everyone will agree about precisely which selections should be called "classics." But we hope that instructors will be pleased to see the work of so many outstanding women and men—carefully edited with under-graduate students in mind—available in a single, affordable source.

Twenty-nine contemporary selections focus on current sociological issues, controversies, and applications. These articles show sociologists at work and demonstrate the importance of ongoing research. They address many of the issues that concern today's students, providing solid data and reasoned analysis. Among the contemporary selections in *Seeing Ourselves* are Patricia Madoo Lengermann and Jill Niebrugge-Brantley on women founders of sociology; Bruce Ravelli on Canadian sociology; Michael Adams on Canadian and American value differences; George Ritzer on McDonaldization and jobs; Daniel Wolf on being a member of a biker gang; Jacqueline Lewis on the organization of strip clubs; Jason Lian and Ralph Matthews on ethnic stratification in Canada; David Ross, Katherine Scott, and Peter Smith from the Canadian Council on Social Development on the prevalence of poverty in Canada; Jean-Paul Restoule on Aboriginal identity; Brenda Beagan and Scott Davies in two separate readings on social class; James Overboe on disability and genetics; Raisa Deber on the Canadian health care system; Donald Clairmont and Dennis Magill on Africville, a Black community in Nova Scotia; and Ronald Wright on the importance of taking care of our environment.

The 23 cross-cultural selections offer sociological insights about the striking cultural diversity of Canada and the larger world. Included are well-known works such as "Body Ritual among the Nacirema" by Horace Miner, "India's Sacred Cow" by Marvin Harris, "The Amish: A Small Society" by John Hostetler, J. M. Carrier's "Homosexuality in Cross-Cultural Perspective." Other articles focus on Arab women and social research; the ways in which global inequality benefits rich countries, including Canada; the practice of female genital mutilation; intercultural marriages in Canada; how courtship and marriage differ around the world; and the central role played by Japanese mothers in their children's schooling. Cross-cultural selections broaden students' understanding of other cultures and, in the process, sharpen their understanding of our own society.

ORGANIZATION OF THE READER

This reader parallels the chapter sequence common to textbooks used in introductory sociology. Instructors can easily and effectively use these articles in a host of other courses and can assign articles in whatever order they wish. For each of the twenty-three general topics, we present a cluster of three to five articles, including at least one classic, at least one contemporary, and at least one cross-cultural selection. The expansive coverage of these seventy-seven articles ensures that instructors can choose readings well suited to their own classes, and at the lowest cost.

The first grouping of articles describes the distinctive sociological perspective, brings to life the promise and pitfalls of sociological research, and demonstrates the discipline's applications to a variety of issues. The selections that follow emphasize key concepts: culture, society, socialization, social interaction, groups and organizations, deviance, and the importance of sexuality to our society. The focus then turns to various dimensions of social inequality, with attention to class, gender, race and ethnicity, and aging. The major social institutions are covered next, including the economy and work; politics, government, and the military; families; religion; education; and health and medicine. The final sets of articles explore dimensions of global transformation—including population growth, urbanization, the natural environment, social movements, and social change.

A NOTE ON LANGUAGE

One of the advantages of using this reader is allowing students to read the exact words of dozens of notable sociologists. The editors have assembled their selections from the sources in their original form; although we have edited some readings for length, we have not altered any author's language. At the same time, we want students and instructors to know that some of the older selections—especially the classics—use male pronouns rather than more contemporary gender-neutral terminology and one article employs the term "Negro." We have not changed the language in any article, wishing not to violate the historical authenticity of any document. That said, we urge faculty and students, with the original articles in hand, to consider the importance of language and how it has changed in their analysis of the author's ideas.

TEACHING FEATURES

Seeing Ourselves, Third Canadian Edition, has two features that enhance the learning of students. First, a brief introduction, placed at the beginning of each selection, summarizes the main argument and highlights important issues to keep in mind while reading the article. Second, at the end of each article are at least three critical-thinking questions which develop the significance of the reading, help students evaluate their own learning, and stimulate class discussion.

SUPPLEMENTS

Instructors using *Seeing Ourselves*, Third Canadian Edition, can take advantage of an Instructor's Manual and Test Item File. These supplements can be downloaded from a password-protected location on Pearson Education Canada's online catalogue (**vig.pearsoned.ca**). Simply search for the text, and then click on "Instructor" under "Resources" in the left-hand menu. You can also contact your local sales representative for further information.

The Instructor's Manual features a guide with suggestions for using readings in *Seeing Ourselves*, Third Canadian Edition, in conjunction with specific chapters typically found in an introductory sociology textbook. The Instructor's Manual also provides brief descriptions and summaries of each of the 77 readings in the text.

The Test Item File offers 6 multiple-choice and 4 essay questions for all 77 readings in *Seeing Ourselves*, Third Canadian Edition.

CHANGES TO THE THIRD CANADIAN EDITION

We are grateful to our colleagues at colleges and universities across Canada who have made *Seeing Ourselves* a part of their courses. In response to this unparalleled reception, the editors have worked especially hard this time around to prepare what we believe is the best and strongest reader available for our discipline. Here are the key changes:

1. Twenty-four new articles appear in the third Canadian edition. This raises the total to 77, an increase of 10 articles from the last edition

2. More attention to important contemporary research. We have kept all of the former classic selections, which, after all, stand up well over time; we supplemented them with some additional classic readings: Charles Horton Cooley's "Primary Groups," Max Weber's "Characteristics of Bureaucracy," and C. Wright Mills's "The Power Elite." However, most of the changes in this edition are new contemporary selections and reflect recent scholarship that has attracted a lot of attention both within and beyond the field of sociology. These new and popular selections include "Invisible Privilege" by Paula Rothenberg," North America's Two Distinct Societies" by Michael Adams, "Disability and Genetics: Affirming the Bare Life" by James Overboe, "Getting What We Pay For: Myths and Realities about Financing Canada's Health Care System" by Raisa Deber, "Experiences of Social Class: Learning from Occupational Therapy Students" by Brenda Beagan, "No Place for Home" by Sean Condon, "Fool's Paradise" by

Ronald Wright, "I'll Scratch your Back if You'll Scratch Mine" by Jacqueline Lewis, and "Stubborn Disparities: Explaining Class Inequalities in Schooling" by Scott Davies.

In addition, this Canadian edition of *Seeing Ourselves* offers four new cross-cultural selections, enriching the anthology's multicultural and global content. The new selections in this category are "India's Sacred Cow" by Marvin Harris, Paul Gecelovsky's "Canadian Cannabis: Marijuana as an Irritant/Problem in Canadian-U.S. Relations," "The Roots of Terrorism" from the 9/11 Commission Report, and "Free Trade and the Third World" by Peter Urmetzer.

3. A greater emphasis on race, class, and gender. Because so much of the research carried out in sociology deals with the causes, the character, and the consequences of social inequality, this new edition of *Seeing Ourselves* offers more on these vital issues than ever before.

We welcome comments and suggestions by faculty, students, and whoever else may happen to read this book. The contact information for the Canadian editor is peter.urmetzer@ubc.ca or Peter Urmetzer, Sociology, Unit 6, University of British Columbia Okanagan, 3333 University Way, Kelowna, British Columbia.

ACKNOWLEDGMENTS

First I would to thank Katie McWhirter from Pearson Education Canada for introducing me to the editorial board and making my participation in this project possible. I would also like to thank Laura Forbes and Victoria Naik for working with me on this project and answering my endless questions and making this an enjoyable experience. Thanks must also go the authors and publishers of the readings included here. Much thought and work has gone into each one of these articles, and a text such as this would not be possible without the ongoing research that is conducted on a daily basis by academics across the country. Thanks must also go to my students for always asking interesting questions and engaging me in sociological issues. Shelley Pacholok suggested one of the readings included here and I thank her for that. A word of appreciation must also go to Rowen Siemens for technical expertise. And last, I would like to thank my partner, Ann McKinnon, for all her support, encouragement, and joy she brings into my life.

PHOTO CREDITS

Reading 1, page 1: Alex Colville (1920–), *To Prince Edward Island*, 1965, acrylic emulsion on masonite, 61.9 3 92.5 cm. National Gallery of Canada, Ottawa. © NGC/MBAC;
Reading 5, p. 19: Doranne Jacobson/International Images;
Reading 8, p. 34: © CLEO/Jeroboam;
Reading 12, p. 57: Corbis/Bettmann;
Reading 15, p. 74: Andy Sacks/Getty Images Inc.—Stone Allstock;
Reading 21, p. 109: Dan Habib Photography;
Reading 25, p. 129: Dan Habib Photography;
Reading 35, p. 194: Bettmann/Corbis;
Reading 38, p. 211: Corbis;
Reading 44, p. 255: U.S. Department of Agriculture;
Reading 48, p. 284: Kenneth Meyer/Pearson Education/PH College;

Reading 51, p. 305: Edward Hopper (1882–1967) *Room in New York* 1932. Oil on canvas, 29 3 36 in. Sheldon Memorial Art Gallery, University of Nebraska-Lincoln. F.M. Hall Collection. 1932.H-166;
Reading 54, p. 327: SP5 Rick Haley/U.S. Army Photo;
Reading 57, p. 345: John Giordano/Corbis/SABA Press Photos, Inc.;
Reading 60, p. 373: U.S. Department of Health and Human Services;
Reading 65, p. 408: New York Convention & Visitors Bureau;
Reading 69, p. 437: Bobbie Kingsley/Photo Researchers, Inc.;
Reading 72, p. 454: Corbis/Bettmann;

About the Editors

John J. Macionis is professor and distinguished scholar of sociology at Kenyon College in Gambier, Ohio. Born and raised in Philadelphia, he earned a bachelor's degree from Cornell University and a doctorate in sociology from the University of Pennsylvania. Macionis has authored a number of best-selling sociology textbooks, including *Sociology*, the leading comprehensive text; *Society: The Basics*, the leading brief textbook; and *Social Problems*, the leading text for that course. Professor Macionis has been active in academic programs in other countries, having travelled to more than 50 nations. In 2002, the American Sociological Association honoured Macionis for his work with textbooks and for pioneering the use of new technology in sociology by bestowing on him the major Award for Distinguished Contributions to Teaching. At Kenyon, Macionis offers a wide range of upper-level courses, but his favourite course is Introduction to Sociology, which he teaches every year. He enjoys extensive contact with students, making an occasional appearance on campus to play oldies rock and roll, and each term inviting his students to enjoy a home-cooked meal. The Macionis family—John, Amy, and children McLean and Whitney—live on a farm in rural Ohio. In his free time, Macionis enjoys playing the Scottish bagpipes, working for environmental organizations, and sharing an adventure with his two children.

Nijole V. Benokraitis is professor of sociology at the University of Baltimore. She earned a B.A. at Emmanuel College (Boston), an M.A. at the University of Illinois at Urbana-Champaign, and a doctorate at the University of Texas at Austin. Professor Benokraitis, who immigrated to the United States from Lithuania with her family when she was six years old, is bilingual and bicultural and is very empathetic of students who try to balance two cultural worlds. She is the author, co-author, editor, and co-editor of seven books, including *Marriages and Families: Changes, Choices, and Constraints*. Benokraitis has published numerous articles and book chapters on topics such as sexism and institutional racism, has received grants and fellowships from many institutions—including the Ford Foundation and the Administration on Aging—and has made numerous appearances on local radio and television shows. She currently serves on the editorial board of Women & Criminal Justice and reviews international fellowship applications for the American Association of University Women's Educational Foundation. Benokraitis and her husband, Vitalius, have two adult children, Gema and Andrius. If she had free time, Benokraitis would read mystery novels, expand her mug collection, have more lunches with her past students, garden, and watch at least two movies every day.

Peter Urmetzer is an associate professor of sociology at the University of British Columbia. He has a B.A. and M.A. from Carleton University in Ottawa and a Ph.D. from the University of British Columbia—all degrees are in sociology. Peter Urmetzer teaches introductory sociology, survey methods, and Canadian society. He is currently conducting research on how values inform economic decision-making. Over the years, his academic interests have consistently leaned toward the distribution of income and wealth. His most recent book, *Globalization Unplugged* (University of Toronto Press), looks at the consequences of globalization on Canada. *From Free Trade to Forced Trade* (Penguin Press Canada) directly speaks to some of the concerns that Canadians have about free trade, in particular the WTO (World Trade Organization). Urmetzer's other academic interests include research methods and what constitutes good evidence.

Bruce Ravelli received his Ph.D. from the University of Victoria in 1997. He has taught introductory sociology for over 20 years, and receives strong teaching evaluations from his students because of his passion for sociology, his dedication to teaching, and his commitment to high academic standards. Bruce has published articles and book chapters on Canadian culture and cross-national value differences as well as students' evaluation of teaching. He has also co-authored *Exploring Sociology: A Canadian Perspective* with Michelle Webber, and edited *Exploring Canadian Sociology: A Reader*, as well as co-authored the brief introduction to sociology text entitled *Core Concepts in Sociology*, Second In-Class Canadian Edition, with Linda Lindsey and Stephen Beach. Bruce is the co-developer of award-winning free online software that allows teachers to anonymously assess their teaching/courses at any point during a course (available at **www.toofast.ca**). He offers workshops and presentations on the software and on anonymous student assessment across North America. Bruce teaches in the Department of Sociology and Anthropology at Mount Royal College in Calgary.

1

The Sociological Imagination

C. WRIGHT MILLS

To C. Wright Mills, the sociological imagination is a special way to engage the world. To think sociologically is to realize that what we experience as personal problems are often widely shared by others like ourselves. Thus, many personal problems are actually social issues. For Mills, one of sociology's most outspoken activists, the sociological imagination encouraged collective action to change the world in some way.

Nowadays men often feel that their private lives are a series of traps. They sense that within their everyday worlds, they cannot overcome their troubles, and in this feeling, they are often quite correct: What ordinary men are directly aware of and what they try to do are bounded by the private orbits in which they live; their visions and their powers are limited to the close-up scenes of job, family, neighborhood; in other milieux, they move vicariously and remain spectators. And the more aware they become, however vaguely, of ambitions and of threats which transcend their immediate locales, the more trapped they seem to feel.

Underlying this sense of being trapped are seemingly impersonal changes in the very structure of continent-wide societies. The facts of contemporary history are also facts about the success and the failure of individual men and women. When a society is industrialized, a peasant becomes a worker; a feudal lord is liquidated or becomes a businessman. When classes rise or fall, a man is employed or unemployed; when the rate of investment goes up or down, a man takes new heart or goes broke. When wars happen, an insurance salesman becomes a rocket launcher; a store clerk, a radar man; a wife

Alex Colville (1920–), *To Prince Edward Island*, 1965, acrylic emulsion on masonite, 61.9 × 92.5 cm. National Gallery of Canada, Ottawa, © NGC/MBAC.

Source: From *The Sociological Imagination* by C. Wright Mills. Copyright © 2000 by Oxford University Press, Inc. Used by permission of Oxford University Press, Inc.

1

lives alone; a child grows up without a father. Neither the life of an individual nor the history of a society can be understood without understanding both.

Yet men do not usually define the troubles they endure in terms of historical change and institutional contradiction. The well-being they enjoy, they do not usually impute to the big ups and downs of the societies in which they live. Seldom aware of the intricate connection between the patterns of their own lives and the course of world history, ordinary men do not usually know what this connection means for the kinds of men they are becoming and for the kinds of history-making in which they might take part. They do not possess the quality of mind essential to grasp the interplay of man and society, of biography and history, of self and world. They cannot cope with their personal troubles in such ways as to control the structural transformations that usually lie behind them.

Surely it is no wonder. In what period have so many men been so totally exposed at so fast a pace to such earthquakes of change? That Americans have not known such catastrophic changes as have the men and women of other societies is due to historical facts that are now quickly becoming "merely history." The history that now affects every man is world history. Within this scene and this period, in the course of a single generation, one-sixth of mankind is transformed from all that is feudal and backward into all that is modern, advanced, and fearful. Political colonies are freed; new and less visible forms of imperialism installed. Revolutions occur; men feel the intimate grip of new kinds of authority. Totalitarian societies rise, and are smashed to bits—or succeed fabulously. After two centuries of ascendancy, capitalism is shown up as only one way to make society into an industrial apparatus. After two centuries of hope, even formal democracy is restricted to a quite small portion of mankind. Everywhere in the underdeveloped world, ancient ways of life are broken up and vague expectations become urgent demands. Everywhere in the overdeveloped world, the means of authority and of violence become total in scope and bureaucratic in form. Humanity itself now lies before us, the super-nation at either pole concentrating its most coordinated and massive efforts upon the preparation of World War III.

The very shaping of history now outpaces the ability of men to orient themselves in accordance with cherished values. And which values? Even when they do not panic, men often sense that older ways of feeling and thinking have collapsed and that newer beginnings are ambiguous to the point of moral stasis. Is it any wonder that ordinary men feel they cannot cope with the larger worlds with which they are so suddenly confronted? That they cannot understand the meaning of their epoch for their own lives? That—in defense of selfhood—they become morally insensible, trying to remain altogether private men? Is it any wonder that they come to be possessed by a sense of the trap?

It is not only information that they need—in this Age of Fact, information often dominates their attention and overwhelms their capacities to assimilate it. It is not only the skills of reason that they need—although their struggles to acquire these often exhaust their limited moral energy.

What they need, and what they feel they need, is a quality of mind that will help them to use information and to develop reason in order to achieve lucid summations of what is going on in the world and of what may be happening within themselves. It is this quality, I am going to contend, that journalists and scholars, artists and publics, scientists and editors are coming to expect of what may be called the sociological imagination.

The sociological imagination enables its possessor to understand the larger historical scene in terms of its meaning for the inner life and the external career of a variety of individuals. It enables him to take into account how individuals, in the welter of their daily experience, often become falsely conscious of their social positions. Within that welter, the framework of modern society is sought, and within that framework the psychologies of a variety of men and women are formulated. By such means the personal uneasiness of individuals is focused upon explicit troubles and the indifference of publics is transformed into involvement with public issues.

The first fruit of this imagination—and the first lesson of the social science that embodies it—is the idea that the individual can understand his own experience and gauge his own fate only by locating himself within his period, that he can know his own chances in life by becoming aware of those of all individuals in his circumstances. In many ways it is a terrible lesson; in many ways a magnificent one. We do not know the limits of man's capacities for supreme effort or willing degradation, for agony or glee, for pleasurable brutality or the sweetness of reason. But in our time we have come to know that the limits of "human nature" are frighteningly broad. We have come to know that every individual lives, from one generation to the next, in some society; that he lives out a biography, and that he lives it out within some historical sequence. By the fact of his living he contributes, however minutely, to the shaping of this society and to the course of its history, even as he is made by society and by its historical push and shove.

The sociological imagination enables us to grasp history and biography and the relations between the two within society. That is its task and its promise. To recognize this task and this promise is the mark of the classic social analyst. It is characteristic of Herbert Spencer—turgid, polysyllabic, comprehensive; of E. A. Ross—graceful, muckraking, upright; of Auguste Comte and Emile Durkheim; of the intricate and subtle Karl Mannheim. It is the quality of all that is intellectually excellent in Karl Marx; it is the clue to Thorstein Veblen's brilliant and ironic insight, to Joseph Schumpeter's many-sided constructions of reality; it is the basis of the psychological sweep of W. E. H. Lecky no less than of the profundity and clarity of Max Weber. And it is the signal of what is best in contemporary studies of man and society.

No social study that does not come back to the problems of biography, of history, and of their intersections within a society has completed its intellectual journey. Whatever the specific problems of the classic social analysts, however limited or however broad the features of social reality they have examined, those who have been imaginatively aware of the promise of their work have consistently asked three sorts of questions:

1. What is the structure of this particular society as a whole? What are its essential components, and how are they related to one another? How does it differ from other varieties of social order? Within it, what is the meaning of any particular feature for its continuance and for its change?

2. Where does this society stand in human history? What are the mechanics by which it is changing? What is its place within and its meaning for the development of humanity as a whole? How does any particular feature we are examining affect, and how is it affected by, the historical period in which it moves? And this period—what are its essential features? How does it differ from other periods? What are its characteristic ways of history-making?

3. What varieties of men and women now prevail in this society and in this period? And what varieties are coming to prevail? In what ways are they selected and formed, liberated and repressed, made sensitive and blunted? What kinds of "human nature" are revealed in the conduct and character we observe in this society in this period? And what is the meaning for "human nature" of each and every feature of the society we are examining?

Whether the point of interest is a great power state or a minor literary mood, a family, a prison, a creed—these are the kinds of questions the best social analysts have asked. They are the intellectual pivots of classic studies of man in society—and they are the questions inevitably raised by any mind possessing the sociological imagination. For that imagination is the capacity to shift from one perspective to another—from the political to the psychological; from examination of a single family to comparative assessment of the national budgets of the world; from the theological school to the military establishment; from considerations of an oil industry to studies of contemporary poetry. It is the capacity to range from the most impersonal and remote transformations to the most intimate features of the human self—and to see the relations between the two. [At the] back of its use there is always the urge to know the social and historical meaning of the individual in the society and in the period in which he has his quality and his being.

That, in brief, is why it is by means of the sociological imagination that men now hope to grasp what is going on in the world, and to understand what is happening in themselves as minute points of the intersections of biography and history within society. In large part, contemporary man's self-conscious view of himself as at least an outsider, if not a permanent stranger, rests upon an absorbed realization of social relativity and of the transformative power of history. The sociological imagination is the most fruitful form of this self-consciousness. By its use men whose mentalities have swept only a series of limited orbits often come to feel as if suddenly awakened in a house with which they had only supposed themselves to be familiar. Correctly or incorrectly, they often come to feel that they can now provide themselves with adequate summations, cohesive assessments, comprehensive orientations. Older decisions that once appeared sound now seem to them products of a mind unaccountably dense. Their capacity for astonishment is made lively again. They acquire a new way of thinking, they experience a transvaluation of values: In a word, by their reflection and by their sensibility, they realize the cultural meaning of the social sciences.

Perhaps the most fruitful distinction with which the sociological imagination works is between "the personal troubles of milieu" and "the public issues of social structure." This distinction

is an essential tool of the sociological imagination and a feature of all classic work in social science.

Troubles occur within the character of the individual and within the range of his immediate relations with others; they have to do with his self and with those limited areas of social life of which he is directly and personally aware. Accordingly, the statement and the resolution of troubles properly lie within the individual as a biographical entity and within the scope of his immediate milieu—the social setting that is directly open to his personal experience and to some extent his willful activity. A trouble is a private matter: Values cherished by an individual are felt by him to be threatened.

Issues have to do with matters that transcend these local environments of the individual and the range of his inner life. They have to do with the organization of many such milieux into the institutions of an historical society as a whole, with the ways in which various milieux overlap and interpenetrate to form the larger structure of social and historical life. An issue is a public matter: Some value cherished by publics is felt to be threatened. Often there is a debate about what that value really is and about what it is that really threatens it. This debate is often without focus if only because it is the very nature of an issue, unlike even widespread trouble, that it cannot very well be defined in terms of the immediate and everyday environments of ordinary men. An issue, in fact, often involves a crisis in institutional arrangements, and often too it involves what Marxists call "contradictions" or "antagonisms."

In these terms, consider unemployment. When, in a city of 100,000, only one man is unemployed, that is his personal trouble, and for its relief we properly look to the character of the man, his skills, and his immediate opportunities. But when in a nation of 50 million employees, 15 million men are unemployed, that is an issue, and we may not hope to find its solution within the range of opportunities open to any one individual. The very structure of opportunities has collapsed. Both the correct statement of the problem and the range of possible solutions require us to consider the economic and political institutions of the society, and not merely the personal situation and character of a scatter of individuals.

Consider war. The personal problem of war, when it occurs, may be how to survive it or how to die in it with honor; how to make money out of it; how to climb into the higher safety of the military apparatus; or how to contribute to the war's termination. In short, according to one's values, to find a set of milieux and within it to survive the war or make one's death in it meaningful. But the structural issues of war have to do with its causes; with what types of men it throws up into command; with its effects upon economic and political, family and religious institutions; with the unorganized irresponsibility of a world of nation-states.

Consider marriage. Inside a marriage a man and a woman may experience personal troubles, but when the divorce rate during the first four years of marriage is 250 out of every 1,000 attempts, this is an indication of a structural issue having to do with the institutions of marriage and the family and other institutions that bear upon them.

Or consider the metropolis—the horrible, beautiful, ugly, magnificent sprawl of the great city. For many upper-class people, the personal solution to "the problem of the city" is to have an apartment with private garage under it in the heart of the city and, forty miles out, a house by Henry Hill, garden by Garrett Eckbo, on a hundred acres of private land. In these two controlled environments—with a small staff at each end and a private helicopter connection—most people could solve many of the problems of personal milieux caused by the facts of the city. But all this, however splendid, does not solve the public issues that the structural fact of the city poses. What should be done with this wonderful monstrosity? Break it up into scattered units, combining residence and work? Refurbish it as it stands? Or, after evacuation, dynamite it and build new cities according to new plans in new places? What should those plans be? And who is to decide and to accomplish whatever choice is made?

These are structural issues; to confront them and to solve them requires us to consider political and economic issues that affect innumerable milieux.

Insofar as an economy is so arranged that slumps occur, the problem of unemployment becomes incapable of personal solution. Insofar as war is inherent in the nation-state system and in the uneven industrialization of the world, the ordinary individual in his restricted milieu will be powerless—with or without psychiatric aid—to solve the troubles this system or lack of system imposes upon him. Insofar as the family as an institution turns women into darling little slaves and men into their chief providers and unweaned dependents, the problem of a satisfactory marriage remains incapable of purely private solution. Insofar as the overdeveloped megalopolis and the overdeveloped automobile are built-in features of the overdeveloped society, the issues of urban living will not be solved by personal ingenuity and private wealth.

What we experience in various and specific milieux, I have noted, is often caused by structural changes. Accordingly, to understand the changes of many personal milieux we are required to look beyond them. And the number and variety of such structural changes increase as the institutions within which we live become more embracing and more intricately connected with one another. To be aware of the idea of social structure and to use it with sensibility is to be capable of tracing such linkages among a great variety of milieux. To be able to do that is to possess the sociological imagination.

CRITICAL THINKING QUESTIONS

1. Why do people tend to think of the operation of society in personal terms?
2. What are the practical benefits of the sociological perspective? Are there liabilities?
3. What does Mills have in mind in suggesting that, by developing the sociological imagination, we learn to assemble *facts* into *social analysis*?

The Sociological Imagination	2
CLASSIC	**Invitation to Sociology**
CONTEMPORARY	PETER L. BERGER
CROSS-CULTURAL	

Using the sociological perspective changes how we perceive the surrounding world and even ourselves. Peter Berger compares thinking sociologically to entering a new and unfamiliar society—one in which "things are not what they seem." This article should lead you to rethink your social world so that you become aware of issues that you may never before have considered.

. . . It can be said that the first wisdom of sociology is this—things are not what they seem. This too is a deceptively simple statement. It ceases to be simple after a while. Social reality turns out to have many layers of meaning. The discovery of each new layer changes the perception of the whole.

Anthropologists use the term "culture shock" to describe the impact of a totally new culture upon a newcomer. In an extreme instance such shock will be experienced by the Western explorer who is told, halfway through dinner, that he is eating the nice old lady he had been chatting with the previous day—a shock with predictable physiological if not moral consequences. Most explorers no longer encounter cannibalism in their travels today. However, the first encounters with polygamy or with puberty rites or even with

the way some nations drive their automobiles can be quite a shock to an American visitor.

With the shock may go not only disapproval or disgust but a sense of excitement that things can really be that different from what they are at home. To some extent, at least, this is the excitement of any first travel abroad. The experience of sociological discovery could be described as "culture shock" minus geographical displacement. In other words, the sociologist travels at home—with shocking results. He is unlikely to find that he is eating a nice old lady for dinner. But the discovery, for instance, that his own church has considerable money invested in the missile industry or that a few blocks from his home there are people who engage in cultic orgies may not be drastically different in emotional impact. Yet we would not want to imply that sociological discoveries are always or even usually outrageous to moral sentiment. Not at all. What they have in common with exploration in distant lands, however, is the

Source: From *Invitation to Sociology* by Peter L. Berger. Copyright © 1963 by Peter L. Berger, Doubleday Dell Group, Inc. Reprinted with permission.

sudden illumination of new and unsuspected facets of human existence in society. This is the excitement and, as we shall try to show later, the humanistic justification of sociology.

People who like to avoid shocking discoveries, who prefer to believe that society is just what they were taught in Sunday school, who like the safety of the rules and the maxims of what Alfred Schuetz has called the "world-taken-for-granted," should stay away from sociology. People who feel no temptation before closed doors, who have no curiosity about human beings, who are content to admire scenery without wondering about the people who live in those houses on the other side of that river, should probably also stay away from sociology. They will find it unpleasant or, at any rate, unrewarding. People who are interested in human beings only if they can change, convert, or reform them should also be warned, for they will find sociology much less useful than they hoped. And people whose interest is mainly in their own conceptual constructions will do just as well to turn to the study of little white mice. Sociology will be satisfying, in the long run, only to those who can think of nothing more entrancing than to watch men and to understand things human. . . .

To ask sociological questions, then, presupposes that one is interested in looking some distance beyond the commonly accepted or officially defined goals of human actions. It presupposes a certain awareness that human events have different levels of meaning, some of which are hidden from the consciousness of everyday life. It may even presuppose a measure of suspicion about the way in which human events are officially interpreted by the authorities, be they political, juridical, or religious in character. If one is willing to go as far as that, it would seem evident that not all historical circumstances are equally favorable for the development of sociological perspective.

It would appear plausible, in consequence, that sociological thought would have the best chance to develop in historical circumstances marked by severe jolts to the self-conception, especially the official and authoritative and generally accepted self-conception of a culture. It is only in such circumstances that perceptive men are likely to be motivated to think beyond the assertions of this self-conception and, as a result, question the authorities. . . .

Sociological perspective can then be understood in terms of such phrases as "seeing through," "looking behind," very much as such phrases would be employed in common speech— "seeing through his game," "looking behind the scenes"—in other words, "being up on all the tricks."

. . . We could think of this in terms of a common experience of people living in large cities. One of the fascinations of a large city is the immense variety of human activities taking place behind the seemingly anonymous and endlessly undifferentiated rows of houses. A person who lives in such a city will time and again experience surprise or even shock as he discovers the strange pursuits that some men engage in quite unobtrusively in houses that, from the outside, look like all the others on a certain street. Having had this experience once or twice, one will repeatedly find oneself walking down a street, perhaps late in the evening, and wondering what may be going on under the bright lights showing through a line of drawn curtains. An ordinary family engaged in pleasant talk with guests? A scene of desperation amid illness or death? Or a scene of debauched pleasures? Perhaps a strange cult or a dangerous conspiracy? The facades of the houses cannot tell us, proclaiming nothing but an architectural conformity to the tastes of some group or class that may not even inhabit the street any longer. The social mysteries lie behind the facades. The wish to penetrate these mysteries is an analogon to sociological curiosity. In some cities that are suddenly struck by calamity this wish may be abruptly realized. Those who have experienced wartime bombings know of the sudden encounters with unsuspected (and sometimes unimaginable) fellow tenants in the air-raid shelter of one's apartment building. Or they can recollect the startling morning sight of a house hit by a bomb during the night, neatly sliced in half, the facade torn away and the previously hidden interior mercilessly revealed in the daylight. But in most cities that one may normally live in, the facades must be penetrated by one's own inquisitive intrusions. Similarly, there are historical situations in which the facades of society are violently torn apart and all but the most incurious are forced to see that there was a reality behind the facades all along. Usually this does not happen, and the facades continue to confront us with seemingly rocklike permanence. The perception of the reality behind the facades then demands a considerable intellectual effort.

A few examples of the way in which sociology "looks behind" the facades of social structures might serve to make our argument clearer. Take, for instance, the political organization of a community. If one wants to find out how a modern American city is governed, it is very easy to get the official information about this subject. The city will have a charter, operating under the laws of the state. With some advice from informed individuals, one may look up various statutes that define the constitution of the city. Thus one may find out that this particular community has a city-manager form of administration, or that party affiliations do not appear on the ballot in municipal elections, or that the city government participates in a regional water district. In similar fashion, with the help of some newspaper reading, one may find out the officially recognized political problems of the community. One may read that the city plans to annex a certain suburban area, or that there has been a change in the zoning ordinances to facilitate industrial development in another area, or even that one of the members of the city council has been accused of using his office for personal gain. All such matters still occur on the, as it were, visible, official, or public level of political life. However, it would be an exceedingly naive person who would believe that this kind of information gives him a rounded picture of the political reality of that community. The sociologist will want to know above all the constituency of the "informal power structure" (as it has been called by Floyd Hunter, an American sociologist interested in such studies), which is a configuration of men and their power that cannot be found in any statutes, and probably cannot be read about in the newspapers. The political scientist or the legal expert might find it very interesting to compare the city charter with the constitutions of other similar communities. The sociologist will be far more concerned with discovering the way in which powerful vested interests influence or even control the actions of officials elected under the charter. These vested interests will not be found in city hall, but rather in the executive suites of corporations that may not even be located in that community, in the private mansions of a handful of powerful men, perhaps in the offices of certain labor unions, or even, in some instances, in the headquarters of criminal organizations. When the sociologist concerns himself with power, he will "look behind" the official mechanisms that are supposed to regulate power in the community. This does not necessarily mean that he will regard the official mechanisms as totally ineffective or their legal definition as totally illusionary. But at the very least he will insist that there is another level of reality to be investigated in the particular system of power. In some cases he might conclude that to look for real power in the publicly recognized places is quite delusional. . . .

Let us take one further example. In Western countries, and especially in America, it is assumed that men and women marry because they are in love. There is a broadly based popular mythology about the character of love as a violent, irresistible emotion that strikes where it will, a mystery that is the goal of most young people and often of the not-so-young as well. As soon as one investigates, however, which people actually marry each other, one finds that the lightning-shaft of Cupid seems to be guided rather strongly within very definite channels of class, income, education, [and] racial and religious background.

If one then investigates a little further into the behavior that is engaged in prior to marriage under the rather misleading euphemism of "courtship," one finds channels of interaction that are often rigid to the point of ritual. The suspicion begins to dawn on one that, most of the time, it is not so much the emotion of love that creates a certain kind of relationship, but that carefully predefined and often planned relationships eventually generate the desired emotion. In other words, when certain conditions are met or have been constructed, one allows oneself "to fall in love." The sociologist investigating our patterns of "courtship" and marriage soon discovers a complex web of motives related in many ways to the entire institutional structure within which an individual lives his life—class, career, economic ambition, aspirations of power and prestige. The miracle of love now begins to look somewhat synthetic. Again, this need not mean in any given instance that the sociologist will declare the romantic interpretation to be an illusion. But, once more, he will look beyond the immediately given and publicly approved interpretations. . . .

We would contend, then, that there is a debunking motif inherent in sociological consciousness. The sociologist will be driven time and again, by the very logic of his discipline, to debunk the social systems he is studying. This unmasking tendency need not necessarily be due to the sociologist's temperament or inclinations.

Indeed, it may happen that the sociologist, who as an individual may be of a conciliatory disposition and quite disinclined to disturb the comfortable assumptions on which he rests his own social existence, is nevertheless compelled by what he is doing to fly in the face of what those around him take for granted. In other words, we would contend that the roots of the debunking motif in sociology are not psychological but methodological. The sociological frame of reference, with its built-in procedure of looking for levels of reality other than those given in the official interpretations of society, carries with it a logical imperative to unmask the pretensions and the propaganda by which men cloak their actions with each other. This unmasking imperative is one of the characteristics of sociology particularly at home in the temper of the modern era. . . .

CRITICAL THINKING QUESTIONS

1. How can we explain the fact that people within any society tend to take their own way of life for granted?

2. What does Berger think is the justification for studying sociology?

3. What is involved in sociological "debunking"? How are others likely to respond to sociological insights?

3

Women and the
Birth of Sociology

PATRICIA MADOO LENGERMANN AND
JILL NIEBRUGGE-BRANTLEY

Most beginning students of sociology know about Karl Marx, Max Weber, and Emile Durkheim; but Harriet Martineau, Ida Wells-Barnett, Anna Julia Cooper, Charlotte Perkins Gilman, and other women were also important founders of the discipline.

The history of sociology's theories is conventionally told as a history of white male agency—an account of the theoretical contributions of a "founding" generation of men, Auguste Comte, Herbert Spencer, and Karl Marx, writing in the middle of the nineteenth century, expanded by a second, "classic" generation of men, Emile Durkheim, Max Weber, Georg Simmel, George Herbert Mead, and Robert E. Park, who wrote between 1890 and 1930. This history is presented as an account of the natural way things occurred, a chronicle beyond the powers of human tellers to change. In contrast, we portray this history as a social construction arising out of the discipline's power arrangements, and like all histories, reflecting an ongoing conflict between exclusionary and inclusionary values and practices (Becker, 1971; Lemert, 1995; D. Smith, 1987). . . .

The claim that a group has been "written out" of history is different from the claim that a group has been "invisible." "Invisibility" suggests not being seen, that is, never having one's presence acknowledged as significant—a concept applied by many African Americans to their experience of marginalization (e.g., Collins, 1990; Cooper, 1892; Du Bois, 1903; Ellison, 1952; Lorde, 1984; Rollins, 1985). "Being written out" suggests having once been seen as a presence in a community and then having been erased from its record. For several reasons, the case of the fifteen women sociologists treated in this volume is an instance of erasure rather than invisibility. First, almost all these women were well-known public figures in their lifetime, larger than the fledgling discipline of sociology they helped create; like the work of Marx, Max Weber, or Durkheim, their work has relevance for all the social sciences. Second, they

Source: From *The Women Founders: Sociology and Theory, 1830–1930*, by Patricia Madoo Lengermann and Jill Niebrugge-Brantley. Copyright © 1998 by McGraw-Hill, Inc.

Figure 3.1   Lifelines of Women and Men Founders of Sociology

1790	1800	1810	1820	1830	1840	1850	1860	1870	1880	1890	1900	1910	1920	1930	1940	1950	1960

```
Auguste Comte 1798–1857 _ _ _ _ _ _ _ _ _
  Harriet Martineau 1802–1876 _ _ _ _ _ _ _ _ _ _ _ _ _
      Karl Marx 1818–1883 _ _ _ _ _ _ _ _ _ _ _ _ _
        Herbert Spencer 1820–1903 _ _ _ _ _ _ _ _ _ _ _ _ _ _ _ _ _ _
                          Anna Julia Cooper 1858–1964 _ _ _ _ _ _ _ _ _ _ _ _ _ _ _ _ _ _ _ _ _ _ _ _ _ _ _ _ _ _
                            Emile Durkheim 1858–1917 _ _ _ _ _ _ _ _ _ _
                            Julia Lathrop 1858–1932 _ _ _ _ _ _ _ _ _ _ _ _ _ _ _ _ _ _ _
                            Georg Simmel 1858–1918 _ _ _ _ _ _ _ _ _ _
                            Marion Talbot 1858–1947 _ _ _ _ _ _ _ _ _ _ _ _ _ _ _ _ _ _ _ _ _ _
                            Beatrice Potter Webb 1858–1943 _ _ _ _ _ _ _ _ _ _ _ _ _ _ _ _ _ _ _ _ _
                             Florence Kelley  1859–1932 _ _ _ _ _ _ _ _ _ _ _ _ _ _ _ _ _ _
                             Jane Addams  1860–1935 _ _ _ _ _ _ _ _ _ _ _ _ _ _ _ _ _ _
                            Charlotte Perkins Gilman 1860–1935 _ _ _ _ _ _ _ _ _ _ _ _ _ _
                              Ida B. Wells-Barnett  1862–1931 _ _ _ _ _ _ _ _ _ _ _ _
                              George Herbert Mead  1863–1931 _ _ _ _ _ _ _ _ _ _ _
                              W. I. Thomas 1863–1947 _ _ _ _ _ _ _ _ _ _ _ _ _ _ _ _ _ _ _ _ _
                               Robert E. Park  1864–1944 _ _ _ _ _ _ _ _ _ _ _ _ _ _ _ _ _ _ _ _
                               Max Weber 1864–1920 _ _ _ _ _ _ _ _ _ _ _ _
                                Sophonisba Breckinridge 1866–1948 _ _ _ _ _ _ _ _ _ _ _ _ _ _ _
                                 Annie Marion MacLean ca. 1870–1934 _ _ _ _ _ _ _
                                Marianne Weber 1870–1954 _ _ _ _ _ _ _ _ _ _ _ _ _ _ _ _ _ _ _ _ _ _
                                  Frances Kellor 1873–1952 _ _ _ _ _ _ _ _ _ _ _ _ _ _ _ _ _ _ _ _
                                   Edith Abbott 1876–1957 _ _ _ _ _ _ _ _ _ _ _ _ _ _ _ _ _ _ _ _ _ _
                                    Grace Abbott 1878–1939 _ _ _ _ _ _ _ _ _ _ _
```

created social theory and did sociology in the same times and places as the male founders (see Figure 3.1). Third, they were widely recognized by their contemporaries, including male sociologists, as significant social analysts. Fourth, they all acted as members of a sociological community, meeting at least one of the following criteria: employment as a sociologist, membership in a national sociological association, publication framed by an explicit concern with sociological principles, self-identification as a sociologist and recognition by contemporaries as a sociologist (Käsler, 1981; Deegan, 1991). We introduce some of the evidence for these claims in the brief descriptions of the women that follow. . . .

Martineau—whose *Illustrations of Political Economy* (1832–1834) outsold even Charles Dickens (Hoecker-Drysdale, 1992)—was Britain's preeminent woman of letters until her death, writing social analysis, journalism, history, novels, children's stories, and travel books. Long identified in the history of sociology for her 1853

translation and abridgement of Comte, she was herself writing sociology as early as 1834, drafting what would become the first major statement of method, *How to Observe Morals and Manners* (1838b) and testing her methodology in her classic study *Society in America* (1836). Addams was the founder of Hull-House, the famous Chicago social settlement; a major spokesperson for Progressive reform on behalf of immigrants, trade unions, women, children, working-class people, and African Americans; and consistently named in public opinion polls as one of the most admired Americans (Davis, 1973; Daniel Levine, 1971). At Hull-House, she administered a major research institution, drawing on her experiences there to formulate a social theory in eight major books and some 200 articles. She self-identified as a sociologist; taught sociology; was a member of the American Sociological Society (ASS)—until 1959 the name of the American Sociological Association (ASA); published in the *American Journal of Sociology (AJS)*; and had significant relationships with Mead, Park, W. I. Thomas, Albion Small, and Ernest Burgess (Deegan, 1988). Gilman was widely regarded as the leading feminist intellectual of her day. Her *Women and Economics* (1898) went through nine printings by 1920, was translated into seven languages, and was the bible of many women's college student bodies (Ceplair, 1991). Besides the classic feminist novella *The Yellow Wallpaper* (1892) and some 2,000 pieces of journalism, poetry, and prose, she wrote six significant works of formal social theory, including *Women and Economics, Human Work* (1904), and *The Man-Made World* (1911). She also published in the *AJS*, was a member of the ASS, and maintained intellectual relationships with Lester Ward and E. A. Ross.

Wells-Barnett spearheaded national and international anti-lynching campaigns, writing major analyses of lynching—*Southern Horrors* (1892) and *A Red Record* (1895)—and carrying the battle to Britain, where she often spoke to crowds in the thousands. She was an active organizer for African American civil rights, helping to found the National Association for the Advancement of Colored People (NAACP). Cooper's major book *A Voice from the South* (1892) received superlative reviews from black and white publications alike, establishing her as a prominent intellectual and spokesperson for African American women; she was one of two women to address the world's first Pan-African Conference in London in 1900. Cooper and Wells-Barnett created a genuine American non-Marxian conflict theory in which they spoke of the sociological framing of their argument; but American racism made tentative any relationship between them and white professional sociology, although both knew and worked with black sociologist W. E. B. Du Bois. Marianne Weber lived at the center of German sociological circles and debated the ideas of both Simmel and her husband Max in her own writings. She was a leading figure in the German feminist movement, the first woman to be elected to a German parliament, and the author of nine books of social

analysis and sociology, including her monumental work on the legal position of women, *Ehefrau und Mutter in der Rechtsentwicklung (Marriage, Motherhood, and the Law)* (1907), and her collected essays, *Frauenfragen und Frauengedanken (Reflections on Women and Women's Issues)* (1919). She secured Max's position within sociology after his death by editing and publishing ten volumes of his work and writing her important interpretive biography of him.

Webb was tutored by Spencer, self-identified as a sociologist, taught sociology, worked as a social investigator on the major empirical study of her age (Charles Booth's *Life and Labour of the People of London*), and did her own independent investigations, leading to the socialist reform classic *The Co-operative Movement in Great Britain* (1891). With her husband Sidney, she researched and co-authored eleven voluminous works of empirical sociology that formed the blueprint for the British welfare state. All the members of the Chicago Women's School of Sociology (hereafter referred to as the Chicago Women's School or the Chicago Women) wrote prolifically as social analysts, all publishing in the *AJS*. Many were prominent public figures: Kelley headed the National Consumers' League (1899–1932); Lathrop (1912–20), and then Grace Abbott (1920–34), served as chief of the Children's Bureau, the highest-ranking woman in the federal government at that time; Edith Abbott and Breckinridge founded the University of Chicago's School of Social Service Administration (1922); Talbot was dean of women at the University of Chicago (1893–1925); Kellor was a founder and executive officer of the American Arbitration League (1926–53). Kelley knew Friedrich Engels, maintained a correspondence with him until his death, and did the first English translation of *The Condition of the Working Class in England in 1844*; MacLean studied with Small, Mead, and Charles Henderson; Kellor also studied with Henderson; Edith Abbott, Grace Abbott, and Breckinridge are all referenced in Park and Burgess's *Introduction to the Science of*

Sociology; Talbot served as an associate editor of the *AJS* from its founding by Small to her retirement in 1925.

These women knew each other or each other's work. Gilman, Webb, Weber, and Wells-Barnett all visited Hull-House, which was, of course, the working base for Addams and most of the Chicago Women. Many of them read Gilman's *Women and Economics*—Webb, Weber, Addams, Kelley, Lathrop, and Talbot. Addams published with Wells-Barnett on lynching on at least two occasions, one of which was in a remarkable issue of *Survey* in February of 1913 in which Addams, Wells-Barnett, Breckinridge, and Du Bois all analyze the problem of race.[1] Addams, Wells-Barnett, Kelley, and Breckinridge participated in the founding of the NAACP. Hull-House residents, including Addams, Lathrop, and Kelley, used Webb's *The Co-operative Movement in Great Britain* in preparation for their own venture into cooperative housing for working women. The persons most outside this network are Martineau, a full generation earlier than the rest of the women, and Cooper, whose life course rarely took her to Chicago. Yet Edith Abbott knew and responded to Martineau's work on women's employment in America, and Gilman refers to Martineau's struggle to overcome gender barriers to her career as a social analyst. And Cooper spoke in Chicago in 1893 at the white feminist Women's Congress, was active, as was Wells-Barnett, in the National Federation of Colored Women's Clubs and the African American settlement house movement, and wrote a sympathetic response to Gilman's suicide.

These women knew that they were part of a larger movement to create a science of society and had their own sense of what that science should be: a project of social critique in which research and theory had as a morally necessary focus the description, analysis, and correction of social inequality. The women vary in terms of the particular inequality focused on—gender, class, race, ethnicity, age, or combinations thereof; the relative balance between research and theory, and

the choice of research strategy and theoretical method. Working out this commitment to critical social theory, these women engaged with sociology and the sociological community at the moment in which the discipline was itself emerging. Their varying relationships to that community thus reflect both the instability of sociology's emerging identity and the effects of gender, class, and race on access to what would become a formal academic enterprise, the province of educated white men. But at the moment these women were writing, sociology was as much their intellectual project as the men's; it is only in the retelling that they have disappeared.

CRITICAL THINKING QUESTIONS

1. What does it mean to say that women have been "written out" of sociology's history? Why did this happen?
2. What issues or ideas did sociology's women founders have in common?
3. What is the importance today of recognizing the contributions of sociology's women founders?

NOTE

1. The *Survey* was a magazine founded in the merger of several social work journals; it was edited by Paul U. Kellogg, and Addams served on its editorial board. This magazine served as a major vehicle for social reformers who saw themselves as engaged in sociology. It also offered a more popular version, *Survey Graphic*, because its editorial board took communication with a general public as a primary duty.

REFERENCES

Becker, Ernest. 1971. *The lost science of man*. New York: Braziller.

Ceplair, Larry (ed.). 1991. *Charlotte Perkins Gilman: A nonfiction reader*. New York: Columbia University Press.

Collins, Randall. 1975. *Conflict sociology*. New York: Academic Press.

Cooper, Anna Julia. 1892. *A voice from the South by a black woman from the South*. Xenia, OH: Aldine Press.

Davis, Allen F. 1973. *American heroine*. New York: Oxford University Press.

Deegan, Mary Jo. 1988. *Jane Addams and the men of the Chicago School, 1892–1918*. New Brunswick, NJ: Transaction Books.

———— (ed.). 1991. *Women in sociology: A bio-bibliographical sourcebook*. Westport, CT: Greenwood Press.

Du Bois, W. E. B. 1903/1989. *The souls of black folk*. New York: Bantam.

Ellison, Ralph. 1952/1972. *Invisible man*. New York: Vintage Books.

Gilman, Charlotte Perkins. 1892/1973. *The yellow wallpaper 1892–1973*. New York: Feminist Press.

————. 1898. *Women and economics*. Boston: Small and Maynard.

————. 1904. *Human work*. New York: McClure and Phillips.

————. 1911. *The man-made world, or our androcentric culture*. New York. Charlton Company.

Hoecker-Drysdale, Susan. 1992. *Harriet Martineau: First woman sociologist*. Oxford, England: Berg Publishers, Inc.

Käsler, Dirk. 1981. "Methodological problems of a sociological history of early German sociology." Paper presented at the Department of Education, University of Chicago, November 5.

Lemert, Charles. 1995. *Sociology after the crisis*. Boulder, CO: Westview Press.

Levine, Daniel. 1971. *Jane Addams and the liberal tradition*. Madison: State Historical Society of Wisconsin.

Lorde, Audre. 1984. *Sister outsider*. Trumansburg, NY: Crossings Press.

Martineau, Harriet. 1832–34. *Illustrations of political economy*. 9 vols. London: Charles Fox.

————. 1836/1837. *Society in America*. 2 vols. New York: Saunders and Otley.

————. 1838b. *How to observe morals and manners*. London: Charles Knight and Company.

Rollins, Judith. 1985. *Between women: Domestics and their employers*. Philadelphia: Temple University Press.

Smith, Dorothy E. 1979. "A sociology for women." In *The prism of sex: Essays in the sociology of knowledge*, ed. J. A. Sherman and E. T. Beck, pp. 135–87. Madison: University of Wisconsin Press.

————. 1987. *The everyday world as problematic: A feminist sociology*. Boston: Northeastern University Press.

Weber, Marianne. 1907. *Ehefrau und mutter in der rechtsentwicklung*. Tübingen: J. C. B. Mohr.

————. 1919. *Frauenfragen und frauengedanken*, Tübingen: J. C. B. Mohr.

Wells-Barnett, Ida B. 1892/1969. *Southern horrors*. Reprinted in *On lynchings*, New York: Arno.

————. 1895. *A red record*. Chicago: Donohue and Henneberry.

4

Body Ritual among the Nacirema

HORACE MINER

Most people take their life for granted; when they think about society at all, it is usually viewed as both natural and good. To help us step back from our society, anthropologist Horace Miner describes the Nacirema, a peculiar people living in North America (whose lives should strike you as familiar). Miner's intellectual sleight-of-hand illustrates how the sociological perspective involves detachment, so that everyday life becomes something new and unusual.

The anthropologist has become so familiar with the diversity of ways in which different peoples behave in similar situations that he is not apt to be surprised by even the most exotic customs. In fact, if all of the logically possible combinations of behavior have not been found somewhere in the world, he is apt to suspect that they must be present in some yet undescribed tribe. This point has, in fact, been expressed with respect to clan organization by Murdock (1949:71). In this light, the magical beliefs and practices of the Nacirema present such unusual aspects that it seems desirable to describe them as an example of the extremes to which human behavior can go.

Professor Linton first brought the ritual of the Nacirema to the attention of anthropologists

twenty years ago (1936:326), but the culture of this people is still very poorly understood. They are a North American group living in the territory between the Canadian Cree, the Yaqui and Tarahumare of Mexico, and the Carib and Arawak of the Antilles. Little is known of their origin, although tradition states that they came from the east. According to Nacirema mythology, their nation was originated by a culture hero, Notgnihsaw, who is otherwise known for two great feats of strength—the throwing of a piece of wampum across the river Pa-To-Mac and the chopping down of a cherry tree in which the Spirit of Truth resided.

Nacirema culture is characterized by a highly developed market economy which has evolved in a rich natural habitat. While much of the people's time is devoted to economic pursuits, a large part of the fruits of these labors and a considerable portion of the day are spent in ritual activity. The focus of this activity is the

Source: "Body Ritual among the Nacirema" by Horace Miner. Reprinted courtesy of the American Anthropological Association from *American Anthropologist,* vol. 58, no. 3, June, 1956.

human body, the appearance and health of which loom as a dominant concern in the ethos of the people. While such concern is certainly not unusual, its ceremonial aspects and associated philosophy are unique.

The fundamental belief underlying the whole system appears to be that the human body is ugly and that its natural tendency is to debility and disease. Incarcerated in such a body, man's only hope is to avert these characteristics through the use of the powerful influences of ritual and ceremony. Every household has one or more shrines devoted to this purpose. The more powerful individuals in this society have several shrines in their houses, and, in fact, the opulence of a house is often referred to in terms of the number of such ritual centers it possesses. Most houses are of wattle and daub construction, but the shrine rooms of the more wealthy are walled with stone. Poorer families imitate the rich by applying pottery plaques to their shrine walls.

While each family has at least one such shrine, the rituals associated with it are not family ceremonies but are private and secret. The rites are normally only discussed with children, and then only during the period when they are being initiated into these mysteries. I was able, however, to establish sufficient rapport with the natives to examine these shrines and to have the rituals described to me.

The focal point of the shrine is a box or chest which is built into the wall. In this chest are kept the many charms and magical potions without which no native believes he could live. These preparations are secured from a variety of specialized practitioners. The most powerful of these are the medicine men, whose assistance must be rewarded with substantial gifts. However, the medicine men do not provide the curative potions for their clients, but decide what the ingredients should be and then write them down in an ancient and secret language. This writing is understood only by the medicine men and by the herbalists who, for another gift, provide the required charm.

The charm is not disposed of after it has served its purpose, but is placed in the charm-box

of the household shrine. As these magical materials are specific for certain ills, and the real or imagined maladies of the people are many, the charm-box is usually full to overflowing. The magical packets are so numerous that people forget what their purposes were and fear to use them again. While the natives are very vague on this point, we can only assume that the idea in retaining all the old magical materials is that their presence in the charm-box, before which the body rituals are conducted, will in some way protect the worshipper.

Beneath the charm-box is a small font. Each day every member of the family, in succession, enters the shrine room, bows his head before the charm-box, mingles different sorts of holy water in the font, and proceeds with a brief rite of ablution. The holy waters are secured from the Water Temple of the community, where the priests conduct elaborate ceremonies to make the liquid ritually pure.

In the hierarchy of magical practitioners, and below the medicine men in prestige, are specialists whose designation is best translated "holy-mouth-men." The Nacirema have an almost pathological horror of and fascination with the mouth, the condition of which is believed to have a supernatural influence on all social relationships. Were it not for the rituals of the mouth, they believe that their teeth would fall out, their gums bleed, their jaws shrink, their friends desert them, and their lovers reject them. They also believe that a strong relationship exists between oral and moral characteristics. For example, there is a ritual ablution of the mouth for children which is supposed to improve their moral fiber.

The daily body ritual performed by everyone includes a mouth-rite. Despite the fact that these people are so punctilious about care of the mouth, this rite involves a practice which strikes the uninitiated stranger as revolting. It was reported to me that the ritual consists of inserting a small bundle of hog hairs into the mouth, along with certain magical powders, and then moving the bundle in a highly formalized series of gestures.

In addition to the private mouth-rite, the people seek out a holy-mouth-man once or twice a year. These practitioners have an impressive set of paraphernalia, consisting of a variety of augers, awls, probes, and prods. The use of these objects in the exorcism of the evils of the mouth involves almost unbelievable ritual torture of the client. The holy-mouth-man opens the client's mouth and, using the above-mentioned tools, enlarges any holes which decay may have created in the teeth. Magical materials are put into these holes. If there are no naturally occurring holes in the teeth, large sections of one or more teeth are gouged out so that the supernatural substance can be applied. In the client's view, the purpose of these ministrations is to arrest decay and to draw friends. The extremely sacred and traditional character of the rite is evident in the fact that the natives return to the holy-mouth-man year after year, despite the fact that their teeth continue to decay.

It is to be hoped that, when a thorough study of the Nacirema is made, there will be careful inquiry into the personality structure of these people. One has but to watch the gleam in the eye of a holy-mouth-man, as he jabs an awl into an exposed nerve, to suspect that a certain amount of sadism is involved. If this can be established, a very interesting pattern emerges, for most of the population shows definite masochistic tendencies. It was to these that Professor Linton referred in discussing a distinctive part of the daily body ritual which is performed only by men. This part of the rite involves scraping and lacerating the surface of the face with a sharp instrument. Special women's rites are performed only four times during each lunar month, but what they lack in frequency is made up in barbarity. As part of this ceremony, women bake their heads in small ovens for about an hour. The theoretically interesting point is that what seems to be a preponderantly masochistic people have developed sadistic specialists.

The medicine men have an imposing temple, or *latipso*, in every community of any size. The more elaborate ceremonies required to treat very sick patients can only be performed at this temple. These ceremonies involve not only the thaumaturge but a permanent group of vestal maidens who move sedately about the temple chambers in distinctive costume and headdress.

The *latipso* ceremonies are so harsh that it is phenomenal that a fair proportion of the really sick natives who enter the temple ever recover. Small children whose indoctrination is still incomplete have been known to resist attempts to take them to the temple because "that is where you go to die." Despite this fact, sick adults are not only willing but eager to undergo the protracted ritual purification, if they can afford to do so. No matter how ill the supplicant or how grave the emergency, the guardians of many temples will not admit a client if he cannot give a rich gift to the custodian. Even after one has gained admission and survived the ceremonies, the guardians will not permit the neophyte to leave until he makes still another gift.

The supplicant entering the temple is first stripped of all his or her clothes. In everyday life the Nacirema avoids exposure of his body and its natural functions. Bathing and excretory acts are performed only in the secrecy of the household shrine, where they are ritualized as part of the body-rites. Psychological shock results from the fact that body secrecy is suddenly lost upon entry into the *latipso*. A man, whose own wife has never seen him in an excretory act, suddenly finds himself naked and assisted by a vestal maiden while he performs his natural functions into a sacred vessel. This sort of ceremonial treatment is necessitated by the fact that the excreta are used by a diviner to ascertain the course and nature of the client's sickness. Female clients, on the other hand, find their naked bodies are subjected to the scrutiny, manipulation, and prodding of the medicine men.

Few supplicants in the temple are well enough to do anything but lie on their hard beds. The daily ceremonies, like the rites of the holy-mouth-men, involve discomfort and torture. With ritual precision, the vestals awaken their miserable charges each dawn and roll them about on their beds of pain while performing ablutions, in the formal movements of which the maidens are highly trained. At other times they insert magic wands in the supplicant's mouth or force him to eat substances which are supposed to be healing. From time to time the medicine men come to their clients and jab magically treated needles into their flesh. The fact that these temple ceremonies may not cure, and may even kill, the neophyte, in no way decreases the people's faith in the medicine men.

There remains one other kind of practitioner, known as a "listener." This witch-doctor has the power to exorcise the devils that lodge in the heads of people who have been bewitched. The Nacirema believe that parents bewitch their own children. Mothers are particularly suspected of putting a curse on children while teaching them the secret body rituals. The counter-magic of the witch-doctor is unusual in its lack of ritual. The patient simply tells the "listener" all his troubles and fears, beginning with the earliest difficulties he can remember. The memory displayed by the Nacirema in these exorcism sessions is truly remarkable. It is not uncommon for the patient to bemoan the rejection he felt upon being weaned as a babe, and a few individuals even see their troubles going back to the traumatic effects of their own birth.

In conclusion, mention must be made of certain practices which have their base in native esthetics but which depend upon the pervasive aversion to the natural body and its functions. There are ritual fasts to make fat people thin and ceremonial feasts to make thin people fat. Still other rites are used to make women's breasts larger if they are small, and smaller if they are large. General dissatisfaction with breast shape is symbolized in the fact that the ideal form is virtually outside the range of human variation. A few women afflicted with almost inhuman hyper-mammary development are so idolized that they make a handsome living by simply going from village to village and permitting the natives to stare at them for a fee.

Reference has already been made to the fact that excretory functions are ritualized, routinized, and relegated to secrecy. Natural reproductive functions are similarly distorted. Intercourse is taboo as a topic and scheduled as an act. Efforts are made to avoid pregnancy by the use of magical materials or by limiting intercourse to certain phases of the moon. Conception is actually very infrequent. When pregnant, women dress so as to hide their condition. Parturition takes place in secret, without friends or relatives to assist, and the majority of women do not nurse their infants.

Our review of the ritual life of the Nacirema has certainly shown them to be a magic-ridden people. It is hard to understand how they have managed to exist so long under the burdens which they have imposed upon themselves. But even such exotic customs as these take on real meaning when they are viewed with the insight provided by Malinowski when he wrote (1948: 70):

Looking from far and above, from our high places of safety in the developed civilization, it is easy to see all the crudity and irrelevance of magic. But without its power and guidance early man could not have mastered his practical difficulties as he has done, nor could man have advanced to the higher stages of civilization.

CRITICAL THINKING QUESTIONS

1. Did you understand that Miner is describing the American—"Nacirema" spelled backwards? Why do we not recognize this right away?

2. Using Miner's approach, describe a baseball game, an auction, shoppers in a supermarket, or a college classroom.

3. What do we gain from being able to "step back" from our way of life as Miner has done here?

REFERENCES

Linton, R. 1936. *The study of man.* New York: Appleton-Century.

Malinowski, B. 1948. *Magic, science and religion.* Glencoe, IL: Free Press.

Murdock, G. P. 1949. *Social structure.* New York: Macmillan.

5

The Case for Value-Free Sociology

MAX WEBER

The following is part of a lecture given in 1918 at Germany's Munich University by Max Weber, one of sociology's pioneers. Weber lived in politically turbulent times, in which the government and other organizations were demanding that university faculty teach the "right" ideas. Weber responded to these pressures by encouraging everyone to be politically involved as citizens; yet, he maintained that the teachers and scholars should prize dispassionate analysis rather than political advocacy. This selection stimulates critical thinking about the mix of fact and value that is found in all sociological research.

Let us consider the disciplines close to me: sociology, history, economics, political science, and those types of cultural philosophy that make it their task to interpret the sciences. It is said, and I agree, that politics is out of place in the lecture-room. It does not belong there on the part of the students. . . . Neither does [it] belong in the lecture-room on the part of the [instructors], and when the [instructor] is scientifically concerned with politics, it belongs there least of all.

Source: Excerpts from *Max Weber: Essays in Sociology by Max Weber,* edited by H. H. Gerth and C. Wright Mills, translated by H. H. Gerth and C. Wright Mills, copyright © 1946, 1958 by H. H. Gerth and C. Wright Mills. Used by permission of Oxford University Press.

To take a practical stand is one thing, and to analyze political structures and party positions is another. When speaking in a political meeting about democracy, one does not hide one's personal standpoint; indeed, to come out clearly and take a stand is one's damned duty. The words one uses in such a meeting are not means of scientific analysis but means of canvassing votes and winning over others. They are not plowshares to loosen the soil of contemplative thought; they are swords against the enemies: Such words are weapons. It would be an outrage, however, to use words in this fashion in a lecture or in the lecture-room. If, for instance, "democracy" is under discussion, one considers its various forms, analyzes them in the way they function, determines what results for the conditions of life the one form has as compared with the other. Then one confronts the forms of democracy with nondemocratic forms of political order and endeavors to come to a position where the student may find the point from which, in terms of his ultimate ideals, he can take a stand. But the true teacher will beware of imposing from the platform any political position upon the student, whether it is expressed or suggested. "To let the facts speak for themselves" is the most unfair way of putting over a political position to the student.

Why should we abstain from doing this? I state in advance that some highly esteemed colleagues are of the opinion that it is not possible to carry through this self-restraint and that, even if it were possible, it would be a whim to avoid declaring oneself. Now one cannot demonstrate scientifically what the duty of an academic teacher is. One can only demand of the teacher that he have the intellectual integrity to see that it is one thing to state facts, to determine mathematical or logical relations or the internal structure of cultural values, while it is another thing to answer questions of the value of culture and its individual contents and the question of how one should act in the cultural community and in political associations. These are quite heterogeneous problems. If he asks further why he should not deal with both types of problems in the lecture-room, the answer is: because the prophet and the demagogue do not belong on the academic platform.

To the prophet and the demagogue, it is said: "Go your ways out into the streets and speak openly to the world," that is, speak where criticism is possible. In the lecture-room we stand opposite our audience, and it has to remain silent. I deem it irresponsible to exploit the circumstance that for the sake of their career the students have to attend a teacher's course while there is nobody present to oppose him with criticism. The task of

the teacher is to serve the students with his knowledge and scientific experience and not to imprint upon them his personal political views. It is certainly possible that the individual teacher will not entirely succeed in eliminating his personal sympathies. He is then exposed to the sharpest criticism in the forum of his own conscience. And this deficiency does not prove anything; other errors are also possible, for instance, erroneous statements of fact, and yet they prove nothing against the duty of searching for the truth. I also reject this in the very interest of science. I am ready to prove from the works of our historians that whenever the man of science introduces his personal value judgment, a full understanding of the facts ceases. . . .

The primary task of a useful teacher is to teach his students to recognize "inconvenient" facts—I mean facts that are inconvenient for their party opinions. And for every party opinion there are facts that are extremely inconvenient, for my own opinion no less than for others. I believe the teacher accomplishes more than a mere intellectual task if he compels his audience to accustom itself to the existence of such facts. I would be so immodest as even to apply the expression "moral achievement," though perhaps this may sound too grandiose for something that should go without saying.

CRITICAL THINKING QUESTIONS

1. Why does Weber seek to set the campus apart from society as an "ivory tower"?

2. How is the classroom a distinctive setting in terms of political neutrality? If instructors cannot be entirely free from value positions, why should they strive to point out "inconvenient facts" to their students?

3. Do you see arguments for instructors presenting passionate advocacy of issues that are of great political and moral significance?

6

Defining Features of Canadian Sociology

BRUCE RAVELLI

Sociological Research
CLASSIC
CONTEMPORARY
CROSS-CULTURAL

In this brief review, Bruce Ravelli looks at some of the defining features of Canadian sociology. This article should inspire you to think about Canadian society and whether you believe it is reflected in Canadian sociology.

Canadian sociology often mirrors the nature of Canada itself: a diverse landscape where Canadians struggle to find their unique voice within a chorus dominated by Americans. In fact, some analysts suggest that Canadian sociology is a product of its experiences with, and at times its resistance to, the larger and more dominant American sociological tradition (see Brym & Saint-Pierre, 1997; Hiller, 2001; Hiller & Di Luzio, 2001). The dominance of the American sociological tradition in Canada is largely due to its longer history[1] and its sheer size.[2] However, at least four elements influence the presence of a distinctly Canadian sociology:

1. Canada's physical geography, defined by its vast and often challenging physical environment, and its regionalism, evidenced in the

important role Quebec plays in Canadian sociology's intellectual development

2. Canadian sociology's focus on the political economy

3. The Canadianization movement of the 1960s and 1970s in response to the number of American faculty in our postsecondary institutions

4. The radical nature of Canadian sociology

CANADA'S GEOGRAPHY AND REGIONALISM

Canada, the world's second-largest country—in terms of total area, not population (Countries of the World, 2002)—is blessed with rich natural resources and a beautiful and diverse landscape. As we will see, these environmental factors have influenced Canadian sociology. According to Hiller (2001), Canadian sociology is not simply

Source: This article was specifically written by the author for an earlier edition of this reader.

a culmination of the varieties of sociology practised in Canada; it is instead the product of Canadian sociologists' efforts to understand the Canadian experience. For Hiller (2001), one of Canadian sociology's defining pursuits has been the attempt to understand a changing national society. Everett Hughes asserted in 1959 that Canadian sociology should be grounded in its own societal context: as society changes, so too should its sociology (cited in Hiller, 2001). Sociology "should reflect both the unique aspects of the society's character as well as the evolution of that society" (Hiller, 2001: 262).

External and internal forces help to shape and define a Canadian sociology. The particular nature of the relationship between Canada's physical landscape and Canadian sociology is seen clearly in Brym and Saint-Pierre (1997). They suggest that one defining characteristic of Canadian sociology is its survivalism (1997: 543) and propose that a core theme of Canadian sociology is the development and maintenance of a community in the face of hostile elements (e.g., geographically, socially) and outside forces (i.e., political and intellectual pressures from the United States and American sociologists). One inside force defining Canadian sociology is the role that regionalism plays in our country's development (e.g., west versus east) and, in particular, Quebec's influence. Quebec has a unique linguistic and cultural influence on Canadian society generally and on Canadian sociology specifically.

The teaching of Canadian francophone sociology began in 1943, when the Faculty of Social Sciences was established at Laval University in Quebec City. Although francophone sociology is comparatively young, it experienced explosive growth from the 1960s to the 1980s, as demonstrated by rising student enrolment and the wealth of research produced by francophone sociologists (Brym & Saint-Pierre, 1997: 544). During the 1960s, a social movement in Quebec called the Quiet Revolution saw the influence of the Catholic Church diminish, replaced by an expanded provincial bureaucracy and, ultimately, a resurgence in nationalistic sentiments (seen in the rising popularity of the separatist movement and the growing influence of the Parti Québécois and its then-leader, René Lévesque).

The Quiet Revolution not only inspired changes in Quebec society and politics, but it also influenced sociologists to focus on issues of social class and social policy (see Brym & Saint-Pierre, 1997; Hiller, 2001). In fact, some Quebec sociologists have played leadership roles in the transformation of francophone society as senior advisors and civil servants for the provincial government (Brym & Saint-Pierre, 1997: 544). This is consistent with Southcott's (1999: 459) position that francophone sociologists are more likely to see themselves as "agents of change" than are their anglophone colleagues. Again, we see that the society in which sociologists work affects their approach to the discipline. One of those approaches involves an interest in the political economy.

CANADIAN FOCUS ON THE POLITICAL ECONOMY

Wallace Clement (2001), a leading figure in Canadian sociology, believes that one of the defining elements of Canadian sociology is its interest in the political economy. The political economy encompasses politics, government, and governing, as well as the social and cultural constitution of markets, institutions, and actors (Clement, 2001: 406). For Clement, this intellectual pursuit is characterized by the attempt to uncover tensions and contradictions within society and use them as the bases for social change.

Arguably, the first Canadian sociologist to investigate Canada's political economy was Harold A. Innis in *The Fur Trade in Canada* (1970/1930) and *The Cod Fisheries* (1954/1940). In these works, Innis develops what has been termed the *staples thesis*, which contends that Canada's development was based on the exploitation of raw materials sent back to European countries to satisfy their industrial thirsts. Innis suggests that each staple (e.g., commercial: cod, fur, timber; industrial: pulp and paper, minerals) had its own characteristics that imposed a particular logic on its individual development (Clement, 2001: 407). As Canada grew and these economic developments continued, these raw materials were sent abroad, refined into more valuable commodities (e.g., furniture, automobiles), and returned to Canada at vastly inflated prices. Innis suggests that since Canada's economic position was subordinate to Britain and to the United States, Canadians were seen as "hewers of wood, drawers of water"—people who performed menial tasks. Certainly, the historical development of Canada's natural resources suggests that Canadian society has been, at least in part, defined by the realization that Canada is not one of the world's major economic or social forces. This underdog mentality was evident in the attempt by Canadian universities in the 1960s and 1970s to Canadianize our postsecondary education system.

THE CANADIANIZATION MOVEMENT

The development of Canadian anglophone sociology was influenced by American sociology as practised at the University of Chicago (see Brym & Saint-Pierre, 1997; Eichler, 2001; Hiller, 2001; Hiller & Di Luzio, 2001; Langlois, 2000; McKay, 1998).

Founded in 1892 by Albion Small, the department of sociology at the University of Chicago defined the American sociological tradition for much of the early twentieth century. The Chicago School of sociology was dominated by the symbolic-interactionist approach, focusing on social reform and collective social responsibility. The Chicago School's influence was most profound on early francophone sociology in Quebec, particularly at Canada's founding department of sociology, McGill. In fact, many influential sociologists in Canada trained at the University of Chicago (such as C. A. Dawson, Everett Hughes,

Harold Innis, A. C. McCrimmon, and Roderick D. McKenzie). The Chicago School was instrumental in defining Canadian sociology, but in the 1950s and 1960s, a movement to increase the number of Canadian faculty teaching at Canadian universities began.

During the late 1960s, Connors and Curtis (1970, cited in Hiller & Di Luzio, 2001: 494) found that more than 60 percent of sociologists in Canada had received their highest degree from a foreign institution. Even in 1971, Hedley and Warburton (1973: 305, cited in Hiller & Di Luzio, 2001: 494) found that in large Canadian sociology departments (those with more than twenty faculty members), more than 50 percent of instructors were American, 20 percent were from other countries, and 30 percent were Canadian. These findings were important as they emphasized the need to hire and train more Canadian sociologists if we ever hoped to investigate and understand Canadian society.

The discipline's Canadianization movement was also prompted by the explosion in the number of university enrolments in Canada beginning in the 1950s. In 1962–63, full-time university enrolment in Canada was 132 681, while only 10 years later (1972–73) it had more than doubled to 284 897. Ten years later (1982–83) the number had reached 640 000 (Hiller & Di Luzio, 2001: 491), and at the end of 1999, the number of full-time Canadian university enrolments hovered around 580 000 (Statistics Canada, 1999). Clearly, the need for Canadian-trained sociologists to teach students about Canadian society was a pressing one. This sentiment was clearly expressed when the Association of Universities and Colleges of Canada appointed a Commission on Canadian Studies in 1972, which resulted in The Symons Report (1975).

The report called on the Canadian academic community to increase its efforts to contribute to the knowledge of their own society. The reaction to this report came in an increase in the number of Canadian society courses taught by sociologists across the country, as well as in an increased focus on publishing sociological materials for Canadian sociology students. The assertion that these measures have worked has some support in the number of part- and full-time students who are undergraduate majors in sociology: the figure rose from 13 638 in 1982–83 to 21 028 in 1996–97 (Hiller & Di Luzio, 2001: 493). These students are making a sociological analysis of their own society, and they are also learning about the comparatively radical nature of Canadian sociology.

THE RADICAL NATURE OF CANADIAN SOCIOLOGY

Brym and Saint-Pierre (1997) suggest that one of the defining features of English-Canadian sociology is its radical nature, seen in its focus on the political economy and feminist ideas and perspectives. The important distinction these authors add, however, is how little of this radicalism is seen by the public (1997: 546). Certainly, Quebec sociologists are more focused on the policy ramifications of their endeavours, but Brym and Saint-Pierre recognize that many leading English-Canadian sociologists (such as Margrit Eichler, Graham Lowe, and Susan McDaniel) are mindful of the impact their ideas have on the larger society (1997: 546). Their investigations into the political economy were instrumental in showing that Canadian sociology was not afraid to uncover the hidden power structures that influence and guide society. Canadian feminist sociologists continue this tradition by looking at how gender acts as a locus of oppression and domination.

Margrit Eichler (2001) suggests that the simultaneous emergence of the Canadianization movement and the feminist movement led to a politics of knowledge that proved helpful to both groups. By expanding university departments by adding Canadian academics during the 1960s and 1970s, the feminist movement found a new voice on university campuses. In Eichler's paper

Women Pioneers in Canadian Sociology: The Effects of a Politics of Gender and a Politics of Knowledge (2001), she attempts to reverse the politics of erasure that she argues effectively allowed the historical contributions of female sociologists in Canada to be written out of the literature. Eichler undertakes the project by conducting interviews with ten of the leading female sociologists born before 1930. Through the interviews, Eichler utilizes a life-history approach, allowing the women to tell their own stories about being female sociologists during a period of rapid growth within the university system in general, and sociology departments in particular, as well as in a period when feminist issues first entered the sociological discourse.

One important finding from Eichler's investigation into these women's lives is the fact that they never had problems finding jobs in academe (2001: 393). The expanding university system, as well as the emerging recognition of feminist issues, allowed these women to begin full-time careers with little effort. Although they all faced sexism in some form during their careers, they were able to initiate significant institutional change by their mere presence on campus (e.g., pay equity measures, sexual harassment policies). Their ability to be a critical social presence within the academic community was an important factor in advancing feminist issues on university campuses and in the larger society as the feminist movement gained momentum in Canada.

That impetus led to the establishment of the Royal Commission on the Status of Women in 1967 to "inquire into and report upon the status of women in Canada, and to recommend what steps might be taken by the Federal Government to ensure for women equal opportunities with men in all aspects of Canadian society" (Cross, 2000). The final report was released in 1970 with 167 recommendations and "became the blueprint for mainstream feminist activism" (Womenspace, 2002). The feminist movement inspired women to reflect differently on their social surroundings and reinforced the need to question social convention.

The influence on early female sociology pioneers was equally important, as it encouraged them to critique their own intellectual foundations generally and sociology specifically. As Dorothy Smith notes about this time, "Because we were free to take up issues for women, we didn't feel committed to reproducing the discipline, . . . it had the effect . . . of really liberating the discipline in general in Canada, so that you now have an orientation where people feel absolutely comfortable in raising current issues, in addressing what's going on in Canada" (cited in Eichler, 2001: 394). The Royal Commission report opened the debate on women's positions in Canadian society and resulted in the formation of the women's caucus at the Canadian Sociology and Anthropology Association, which still exists today. The feminist movement, and sociology's role within it, is just one example of Canadian sociology's critical foundation and how Canada continues to influence the discipline today.

CONCLUSION

Canadian sociology is defined by its geography, focus on the political economy, the Canadianization movement, and its radical approach to social issues. This brief review should give you some appreciation for the flavour of Canadian sociology and how it represents a unique approach to the discipline and to our understanding of what it means to be Canadian.

CRITICAL THINKING QUESTIONS

1. Do you believe that social forces influence how academics in a given country see the world? Support your answer.

2. Provide examples of how Canadian winters influence the way Canadians think about themselves. Can similar examples be found for how Canadian summers influence our national identity?

3. In your opinion, was the Canadianization movement at universities and colleges necessary? Why or why not?

NOTES

1. The University of Chicago established the first American department of sociology in 1892 and McGill University established the first Canadian one in 1924.

2. The American postsecondary system serves more than 14 800 000 students and the Canadian system around 827 000 (NCES, 2002; Statistics Canada, 1999). In 1999 more than 2400 departments of sociology existed in the United States (ASA, 2002). Canada had around 45 university departments of sociology—including joint sociology/anthropology departments—(McMaster, 2002) and approximately 150 colleges, the majority of which offered at least introductory sociology (ACCC, 2002).

REFERENCES

ACCC (Association of Canadian Community Colleges). 2002. Membership list. [Online]: Available: **http://www.accc.ca/english/colleges/membership_list.cfm.** Accessed October 27, 2002.

ASA (American Sociological Association). 2002. Departmental listings for 1999. [Online]. Available: **http://www.asanet.org/pubs/dod.html.** Accessed October 27, 2002.

Brym, R., and C. Saint-Pierre. 1997. Canadian sociology. *Contemporary Sociology*, 26(5): 543–46.

Clement, W. 2001. Canadian political economy's legacy for sociology. *Canadian Journal of Sociology*, 26(3): 405–20.

Connor, D. M., and E. Curtis. 1970. *Sociology and anthropology in Canada: Some characteristics of the disciplines and their current university programs.* Montreal: Canadian Sociology and Anthropology Association.

Countries of the World. 2002. Country statistics at a glance. [Online]. Available: **http://www.infoplease.com/ipa/A0762380.html.** Accessed July 17, 2002.

Cross, P. 2000. *Report of the Royal Commission on the Status of Women: Where are we after thirty years?* [Online]. Available: **http://www.owjn.org/issues/equality/thirty.htm.** Accessed January 31, 2003.

Eichler, M. 2001. Women pioneers in Canadian sociology: The effects of a politics of gender and a politics of knowledge. *Canadian Journal of Sociology*, 26(3): 375–403.

Hedley, R. A., and R. T. Warburton. 1973. The role of national courses in the teaching and development of sociology: The Canadian case. *Sociological Review*, 21(2): 299–319.

Hiller, H. H. 2001. Legacy for a new millennium: Canadian sociology in the twentieth century as seen through its publications. *Canadian Journal of Sociology*, 26(3): 257–63.

Hiller, H. H., and L. Di Luzio. 2001. Text and context: Another "chapter" in the evolution of sociology in Canada. *Canadian Journal of Sociology*, 26(3): 487–512.

Innis, H. A. 1954. *The cod fisheries: The history of an international economy.* University of Toronto Press (original work published 1940).

———. 1970. *The fur trade in Canada.* Toronto: University of Toronto Press (original work published 1930).

Langlois, S. 2000. A productive decade in the tradition of Canadian sociology. *Canadian Journal of Sociology,* 25(3): 391–97.

McKay, I. 1998. Changing the subject(s) of the "History of Canadian sociology": The case of Colin McKay and Spencerian Marxism, 1890–1940. *Canadian Journal of Sociology,* 23(4): 389–426.

McMaster University. 2002. Sociology institutions—departments. [Online]. Available: **http://www.mcmaster. ca/socscidocs/w3virtsoclib/cansoc.htm.** Retrieved October 27, 2002.

NCES (National Center for Education Statistics). 2002. Digest of education statistics, 2001—Chapter 3: Postsecondary education. [Online]. Available: **http://nces.ed. gov//pubs2002/digest2001/ch3.asp#1.** Accessed January 31, 2003.

Southcott, C. 1999. The study of regional inequality in Quebec and English Canada: A comparative analysis of perspectives. *Canadian Journal of Sociology,* 24(4): 457–84.

Statistics Canada. 1999. University enrolment, full-time and part-time, by sex. [Online]. Available: **http://www. statcan.ca/english/Pgdb/educ03a.htm.** Accessed October 27, 2002.

Womenspace. 2002. *Since the Royal Commission on the Status of Women.* [Online]. Available: **http://herstory. womenspace.ca/RCSW.html.** Retrieved October 23.

7

Arab Women in the Field

SORAYA ALTORKI

Sociological
Research

CLASSIC

CONTEMPORARY

CROSS-CULTURAL

Social scientists often rely on ethnography—the study of people using observation or interviews—to provide detailed descriptions of groups, organizations, and communities. Such fieldwork, like other data collection methods, has both strengths and limitations. As Soraya Altorki shows, a major advantage of studying one's own culture includes a familiarity with the people and the environment. The researcher also encounters a number of problems. One of Altorki's challenges, for example, involved resocializing herself into her culture, having been abroad for a number of years. She also had to overcome the informants' reluctance to address sensitive questions about their religious practices and family life to an "outsider."

AT HOME IN THE FIELD

Having been socialized many years in Egypt and identifying with its people, I had regarded it, on one level, to be my home. On another level, however, I had been brought up in a Saudi Arabian family committed in great measure to that country's cultural heritage and the observance of its cultural norms, even while selectively observing certain Egyptian values and practices. Throughout my college days, I had been reminded that I could not do what my Egyptian girlfriends could do, because "our" traditions were different and for "us" such behavior was unacceptable.

Besides, it was not only the constraining elements of Saudi Arabian culture that molded my

growing-up experiences in Egypt, but also the rich rewards that I reaped from kinship support and shared cultural knowledge. These provided for me the security of a closure that was not attainable in Egypt. Thus, Saudi Arabia was home for me on a more fundamental level.

Arriving in Jiddah [Saudi Arabia], my native city, I knew I wanted to study urban life. Although the entire northern portion of the Arabian Peninsula was virtually unknown to social scientists, yet early travelers and even scholars avoided its study in favor of the nomad and the camel. Barring Hürgrouje and Burton, almost nothing was known about urban life. In retrospect, I believe that my choice to focus on urban society was partly a reaction to the stereotypical view of Saudi Arabia as a society of nomads and oil wells.

There were also social constraints to my choice. I knew that, as an unmarried woman, I could neither travel alone in the country nor

Source: "At Home in the Field," by Soraya Altorki, in *Arab Women in the Field: Studying Your Own Society,* eds. Soraya Altorki and Camillia Fawzi El-Solh, pp. 51–59. New York: Syracuse University Press, 1998. Reprinted by permission.

wander around with the nomads. Living alone, anywhere in the country, was out of the question. Thus, for many considerations, an urban-based study seemed most appropriate, and the city of Jiddah the most convenient.

The realities of being an unmarried woman in many ways dictated my field of research, although it did not determine my choice of research topic within that field (Altorki, 1986). This essentially meant that I could work with women and that I had limited access to men. Within these bounds, my choice was absolutely free. . . .

INSIDER/OUTSIDER

Being literally at home in Jiddah, I was spared having to worry about the problems of settling in that most anthropologists face when entering the field. Furthermore, I needed no research permit (or if I did, I never bothered to find out) and no letters of guarantee. Neither was I required to make commitments to local authorities and research institutes concerning the conduct of my work and the use and distribution of my data.

The people I studied saw me as one of themselves. Some of them had ties of kinship and friendship to my family. Others knew my family members by name. This state of affairs provided me with significant advantages. Others, working in their own society, have observed similar benefits in knowing the culture and consequently being able to select their research agenda in consonance with what is most expedient for the research task and what is most feasible within the limits of what will be allowed by the subjects under investigation (see Stephenson and Greer 1981:126).

However, some facets of my life concerned my informants. Why, for example, was I not a married woman with children, like all my peers? And why was I still living abroad rather than residing in Jiddah, awaiting marriage? My unmarried status at the age of twenty-two made me somewhat of an anomaly. More distressing to the

older women among whom I worked was the conclusion that I was more interested in following my studies than in settling down to married life. Although the role of an educated woman had come to be accepted by the community at large and the elite in particular, the problem was in the priorities this role took over what was perceived to be the more important aspect of gender role, namely the status that marriage and motherhood bring. According to both men and women, it is these dimensions of womanhood that are primary. In fact, given the segregation of Saudi Arabian women from men, and their isolation from public life, marriage and motherhood become a woman's avenues to maturity, security, and greater prestige. Being a member of the society, I anticipated this and was well prepared to deal with its consequences.

Although women come of age with marriage, and prestige for them is attained by motherhood, my status within the community had to rest on other things: It relied greatly on my education. Lacking husband and child, I predicated my adulthood on education and depended on the community's acceptance of it as a legitimate goal for women to attain. Men and women alike respected this, although never failing to remind me of the fundamentals of my role as a woman. As one older woman put it to me: "Education is good, but women are weak. No matter how much money they have, no matter their education, they cannot manage without men. May Allah save your father and your brother. But you have to start your own family." That statement accurately reflects the dependence of women on men, a dependence that also correlates with their segregation in Saudi Arabian society. But my role as a Saudi Arabian woman, educated abroad, permitted me more flexibility and autonomy. For one thing, my interaction with men who were not my relatives was tolerated.

My long absence abroad was an additional factor leading to more mobility. While abroad, I had been immersed in a different way of life, and hence women and men alike did not expect me to conform totally to the cultural norms governing the relationship of men and women in Saudi Arabian society. My absence had a complex effect on my reentry into my own community. On the one hand, it allowed more maneuverability in my role as an unmarried woman, and, on the other hand, it made conformity especially expedient in strengthening my ties to my informants.

Repeatedly, men and women expressed their surprise and approval when my behavior showed conformity to Saudi Arabian culture. They were, for example, delighted that my many years in Egypt had not changed my accent to Egyptian. Whenever I showed observance of norms that young people my age had begun to modify, members of the older generation were astonished and particularly delighted. Those of the younger generation, however, saw such conformity as awkward and continued to remind me that times had changed: "Nobody is observing such things these days."

For example, norms of deference to older siblings necessitate that they be addressed in specific terms. To an older brother and kinsmen his age the term is *sidi*, which means "my master." My use of these terms of address was welcomed by all, barring girls of my age who by then were seeking to substitute as equivalent for the term *sidi* those of *akhuya* (my brother) and the sobriquet *abu flan* (father of). In doing this, I took my cues from young men who had obtained their college education abroad, sometimes through graduate school, and who continued to use traditional terms of reference in addressing older female siblings and other kinswomen in their age group.

It was in the same spirit that I observed some norms of modesty, particularly those related to veiling. Such practices were changing at the time of my fieldwork, so that the families I studied showed the whole spectrum of veiling practices, from those who had considerably modified its use to leave the face bare, to those who still observed the traditional practice of covering the face as well. While visiting the homes of the latter, I made sure to conform and to cover my face

carefully. This gesture of respect did not go unnoticed: Women and men alike commented that my many years abroad had not made me behave like a "foreigner."

The years abroad had been spent as a student, and now I had come back as a researcher with the intention of recording a way of life that had not previously been studied. Everyone understood that role. Female education was not a novelty. Girls were sent to *faqihas* (informal traditional schools) as far back as older informants could remember; and formal girls' schools were opened by the government in 1960. By the time I went to the field, the first women's university had already opened in Jiddah. College education was thoroughly acceptable for women; indeed, it had become greatly valued.

Thus, I had no problem in defining part of my role to the subjects of my research. I wanted to study social life, family organization, rituals, beliefs, and customs, and to document how these have changed for the younger people in the study. In another way, my role was more ascribed. My return to Jiddah meant taking my place in a family and getting involved in the various ramifications of family life. It also meant belonging to a class with the task of conforming to the behavior of that class. I was aware that I could in fact not conform to that behavior, but I had little choice with regard to involvement in family life.

The ascribed aspects of my role, i.e., gender, age, and kinship, were more fundamental in people's perception of me, which may be unavoidable in doing research among one's own people. My education was important in allowing me to explore areas of social life (e.g., more access to the world of men) that other women could not undertake. Despite my research objective, known and accepted to all the families, I remained primarily a Saudi Arabian woman. As such, I was known to some as the daughter or a sister of a friend, while to others as a member of a lineage they knew from other mutual friends. These considerations were always present in my interaction with others. While criteria centering on the individual are not without relevance in structuring relations, the world of these elite families was in the first instance structured by consanguineous and marital ties, and in the second place by friendship and business networks.

Within this world an individual—whether man or woman—is deeply embedded in the *'aila* (family). One's status is, to a considerable degree, ascribed by the status of the *'aila*. Individual achievement is an avenue to mobility, but clearly it is the achievement of men and not of women that is associated with family prestige. Recent changes in the wider society have introduced more emphasis on individuality and an increase of distance from the *'aila*. This is evidenced in neolocal residence patterns, more individual involvement in marriage choice, relative reduction of parental authority, independent career choices for men, and less observance of traditional obligations to kinsmen (Altorki, 1986).

On the whole, I experienced no problems in establishing rapport—that quality in the relationship between the ethnographer and the host community that the introductions to ethnographic monographs rarely fail to mention, but which probably involves the most enigmatic aspect of our methodological trademark: participant observation. I spoke the language, and the trademark itself had no special meaning for me, although, as I will explain, it had very special implications in my case.

In short, I found practical advantages in my particular field situation: Unencumbered by bureaucratic impediments, comfortably set up in my family's home, fluent in the vernacular, and personally known in some of the households I was to study, I could begin my research under very auspicious circumstances—or so it seemed until I realized the implications of being an indigenous anthropologist. I discovered that almost every one of the advantages had its negative side.

In a very real sense, my fieldwork experience was a process of resocialization into my own society. Although I was raised in a Saudi Arabian family, my long years of residence abroad had established considerable distance between me and my society. The advantages were that much of the culture was not so familiar that it could easily escape my notice. This problem in the collection of data has been observed by other ethnographers working under similar conditions (cf. Spradley and McCurdy, 1972; Ablon, 1977; Stephenson and Greer, 1981), but it is one that can be overcome by rigorous training. The researcher can counteract familiarity by close observation, meticulous recording of ethnographic scenes, and detailed probing to uncover the "taken-for-granted" world he or she may share with members of the community being studied.

Living at home meant that I had to assume the role expected of a family member in my position within the household group. The ordinary field situation reversed itself in my case. I became what may best be described as an observant participant. My primary duty was to participate. To observe became an incidental privilege.

My status did not afford me immunity from observing all the taboos and attending to all the obligations my culture prescribed for me—an immunity usually granted to foreign anthropologists. I had to accept severe restrictions on my movements and on my interaction with other people. For example, I had no freedom to move in public on my own, and challenging any norms of conduct would have jeopardized my relationships with the families I had decided to study. Had I not conformed, I would have risked ostracism and termination of my research. Persistently, if slowly, I achieved a precarious balance of roles that allowed me mobility and freedom to do my research as well as to be accepted and taken seriously. I became a conscious witness to my own resocialization as an Arab woman in my society and thus learned and comprehended many aspects of this role in the best possible manner.

This, perhaps, is one of the hidden advantages of being an insider. For example, veiling norms can be observed and described by an outsider, and one can also learn about the meaning of veiling by soliciting relevant information from informants. Yet the participant charged with the task of abiding by the norms experiences the constraints, to be sure, but also the rewards of these norms on a more basic level. In that sense, my re-socialization generated data on an experiential level different from that to which an outsider could bear witness. This point has also been observed as a merit of indigenous research elsewhere. Aguilar, for example, summarizing the pros and cons of this kind of research, mentions that its advocates insist "that the covert culture of the insider has the heuristic value of lending psychological reality (or cultural reality) to ethnographic analyses" (1981:16).

My status affected my research in another way. Restricted possibilities for movement outside the house and pervasive segregation of men and women in public confined the research predominantly to the world of women. These realities affected the choice of topic for investigation. I could not study market or political relations, for example. Neither could I investigate any other subject in which men, rather than women, are the dominant actors. Family organization seemed the most accessible for a female researcher, and elites became my focus. Within that, my emphasis was on how ideology and practice affect and are influenced by one another. But, as noted elsewhere, elites are the least accessible to inquiry, especially through the technique of prolonged participant observation. The families I elected to study formed closed groups, and although the observation of and participation in their daily lives was possible for me as a member of the group, even I could gain their confidence only through patient approaches along the lines of friendship.

Although generous hospitality is highly valued behavior, there remain degrees of formality that the families must always maintain vis-à-vis the whole community. Only with considerable caution can a nonmember see their lives as they live them, as opposed to how they want the rest of the community to perceive them. For example, it takes a long time, coupled with intensive interaction, before people allow a friend to move within

their home free of the facade of formality exhibited to outsiders. Indeed, it took between six and eight months before I could develop the friendships that made close observation of their daily lives possible to the degree that my presence was more or less ignored. Being an insider has even more serious consequences for research. Information may be withheld when it relates to behavior that must be concealed from public knowledge. If one is outside the system, one's awareness of goings-on may not be problematical. But as a participant, the researcher constitutes a threat of exposure and judgment. Lewis (1973:588) explains this situation very well:

> There is a growing fear that the information collected by an outsider, someone not constrained by group values and interests, will expose the group to outside manipulation and control. . . . The insider, on the other hand, is accountable; s/he must remain in the community and take responsibility for her/his actions. Thus, s/he is forced through self-interest to exercise discretion.

This was one of the hardest areas to overcome in doing research among one's own people. For example, family solidarity and cohesion are greatly valued. Verbally, men and women endorse the ideal of love and support between siblings; respect and obedience in filial relations; and honoring family duties of financial support to the needy and maintenance of elderly parents. In practice, the older generations approximated many of these ideals (Altorki, 1986).

But family conflict does occur, and younger generation members have begun to modify family obligations in general. Differences over inheritance constitute the most serious threat to family solidarity—a threat that mounts as the stakes become higher and people's wealth increases. The ideal remains that such differences must be kept out of the public eye and should be reconciled between family members without recourse to the courts. So important is this family ideal that information about conflict, especially that considered to be serious, was at first not revealed to me. I learned about such conflicts indirectly from domestic servants working in these homes who, by coincidence, happened to be related to women working in my family's household. On other occasions, I obtained relevant information from women with whom I had established such strong ties of friendship that we had come to be considered "sisters." This family idiom symbolized our enclosure in the same kinship group and, by implication, showed our interest in protecting that group and shielding it from public criticism.

On one point, my learning about family conflicts was fortuitous. Is it conceivable that I would have returned from the field with the belief that the ideal of family solidarity was the reality? By being an insider, and from my own kinship network, I "experienced" the fact that reality was different and that disagreement can escalate to conflicts between family members. The problem, however, was in collecting data about conflict from the other families to uncover patterns in its expression and management. What, for example, were the patterns for the expression of intrafamily conflict? How was it managed, and what are the patterns for its resolution?

In this respect, my status as an insider prevented people from divulging such information for fear of having it exposed to the wider community. Obviously, disseminating information about intrafamilial conflict to the community also implies that the disseminator, i.e., the indigenous anthropologist, has judged it negatively and is now taking an active role in censoring the behavior it bespeaks. While the question of exposure to the public can be bridged by trust and confidence in the researcher, the threat of judgment is harder to overcome. Being a participating family member implies, of course, subscribing to the cultural norms and values of the group and to the sanctions that follow a breach of valued behavior.

These considerations are different for a foreign anthropologist. As an outsider investigating family organization and interfamilial conflict, she or he must gain the confidence of the people and be trusted not to expose family differences to the community. But outsider status does not imply shared cultural knowledge, and thus protects the outsider from applying the same moral judgments. The non-indigenous researcher is outside the system, and for this very reason people may not conceal family differences to the same degree as they would from a member of their own group. In collecting relevant data, the indigenous researcher is twice bound and must be able to overcome barriers to confidence and to potential value judgment.

Other social scientists have made similar observations. Aguilar, for example, highlights the constraints indigenous status may place on access to data (1981:21), although, as he points out, other anthropologists claim the opposite (1981:18). However, the Saudi Arabian case indicates that while confidence can be established, a morally neutral judgment is harder to demonstrate. An effective strategy is to be drawn into the same closure that allows sharing of such delicate information. In my case, the idiom of kinship and the ties of close friendships provided such a closure.

My general familiarity with these families had another irksome drawback. My informants presumed that I knew my own culture, and for a long time they either misinterpreted my questions as implying an unbecoming skepticism or failed to appreciate that I truly did not know what I had asked them to explain. This was especially true for knowledge of religious beliefs and rituals, which for me was a difficult area to explore. Such knowledge is essential to an adult Muslim, and any queries about it reveal a lapse in religious duties. Fed up with my questions, an older woman put it to me this way: "Are you not ashamed that you do not know how to pray at your age? What then did they teach you abroad?"

This revealed to me the cultural givens of the community and the cultural repertoire indispensable to membership in it. The best research strategy to circumvent this role was to openly admit my ignorance and to blame it all on my long absence abroad. Women and men patiently explained matters to me in a desire to resocialize me as a Muslim Arab woman. In fact, it was especially pleasing to the older women, often illiterate, to instruct me despite my higher formal education.

These considerations have been well described by Stephenson and Greer. They note that while familiarity with the culture under study can be a bonus, prior knowledge of the people studied provides no guaranteed advantage. The expectations people may have of the investigator could make it more difficult for her or him to break out of fixed patterns and thus serve to restrict the work at hand (1981:129). The role that the community attributes to the researcher may inhibit other relationships and bias the researcher's thoughts. Moreover, the role ascribed by kinship to the indigenous anthropologist may forcefully draw that person into factionalism within the community and thereby limit the work that can be accomplished. Sometimes, such problems can be circumvented by conscious strategy. As Stephenson and Greer observe, "the researcher can mitigate the effects of already established roles by emphasizing some over others" (1981:127).

CRITICAL THINKING QUESTIONS

1. How did Altorki's sex and background influence her decisions about where and how to conduct her research on Arab society?

2. Field researchers must often balance the advantages and disadvantages of playing "insider" and "outsider" roles. How did being an insider both benefit and limit Altorki's research? What barriers did she have to overcome?

3. What strengths and weaknesses did Altorki encounter as an outsider? Is it possible for researchers who are outsiders to offer information and valid insights about the societies they study? Explain your answer.

REFERENCES

Ablon, J. 1977. Field methods in working with middle class Americans: New issues of values, personality and reciprocity. *Human Organization*, 36(1): 69–72.

Aguilar, J. 1981. Insider research: An ethnography of a debate. In *Anthropologists at home in North America: Methods and issues in the study of one's own society*, ed. D. A. Messerschmidt. Cambridge: Cambridge University Press.

Altorki, S. 1986. *Women in Saudi Arabia: Ideology and behavior among the elite.* New York: Columbia University Press.

Lewis, D. 1973. Anthropology and colonialism. *Current Anthropology*, 14(12): 581–602.

Spradley, J. P., and D. W. McCurdy. 1972. *The cultural experience.* Chicago: Science Research Association.

Stephenson, J. B., and L. S. Greer. 1981. Ethnographers in their own cultures: Two Appalachian cases. *Human Organization*, 40(2): 123–30.

8

Symbol: The Basic Element of Culture

LESLIE A. WHITE

Leslie A. White, a noted anthropologist, argues in this selection that the key to human existence is the ability to use symbols. While all animals are capable of complex behaviour, only humanity depends on symbolic activity. This is the special power that underlies our autonomy as the only creatures who live according to meanings we set for ourselves. Thus symbols convert our animal species into humanity, in the process transforming social behaviour into true civilization.

All human behavior originates in the use of symbols. It was the symbol which transformed our anthropoid ancestors into men and made them human. All civilizations have been generated, and are perpetuated, only by the use of symbols. It is the symbol which transforms an infant of *Homo sapiens* into a human being; deaf mutes who grow up without the use of symbols are not human beings. All human behavior consists of, or is dependent upon, the use of symbols. Human behavior is symbolic behavior; symbolic

behavior is human behavior. The symbol is the universe of humanity. . . .

That there are numerous and impressive similarities between the behavior of man and that of ape is fairly obvious; it is quite possible that chimpanzees and gorillas in zoos have noted and appreciated them. Fairly apparent, too, are man's behavioral similarities to many other kinds of animals. Almost as obvious, but not easy to define, is a difference in behavior which distinguishes man from all other living creatures. I say "obvious" because it is quite apparent to the common man that the nonhuman animals with which he is familiar do not and cannot enter, and participate in, the world in which he, as a human being, lives. It is impossible for a

Source: From "The Symbol: The Origin and the Basis of Human Behavior," in *The Science of Culture: A Study of Man and Civilization* by Leslie White. Copyright © 1949 by Leslie White. Copyright renewed by Crocker National Bank. Reprinted by permission of Farrar, Straus & Giroux, Inc.

dog, horse, bird, or even an ape, to have any understanding of the meaning of the sign of the cross to a Christian, or of the fact that black (white among the Chinese) is the color of mourning. No chimpanzee or laboratory rat can appreciate the difference between Holy water and distilled water, or grasp the meaning of *Tuesday*, *3*, or *sin*. No animal save man can distinguish a cousin from an uncle, or a cross cousin from a parallel cousin. Only man can commit the crime of incest or adultery; only he can remember the Sabbath and keep it Holy. It is not, as we well know, that the lower animals can do these things but to a lesser degree than ourselves; they cannot perform these acts of appreciation and distinction at all. It is, as Descartes said long ago, "not only that the brutes have less Reason than man, but that they have none at all." . . .

A symbol may be defined as a thing the value or meaning of which is bestowed upon it by those who use it. I say "thing" because a symbol may have any kind of physical form; it may have the form of a material object, a color, a sound, an odor, a motion of an object, a taste.

The meaning, or value, of a symbol is in no instance derived from or determined by properties intrinsic in its physical form: The color appropriate to mourning may be yellow, green, or any other color; purple need not be the color of royalty; among the Manchu rulers of China it was yellow. . . . The meaning of symbols is derived from and determined by the organisms who use them; meaning is bestowed by human organisms upon physical things or events which thereupon become symbols. Symbols "have their signification," to use John Locke's phrase, "from the arbitrary imposition of men."

All symbols must have a physical form; otherwise they could not enter our experience. . . . But the meaning of a symbol cannot be discovered by mere sensory examination of its physical form. One cannot tell by looking at an *x* in an algebraic equation what it stands for; one cannot ascertain with the ears alone the symbolic value of the phonetic compound *si*; one cannot tell merely by

weighing a pig how much gold he will exchange for; one cannot tell from the wavelength of a color whether it stands for courage or cowardice, "stop" or "go"; nor can one discover the spirit in a fetish by any amount of physical or chemical examination. The meaning of a symbol can be grasped only by nonsensory, symbolic means. . . .

Thus Darwin says: "That which distinguishes man from the lower animals is not the understanding of articulate sounds, for as everyone knows, dogs understand many words and sentences."[1] . . .

The man differs from the dog—and all other creatures—in that *he can and does play an active role in determining what value the vocal stimulus is to have, and the dog cannot*. The dog does not and cannot play an active part in determining the value of the vocal stimulus. Whether he is to roll over or go fetch at a given stimulus, or whether the stimulus for roll over be one combination of sounds or another is a matter in which the dog has nothing whatever to "say." He plays a purely passive role and can do nothing else. He learns the meaning of a vocal command just as his salivary glands may learn to respond to the sound of a bell. But man plays an active role and thus becomes a creator: Let *x* equal three pounds of coal and it does equal three pounds of coal; let removal of the hat in a house of worship indicate respect and it becomes so. This creative faculty, that of freely, actively, and arbitrarily bestowing value upon things, is one of the most commonplace as well as *the* most important characteristic of man. Children employ it freely in their play: "Let's pretend that this rock is a wolf." . . .

All culture (civilization) depends upon the symbol. It was the exercise of the symbolic faculty that brought culture into existence, and it is the use of symbols that makes the perpetuation of culture possible. Without the symbol there would be no culture, and man would be merely an animal, not a human being.

Articulate speech is the most important form of symbolic expression. Remove speech from culture and what would remain? Let us see.

Without articulate speech we would have no *human* social organization. Families we might have, but this form of organization is not peculiar to man; it is not, *per se*, human. But we would have no prohibitions of incest, no rules prescribing exogamy and endogamy, polygamy, monogamy. How could marriage with a cross cousin be prescribed, marriage with a parallel cousin proscribed, without articulate speech? How could rules which prohibit plural mates possessed simultaneously, but permit them if possessed one at a time, exist without speech?

Without speech we would have no political, economic, ecclesiastic, or military organization; no codes of etiquette or ethics; no laws; no science, theology, or literature; no games or music, except on an ape level. Rituals and ceremonial paraphernalia would be meaningless without articulate speech. Indeed, without articulate speech we would be all but toolless: We would have only the occasional and insignificant use of the tool such as we find today among the higher apes, for it was articulate speech that transformed the nonprogressive tool-using of the ape into the progressive, cumulative tool-using of man, the human being.

In short, without symbolic communication in some form, we would have no culture. "In the Word was the beginning" of culture—and its perpetuation also.

To be sure, with all his culture man is still an animal and strives for the same ends that all other living creatures strive for: the preservation of the individual and the perpetuation of the [species]. In concrete terms these ends are food, shelter from the elements, defense from enemies, health, and offspring. The fact that man strives for these ends just as all other animals do has, no doubt, led many to declare that there is "no fundamental difference between the behavior of man and of other creatures." But man does differ, not in *ends* but in *means*. Man's means are cultural means: Culture is simply the human animal's way of living. And, since these means, culture, are dependent upon a faculty possessed by man alone, the ability to use symbols, the difference between the behavior of man and of all other creatures is not merely great, but basic and fundamental.

The behavior of man is of two distinct kinds: symbolic and nonsymbolic. Man yawns, stretches, coughs, scratches himself, cries out in pain, shrinks with fear, "bristles" with anger, and so on. Nonsymbolic behavior of this sort is not peculiar to man; he shares it not only with the other primates but with many other animal species as well. But man communicates with his fellows with articulate speech, uses amulets, confesses sins, makes laws, observes codes of etiquette, explains his dreams, classifies his relatives in designated categories, and so on. This kind of behavior is unique; only man is capable of it; it is peculiar to man because it consists of, or is dependent upon, the use of symbols. The nonsymbolic behavior of *Homo sapiens* is the behavior of man the animal; the symbolic behavior is that of man the human being. It is the symbol which has transformed man from a mere animal to a human animal. . . .

The infant of the species *Homo sapiens* becomes human only when and as he exercises his symbol faculty. Only through articulate speech—not necessarily vocal—can he enter the world of human beings and take part in their affairs. The questions asked earlier may be repeated now. How could a growing child know and appreciate such things as social organization, ethics, etiquette, ritual, science, religion, art, and games without symbolic communication? The answer is of course that he could know nothing of these things and have no appreciation of them at all. . . .

Children who have been cut off from human intercourse for years by blindness and deafness but who have eventually effected communication with their fellows on a symbolic level are exceedingly illuminating. The case of Helen Keller is exceptionally instructive. . . .

Helen Keller was rendered blind and deaf at an early age by illness. She grew up as a child without symbolic contact with anyone. Descriptions of her at the age of seven, the time at which her teacher, Miss Sullivan, came to her home, disclosed no *human* attributes of Helen's behavior at all. She was a headstrong, undisciplined, and unruly little animal.

Within a day or so after her arrival at the Keller home, Miss Sullivan taught Helen her first word, spelling it into her hand. But this word was merely a sign, not a symbol. A week later Helen knew several words but, as Miss Sullivan reports, she had "no idea how to use them or that everything has a name." Within three weeks Helen knew eighteen nouns and three verbs. But she was still on the level of signs; she still had no notion "that everything has a name."

Helen confused the word signs for "mug" and "water" because, apparently, both were associated with drinking. Miss Sullivan made a few attempts to clear up this confusion but without success. One morning, however, about a month after Miss Sullivan's arrival, the two went out to the pump in the garden. What happened then is best told in their own words:

I made Helen hold her mug under the spout while I pumped. As the cold water gushed forth, filling the mug, I spelled "w-a-t-e-r" into Helen's free hand. The word coming so close upon the sensation of cold water rushing over her hand seemed to startle her. She dropped the mug and stood as one transfixed. A new light came into her face. She spelled "water" several times. Then she dropped on the ground and asked for its name and pointed to the pump and the trellis, and suddenly turning round she asked for my name. . . . *In a few hours she had added thirty new words to her vocabulary.*

But these words were now more than mere signs as they are to a dog and as they had been to Helen up to then. They were *symbols*. Helen had at last grasped and turned the key that admitted her for the first time to a new universe: the world of human beings. Helen describes this marvelous experience herself:

We walked down the path to the well-house, attracted by the fragrance of the honeysuckle with which it was covered. Someone was drawing water and my teacher placed my hand under the spout. As the cool stream gushed over one hand she spelled into the other the word *water*, first slowly, then rapidly. I stood still, my whole attention fixed upon the motion of her fingers.

Suddenly I felt a misty consciousness as of something forgotten—a thrill of returning thought; and *somehow the mystery of language was revealed to me*. I knew then that "w-a-t-e-r" meant the wonderful cool something that was flowing over my hand. That living word awakened my soul, gave it light, hope, joy, set it free!

Helen was transformed on the instant by this experience. Miss Sullivan had managed to touch Helen's symbol mechanism and set it in motion. Helen, on her part, grasped the external world with this mechanism that had lain dormant and inert all these years, sealed in dark and silent isolation by eyes that could not see and ears that heard not. But now she had crossed the boundary and entered a new land. Henceforth the progress would be rapid.

"I left the well-house," Helen reports, "eager to learn. Everything had a name, and each name gave birth to a new thought. As we returned to the house every object which I touched seemed to quiver with life. That was because I saw everything with the strange new sight that had come to me."

Helen became humanized rapidly. "I see an improvement in Helen from day to day," Miss Sullivan wrote in her diary, "*almost from hour to hour*. Everything must have a name now. . . . She drops the signs and pantomime she used before as soon as she has words to supply their place. . . . We notice her face grows more expressive each day. . . ."

A more eloquent and convincing account of the significance of symbols and of the great gulf between the human mind and that of minds without symbols could hardly be imagined.

The natural processes of biologic evolution brought into existence in man, and man alone, a new and distinctive ability; the ability to use symbols. The most important form of symbolic expression is articulate speech. Articulate speech means communication of ideas; communication means preservation—tradition—and preservation means accumulation and progress. The emergence of the faculty of symboling has resulted in the genesis of a new order of phenomena: an extrasomatic, cultural order. All civilizations are born of, and are perpetuated by, the use of symbols. A culture, or civilization, is but a particular kind of form which the biologic, life-perpetuating activities of a particular animal, man, assume.

Human behavior is symbolic behavior; if it is not symbolic, it is not human. The infant of the genus *Homo* becomes a human being only as he is introduced into and participates in that order of phenomena which is culture. And the key to this world and the means of participation in it is—the symbol.

CRITICAL THINKING QUESTIONS

1. Why does White argue that a deaf mute unable to communicate symbolically is not fully human? What opposing argument might be made? What position would White take in the pro-choice versus pro-life abortion controversy?

2. Because the reality we experience is based on a particular system of symbols, how do we tend to view members of other cultures? What special efforts are needed to overcome the tendency to treat people of different cultures as less worthy than we are?

3. How did gaining the capacity to use symbols transform Helen Keller? How did this ability alter her capacity for further learning?

NOTE

1. Charles Darwin, *The Descent of Man*, chap. 3.

9

Investigating Canadian and American Value Differences Through an Analysis of Media Portrayals of Native Issues

BRUCE RAVELLI

Culture

CLASSIC

CONTEMPORARY

CROSS-CULTURAL

In this article, Bruce Ravelli tests Seymour Martin Lipset's predictions about the differences between Canadian and American values by analyzing each country's print media presentations of Native issues. The analysis fails to find support for many of Lipset's arguments but does reveal some interesting differences between media portrayals.

CULTURE

One of sociology's defining interests is the study of the relationship between the individual and society (Brym with Fox, 1989: 4). A critical component of this investigation is the attempt to understand the role culture plays in defining people's perception of their social environment.

The first section of this article reviews the defining characteristics of culture and many of the concepts that sociologists use to analyze and study it. The second section investigates Canadian and American cultural values, to determine whether they are different. The purpose of this article then is twofold: the first is to acquaint you with the sociological analyses of culture, and the

second is to compare and contrast Canadian and American cultures in the hope of helping you appreciate what it means to be Canadian.

DEFINING ELEMENTS OF CANADIAN CULTURE

Before we begin our analysis, it is important to define what sociologists mean when they refer to a society's *culture* and *values*.[1] *Culture* is defined as a broad spectrum of beliefs, values, and material objects that help people define their way of life. For example, Canadians' appreciation of multiculturalism and support for universal health care are two defining attributes of what it means to be Canadian. *Values* are defined in more general terms and involve standards, principles, and broad guidelines as to how people should try to live their lives. For example, a Canadian value might be the belief that it is better to compete

Source: Consolidated from Bruce Ravelli, 1997, "Canadian–American Value Differences: Media Portrayals of Native Issues," Victoria, BC: unpublished manuscript, Department of Sociology, University of Victoria.

fairly and lose than to cheat and win. As we will see, Canadian culture and values are shaped by an intricate and diverse set of physical and social circumstances.

Physically, Canada is the second-largest country in the world (Countries of the World, 2002). Although it boasts a rich and diverse supply of natural resources, it also endures challenging, cold winters. Noted Canadian writer Margaret Atwood believes that Canada's adaptation to its harsh physical environment defines Canadian culture and, to some extent, what it means to be Canadian (Atwood, 1970: 33, cited in Lipset, 1986: 124). Socially, Canadian culture has been defined by the coexistence of, and at times conflict between, the English and the French (Hiller, 1996). The fact that 87 percent of the people living in Quebec identify French as their mother tongue suggests that on this criterion at least, Quebec is certainly *distinct* from the rest of the country (Statistics Canada, 2002). However, Quebec's distinctiveness does not rest solely on language; it also rests on its people's shared history, symbols, ideas, and perceptions of reality (McGuigan, 1997: 52). Clearly, Canada's physical and social environments have influenced its culture, but arguably, they have also influenced its values as well.

Canadian values were of primary interest to a 1991 federal commission called the Citizens' Forum on Canada's Future, or the Spicer Commission (CFCF, 1991: 35–45). In its report, the commission identified seven primary cultural values:

1. *Equality and fairness in a democratic society:* Canadians believe in treating all citizens equally (e.g., people with disabilities).

2. *Consultation and dialogue:* Canadians try to settle differences peacefully through discussion and collective problem solving (e.g., Aboriginal self-government initiatives).

3. *Importance of accommodation and tolerance:* Canadians attempt to accommodate the traditions and customs of various ethnic populations (e.g., Aboriginal peoples and the French in Quebec).

4. *Appreciation for diversity:* Canadians support diversity (e.g., regional, ethnic, linguistic, or cultural differences).

5. *Compassion and generosity:* Canadians value their social safety net as an attempt to provide a fair and accessible society for all (e.g., universal health care, pension plans, economic development programs, openness to refugees, and commitment to reducing regional disparities).

6. *Attachment to Canada's natural beauty:* Canadians believe they have a close connection to the natural environment and feel that governments should do more to protect it from pollution and other forms of industrialization (e.g., environmental protection legislation).

7. *Commitment to freedom, peace, and nonviolent change:* Canadians see themselves as peaceful people who maintain an active role in international peacekeeping (e.g., Canada's support for UN-sponsored peacekeeping initiatives) (Macionis, Jansson, & Benoit, 2002: 36).

Clearly, Canadian culture and values are a culmination of many physical and social forces, and studying Canadian–American differences fascinates Canadians (Lipset, 1999: 124; 1990: 53; 1986: 123) and Canadian sociologists in particular (Arnold & Tigert, 1974; Brym & Saint-Pierre, 1997; Clark, 1942; Clement, 1975; Hull, 1998: 4; Porter, 1965; Ravelli, 1994; Reitz & Breton, 1994). Seymour Martin Lipset (an American) has based his career on the study of what makes Canadians and Americans different (Tiryakian, 1991: 1040; Waller, 1990: 380). Lipset's book *Continental Divide* (1990) summarizes and consolidates his almost forty-five years of research on Canadian–American differences; in it he justifies his research, arguing that

Knowledge of Canada or the United States is the best way to gain insight into the other North American country. Nations can only be understood in comparative perspective. And the more similar the units being compared, the more possible it should be to isolate the factors responsible for differences between them. Looking intensively at Canada and the United States sheds light on both of them. (1990: xiii)

Canadians, historically at least, defined themselves by what they were not—Americans (Lipset: 1990: 53; 1986: 123). For Lipset, the primordial event that generated the different founding ideologies of Canada and the United States was the American Revolution (Lipset, 1990: 8; 1986: 114; 1985: 160; 1963: 239). The United States emerged from the Revolution as a manifestation of the classic liberal state, rejecting all ties to the throne, ascriptive elitism, noblesse oblige, and communitarianism (1986: 114). English Canada, however, fought to maintain its imperial ties through the explicit rejection of liberal revolutions (Lipset, 1986: 115). Canadian identity was not defined by a successful revolution, but instead a successful counterrevolution (Lipset, 1993: 161; 1990: 42). America, conversely, was defined by a rigid and stable ideology Lipset called Americanism (1950: 181).[2]

Lipset offers evidence that Canadian and American founding ideologies are present in each country's literature (1986: 123). For example, American literature concentrates on themes of winning, opportunism, and confidence, while Canadian writing focuses on defeat, difficult physical circumstances, and abandonment by Britain (Lipset, 1990: 1; 1986: 123). Lipset cites well-known Canadian novelist Margaret Atwood, who suggests that national symbols reveal a great deal about the cultural values a nation embraces. For Atwood, the defining symbol for America was "the frontier," which inspired images of vitality and unrealized potential, while the symbol of "survival" summed up Canada's national character: "Canadians are forever taking the national pulse like doctors at a sickbed; the aim is not to see whether the patient will live well but simply

whether he will live at all" (Atwood, 1970: 33, cited in Lipset, 1986: 124). Lipset suggests that the symbols, attitudes, and values of a people do not exist in a vacuum; rather, social and political institutions embody and reinforce them (Lipset, 1990: xiv, 225; 1986: 114, 119; Baer, Grabb, & Johnston, 1990a: 693). For Lipset, values are the basis on which society builds its social and political structures, and different value systems manifest themselves in all social realms, not just literature (Lipset, 1990: xiv).

Lipset argues that social structures reflect a society's values and beliefs (Baer, Grabb, & Johnston, 1990a: 693; Grabb & Curtis, 1988: 129, 137; Lipset, 1963: 210). To understand the importance of culture in determining a society's social structure, Lipset incorporated Talcott Parsons' (1952) pattern variables typology into his research (Lipset, 1963: 210). Parsons' pattern variables provide researchers with a method for classifying social values that is more sensitive to cultural variation than the older polar concepts of sociology, such as core–periphery, folk–urban, mechanical–organic, and primary–secondary.

Lipset's thesis of cross-national value differences suggests that Canadians are more elitist and ascriptive; appreciate racial and ethnic variation; and are more community-oriented than Americans. Although Lipset is a dominant figure in North American sociology,[3] his Canadian–American research has been the subject of much interest and debate. Various researchers (see Baer, Grabb, & Johnston, 1990a, 1990b, 1990c, 1993; Curtis, Grabb, & Baer, 1992; Grabb & Curtis, 1988) have attempted to test Lipset's thesis but have faced several difficulties, the most challenging being the following:

- Lipset's research is based on subjective data that are difficult, if not impossible, to test systematically.
- Lipset's pattern variables are at times contradictory and often suggest Canadian–American differences that are opposite to what his thesis would predict.

- Lipset fails to recognize how contemporary social change may influence Canadian and American values.
- Lipset's approach ignores regional variations.
- Lipset fails to offer alternative explanations for Canadian and American value differences.

In spite of such pointed criticism, sociologists generally agree that Lipset's fundamental proposition[,] that Canadian and American cultural values are different, is sound (see Brym with Fox, 1989: 16–8; Clark, 1975: 26; Baer, Grabb, & Johnston, 1990a: 708; 1990c: 276; McGuigan, 1990: 127; Ogmundson & Fisher, 1994: 196). One area of investigation that may shed a contemporary light on Canadian–American differences is an analysis of each country's media, looking for evidence of national value differences.[4]

THE MEDIA'S INFLUENCE ON DEFINING CULTURE

In *Inventing Reality* (1993), Michael Parenti argues that although the media may not mould our every opinion, they do mould *opinion visibility* (Parenti, 1993: 23; see also Gamson & Modigliani, 1989: 3). In effect, journalists, reporters, and news anchors set our *perceptual agenda* (a view shared by Adams, 1978: 30; and Smith, 1992: 210). Parenti states, "The media may not always be able to tell us what to think, but they are strikingly successful in telling us what to think about" (1993: 23; see also Smith, 1992: 210). It is not so much that the media construct opinion; it is enough that they give legitimacy to certain views and illegitimacy to others (Parenti, 1993: 24). This ability has important implications for how the media define and reflect our perceptions and guide our interactions with the social world by effectively constructing news that reflects dominant values (Parenti, 1993: 69). Edward Herman and Noam Chomsky explore this issue in *Manufacturing Consent* (1988).

Herman and Chomsky suggest that the media intentionally create a social environment favourable to the dominant classes by *manufacturing consent* through the filtering of stories (Herman & Chomsky, 1988: xi, 2). This filtering takes two forms: (1) deciding not to cover a story and (2) presenting a story in such a way as to diffuse or bias its objective content. This filtering influences how people see and interpret the social world because it defines their reality. Herman and Chomsky suggest that the primary role of mainstream media is to ensure popular support for the economic, social, and political agenda of the privileged classes (1988: 298). Their *propaganda* model reveals many of the techniques media use to manufacture consent.

One way to find evidence for Canadian and American cultural differences would be to study a single social phenomenon common to both countries, such as how the media present a common and familiar issue. This brief review of how the media reflect and define a society's values reinforces the selection of media as one avenue by which to investigate Lipset's thesis of cross-national value differences in more detail. As argued by many, the media are becoming *the* conduit through which much of the world defines and reflects its cultural values (see Adams, 1978: 30; Campbell, 1999; Gamson & Modigliani, 1989: 3; Gitlin, 1980; Herman & Chomsky, 1988: 2; Parenti, 1993: 23; Smith, 1992: 210; Tetzlaff, 1992). My approach uses Native issues as a social phenomenon for study since both Canada and the United States have a long history of Native–White contact (see Berelson & Salter, 1946; Grenier, 1993; Singer, 1982; Skea, 1993).[5]

To test Lipset's thesis, I employed a fifty-year longitudinal study of Canadian and American media and how they presented Native issues. The medium I chose for the comparison was newsmagazines, in particular, *Maclean's* in Canada and *Newsweek* in the United States.[6] These newsmagazines were selected because they are regarded as journalistic leaders (see Roy, 1990: 510; van Driel & Richardson, 1988: 38) and attract national audiences. Thus, they should present national values to the extent that they exist. To test Lipset's theory, I formulated seven hypotheses flowing directly out of his four pattern variables (see Table 9.1).

My sampling frame included all articles referring to Natives in *Maclean's* and *Newsweek* from 1943 to 1993.[7] After locating the articles, I conducted a content analysis to determine whether there were systematic differences between each magazine's coverage of Native issues.

My analysis of *Maclean's* and *Newsweek* incorporated two complementary perspectives, the first a quantitative examination testing whether Lipset's value differences were evident (see Appendix A), and the second a qualitative exploration to detect themes speaking to Lipset's thesis (see Appendix B). The quantitative analysis provides a rudimentary statistical assessment of Lipset's thesis, while the qualitative has greater sensitivity to themes appearing in the articles pertaining to cultural differences. By coding the articles from both quantitative and qualitative perspectives, I hoped to gain a more complete appreciation of their portrayals of Native issues than would be possible by using either approach independently.

Results suggest little quantitative or qualitative support for Lipset's thesis of Canadian–American value differences (see Table 9.2).

TABLE 9.1   Testing Lipset's Thesis

Lipset's Pattern Variable	Hypothesis
Elitism–Egalitarianism	1a: Canadians will view political leaders more positively than Americans. 1b: Canadians will view minority leaders more critically than Americans.
Ascription–Achievement	2a: Canadians will support government-sponsored redistribution programs more than Americans. 2b: Canadians will criticize lawlessness more than Americans.
Particularism–Universalism	3: Canadians will support the mosaic perspective more than Americans.
Diffuseness–Specificity	4a: Canadians will support the collectivist perspective more than Americans. 4b: Canadians will criticize minority challenges to the collective more than Americans

TABLE 9.2   Qualitative/Quantitative Results Summary

Pattern Variable	Hypothesis	Quantitative Results	Qualitative Results
Elitism versus Egalitarianism	1a: Political Leadership 1b: Native Leadership	Reject Reject	Reject Reject
Ascription versus Achievement	2a: Redistribution Programs 2b: Native Lawlessness	Reject Reject	Support Reject
Particularism versus Universalism	3: Mosaic Perspective	Support	Support
Diffuseness versus Specificity	4a: Collectivist Perspective 4b: Native Challenge to the Collective	Reject Reject	Support Reject

Table 9.2 illustrates that six of the seven quantitative results fail to support Lipset's thesis. Statistical differences existed between *Maclean's* and *Newsweek* and their presentation of Native issues, but the differences were often in the opposite direction of what Lipset's thesis would predict. Qualitative results were similar to the quantitative in that four of the seven hypotheses rejected Lipset's thesis.

1. Elitism versus Egalitarianism is **not supported** as all four tests reject Lipset's hypothesis.

2. Ascription versus Achievement is **not supported** as three of the four tests refute Lipset's hypothesis.

3. Particularism versus Universalism is **supported** as both tests support Lipset's hypothesis.

4. Diffuseness versus Specificity is **not supported** as three of the four tests reject Lipset's hypothesis.

My findings suggest that Canadian and American cultural values do vary, but not in a manner consistent with Lipset's pattern variable thesis. The only pattern variable to be supported was *Particularism versus Universalism*, which suggests that Canadians do recognize and encourage racial and ethnic diversity more than Americans. Although my research found little support for the three remaining pattern variables, it did find evidence to support the common experience that Canadian and American cultures differ (see Reitz & Breton, 1994).

CONCLUSION

After reading almost 400 magazine articles, on at least three separate occasions, I was struck by how often *Maclean's* presented Native issues with emotion and passion and how rarely any empathy was shown for the plight of American Natives in *Newsweek*. For me, this suggests one of the defining differences between Canadians and Americans—the belief in, and support for, multiculturalism. Granted, Canada's record of dealing with Native populations has often been strained and difficult; however, the dialogue between the parties has played a central and defining role in constructing our national value systems. This level of public debate and discussion between American Natives and the larger American society has not yet occurred. Canadians, however, must appreciate that just saying that Canada is a multicultural society is not enough. All people in Canada need to know, and be shown, that for Canadians, multiculturalism is not just an abstract philosophy; it is one of the defining elements of who we are as a people—multiculturalism means nothing if we don't practise what we preach.

APPENDIX A

My quantitative coding tested Lipset's overall thesis of cross-national value differences by comparing how each article portrayed issues that were relevant to Lipset's pattern variables. For example, when an article discussed political leaders (pertinent to hypothesis 1a), I noted every reference to political leaders as positive, negative, or indeterminate in the margins of the article. Positive statements about political leaders were coded as PL+, negative as PL−, and indeterminate as PL? When I completed the coding, I added the number of positive, negative, and indeterminate references and determined an overall coding for that article. That is, if the article had 15 positive statements about the political leader, 3 negative, and 0 indeterminate, I concluded that the article presented a supportive portrayal of political leaders. The statistical analyses were based on these comparisons. An obvious concern at this point is how confident I am that my coding of the articles was reliable.

Research is deemed reliable when the particular research technique, applied repeatedly to the same phenomenon, yields the same results (Babbie, 1995: 124). I am confident that my coding was reliable for two reasons. First, totals for the three possible codings (i.e., PL+, PL−, PL?) were never within 10 percent of each other. This indicates that the article's editorial bias (or lack of one) was readily apparent. Second, even though I was the only person coding the articles, I re-coded a 10 percent random sample of the articles (30 articles from *Maclean's*, 10 from *Newsweek*) six months after I completed my initial coding. The coefficient of reliability between the codings was 72 percent (coefficient of reliability = number of units in identical category/total number of units). Since coefficient values higher than 60 percent are deemed reliable (Jackson, 1995: 72), I am confident that my coding reliably reflects the articles' (and by extension, the newsmagazines') editorial bias.

APPENDIX B

Content analysis is a set of procedures used to study text (Weber, 1990: 9) and is appropriate for most forms of communication (Babbie, 1995: 307). Using content analysis I was able to investigate themes in media content that went beyond those explicitly stated. Robert Weber (1990: 9) suggests that content analysis of media can reveal international differences and uncover the cultural patterns of groups, institutions, or societies. The ability to look beyond the text makes content analysis well suited for a cross-national analysis of culture differences in media (Babbie, 1995: 315).

CRITICAL THINKING QUESTIONS

1. What are pattern variables? Do you feel they are useful concepts when investigating national value differences? Why?

2. Mass media play an important role in our lives today. What are some ways in which mass media influence your world view that was not possible in your parents' generation?

3. An ongoing debate for researchers is whether media actively *define* our reality or, alternatively, simply *reflect* it. Which do you feel is the more convincing position? Why?

NOTES

1. The majority of the following analysis is a consolidation of my doctoral dissertation, "Canadian–American Value Differences: Media Portrayals of Native Issues" (1997), unpublished manuscript, Department of Sociology, University of Victoria.

2. An ideology is a system of beliefs, common ideas, perceptions, and values held in common by members of a collective (Parsons, 1952: 349). Ideology can be thought of as the filter through which we interpret our social world.

3. As demonstrated, in part, by his election as president of the American Sociological Association for 1993–94.

4. My working assumption behind this analysis is the belief that media content will reflect national values to secure the widest audience possible and, by extension, the greatest financial benefit for its shareholders.

5. The term "Native" is used to describe the indigenous populations of North America. This terminology was selected over others (e.g., Aboriginal, First Nations, Amerindian, Indian) as it is the standard in contemporary literature (see Francis, 1992: 9).

6. Electronic media are too recent to study and print media lend themselves to better contextual analysis (see Neumann, Just, & Crigler, 1992: 58–9; Vipond, 1992: 27, 78, 128).

7. To locate the articles, I first consulted the Library of Congress subject heading Indians of North America. I then manually searched the *Reader's Guide to Periodical Literature* (Reader's Guide) and the *Canadian Periodical Index* (CPI) for references to the subject title. This strategy located 296 articles in *Maclean's* and 96 in *Newsweek*.

REFERENCES

Adams, W. C. 1978. Network news research in perspective: A bibliographic essay. In *Television network news: Issues in content research*. Washington, DC: George Washington University Press.

Arnold, S. J., and D. J. Tigert. 1974. Canadians and Americans: A comparative analysis. *International Journal of Comparative Sociology*, 15: 68–83.

Atwood, M. 1970. *The journals of Susanna Moodie: Poems*. Toronto: Oxford University Press.

Babbie, E. 1995. *The practice of social research*, 7th ed. Belmont, CA: Wadsworth Publishing Company.

Baer, D., E. Grabb, and W. A. Johnston. 1990a. *The values of Canadians and Americans: A critical analysis and reassessment*. Social Forces, 68(3): 693–713.

———. 1990b. Reassessing differences in Canadian and American values. In *Images of Canada: The sociological tradition*, eds. J. Curtis and L. Tepperman, 86–97. Scarborough, ON: Prentice-Hall Canada.

———. 1990c. The values of Canadians and Americans: A rejoinder. *Social Forces*, 69(1): 273–77.

———. 1993. National character, regional culture, and the values of Canadians and Americans. *Canadian Review of Sociology and Anthropology*, 30(1): 13–36.

Berelson, B., and P. J. Salter. 1946. Majority and minority Americans: An analysis of magazine fiction. *Public Opinion Quarterly*, 10.

Brym, R. J., with B. J. Fox. 1989. *From culture to power: The sociology of English Canada*. Toronto: Oxford University Press.

Brym, R., and C. Saint-Pierre. 1997. Canada: Canadian sociology. *Contemporary Sociology*, 26(5): 543–46.

Campbell, K. 1999. Why we must protect Canadian culture from the U.S. juggernaut. In *Canadian communications: Issues in contemporary media culture*, eds. B. Szuchewycz, and J. Sloniowski, 214–18. Scarborough, ON: Prentice Hall/Allyn and Bacon Canada.

CFCF (Citizen's Forum on Canada's Future). 1991. *Report to the People and Government of Canada*. Ottawa: Supply and Services Canada.

Clark, S. D. 1942. *The social development of Canada: An introductory study with select documents*. Toronto: University of Toronto Press.

———. 1975. The post–Second World War Canadian society. *Canadian Review of Sociology and Anthropology*, 12(1).

Clement, W. 1975. *The Canadian corporate elite: An analysis of economic power*. Toronto: McClelland and Stewart.

Countries of the World. 2002. Country statistics at a glance. [Online]. Available: **http://www.infoplease.com/ipa/ A0762380.html.** Accessed July 17, 2002.

Curtis, J. E., E. G. Grabb, and D. E. Baer. 1992. Voluntary association membership in fifteen countries: A comparative analysis. *American Sociological Review*, 57(April): 139–52.

Francis, D. 1992. *The imaginary Indian: The image of the Indian in Canadian culture.* Vancouver: Arsenal Pulp Press.

Gamson, W. A., and A. Modigliani. 1989. Media discourse and public opinion on nuclear power: A constructionist approach. *American Journal of Sociology*, 95(1): 1–37.

Gitlin, T. 1980. *The whole world is watching.* Berkeley: University of California Press.

Grabb, E. G., and J. E. Curtis. 1988. English Canadian–American differences in orientation toward social control and individual rights. *Sociological Focus*, 21(2): 127–40.

Grenier, M. 1993. Native Indians in the English-Canadian press: The case of the Oka Crisis. *Media, Culture and Society*, 16 (April): 313–36.

Herman, E. S., and N. Chomsky. 1988. *Manufacturing consent: The political economy of the mass media.* New York: Pantheon Books.

Hiller, H. 1996. *Canadian society: A macro analysis*, 3rd ed. Scarborough, ON: Prentice Hall Canada.

Hull, J. P. 1998. From many, two: A bibliographic history of Canadian–American relations. *American Studies International*, 36(2): 4–22.

Jackson, W. 1995. *Methods: Doing social research.* Scarborough, ON: Prentice Hall Canada.

Lipset, S. M. 1950. *Agrarian socialism: The Cooperative Commonwealth Federation in Saskatchewan.* Berkeley and Los Angeles: University of California Press.

———. 1963. *The first new nation: The United States in historical and comparative perspective.* New York: Basic Books.

———. 1985. Canada and the United States: The cultural dimension. *In Canada and the United States*, eds. C. F. Doran, and J. H. Sigler, 109–60. Englewood Cliffs, NJ: Prentice Hall.

———. 1986. Historical traditions and national characteristics: A comparative analysis of Canada and the United States. *Canadian Journal of Sociology* 11(2): 113–55.

———. 1990. *Continental divide: The values and institutions of the United States and Canada.* New York: Routledge.

———. 1993. Revolution and counterrevolution: The United States and Canada. In *A passion for identity: An introduction to Canadian studies*, eds. D. Taras, B. Rasporich, and E. Mandel, 150–61. Scarborough, ON: Nelson Canada.

———. 1999. American union density in comparative perspective. *Contemporary Sociology*, 27(2): 123–25.

Macionis, J. J., S. M. Jansson, and C. M. Benoit. 2002. *Society: The basics*, 2nd Cdn ed. Toronto: Pearson Education Canada.

McGuigan, B. 1990. The comparative sociology of Seymour Martin Lipset: An analysis and critique. Unpublished master's thesis. University of Calgary.

———. 1997. Issues in Canadian culture. In *Issues in Canadian sociology*, 2nd ed., eds. M. Kanwar and D. Swenson, 35–60. Dubuque, IA: Kendall/Hunt Publishing.

Neumann, R. W., M. R. Just, and A. N. Crigler. 1992. *Common knowledge: News and the construction of political meaning.* Chicago: University of Chicago Press.

Ogmundson, R. L., and L. Fisher. 1994. Beyond Lipset and his critics: An initial reformulation. *Canadian Review of Sociology and Anthropology*, 31(2): 196–99.

Parenti, M. 1993. *Inventing the politics of news media reality*, 2nd ed. New York: St. Martin's Press.

Parsons, T. 1952. *The social system.* London: Tavistock Publications Ltd.

Porter, J. 1965. *The vertical mosaic: An analysis of social class and power in Canada.* Toronto: University of Toronto Press.

Ravelli, B. 1994. Health care in the United States and Canada. In *The sociological outlook: A text with readings*, 4th ed., ed. R. Luhman, 467–68. San Diego: Collegiate Press.

Reitz, J. G., and R. Breton. 1994. *The illusion of difference: Realities of ethnicity in Canada and the United States.* Toronto: C.D. Howe Institute.

Roy, D. 1990. The U.S. print media and the conventional military balance in Europe. *Armed Forces & Society*, 16(4): 509–28.

Singer, B. D. 1982. Minorities in the media: A content analysis of Native Canadians in the daily press. *Canadian Review of Sociology and Anthropology*, 19(3): 348–59.

Skea, W. H. 1993. The Canadian newspaper industry's portrayal of the Oka Crisis. *Native Studies Review*, 9(1): 15–31.

Smith, R. L. 1992. Media networking: Toward a model for the global management of sociocultural change. In *Mass media effects across cultures*, eds. F. Korzenny et al., 201–28. Newbury Park, CA.: Sage.

Statistics Canada. 2002. Population by home language, 2001 Census. [Online]. Available: **http://www.statcan. ca/english/Pgdb/demo29b.htm.** Accessed July 16, 2002.

Tetzlaff, D. 1992. Popular culture and social control in late capitalism. In *Culture and power: A media, culture and society reader*, eds. P. Scannell, P. Schlesinger, and C. Sparks, 48–72. London: Sage.

Tiryakian, E. A. 1991. Book review of *Continental divide: The values and institutions of the United States and Canada* by S. M. Lipset. *American Journal of Sociology*, 96(4): 1040–42.

Van Driel, B., and Richardson, J. T. 1988. Print media coverage of new religious movements: A longitudinal study. *Journal of Communication*, 38(3): 37–61.

Vipond, M. 1992. *The mass media in Canada.* Toronto: James Lorimer & Company.

Waller, H. M. 1990. Book review of *Continental divide: The values and institutions of the United States and Canada* by S. M. Lipset. *Canadian Journal of Political Science*, 23: 380–81.

Weber, R. P. 1990. *Basic content analysis*, 2nd ed. Newbury Park, CA: Sage Publications.

10

North America's Two Distinct Societies

MICHAEL ADAMS (WITH AMY LANGSTAFF AND DAVID JAMIESON)

Culture

CLASSIC

CONTEMPORARY

CROSS-CULTURAL

A sizable proportion of Canada's population, particularly among the left, is concerned that economic and political integration with the United States will inevitably result in cultural homogenization. In the minds of many, Canadians are becoming more like their American counterparts. This excerpt dispels some of those fears and discusses some of the characteristics that make Canadians distinct from their neighbours to the south.

Canada and the United States have reached the point where we can no longer think of each other as foreign countries.

—Harry S. Truman, U.S. president, address, joint sitting of the Canadian Senate and House of Commons, 11 June 1947

He understands I want to make sure our relations with our most important neighbour to the north of us, the Canadians, is strong. . . .

—George W. Bush, reacting to a statement of support for his presidential bid from "Canadian Prime Minister Jean Poutine"; Poutine's thumbs-up was relayed to President Bush at a 2000 campaign stop by Canadian comic and *This Hour Has 22 Minutes* "reporter" Rick Mercer

Source: Michael Adams, with Amy Langstaff and David Jamieson. 2003. *Fire and Ice: The United States, Canada and the Myth of Converging Values*, pp. 47–56. Toronto: Penguin Canada.

Canada is the largest country in the world that doesn't exist.

—Richard Rodriguez, American social commentator of Mexican-Indian descent, commenting on the notion that minority groups overtake majority groups, in an interview by Neil Bissoondath on TVO's *Markings*, 3 July 1995

In the days and weeks following 11 September, Canadians' feelings of sympathy for and solidarity with the United States were expressed again and again. Canadian firefighters and medical professionals travelled to New York City to offer assistance to those affected by the terrorist attacks. Families in Newfoundland opened their homes to fearful and distraught Americans whose planes had been diverted into Canada after news of the disaster had spread through airline communication systems. On 14 September, 100,000 Canadians gathered on Parliament Hill to express their grief over the tragedies that had befallen their neighbours.

The reaction was more immediate and heart-felt than in any other nation. It brought to mind a child in a schoolyard tearfully rushing to the aid of an older sibling in serious distress, affection and fellow feeling blotting out all the usual resentment over quotidian bullying or petty squabbles. Certainly, after things had settled down somewhat, some of the usual fault lines between the two countries began to reappear: Canadians began to wonder about what the U.S. response to the attacks would be, and some eventually began to fret openly (if gingerly) about how Canadians would be drawn into the conflict. But for a short time, the differences between Canada and the United States seemed to dissolve.

As the horror receded and daily life slowly resumed, the differences that had seemed so trivial as to be almost non-existent on that Tuesday morning began to reassert themselves little by little. As 2001 wound shakily down and 2002 began, many Canadians once again found themselves beginning to roll their eyes at phrases like "axis of evil" and shake their heads at George W. Bush's repeated references to the women of Afghanistan as "women of cover." Without losing any of our sympathy for the lives lost or irrevocably altered on 11 September, Canadians began to regain some of their sense of distance and difference from the United States and its worldview.

This slow, tentative process was accelerated very suddenly on 17 April 2002, when news of the deaths of four Canadian soldiers in Afghanistan reached North America (or at least, the news *seemed* to reach North America, but for all the attention it received south of the border it might as well have been lost in transit). The four soldiers were killed (and eight others injured) by "friendly fire"; a U.S. fighter pilot dropped a bomb on the Canadians (whom he mistook for enemy soldiers) as they were carrying out a training exercise on the ground.

"Accidents happen in wars," all voices seemed to concede sadly. "Nobody wanted this to happen." But as President Bush made his first,

second, third, fourth, and fifth public appearances the next day without ever mentioning the incident—and even ignoring a question shouted by a Canadian reporter as Bush scuttled away from one press conference—sadness turned to anger. Was it really too much to expect that the United States might have been saddened at having killed and wounded a group of young Canadians who were doing their best to help America fight its war? Was it too much to expect that the American president would at least *pretend* to be dismayed, expressing at least some modest words of empathy and regret? Or that the *New York Times* might have spared a little space somewhere ahead of page fourteen on the day following the incident?

Now Canadians were beginning to recall the old simmering resentments of life in Uncle Sam's backyard. Though the feeling of fraternity that had permeated the country in the period immediately following September 11 had been entirely genuine, this familiar feeling of ill use was no less so. Canadians seemed to recall, in April of 2002, that although it may sometimes seem that Canada and the U.S. are "on the same page," that's usually because we're reading over their shoulder.

Because the cultural differences between Canada and the United States tend to exist beneath the consciousness of our daily lives, it is sometimes possible to imagine that those differences do not exist. After all, on any given day, most Canadians, like most Americans, can be spotted in their natural habitats driving cars, consuming too much energy and water, spending a little less time with their nuclear families than they would like, working a little more than is healthy, watching television, and buying some things they could probably survive without. But differences—both subtle and marked—do exist, and do endure. Some are external (gun control, bilingualism, health care), but many exist only inside the minds of Canadians and Americans—in how they see the world, how they engage with it, and how they hope to shape it.

In this chapter, I will offer a closer look at Canadians' and Americans' responses to individual survey questions—responses that attest, one by one, to a broad trend of cultural *divergence*.

But before the big picture, I'd like to share some raw numbers. We begin our portrait of these two neighbours with a comparison of their religious convictions. Canadians are by now quite familiar with evangelists Jerry Falwell, Pat Robertson, Jimmy Swaggart, Jim and Tammy Faye Bakker (who are slowly getting back to the business), and even William Jennings Bryan, who defended creationism in the famous Scopes Monkey trial in the 1920s. We know that Christian fundamentalism has far deeper and more enduring roots in the United States, particularly in the Bible Belt, than here in Canada. What we sometimes fail to remember is that not so long ago, Canadians were more conventionally religious than Americans. In the mid-1950s, 60 per cent of Canadians told pollsters they went to church each Sunday; the proportion in the U.S. at that time was only 50 per cent. Today, only a fifth of Canadians claim weekly church attendance (22 per cent, according to Ekos), whereas the proportion in the U.S. is 42 per cent. A 2002 Pew Research Center poll found religion to be important to 59 per cent of Americans—the highest proportion in all the developed nations surveyed—and to only 30 per cent of Canadians, a rate similar to that found in Great Britain and Italy. Nearly four in ten Canadians do not consider themselves to be members of a religious faith. In the U.S. the proportion of atheists, agnostics, or secular humanists is only 25 per cent. In less than a generation, Canadians have evolved from being much more religious than Americans to being considerably less so.

Canadians have not only rejected in large numbers the authority of religious institutions, but have brought this questioning of traditional authority closer to home. Our research shows Canadians to be far less likely than Americans to agree with the statement, "The father of the family

Figure 10.1 Father of Family Must Be Master in His Own House: Canada and the United States: Agree 1992, 1996, & 2000

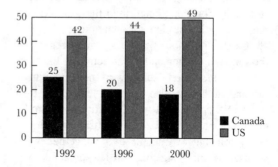

must be master in his own home." In 1992 we found that 26 per cent of Canadians believed Father must be master (down from 42 per cent in 1983). In 1992, 42 per cent of Americans told us Dad should be on top. Since then the gap has widened: down to 20 per cent in Canada and up to 44 per cent in the U.S. in 1996, and then down even further (to 18 per cent) in Canada in 2000 and up further still (to 49 per cent) in the U.S. in that year. The widening gap between the two countries now stands at an astonishing thirty-one points, with Canadians becoming ever less deferential to patriarchal authority and Americans becoming more and more willing to Wait Till Their Father Comes Home to find out if it's okay to watch *The Simpsons*.

Paralleling this differing orientation to patriarchal authority are the two populations' attitudes toward the relative status of the sexes. In a word, Americans are more predisposed to male chauvinism than Canadians, and here again the gap is widening. In 1992, 26 per cent of Canadians told us that men are naturally superior to women, while 30 per cent of Americans felt the same way. Four years later in 1996, the proportion of Canadians believing in the innate superiority of men declined to 23 per cent while the U.S. proportion rose to 32 per cent. By 2000, the proportion in Canada stood at 24 per cent while that in the U.S. shot up to 38 per cent. It only stands to reason, many Americans seem to be telling us, that if God-fearing men are the superior beings on this planet, then they should certainly be the bosses in their own homes.

Canadians' more egalitarian views regarding the status of women and the structure of the family, plus a more skeptical view of traditional institutional authority, also seem to lead them to a more relaxed view of what constitutes a family. Over the past decade, Canadians have consistently felt that two people living together, what we used to call living common-law, in fact constitutes a family. In 2000, 71 per cent of Canadians felt a couple that shared a home were a family, up from 66 per cent in 1992. Only 54 per cent of Americans shared this view, albeit up from 49 per cent in 1992. It is almost impossible to imagine a governor of any U.S. state daring to brazenly "live in sin" with his or her "life partner" as can Ontario Premier Ernie Eves. When in 1942 the Conservatives added the adjective "Progressive" to their party name, I doubt they had common-law cohabitation in mind.

What emerges so far is a portrait of two nations evolving in unexpected directions: the once shy and deferential Canadians, who used to wait to be told by their betters what to do and how to think, have become more skeptical of traditional authority and more confident about their own personal decisions and informal arrangements. Americans, by contrast, seeking a little of the "peace and order" that Canadians hoped "good government" would provide, seem inclined to latch on to traditional institutional practices, beliefs, and norms as anchors in a national environment that is more intensely competitive, chaotic, and even violent.

Attitudes toward violence are, in fact, among the features that most markedly differentiate Canadians from Americans. In the year 2000, 50 per cent of Canadians told us they felt violence to be all around them, a high figure to be sure, but nowhere near the 76 per cent of Americans who felt the same way. Americans' responses to our questions about violence suggest that they may even be becoming inured to the violence they perceive to be ubiquitous. In 1992, 9 per cent of Canadians and 10 per cent of Americans told us that violence is a normal part of life, nothing to be concerned about. In 1996, the figure in Canada was still 9 per cent, but had grown to 18 per cent in the U.S. In 2000, 12 per cent of Canadians felt that violence in everyday life was normal, but in the same year 24 per cent of Americans felt the same way. For one American in four, representing 70 million people, violence is perceived as a normal part of one's daily routine. The other three-quarters of the population, presumably, are doing all they can to avoid those 70 million, particularly if alone on the street after dark.

We found further evidence that violence is becoming more, not less, normative in America when we asked Americans to agree or disagree that when one is extremely tense or frustrated, a little violence can offer relief, and that "it's no big deal." In 1992, 14 per cent of Americans agreed with this sentiment, as did 14 per cent of Canadians we polled. In 1996, the proportion was 10 per cent in Canada but zoomed to 27 per cent in the U.S. By 2000, the proportion in Canada was back up to 14 per cent, but had surged further to 31 per cent in America, nearly one-third of the population. Again, you might not want to confront one of these folks when they're feeling a bit on edge, particularly when you remember that many of them (including the U.S. Attorney General) believe their Constitution guarantees them the right to bear firearms.

America is and always has been a very competitive society, nurtured by the myth of the American Dream, which suggests that anyone with a little vision and a lot of hard work can achieve material success. Sociologist Seymour Martin Lipset points out that in all categories, crime rates in America are about three times higher than they are in other industrialized countries. Lipset suggests as an explanation for this phenomenon the following: the American Dream, and the concomitant imperative to achieve material success, are so strong in America that many people pursue the goals of wealth and status in reckless, sometimes even criminal, ways. The end is of such monumental importance that the means become almost irrelevant.

Our polling found some interesting results in this area. In 1992, we asked Canadians and Americans whether they would be prepared to take "great risks" in order to get what they want. That year, nearly equal proportions of Canadians (25 per cent) and Americans (26 per cent) reported that they would indeed be prepared to rake great risks to get what they wanted. The same in 1996. But by 2000 still only a quarter of Canadians were prepared to take great risks while the proportion in the U.S. increased to 38 per cent—a full eleven points higher than in Canada.

Americans are prepared to put a lot more on the line than Canadians to achieve their version of the American Dream, including personal risks to life and limb. They are also, as it turns out, more willing than Canadians to risk the lives and limbs of others to achieve the same ends. In 1992, 10 per cent of Canadians and only 9 per cent of Americans told us that it is acceptable to use violence to get what you want. In 1996, 11 per cent of Canadians felt this way, but the proportion of Americans rose to 17 per cent. By 2000, 13 per cent of Canadians felt the use of violence, presumably on or off the ice, was an acceptable way of achieving one's objectives, while the proportion in the U.S. was 23 per cent, nearly one in four and almost double the figure in Canada.

Lipset's hypothesis about the possible relationship between crime and the deep-rooted imperative of the American Dream illuminates an interesting contradiction: frustrated by their inability to achieve the Dream by socially acceptable means, those who obtain the trappings of success unlawfully exercise excessive individualism precisely *in order* to conform.

The idea that America's ostensible commitment to individualism may mask a deep impulse toward conformity is borne out in our polling data. We find that Americans are in fact more prone to conformity than their neighbours to the north, who reside in a land that not only tolerates but actually celebrates linguistic, ethnic, and regional group identities. We track three items that shed light on this intriguing question: do people mind changing their habits, do they relate to people who show originality in dress and behaviour, and do they relate to people who repress rather than show their emotions. Our findings are surprising. In 1992, 51 per cent of Canadians and 56 per cent of Americans reported that they did not like changing their habits. In 1996, 48 per cent of Canadians reported being stuck in their ways—a decline of three points—and 58 per cent of Americans said the same thing, an increase of two points. By 2000, we had a widening and quite significant gap: only 42 per cent of Canadians said they don't like changing their habits while 54 per cent of Americans reported the same, now a gap of twelve points showing Canadians to be less conservative and more flexible than Americans in their day-to-day routines.

How about conformity of dress and behaviour: wearing the right costume or uniform for the occasion, not saying or doing anything politically incorrect? Who are the conformists? Who are the rebels? In 1992, 1996, and 2000 a consistent two-thirds of Canadians (68, 68, and 67 per cent) told us that they relate to nonconformists. Conversely, in each year, the proportion of Americans who do so dropped: from 64 per cent in 1992 to 61 per cent in 1996 to 52 per cent in 2000. Overall, the gap between the U.S. and Canada stands at 15 per cent. That George W. Bush, after his election, instantly reinstated a strict suit-and-tie dress code at the White House illustrates this penchant for order and decorum, in stark contrast to the Clinton-era "work casual" image. Meanwhile, Canada's male politicians go out of their way to dress informally, almost invariably replacing their blue suits with open-collared sports shirts when on the campaign trail. One of the truly remarkable silent social revolutions in Canada has been the rapid death of the dress code. Dress-down Friday became dress-down every day in the Canadian workplace in a matter of months. In New York many upscale restaurants still strictly enforce a jacket-and-tie dress code; in Toronto only the stuffiest of private clubs have a store of apparel for the uncouth who show up improperly attired.

And finally, what about emotional informality and openness? Who are more open: the famously friendly "y'all come back real soon" Americans or the reputedly reserved, understated (even cold?) Canadians? In 1992, 32 per cent of Canadians told us that they relate best to people who do not show their emotions. In 1996 we found a similar proportion (28 per cent), and in 2000 30 per cent—essentially no change over the decade. In 1992, the proportion of Americans who preferred the stiff-upper-lip type was 27 per cent—five points lower than in Canada, as expected. But in 1996 that proportion rose to 35 per cent, and then in 2000 shot up even further to 44 per cent—an astounding fourteen-point gap. It's hard to get your head around the idea of a touchy-feely Canadian in contrast to the emotionally restrained, uptight American. But think back—way back—to the strong, silent heroes of American westerns who let their guns do the talking and held their liquor as if it were Ovaltine. The late 90s have seen a tremendous backlash in the U.S. against the early trend toward "feminization." Today that forgotten cowboy, the one who doesn't have much time for fancy language or womanish diplomacy but sure knows what to do with an axis of evil when he sees one, is back in style.

Soon after 9/11, President George Bush and then New York Mayor Rudolph Giuliani urged Americans to demonstrate their patriotism in defiance of the forces of evil who "wish to destroy our way of life." The president and the mayor urged their fellow Americans to go out shopping. This the people did, thus saving the U.S. (and Canada) from recession. These leaders knew they were addressing receptive audiences: hordes of people who not only felt a genuine desire to do something, anything, to respond to those deeply traumatic events in a helpful way, but who had also been weaned on the idea that material possessions are among the most important expressions of one's status, interests, personality, and citizenship in the greatest country on earth. In 1992, 38 per cent of Americans told us it was important that people admire the things they own. Similar proportions in 1996 (37 per cent) and 2000 (36 per cent) said the same thing. In Canada, meanwhile, ostentatious consumption has been in gentle decline: from 34 per cent in 1992, to 32 percent in 1996, and down to 29 per cent in 2000. Many Canadians are still conspicuous consumers, but they lag behind their American cousins and seem to be drifting away from consuming "things" toward enjoying "experience." Americans brag about the new car they just bought; Canadians are more likely to boast about the trips they have taken.

CRITICAL THINKING QUESTIONS

1. Do you think that people from Canada and the United States are generally the same, or are there significant differences? What are those differences? How would you go about measuring those differences? And finally, what do you think lies at the root of those differences?

2. Studying the differences between Canadians and Americans has been a topic of social research for decades. What kind of evidence does Adams have to offer that our two cultures are not becoming more similar? Give specific examples. What research method does he apply?

3. One fear that persists among Canadians is that as the North American economy becomes more integrated, culture will follow. What is meant by *culture* in this instance? Can you give some examples of cultural products? Do you think that there is a connection between the economy and culture?

11

India's Sacred Cow

MARVIN HARRIS

Anthropologist Marvin Harris uses the approach of cultural ecology to investigate how exotic and seemingly inexplicable cultural patterns may turn out to be everyday strategies for human survival in a particular natural environment. In this article, he offers his own favourite example: Why do people in India—many of whom are hungry—refuse to eat beef from the "sacred cows" that are found almost everywhere?

Whenever I get into discussions about the influence of practical and mundane factors on lifestyles, someone is sure to say, "But what about all those cows the hungry peasants in India refuse to eat?" The picture of a ragged farmer starving to death alongside a big fat cow conveys a reassuring sense of mystery to Western observers. In countless learned and popular allusions, it confirms our deepest conviction about how people with inscrutable Oriental minds ought to act. It is comforting to know—somewhat like "there will always be an England"—that in India spiritual values are more precious than life itself. And at the same time it makes us feel sad. How can we ever hope to understand people so different from ourselves? Westerners

find the idea that there might be a practical explanation for Hindu love of the cow more upsetting than Hindus do. The sacred cow—how else can I say it?—is one of our favorite sacred cows.

Hindus venerate cows because cows are the symbol of everything that is alive. As Mary is to Christians the mother of God, the cow to Hindus is the mother of life. So there is no greater sacrilege for a Hindu than killing a cow. Even the taking of human life lacks the symbolic meaning, the unutterable defilement, that is evoked by cow slaughter.

According to many experts, cow worship is the number one cause of India's hunger and poverty. Some Western-trained agronomists say that the taboo against cow slaughter is keeping 100 million "useless" animals alive. They claim that cow worship lowers the efficiency of agriculture because the useless animals contribute neither milk nor meat while competing for croplands and food-stuff with useful animals and hungry human beings. . . .

Source: From *Cows, Pigs, Wars, and Witches: The Riddles of Culture* by Marvin Harris. Copyright © 1974 by Marvin Harris, Random House. Reprinted with permission of Random House, Inc.

It does seem that there are enormous numbers of surplus, useless, and uneconomic animals, and that this situation is a direct result of irrational Hindu doctrines. Tourists on their way through Delhi, Calcutta, Madras, Bombay, and other Indian cities are astonished at the liberties enjoyed by stray cattle. The animals wander through the streets, browse off the stalls in the market place, break into private gardens, defecate all over the sidewalks, and snarl traffic by pausing to chew their cuds in the middle of busy intersections. In the countryside, the cattle congregate on the shoulders of every highway and spend much of their time taking leisurely walks down the railroad tracks.

To Western observers familiar with modern industrial techniques of agriculture and stock raising, cow love seems senseless, even suicidal. The efficiency expert yearns to get his hands on all those useless animals and ship them off to a proper fate. And yet one finds certain inconsistencies in the condemnation of cow love. When I began to wonder if there might be a practical explanation for the sacred cow, I came across an intriguing government report. It said that India had too many cows but too few oxen. With so many cows around, how could there be a shortage of oxen? Oxen and male water buffalo are the principal source of traction for plowing India's fields. For each farm of ten acres or less, one pair of oxen or water buffalo is considered adequate. A little arithmetic shows that as far as plowing is concerned, there is indeed a shortage rather than a surplus of animals. India has 60 million farms, but only 80 million traction animals. If each farm had its quota of two oxen or two water buffalo, there ought to be 120 million traction animals—that is, 40 million more than are actually available.

The shortage may not be quite so bad, since some farmers rent or borrow oxen from their neighbors. But the sharing of plow animals often proves impractical. Plowing must be coordinated with the monsoon rains, and by the time one farm has been plowed, the optimum moment for plowing another may already have passed. Also, after plowing is over, a farmer still needs his own pair of oxen to pull his oxcart, the mainstay of the bulk transport throughout rural India. Quite possibly private ownership of farms, livestock, plows, and oxcarts lowers the efficiency of Indian agriculture, but this, I soon realized, was not caused by cow love.

The shortage of draft animals is a terrible threat that hangs over most of India's peasant families. When an ox falls sick a poor farmer is in danger of losing his farm. If he has no replacement for it, he will have to borrow money at usurious rates. Millions of rural households have in fact lost all or part of their holdings and have gone into sharecropping or day labor as a result of such debts. Each year hundreds of thousands of destitute farmers end up migrating to the cities, which already teem with unemployed and homeless persons.

The Indian farmer who can't replace his sick or deceased ox is in much the same situation as an American farmer who can neither replace nor repair his broken tractor. But there is an important difference: Tractors are made by factories, but oxen are made by cows. A farmer who owns a cow owns a factory for making oxen. With or without cow love, this is a good reason for him not to be too anxious to sell his cow to the slaughterhouse. One also begins to see why Indian farmers might be willing to tolerate cows that give only 500 pounds of milk per year. If the main economic function of the zebu cow is to breed male traction animals, then there's no point in comparing her with specialized American dairy animals, whose main function is to produce milk. Still, the milk produced by zebu cows plays an important role in meeting the nutritional needs of many poor families. Even small amounts of milk products can improve the health of people who are forced to subsist on the edge of starvation.

Agriculture is part of a vast system of human and natural relationships. To judge isolated portions of this "ecosystem" in terms that are relevant to the conduct of American agribusiness leads to some very strange impressions. Cattle figure in the Indian ecosystem in ways that are easily overlooked or demeaned by observers from industrialized, high-energy societies. In the United States, chemicals have almost completely replaced animal manure as the principal source of farm fertilizer. American farmers stopped using manure when they began to plow with tractors rather than mules or horses. Since tractors excrete poisons rather than fertilizers, a commitment to large-scale machine farming is almost of necessity a commitment to the use of chemical fertilizers. And around the world today there has in fact grown up a vast integrated petrochemical-tractor-truck industrial complex that produces farm machinery, motorized transport, oil and gasoline, and chemical fertilizers and pesticides upon which new high-yield production techniques depend.

For better or worse, most of India's farmers cannot participate in this complex, not because they worship their cows, but because they can't afford to buy tractors. Like other underdeveloped nations, India can't build factories that are competitive with the facilities of the industrialized nations nor pay for large quantities of imported industrial products. To convert from animals and manure to tractors and petrochemicals would require the investment of incredible amounts of capital. Moreover, the inevitable effect of substituting costly machines for cheap animals is to reduce the number of people who can earn their living from agriculture and to force a corresponding increase in the size of the average farm. We know that the development of large-scale agribusiness in the United States has meant the virtual destruction of the small family farm. Less than 5 percent of U.S. families now live on farms, as compared with 60 percent about a hundred years ago. If agribusiness were to develop along similar lines in India, jobs and housing would soon have to be found for a quarter of a billion displaced peasants.

Since the suffering caused by unemployment and homelessness in India's cities is already intolerable, an additional massive build-up of the urban population can only lead to unprecedented upheavals and catastrophes.

With this alternative in view, it becomes easier to understand low-energy, small-scale, animal-based systems. As I have already pointed out, cows and oxen provide low-energy substitutes for tractors and tractor factories. They also should be credited with carrying out the functions of a petrochemical industry. India's cattle annually excrete about 700 million tons of recoverable manure. Approximately half of this total is used as fertilizer, while most of the remainder is burned to provide heat for cooking. The annual quantity of heat liberated by this dung, the Indian housewife's main cooking fuel, is the thermal equivalent of 27 million tons of kerosene, 35 million tons of coal, or 68 million tons of wood. Since India has only small reserves of oil and coal and is already the victim of extensive deforestation, none of these fuels can be considered practical substitutes for cow dung. The thought of dung in the kitchen may not appeal to the average American, but Indian women regard it as a superior cooking fuel because it is finely adjusted to their domestic routines. Most Indian dishes are prepared with clarified butter known as ghee, for which cow dung is the preferred source of heat since it burns with a clean, slow, long-lasting flame that doesn't scorch the food. This enables the Indian housewife to start cooking her meals and to leave them unattended for several hours while she takes care of the children, helps out in the fields, or performs other chores. American housewives achieve a similar effect through a complex set of electronic controls that come as expensive options on late-model stoves.

Cow dung has at least one other major function. Mixed with water and made into a paste, it is used as a household flooring material. Smeared over a dirt floor and left to harden into a smooth surface, it keeps the dust down and can be swept clean with a broom.

Because cattle droppings have so many useful properties, every bit of dung is carefully collected. Village small fry are given the task of following the family cow around and of bringing home its daily petrochemical output. In the cities, sweeper castes enjoy a monopoly on the dung deposited by strays and earn their living by selling it to housewives. . . .

During droughts and famines, farmers are severely tempted to kill or sell their livestock. Those who succumb to this temptation seal their doom, even if they survive the drought, for when the rains come, they will be unable to plow their fields. I want to be even more emphatic: Massive slaughter of cattle under the duress of famine constitutes a much greater threat to aggregate welfare than any likely miscalculation by particular farmers concerning the usefulness of their animals during normal times. It seems probable that the sense of unutterable profanity elicited by cow slaughter has its roots in the excruciating contradiction between immediate needs and long-term conditions of survival. Cow love with its sacred symbols and holy doctrines protects the farmer against calculations that are "rational" only in the short term. To Western experts it looks as if "the Indian farmer would rather starve to death than eat his cow.". . . They don't realize that the farmer would rather eat his cow than starve, but that he will starve if he does eat it. . . .

Do I mean to say that cow love has no effect whatsoever on . . . the agricultural system? No. What I am saying is that cow love is an active element in a complex, finely articulated material and cultural order. Cow love mobilizes the latent capacity of human beings to persevere in a low-energy ecosystem in which there is little room for waste or indolence. Cow love contributes to the adaptive resilience of the human population by preserving temporarily dry or barren but still useful animals; by discouraging the growth of an energy-expensive beef industry; by protecting cattle that fatten in the public domain or at landlord's expense; and by preserving the recovery potential of the cattle population during droughts and famines. . . .

Wastefulness is more a characteristic of modern agribusiness than of traditional peasant economies. . . .

Automobiles and airplanes are faster than oxcarts, but they do not use energy more efficiently. In fact, more calories go up in useless heat and smoke during a single day of traffic jams in the United States than is wasted by all the cows of India during an entire year. The comparison is even less favorable when we consider the fact that the stalled vehicles are burning up irreplaceable reserves of petroleum that it took the earth tens of millions of years to accumulate. If you want to see a real sacred cow, go out and look at the family car.

CRITICAL THINKING QUESTIONS

1. What evidence does Harris offer to support his argument that defining the cow as sacred is a necessary strategy for human survival in India?

2. If survival strategies make sense when we take a close look at them, why do they become so "encased" in elaborate cultural explanations?

3. Does India's recognition of the sacred cow help or hurt that nation's natural environment?

4. Following Harris's logic, can you think of reasons that people in some parts of the world (the Middle East, for instance) do not eat pork?

12

Manifesto of the Communist Party

KARL MARX AND FRIEDRICH ENGELS

Society

CLASSIC

CONTEMPORARY

CROSS-CULTURAL

Karl Marx, collaborating with Friedrich Engels, produced the "Manifesto" in 1848. This document is a well-known statement about the origin of social conflict in the process of material production. The ideas of Marx and Engels have been instrumental in shaping the political lives of more than one-fifth of the world's population, and, of course, they have also been instrumental in the development of the social-conflict paradigm in sociology.

BOURGEOIS AND PROLETARIANS[1]

The history of all hitherto existing society[2] is the history of class struggles.

Freeman and slave, patrician and plebeian, lord and serf, guild-master[3] and journeyman, in a word, oppressor and oppressed, stood in constant opposition to one another, carried on an uninterrupted, now hidden, now open fight, a fight that each time ended, either in a revolutionary reconstitution of society at large, or in the common ruin of the contending classes.

Source: From *Manifesto of the Communist Party*, Part I, by Karl Marx and Friedrich Engels.

In the earlier epochs of history, we find almost everywhere a complicated arrangement of society into various orders, a manifold gradation of social rank. In ancient Rome we have patricians, knights, plebeians, slaves; in the Middle Ages, feudal lords, vassals, guild-masters, journeymen, apprentices, serfs; in almost all of these classes, again, subordinate gradations.

The modern bourgeois society that has sprouted from the ruins of feudal society has not done away with class antagonisms. It has but established new classes, new conditions of oppression, new forms of struggle in place of the old ones.

Our epoch, the epoch of the bourgeoisie, possesses, however, this distinctive feature; it has simplified the class antagonisms. Society as a whole is more and more splitting up into two great hostile camps, into two great classes directly facing each other: Bourgeoisie and Proletariat.

From the serfs of the Middle Ages sprang the chartered burghers of the earliest towns. From these burgesses the first elements of the bourgeoisie were developed.

The discovery of America, the rounding of the Cape, opened up fresh ground for the rising bourgeoisie. The East Indian and Chinese markets, the [colonization] of America, trade with the colonies, the increase in the means of exchange and in commodities generally, gave to commerce, to navigation, to industry, an impulse never before known, and thereby, to the revolutionary element in the tottering feudal society, a rapid development.

The feudal system of industry, under which industrial production was monopolized by close guilds, now no longer sufficed for the growing wants of the new markets. The manufacturing system took its place. The guild-masters were pushed on one side by the manufacturing middle class; division of labor between the different corporate guilds vanished in the face of division of labor in each single workshop.

Meantime the markets kept ever growing, the demand, ever rising. Even manufacture no longer sufficed. Thereupon, steam and machinery revolutionized industrial production. The place of manufacture was taken by the giant, Modern Industry, the place of the industrial middle class, by industrial millionaires, the leaders of whole industrial armies, the modern bourgeois.

Modern industry has established the world-market, for which the discovery of America paved the way. This market has given an immense development to commerce, to navigation, to communication by land. This development has, in its turn, reacted on the extension of industry; and in proportion as industry, commerce, navigation, railways extended, in the same proportion the bourgeoisie developed, increased its capital, and pushed into the background every class handed down from the Middle Ages.

We see, therefore, how the modern bourgeoisie is itself the product of a long course of development, of a series of revolutions in the modes of production and of exchange.

Each step in the development of the bourgeoisie was accompanied by a corresponding political advance of that class. An oppressed class under the sway of the feudal nobility, an armed and self-governing association in the mediæval commune,[4] here independent urban republic (as in Italy and Germany), there taxable "third estate" of the monarchy (as in France), afterwards, in the period of manufacture proper, serving either the semi-feudal or the absolute monarchy as a counterpoise against the nobility, and, in fact, cornerstone of the great monarchies in general, the bourgeoisie has at last, since the establishment of modern industry and of the world-market, conquered for itself, in the modern representative State, exclusive political sway. The executive of the modern State is but a committee for managing the common affairs of the whole bourgeoisie.

The bourgeoisie, historically, has played a most revolutionary part.

The bourgeoisie, wherever it has got the upper hand, has put an end to all feudal, patriarchal, idyllic relations. It has pitilessly torn asunder the motley feudal ties that bound man to his "natural superiors," and has left remaining no other nexus between man and man than naked self-interest, than callous "cash payment." It has drowned the most heavenly ecstasies of religious fervour, of chivalrous enthusiasm, of philistine sentimentalism, in the icy water of egotistical calculation. It has resolved personal worth into exchange value, and in place of the numberless indefeasible chartered freedoms, has set up that single, unconscionable freedom—Free Trade. In one word, for exploitation, veiled by religious and political illusions, it has substituted naked, shameless, direct, brutal exploitation.

The bourgeoisie has stripped of its halo every occupation hitherto honoured and looked up to with reverent awe. It has converted the physician, the lawyer, the priest, the poet, the man of science, into its paid [wage-laborers].

The bourgeoisie has torn away from the family its sentimental veil, and has reduced the family relation to a mere money relation.

The bourgeoisie has disclosed how it came to pass that the brutal display of vigour in the Middle Ages, which reactionists so much admire, found its fitting complement in the most slothful indolence. It has been the first to show what man's activity can bring about. It has accomplished wonders far surpassing Egyptian pyramids, Roman aqueducts, and Gothic cathedrals; it has conducted expeditions that put in the shade all former Exoduses of nations and crusades.

The bourgeoisie cannot exist without constantly revolutionizing the instruments of production, and thereby the relations of production, and with them the whole relations of society. Conservation of the old modes of production in unaltered form, was, on the contrary, the first condition of existence for all earlier industrial classes. Constant revolutionizing of production, uninterrupted disturbance of all social conditions, everlasting uncertainty and agitation distinguish the bourgeois epoch from all earlier ones. All fixed, fast-frozen relations, with their train of ancient and venerable prejudices and opinions, are swept away, all new-formed ones become antiquated before they can ossify. All that is solid melts into air, all that is holy is profaned, and man is at last compelled to face with sober senses, his real conditions of life, and his relations with his kind.

The need of a constantly expanding market for its products chases the bourgeoisie over the whole surface of the globe. It must nestle everywhere, settle everywhere, establish [connections] everywhere.

The bourgeoisie has through its exploitation of the world-market given a cosmopolitan character to production and consumption in every country. To the great chagrin of reactionists, it has drawn from under the feet of industry the national ground on which it stood. All old-established national industries have been destroyed or are daily being destroyed. They are dislodged by new industries, whose introduction becomes a life and death question for all civilised nations, by industries that no longer work up indigenous raw material, but raw material drawn from the remotest zones; industries whose products are consumed, not only at home, but in every quarter of the globe. In place of the old wants, satisfied by the productions of the country, we find new wants, requiring for their satisfaction the products of distant lands and climes. In place of the old local and national seclusion and self-sufficiency, we have intercourse in every direction, universal interdependence of nations. And as in material, so also in intellectual production. The intellectual creations of individual nations become common property. National one-sidedness and narrow-mindedness become more and more impossible, and from the numerous national and local literatures there arises a world-literature.

The bourgeoisie, by the rapid improvement of all instruments of production, by the immensely facilitated means of communication, draws all, even the most barbarian, nations into civilization. The cheap prices of its commodities are the heavy artillery with which it batters down all Chinese walls, with which it forces the barbarians' intensely obstinate hatred of foreigners to capitulate. It compels all nations, on pain of extinction, to adopt the bourgeois mode of production; it compels them to introduce what it calls civilization into their midst, i.e., to become bourgeois themselves. In a word, it creates a world after its own image.

The bourgeoisie has subjected the country to the rule of the towns. It has created enormous cities, has greatly increased the urban population as compared with the rural, and has thus rescued a considerable part of the population from the idiocy of rural life. Just as it has made the country dependent on the towns, so it has made barbarian and semi-barbarian countries dependent on the civilised ones, nations of peasants on nations of bourgeois, the East on the West.

The bourgeoisie keeps more and more doing away with the scattered state of the population, of the means of production, and of property. It has agglomerated population, centralized means of production, and has concentrated property in a few hands. The necessary consequence of this was political centralization. Independent, or but loosely connected provinces, with separate interests, laws, governments and systems of taxation, became lumped together in one nation, with one government, one code of laws, one national class-interest, one frontier and one customs-tariff.

The bourgeoisie, during its rule of scarce one hundred years, has created more massive and more colossal productive forces than have all preceding generations together. Subjection of Nature's forces to man, machinery, application of chemistry to industry and agriculture, steam-navigation, railways, electric telegraphs, clearing of whole continents for cultivation, canalization of rivers, whole populations conjured out of the ground—what earlier century had even a presentiment that such productive forces slumbered in the lap of social labor?

We see then: The means of production and of exchange on whose foundation the bourgeoisie built itself up, were generated in feudal society. At a certain stage in the development of these means of production and of exchange, the conditions under which feudal society produced and exchanged, the feudal organization of agriculture and manufacturing industry, in one word, the feudal relations of property became no longer compatible with the already developed productive forces; they became so many fetters. They had to burst asunder; they were burst asunder.

Into their places stepped free competition, accompanied by a social and political constitution adapted to it, and by the economical and political sway of the bourgeois class.

A similar movement is going on before our own eyes. Modern bourgeois society with its relations of production, of exchange and of property, a society that has conjured up such gigantic means of production and of exchange, is like the sorcerer, who is no longer able to control the powers of the nether world whom he has called up by his spells. For many a decade past the history of industry and commerce is but the history of the revolt of modern productive forces against modern conditions of production, against the property relations that are the conditions for the existence of the bourgeoisie and of its rule. It is enough to mention the commercial crises that by their periodical return put on its trial, each time more threateningly, the existence of the entire bourgeois society. In these crises a great part not only of the existing products, but also of the previously created productive forces, are periodically destroyed. In these crises there breaks out an epidemic that, in all earlier epochs, would have seemed an absurdity—the epidemic of overproduction. Society suddenly finds itself put back into a state of momentary barbarism; it appears as if a famine, a universal war of devastation had cut off the supply of every means of subsistence; industry and commerce seem to be destroyed; and why? Because there is too much civilization, too much means of subsistence, too much industry, too much commerce. The productive forces at the disposal of society no longer tend to further the development of the conditions of bourgeois property; on the contrary, they have become too powerful for these conditions, by which they are fettered, and so [as] soon as they overcome these fetters, they bring disorder into the whole of bourgeois society, endanger the existence of bourgeois property. The conditions of bourgeois society are too narrow to comprise the wealth created by them. And how does the bourgeoisie get over these crises? On the one hand by enforced destruction of a mass of productive forces; on the other, by the conquest of new markets, and by the more thorough exploitation of the old ones. That is to say, by paving the way for more extensive and more destructive crises, and by diminishing the means whereby crises are prevented.

The weapons with which the bourgeoisie felled feudalism to the ground are now turned against the bourgeoisie itself.

But not only has the bourgeoisie forged the weapons that bring death to itself; it has also called into existence the men who are to wield those weapons—the modern working class—the proletarians.

In proportion as the bourgeoisie, i.e., capital, is developed, in the same proportion is the proletariat, the modern working class, developed, a class of laborers, who live only so long as they find work, and who find work only so long as their labor increases capital. These laborers, who must sell themselves piecemeal, are a commodity, like every other article of commerce, and are consequently exposed to all the vicissitudes of competition, to all the fluctuations of the market.

Owing to the extensive use of machinery and to division of labor, the work of the proletarians has lost all individual character, and, consequently, all charm for the workman. He becomes an appendage of the machine, and it is only the most simple, most monotonous and most easily acquired knack that is required of him. Hence, the cost of production of a workman is restricted, almost entirely, to the means of subsistence that he requires for his maintenance, and for the propagation of his race. But the price of a commodity, and also of labor, is equal to its cost of production. In proportion, therefore, as the repulsiveness of the work increases, the wage decreases. Nay more, in proportion as the use of machinery and division of labor increases, in the same proportion the burden of toil also increases, whether by prolongation of the working hours, by increase of the work enacted in a given time, or by increased speed of the machinery, etc.

Modern industry has converted the little workshop of the patriarchal master into the great factory of the industrial capitalist. Masses of laborers, crowded into the factory, are organized like soldiers. As privates of the industrial army they are placed under the command of a perfect hierarchy of officers and sergeants. Not only are they the slaves of the bourgeois class, and of the bourgeois State, they are daily and hourly enslaved by the machine, by the over-looker, and,

above all, by the individual bourgeois manufacturer himself. The more openly this despotism proclaims gain to be its end and aim, the more petty, the more hateful and the more embittering it is.

The less the skill and exertion or strength implied in manual labor, in other words, the more modern industry becomes developed, the more is the labor of men superseded by that of women. Differences of age and sex have no longer any distinctive social validity for the working class. All are instruments of labor, more or less expensive to use, according to their age and sex.

No sooner is the exploitation of the laborer by the manufacturer, so far, at an end, that he receives his wages in cash, than he is set upon by the other portions of the bourgeoisie, the landlord, the shopkeeper, the pawnbroker, etc.

The lower strata of the middle class—the small tradespeople, shopkeepers, and retired tradesmen generally, the handicraftsmen and peasants—all these sink gradually into the proletariat, partly because their diminutive capital does not suffice for the scale on which Modern Industry is carried on, and is swamped in the competition with the large capitalists, partly because their specialised skill is rendered worthless by new methods of production. Thus the proletariat is recruited from all classes of the population.

The proletariat goes through various stages of development. With its birth begins its struggle with the bourgeoisie. At first the contest is carried on by individual laborers, then by the workpeople of a factory, then by the operatives of one trade, in one locality, against the individual bourgeois who directly exploits them. They direct their attacks not against the bourgeois conditions of production, but against the instruments of production themselves; they destroy imported wares that compete with their labor, they smash to pieces machinery, they set factories ablaze, they seek to restore by force the vanished status of the workman of the Middle Ages.

At this stage the laborers still form an incoherent mass scattered over the whole country, and broken up by their mutual competition. If anywhere they unite to form more compact bodies, this is not yet the consequence of their own active union, but of the union of the bourgeoisie, which class, in order to attain its own political ends, is compelled to set the whole proletariat in motion, and is moreover yet, for a time, able to do so. At this stage, therefore, the proletarians do not fight their enemies, but the enemies of their enemies, the remnants of absolute monarchy, the landowners, the non-industrial bourgeois, the petty bourgeoisie. Thus the whole historical movement is concentrated in the hands of the bourgeoisie; every victory so obtained is a victory for the bourgeoisie.

But with the development of industry the proletariat not only increases in number, it becomes concentrated in greater masses, its strength grows, and it feels that strength more. The various interests and conditions of life within the ranks of the proletariat are more and more equalized, in proportion as machinery obliterates all distinctions of labor, and nearly everywhere reduces wages to the same low level. The growing competition among the bourgeois, and the resulting commercial crises, make the wages of the workers ever more fluctuating. The unceasing improvement of machinery, ever more rapidly developing, makes their livelihood more and more precarious; the collisions between individual workmen and individual bourgeois take more and more the character of collisions between two classes. Thereupon the workers begin to form combinations (Trades' Unions) against the bourgeois; they club together in order to keep up the rate of wages; they found permanent associations in order to make provision beforehand for these occasional revolts. Here and there the contest breaks out into riots.

Now and then the workers are victorious, but only for a time. The real fruit of their battles lies, not in the immediate result, but in the ever expanding union of the workers. This union is helped on by the improved means of communication that are created by modern industry, and that

place the workers of different localities in contact with one another. It was just this contact that was needed to centralize the numerous local struggles, all of the same character, into one national struggle between classes. But every class struggle is a political struggle. And that union, to attain which the burghers of the Middle Ages, with their miserable highways, required centuries, the modern proletarians, thanks to railways, achieve in a few years.

This organization of the proletarians into a class, and consequently into a political party, is continually being upset again by the competition between the workers themselves. But it ever rises up again, stronger, firmer, mightier. It compels legislative recognition of particular interests of the workers, by taking advantage of the divisions among the bourgeoisie itself. Thus the ten-hours'-bill in England was carried.

Altogether collisions between the classes of the old society further, in many ways, the course of development of the proletariat. The bourgeoisie finds itself involved in a constant battle. At first with the aristocracy; later on, with those portions of the bourgeoisie itself, whose interests have become antagonistic to the progress of industry; at all times, with the bourgeoisie of foreign countries. In all these battles it sees itself compelled to appeal to the proletariat, to ask for its help, and thus, to drag it into the political arena. The bourgeoisie itself, therefore, supplies the proletariat with its own elements of political and general education, in other words, it furnishes the proletariat with weapons for fighting the bourgeoisie.

Further, as we have already seen, entire sections of the ruling classes are, by the advance of industry, precipitated into the proletariat, or are at least threatened in their conditions of existence. These also supply the proletariat with fresh elements of enlightenment and progress.

Finally, in times when the class-struggle nears the decisive hour, the process of dissolution going on within the ruling class, in fact within the whole range of old society, assumes such a violent, glaring character, that a small section of the ruling class cuts itself adrift, and joins the revolutionary class, the class that holds the future in its hands. Just as, therefore, at an earlier period, a section of the nobility went over to the bourgeoisie, so now a portion of the bourgeoisie goes over to the proletariat, and in particular, a portion of the bourgeois ideologists, who have raised themselves to the level of comprehending theoretically the historical movements as a whole.

Of all the classes that stand face to face with the bourgeoisie today, the proletariat alone is a really revolutionary class. The other classes decay and finally disappear in the face of modern industry; the proletariat is its special and essential product.

The lower-middle class, the small manufacturer, the shopkeeper, the artisan, the peasant, all these fight against the bourgeoisie, to save from extinction their existence as fractions of the middle class. They are therefore not revolutionary, but conservative. Nay more, they are reactionary, for they try to roll back the wheel of history. If by chance they are revolutionary, they are so, only in view of their impending transfer into the proletariat, they thus defend not their present, but their future interests, they desert their own standpoint to place themselves at that of the proletariat.

The "dangerous class," the social scum, that passively rotting mass thrown off by the lowest layers of old society, may, here and there, be swept into the movement by a proletarian revolution; its conditions of life, however, prepare it far more for the part of a bribed tool of reactionary intrigue.

In the conditions of the proletariat, those of old society at large are already virtually swamped. The proletarian is without property; his relation to his wife and children has no longer anything in common with the bourgeois family-relations; modern industrial labor, modern subjection to capital, the same in England as in France, in America as in Germany, has stripped him of every trace of national character. Law, morality, religion, are to him so many bourgeois

prejudices, behind which lurk in ambush just as many bourgeois interests.

All the preceding classes that got the upper hand sought to fortify their already acquired status by subjecting at large to their conditions of appropriation. The proletarians cannot become masters of the productive forces of society, except by abolishing their own previous mode of appropriation, and thereby also every other previous mode of appropriation. They have nothing of their own to secure and to fortify; their mission is to destroy all previous securities for, and insurances of, individual property.

All previous historical movements were movements of minorities, or in the interest of minorities. The proletarian movement is the self-conscious, independent movement of the immense majority, in the interest of the immense majority. The proletariat, the lowest stratum of our present society, cannot stir, cannot raise itself up, without the whole superincumbent strata of official society being sprung into the air.

Though not in substance, yet in form, the struggle of the proletariat with the bourgeoisie is at first a national struggle. The proletariat of each country must, of course, first of all settle matters with its own bourgeoisie.

In depicting the most general phases of the development of the proletariat, we traced the more or less veiled civil war, raging within existing society, up to the point where that war breaks out into open revolution, and where the violent overthrow of the bourgeoisie, lays the foundation for the sway of the proletariat.

Hitherto, every form of society has been based, as we have already seen, on the antagonism of oppressing and oppressed classes. But in order to oppress a class, certain conditions must be assured to it under which it can, at least, continue its slavish existence. The serf, in the period of serfdom, raised himself to membership in the commune, just as the petty bourgeois, under the yoke of feudal absolutism, managed to develop into a bourgeois. The modern laborer, on the contrary, instead of rising with the progress of industry, sinks deeper and deeper below the conditions of existence of his own class. He becomes a pauper, and pauperism develops more rapidly than population and wealth. And here it becomes evident, that the bourgeoisie is unfit any longer to be the ruling class in society, and to impose its conditions of existence upon society as an overriding law. It is unfit to rule, because it is incompetent to assure an existence to its slave within his slavery, because it cannot help letting him sink into such a state, that it has to feed him, instead of being fed by him. Society can no longer live under this bourgeoisie, in other words, its existence is no longer compatible with society.

The essential condition for the existence, and for the sway of the bourgeois class, is the formation and augmentation of capital; the condition for capital is wage-labor. Wage-labor rests exclusively on competition between the laborers. The advance of industry, whose involuntary promoter is the bourgeoisie, replaces the isolation of the laborers, due to competition, by their involuntary combination, due to association. The development of modern industry, therefore, cuts from under its feet the very foundation on which the bourgeoisie produces and appropriates products. What the bourgeoisie therefore produces, above all, are its own grave-diggers. Its fall and the victory of the proletariat are equally inevitable.

CRITICAL THINKING QUESTIONS

1. What are the distinguishing factors of "class conflict"? How does this differ from other kinds of conflict, as between individuals or nations?

2. Why do Marx and Engels argue that understanding society in the present requires investigating the society of the past?

3. On what grounds did Marx and Engels *praise* industrial capitalism? On what grounds did they *condemn* the system?

NOTES

1. By *bourgeoisie* is meant the class of modern capitalists, owners of the means of social production and employers of wage-labor; by *proletariat*, the class of modern wage-laborers who, having no means of production of their own, are reduced to selling their labor-power in order to live.

2. That is, all written history. In 1847, the prehistory of society, the social organization existing previous to recorded history, was all but unknown. Since then, Haxthausen discovered common ownership of land in Russia. Maurer proved it to be the social foundation from which all Teutonic races started in history, and by and by village communities were found to be, or to have been, the primitive form of society everywhere from India to Ireland. The inner organization of this primitive Communistic society was laid bare, in its typical form, by Morgan's crowning discovery of the true nature of the gens and its relation to the tribe. With the dissolution of these primæval communities society begins to be differentiated into separate and finally antagonistic classes. I have attempted to retrace this process of dissolution in "Der Ursprung der Familie, des Privateigenthums und des Staats," 2d ed. Stuttgart 1886.

3. Guild-master, that is, a full member of a guild, a master within, not a head of, a guild.

4. "Commune" was the name taken, in France, by the nascent towns even before they had conquered from their feudal lords and masters, local self-government and political rights as "the Third Estate." Generally speaking, for the economical development of the bourgeoisie, England is here taken as the typical country, [and] for its political development, France.

13

Society

CLASSIC

CONTEMPORARY

CROSS-CULTURAL

Marx, Globalization, and Modernity: What Is Old Becomes New Again

PETER URMETZER

In the beginning of the 21st century, people are generally awed by the pace of technological progress. This has resulted in all kinds of pronouncements about how we are living in an era of unprecedented change. But exactly how novel are such observations? This reading uses the Communist Manifesto (featured in the previous reading) as a basis to illustrate that many of the uncertainties that are commonly associated with globalization are remarkably similar to observations made by Marx and Engels in the middle of the 1800s in Europe.

Everything has been thought of before, but the problem is to think of it again.

—Johann W. von Goethe

Hegel remarks somewhere that all great world historic facts and personages appear, so to speak, twice. He forgot to add: the first time as tragedy, the second time as farce.

—Karl Marx

WHAT'S NEW?

Is it true, as Hegel and then Marx observed, that everything happens twice? With respect to globalization, then, are we living amid tragedy or farce? Or as Goethe would suggest, has the idea of globalization been thought of before? In this

Source: Peter Urmetzer. 2005. In *Globalization Unplugged: Sovereignty and the Canadian State in the Twenty-First Century*, pp. 39–41, 42–47. Toronto: University of Toronto Press.

chapter I argue that globalization has been thought of before and that it was identified in everything but name by Marx and Engels more than 150 years ago in their *Manifesto of the Communist Party*. At the time of writing, 1848, the ideas embraced by communists were disseminated in the *Manifesto* to warn of the drastic consequences of capitalism, a mode of production that the authors predicted would eventually collapse under its own weight and open the way to socialism. More than a century and a half later, socialism has come and gone while capitalism reigns (notwithstanding exceptions such as North Korea, Cuba, and China). In an ironic twist, in what could only be described as farce, the political right has now appropriated some of the ideas from the *Manifesto* and used a similar kind of logic to predict not the collapse of capitalism but its final triumph.

First, I take a close look at the language of the *Manifesto* to highlight the similarities between it and current accounts of globalization. The section following again uses the *Manifesto* for comparative purposes, this time as a *Zeitdiagnose* originating in cultural studies that attempts to capture the mood of the current age. Here it is argued that we've had this feeling before.

GLOBALIZATION, *DER WELTMARKT*, *LE MONDE*

Many authors have tried to link the novelty of the process of globalization to the newness of the word itself. Albrow (1996) has traced the genealogy of 'globalization' to the postwar period. In this respect, we can be reasonably sure that the word 'globalization' is new. *Merriam Webster's Dictionary* traces the first use of 'globalize' to 1944, and the *Oxford English Dictionary* dates the first use of 'globalization' to only 1962. The novelty of the word, however, should not be overemphasized, as this equates the process to the word, and even some staunch advocates of globalization insist that the process has been unfolding for centuries. Since the globalization perspective is proudly anti-Westerncentric, it should pay heed to the fact that other languages or cultures may have incorporated this concept, a fact automatically precluded by an approach focusing on the brief history of its use since the Second World War.

In other words, presenting the word's etymology as equivalent to its history constitutes too literal an interpretation, as it ignores the fact that the concept of global markets has existed for a long time. Using selected passages from the *Manifesto,* I am going to argue that Marx and Engels painted a picture of society that is remarkably similar to that presented by globalists today. It is essential to keep in mind that Marx and Engels wrote primarily in German, and that the word 'globalization' is, after all, English. In fact a case can be made that had the word 'globalization' existed in the mid-eighteen hundreds, Marx and Engels would have used it. The *Manifesto*

provides many examples of how capitalism uses the globe as its stage, revealing that this idea can lay claim to an ancestry that goes back at least a century and a half. The following passage might well be found in a contemporary account of globalization:

> The need of a constantly expanding market for its products chases the bourgeoisie over the whole surface of the globe. It must nestle everywhere, settle everywhere, establish connexion everywhere. (Marx and Engels 1986: 37)

Compare this to a definition of globalization offered by the *Fortune Encyclopedia of Economics.* 'The owners of these mobile production factors . . . are increasingly "shopping around" the world for the labor and the style of government administration that promise them a high rate of return (and low risks) . . . Internationally, this has led to the phenomenon of globalization . . . ' (Kasper 1993: 84). The general thrust of the two arguments is strikingly similar, although the terminology is not. In contemporary discussions about globalization, 'bourgeoisie' is replaced by 'capital' or 'multinational corporations.' Reference in the *Manifesto* to an 'expanding market' leaves little doubt not only that unfettered capitalism has long been recognized, but that it has invited criticism as well. The frequent use of the word 'globe' itself brings into sharp focus the long-term historical awareness (the phenomenological aspect) of the process of globalization that Robertson (1992) and Waters (2001) contend differentiates our age from those past.

The use of the word 'globe' is not the only reference to this worldly consciousness. Allusions to the 'world as one place' set the tone for much of the *Manifesto:* 'The bourgeoisie has through its exploitation of the world market given a cosmopolitan character to production and consumption in every country' (Marx and Engels 1986: 37). The emphasis here is on a process that is greater than an individual country. The word 'cosmopolitan' (*kosmopolitisch* in German), derived from the Greek *cosmo,* meaning 'world,' could easily serve as a synonym for 'global.' The word 'world' is used nine times throughout the *Manifesto* and is indicative of the inclusive and expansive world-view adopted by the authors. In German the word for 'world' is *Welt*, where it can mean many things, not only the world, but also the universe or the globe (Marx and Engels 1989). Recognition of a 'world market' (Marx and Engels 1986: 36, 37) serves as strong evidence that the consciousness of the 'globe' as a single society has been with us for some time.

Even some of the geographical regions highlighted in the *Manifesto,* such as China, are identical to those identified as major players in today's global economy. The references to distant locales around the globe, their connection to technology, and the rise of the bourgeoisie are strikingly similar to current observations about 'globalization.'

The discovery of America, the rounding of the Cape, opened up fresh ground for the rising bourgeoisie. The East-Indian and Chinese markets, the colonisation of America, trade with the colonies, the increase in the means of exchange and in commodities generally, gave to commerce, to navigation, to industry, an impulse never before known, and thereby, to the revolutionary element in the tottering feudal society, a rapid development. (Marx and Engels 1986: 33)

The fact that Marx and Engels attributed this 'impulse' to the forces of capitalism is less critical than their consciousness of the process, and of the general climate of instability and insecurity it created. . . .

Marx, Modernity, and the New

The *Manifesto,* however, is significant not only as a harbinger of contemporary accounts of globalization but also as a snapshot of modernity. Here I argue that globalization is neither new nor distinct from modernism but is merely modernism by another name. The *Manifesto* has been identified as 'the first major sociopolitical affirmation of modernity' (Therborn 1995: 125), and in this sense it has proved to be an enduring document. In their overall tenor, contemporary accounts of globalization are strangely similar to the *Zeit-diagnose* identified by Marx and Engels 150 years ago, a climate of change that the two German expatriates attributed to 'Modern Industry' and the 'Modern State.' Use of the word 'modern' is key here; it appears thirty-two times in the approximately thirty-page document. The argument that follows makes the case that observations about globalization in contemporary society are not distinct enough from observations about modernism to qualify as a new theory.

The critical question that needs to be asked is whether globalization is a useful concept or theory. In order for a concept to meet such criteria, a *new* concept should correspondingly explain something *new* about the world. Most importantly, to be valuable, the concept of globalization should refer to processes that are clearly different from those that fall under the rubric of 'modernity,' a concept to which 'globalization' ostensibly stands in contrast. The impact of technology, the increased interconnection of different peoples, and the phenomenon of time-space compression have all been commented on by a multitude of observers and are often recognized as hallmarks of modernity. The emphasis of modernity has long been to differentiate our society from those of a preceding age, to identify the new (Kumar 1994: 392). Ideally a useful theory of globalization would identify new institutions and processes that separate it from modernity without relying on modernist conceptual tools (e.g., time-space compression, technology). At a minimum, a theory of globalization should make a convincing case for why an acceleration in this process amounts to a qualitative transformation. In short, a new theory should be more than simply anti-modern in sentiment and should provide evidence of how the rejection of modernism is manifested in the social world.

Further analysis of the *Manifesto* shows that the globalization theory fails on both counts: (1) it fails to isolate new institutions, and (2) it fails to provide convincing evidence of how this process has qualitatively changed. Similarities between contemporary accounts of globalization and modernism are not confined to the political project but spill over and incorporate the *Zeitdiagnose*. One resemblance between early modernist and the current literature on globalization is an ambivalent attitude towards technology. Throughout the globalization literature there exists an awe towards, even reverence for, technology. In much the same way that Marx and Engels saw the spread of capitalism and technology beyond the reach of 'national one-sidedness and narrow-mindedness,' technology is implicated in today's events.

[The] *flows* of ideas, commodities, symbols, people, images and money on a global scale ... are disjunctive and fragmenting, anarchical and disordered ... unbounded by spatial borders ... Many institutions of existing nation-states are now a fetter upon the emerging glocal modes of productions ... Borders today are highly porous, and the pressure of glocal flows of goods and services are continuously eroding them even more every day. (Luke 1995: 99; italics in original)

Compare this to the following passage from the *Manifesto*.

The bourgeoisie, during its rule of scarce one hundred years, has created more massive and more colossal productive forces than have all preceding generations together. Subjection of Nature's forces to man, machinery, application of chemistry to industry and agriculture, steam-navigation, railways, electric telegraphs, clearing of whole continents for cultivation, canalisation of rivers, whole populations conjured out of the ground—what earlier century had even a presentiment that such productive forces slumbered in the lap of social labour? (Marx and Engels 1986: 38, 39)

The global consequences of this process are also noted by Marx and Engels: 'The bourgeoisie, by the rapid improvement of all instruments of production, by the immensely facilitated means of communication, draw all, even the most barbarian, nations into civilisation ... It compels all nations, on pain of extinction, to adopt the bourgeois mode of production ... In one word, it creates a world after its own image' (Marx and Engels 1986: 38). This passage was written more

than 150 years ago. The phenomena it describes have been incorporated into contemporary theories of globalization, but with the important proviso that these changes are now qualitatively different.

Plainly, a 'transnational' flow of goods, capital, people and ideas has existed for centuries; it antedates even the rise of nation-states. However, this historical flow, at least until the 1950s and 1960s, tended to move more slowly, move less and more narrowly than the rush of products, ideas, persons and money that develops with jet transportation, electronic telecommunications, massive decolonization and extensive computerization after 1960. It is these greater intensities, rates, densities, levels and velocities of the post-historical flows, which have transmuted it quantitatively into something qualitatively new, complex and different. (Luke 1995: 99)

Here again we encounter an emphasis on technology as a primary impetus for globalization. Most interesting is how adamant the author is about the novelty of this process. Jet engines, computerization, and electronic telecommunications, all of which are relatively recent inventions, are introduced to stress just how far technology has advanced, an advance that, in the eyes of the author, serves as a justification to announce the advent of a new age. But as Harvey (1995: 9) points out, 'the newness of the railroad and the telegraph, the automobile, the radio, and the telephone in their day impressed equally.' To put it in everyday language, if it's not one thing, it's another.

Two further comments can be made with respect to contemporary observations about technology and globalization. First, in light of Marx and Engels's work, the emphasis on technology and how it is implicated in the acceleration of globalization borders on the hackneyed. Only a fool would argue that technology is less advanced now than it was around Marx's time, but this misses the bigger point. The more important observation is that this relentless accumulation of technology, commonly called progress, is a constant by-product of modernity. It is far from new, and it differs merely in degree.

Second, as is only too common in cultural accounts, there is scant evidence presented for these increased flows. The overall thrust of the passage is a combination of enthusiasm for and unease about contemporary changes, yet there is no evidence of the degree to which these flows have increased, despite a claim of a transformation from the quantitative to the qualitative. Furthermore . . . a focus on international flows completely ignores national flows, which may well counteract the denationalizing effects of international flows. And finally, these flows are far from unrestricted, as the movement of goods, services, ideas, and people continues to be tightly controlled by states. Massey has properly noted that globalization is primarily written about by people who are able to enjoy intercontinental travel: academics and journalists. Such an approach ignores how 'differential mobility can weaken the leverage of the already weak' (Massey 1994: 150).

A theory that attempts to distinguish itself from modernity, as globalization does, would have to spell out how the world is moving away from its reverence for technology. In other words, in order to eclipse modernism, such a theory would have to successfully escape the straitjacket of technology and reject the allure of the new. Postmodernism spelled out what some of these conditions might be—a rejection of the institutions of modernism (see Giddens 1990)—but postmodernism remains primarily a vision about how society ought to be and not about what it is. Similar charges can be made against visions of globalization. And when it comes to how contemporary society *is,* it continues to be very much modern.

Similarities between the *Manifesto* and contemporary writings indicate that globalists continue the old modernist admiration for the new. Often this new world is simultaneously revered and feared. Moreover, control over new technology is perceived to be out of our hands. Flows of money, people, goods, and so on, are so chaotic and uncontrollable that they cause us to experience a general sense of unease or 'ontological insecurity' (Giddens 1990). This admiration of the new and at the same time the anxiety it engenders are hallmarks of the 'juggernaut of modernity,' an analogy used by Giddens. In powerful language, Marx and Engels write about the turbulent times that accompany modernism, their account sounding strangely similar to present-day observations about the novel characteristics of globalization.

Constant revolutionising of production, uninterrupted disturbance of all social conditions, everlasting uncertainty and agitation distinguish the bourgeois epoch from earlier ones. All fixed, fast-frozen relations, with their train of ancient and venerable prejudices and opinions, are swept away, all new-formed ones become antiquated before they can ossify. All that is solid melts into air, all that is holy is profaned, and man is at last compelled to face, with sober senses, his real conditions of life, and his relations with his kind. (Marx and Engels 1986: 37)

In his incisive account of modernism, Berman puts contemporary observations that echo these sentiments into perspective: 'People who find themselves in the midst of this maelstrom are apt to feel that they are the first ones, and maybe the only ones, that are going through it . . . In fact, however, great and ever-increasing numbers of people have been going through it for close to five hundred years' (Berman 1982: 16). This suggests that the subjective component of globalization, the increased consciousness of the new, may not be all that good an indicator of a new age. The excitement generated by the perceived novelty of our world is a faithful, often silent, companion of modernism. According to Therborn (1995) modernism is, more than anything, an experience, and this experience is remarkably similar to that described by globalists. For that reason, we cannot rely on general impressions as evidence of globalization. In the end, evidence of globalization amounts to no more than impressions, impressions that appear to be not particularly original. To perceive these observations as new is no more than a globalist's conceit; these characteristics are already emblematic of another age: modernism.

Optimally we might expect similar features from a theory of globalization to what we find with modernity. That is, a theory that identifies, and preferably explains, a break similar to the break from traditional society that characterizes modernity. A theory of globalization should set itself apart from modernity not only by being anti-modern, that is, by rejecting ideas of modernism (as do the Club of Rome and many environmental movements, for example), but also by presenting evidence of how the world has made concrete changes in an anti-modern direction. The fact is that people and governments are still very much bound by the principles and beliefs of modernity. The continual attention paid to growth, the persistence of a consumer culture, and the unwillingness to change in the face of potential environmental disaster indicate that anti-modernism exists only in spirit and is not manifested in action.

It is easy to see why the *Manifesto* continues to inspire so many people. Its language is uncompromising, concise, and forceful—its observations timeless. A reading of the *Manifesto* reveals that the ideas associated with globalization—ideas about its power, inevitability, and intractability—are already more than a century and a half old and may be as old as capitalism itself. It is no small irony that those on the right, who in the past have derided Marx as deterministic and rigid, have now adopted a similar approach when they portray contemporary markets. Marx regarded what he identified as the tumultuous circumstances surrounding capitalism as tragedy. One hundred and fifty-seven years later, the same ideas are used to celebrate the victory of capitalism. As Marx said, first there was tragedy, then there was farce.

CRITICAL THINKING QUESTIONS

1. Think about the twentieth century and the changes (social and technological) that occurred. Think about the consequences of those events. Which do you think was the more eventful era, the first half or the second half of the century?

2. Do you agree with Berman's observation that the feeling of the new is a steady companion of modernity, or do you think that there is something fundamentally different and new about globalization?

3. When you hear or read about globalization what processes do you think about? How new are these processes? Why do you think the concept of globalization has become so popular?

REFERENCES

Albrow, Martin. 1994. "Globalization," (248–49) in *The Blackwell Dictionary of Twentieth-Century Social Thought* (eds. Outhwaite and Bottomore). Oxford: Blackwell.

Berman, Marshall. 1982. *All that is Solid Melts into Air.* New York: Penguin.

Giddens, Anthony. 1990. *The Consequences of Modernity.* Stanford: Stanford University Press.

Harvey, David. 1995. "Globalization in Question," (1–17) in *Rethinking Marxism,* Vol. 8 No. 4.

Kasper, Wolfgang. 1993. "Spatial Economics," (82–85) in *The Fortune Encyclopaedia of Economics* (ed. D.R. Henderson). New York: Warner Books.

Kumar, Krishan. 1994. "Modernity," (391–92), in *The Blackwell Dictionary of Twentieth-Century Social Thought* (eds. Outhwaite and Bottomore). Oxford: Blackwell.

Luke, T.W. 1995. "New World Order or Neoworld Orders: Power, Politics, and Ideology in Informationalizing Glocalities," in *Global Modernities* (eds. Featherstone *et al*). London: Sage.

Massey, Doreen. 1994. *Space, Place, and Gender*. Minneapolis: University of Minnesota Press.

Marx, Karl; Engels, Friedrich. 1986. *Manifesto of the Communist Party.* Moscow: Progress Publishers.

Marx, Karl; Engels, Friedrich. 1989. *Manifest der Kommunistischen Partei.* Stuttgart: Reclam.

Robertson, Roland. 1992. *Globalization: Social Theory and Global Culture.* London: Sage.

Therborn, Goran. 1995. "Routes to/through Modernity," in *Global Modernities* (eds. Featherstone *et al*). London: Sage.

Waters, Malcolm. 2001. *Globalization* (2nd ed.). New York: Routledge.

14

The Amish: A Small Society

JOHN A. HOSTETLER

Society

CLASSIC

CONTEMPORARY

CROSS-CULTURAL

Some 100,000 Old Order Amish live in the rolling farmland of Pennsylvania, Ohio, Indiana, and southern Ontario. These descendants of 16th-century Germans, who fled persecution for their religious beliefs, constitute a distinctive "small society" that keeps the larger world at arm's length. This description of the Amish suggests the extent of cultural diversity within North America and raises questions about why some people would reject the "advantages" that many others take for granted.

Small communities, with their distinctive character—where life is stable and intensely human—are disappearing. Some have vanished from the face of the earth, others are dying slowly, but all have undergone changes as they have come into contact with an expanding machine civilization. The merging of diverse peoples into a common mass has produced tension among members of the minorities and the majority alike.

The Old Order Amish, who arrived on American shores in colonial times, have survived in the modern world in distinctive, viable, small communities. They have resisted the homogenization process more successfully than others. In planting and harvest time one can see their bearded men working the fields with horses and their women hanging out the laundry in neat rows to dry.

Many American people have seen Amish families, with the men wearing broad-brimmed black hats and the women in bonnets and long dresses, in railway depots or bus terminals. Although the Amish have lived with industrialized America for over two and a half centuries, they have moderated its influence on their personal lives, their families, communities, and their values.

The Amish are often perceived by other Americans to be relics of the past who live an austere, inflexible life dedicated to inconvenient and archaic customs. They are seen as renouncing both modern conveniences and the American dream of success and progress. But most people have no quarrel with the Amish for doing things the old-fashioned way. Their conscientious objection was tolerated in wartime, for after all, they are meticulous farmers who practice the virtues of work and thrift.

. . . The Amish are a church, a community, a spiritual union, a conservative branch of Christianity, a religion, a community whose

Source: From *Amish Society*, 3rd ed., by John A. Hostetler (Baltimore: The Johns Hopkins University Press, 1980), pp. 3–12. Reprinted with permission.

members practice simple and austere living, a familistic entrepreneuring system, and an adaptive human community. . . .

The Amish are in some ways a little commonwealth, for their members claim to be ruled by the law of love and redemption. The bonds that unite them are many. Their beliefs, however, do not permit them solely to occupy and defend a particular territory. They are highly sensitive in caring for their own. They will move to other lands when circumstances force them to do so.

Commonwealth implies a place, a province, which means any part of a national domain that geographically and socially is sufficiently unified to have a true consciousness of its unity. Its inhabitants feel comfortable with their own ideas and customs, and the "place" possesses a sense of distinction from other parts of the country. Members of a commonwealth are not foot-loose. They have a sense of productivity and accountability in a province where "the general welfare" is accepted as a day-to-day reality. Commonwealth has come to have an archaic meaning in today's world, because when groups and institutions become too large, the sense of commonwealth or the common good is lost. Thus it is little wonder that the most recent dictionaries of the American English language render the meaning of commonwealth as "obsolescent." In reality, the Amish are in part a commonwealth. There is, however, no provision for outcasts.

It may be argued that the Amish have retained elements of wholesome provincialism, a saving power to which the world in the future will need more and more to appeal. Provincialism need not turn to ancient narrowness and ignorance, confines from which many have sought to escape. A sense of province or commonwealth, with its cherished love of people and self-conscious dignity, is a necessary basis for relating to the wider world community. Respect for locality, place, custom, and local idealism can go a long way toward checking the monstrous growth of consolidation in the nation and thus help to save human freedom and individual dignity. . . . Anthropologists, who have compared societies all over the world, have tended to call semi-isolated peoples "folk societies," "primitives,"

or merely "simple societies." These societies constitute an altogether different type in contrast to the industrialized, or so-called civilized, societies.

The "folk society," as conceptualized by Robert Redfield,[1] is a small, isolated, traditional, simple, homogeneous society in which oral communication and conventionalized ways are important factors in integrating the whole life. In such an ideal-type society, shared practical knowledge is more important than science, custom is valued more than critical knowledge, and associations are personal and emotional rather than abstract and categoric.

Folk societies are uncomfortable with the idea of change. Young people do what the old people did when they were young. Members communicate intimately with one another, not only by word of mouth but also through custom and symbols that reflect a strong sense of belonging to one another. A folk society is *Gemeinschaft*-like; there is a strong sense of "we-ness." Leadership is personal rather than institutionalized. There are no gross economic inequalities. Mutual aid is characteristic of the society's members. The goals of life are never stated as matters of doctrine, but neither are they questioned. They are implied by the acts that constitute living in a small society. Custom tends to become sacred. Behavior is strongly patterned, and acts as well as cultural objects are given symbolic meaning that is often pervasively religious. Religion is diffuse and all-pervasive. In the typical folk society, planting and harvesting are as sacred in their own ways as singing and praying.

The folk model lends itself well to understanding the tradition-directed character of Amish society. The heavy weight of tradition can scarcely be explained in any other way. The Amish, for example, have retained many of the customs and small-scale technologies that were common in rural society in the nineteenth century. Through a process of syncretism, Amish religious values have been fused with an earlier period of simple country living when everyone farmed with horses and on a scale where family members could work together. The Amish exist as a folk or "little" community in a rural subculture within the modern state. . . . The outsider who drives through an Amish settlement cannot help but recognize them by their clothing, farm homes, furnishings, fields, and other material traits of culture. Although they speak perfect English with outsiders, they speak a dialect of German among themselves.

Amish life is distinctive in that religion and custom blend into a way of life. The two are inseparable. The core values of the community are religious beliefs. Not only do the members worship a deity they understand through the revelation of Jesus Christ and the Bible, but their patterned behavior [also] has a religious dimension. A distinctive way of life permeates daily life, agriculture, and the application of energy to economic ends. Their beliefs determine their conceptions of the self, the universe, and man's place in it. The Amish world view recognizes a certain spiritual worth and dignity in the universe in its natural form. Religious considerations determine hours of work and the daily, weekly, seasonal, and yearly rituals associated with life experience. Occupation, the means and destinations of travel, and choice of friends and mate are determined by religious considerations. Religious and work attitudes are not far distant from each other. The universe includes the divine, and Amish society itself is considered divine insofar as the Amish recognize themselves as "a chosen people of God." The Amish do not seek to master nature or to work against the elements, but try to work with them. The affinity between Amish society and nature in the form of land, terrain, and vegetation is expressed in various degrees of intensity.

Religion is highly patterned, so one may properly speak of the Amish as a tradition-directed group. Though allusions to the Bible play an important role in determining their outlook on the world, and on life after death, these beliefs have been fused with several centuries of struggling to survive in [a] community. Out of intense religious experience, societal conflict, and intimate agrarian experience, a mentality has developed that prefers the old rather than the new. While the principle seems to apply especially to religion, it

has also become a charter for social behavior. "The old is the best, and the new is of the devil" has become a prevalent mode of thought. By living in closed communities where custom and a strong sense of togetherness prevail, the Amish have formed an integrated way of life and a folklike culture. Continuity of conformity and custom is assured and the needs of the individual from birth to death are met within an integrated and shared system of meanings. Oral tradition, custom, and conventionality play an important part in maintaining the group as a functioning whole. To the participant, religion and custom are inseparable. Commitment and culture are combined to produce a stable human existence.

. . . A century ago, hardly anyone knew the Amish existed. A half-century ago they were viewed as an obscure sect living by ridiculous customs, as stubborn people who resisted education and exploited the labor of their children. Today the Amish are the unwilling objects of a thriving tourist industry on the eastern seaboard. They are revered as hard-working, thrifty people with enormous agrarian stamina, and by some, as islands of sanity in a culture gripped by commercialism and technology run wild.

CRITICAL THINKING QUESTIONS

1. In what ways does this description of the Amish way of life make you think about your own way of life differently?

2. Why would the Amish reject technological advances that most members of our society hold to be invaluable?

3. What might the majority of the North American population learn from the Amish?

NOTE

1. Robert Redfield, "The Folk Society," *American Journal of Sociology*. 52 (Jan. 1947), 293–308. See also his book *The Little Community* (Chicago: University of Chicago Press, 1955).

Socialization

CLASSIC

CONTEMPORARY

CROSS-CULTURAL

15

The Self

GEORGE HERBERT MEAD

The self is not the body but arises in social experience. Explaining this insight is perhaps the greatest contribution of George Herbert Mead. Mead argues that the basic shape of our personalities is derived from the social groupings in which we live. Note, too, that even the qualities that distinguish each of us from others emerge only within a social community.

In our statement of the development of intelligence we have already suggested that the language process is essential for the development of the self. The self has a character which is different from that of the physiological organism proper. The self is something which has a development; it is not initially there, at birth, but arises in the process of social experience and activity, that is, develops in the given

Source: From *Mind, Self and Society: From the Standpoint of a Social Behaviorist* by George Herbert Mead (Chicago: University of Chicago Press, 1934), pp. 135–42, 144, 149–56, 158, 162–64. Copyright © 1934 by the University of Chicago Press. Reprinted with permission of the University of Chicago Press.

individual as a result of his relations to that process as a whole and to other individuals within that process. . . .

We can distinguish very definitely between the self and the body. The body can be there and can operate in a very intelligent fashion without there being a self involved in the experience. The self has the characteristic that it is an object to itself, and that characteristic distinguishes it from other objects and from the body. It is perfectly true that the eye can see the foot, but it does not see the body as a whole. We cannot see our backs; we can feel certain portions of them, if we are agile, but we cannot get an experience of our whole body.

There are, of course, experiences which are somewhat vague and difficult of location, but the bodily experiences are for us organized about a self. The foot and hand belong to the self. We can see our feet, especially if we look at them from the wrong end of an opera glass, as strange things which we have difficulty in recognizing as our own. The parts of the body are quite distinguishable from the self. We can lose parts of the body without any serious invasion of the self. The mere ability to experience different parts of the body is not different from the experience of a table. The table presents a different feel from what the hand does when one hand feels another, but it is an experience of something with which we come definitely into contact. The body does not experience itself as a whole, in the sense in which the self in some way enters into the experience of the self.

It is the characteristic of the self as an object to itself that I want to bring out. This characteristic is represented in the word "self," which is a reflexive, and indicates that which can be both subject and object. This type of object is essentially different from other objects, and in the past it has been distinguished as conscious, a term which indicates an experience with, an experience of, one's self. It was assumed that consciousness in some way carried this capacity of being an object to itself. In giving a behavioristic statement of consciousness we have to look for some sort of experience in which the physical organism can become an object to itself.[1]

When one is running to get away from someone who is chasing him, he is entirely occupied in this action, and his experience may be swallowed up in the objects about him, so that he has, at the time being, no consciousness of self at all. We must be, of course, very completely occupied to have that take place, but we can, I think, recognize that sort of a possible experience in which the self does not enter. We can, perhaps, get some light on that situation through those experiences in which in very intense action there appear in the experience of the individual, back of this intense action, memories and anticipations. Tolstoi as an officer in the war gives an account of having pictures of his past experience in the midst of his most intense action. There are also the pictures that flash into a person's mind when he is drowning. In such instances there is a contrast between an experience that is absolutely wound up in outside activity in which the self as an object does not enter, and an activity of memory and imagination in which the self is the principal object. The self is then entirely distinguishable from an organism that is surrounded by things and acts with reference to things, including parts of its own body. These latter may be objects like other objects, but they are just objects out there in the field, and they do not involve a self that is an object to the organism. This is, I think, frequently overlooked. It is that fact which makes our anthropomorphic reconstructions of animal life so fallacious. How can an individual get outside himself (experientially) in such a way as to become an object to himself? This is the essential psychological problem of selfhood or of self-consciousness; and its solution is to be found by referring to the process of social conduct or activity in which the given person or individual is implicated. The apparatus of reason would not be complete unless it swept itself into its own analysis of the field of experience; or unless the individual brought himself into the same experiential field as that of the other individual selves in relation to whom he acts in any given social situation. Reason cannot become impersonal unless it takes an objective, noneffective attitude toward itself; otherwise we have just consciousness, not *self-consciousness*. And it is necessary to rational conduct that the individual should thus take an objective, impersonal attitude toward himself, that he should become an object to himself. For the individual organism is obviously an essential and important fact or constituent element of the empirical situation in which it acts; and without taking objective account of itself as such, it cannot act intelligently, or rationally.

The individual experiences himself as such, not directly, but only indirectly, from the particular standpoints of other individual members of the same social group, or from the generalized standpoint of the social group as a whole to which he belongs. For he enters his own experience as a self or individual, not directly or immediately, not by becoming a subject to himself, but only insofar as he first becomes an object to himself just as other individuals are objects to him or in his experience; and he becomes an object to himself only by taking the attitudes of other individuals toward himself within a social environment or context of experience and behavior in which both he and they are involved.

The importance of what we term "communication" lies in the fact that it provides a form of behavior in which the organism or the individual may become an object to himself. It is that sort of communication which we have been discussing—not communication in the sense of the cluck of the hen to the chickens, or the bark of a wolf to the pack, or the lowing of a cow, but communication in the sense of significant symbols, communication which is directed not only to others but also to the individual himself. So far as that type of communication is a part of behavior it at least introduces a self. Of course, one may hear without listening; one may see things that he does not realize; do things that he is not really aware of. But it is where one does respond to that which he addresses to another and where that response of his own becomes a part of his conduct, where he not only hears himself but responds to himself, talks and replies to himself as truly as the other person replies to him, that we have behavior in which the individuals become objects to themselves. . . .

The self, as that which can be an object to itself, is essentially a social structure, and it arises in social experience. After a self has arisen, it in a certain sense provides for itself its social experiences, and so we can conceive of an absolutely solitary self. But it is impossible to conceive of a self arising outside of social experience. When it has arisen we can think of a person in solitary confinement for the rest of his life, but who still has himself as a companion, and is able to think and to converse with himself as he had communicated with others. That process to which I have just referred, of responding to one's self as another responds to it, taking part in one's own conversation with others, being aware of what one is saying and using that awareness of what one is saying to determine what one is going to say thereafter—that is a process with which we are all familiar. We are continually following up our own address to other persons by an understanding of what we are saying, and using that understanding in the direction of our continued speech. We are finding out what we are going to say, what we are going to do, by saying and doing, and in the process we are continually controlling the process itself. In the conversation of gestures what we say calls out a certain response in another and that in turn changes our own action, so that we shift from what we started to do because of the reply the other makes. The conversation of gestures is the beginning of communication. The individual comes to carry on a conversation of gestures with himself. He says something, and that calls out a certain reply in himself which makes him change what he was going to say. One starts to say something, we will presume an unpleasant something, but when he starts to say it he realizes it is cruel. The effect on himself of what he is saying checks him; there is here a conversation of gestures between the individual and himself. We mean by significant speech that the action is one that affects the individual himself, and that the effect upon the individual himself is part of the intelligent carrying-out of the conversation with others. Now we, so to speak, amputate that social phase and dispense with it for the time being, so that one is talking to one's self as one would talk to another person.[2]

This process of abstraction cannot be carried on indefinitely. One inevitably seeks an audience, has to pour himself out to somebody. In reflective intelligence one thinks to act, and to act solely so that this action remains a part of a social process. Thinking becomes preparatory to social action.

The very process of thinking is, of course, simply an inner conversation that goes on, but it is a conversation of gestures which in its completion implies the expression of that which one thinks to an audience. One separates the significance of what he is saying to others from the actual speech and gets it ready before saying it. He thinks it out, and perhaps writes it in the form of a book; but it is still a part of social intercourse in which one is addressing other persons and at the same time addressing one's self, and in which one controls the address to other persons by the response made to one's own gesture. That the person should be responding to himself is necessary to the self, and it is this sort of social conduct which provides behavior within which that self appears. I know of no other form of behavior than the linguistic in which the individual is an object to himself, and, so far as I can see, the individual is not a self in the reflexive sense unless he is an object to himself. It is this fact that gives a critical importance to communication, since this is a type of behavior in which the individual does so respond to himself.

We realize in everyday conduct and experience that an individual does not mean a great deal of what he is doing and saying. We frequently say that such an individual is not himself. We come away from an interview with a realization that we have left out important things, that there are parts of the self that did not get into what was said. What determines the amount of the self that gets into communication is the social experience itself. Of course, a good deal of the self does not need to get expression. We carry on a whole series of different relationships to different people. We are one thing to one man and another thing to another. There are parts of the self which exist only for the self in relationship to itself. We divide ourselves up in all sorts of different selves with reference to our acquaintances. We discuss politics with one and religion with another. There are all sorts of different selves answering to all sorts of different social reactions. It is the social process itself that is responsible for the appearance of the self;

it is not there as a self apart from this type of experience.

A multiple personality is in a certain sense normal, as I have just pointed out. . . .

The unity and structure of the complete self reflects the unity and structure of the social process as a whole; and each of the elementary selves of which it is composed reflects the unity and structure of one of the various aspects of that process in which the individual is implicated. In other words, the various elementary selves which constitute, or are organized into, a complete self are the various aspects of the structure of that complete self answering to the various aspects of the structure of the social process as a whole; the structure of the complete self is thus a reflection of the complete social process. The organization and unification of a social group is identical with the organization and unification of any one of the selves arising within the social process in which that group is engaged, or which it is carrying on.[3]

. . . Another set of background factors in the genesis of the self is represented in the activities of play and the game. . . . We find in children . . . imaginary companions which a good many children produce in their own experience. They organize in this way the responses which they call out in other persons and call out also in themselves. Of course, this playing with an imaginary companion is only a peculiarly interesting phase of ordinary play. Play in this sense, especially the stage which precedes the organized games, is a play at something. A child plays at being a mother, at being a teacher, at being a policeman; that is, it is taking different roles, as we say. We have something that suggests this in what we call the play of animals: A cat will play with her kittens, and dogs play with each other. Two dogs playing with each other will attack and defend, in a process which if carried through would amount to an actual fight. There is a combination of responses which checks the depth of the bite. But we do not have in such a situation the dogs taking a definite role in the sense that a child deliberately takes the role of another. This tendency on the part of children is what we are working with in the kindergarten where the roles which the children assume are made the basis for training. When a child does assume a role he has in himself the stimuli which call out that particular response or group of responses. He may, of course, run away when he is chased, as the dog does, or he may turn around and strike back just as the dog does in his play. But that is not the same as playing at something. Children get together to "play Indian." This means that the child has a certain set of stimuli that call out in itself the responses that they would call out in others, and which answer to an Indian. In the play period the child utilizes his own responses to these stimuli which he makes use of in building a self. The response which he has a tendency to make to these stimuli organizes them. He plays that he is, for instance, offering himself something, and he buys it; he gives a letter to himself and takes it away; he addresses himself as a parent, as a teacher; he arrests himself as a policeman. He has a set of stimuli which call out in himself the sort of responses they call out in others. He takes this group of responses and organizes them into a certain whole. Such is the simplest form of being another to one's self. It involves a temporal situation. The child says something in one character and responds in another character, and then his responding in another character is a stimulus to himself in the first character, and so the conversation goes on. A certain organized structure arises in him and in his other which replies to it, and these carry on the conversation of gestures between themselves.

If we contrast play with the situation in an organized game, we note the essential difference that the child who plays in a game must be ready to take the attitude of everyone else involved in that game, and that these different roles must have a definite relationship to each other. Taking a very simple game such as hide-and-seek, everyone with the exception of the one who is hiding is a person who is hunting. A child does not require more than the person who is hunted and the one

who is hunting. If a child is playing in the first sense he just goes on playing, but there is no basic organization gained. In that early stage he passes from one to another just as a whim takes him. But in a game where a number of individuals are involved, then the child taking one role must be ready to take the role of everyone else. If he gets in a ball game he must have the responses of each position involved in his own position. He must know what everyone else is going to do in order to carry out his own play. He has to take all of these roles. They do not all have to be present in consciousness at the same time, but at some moments he has to have three or four individuals present in his own attitude, such as the one who is going to throw the ball, the one who is going to catch it, and so on. These responses must be, in some degree, present in his own make-up. In the game, then, there is a set of responses of such others so organized that the attitude of one calls out the appropriate attitudes of the other.

This organization is put in the form of the rules of the game. Children take a great interest in rules. They make rules on the spot in order to help themselves out of difficulties. Part of the enjoyment of the game is to get these rules. Now, the rules are the set of responses which a particular attitude calls out. You can demand a certain response in others if you take a certain attitude. These responses are all in yourself as well. There you get an organized set of such responses as that to which I have referred, which is something more elaborate than the roles found in play. Here there is just a set of responses that follow on each other indefinitely. At such a stage we speak of a child as not yet having a fully developed self. The child responds in a fairly intelligent fashion to the immediate stimuli that come to him, but they are not organized. He does not organize his life as we would like to have him do, namely, as a whole. There is just a set of responses of the type of play. The child reacts to a certain stimulus, and the reaction is in himself that is called out in others, but he is not a whole self. In his game he has to have an organization of these roles; otherwise he cannot play the game. The game represents the passage in the life of the child from taking the role of others in play to the organized part that is essential to self-consciousness in the full sense of the term.

. . . The fundamental difference between the game and play is that in the former the child must have the attitude of all the others involved in that game. The attitudes of the other players which the participant assumes organize into a sort of unit, and it is that organization which controls the response of the individual. The illustration used was of a person playing baseball. Each one of his own acts is determined by his assumption of the action of the others who are playing the game. What he does is controlled by his being everyone else on that team, at least insofar as those attitudes affect his own particular response. We get then an "other" which is an organization of the attitudes of those involved in the same process.

The organized community or social group which gives to the individual his unity of self may be called "the generalized other." The attitude of the generalized other is the attitude of the whole community.[4] Thus, for example, in the case of such a social group as a ball team, the team is the generalized other insofar as it enters—as an organized process or social activity—into the experience of any one of the individual members of it.

If the given human individual is to develop a self in the fullest sense, it is not sufficient for him merely to take the attitudes of other human individuals toward himself and toward one another within the human social process, and to bring that social process as a whole into his individual experience merely in these terms: He must also, in the same way that he takes the attitudes of other individuals toward himself and toward one another, take their attitudes toward the various phases or aspects of the common social activity or set of social undertakings in which, as members of an organized society or social group, they are all engaged; and he must then, by generalizing these individual attitudes of that organized

society or social group itself, as a whole, act toward different social projects which at any given time it is carrying out, or toward the various larger phases of the general social process which constitutes its life and of which these projects are specific manifestations. This getting of the broad activities of any given social whole or organized society as such within the experiential field of any one of the individuals involved or included in that whole is, in other words, the essential basis and prerequisite of the fullest development of that individual's self: Only insofar as he takes the attitudes of the organized social group to which he belongs toward the organized, cooperative social activity or set of such activities in which that group as such is engaged, does he develop a complete self or possess the sort of complete self he has developed. And on the other hand, the complex cooperative processes and activities and institutional functionings of organized human society are also possible only insofar as every individual involved in them or belonging to that society can take the general attitudes of all other such individuals with reference to these processes and activities and institutional functionings, and to the organized social whole of experiential relations and interactions thereby constituted—and can direct his own behavior accordingly.

It is in the form of the generalized other that the social process influences the behavior of the individuals involved in it and carrying it on, i.e., that the community exercises control over the conduct of its individual members; for it is in this form that the social process or community enters as a determining factor into the individual's thinking. In abstract thought the individual takes the attitude of the generalized other[5] toward himself, without reference to its expression in any particular other individuals; and in concrete thought he takes that attitude insofar as it is expressed in the attitudes toward his behavior of those other individuals with whom he is involved in the given social situation or act. But only by taking the attitude of the generalized other toward himself, in one or another of these ways, can he think at all; for only thus can thinking—or the internalized conversation of gestures which constitutes thinking—occur. And only through the taking by individuals of the attitude or attitudes of the generalized other toward themselves is the existence of a universe of discourse, as that system of common or social meanings which thinking presupposes at its context, rendered possible.

. . . I have pointed out, then, that there are two general stages in the full development of the self. At the first of these stages, the individual's self is considered simply by an organization of the particular attitudes of other individuals toward himself and toward one another in the specific social acts in which he participates with them. But at the second stage in the full development of the individual's self that self is constituted not only by an organization of these particular individual attitudes, but also by an organization of the social attitudes of the generalized other or the social group as a whole to which he belongs. . . . So the self reaches its full development by organizing these individual attitudes of others into the organized social or group attitudes, and by thus becoming an individual reflection of the general systematic pattern of social or group behavior in which it and the others are all involved—a pattern which enters as a whole into the individual's experience in terms of these organized group attitudes which, through the mechanism of his central nervous system, he takes toward himself, just as he takes the individual attitudes of others.

. . . A person is a personality because he belongs to a community, because he takes over the institutions of that community into his own conduct. He takes its language as a medium by which he gets his personality, and then through a process of taking the different roles that all the others furnish he comes to get the attitude of the members of the community. Such, in a certain sense, is the structure of a man's personality. There are certain common responses which each individual has toward certain common things, and insofar as those common responses are awakened in the individual when he is affecting other persons he arouses his own self. The structure, then, on which the self is built is this response which is common to all, for one has to be a member of a community to be a self. Such responses are abstract attitudes, but they constitute just what we term a man's character. They give him what we term his principles, the acknowledged attitudes of all members of the community toward what are the values of that community. He is putting himself in the place of the generalized other, which represents the organized responses of all the members of the group. It is that which guides conduct controlled by principles, and a person who has such an organized group of responses is a man who we say has character, in the moral sense.

. . . I have so far emphasized what I have called the structures upon which the self is constructed, the framework of the self, as it were. Of course we are not only what is common to all: Each one of the selves is different from everyone else; but there has to be such a common structure as I have sketched in order that we may be members of a community at all. We cannot be ourselves unless we are also members in whom there is a community of attitudes which control the attitudes of all. We cannot have rights unless we have common attitudes. That which we have acquired as self-conscious persons makes us such members of society and gives us selves. Selves can only exist in definite relationships to other selves. No hard-and-fast line can be drawn between our own selves and the selves of others, since our own selves exist and enter as such into our experience only insofar as the selves of others exist and enter as such into our experience also. The individual possesses a self only in relation to the selves of the other members of his social group; and the structure of his self expresses or reflects the general behavior pattern of this social group to which he belongs, just as does the structure of the self of every other individual belonging to this social group.

CRITICAL THINKING QUESTIONS

1. How does Mead distinguish between body and the self? What makes this a radically *social* view of the self?

2. How is the self both a subject and an object to itself? How is the ability to assume "the role of the other" vital to our humanity?

3. The idea that socialization produces conformity is easy to understand, but explain Mead's argument that individual distinctiveness is also a result of social experience.

NOTES

1. Man's behavior is such in his social group that he is able to become an object to himself, a fact which constitutes him a more advanced product of evolutionary development than are the lower animals. Fundamentally it is this social fact—and not his alleged possession of a soul or mind with which he, as an individual, has been mysteriously and supernaturally endowed, and with which the lower animals have not been endowed—that differentiates him from them.

2. It is generally recognized that the specifically social expressions of intelligence, or the exercise of what is often called "social intelligence," depend upon the given individual's ability to take the roles of, or "put himself in the place of," the other individuals implicated with him in given social situations; and upon his consequent sensitivity to their attitudes toward himself and toward one another. These specifically social expressions of intelligence, of course, acquire unique significance in terms of our view that the whole nature of intelligence is social to the very core—that this putting of one's self in the places of others, this taking by one's self of their roles or attitudes, is not merely one of the various aspects or expressions of intelligence or intelligent behavior, but is the very essence of its character. Spearman's "X factor" in intelligence—the unknown factor which, according to him, intelligence contains—is simply (if our social theory of intelligence is correct) this ability of the intelligent individual to take the attitude of the other, or the attitudes of others, thus realizing the significations or grasping the meanings of the symbols or gestures in terms of which thinking proceeds; and thus being able to carry on with himself the internal conversation with these symbols or gestures which thinking involves.

3. The unity of the mind is not identical with the unity of the self. The unity of the self is constituted by the unity of the entire relational pattern of social behavior and experience in which the individual is implicated, and which is reflected in the structure of the self; but many of the aspects or features of this entire pattern do not enter into consciousness, so that the unity of the mind is in a sense an abstraction from the more inclusive unity of the self.

4. It is possible for inanimate objects, no less than for other human organisms, to form parts of the generalized and organized—the completely socialized—other for any given human individual, insofar as he responds to such objects socially or in a social fashion (by means of the mechanism of thought, the internalized conversation of gestures). Any thing—any object or set of objects, whether animate or inanimate, human or animal, or merely physical—toward which he acts, or to which he responds, socially, is an element in what for him is the generalized other; by taking the attitudes of which toward himself he becomes conscious of himself as an object or individual, and thus develops a self or personality. Thus, for example, the cult, in its primitive form, is merely the social embodiment of the relation between the given social group or community and its physical environment—an organized social means, adopted by the individual members of that group or community, of entering into social relations with that environment, or (in a sense) of carrying on conversations with it; and in this way that environment becomes part of the total generalized other for each of the individual members of the given social group or community.

5. We have said that the internal conversation of the individual with himself in terms of words or significant gestures—the conversation which constitutes the process or activity of thinking—is carried on by the individual from the standpoint of the "generalized other." And the more abstract that conversation is, the more abstract thinking happens to be, the further removed is the generalized other from any connection with particular individuals. It is especially in abstract thinking, that is to say, that the conversation involved is carried on by the individual with the generalized other, rather than with any particular individuals. Thus it is, for example, that abstract concepts are concepts stated in terms of the attitudes of the entire social group or community; they are stated on the basis of the individual's consciousness of the attitudes of the generalized other toward them, as a result of his taking these attitudes of the generalized other and then responding to them. And thus it is also that abstract propositions are stated in a form which anyone—any other intelligent individual—will accept.

16

Socialization and the Power of Advertising

JEAN KILBOURNE

Can parents just turn off the TV to protect their kids from the negative impact of advertising? No, claims Jean Kilbourne. Because advertising permeates our environment, she claims, "We cannot escape it." Advertisers customize ads for subscribers of the same magazine, attract children to websites with games and prizes, and bombard us with products on billboards, public transportation systems, and the sides of buildings, trucks, and shopping carts. As a result, Kilbourne argues, advertising continues to persuade people of all ages that the way to be happy is to buy, buy, buy.

If you're like most people, you think that advertising has no influence on you. This is what advertisers want you to believe. But, if that were true, why would companies spend over $200 billion a year on advertising? Why would they be willing to spend over $250,000 to produce an average television commercial and another $250,000 to air it? If they want to broadcast their commercial during the Super Bowl, they will gladly spend over a million dollars to produce it and over one and a half million to air it. After all, they might have the kind of success that Victoria's Secret did during the 1999 Super Bowl. When they paraded bra-and-panty-clad models across TV screens for a mere thirty seconds,

Source: Reprinted with the permission of The Free Press, a Division of Simon & Schuster Adult Publishing Group, from *Deadly Persuasion: Why Women and Girls Must Fight the Addictive Power of Advertising* by Jean Kilbourne. Copyright © 1999 by Jean Kilbourne.

1 million people turned away from the game to log on to the Web site promoted in the ad. No influence? . . .

Through focus groups and depth interviews, psychological researchers can zero in on very specific target audiences—and their leaders. "Buy this twenty-four-year-old and get all his friends absolutely free," proclaims an ad for MTV directed to advertisers. MTV presents itself publicly as a place for rebels and nonconformists. Behind the scenes, however, it tells potential advertisers that its viewers are lemmings who will buy whatever they are told to buy.

The MTV ad gives us a somewhat different perspective on the concept of "peer pressure." Advertisers, especially those who advertise tobacco and alcohol, are forever claiming that advertising doesn't influence anyone, that kids smoke and drink because of peer pressure. Sure, such pressure exists and is an important influence, but a lot of it is created by advertising. Kids who exert peer pressure don't drop into high schools like Martians. They are kids who tend to be leaders, whom other kids follow for good or for bad. And they themselves are mightily influenced by advertising, sometimes very deliberately, as in the MTV ad. As an ad for *Seventeen* magazine, picturing a group of attractive young people, says, "Hip doesn't just happen. It starts at the source: *Seventeen.*" In the global village, the "peers" are very much the same, regardless of nationality, ethnicity, culture. In the eyes of the media, the youths of the world are becoming a single, seamless, soulless target audience—often cynically labeled Generation X, or, for the newest wave of teens, Generation Y. "We're helping a soft drink company reach them, even if their parents can't," says [a newspaper ad] featuring a group of young people. The ad continues, "If you think authority figures have a hard time talking to Generation X, you should try being an advertiser," and goes on to suggest placing ads in the television sections of newspapers. . . .

Home pages on the World Wide Web hawk everything from potato chips to cereal to fast food—to drugs. Alcohol and tobacco companies, chafing under advertising restrictions in other media, have discovered they can find and woo young people without any problem on the Web. Indeed, children are especially vulnerable on the Internet, where advertising manipulates them, invades their privacy, and transforms them into customers without their knowledge. Although there are various initiatives pending, there are as yet no regulations against targeting children online. Marketers attract children to Web sites with games and contests, and then extract from them information that can be used in future sales pitches to the child and the child's family. They should be aware that this information might be misleading. My daughter recently checked the "less than $20,000" household income box because she was thinking of her allowance.

Some sites offer prizes to lure children into giving up the email addresses of their friends too. Online advertising targets children as young as

four in an attempt to develop "brand loyalty" as early as possible. Companies unrelated to children's products have Web sites for children, such as Chevron's site, which features games, toys, and videos touting the importance of—surprise!—the oil industry. In this way, companies can create an image early on and can also gather marketing data. As one ad says to advertisers, "Beginning this August, Kidstar will be able to reach every kid on the planet. And you can, too."

The United States is one of the few industrialized nations in the world that thinks that children are legitimate targets for advertisers. Belgium, Denmark, Norway, and the Canadian province of Quebec ban all advertising to children on television and radio, and Sweden and Greece are pushing for an end to all advertising aimed at children throughout the European Union. An effort to pass similar legislation in the United States in the 1970s was squelched by a coalition of food and toy companies, broadcasters, and ad agencies. Children in America appear to have value primarily as new consumers. As an ad for juvenile and infant bedding and home accessories says, "Having children is so rewarding. You get to buy childish stuff and pretend it's for them." Our public policy—or lack thereof—on every children's issue, from education to drugs to teen suicide to child abuse, leaves many to conclude that we are a nation that hates its children.

However, the media care about them. The Turner Cartoon Network tells advertisers, "Today's kids influence over $130 billion of their parent's spending annually. Kids also spend $8 billion of their own money. That makes these little consumers big business." Not only are children influencing a lot of spending in the present, they are developing brand loyalty and the beginnings of an addiction to consumption that will serve corporations well in the future. According to Mike Searles, president of Kids 'R' Us, "If you own this child at an early age, you can own this child for years to come. Companies are saying, 'Hey, I want to own the kid younger and younger.'" No wonder Levi Strauss & Co. finds it worthwhile to send a direct mailing to seven- to twelve-year-old girls to learn about them when they are starting to form brand opinions. According to the senior advertising manager, "This is more of a long-term relationship that we're trying to explore." There may not seem much harm in this until we consider that the tobacco and alcohol industries are also interested in long-term relationships beginning in childhood—and are selling products that can indeed end up "owning" people.

Advertisers are willing to spend a great deal on psychological research that will help them target children more effectively. Nintendo U.S. has a research center which interviews at least fifteen hundred children every week. Kid Connection, a unit of the advertising agency Saatchi & Saatchi, has commissioned what the company calls "psychocultural youth research" studies from cultural anthropologists and clinical psychologists. In a recent study, psychologists interviewed young people between the ages of six and twenty and then analyzed their dreams, drawings, and reactions to symbols. Meanwhile, the anthropologists spent over five hundred hours watching other children use the Internet.

Children are easily influenced. Most little children can't tell the difference between the shows and the commercials (which basically means they are smarter than the rest of us). The toys sold during children's programs are often based on characters in the programs. Recently, the Center for Media Education asked the Federal Trade Commission to examine "kidola," a television marketing strategy in which toy companies promise to buy blocks of commercial time if a local broadcast station airs programs associated with their toys.

One company has initiated a program for advertisers to distribute samples, coupons, and promotional materials to a network of twenty-two thousand day care centers and 2 million preschool children. The editor-in-chief of *KidStyle*, a kids' fashion magazine that made its debut in 1997, said, "It's not going to be another parenting magazine. This will be a pictorial magazine focusing on products."

Perhaps most troubling, advertising is increasingly showing up in our schools, where ads are emblazoned on school buses, scoreboards, and book covers, where corporations provide "free" material for teachers, and where many children are a captive audience for the commercials on Channel One, a marketing program that gives video equipment to desperate schools in exchange for the right to broadcast a "news" program studded with commercials to all students every morning. Channel One is hardly free, however—it is estimated that it costs taxpayers $1.8 billion in lost classroom time. But it certainly is profitable for the owners[,] who promise advertisers "the largest teen audience around" and "the undivided attention of millions of teenagers for twelve minutes a day." Another ad for Channel One boasts, "Our relationship with 8.1 million teenagers lasts for six years (rather remarkable considering most of theirs last for . . . like six days)." Imagine the public outcry if a political or religious group offered schools an information package with ten minutes of news and two minutes of political or religious persuasion. Yet we tend to think of commercial persuasion as somehow neutral, although it certainly promotes beliefs and behavior that have significant and sometimes harmful effects on the individual, the family, the society, and the environment.

"Reach him at the office," says an ad featuring a small boy in a business suit, which continues, "His first day job is kindergarten. Modern can put your sponsored educational materials in the lesson plan." Advertisers are reaching nearly 8 million public-school students each day.

Cash-strapped and underfunded schools accept this dance with the devil. And they are not alone. As many people become less and less willing to pay taxes to support public schools and other institutions and services, corporations are only too eager to pick up the slack—in exchange for a captive audience, of course. As one good corporate citizen, head of an outdoor advertising agency, suggested, "Perhaps fewer libraries would be closing their doors or reducing their services if they wrapped their buildings in tastefully done outdoor ads."

According to the Council for Aid to Education, the total amount corporations spend on "educational" programs from kindergarten through high school has increased from $5 million in 1965 to about $500 million today. The Seattle School Board recently voted to aggressively pursue advertising and corporate sponsorship. "There can be a Nike concert series and a Boeing valedictorian," said the head of the task force. We already have market-driven educational materials in our schools, such as Exxon's documentary on the beauty of the Alaskan coastline or the McDonald's Nutrition Chart and a kindergarten curriculum that teaches children to "Learn to Read through Recognizing Corporate Logos."

No wonder so many people fell for a "news item" in *Adbusters* (a Canadian magazine that critiques advertising and commercialism) about a new program called "Tattoo You Too!", which pays schools a fee in exchange for students willing to be tattooed with famous corporate logos, such as the Nike "swoosh" and the Guess question mark. Although the item was a spoof, it was believable enough to be picked up by some major media. I guess nothing about advertising seems unbelievable these days.

There are penalties for young people who resist this commercialization. In the spring of 1998 Mike Cameron, a senior at Greenbrier High School in Evans, Georgia, was suspended from school. Why? Did he bring a gun to school? Was he smoking in the boys' room? Did he assault a teacher? No. He wore a Pepsi shirt on a school-sponsored Coke day, an entire school day dedicated to an attempt to win ten thousand dollars in a national contest run by Coca-Cola.

Coke has several "partnerships" with schools around the country in which the company gives several million dollars to the school in exchange for a longterm contract giving Coke exclusive rights to school vending machines. John Bushey, an area superintendent for thirteen schools in Colorado Springs who signs his correspondence

"The Coke Dude," urged school officials to "get next year's volume up to 70,000 cases" and suggested letting students buy Coke throughout the day and putting vending machines "where they are accessible all day." Twenty years ago, teens drank almost twice as much milk as soda. Today they drink twice as much soda as milk. Some data suggest this contributes to broken bones while they are still teenagers and to osteoporosis in later life. . . .

ADVERTISING IS OUR ENVIRONMENT

Advertisers like to tell parents that they can always turn off the TV to protect their kids from any of the negative impact of advertising. This is like telling us that we can protect our children from air pollution by making sure they never breathe. Advertising is our *environment*. We swim in it as fish swim in water. We cannot escape it. Unless, of course, we keep our children home from school and blindfold them whenever they are outside of the house. And never let them play with other children. Even then, advertising's messages are inside our intimate relationships, our homes, our hearts, our heads.

Advertising not only appears on radio and television, in our magazines and newspapers, but also surrounds us on billboards, on the sides of buildings, plastered on our public transportation. Buses now in many cities are transformed into facsimiles of products, so that one boards a bus masquerading as a box of Dunkin' Donuts (followed, no doubt, by a Slimfast bus). The creators of this atrocity proudly tell us in their ad in *Advertising Age*, "In your face . . . all over the place!" Indeed.

Trucks carry advertising along with products as part of a marketing strategy. "I want every truck we have on the road making folks thirsty for Bud Light," says an ad in *Advertising Age*, which refers to a truck as a "valuable moving billboard." Given that almost half of all automobile crashes are alcohol-related, it's frightening to think of people becoming thirsty for Bud Light while driving their cars. A Spanish company has paid the drivers of seventy-five cars in Madrid to turn their cars into Pall Mall cigarette packages, and hopes to expand its operation throughout Spain. Imagine cars disguised as bottles of beer zipping along our highways. If we seek to escape all this by taking a plane, we become a captive audience for in-flight promotional videos.

Ads are on the videos we rent, the shopping carts we push through stores, the apples and hot dogs we buy, the online services we use, and the navigational screens of the luxury cars we drive. A new device allows advertisers to print their messages directly onto the sand of a beach. "This is my best idea ever—5,000 imprints of Skippy Peanut Butter jars covering the beach," crowed the inventor. Added the promotion director, "I'm here looking at thousands of families with kids. If they're on the beach thinking of Skippy, that's just what we want." Their next big idea is snow imprinting at ski resorts. In England the legendary white cliffs of Dover now serve as the backdrop for a laser-projected Adidas ad. American consumers have recently joined Europeans in being offered free phone calls if they will also listen to commercials. Conversations are interrupted by brief ads, tailored to match the age and social profiles of the conversants. And beer companies have experimented with messages posted over urinals, such as "Time for more Coors" or "Put used Bud here."

The average American is exposed to at least three thousand ads every day and will spend three years of his or her life watching television commercials. Advertising makes up about 70 percent of our newspapers and 40 percent of our mail. Of course, we don't pay direct attention to very many of these ads, but we are powerfully influenced, mostly on an unconscious level, by the experience of being immersed in an advertising culture, a market-driven culture, in which all our institutions, from political to religious to educational, are increasingly for sale to the highest bidder. According to Rance Crain, editor-in-chief of *Advertising Age*, the major publication of the advertising industry, "Only eight percent of an ad's message is received by the conscious mind; the rest is worked and reworked deep within the recesses of the brain, where a product's positioning and repositioning takes shape." It is in this sense that advertising is subliminal: not in the sense of hidden messages embedded in ice cubes, but in the sense that we aren't consciously aware of what advertising is doing.

Commercialism has no borders. There is barely any line left between advertising and the rest of the culture. The prestigious Museum of Fine Arts in Boston puts on a huge exhibit of Herb Ritts, fashion photographer, and draws one of the largest crowds in its history. In 1998 the museum's Monet show was the most popular exhibit in the world. Museum officials were especially pleased by results of a survey showing 74 percent of visitors recognized that the show's sponsor was Fleet Financial Group, which shelled out $1.2 million to underwrite the show.

Bob Dole plays on his defeat in the presidential election in ads for Air France and Viagra, while Ed Koch, former mayor of New York City, peddles Dunkin' Donuts' bagels. Dr. Jane Goodall, doyenne of primatology, appears with her chimpanzees in an ad for Home Box Office, and Sarah Ferguson, the former duchess of York, gets a million dollars for being the official spokeswoman for Weight Watchers (with a bonus if she keeps her weight down). . . .

The unintended effects of advertising are far more important and far more difficult to measure than those effects that are intended. The important question is not "Does this ad sell the product?" but rather "What else does this ad sell?" An ad for Gap khakis featuring a group of acrobatic swing dancers probably sold a lot of pants, which, of course, was the intention of the advertisers. But it also contributed to a rage for swing dancing. This is an innocuous example of advertising's powerful unintended effects. Swing dancing is not binge drinking, after all.

Advertising often sells a great deal more than products. It sells values, images, and concepts of love and sexuality, romance, success, and, perhaps most important, normalcy. To a great extent, it tells us who we are and who we should be. We are increasingly using brand names to create our identities. James Twitchell argues that the label of our shirt, the make of our car, and our favorite laundry detergent are filling the vacuum once occupied by religion, education, and our family name.

CRITICAL THINKING QUESTIONS

1. Advertisers maintain that people rely on commercials and ads to make informed decisions about the products and services they buy. Using the material in this chapter, discuss whether you agree or disagree with advertisers' claims that they are providing a service to consumers by educating them about their market choices.

2. What does Kilbourne mean when she says that advertising "sells a great deal more than products"? How, for example, does advertising influence our values and lifestyles? What about children's and adolescents' attitudes about tobacco, alcohol, food, and their self-image?

3. Belgium, Denmark, Norway, and other countries ban all television and radio advertising directed at children. Should Canada pass similar legislation?

REFERENCES

Angier, N. 1996. Who needs this ad most? *New York Times* (November 24): 4E.

Associated Press. 1998. Pepsi prank goes flat. *Boston Globe* (March 26): A3.

Austen, I. 1999. But first, another word from our sponsors. *New York Times* (February 18): E1, E8.

Bidlake, S. 1997. Commercials support free phone calls. *Advertising Age International* (September): 147, 149.

Carroll, J. 1996. Adventures into new territory. *Boston Globe* (November 24): D1, D5.

Cortissoz, A. 1998. For young people, swing's the thing. *Boston Globe* (July 25): A2, A10.

Crain, R. 1997. Who knows what ads lurk in the hearts of consumers? The inner mind knows. *Advertising Age* (June 9): 25.

Foreman, J. 1999. Sugar's "empty calories" pile up. *Boston Globe* (March 1): C1, C4.

Grunwald, M. 1997. Megamall sells stimulation. *Boston Globe* (December 9): A1, A26.

Harris, R. 1989. Children who dress for excess: Today's youngsters have become fixated with fashion. *Los Angeles Times* (November 12): A1.

Jacobson, M. F., and L. A. Mazur. 1995. *Marketing madness: A survival guide for a consumer society.* Boulder, CO: Westview Press.

Jhally, S. 1998. *Advertising and the end of the world* (a video). Northampton, MA: Media Education Foundation.

Kerwin, A. M. 1997. "KidStyle" crafts customized ad opportunities. *Advertising Age* (April 28): 46.

Koranteng, J. 1999. Sweden presses EU for further ad restrictions. *Advertising Age International* (April 12): 2.

Krol, C. 1998. Levi's reaches girls as they develop opinions on brands. *Advertising Age* (April 20): 29.

Lewis, M. 1997. Royal scam. *New York Times Magazine* (February 9): 22.

Liu, E. 1999. Remember when public space didn't carry brand names? *USA Today* (March 25): 15A.

McCarthy, C. 1990. In thingdom, laying waste our powers. *Washington Post* (November 11): F3.

McLaren, C. 1997. The babysitter's club. *Stay Free!* (Spring): 8–11.

Mohl, B. 1999. Lend them your ear, and your call is free. *Boston Globe* (January 13): AI, A10.

Monet show sets world record 1999. *Boston Globe* (February 2): E2.

Not for Sale! 1997. Oakland, CA: Center for Commercial-Free Public Education. (Spring).

Not for Sale! 1999. Oakland, CA: Center for Commercial-Free Public Education. (Winter).

Orlando, S. 1999. A material world: Defining ourselves by consumer goods. [Online]. Available: **http://www.sciencedaily.com/releases/1999/05/990518114815.htm**.

Reading, Writing . . . and TV commercials. 1999. *Enough!* 7(10) (Spring).

Rich, F. 1997. howdydoody.com. *New York Times* (June 8): E15.

Rosenberg, A. S. 1999. Ad ideas etched in sand. *Boston Globe* (February 1): A3.

Sharkey, J. 1998. Beach-blanket babel: Another reason to stay at the pool. *New York Times* (July 5): 2.

Twitchell, J. B. 1996. *Adcult USA: The triumph of advertising in American culture.* New York: Columbia University Press.

U.S. Department of Transportation. 1999. National Highway Traffic Safety Administration. [Online]. Available: **http://www.nhtsa.dot.gov/people/ncsa/FactPreve/alc96.html**.

Wallace, D. F. 1996. *Infinite jest.* Boston: Little Brown.

Weber, J. 1997. Selling to kids: At what price? *Boston Globe* (May 18): F4.

17

Parents' Socialization of Children in Global Perspective

D. TERRI HEATH

One of the most important functions of the family worldwide is the socialization of children. Although parents might receive help from others (such as relatives, neighbours, and professional caregivers), most communities expect parents themselves to raise their children to be productive and responsible adults. Across vastly different cultural environments, D. Terri Heath shows the universal importance of closeness with parents in affecting the academic achievement, psychological well-being, substance use and juvenile delinquency, and general behaviour of children worldwide.

THE BENEFITS OF CLOSE PARENT–YOUTH RELATIONSHIPS IN ADOLESCENCE

This article . . . [describes] how a positive relationship between parents and children later enhances the life satisfaction and psychological well-being of older youths and protects them from juvenile delinquency and substance abuse. As the cross-cultural examples illustrate, youth who perceive a close relationship with their parents exhibit more positive outcomes in each of these four areas. Life satisfaction and psychological well-being are described first, followed by illustrative cross-cultural examples. Next is a description of the impact of close parent-child relationships and their protective value on the

Source: From *Families in Multicultural Perspective,* eds. Bron B. Ingoldsby and Suzanna Smith, pp. 161–86. Copyright © 1995 Guilford Press, NY. Reprinted with permission.

substance abuse and juvenile delinquency of adolescents. Relevant, illustrative cross-cultural examples conclude this section.

Life satisfaction is a subjective measure of an individual's perception of his/her quality of life. Rather than objective measures of income, education, accumulation of wealth, and home ownership, life satisfaction is the level of individual satisfaction each person perceives in his/her own life: that which is privately known and privately evaluated. A multitude of factors influence life satisfaction, and because it is a personal evaluation, these factors differ for individuals. A study of life satisfaction among Hong Kong adolescents illustrates the profound effects peers and parents can exert on an adolescent's life satisfaction.

Psychological well-being is a measure of multiple submissions: self-esteem, locus of control, anxiety, loneliness, and sociability. Persons who exhibit high self-esteem, an internal locus of control, low anxiety and loneliness, and high sociability are considered to have strong psychological well-being. Just as with life satisfaction, many factors can influence psychological well-being, but this section focuses specifically on the association between strong relationships with parents and positive outcomes for youth and young adults.

Hong Kong

Adolescence is a transitional period in the life cycle. Associations with family and peers are changing, and adolescents often feel increased pressure to succeed in social relationships outside their families. Their level of attachment, identification, and frequency of consultation with parents relative to that with peers influences the life satisfaction of adolescents in general and, specifically, their satisfaction with school, family, and others. Hong Kong, on the south coast of China, is heavily influenced by current political and economic changes in China. Chinese culture, with its emphasis on family and community over individual independence, continues to play a significant role in the culture of Hong Kong. Because the orientation of adolescents toward their peers and parents has important implications for their satisfaction with life, Hong Kong offers a unique look at this relationship in a rapidly developing society. In a study of 1,906 students, ages thirteen to sixteen, adolescents who were more oriented toward their parents, as well as those who were more oriented toward their peers, were equally satisfied with school, their acceptance by others, the government, and the media. However, those adolescents who are most oriented toward their parents were additionally satisfied with life in general, their families, and the environment (Man, 1991). Man (1991) concludes that "in a predominantly Chinese society like Hong Kong, the family remains a highly important determinant of the adolescents' life satisfaction" (p. 363).

Iran

Parents continue to influence the lives of their children as young adults through parental interactions, guidance, and shared history. When young adults are dissatisfied with their parents, their adult psychological well-being appears to be negatively influenced. When Iranian students, ages seventeen to thirty-nine, studying at universities in Iran and the United States, were asked about their childhood dissatisfactions with their parents, an interesting pattern emerged. Those adults who perceived the most childhood dissatisfaction with parents were most likely to experience current loneliness, anxiety, external locus of control, misanthropy, neurosis, and psychosis when compared to adults who scored low on the dissatisfaction scale. They were also more likely to experience lower self-esteem and lower sociability, as well as decreased satisfaction with peer relationships, than were adults who had perceptions of childhood satisfaction with parents (Hojat, Borenstein, & Shapurian, 1990). There were no differences between the Iranian students studying at U.S. universities and those studying at Iranian institutions. The authors conclude that when a child's needs for closeness, attachment, and intimacy are not fulfilled to the child's satisfaction in early childhood, the result can be adult dissatisfactions with peer relationships and decreased psychological well-being in adulthood.

Puerto Rico

Can a child's need for closeness and intimacy be adequately fulfilled when the parents of the child are either alcohol dependent or mentally ill? By comparing three groups of children—those with an alcoholic parent, with a mentally ill parent, and with other parents without obvious diagnoses—researchers in Puerto Rico believe that children and adolescents, ages four to sixteen, with alcoholic or mentally ill parents are more likely than other children to be exposed to adverse family environments, such as stressful life events, marital discord, and family dysfunction. In addition, the children in these families were more maladjusted than were children in families without a diagnosed parent, according to reports by psychiatrists, parents, and the children themselves (Rubio-Stipec et al., 1991). (However, the teachers of these three groups of children were unable to detect differences in child behavior, probably because 43 percent of them rated their familiarity with the child as "not good.") It appears from this research that children of alcoholic or mentally ill parents suffer negative consequences during childhood, and these consequences are readily apparent to psychiatrists, their parents, and even the children themselves.

In many cultures, adolescence is a period of rapid psychological growth and a shift in orientation from parents to peers. Adolescents move through this period from childhood at the beginning to adulthood at the end. Most choose educational and career paths during this period. Many choose marriage partners. They move from residing with their parents to residing with peers, with spouses, or by themselves. Because this is a time of such change, some adolescents cope with the transitions by engaging in problematic behaviors (e.g., drug and alcohol abuse and juvenile delinquency). This section presents some of the factors that contribute to problematic behaviors for youth in Canada and three subcultures in the United States: Native American, white, and Hispanic.

Canada

Social control theorists contend that adolescent alcohol consumption is influenced by the degree to which youth are influenced by peers more than parents. A study of alcohol consumption by Canadian eleventh and twelfth graders demonstrates this relationship (Mitic, 1990). Students were divided into three groups: (1) those who

drank only with their parents, (2) those who drank only with their peers, and (3) those who drank both with and without their parents. The consumption rates of this last group were further divided into the amount of drinking with and without parents. As might be expected, students who drank only with parents consumed the least amount of alcohol. Those who drank with both parents and peers consumed the most alcohol and drank more heavily when they were with peers. It appears that what parents model for their children regarding alcohol consumption has only a small influence in the youths' consumption behaviors when the parents are not present.

Hispanics and Whites in the United States

Researchers found that Hispanic and white youth (ages nine to seventeen) in the United States are also significantly influenced in their drug and alcohol consumption by their relationships with friends and parents. For white and Hispanic adolescents who used either licit substances (e.g., cigarettes and alcohol), marijuana, or other illicit substances (e.g., cocaine, heroin, and prescription drugs used for recreational purposes), the single most important influence was the percentage of friends who used marijuana. Those youths who had higher percentages of friends who used marijuana were more likely to use each category of drug (licit, marijuana, and other illicit) than were youths who had fewer friends who used marijuana; this is equally true for both Hispanic and white youth. Although both users and abstainers were more affiliated with their parents than their peers, users were more strongly influenced by their peers; more likely to believe that their friends, rather than their parents, understand them best; and more likely to respect the ideas of their friends in different situations. The only cultural difference was that, in general, Hispanic youths respected their parents' views more than did white youths, regardless of whether they used or abstained from drugs and alcohol (Coombs, Paulson, & Richardson, 1991). Coombs et al. conclude that "youths having viable relationships with parents are less involved with drugs and drug-oriented peers" (p. 87).

Ojibway Native Americans

Delinquent behavior represents a dysfunctional response to stressors and strains in adolescence. On Native American reservations in the United States, an orientation toward parents and tribal elders appears to protect some youth from these negative behaviors. High percentages of Native American Ojibway adolescents, ages twelve to eighteen, reported inappropriate or illegal activities, such as using alcohol (85 percent), stealing something (70 percent), skipping school (64 percent), smoking marijuana (53 percent), and intentional damage to property (45 percent). However, those who spent more time with their family in chores, recreation, family discussions, and meals were less involved in negative behaviors. As expected, those youth who spent more time in activities away from their families—such as listening alone to the radio, and partying with drugs and alcohol—were at greatest risk for delinquent behaviors and court adjudications (Zitzow, 1990). Ojibway youths who spent more time in activities with parents and tribal elders were less likely to engage in delinquent behaviors resulting in court adjudications.

Summary

This last section focuses on how close parent-youth relationships are associated with the life satisfaction, psychological well-being, lack of substance use, and absence of delinquent behavior in adolescents. Without exception, adolescents in all six studies benefit from increased involvement with healthy parents. Parental involvement enhanced life satisfaction among

adolescents in Hong Kong and contributed to psychological well-being among Iranian college students and Puerto Rican youths. The presence of parents was associated with less alcohol consumption among Canadian adolescents, a strong bond with parents was associated with less drug consumption by Hispanic and white youth in the United States, and spending time with parents and tribal elders was associated with less involvement in delinquent behaviors for Native American adolescents in the United States.

CONCLUSION

In reviewing the literature on cross-cultural research on parent-child relations for this chapter, a clear trend became increasingly apparent. When parents are more involved and/or have greater expectations of their children's behavior, children demonstrate better outcomes. As is apparent from the illustrative examples, greater parental involvement is an active involvement, not a passive one. It is acquired not simply by the amount of time parents and children spend together but rather by how the time is spent. An involved parent is not one who spends the majority of the day near his/ her child but rarely interacting with the child. It is, instead, the parent who uses opportunities to share activities such as teaching the child a local trade, reading together, or fostering a close, supportive relationship through companionship. This active, involved parent appears much more likely to rear a successful child. Illustrative cross-cultural examples presented here of high-quality interaction between parents and children, such as . . . establishing firm limits and offering support in China, and engaging adolescents in activities with parents and tribal elders in the United States, has been associated with better child outcomes. These patterns emerged even when examining parent-son versus parent-daughter relations, relationships among family members in developing versus developed countries, or parent-child relationships in families that resided in Western cultures versus Eastern ones.

CRITICAL THINKING QUESTIONS

1. According to Heath, are there greater differences or similarities across cultures in the relationship between parent–child closeness and adolescent behaviour?

2. What are some of the factors that contribute to the problematic behaviour of adolescents both cross-culturally and within Canada?

3. What does Heath mean by "parental involvement"? What other variables might also have an impact on parent–child relationships that are not discussed in this selection?

REFERENCES

Coombs, R. H., M. J. Paulson, and M. A. Richardson. 1991. Peer versus parental influence in substance use among Hispanic and Anglo children and adolescents. *Journal of Youth and Adolescence*, 20(1): 73–88.

Hojat, M., B. D. Borenstein, and R. Shapurian. 1990. Perception of childhood dissatisfaction with parents and selected personality traits in adulthood. *Journal of General Psychology*, 117(3): 241–53.

Man, P. 1991. The influence of peers and parents on youth life satisfaction in Hong Kong. *Social Indicators Research*, 24(4): 347–65.

Mitic, W. 1990. Parental versus peer influence on adolescents' alcohol consumption. *Psychological Reports*, 67: 1273–74.

Rubio-Stipec, M., H. Bird, G. Canino, and M. Alegria. 1991. Children of alcoholic parents in the community. *Journal of Studies on Alcohol*, 52(1): 78–88.

Zitzow, D. 1990. Ojibway adolescent time spent with parents/elders as related to delinquency and court adjudication experiences. *American Indian and Alaska Native Mental Health Research*, 4(1): 53–63.

18

The Presentation of Self

ERVING GOFFMAN

Social Interaction in Everyday Life

CLASSIC

CONTEMPORARY

CROSS-CULTURAL

Face-to-face interaction is a complex process by which people both convey and receive information about each other. In this selection, Erving Goffman presents basic observations about how everyone tries to influence how others perceive them. In addition, he suggests ways in which people can evaluate how honestly others present themselves.

When an individual enters the presence of others, they commonly seek to acquire information about him or to bring into play information about him already possessed. They will be interested in his general socioeconomic status, his conception of self, his attitude toward them, his competence, his trustworthiness, etc. Although some of this information seems to be sought almost as an end in itself, there are usually quite practical reasons for acquiring it. Information about the individual helps to define the situation, enabling others to know in advance what he will expect of them and what they may expect of him. Informed in these ways, the others will know how best to act in order to call forth a desired response from him.

Source: From *The Presentation of Self in Everyday Life* by Erving Goffman, copyright © 1959 by Erving Goffman, Bantam Doubleday Dell Publishing Group, Inc. Reprinted with permission.

For those present, many sources of information become accessible and many carriers (or "sign-vehicles") become available for conveying this information. If unacquainted with the individual, observers can glean clues from his conduct and appearance which allow them to apply their previous experience with individuals roughly similar to the one before them or, more important, to apply untested stereotypes to him. They can also assume from past experience that only individuals of a particular kind are likely to be found in a given social setting. They can rely on what the individual says about himself or on documentary evidence he provides as to who and what he is. If they know, or know of, the individual by virtue of experience prior to the interaction, they can rely on assumptions as to the persistence and generality of psychological traits as a means of predicting his present and future behavior.

However, during the period in which the individual is in the immediate presence of the others, few events may occur which directly provide the others with the conclusive information they will need if they are to direct wisely their own activity. Many crucial facts lie beyond the time and place of interaction or lie concealed within it. For example, the "true" or "real" attitudes, beliefs, and emotions of the individual can be ascertained only indirectly, through his avowals or through what appears to be involuntary expressive behavior. Similarly, if the individual offers the others a product or service, they will often find that during the interaction there will be no time and place immediately available for eating the pudding that the proof can be found in. They will be forced to accept some events as conventional or natural signs of something not directly available to the senses. In Ichheiser's terms,[1] the individual will have to act so that he intentionally or unintentionally *expresses* himself, and the others will in turn have to be *impressed* in some way by him.

The expressiveness of the individual (and therefore his capacity to give impressions) appears to involve two radically different kinds of sign activity: the expression that he *gives*, and the expression that he *gives off*. The first involves verbal symbols or their substitutes which he uses admittedly and solely to convey the information that he and the others are known to attach to these symbols. This is communication in the traditional and narrow sense. The second involves a wide range of action that others can treat as symptomatic of the actor, the expectation being that the action was performed for reasons other than the information conveyed in this way. As we shall have to see, this distinction has an only initial validity. The individual does of course intentionally convey misinformation by means of both of these types of communication, the first involving deceit, the second feigning.

. . . Let us now turn from the others to the point of view of the individual who presents himself before them. He may wish them to think highly of him, or to think that he thinks highly of them, or to perceive how in fact he feels toward them, or to obtain no clear-cut impression; he may wish to ensure sufficient harmony so that the interaction can be sustained, or to defraud, get rid of, confuse, mislead, antagonize, or insult them. Regardless of the particular objective which the individual has in mind and of his motive for having this objective, it will be in his interests to control the conduct of the others, especially their responsive treatment of him. This control is achieved largely by influencing the definition of the situation which the others come to formulate, and he can influence this definition by expressing himself in such a way as to give them the kind of impression that will lead them to act voluntarily in accordance with his own plan. Thus, when an individual appears in the presence of others, there will usually be some reason for him to mobilize his activity so that it will convey an impression to others which it is in his interests to convey. Since a girl's dormitory mates will glean evidence of her popularity from the calls she receives on the phone, we can suspect that some girls will arrange for calls to be made, and Willard Waller's finding can be anticipated:

It has been reported by many observers that a girl who is called to the telephone in the dormitories will often allow herself to be called several times, in order to give all the other girls ample opportunity to hear her paged.[2]

Of the two kinds of communication—expressions given and expressions given off—this report will be primarily concerned with the latter, with the more theatrical and contextual kind, the nonverbal, presumably unintentional kind, whether this communication be purposely engineered or not. As an example of what we must try to examine, I would like to cite at length a novelistic incident in which Preedy, a vacationing Englishman, makes his first appearance on the beach of his summer hotel in Spain:

But in any case he took care to avoid catching anyone's eye. First of all, he had to make it clear to those potential companions of his holiday that they were of no concern to him whatsoever. He stared through them, round them, over them—eyes lost in space. The beach might have been empty. If by chance a ball was thrown his way, he looked surprised; then let a smile of amusement lighten his face (Kindly Preedy), looked round dazed to see that there were people on the beach, tossed it back with a smile to himself and not a smile at the people, and then resumed carelessly his nonchalant survey of space.

But it was time to institute a little parade, the parade of the Ideal Preedy. By devious handlings he gave any who wanted to look a chance to see the title of his book—a Spanish translation of Homer, classic thus, but not daring, cosmopolitan too—and then gathered together his beach-wrap and bag into a neat sand-resistant pile (Methodical and Sensible Preedy), rose slowly to stretch at ease his huge frame (Big-Cat Preedy), and tossed aside his sandals (Carefree Preedy, after all).

The marriage of Preedy and the sea! There were alternative rituals. The first involved the stroll that turns into a run and a dive straight into the water, thereafter smoothing into a strong splashless crawl towards the horizon. But of course not really to the horizon. Quite suddenly he would turn on to his back and thrash great white splashes with his legs, somehow thus showing that he could have swum further had he wanted to, and then would stand up a quarter out of water for all to see who it was.

The alternative course was simpler, it avoided the cold-water shock and it avoided the risk of appearing too high-spirited. The point was to appear to be so used to the sea, the Mediterranean, and this particular beach, that one might as well be in the sea as out of it. It involved a slow stroll down and into the edge of the water—not even noticing his toes were wet, land and water all the same to *him*!—with his eyes up at the sky gravely surveying portents, invisible to others, of the weather (Local Fisherman Preedy).[3]

The novelist means us to see that Preedy is improperly concerned with the extensive impressions he feels his sheer bodily action is giving off to those around him. We can malign Preedy further by assuming that he has acted merely in order to give a particular impression, that this is a false impression, and that the others present receive either no impression at all, or, worse still, the impression that Preedy is affectedly trying to cause them to receive this particular impression. But the important point for us here is that the kind of impression Preedy thinks he is making is

in fact the kind of impression that others correctly and incorrectly glean from someone in their midst. . . .

There is one aspect of the others' response that bears special comment here. Knowing that the individual is likely to present himself in a light that is favorable to him, the others may divide what they witness into two parts; a part that is relatively easy for the individual to manipulate at will, being chiefly his verbal assertions, and a part in regard to which he seems to have little concern or control, being chiefly derived from the expressions he gives off. The others may then use what are considered to be the ungovernable aspects of his expressive behavior as a check upon the validity of what is conveyed by the governable aspects. In this a fundamental asymmetry is demonstrated in the communication process, the individual presumably being aware of only one stream of his communication, the witnesses of this stream and one other. For example, in Shetland Isle one crofter's wife, in serving native dishes to a visitor from the mainland of Britain, would listen with a polite smile to his polite claims of liking what he was eating; at the same time she would take note of the rapidity with which the visitor lifted his fork or spoon to his mouth, the eagerness with which he passed food into his mouth, and the gusto expressed in chewing the food, using these signs as a check on the stated feelings of the eater. The same woman, in order to discover what one acquaintance (A) "actually" thought of another acquaintance (B), would wait until B was in the presence of A but engaged in conversation with still another person (C). She would then covertly examine the facial expressions of A as he regarded B in conversation with C. Not being in conversation with B, and not being directly observed by him, A would sometimes relax usual constraints and tactful deceptions, and freely express what he was "actually" feeling about B. This Shetlander, in short, would observe the unobserved observer.

Now given the fact that others are likely to check up on the more controllable aspects of behavior by means of the less controllable, one can expect that sometimes the individual will try to exploit this very possibility, guiding the impression he makes through behavior felt to be reliably informing.[4] For example, in gaining admission to a tight social circle, the participant observer may not only wear an accepting look while listening to an informant, but may also be careful to wear the same look when observing the informant talking to others; observers of the observer will then not as easily discover where he actually stands. A specific illustration may be cited from Shetland Isle. When a neighbor dropped in to have a cup of tea, he would ordinarily wear at least a hint of an expectant warm smile as he passed through the door into the cottage. Since lack of physical obstructions outside the cottage and lack of light within it usually made it possible to observe the visitor unobserved as he approached the house, islanders sometimes took pleasure in watching the visitor drop whatever expression he was manifesting and replace it with a sociable one just before reaching the door. However, some visitors, in appreciating that this examination was occurring, would blindly adopt a social face a long distance from the house, thus ensuring the projection of a constant image.

This kind of control upon the part of the individual reinstates the symmetry of the communication process, and sets the stage for a kind of information game—a potentially infinite cycle of concealment, discovery, false revelation, and rediscovery. It should be added that since the others are likely to be relatively unsuspicious of the presumably unguided aspects of the individual's conduct, he can gain much by controlling it. The others of course may sense that the individual is manipulating the presumably spontaneous aspects of his behavior, and seek in this very act of manipulation some shading of conduct that the individual has not managed to control. This again provides a check upon the individual's behavior, this time his presumably uncalculated behavior, thus re-establishing the asymmetry of the communication process. Here I would like only to add

the suggestion that the arts of piercing an individual's effort at calculated unintentionality seem better developed than our capacity to manipulate our own behavior, so that regardless of how many steps have occurred in the information game, the witness is likely to have the advantage over the actor, and the initial asymmetry of the communication process is likely to be retained. . . .

In everyday life, of course, there is a clear understanding that first impressions are important. Thus, the work adjustment of those in service occupations will often hinge upon a capacity to seize and hold the initiative in the service relation, a capacity that will require subtle aggressiveness on the part of the server when he is of lower socioeconomic status than his client. W. F. Whyte suggests the waitress as an example:

The first point that stands out is that the waitress who bears up under pressure does not simply respond to her customers. She acts with some skill to control their behavior. The first question to ask when we look at the customer relationship is, "Does the waitress get the jump on the customer, or does the customer get the jump on the waitress?" The skilled waitress realizes the crucial nature of this question. . . .

The skilled waitress tackles the customer with confidence and without hesitation. For example, she may find that a new customer has seated himself before she could clear off the dirty dishes and change the cloth. He is now leaning on the table studying the menu. She greets him, says, "May I change the cover, please?" and, without waiting for an answer, takes his menu away from him so that he moves back from the table, and she goes about her work. The relationship is handled politely but firmly, and there is never any question as to who is in charge.[5]

When the interaction that is initiated by "first impressions" is itself merely the initial interaction in an extended series of interactions involving the same participants, we speak of "getting off on the right foot" and feel that it is crucial that we do so. Thus, one learns that some teachers take the following view:

You can't ever let them get the upper hand on you or you're through. So I start out tough. The first day I get a new class in, I let them know who's boss. . . . You've got to start off tough, then you can ease up as you go along. If you start out easy-going, when you try to get tough, they'll just look at you and laugh.[6]

. . . In stressing the fact that the initial definition of the situation projected by an individual tends to provide a plan for the cooperative activity that follows—in stressing this action point of view—we must not overlook the crucial fact that any projected definition of the situation also has a distinctive moral character. It is this moral character of projections that will chiefly concern us in this report. Society is organized on the principle that any individual who possesses certain social characteristics has a moral right to expect that others will value and treat him in an appropriate way. Connected with this principle is a second, namely that an individual who implicitly or explicitly signifies that he has certain social characteristics ought in fact to be what he claims he is. In consequence, when an individual projects a definition of the situation and thereby makes an implicit or explicit claim to be a person of a particular kind, he automatically exerts a moral demand upon the others, obliging them to value and treat him in the manner that persons of his kind have a right to expect. He also implicitly foregoes all claims to be things he does not appear to be[7] and hence foregoes the treatment that would be appropriate for such individuals. The others find, then, that the individual has informed them as to what is and as to what they *ought* to see as the "is."

One cannot judge the importance of definitional disruptions by the frequency with which they occur, for apparently they would occur more frequently were not constant precautions taken. We find that preventive practices are constantly employed to avoid these embarrassments and that corrective practices are constantly employed to compensate for discrediting occurrences that have not been successfully avoided. When the individual employs these strategies and tactics to protect his own projections, we may refer to them as "defensive practices"; when a participant employs them to save the definition of the situation projected by another, we speak of "protective practices" or "tact." Together, defensive and protective practices comprise the techniques employed to safeguard the impression fostered by an individual during his presence before others. It should be added that while we may be ready to see that no fostered impression would survive if defensive practices were not employed, we are less ready perhaps to see that few impressions could survive if those who received the impression did not exert tact in their reception of it.

In addition to the fact that precautions are taken to prevent disruption of projected definitions, we may also note that an intense interest in these disruptions comes to play a significant role in the social life of the group. Practical jokes and social games are played in which embarrassments which are to be taken unseriously are purposely engineered.[8] Fantasies are created in which devastating exposures occur. Anecdotes from the past—real, embroidered, or fictitious—are told and retold, detailing disruptions which occurred, almost occurred, or occurred and were admirably resolved. There seems to be no grouping which does not have a ready supply of these games, reveries, and cautionary tales, to be used as a source of humor, a catharsis for anxieties, and a sanction for inducing individuals to be modest in their claims and reasonable in their projected expectations. The individual may tell himself through dreams of getting into impossible positions. Families tell of the time a guest got his dates mixed and arrived when neither the house nor anyone in it was ready for him. Journalists tell of times when an all-too-meaningful misprint occurred, and the paper's assumption of objectivity or decorum was humorously discredited. Public servants tell of times a client ridiculously misunderstood form instructions, giving answers which implied an unanticipated and bizarre definition of the situation.[9] Seamen, whose home away from home is rigorously he-man, tell stories of coming back home and inadvertently asking mother to "pass the fucking butter."[10] Diplomats tell of the time a near-sighted queen asked a republican ambassador about the health of his king.[11]

To summarize, then, I assume that when an individual appears before others he will have many motives for trying to control the impression they receive of the situation.

CRITICAL THINKING QUESTIONS

1. How does the "presentation of self" contribute to a definition of a situation in the minds of participants? How does this definition change over time?

2. Apply Goffman's approach to the classroom. What are the typical elements of the instructor's presentation of self? A student's presentation of self?

3. Can we evaluate the validity of people's presentations? How?

NOTES

1. Gustav Ichheiser, "Misunderstandings in Human Relations," supplement to *The American Journal of Sociology* 55 (Sept., 1949), 6–7.

2. Willard Waller, "The Rating and Dating Complex," *American Sociological Review* 2 (1937), 730.

3. William Sansom, *A Contest of Ladies* (London: Hogarth, 1956), pp. 230–32.

4. The widely read and rather sound writings of Stephen Potter are concerned in part with signs that can be engineered to give a shrewd observer the apparently incidental cues he needs to discover concealed virtues the gamesman does not in fact possess.

5. W. F. Whyte, "When Workers and Customers Meet," chap. 7, *Industry and Society*, ed. W. F. Whyte (New York: McGraw-Hill, 1946), pp. 132–33.

6. Teacher interview quoted by Howard S. Becker, "Social Class Variations in the Teacher-Pupil Relationship," *Journal of Educational Sociology* 25, p. 459.

7. This role of the witness in limiting what it is the individual can be has been stressed by Existentialists, who see it as a basic threat to individual freedom. See Jean-Paul Sartre, *Being and Nothingness*, trans. Hazel E. Barnes (New York: Philosophical Library, 1956), pp. 365ff.

8. Goffman, op. cit., pp. 319–27.

9. Peter Blau, "Dynamics of Bureaucracy" (Ph.D. dissertation, Department of Sociology, Columbia University, forthcoming, University of Chicago Press), pp. 127–29.

10. Walter M. Beattie, Jr., "The Merchant Seaman" (unpublished M.A. Report, Department of Sociology, University of Chicago, 1950), p. 35.

11. Sir Frederick Ponsonby, *Recollections of Three Reigns* (New York: Dutton, 1952), p. 46.

19

Invisible Privilege

PAULA S. ROTHENBERG

In this article, mother and feminist scholar Paula Rothenberg explains how class and race affect friendship in the life of her daughter.

Perhaps it will be instructive to tell the story of the friendship between my daughter, Andrea, who is white[,] and her onetime friend, Jewel, who is Black. Although it is simply the story of two little girls who managed to be best friends for a very brief time and is highly specific to them, it sheds light on the complex nature of relations across race/ethnicity and class in the suburbs.

Jewel and Andrea met in kindergarten and were kindred spirits from the start. Both were smart and spunky, and both loved to be silly. The girls wanted to play together after school, but that was easier said than done. They managed to trade phone numbers, but whenever I called Jewel's house her grandmother answered and said that Jewel's parents were not available and she was not able to make arrangements for a play date in their absence.

After several weeks of fruitless calls, persistence finally paid off; one day, Jewel's mother, Carol, called back. Yes, Jewel could play at our house after school as long as I didn't mind keeping her until after dinner. Her mother worked late and wouldn't be able to come by until 7:30 or so. Since that was no problem, I picked up both girls at school the very next day. What I remember about the visit was Jewel's amazement as she explored our house for the first time and discovered that we had more than one bathroom.

After a series of other play dates and several conversations over coffee, Carol told me what I suspected. It was so difficult to reach her and so hard to coordinate play dates for the girls because Carol and her husband did not live in Montclair and Jewel managed to go to the Montclair public schools by claiming her grandmother's house as her residence.

Source: From *Invisible Privilege: A Memoir about Race, Class, and Gender* by Paula S. Rothenberg, University Press of Kansas, 2000.

This practice is not uncommon. Taxes in Montclair are very high, and many African-Americans who were raised in town and whose parents still live here can't afford either the price of a house or the taxes they would have to pay as residents. A common solution is to live in East Orange or some other surrounding community in a neighborhood where the schools are inferior but the taxes and property values are much lower and use a parent's or relative's address to claim residency and gain access to the Montclair school system.

Obviously people react to this subterfuge in different ways, depending largely on their race and their class. Many whites in town are angered by the fact that some children, mostly Black, who don't actually live in town attend the public schools, thereby raising their tax burden, while many Blacks see nothing very wrong with the practice. They question why education should be funded by local property taxes in the first place instead of on a statewide basis, which could ensure equal education for all children. Besides, having grown up here, they think of themselves as part of the town—quite apart from the technicality of their legal residence. While many of the white homeowner/tax payers are recent arrivals to Montclair, many of the African-Americans who resort to the subterfuge are members of families that have lived in the town for several generations. In many cases, they attended the same schools that their children now attend. What seems like a gross violation of law and justice to some of the whites, who focus on whether the parents of the children actually live in town, hardly seems that way to many of the African-Americans whose sense of family is much more inclusive. Children and grandchildren, cousins and nieces are understood to be part of the extended family of the relatives who are Montclair residents and taxpayers. These relatives care for the children at their homes on a regular basis, often having the children spend nights as well as days with them. The children's parents and other family members see the house itself as part of their extended residence, frequently eating and socializing with one another there, dropping in to use the phone or to help with home repairs. Legal residency often seems like a procedural technicality rather than an accurate indicator of who is part of town life. In fact, according to some criteria, these Black Montclairions, whose roots are firmly planted in the town, have more claim to being part of it than the newly arrived white professionals who simply sleep here, commuting to work in New York each day and spending their weekends playing golf at the country club in Glen Ridge.

When Carol finally gave me the family's address and phone number in another town, it was a real sign of trust. The first priority in her life was keeping Jewel in a good school system, arranging afternoon play dates with a white classmate was low on the list. But as the girls' friendship blossomed, Carol, like me, was eager to let them enjoy time together.

And then the inevitable happened. During one of the periodic efforts that the town officials make to track down children who are attending public school illegally, Jewel's illegal status was discovered. Carol never asked whether I had provided the school officials with the information—of course, I had not—but it's difficult to imagine that the idea didn't cross her mind. How could she ever be sure? Through some special arrangement, Jewel was allowed to finish up the school year, which was almost over. During the summer, her family moved out of their apartment and into a small house on the outskirts of Newark, about twenty minutes away. The following September, Jewel began attending parochial school. For her family, as for others like them, parochial school provided the only viable alternative to the inferior and dangerous public school near their home.

Jewel attended Andrea's birthday party that September, as she had in the past, and in January, Carol called to invite Andrea to Jewel's birthday party a week later. Andrea was thrilled with the prospect of seeing Jewel again and of visiting Jewel's house for the first time. She could talk of nothing else.

Jewel's new house was located in a fairly rundown Black neighborhood of small, single-family, urban-style homes. In spite of its appearance, I knew that it would be classified as a middle-class neighborhood by other Black families, since definitions of what counts as "middle class" are themselves race specific, and it is informal residential segregation that often determines how neighborhoods are defined and who gets to live in them. The front door of the house opened into a tiny living room that, in turn, opened into a larger, but still small, dining alcove. Sitting around a large wood table, filling all the space in the room, was a gaggle of aunts and uncles, grandparents and cousins. Apart from Jewel's young cousins, Andrea was the only child present, and she and I were the only white people. Conversation among the adults was friendly, if labored, with everyone trying hard to make us feel welcome. I tried hard not to cramp their good time.

But Andrea was very uncomfortable. Many of the social cues that she counted on to negotiate such events were missing, and she had not had the opportunity to learn the ones that were in place. People talked to each other in unfamiliar ways, and, at times, what I recognized as affectionate teasing must have sounded to her like sharp criticism or argument. She was frightened by how dark the house was and couldn't understand why only one lightbulb was burning on such a dark day. Coming from a world where people have enough money to use lighting as much for decoration as to be functional, she couldn't know that for most of the world, electric lights are a luxury or at least a carefully conserved resource.

A special point of pride for Jewel was the second toilet—literally a water closet—her dad had rigged up in the basement of the house to supplement the full bath upstairs. It consisted of a four-sided wooden cabinet set on a platform in the middle of a dark basement. The cabinet itself had no electric light, but some open space had been left between the ceiling and one side of the cabinet to allow light to enter. Jewel's pride was my daughter's terror. She went to the bathroom only after it was clear that one more postponement would have dire consequences, and she could use the bathroom at all only because I stayed in the cabinet with her.

As we drove home, I knew it was unlikely that the girls would continue their friendship. And in fact, they did not. It was just too difficult. Although Carol and I had tried to help the girls be friends, perhaps because we wanted the possibility of friendship for ourselves as well, the odds against it were too overwhelming and the differences separating the girls were just too great to bridge. In the end, personal relations occur within social contexts, and, in this case, it was unreasonable to expect two eight-year-old girls to be able to negotiate each other's worlds.

Different people will make different things out of this story. Some will see class as the villain here and argue, along with William Julius Wilson and others, that it is class, not race, that separates whites and Blacks today. This I think is an oversimplification. Jewel and Andrea carried with them the combined history of three hundred years of race, class, and gender oppression and privilege, and the differences created by them were just too great to overcome. For example, why was I able to live in the town and have legitimate access to the schools for my children while Jewel's mother, who had grown up there, could no longer claim access to her own community? Both Jewel's mother and I worked full time, but my job as a college teacher allowed me flexible hours with good pay. Carol worked in the accounting department of a large supermarket corporation in a job that often required her to stay until 11 p.m. Although both she and her husband worked full time, as did Andrea's father and I, their combined income was a fraction of ours. This was not surprising, since statistics indicate that in 1996 annual income for the typical Black family was about half of the $47,000 a year enjoyed by white families. In fact, according to a report issued by the White House's Council of Economic Advisers,

Black and Hispanic family incomes are farther behind those of whites today than they were twenty years ago.* For so many years, while I was fortunate enough to be paying off a mortgage on a home I obtained because my in-laws could afford to provide a down payment, Carol and her husband were paying rent and working overtime to save up for a house. Their down payment ultimately bought them a poorly constructed home in a marginal urban neighborhood with inadequate schools, dirty streets, and food stores that overcharge. Some little white girl, a mirror image of my long-ago self, drives through those streets today, and her parents caution her to roll up her window and lock her door. They shake their heads over the way some people choose to live when nothing more than hard work and ability are required to earn us all a piece of the American dream. They do not know that for Jewel's family, this is their piece of the American dream and they

have had to work very hard to achieve it. They do not understand that those of us who have more have drawn on the privileges of our race, our class, our gender, or some combination of them and have done so at the expense of the very people we denigrate.

CRITICAL THINKING QUESTIONS

1. Why is privilege often invisible? What categories of people are more and less likely to be aware of privilege?

2. Why was Andrea so uncomfortable in Jewel's Newark home? Do you think people can overcome the type of social differences described here? Explain.

3. Can you identify elements of privilege in your own life? How have they affected your relationships with others?

---

* *New York Times,* February 17, 1998, A18.

20

The DOs and TABOOs of Body
Language Around the World

ROGER E. AXTELL

In a world that grows smaller every year, it is easy to offend others simply by being ourselves—gestures that we take as innocent may be seen by someone else as deeply insulting. This selection suggests the extent of the problem and, in an age of global business dealings, the need to cultivate cultural sensitivity.

THREE GREAT GAFFES OR ONE COUNTRY'S GOOD MANNERS, ANOTHER'S GRAND FAUX PAS

In Washington they call protocol "etiquette with a government expense account." But diplomacy isn't just for diplomats. How you behave in other people's countries reflects on more than you alone. It also brightens—or dims—the image of where you come from and whom you work for. The Ugly American about whom we used to read so much may be dead, but here and there the ghost still wobbles out of the closet.

Source: "The DOs and TABOOs of Body Language around the World," by Roger E. Axtell, from *The DOs and TABOOs around the World*, 3rd ed., by Roger E. Axtell. Copyright © 1993 by Parker Pen Company. A Benjamin Book distributed by John Wiley & Sons, Inc. This material is used by permission of John Wiley & Sons, Inc.

Three well-traveled Americans tell how even an old pro can sometimes make the wrong move in the wrong place at the wrong time.

A Partner in One of New York's Leading Private Banking Firms

When the board chairman is Lo Win Hao, do you smile brightly and say, "How do you do, Mr. Hao?" or "Mr. Lo"? Or "Mr. Win"?

I traveled nine thousand miles to meet a client and arrived with my foot in my mouth. Determined to do things right, I'd memorized the names of the key men I was to see in Singapore. No easy job, inasmuch as the names all came in threes. So, of course, I couldn't resist showing off that I'd done my homework. I began by addressing top man Lo Win Hao with plenty of well placed Mr. Hao's—and sprinkled the rest of my remarks with a Mr. Chee this and a Mr. Woon that. Great show. Until a note was passed to me from one man I'd met before, in New York. Bad news. "Too friendly too soon, Mr. Long," it said. Where diffidence is next to godliness, there I was, calling a roomful of VIPs, in effect, Mr. Ed and Mr. Charlie. I'd remembered everybody's name—but forgotten that in Chinese the surname comes *first* and the given name *last*.

An Associate in Charge of Family Planning for an International Human Welfare Organization

The lady steps out in her dazzling new necklace and everybody dies laughing. (Or what not to wear to Togo on a Saturday night.)

From growing up in Cuba to joining the Peace Corps to my present work, I've spent most of my life in the Third World. So nobody should know better than I how to dress for it. Certainly one of the silliest mistakes an outsider can make is to dress up in "native" costume, whether it's a sari or a sombrero, unless you really know what you're doing. Yet, in Togo, when I found some of the most beautiful beads I'd ever seen, it never occurred to me not to wear them. While I was up-country, I seized the first grand occasion to flaunt my new find. What I didn't know is that locally the beads are worn not at the neck but at the waist—to hold up a sort of loincloth under the skirt. So, into the party I strutted, wearing around my neck what to every Togolese eye was part of a pair of underpants.

An Account Executive at an International Data Processing and Electronics Conglomerate

Even in a country run by generals, would you believe a runny nose could get you arrested?

A friend and I were coming into Colombia on business after a weekend in the Peruvian mountains touring Machu Picchu. What a sight that had been. And what a head cold the change in temperature had given my friend. As we proceeded through customs at the airport, he was wheezing and blowing into his handkerchief like an active volcano. Next thing I knew, two armed guards were lockstepping him through a door. I tried to intercede before the door slammed shut, but my spotty Spanish failed me completely. Inside a windowless room with the guards, so did his. He shouted in English. They shouted in Spanish. It was beginning to look like a bad day in Bogotá when a Colombian woman who had seen what happened burst into the

room and finally achieved some bilingual understanding. It seems all that sniffling in the land of the infamous coca leaf had convinced the guards that my friend was waltzing through their airport snorting cocaine.

CUDDLY ETHNOCENTRICS

If only the world's customs inspectors could train their German shepherds to sniff out the invisible baggage we all manage to slip with us into foreign countries. They are like secret little land mines of the mind. Set to go off at the slightest quiver, they can sabotage a five-minute stroll down the Champs-Élysées or a $5 million tractor sale to Beijing. Three of our most popular national take-alongs:

Why Don't They Speak English? For the same reason we don't speak Catalan or Urdu. The wonder, in fact, is that so many people do speak so many languages. Seldom is a Continental European fluent in fewer than three, often more. Africans grow up with language of the nation that once colonized theirs plus half a dozen different tribal dialects. Japan has three distinct Japanese languages, which even the lowliest street sweeper can understand. Middle Eastern businesspeople shift effortlessly from their native tongue(s) to Oxford English to Quai d'Orsay French. Yet most of the English-speaking world remains as cheerfully monolingual as Queen Victoria's parakeet. If there are any complaints, then, it is clear they should not be coming from the American/English-speaking traveler.

Take Me to Your Burger King. In Peoria a Persian does not go looking for pot-au-feu. Alone among travelers, Americans seem to embark like astronauts—sealed inside a cozy life-support system from home. Scrambled eggs. Rent-a-cars. Showers. TV. Nothing wrong with any of it back home, but to the rest of the universe it looks sadly like somebody trying to read a book with the cover closed. Experiment! Try the local specialties.

American Know-How to the Rescue! Our brightest ideas have taken root all over the world—from assembling lines in Düsseldorf to silicon chips in Osaka to hybrid grains that are helping to nourish the Third World. Nonetheless, bigger, smarter, and faster do not inevitably add up to better. Indeed, the desire to take on shiny new American ways has been the downfall of nations whose cultures were already rich in art and technology when North America was still a glacier. As important as the idea itself is the way it is presented.

A U.S. doctor of public health recently back from West Africa offers an example of how to make the idea fit the ideology. "I don't just pop over and start handing out antimalarial pills on the corner," she says. "First I visit with the village chief. After he gives his blessing, I move in with the local witch doctor. After she shows me her techniques and I show her mine—and a few lives are saved—maybe then we can get the first native to swallow the first pill."

This is as true at the high-tech level as at the village dispensary. "What is all this drinking of green tea before the meeting with Mitsubishi?" The American way is to get right down to business. Yet if you look at Mitsubishi's bottom line, you have to wonder if green tea is such a bad idea after all.

It should come as no surprise that people surrounded by oceans rather than by other people end up ethnocentric. Even our biggest fans admit that America often strikes the rest of the world as a sweet-but-spoiled little darling, wanting desperately to please, but not paying too much attention to how it is done. Ever since the Marshall Plan, we seemed to believe that *our* games and *our* rules were the only ones in town. Any town. And that all else was the Heart of Darkness.

Take this scene in a Chinese cemetery. Watching a Chinese reverently placing fresh fruit on a grave, an American visitor asked, "When do you expect your ancestors to get up and eat the fruit?" The Chinese replied, "As soon as your ancestors get up and smell the flowers."

HANDS ACROSS THE ABYSS

Our bad old habits are giving way to a new when-in-Rome awareness. Some corporations take it so seriously that they put employees into a crash course of overseas cultural immersion. AT&T, for instance, encourages—and pays for—the whole family of an executive on the way to a foreign assignment to enroll in classes given by experts in the mores and manners of other lands.

Among the areas that cry out loudest for international understanding are how to say people's names, eat, dress, and talk. Get those four basics right and the rest is a piece of kuchen.

Basic Rule #1: What's in a Name?

. . . The first transaction between even ordinary citizens—and the first chance to make an impression for better or worse—is, of course, an exchange of names. In America there usually is not very much to get wrong. And even if you do, so what?

Not so elsewhere. Especially in the Eastern Hemisphere, where name frequently denotes social rank or family status, a mistake can be an outright insult. So can switching to a given name without the other person's permission, even when you think the situation calls for it.

"What would you like me to call you?" is always the opening line of one overseas deputy director for an international telecommunications corporation. "Better to ask several times," he advises, "than to get it wrong." Even then, "I err on the side of formality until asked to 'Call me Joe.'" Another frequent traveler insists his company provide him with a list of key people he will meet, country by country, surnames underlined, to be memorized on the flight over.

Don't Trust the Rules. Just when you think you have broken the international name code, they switch the rules on you. Take Latin America. Most people's names are a combination of the father's and mother's, with only the father's name used in conversation. In the Spanish-speaking countries the father's name comes first. Hence, Carlos Mendoza-Miller is called Mr. Mendoza. But in Portuguese-speaking Brazil it is the other way around, with the mother's name first.

In the Orient the Chinese system of surname first, given name last does not always apply. The Taiwanese, many of whom were educated in missionary schools, often have a Christian first name, which comes before any of the others—as in Tommy Ho Chin, who should be called Mr. Ho or, to his friends, Tommy Ho. Also, given names are often officially changed to initials, and a Y.Y. Lang is Y.Y.; never mind what it stands for. In Korea, which of a man's names takes a Mr. is determined by whether he is his father's first or second son. Although in Thailand names run backwards, Chinese style, the Mr. is put with the *given* name, and to a Thai it is just as important to be called by his given name as it is for a Japanese to be addressed by his surname. With the latter, incidentally, you can in a very friendly relationship respond to his using *your* first name by dropping the Mr. and adding *san* to his last name, as in Ishikawa-san.

Hello. Are you still there? Then get ready for the last installment of the name game, which is to disregard all of the above—sometimes. The reason is that many Easterners who deal regularly with the West are now changing the order of their names to un-confuse us. So, while to one another their names remain the same, to us the given name may come before the surname. Then again, it may not.

The safest course remains: Ask.

Basic Rule #2: Eat, Drink, and Be Wary

. . . [M]ealtime is no time for a thanks-but-no-thanks response. Acceptance of what is on your plate is tantamount to acceptance of host, country, and company. So, no matter how tough things may be to swallow, swallow. Or, as one veteran globe-girdler puts it, "Travel with a cast-iron stomach and eat everything everywhere."

Tastiness Is in the Eye of the Beholder. Often, what is offered constitutes your host country's proudest culinary achievements. What would we Americans think of a Frenchman who refused a bite of homemade apple pie or sizzling sirloin? Squeamishness comes not so much from the thing itself as from our unfamiliarity with it. After all, an oyster has remarkably the same look and consistency as a sheep's eye, and at first encounter a lobster would strike almost anybody as more a creature from science fiction than something you dip in melted butter and pop into your mouth.

Incidentally, in Saudi Arabia sheep's eyes are a delicacy, and in China it's bear's paw soup.

Perhaps the ultimate in exotic dining abroad befell a family planning expert on a trip for an international human welfare organization. It was a newly emerged African country where the national dish—in fact, the *only* dish eleven months of the year—is yam. The visitor's luck, however, was to be there the *other* month, when gorillas come in from the bush to steal the harvest. Being the only available protein, gorilla meat is as prized as sirloin is over here, and the village guest of honor was served a choice cut. Proudly, a platter of the usual mashed yams was placed before her—but with a roast gorilla hand thrusting artfully up from the center.

Is there any polite way out besides the back door?

Most experienced business travelers say no, at least not before taking at least a few bites. It helps, though, to slice whatever the item is very thin. This way, you minimize the texture—gristly, slimy, etc.—and the reminder of whence it came. Or, "Swallow it quickly," as one traveler recommends. "I still can't tell you what sheep's eyeballs taste like." As for dealing with taste, the old canard that "it tastes just like chicken" is often mercifully true. Even when the "it" is rodent, snake—or gorilla.

Another useful dodge is not knowing what you are eating. What's for dinner? Don't ask. Avoid poking around in the kitchen or looking at English-language menus. Your host will be flattered that you are following his lead, and who knows? Maybe it really is chicken in that stew. . . .

Bottoms Up—or Down? Some countries seem to do it deliberately, some inadvertently, except for Islam, where they don't do it at all. Either way, getting visitors as tipsy as possible as fast as possible stands as a universal sign of hospitality, and refusal to play your part equals rebuff. Wherever you go, toasts are as reciprocal as handshakes: If one does, all do. "I don't drink, thank you" rarely gets you off gracefully. Neither does protesting that you must get up early. (So must everyone else.)

"I try to wangle a glass of wine instead of the local firewater," one itinerant American says. "The only trouble is, the wine is usually stronger than the hard stuff." Mao-tai, Chinese wine made from sorghum, is notorious for leaving the unsuspecting thoroughly shanghaied. The Georgian wine so popular in Russia is no ladylike little Chablis either. In Nordic lands proper form for the toast is to raise the glass in a sweeping arc from belt buckle to lips while locking stares with your host. It takes very few akvavit-with-beer-chasers before you both start seeing northern lights.

In Africa, where all the new countries were once old European colonies, it is often taken for granted that if you are white you must have whiskey or gin or whatever the colonials used to like. A traveler to a former French possession describes the dilemma of being served a large gourdful of Johnnie Walker Red at nine in the morning. The host was simply remembering how the French had always loved their Scotch. *When* they drank it and *how much* were details he had never noticed. Yet there was no saying no without giving offense. A few sips had to be taken and a promise made to finish the rest later.

Basic Rule #3: Clothes Can Also *Un*make the Man

. . . Wherever you are, what you wear among strangers should not look strange to *them*. Which does not mean, "When in Morocco wear djellabas," etc. It means wear what you look natural in—and know how to wear—that also fits in with your surroundings.

For example, a woman dressed in a tailored suit, even with high heels and flowery blouse, looks startlingly masculine in a country full of diaphanous saris. More appropriate, then, is a silky, loose-fitting dress in a bright color—as opposed to blue serge or banker's gray.

In downtown Nairobi, a safari jacket looks as out of place as in London. With a few exceptions (where the weather is just too steamy for it), the general rule everywhere is that for business, for eating out, even for visiting people at home, you should be very buttoned up: conservative suit and tie for men, dress or skirt-suit for women. To be left in the closet until you go on an outdoor sightseeing trek:

jeans, however haute couture
jogging shoes
tennis and T-shirts
tight-fitting sweaters (women)
open-to-the-navel shirts (men)
funny hats (both)

Where you *can* loosen up, it is best to do it the way the indigines do. In the Philippines men wear the *barong tagalog*—a loose, frilly, usually white or cream-colored shirt with tails out, no jacket or tie. In tropical Latin American countries the counterpart to the barong is called a *guayabera* and, except for formal occasions, is acceptable business attire. In Indonesia they wear *Batiks*—brightly patterned shirts that go tieless and jacketless everywhere. In Thailand the same is true for the collarless Thai silk shirt. In Japan dress is at least as formal as in Europe (dark suit and tie for a man, business suit or tailored dress for a woman) except at country inns (called *ryokans*), where even big-city corporations sometimes hold meetings. Here you are expected to wear a kimono. Not to daytime meetings but to dinner, no matter how formal. (Don't worry—the inn always provides the kimono.)

One thing you notice wherever you go is that polyester is the mark of the tourist. The less drip-dry you are, the more you look as if you have come to do serious business, even if it means multiple dry-cleaning bills along the way.

Take It Off or Put It On—Depending. What you do or do not wear can be worse than bad taste—ranging from insulting to unhygienic to positively sinful. Shoes are among the biggest offenders in the East, even if you wear a 5AAA. They are forbidden within Muslim mosques and Buddhist temples. Never wear them into Japanese homes or restaurants unless the owner insists, and in Indian and Indonesian homes, if the host goes shoeless, do likewise. And wherever you take your shoes off, remember to place them neatly together facing the door you came in. This is particularly important in Japan. . . .

In certain conservative Arab countries, the price for wearing the wrong thing can hurt more than feelings. Mullahs have been known to give a sharp whack with their walking sticks to any woman whom they consider immodestly dressed. Even at American-style hotels there, do not wear shorts, skirts above the knee, sleeveless blouses, or low necklines—much less a bikini at the pool. . .

CRITICAL THINKING QUESTIONS

1. Historically, people in North America have been rather indifferent to the dangers of inadvertently offending others. Why do you think this has been the case?

2. Have you ever offended others—or been offended—in the way depicted by Axtell? If so, how? How did you and others respond?

3. Can the type of cultural conflict Axtell describes occur right here in Canada? How?

21

Primary Groups

CHARLES HORTON COOLEY

Charles Horton Cooley argues that human nature is a social nature and is clearly expressed in group life. Cooley describes primary groups as "spheres of intimate association and cooperation" that are vital to the process of socialization.

By primary groups I mean those characterized by intimate face-to-face association and cooperation. They are primary in several senses, but chiefly in that they are fundamental in forming the social nature and ideals of the individual. The result of intimate association, psychologically, is a certain fusion of individualities in a common whole, so that one's very self, for many purposes at least, is the common life and purpose of the group. Perhaps the simplest way of describing this wholeness is by saying that it is a "we"; it involves the sort of sympathy and mutual identification for

Source: From *Social Organization: A Study of the Larger Mind* by Charles Horton Cooley (New York: Schocken Books, a subsidiary of Pantheon Books, 1962; orig. 1909), pp. 23–31. Reprinted with permission.

which "we" is the natural expression. One lives in the feeling of the whole and finds the chief aims of his will in that feeling.

It is not to be supposed that the unity of the primary group is one of mere harmony and love. It is always a differentiated and usually a competitive unity, admitting of self-assertion and various appropriative passions; but these passions are socialized by sympathy, and come, or tend to come, under the discipline of a common spirit. The individual will be ambitious, but the chief object of his ambition will be some desired place in the thought of the others, and he will feel allegiance to common standards of service and fair play. So the boy will dispute with his fellows a place on the team, but above such

disputes will place the common glory of his class and school.

The most important spheres of this intimate association and cooperation—though by no means the only ones—are the family, the play-group of children, and the neighborhood or community group of elders. These are practically universal, belonging to all times and all stages of development; and are accordingly a chief basis of what is universal in human nature and human ideals. The best comparative studies of the family, such as those of Westermarck[1] or Howard,[2] show it to us as not only a universal institution, but as more alike the world over than the exaggeration of exceptional customs by an earlier school had led us to suppose. Nor can anyone doubt the general prevalence of play-groups among children or of informal assemblies of various kinds among their elders. Such association is clearly the nursery of human nature in the world about us, and there is no apparent reason to suppose that the case has anywhere or at any time been essentially different.

As regards play, I might, were it not a matter of common observation, multiply illustrations of the universality and spontaneity of the group discussion and cooperation to which it gives rise. The general fact is that children, especially boys after about their twelfth year, live in fellowships in which their sympathy, ambition, and honor are engaged even more often than they are in the family. Most of us can recall examples of the endurance by boys of injustice and even cruelty, rather than appeal from their fellows to parents or teachers—as, for instance, in the hazing so prevalent at schools, and so difficult, for this very reason, to suppress. And how elaborate the discussion, how cogent the public opinion, how hot the ambitions in these fellowships.

Nor is this facility of juvenile association, as is sometimes supposed, a trait peculiar to English and American boys; since experience among our immigrant population seems to show that the offspring of the more restrictive civilizations of the continent of Europe form self-governing play-groups with almost equal readiness. Thus Miss Jane Addams, after pointing out that the "gang" is almost universal, speaks of the interminable discussion which every detail of the gang's activity receives, remarking that "in these social folk-motes, so to speak, the young citizen learns to act upon his own determination."[3]

Of the neighborhood group it may be said, in general, that from the time men formed permanent settlements upon the land, down, at least, to the rise of modern industrial cities, it has played a main part of the primary, heart-to-heart life of the people. Among our Teutonic forefathers the village community was apparently the chief sphere of sympathy and mutual aid for the commons all through the "Dark" and Middle Ages, and for many purposes it remains so in rural districts at the present day. In some countries we still find it with all its ancient vitality, notably in Russia, where the *mir*, or self-governing village group, is the main theatre of life, along with the family, for perhaps fifty million peasants.

In our own life the intimacy of the neighborhood has been broken up by the growth of an intricate mesh of wider contacts which leaves us strangers to people who live in the same house. And even in the country the same principle is at work, though less obviously, diminishing our economic and spiritual community with our neighbors. How far this change is a healthy development, and how far a disease, is perhaps still uncertain.

Besides these almost universal kinds of primary association, there are many others whose form depends upon the particular state of civilization; the only essential thing, as I have said, being a certain intimacy and fusion of personalities. In our own society, being little bound by place, people easily form clubs, fraternal societies and the like, based on congeniality, which may give rise to real intimacy. Many such relations are formed at school and college, and among men and women brought together in the first instance by their occupations—as workmen in the same trade, or the like. Where there is a little common interest and activity, kindness grows like weeds by the roadside.

But the fact that the family and neighborhood groups are ascendant in the open and plastic time of childhood makes them even now incomparably more influential than all the rest.

Primary groups are primary in the sense that they give the individual his earliest and completest experience of social unity, and also in the sense that they do not change in the same degree as more elaborate relations, but form a comparatively permanent source out of which the latter are ever springing. Of course they are not independent of the larger society, but to some extent reflect its spirit; as the German family and the German school bear somewhat distinctly the print of German militarism. But this, after all, is like the tide setting back into creeks, and does not commonly go very far. Among the German, and still more among the Russian, peasantry are found habits of free cooperation and discussion almost uninfluenced by the character of the state; and it is a familiar and well-supported view that the village commune, self-governing as regards local affairs and habituated to discussion, is a very widespread institution in settled communities, and the continuator of a similar autonomy previously existing in the clan. "It is man who makes monarchies and establishes republics, but the commune seems to come directly from the hand of God."[4]

In our own cities the crowded tenements and the general economic and social confusion have sorely wounded the family and the neighborhood, but it is remarkable, in view of these conditions, what vitality they show; and there is nothing upon which the conscience of the time is more determined than upon restoring them to health.

These groups, then, are springs of life, not only for the individual but for social institutions. They are only in part moulded by special traditions, and, in larger degree, express a universal nature. The religion or government of other civilizations may seem alien to us, but the children or the family group wear the common life, and with them we can always make ourselves at home.

By human nature, I suppose, we may understand those sentiments and impulses that are human in being superior to those of lower animals, and also in the sense that they belong to mankind at large, and not to any particular race or time. It means, particularly, sympathy and the innumerable sentiments into which sympathy enters, such as love, resentment, ambition, vanity, hero-worship, and the feeling of social right and wrong.

Human nature in this sense is justly regarded as a comparatively permanent element in society. Always and everywhere men seek honor and dread ridicule, defer to public opinion, cherish their goods and their children, and admire courage, generosity, and success. It is always safe to assume that people are and have been human.

To return to primary groups: The view here maintained is that human nature is not something existing separately in the individual, but a *group-nature* or *primary phase of society*, a relatively simple and general condition of the social mind. It is something more, on the one hand, than the mere instinct that is born in us—though that enters into it—and something else, on the other, than the more elaborate development of ideas and sentiments that makes up institutions. It is the nature which is developed and expressed in those simple, face-to-face groups that are somewhat alike in all societies; groups of the family, the playground, and the neighborhood. In the essential similarity of these is to be found the basis, in experience, for similar ideas and sentiments in the human mind. In these, everywhere, human nature comes into existence. Man does not have it at birth; he cannot acquire it except through fellowship, and it decays in isolation.

If this view does not recommend itself to common sense I do not know that elaboration will be of much avail. It simply means the application at this point of the idea that society and individuals are inseparable phases of a common whole, so that wherever we find an individual fact we may look for a social fact to go with it. If there is a universal nature in persons there must be something universal in association to correspond to it.

What else can human nature be than a trait of primary groups? Surely not an attribute of the separate individual—supposing there were any such thing—since its typical characteristics, such as affection, ambition, vanity, and resentment, are inconceivable apart from society. If it belongs, then, to man in association, what kind or degree of association is required to develop it? Evidently nothing elaborate, because elaborate phases of society are transient and diverse, while human nature is comparatively stable and universal. In short the family and neighborhood life is essential to its genesis and nothing more is.

Here as everywhere in the study of society we must learn to see mankind in psychical wholes, rather than in artificial separation. We must see and feel the communal life of family and local groups as immediate facts, not as combinations of something else. And perhaps we shall do this best by recalling our own experience and extending it through sympathetic observation. What, in our life, is the family and the fellowship; what do we know of the we-feeling? Thought of this kind may help us to get a concrete perception of that primary group-nature of which everything social is the outgrowth.

CRITICAL THINKING QUESTIONS

1. Are primary groups necessarily devoid of conflict? How does Cooley address this issue?

2. Why does Cooley employ the term primary in his analysis? What are the characteristics of the implied opposite of primary groups: "secondary groups"?

3. What is Cooley's view of human nature? Why does he think that society cannot be reduced to the behaviour of many distinct individuals?

NOTES

1. *The History of Human Marriage.*
2. *A History of Matrimonial Institutions.*
3. *Newer Ideals of Peace,* p. 177.
4. De Tocqueville, *Democracy in America,* vol. 1, chap 5.

22

The Characteristics of Bureaucracy

MAX WEBER

According to Max Weber, human societies have historically been oriented by tradition of one kind or another. Modernity, in contrast, is marked by a different form of human consciousness: a rational world view. For Weber, there is no clearer expression of modern rationality than bureaucracy. In this selection, Weber identifies the characteristics of this organizational form.

Modern officialdom functions in the following specific manner:

I. There is the principle of fixed and official jurisdictional areas, which are generally ordered by rules, that is, by laws or administrative regulations. (1) The regular activities required for the purposes of the bureaucratically governed structure are distributed in a fixed way as official duties. (2) The authority to give the commands required for the discharge of these duties is distributed in a stable way and is strictly delimited by rules concerning the coercive means, physical, sacerdotal, or otherwise, which may be placed at the disposal of officials. (3) Methodical

Source: From *Max Weber: Essays in Sociology*, by Max Weber, edited by H. H. Gerth and C. Wright Mills, translated by H. H. Gerth and C. Wright Mills. Copyright © 1946, 1958 by H. H. Gerth and C. Wright Mills. Used by permission of Oxford University Press.

provision is made for the regular and continuous fulfillment of these duties and for the execution of the corresponding rights; only persons who have the generally regulated qualifications to serve are employed.

In public and lawful government these three elements constitute "bureaucratic authority." In private economic domination, they constitute bureaucratic "management." Bureaucracy, thus understood, is fully developed in political and ecclesiastical communities only in the modern state, and, in the private economy, only in the most advanced institutions of capitalism. Permanent and public office authority, with fixed jurisdiction, is not the historical rule but rather the exception. This is so even in large political structures such as those of the ancient Orient, the Germanic, and Mongolian empires of conquest, or of many feudal structures of state. In all these cases, the ruler executes the most important measures through personal trustees, table-companions, or court-servants. Their commissions and authority are not precisely delimited and are temporarily called into being for each case.

II. The principles of office hierarchy and of levels of graded authority mean a firmly ordered system of super- and subordination in which there is a supervision of the lower offices by the higher ones. Such a system offers the governed the possibility of appealing the decision of a lower office to its higher authority, in a definitely regulated manner. With the full development of the bureaucratic type, the office hierarchy is monocratically organized. The principle of hierarchical office authority is found in all bureaucratic structures: in state and ecclesiastical structures as well as in large party organizations and private enterprises. It does not matter for the character of bureaucracy whether its authority is called "private" or "public."

When the principle of jurisdictional "competency" is fully carried through, hierarchical subordination—at least in public office—does not mean that the "higher" authority is simply authorized to take over the business of the "lower." Indeed, the opposite is the rule. Once established and having fulfilled its task, an office tends to continue in existence and be held by another incumbent.

III. The management of the modern office is based upon written documents ("the files"), which are preserved in their original or draft form. There is, therefore, a staff of subaltern officials and scribes of all sorts. The body of officials actively engaged in a "public" office, along with the respective apparatus of material implements and the files, make up a "bureau." In private enterprise, "the bureau" is often called "the office."

In principle, the modern organization of the civil service separates the bureau from the private domicile of the official, and, in general, bureaucracy segregates official activity as something distinct from the sphere of private life. Public monies and equipment are divorced from the private property of the official. . . . In principle, the executive office is separated from the household, business from private correspondence, and business assets from private fortunes. The more consistently the modern type of business management has been carried through, the more are these separations the case. The beginnings of this process are to be found as early as the Middle Ages.

It is the peculiarity of the modern entrepreneur that he conducts himself as the "first official" of his enterprise, in the very same way in which the ruler of a specifically modern bureaucratic state spoke of himself as "the first servant" of the state. The idea that the bureau activities of the state are intrinsically different in character from the management of private economic offices is a continental European notion and, by the way of contrast, is totally foreign to the American way.

IV. Office management, at least all specialized office management—and such management is distinctly modern—usually presupposes a thorough and expert training. This increasingly holds for the modern executive and employee of private enterprises, in the same manner as it holds for the state official.

V. When the office is fully developed, official activity demands the full working capacity of the official, irrespective of the fact that his obligatory time in the bureau may be firmly delimited. In the normal case, this is only the product of a long development, in the public as well as in the private office. Formerly, in all cases, the normal state of affairs was reversed: Official business was discharged as a secondary activity.

VI. The management of the office follows general rules, which are more or less stable, more or less exhaustive, and which can be learned. Knowledge of these rules represents a special technical learning which the officials possess. It involves jurisprudence, or administrative or business management.

VII. The reduction of modern office management to rules is deeply embedded in its very nature. The theory of modern public administration, for instance, assumes that the authority to order certain matters by decree—which has been legally granted to public authorities—does not entitle the bureau to regulate the matter by commands given for each case, but only to regulate the matter abstractly. This stands in extreme contrast to the regulation of all relationships through individual privileges and bestowals of favor, which is absolutely dominant in patrimonialism, at least insofar as such relationships are not fixed by sacred tradition.

All this results in the following for the internal and external position of the official.

I. Office holding is a "vocation." This is shown, first, in the requirement of a firmly prescribed course of training, which demands the entire capacity for work for a long period of time, and in the generally prescribed and special examinations which are prerequisites of employment. Furthermore, the position of the official is in the nature of a duty. This determines the internal structure of his relations, in the following manner: Legally and actually, office holding is not considered a source to be exploited for rents or emoluments, as was normally the case during the Middle Ages and frequently up to the threshold of recent times. . . . Entrances into an office, including one in the private economy, is considered an acceptance of a specific obligation of faithful management in return for a secure existence. It is decisive for the specific nature of modern loyalty to an office that, in the pure type, it does not establish a relationship to a *person*, like the vassal's or disciple's faith in feudal or in patrimonial relations and authority. Modern loyalty is devoted to impersonal and functional purposes. . . .

II. The personal position of the official is patterned in the following way:

(1) Whether he is in a private office or a public bureau, the modern official always strives and usually enjoys a distinct *social esteem* as compared with the governed. His social position is guaranteed by the prescriptive rules of rank order and, for the political official, by special definitions of the criminal code against "insults of officials" and "contempt" of state and church authorities.

The actual social position of the official is normally highest where, as in old civilized countries, the following conditions prevail: a strong demand for administration by trained experts; a strong and stable social differentiation, where the official predominantly derives from socially and economically privileged strata because of the social distribution of power; or where the costliness of the required training and status conventions are binding upon him. The possession of educational certificates—to be discussed elsewhere—are usually linked with qualification for office. Naturally, such certificates or patents enhance the "status element" in the social position of the official. . . .

Usually the social esteem of the officials as such is especially low where the demand for expert administration and the dominance of status conventions are weak. This is especially the case in the United States; it is often the case in new settlements by virtue of their wide fields for profit-taking and the great instability of their social stratification.

(2) The pure type of bureaucratic official is *appointed* by a superior authority. An official elected by the governed is not a purely bureaucratic figure. Of course, the formal existence of an election does not by itself mean that no appointment hides behind the election—in the state, especially, appointment by party chiefs. Whether or not this is the case does not depend upon legal statutes but upon the way in which the party

mechanism functions. Once firmly organized, the parties can turn a formally free election into the mere acclamation of a candidate designated by the party chief. As a rule, however, a formally free election is turned into a fight, conducted according to definite rules, for votes in favor of one of two designated candidates. . . .

(3) Normally, the position of the official is held for life, at least in public bureaucracies; and this is increasingly the case for all similar structures. As a factual rule, *tenure for life* is presupposed, even where the giving of notice or periodic reappointment occurs. In contrast to the worker in a private enterprise, the official normally holds tenure. Legal or actual life-tenure, however, is not recognized as the official's right to the possession of office, as was the case with many structures of authority in the past. Where legal guarantees against arbitrary dismissal of transfer are developed, they merely serve to guarantee a strictly objective discharge of specific office duties free from all personal considerations. . . .

(4) The official receives the regular *pecuniary* compensation of a normally fixed *salary* and the old age security provided by a pension. The salary is not measured like a wage in terms of work done, but according to "status," that is, according to the kind of function (the "rank") and, in addition, possibly, according to the length of service. The relatively great security of the official's income, as well as the rewards of social esteem, make the office a sought-after position. . . .

(5) The official is set for a "*career*" within the hierarchical order of the public service. He moves from the lower, less important, and lower paid to the higher positions. The average official naturally desires a mechanical fixing of the conditions of promotion: if not of the offices, at least of the salary levels. He wants these conditions fixed in terms of "seniority," or possibly according to grades achieved in a developed system of expert examinations.

CRITICAL THINKING QUESTIONS

1. In what respects is bureaucracy impersonal? What are some of the advantages and disadvantages of this impersonality?

2. Through most of human history, kinship has been the foundation of social organization. Why is kinship missing from Weber's analysis of bureaucracy? On what other basis are people selected for bureaucratic positions?

3. Why does bureaucracy take a hierarchical form? Do you think formal organization must be hierarchical?

23

McJobs: McDonaldization and the Workplace

CONTEMPORARY

CONTEMPORARY

CROSS-CULTURAL

GEORGE RITZER

About a decade ago, George Ritzer coined the term "McDonaldization" to refer to a set of organizational principles—including efficiency, uniformity, predictability, and control—that play an important part in today's society. Here, he describes the way McDonald's and similar organizations control not just their workers, but also their customers.

In recent years the spread of McDonaldized systems has led to the creation of an enormous number of jobs. Unfortunately, the majority of them can be thought of as McDonaldized jobs, or "McJobs." While we usually associate these types of positions with fast-food restaurants, and in fact there are many such jobs in that setting (over 2.5 million people worked in that industry in the United States in 1992 [Van Giezen, 1994]), McJobs have spread throughout much of the economy with the growing impact of McDonaldization on work settings which had previously experienced relatively little rationalization.

It is worth outlining some of the basic realities of employment in the fast-food industry in the United States since those jobs serve as a model for employment in other McDonaldized settings

Source: From *The McDonaldization Thesis: Explorations and Extensions,* by George Ritzer, pp. 59–65, 68. Copyright © 1998 Sage Publications. Reprinted with permission.

(Van Giezen, 1994). The large number of people employed in fast-food restaurants accounts for over 40 percent of the approximately six million people employed in restaurants of all types. Fast-food restaurants rely heavily on teenage employees—almost 70 percent of their employees are twenty years of age or younger. For many, the fast-food restaurant is likely to be their first employer. It is estimated that the first job for one of every fifteen workers was at McDonald's; one of every eight Americans has worked at McDonald's at some time in his or her life. The vast majority of employees are part-time workers: The average work week in the fast-food industry is 29.5 hours. There is a high turnover rate: Only slightly more than half the employees remain on the job for a year or more. Minorities are overrepresented in these jobs—almost two-thirds of employees are women and nearly a quarter are non-white. These are low-paid occupations, with many earning the minimum wage, or slightly more. As a result, these jobs are greatly affected by changes in the minimum wage: An upward revision has an important effect on the income of these workers. However, there is a real danger that many workers would lose their positions as a result of such increases, especially in economically marginal fast-food restaurants.[1]

Although the McDonaldization of society is manifest at all levels and in all realms of the social world, the work world has played a particularly pivotal role in this. On the one hand, it is the main source of many of the precursors of McDonaldization, including bureaucracies, scientific management, assembly lines, and so on. More contemporaneously, the kinds of jobs, work procedures, and organizing principles that have made McDonald's so successful have affected the way in which many businesses now organize much of their work. In fact, it could well be argued that the primary root of the McDonaldization of the larger society is the work world. On the other hand, the McDonaldization of the larger society has, in turn, served to further rationalize the work world. We thus have a self-reinforcing and enriching process that is speeding the growth and spread of McDonaldization.

The process of McDonaldization is leading to the creation of more and more McJobs.[2] The service sector, especially at its lower end, is producing an enormous number of jobs, most of them requiring little or no skill. There is no better example of this than the mountain of jobs being produced by the fast-food industry. However, new occupational creation is not the only source of McJobs: Many extant low-level jobs are being McDonaldized. More strikingly, large numbers of middle-level jobs are also being deskilled and transformed into McJobs.

McJobs are characterized by the five dimensions of McDonaldization. The jobs tend to involve a series of simple tasks in which the emphasis is on performing each as efficiently as possible. Second, the time associated with many of the tasks is carefully calculated and the emphasis on the quantity of time a task should take tends to diminish the quality of the work from the point of view of the worker. That is, tasks are so simplified and streamlined that they provide little or no meaning to the worker. Third, the work is predictable: employees do and say essentially the same things hour after hour, day after day. Fourth, many nonhuman technologies are employed to control workers and reduce them to robotlike actions. Some technologies are in place, and others are in development, that will lead to the eventual replacement of many of these "human robots" with computerized robots. Finally, the rationalized McJobs lead to a variety of irrationalities, especially the dehumanization of work. The result is the extraordinarily high turnover rate described above and difficulty in maintaining an adequate supply of replacements.[3]

The claim is usually made by spokespeople for McDonaldized systems that they are offering a large number of entry-level positions that help give employees basic skills they will need in order to move up the occupational ladder within such systems (and many of them do). This is likely to be true in the instances in which the middle-level jobs to which they move—for example, shift leader, assistant manager, or manager of a fast-food restaurant—are also routinized and scripted. In fact, it turns out that this even holds for the positions held by the routinized and scripted instructors at [McDonald's training program at] Hamburger University who teach the managers, who teach the employees, and so on. However, the skills acquired in McJobs are not likely to prepare one for, help one to acquire, or help one to function well in, the far more desirable postindustrial occupations which are highly complex and require high levels of skill and education. Experience in routinized actions and scripted interactions do not help much when occupations require thought and creativity. . . .

At the cultural level, large numbers of people in the United States, and increasingly throughout much of the rest of the world, have come to value McDonaldization in general, as well as its fundamental characteristics. McDonaldization, as well as its various principles, has become part of our value system. That value system has, in turn, been translated into a series of principles that have been exported to, adopted by, and adapted to, a wide range of social settings. . . .

. . . For example, the behavior of customers at fast-food restaurants is being affected in much the same way as the behavior of those who work in those restaurants. . . .

The constraints on the behavior of employees and customers in McDonaldized systems are of both a structural and a cultural nature. Employees and customers find themselves in a variety of McDonaldized structures that demand that they behave in accord with the dictates of those structures. For example, the drive-through window associated with the fast-food restaurant (as well as other settings such as banks) structures both what customers in their cars and employees in their booths can and cannot do. They can efficiently exchange money for food, but their positions (in a car and a booth) and the press of other cars in the queue make any kind of personal interaction virtually impossible. Of course, many other kinds of behavior are either made possible, or prohibited, by such structures. In Giddens's (1984) terms, such structures are both enabling and constraining.

At a cultural level, both employees and customers are socialized into, and have internalized, the norms and values of working and living in a McDonaldized society. Employees are trained by managers or owners who are likely, themselves, to have been trained at an institution like McDonald's Hamburger University (Schaaf, 1994). Such institutions are as much concerned with inculcating norms and values as they are with the teaching of basic skills. For their part, customers are not required to attend Hamburger University, but they are "trained" by the employees themselves, by television advertisements, and by their own children who are often diligent students, teachers, and enforcers of the McDonald's way. This "training," like that of those employees who attend Hamburger University, is oriented not only to teaching the "skills" required to be a customer at a fast-food

restaurant (e.g., how to queue up in order to order food), but also the norms and values of such settings as they apply to customers (e.g., customers are expected to dispose of their own debris; they are not expected to linger after eating). As a result of such formal and informal training, both employees and customers can be relied on to do what they are supposed to, and what is expected of them, with little or no personal supervision. . . .

. . . McJobs are not simply the deskilled jobs of our industrial past in new settings; they are jobs that have a variety of new and distinctive characteristics. . . . Industrial and McDonaldized jobs both tend to be highly routinized in terms of what people do on the job. However, one of the things that is distinctive about McDonaldized jobs, especially since so many of them involve work that requires interaction and communication, especially with consumers, is that what people say on the job is also highly routinized. To put this another way, McDonaldized jobs are tightly scripted: They are characterized by *both* routinized actions (for example, the way McDonald's hamburgers are to be put down on the grill and flipped [Love, 1986: 141–2]) and scripted interactions (examples include "May I help you?"; "Would you like a dessert to go with your meal?"; "Have a nice day!"). Scripts are crucial because, as Leidner (1993) points out, many of the workers in McDonaldized systems are interactive service workers. This means that they not only produce goods and provide services, but they often do so in interaction with customers.

The scripting of interaction leads to new depths in the deskilling of workers. Not only have employee actions been deskilled; employees' ability to speak and interact with customers is now being limited and controlled. There are not only scripts to handle general situations, but also a range of subscripts to deal with a variety of contingencies. Verbal and interactive skills are being taken away from employees and built into the scripts in much the same way that manual skills were taken and built into various technologies. At one time distrusted in their ability to *do* the right thing, workers now find themselves no longer trusted to *say* the right thing. Once able to create distinctive interactive styles, and to adjust them to different circumstances, employees are now asked to follow scripts as mindlessly as possible. . . .

One very important, but rarely noted, aspect of the labor process in the fast-food restaurant and other McDonaldized systems is the extent to which customers are being led, perhaps even almost required, to perform a number of tasks without pay that were formerly performed by paid employees. For example, in the modern gasoline station the driver now does various things for free (pumps gas, cleans windows, checks oil, even pays through a computerized credit card system built into the pump) that were formerly done by paid attendants. In these and many other settings, McDonaldization has brought the customer *into* the labor process: The customer is the laborer! This has several advantages for employers, such as lower (even nonexistent) labor costs, the need for fewer employees, and less trouble with personnel problems: Customers are far less likely to complain about a few seconds or minutes of tedious work than employees who devote a full work day to such tasks. Because of its advantages, as well as because customers are growing accustomed to and accepting of it, I think customers are likely to become even more involved in the labor process.

This is the most revolutionary development, at least as far as the labor process is concerned, associated with McDonaldization. As a result of this dramatic change, the analysis of the labor process must be extended to what customers do in McDonaldized systems. The distinction between customer and employee is eroding, or in postmodern terms "imploding," and one can envision more and more work settings in which customers are asked to do an increasing amount of "work." More dramatically, it is also likely that we will see more work settings in which there are no employees at all! In such settings customers, in interaction with nonhuman technologies, will do *all* of the human labor. A widespread example

is the ATM in which customers (and the technology) do all of the work formerly done by bank tellers. More strikingly, we are beginning to see automated loan machines which dispense loans as high as $10,000 (Singletary, 1996). Again, customers and technologies do the work and, in the process, many loan-officer positions are eliminated. Similarly, the new automated gasoline pumps allow (or force) customers to do all of the required tasks; in some cases and at certain times (late at night) no employees at all are present.

In a sense, a key to the success of McDonaldized systems is that they have been able to supplement the exploitation of employees with the exploitation of customers. Lest we forget, Marx "put at the heart of his sociology—as no other sociology does—the theme of exploitation" (Worsley, 1982: 115). In Marxian theory, the capitalists are seen as simply paying workers less than the value produced by the workers, and as keeping the rest for themselves. This dynamic continues in contemporary society, but capitalists have learned that they can ratchet up the level of exploitation not only by exploiting workers more, but also by exploiting a whole new group of people—consumers. In Marxian terms, customers create value in the tasks they perform for McDonaldized systems. And they are not simply paid less than the value they produce, they are paid *nothing at all*. In this way, customers are exploited to an even greater degree than workers. . . .

While no class within society is immune to McDonaldization, the lower classes are the most affected. They are the ones who are most likely to go to McDonaldized schools, live in inexpensive, mass-produced tract houses, and work in McDonaldized jobs. Those in the upper classes have much more of a chance of sending their children to non-McDonaldized schools, living in custom-built homes, and working in occupations in which they impose McDonaldization on others while avoiding it to a large degree themselves.

Also related to the social class issue is the fact that the McDonaldization of a significant portion of the labor force does not mean that all, or even most, of the labor force is undergoing this process. In fact, the McDonaldization of some of the labor force is occurring at the same time that another large segment is moving in a postindustrial, that is, more highly skilled, direction (Hage & Powers, 1992). Being created in this sector of society are relatively high-status, well-paid occupations requiring high levels of education and training. In the main, these are far from McJobs and lack most, or all, of the dimensions discussed at the beginning of this [reading]. The growth of such postindustrial occupations parallels the concern in the labor process literature with flexible specialization occurring side by side with the deskilling of many other jobs. This points to a bifurcation in the class system. In spite of appearances, there is no contradiction here; McDonaldization and postindustrialization tend to occur in different sectors of the labor market. However, the spread of McJobs leads us to be dubious of the idea that we have moved into a new postindustrial era and have left behind the kind of deskilled jobs we associate with industrial society.

CRITICAL THINKING QUESTIONS

1. Describe ways in which McDonaldization is evident in a number of familiar settings (not just the workplace, but perhaps shopping malls and even the college campus). What elements of McDonaldization can you find?

2. In what ways does a McDonaldized setting control not just workers but customers as well? Why do organizations want to control customers?

3. Why does McDonaldization seem to appeal to many people? Do you think this process is good for society as a whole or harmful? Why?

NOTES

This chapter combines a paper, "McJobs," published in Rich Feller and Garry Walz (eds.), *Career Transitions in Turbulent Times* (Greensboro, N.C.: ERIC/CASS Publications, 1996) and the Invited Plenary Address, International Labour Process Conference, Blackpool, England, April, 1995.

1. Although a study by Katz and Krueger (1992) indicates an employment increase accompanying a rise in the minimum wage.
2. As we will see below, other kinds of high-status, high-paying postindustrial occupations are also growing.
3. There are, of course, many other factors involved in turnover.

REFERENCES

Giddens, Anthony. 1984. *The constitution of society: Outline of the theory of structuration.* Berkeley, CA: University of California Press.

Hage, Jerald, and Charles H. Powers. 1992. *Post-industrial lives: Roles and relationships in the 21st century.* Newbury Park, CA: Sage.

Leidner, Robin. 1993. *Fast food, fast talk: Service work and the routinization of everyday life.* Berkeley, CA: University of California Press.

Love, John. 1986. *McDonald's: Behind the arches.* Toronto: Bantam Books.

Schaaf, Dick. 1994. Inside Hamburger University. *Training*, December: 18–24.

Singletary, Michelle. 1996. Borrowing by the touch. *Washington Post*, 30 March: C1, C2.

Van Giezen, Robert W. 1994. Occupational wages in the fast-food restaurant industry. *Monthly Labor Review*, August: 24–30.

Worsley, Peter. 1982. *Marx and Marxism.* Chichester, UK: Ellis Horwood.

24

"Even If I Don't Know What I'm Doing, I Can Make It Look Like I Do": Becoming a Doctor in Canada

BRENDA L. BEAGAN

Sociologists use the term "social structure" to refer to the relatively stable patterns of social interaction and organized relationships that persist over time. Brenda Beagan's article shows how medical students who are trained at Canadian universities are social-ized to fit into existing social structures rather than to change them. Notice how medical students incorporate their new professional identity as they move through their studies.

When students enter medical school they are lay people with some science background. When they leave four years later they have become physicians; they have acquired specialized knowledge and taken on a new identity of medical professional. What happens in those four years? What processes of socialization go into the making of a doctor?. . .

This study draws on survey and interview data from students and faculty at one Canadian medical school to examine the processes of professional identity formation and how they are experienced by diverse undergraduate medical students in the late 1990s. As the results will show, the processes are remarkably unchanged from the processes doc-umented forty years ago. . . .

Source: Brenda L. Beagan. 2001. "Even If I Don't Know What I'm Doing I Can Make It Look Like I Know What I'm Doing": Becoming a Doctor in the 1990s. *The Canadian Review of Sociology and Anthropology*, 38(3), 275–92.

FIRST EXPERIENCES BECOME COMMONPLACE

When identifying how they came to think of them-selves as medical students, participants described a process whereby what feels artificial and unnatu-ral initially comes to feel natural simply through repetition. For many students, a series of "first times" were transformative moments.

Denise:[1] I think there are sort of seminal experiences. The first cut in anatomy, the first time you see a patient die, first time you see a treatment that was really ag-gressive and didn't work. . . . First few procedures that I conducted myself, first time I realized that I really did have somebody's life in my hands. . . . It seems like a whole lot of first times. The first time you take a his-tory, the first time you actually hear the murmur. There are a lot of "Ah-ha!" sort of experiences.

Part of the novelty is the experience of being entitled—even required—to violate conventional social norms, touching patients' bodies, inquiring about bodily functions, probing emotional states: "You have to master a sense that you're invading somebody, and to feel like it's all right to do that, to invade their personal space. . . ."

CONSTRUCTING A PROFESSIONAL APPEARANCE

Students are quite explicitly socialized to adopt a professional appearance: "When people started to relax the dress code a letter was sent to everybody's mailbox, commenting that we were not to show up in jeans, and a tie is appropriate for men." Most students, however, do not require such reminders; they have internalized the requisite standards.

Dressing neatly and appropriately is important to convey respect to patients, other medical staff, and the profession. It probably also helps in patients taking students seriously (survey comment).

Asked whether or not they ever worry about their appearance or dress at the hospital, 41 percent of the survey respondents said they do not, while 59 percent said they do.

There were no statistically significant differences by gender, class background or "minority" status, yet gendered patterns emerged when students detailed their concerns in an open-ended question. Most of the men satisfied their concerns about professional appearance with a shave and a collared shirt, perhaps adding a tie: "I do make sure that I am dressed appropriately when I see patients i.e. well-groomed, collared shirt (but no tie)." Women, on the other hand, struggled with the complex messages conveyed by their clothing, trying to look well-dressed yet not convey sexual messages. For women, "dressed up" normally means feminine while a professional image is intended to convey competence. Striking a balance at the intersection can be difficult: "Is it professional enough? Competent looking? . . . I do not want to appear 'sexy' on the job." As one student noted, while both men and women sometimes violate standards of professional dress, men's violations tend to involve being too informal; women's may involve dressing too provocatively, thereby sexualizing a doctor–patient encounter.

CHANGES IN LANGUAGE, THINKING AND COMMUNICATION SKILLS

Acquiring a huge vocabulary of new words and old words with new meanings—what one student called "medical-ese"—is one of the central tasks facing medical students, and one of the major bases for examining them (Sinclair, 1997). Students were well aware of adopting the formal language of medicine.

Dawna: All of a sudden all I can think of is this lingo that people won't understand. My brother told me the other day, "Sometimes I just don't understand what you are talking about anymore." I don't realize it! I'll use technical terms that I didn't think that other people wouldn't know.

The language of medicine is the basis for constructing a new social reality. Even as it allows communication, language constructs "zones of meaning that are linguistically circumscribed" (Berger & Luckmann, 1966: 39). Medical language encapsulates and constructs a worldview wherein reducing a person to body parts, tissues, organs and systems becomes normal, natural, "the only reasonable way to think" (Good & Good, 1993: 98–9). Students described this as learning to pare away "extraneous" information about a patient's life to focus on what is clinically relevant.

Becky: I see how it happens. . . . The first day of medicine we're just people. We relate by asking everything about a person, just like you'd have a conversation with anybody. And then that sort of changes and you become focused on the disease . . . because right now there's just too much. It's overwhelming. I'm hoping that as I learn more and become more comfortable with what I know and I can apply it without having to consciously go through every step in my mind, that I'll be able to focus on the *person* again.

In part through the language of medicine students learn a scientific gaze that reduces patients to bodies, allowing them to concentrate on what is medically important—disease, procedures, and techniques (Haas & Shaffir, 1987).

Not surprisingly, students may simultaneously lose the communication abilities they had upon entering medical school.

Dr. W.: Their ability to talk to people becomes corrupted by the educational process. They learn the language of medicine but they give up some of the knowledge that they brought in. . . . The knowledge of how to listen to somebody, how to be humble, how to hear somebody else's words. . . . It gets overtaken by the agenda of medical interviewing.

Another faculty member noted that students' communication skills improved significantly during their first term of first year, but "by the end of fourth year they were worse than they had been before medical school."

LEARNING THE HIERARCHY

Key to becoming a medical student is learning to negotiate the complex hierarchy within medicine, with students positioned at the bottom. A few faculty saw this hierarchy as a fine and important tradition facilitating students' learning.

Dr. U.: You're always taught by the person above you. Third-year medical students taught by the fourth-year student. . . . Fourth-year student depends on the resident to go over his stuff. Resident depends on maybe the senior or the chief resident or the staff person. So they all get this hierarchy which is wonderful for learning because the attendings can't deal with everybody.

Students, and most faculty, were far less accepting of this traditional hierarchy—particularly of students' place in it.

Both faculty and students pointed out the compliance the hierarchical structure inculcates in students, discouraging them from questioning those above them.

Dr. G.: If they don't appear compliant and so on they will get evaluated poorly. And if you get evaluated

poorly then you might not get a good residency position. There's that sort of thing over their shoulders all of the time . . . the fear.

For students being a "good medical student" means not challenging clinicians.

Valerie: If I ever saw something blatantly sexist or racist or wrong I hope that I would say something. But you get so caught up in basically clamming up, shutting up, and just taking it. . . . Is it going to ruin my career, am I going to end up known as the fink, am I going to not get the [residency] spot that I want because I told?

Though virtually every student described seeing things on the wards that they disagreed with, as long as there was no direct harm to a patient they stayed silent and simply filed away the incident in their collection of "things not to do when I am a doctor."

Other researchers have noted that medical students develop an approach geared to getting along with faculty, pleasing them whatever their demands (Becker et al., 1961: 281; Bloom, 1973: 20; Sinclair, 1997: 29). Some students, however, had internalized the norm of not criticizing clinicians, adopting an unspoken "code of silence" not just to appease faculty, but as part of being a good physician. In particular, one should never critique a colleague in front of patients.

Mark: As students we all critique the professors and our attendings. . . . But I don't think we'd ever do that in front of a patient. It's never been told to us not to. But most of us wouldn't do that. Even if a patient describes something their doctor has prescribed to them or a treatment they've recommended which you know is totally wrong, maybe even harmful, I think most of us, unless it was really harmful, would tend to ignore it and just accept, "This is the doctor and his patient. What happens between them is okay."

These students had developed a sense of alliance with other members of the profession rather than with lay people and patients—a key to professional socialization. Several faculty referred to good medical students as "good team players" (cf. Sinclair, 1997), invoking a notion of belonging.

Dr. M.: That sense of belonging, I think, is a sense of belonging to the profession. . . . You're part of the process of health care. . . . I mean, you haven't a lot of the responsibility, but at least you're connected with the team.

For some students, too, the desire to present a united front for patients was expressed as being a good team player: "You have to go along with some things. . . in front of the patient. For teams it wouldn't be good to have the ranks arguing amongst themselves about the best approach for patient care." To remain good team players, many students, residents and physicians learn to say nothing even when they see colleagues and superiors violating the ethics and standards of the profession; such violations are disregarded as matters of personal style (Light, 1988).

RELATIONSHIP TO PATIENTS

As students are learning their place in the hierarchy within medicine, they are simultaneously learning an appropriate relationship to patients. Within the medical hierarchy students feel powerless at the bottom. Yet in relation to patients even students hold a certain amount of power. In the interviews there were widely diverging views on the degree of professional authority physicians and student-physicians should display.

Some faculty drew a very clear connection between professionalism and the "emotional distancing" Fox documented in medicine in 1957, describing students developing a "hard shell" as a "way of dealing with feelings" to prevent over-identifying with patients. Emotional involvement and over-identification are seen as dangerous; students must strike a balance between empathy and objectivity, learning to overcome or master their emotions (Conrad, 1988; Haas & Shaffir, 1987): "I only become of use if I can create some distance so that I can function."

Dr. E.: Within the professional job that you have to do, one can be very nice to patients but there's a distancing that says you're not their friend, you're their doctor.

In contrast, several faculty members rejected the "emotional distancing" approach to medicine in favour of one based in egalitarian connection.

Dr. V.: I reject that way of dealing with it. . . . When I'm seeing a patient I have to try to get into understanding what's bothering them. And in fact it's a harder job, I mean I need to understand well enough so I can help them to understand. 'Cause the process of healing is self-understanding.

These faculty members talked about recognizing and levelling power or sharing power. They saw professional distancing as the loss of humanitarianism, the adoption of a position of superiority, aloofness, emphasizing that clinicians need to know their patients as something more than a diagnosis. Women were slightly over-represented among those expressing the egalitarian perspective, but several male clinicians also advocated this position.

PLAYING A ROLE GRADUALLY BECOMES REAL

Along with emotional distancing, Fox (1957) identified "training for uncertainty" as key to medical socialization, including the uncertainty arising from not knowing everything, and not knowing enough. Alongside gathering the knowledge and experience that gradually reduces feelings of uncertainty, students also grow to simply tolerate high levels of uncertainty. At the same time they face routine expectations of certainty— from patients who expect them "to know it all" and faculty who often expect them to know far more than they do and who evaluate the students' competence (Haas & Shaffir, 1987). Students quickly learn it is risky to display lack of certainty; impression management becomes a central feature of clinical learning (Conrad, 1988). Haas and Shaffir (1987: 110) conclude that the process of professionalization involves above all the successful adoption of a cloak of competence such that audiences are convinced of the legitimacy of claims to competence.

Robert Coombs argues that medical professional socialization is partly a matter of playing the role of doctor, complete with the props of white coat, stethoscope, name tag, and clipboard (1978: 222). The symbols mark medical students off as distinct from lay people and other hospital staff, differentiating between We and They. Students spoke of "taking on a role" that initially made them feel like "total frauds," "impostors."

Erin: It was really role-playing. You were doing all these examinations on these patients which were not going to go into their charts, were not going to ever be read by anybody who was treating the people so it really was just practice. Just play-acting.

They affirmed the importance of the props to successful accomplishment of their role play—even as it enhanced the feeling of artifice: "During third year when we got to put the little white coat on and carry some instruments around the hospital, have a name tag . . . it definitely felt like role-playing."

Despite feeling fraudulent, the role play allows students to meet a crucial objective: demonstrating to faculty, clinical instructors, nurses and patients that they know something. They quickly learn to at least look competent.

Nancy: Even if I don't know what I'm doing I can make it *look* like I know what I'm doing. . . . It was my acting in high school. . . . I get the trust of the patient. . . .

RESPONSES FROM OTHERS

The more students are treated by others as if they really were doctors the more they feel like doctors (cf. Coombs, 1978). In particular, the response from other hospital personnel and patients can help confirm the student's emerging medical professional identity.

Rina: The more the staff treats you as someone who actually belongs there, that definitely adds to your feeling like you do belong there. . . . It's like, "Wow! This nurse is paging me and wants to know *my* opinion on why this patient has no urine output?!"

For many students, patients were the single most important source of confirmation for their emerging identity as physicians. With doctors and nurses, students feel they can easily be caught out for what they don't know; with patients they feel fairly certain they can pull off a convincing performance, and they often realize they do know more than the average person.

One response from others that has tremendous impact is simply being called doctor by others (Konner, 1987; Shapiro, 1987). Survey results show 68 percent ($n = 48$) of students had been called doctor at least occasionally by people other than family or friends. All but two fully recalled the first time they were called doctor and how they felt about it. Not being called doctor—especially when your peers are—can be equally significant. In previous accounts, being white and being male have greatly improved a medical student's chances of being taken for a doctor (Dickstein, 1993; Gamble, 1990; Kirk, 1994; Lenhart, 1993). In this study, although social class background, minority status and first language made no difference, significantly more men than women were *regularly* called doctor and significantly more women had *never* been called doctor.[2]

These data suggest a lingering societal assumption that the doctor is a man. According to the interviews, women medical students and physicians are still often mistaken for nurses. Two of the male students suggested the dominant assumption that a doctor is a man facilitates their establishing rapport with patients and may ease their relationships with those above them in the medical hierarchy: "I've often felt because I fit like a stereotypical white male, that patients might see me as a bit more trustworthy. A bit more what they'd like to see. Who they want to see." Goffman notes that the part of a social performance intended to impress others, which he calls the "front," and which includes clothing, gender, appearance and manner, is predetermined: "When an actor takes on an established social role, usually he finds that a particular front has already been established for it" (1959: 27). In this case it appears that the role doctor, or medical student, still carries an attached assumption of maleness. . . .

CONCLUSION

What is perhaps most remarkable about these findings is how little has changed since the publication of *Boys in White* (Becker et al., 1961) and *Student Physician* (Merton et al., 1957), despite the passage of forty years and the influx of a very different student population. The basic processes of socializing new members into the profession of medicine remain remarkably similar, as students encounter new social norms, a new language, new thought processes, and a new world view that will eventually enable them to become full-fledged members of "the team" taking the expected role in the medical hierarchy.

Yet, with the differences in the 1990s student population, there are also some important differences in experiences. The role of medical student continues to carry with it certain expectations of its occupant. At a time when medical students were almost exclusively white, heterosexually identified, upper- or middle-class men, the identity may have "fit" more easily than it does for students who are women, who are from minority racial groups, who identify as gay or lesbian or working-class. If role-playing competence and being reflected back to yourself as "doctor" are as central to medical socialization as Haas and Shaffir (1987) suggest, what does it mean that women students are less likely than their male peers to be called doctor? This research has indicated the presence of a lingering societal assumption that Doctor = Man. Women students struggle to construct a professional appearance that male students find a straightforward accomplishment. Women search for ways to be in a relationship with their patients that are unmarked by gender. Despite the fact that they make up half of all medical students in Canada, women's experiences of medical school remain different. In this research, almost half (six of fourteen) of the women students interviewed indicated that they do not identify themselves as medical students in casual social settings outside school lest they be seen as putting on airs; none of the male students indicated this. It remains for future research to determine whether gender differences in the "fit" of the physician role make a difference to medical practice. . . .

CRITICAL THINKING QUESTIONS

1. One new experience for medical students is learning *medical-ese*. Have you faced a similar process during your college education? Explain.

2. Why do you think that the traditional hierarchy in medical schools (i.e., faculty at the top, students at the bottom) is seen by many as a good thing?

3. Which groups of students were most likely to resist professional socialization? Why would this be the case?

NOTES

1. All names are pseudonyms.
2. Never been called doctor, 14 percent of women, 0 percent of men; occasionally or regularly, 57 percent of women, 78 percent of men (Cramer's V = 0.32).

REFERENCES

Becker, H. S., B. Geer, A. L. Strauss, and F. C. Hughes. 1961. *Boys in white: Student culture in medical school.* Chicago: University of Chicago Press.

Berger, P. L., and T. Luckmann. 1966. The social construction of reality: A treatise in the sociology of knowledge. New York: Doubleday and Co.

Bloom, S. W. 1973. *Power and dissent in the medical school.* New York: The Free Press.

———. 1988. Structure and ideology in medical education: An analysis of resistance to change. *Journal of Health and Social Behavior*, 29: 294–306.

Conrad, E. 1988. Learning to doctor: Reflections on recent accounts of the medical school years. *Journal of Health and Social Behavior*, 29: 323–32.

Coombs, R. H. 1978. *Mastering medicine*. New York: Free Press.

Dickstein, L. J. 1993. Gender bias in medical education: Twenty vignettes and recommended responses. *Journal of the American Medical Women's Association*, 48(5): 152–62.

Fox, R. C. 1957. Training for uncertainty. In *The student-physician: Introduction studies in the sociology of medical education*, eds. R. K. Merton, G. G. Reader, and E. L. Kendall, 207–44. Cambridge, MA: Harvard University Press.

Gamble, V. N. 1990. On becoming a physician: A dream not deferred. In *The black women's health book: Speaking for ourselves*, ed. E. C. White, 52–64. Seattle, WA: Seal Press.

Goffman, E. 1959. *The presentation of self in everyday life*. New York: Doubleday.

Good, B. J., and M. J. DelVecchio Good. 1993. "Learning medicine." The constructing of medical knowledge at Harvard medical school. In *Knowledge, power, and practice: The anthropology of medicine and everyday life*, eds. S. Lindbaum, and M. Lock, 81–107. Berkeley: University of California Press.

Haas, J., and W. Shaffir. 1987. *Becoming doctors: The adoption of a cloak of competence*. Greenwich, CT: JAI Press.

Kirk, J. 1994. A feminist analysis of women in medical schools. In *Health, illness, and health care in Canada*, 2nd ed., eds. B. S. Bolaria, and H. D. Dickenson, 158–82. Toronto: Harcourt Brace.

Konner, M. 1987. *Becoming a doctor: A journey of initiation in medical school*. New York: Viking.

Lenhart, S. 1993. Gender discrimination: A health and career development problem for women physicians. *Journal of the American Medical Women's Association*, 48(5): 155–59.

Light, D. W. 1988. Toward a new sociology of medical education. *Journal of Health and Social Behavior*, 29: 307–22.

Merton, R. K., G. G. Reader, and P. L. Kendall. 1957. *The student physician: Introductory studies in the sociology of medical education*. Cambridge, MA: Harvard University Press.

Shapiro, M. 1987. *Getting doctored: Critical reflections on becoming a physician*. Toronto: Between the Lines.

Sinclair, S. 1997. *Making doctors: An institutional apprenticeship*. New York: Berg.

25

The Functions of Crime

EMILE DURKHEIM

Common sense leads us to view crime, and all kinds of deviance, as pathological—that is, as harmful to social life. Despite the obvious social costs of crime, however, Durkheim argues that crime is normal because it is part of all societies. Furthermore, he claims that crime makes important contributions to the operation of a social system.

Crime is present not only in the majority of societies of one particular species but in all societies of all types. There is no society that is not confronted with the problem of criminality. Its form changes; the acts thus characterized are not the same everywhere; but, everywhere and always, there have been men who have behaved in such a way as to draw upon themselves penal repression. . . . There is, then, no phenomenon that presents more indisputably all the symptoms of normality, since it appears closely connected with the conditions of all collective life. To make of crime a form of social morbidity would be to admit that morbidity is not something accidental, but, on the contrary, that in certain cases it grows out of the fundamental constitution of the living organism; it would result in wiping out all distinction between the physiological and the pathological. No doubt it is possible that crime itself will have abnormal forms, as, for example, when its rate is unusually high. This excess is, indeed, undoubtedly

Source: Reprinted with permission of The Free Press, a Division of Simon & Schuster Adult Publishing Group, from *The Rules of Sociological Method* by Emile Durkheim, translated by Sarah A. Solovay and John H. Mueller. Edited by George E. G. Catlin. Copyright © 1938 by George E. G. Catlin; copyright renewed 1966 by Sarah A. Solovay, John H. Mueller, and George E. G. Catlin.

morbid in nature. What is normal, simply, is the existence of criminality. . . .

Here we are, then, in the presence of a conclusion in appearance quite paradoxical. Let us make no mistake. To classify crime among the phenomena of normal sociology is not to say merely that it is an inevitable, although regrettable, phenomenon, due to the incorrigible wickedness of men; it is to affirm that it is a factor in public health, an integral part of all healthy societies. This result is, at first glance, surprising enough to have puzzled even ourselves for a long time. Once this first surprise has been overcome, however, it is not difficult to find reasons explaining this normality and at the same time confirming it.

In the first place crime is normal because a society exempt from it is utterly impossible. Crime . . . consists of an act that offends certain very strong collective sentiments. In a society in which criminal acts are no longer committed, the sentiments they offend would have to be found without exception in all individual consciousnesses, and they must be found to exist with the same degree as sentiments contrary to them. Assuming that this condition could actually be realized, crime would not thereby disappear; it would only change its form, for the very cause which would thus dry up the sources of criminality would immediately open up new ones.

Indeed, for the collective sentiments which are protected by the penal law of a people at a specified moment of its history to take possession of the public conscience or for them to acquire a stronger hold where they have an insufficient grip, they must acquire an intensity greater than that which they had hitherto had. The community as a whole must experience them more vividly, for it can acquire from no other source the greater force necessary to control these individuals who formerly were the most refractory. For murderers to disappear, the horror of bloodshed must become greater in those social strata from which murderers are recruited; but, first it must become greater throughout the entire society. Moreover,

the very absence of crime would directly contribute to produce this horror; because any sentiment seems much more respectable when it is always and uniformly respected.

One easily overlooks the consideration that these strong states of the common consciousness cannot be thus reinforced without reinforcing at the same time the more feeble states, whose violation previously gave birth to mere infraction of convention—since the weaker ones are only the prolongation, the attenuated form, of the stronger. Thus robbery and simple bad taste injure the same single altruistic sentiment, the respect for that which is another's. However, this same sentiment is less grievously offended by bad taste than by robbery; and since, in addition, the average consciousness has not sufficient intensity to react keenly to the bad taste, it is treated with greater tolerance. That is why the person guilty of bad taste is merely blamed, whereas the thief is punished. But, if this sentiment grows stronger, to the point of silencing in all consciousnesses the inclination which disposes man to steal, he will become more sensitive to the offenses which, until then, touched him but lightly. He will react against them, then, with more energy; they will be the object of greater opprobrium, which will transform certain of them from the simple moral faults that they were and give them the quality of crimes. For example, improper contracts, or contracts improperly executed, which only incur public blame or civil damages, will become offenses in law.

Imagine a society of saints, a perfect cloister of exemplary individuals. Crimes, properly so called, will there be unknown; but faults which appear venial to the layman will create there the same scandal that the ordinary offense does in ordinary consciousnesses. If, then, this society has the power to judge and punish, it will define these acts as criminal and will treat them as such. For the same reason, the perfect and upright man judges his smallest failings with a severity that the majority reserve for acts more truly in the nature of an offense. Formerly, acts of violence against persons were more frequent than they are today, because respect for individual dignity was less strong. As this has increased, these crimes have become more rare; and also, many acts violating this sentiment have been introduced into the penal law which were not included there in primitive times. . . .[1]

Crime is, then, necessary; it is bound up with the fundamental conditions of all social life, and by that very fact it is useful, because these conditions of which it is a part are themselves indispensable to the normal evolution of morality and law.

Indeed, it is no longer possible today to dispute the fact that law and morality vary from one social type to the next, nor that they change within the same type if the conditions of life are modified. But, in order that these transformations may be possible, the collective sentiments at the basis of morality must not be hostile to change, and consequently must have but moderate energy. If they were too strong, they would no longer be plastic. Every pattern is an obstacle to new patterns, to the extent that the first pattern is inflexible. The better a structure is articulated, the more it offers a healthy resistance to all modification; and this is equally true of functional, as of anatomical, organization. If there were no crimes, this condition could not have been fulfilled; for such a hypothesis presupposes that collective sentiments have arrived at a degree of intensity unexampled in history. Nothing is good indefinitely and to an unlimited extent. The authority which the moral conscience enjoys must not be excessive; otherwise no one would dare criticize it, and it would too easily congeal into an immutable form. To make progress, individual originality must be able to express itself. In order that the originality of the idealist whose dreams transcend his century may find expression, it is necessary that the originality of the criminal, who

is below the level of his time, shall also be possible. One does not occur without the other.

Nor is this all. Aside from this indirect utility, it happens that crime itself plays a useful role in this evolution. Crime implies not only that the way remains open to necessary changes but that in certain cases it directly prepares these changes. Where crime exists, collective sentiments are sufficiently flexible to take on a new form, and crime sometimes helps to determine the form they will take. How many times, indeed, it is only an anticipation of future morality—a step toward what will be! According to Athenian law, Socrates was a criminal, and his condemnation was no more than just. However, his crime, namely, the independence of his thought, rendered a service not only to humanity but to his country. . . .

From this point of view the fundamental facts of criminality present themselves to us in an entirely new light. Contrary to current ideas, the criminal no longer seems a totally unsociable being, a sort of parasitic element, a strange and unassimilable body, introduced into the midst of society. On the contrary, he plays a definite role in social life.

CRITICAL THINKING QUESTIONS

1. On what grounds does Durkheim argue that crime should be considered a "normal" element of society?

2. Why is a society devoid of crime an impossibility?

3. What are the functional consequences of crime and deviance?

NOTE

1. Calumny, insults, slander, fraud, etc.

26

The Rebels: A Brotherhood of Outlaw Bikers

DANIEL R. WOLF

Using a classic social research strategy, fieldwork, Wolf reviews his experiences as a member of the outlaw biker gang, the Rebels.

ENTERING THE WORLD OF THE OUTLAW

"All the world likes an outlaw. For some damn reason they remember 'em."

—Jesse James

A midnight run shatters the night air. Thirty Harley-Davidson motorcycles stretch out for a quarter-mile, thundering down the highway. The pack moves in tight formation, advancing as a column of staggered twos. Veteran riders make sure there are fifteen yards between themselves and the bikes they are riding behind, three yards and a 45-degree angle between themselves and the bikes they are riding beside. Thirty men ride in boots and jeans, leathers and cut-off denim jackets, beards and long hair, tattoos and

Source: From *The Rebels: A Brotherhood of Outlaw Bikers* by Daniel R. Wolf. Toronto: University of Toronto Press, 1991, pp. 3–21. Reprinted by permission of the publisher.

earrings, buck knives and chain belts. Each rider follows the grimacing skull on the back patch of the rider in front of him. Some ride with their ol' ladies, "jamming in the wind" with a laid-back coolness bordering on arrogance, a combination of speed, grace, and power. The lead biker snaps his wrist to full throttle and the supercharged V-twin engines heat up and pound out the challenge. Each biker is locked into the tunnel vision of his own world. He feels the heavy metal vibrations in every joint of his body, but he can no longer hear the rumble of his own machine, just a collective roar. Headlamps slice open just enough darkness to let the sculptured metal of extended front ends slide through. Cool blackness clips over high-rise handlebars, whips their faces, then quickly swallows the red glare of tail-lights. A grey blur of pavement that represents instant oblivion passes six inches beneath the soles of their boots. At a hundred miles an hour the inflections of the road surface disappear, eye sockets are pushed back, and tears flow. Riders hurtle down the highway, in total control of their own destinies, wrapped in the freedom of high sensation. They are the Rebels: Caveman, Blues, Tiny, Wee Albert, Gerry, Slim, Tramp, Danny, Onion, Jim Raunch, Ken, Voodoo, Larry, Killer, Whimpy, Clayton, Steve, Indian, Armand, Crash, Big Mike, Smooth Ed, Yesnoski, Snake, Dale the Butcher, Saint, and Terrible Tom.

Outlaw motorcycle clubs originated on the American west coast following the Second World War. With names such as the Booze Fighters and their parent club the 13 Rebels, the Galloping Gooses, Satan's Sinners, and the Winos, they rapidly spread across the United States and into Canada in the early 1950s; Canada's first outlaw club was the Canadian Lancers in Toronto, Ontario. Today, outlaw motorcycle clubs are an international social phenomenon. As of 1990 the outlaw club subculture had spread into eleven other countries, including the European nations of Great Britain, West Germany, France, Switzerland, Austria, Belgium, Denmark, and the Netherlands in the mid-sixties and early seventies, and then into Australia, New Zealand, and Brazil in the mid-seventies and early eighties.

What is or is not considered deviant by society, and how society reacts to that deviance, always involves the process of social definition. Technically, the label "outlaw motorcycle club" designates a club that is not registered with the American Motorcycle Association (AMA) or the Canadian Motorcycle Association (CMA), which are the respective governing bodies for the sport of motorcycling in the United States and Canada. The AMA and CMA are themselves affiliated with the Fédération Internationale Motorcycliste (FIM), the international coordinating body for motorcycling whose headquarters are located in Paris, France. A motorcycle club that is registered with the AMA or CMA obtains a club charter from those parent bodies that allows the club and its members to participate in or sponsor sanctioned motorcycle events—mainly racing

competitions. AMA or CMA registration further aligns the club with the legal and judicial elements of the host society; some clubs will go one step further and incorporate themselves as "registered societies" with the local state or provincial authorities. Non-registered clubs are labelled "outlaw" and considered as the 1 per cent deviant fringe that continues to tarnish the public image of both motorcycles and motorcyclists. For its part, the outlaw-biker community graciously accepted the AMA's "one percenter" label as a means of identifying a "righteous outlaw." Today, many outlaw club members wear 1% badges as a supplement to their club colours; or, as Sonny Barger, president of the Hell's Angels, first did in the sixties, they make a very personal and uncompromising statement on where they stand on the issue of being an outlaw by having the 1% logo tattooed on their shoulders.

Historically, the initial and most dramatic definition of outlaw clubs occurred in response to the world's first motorcycle riot in the rural town of Hollister, California, on 4 July 1947. Approximately five hundred non-affiliated bikers disrupted an AMA-sponsored Gypsy Tour and competition events involving 2500 affiliated bikers by drinking and racing in the streets of the host town of Hollister. The ineffective efforts of a numerically insufficient seven-man police force, in conjunction with the sometimes provocative vigilante tactics of indignant local residents, caused the motorcyclists to coalesce as a mob. At the height of the riot, bikers rode their motorcycles into bars and restaurants and through traffic lights, tossed bottles out of upper-floor windows, and got rid of the beer they had been drinking in the streets (indecent exposure). The unruly behaviour lasted for approximately thirty-six hours, from July 4th to 5th; the world's first motorcycle riot ended with the departure of many of the partyers on the evening of the first day and the arrival on the second of an auxiliary police force of thirty-two officers.

The national exposure that was given the Hollister incident by *Life* magazine and others resulted in the stigmatization of an image: the motorcyclist as deviant. *Life's* account started a mass-media chain reaction that saw the Hollister incident grow considerably in its sensationalistic portrayal, and, as a result, the image of the motorcyclist as deviant become more defined and immutable. In 1949, Frank Rooney wrote a short narrative entitled "Cyclist Raid," based on *Life's* one-hundred-and-fifteen-word documentary; in 1951, "Cyclist Raid" was published in *Harper's* magazine. The *Harper's* serial was read by Stanley Kramer, a Hollywood producer, who immortalized the "motorcycle riot" in the movie *The Wild One,* released in 1953. The anti-hero image of the motorcyclist was cast in the person of Marlon Brando, while Lee Marvin personified the motorcyclist as villain. Interestingly enough, the striped shirt that Lee Marvin wore in the movie was later bought by a member of the Hell's Angels Motorcycle Club (MC)—a symbolic indication of events to come. The movie was to titillate the North American media with its "factual" account of a "menacing element of modern youth": A little bit of the surface of contemporary American life is scratched in Stanley Kramer's "The Wild One" . . . and underneath is opened an ugly, debauched and frightening view of a small, but particularly significant and menacing element of modern youth. . . .

The subject of its examination is a swarm of youthful motorcyclists who ride through the country in wolf-pack fashion and terrorize the people of one small town. . . . These "wild ones" resent discipline and show an aggressive contempt for common decency and the police. Reckless and vandalistic, they live for sensations, nothing more—save perhaps the supreme sensation of defying the normal world. (Crowther, *New York Times,* 31 December 1953)

Audiences who like their facts dished up with realism, no matter how painful, might pay attention to "The Wild One"—a picture that is factual. . . . It displays a group of hoodlums, motorcyclists who ride around the country with a contempt for the law and a fondness for annoying people, who take over a small town . . . a slice of contemporary Americana at its worst. (Hartung, *Commonweal,* 3 February 1954)

The above "factual" accounts were based on viewing a Stanley Kramer movie production whose script was written by John Paxton; Paxton's script was based on Kramer's reading of Frank Rooney's serialized story in *Harper's* magazine; Rooney's short story was in turn based on his reading of *Life's* one-hundred-and-fifteen-word report—complete with photo—which itself was originally construed [*sic*] by adding four major distortions to a brief press-wire release.

By contemporary standards the amount of property damage and civic duress incurred in Hollister was minimal. In actuality there were only thirty-eight arrests (out of approximately three or four thousand bikers), fighting was mostly confined to the bikers, and no one was killed, maimed, or even gang-kissed. "Wino Willie" Forkner is a biker who has ridden Harleys since he was a teenager in the 1930s. He had returned from the Second World War after fighting the Japanese as a waist gunner and engineer for the American Seventh Air Force. He attended the Hollister incident as a charter member of the Booze Fighters MC:

The worst thing that happened was that a bunch of guys wanted to break Red Daldren out of jail. I was in a bar and somebody came in and said there were about 500 bikers ready to break him out, and I thought, "Shit, that's all we need, something like that." So I ran down to where the crowd was assembling and told 'em, "Hell, old Red's drunk and he needs a good night's sleep. Leave him stay—he'll be out in the morning." Then I turned around and went back to the bar, and damned if the cops didn't come and nail me for inciting a riot [the charges were dropped] . . . but no big bad things happened. There were a few broken windows that we paid for. ("Wino Willie" Faukner, interview in *Easyriders,* September 1986: 107)

However, as *Life* was to point out twenty-five years after the Hollister riot, the significance of the media chain reaction was its very real consequences: "The *Wild One* became a milestone in movie history, launching the cult of gang violence in films. It also helped create an image of motorcycling that non-violent bike riders have been trying to live down for a quarter of a century now" (*Life,* September 1972: 32). After the Hollister incident and, more to the point, after the movie, the AMA issued its now famous statement about 1 per cent of the motorcycling public, specifically clubs like the Booze Fighters, being a deviant criminal fringe element.

There is a tendency to view the Hollister motorcycle riot and its subsequent national media coverage as the genesis of the "outlaw biker"—it was the birth of an image. In effect, the outlaw biker image that was created served as a frame of reference for many young and restless rebels who copied the celluloid vision in search of both a thrill and a cause. Historically, outlaw motorcycle clubs have operated in the shadows of several different media stereotypes, all of which have been variations on the theme of "social menace." In the 1950s bikers were depicted as social rebels and deviants; in the sixties and seventies the clubs were seen as subcultures of violence and drugs. The contemporary image adds a spectre of organized crime. In 1984 the Criminal Intelligence Service of Canada (CISC) declared that outlaw motorcycle gangs had become as much of an organized-crime threat to Canada as the traditional Mafia. According to the CISC report, outlaw clubs "are involved in practically all major crime activities from murder to white-collar crime." At the annual meeting of Canadian police chiefs in 1985, outlaw motorcycle clubs were again acknowledged as the number-one concern in the area of organized crime; media headlines carried the claim: "Bikers more powerful than Mafia" (Canadian Press release, *Edmonton Journal,* 15 August 1985: A12). How law-enforcement agencies have come to view outlaw motorcycle clubs is summarized in the following profile contained in an application for a search warrant made out by a member of the City of Calgary police department's Special Strike Force:

Outlaw Motorcycle Gangs have over the years evolved into highly sophisticated "organized crime" bodies, involved in drug manufacture/distribution/trafficking, prostitution, "gun running," fencing of stolen property and strong arm debt collection.

Law enforcement agencies across Canada have recognized that outlaw motorcycle gangs as "organized crime" bodies pose the single most serious threat to the country.

An outlaw motorcycle gang is "Any group of motorcycle enthusiasts who have voluntarily made a commitment to band together and abide by their organization's rigorous rules enforced by violence, who engage in activities that bring them and their club into serious conflict with society and the law."

It is their involvement as a group in criminal activities and antisocial behaviour which sets them apart from other organized groups. (Detective Brendan Alexander Kapuscinski, City of Calgary police force, "Application for Warrant to Search and Seize," 1988: 2)

"If the Cops are the Good Guys," writes the representative of an American federal law-enforcement training centre, "then it's hard to imagine a more archetypal Bad Guy than the outlaw motorcyclist!" (Ayoob, 1982: 26). North Americans typically react with an interesting mixture of apprehension and fascination to the fearsome images of aggression, revolt, anarchy, and criminal abandon that are used to portray outlaw-biker gangs.

Ironically, the appeal of outlaw clubs to their members is very different from what the public understands. Outlaw bikers view themselves as nothing less than frontier heroes, living out the "freedom ethic" that they feel the rest of society has largely abandoned. They acknowledge that they are antisocial, but only to the extent that they seek to gain their own unique experiences and express their individuality through their motorcycles. Their "hogs" become personal charms against the regimented world of the "citizen." They view their club as collective leverage that they can use against an establishment that threatens to crush those who find conventional society inhibiting and destructive of individual character. In an interesting twist of stereotypes the citizen becomes the bad guy, or at least weak, and the outlaw becomes the hero. Bikers make much of the point that the differential treatment—harassment—accorded outlaw clubs by law-enforcement agencies runs counter to the basic principles of self-determination. They protest that a truly democratic society should be able to tolerate diversity and accommodate an awareness that drifting away from society's conventions is very different from opting out of society's laws. Somewhere between the convenient stereotype of "criminal deviants" used by the police and the stylized self-conscious image outlaws have of themselves as "frontier heroes" lies the story of real people.

The Rebels Motorcycle Club is an outlaw club. It began in 1969 as a small club of motorcycle enthusiasts who rode their Harley-Davidsons on the streets of Edmonton, Alberta, a mid-sized Canadian city with a population of approximately 700,000 people. Today (1990), the Rebels MC is a federation of four clubs—located in the provinces of Alberta and Saskatchewan—that maintains informal social and political ties with the Hells Angels MC. Becoming a Rebel means being part of a tightly knit voluntary association that operates as a secret society within an organizational framework that includes a political structure, a financial base, a geographical territory, a chain of command, a constitution, an elaborate set of rules, and internal mechanisms for enforcing justice and compliance from within.

At its best a veteran club will operate with the internal discipline and precision of a paramilitary organization, which is completely necessary if it hopes to beat the odds and survive. These men close their world to the outside, turning to each other for help and guidance. They protect themselves with a rigid code of silence that cloaks their world in secrecy. Thus, despite the fact that outlaw motorcycle clubs are found in every major urban centre in Canada and the United States— there are approximately 900 clubs—*the subculture had remained ethnographically unexplored.*

As a doctoral graduate student in anthropology at the University of Alberta, Edmonton, I wanted to study the "Harley tribe." It was my intent to obtain an insider's perspective on the emotions and the mechanics that underlie the outlaw bikers' creation of a subcultural alternative. My

interest in outlaw motorcycle clubs was not entirely theoretical; it was also a personal challenge. Brought up on the streets of a lower-class neighbourhood, I saw my best friend—with whom I broke into abandoned buildings as a kid—sent to prison for grand theft auto, and then shot down in an attempted armed robbery. Rather than be crushed like that, I worked in meat-packing plants and factories for thirteen hours a day and put myself through university. I also bought myself a British-made Norton motorcycle. My Norton Commando became a "magic carpet ride" of thrills and excitement that I rode with lean women who were equally hungry to get their share. But it was more than that. I rode my motorcycle in anger; for me it became a show of contempt and a way of defying the privileged middle class that had put me down and had kept my parents "in their place." I felt that the Establishment had done me no favours and that I owed it even less. At that time I saw outlaw bikers as a reflection of my own dark side. I made them the embodiment of my own youthful rebellion and resentment. In retrospect, I believe that it was this aspect of my non-academic background—the fact that I had learned to ride and beat the streets—that made it possible for me to contemplate such a study, and eventually to ride with the Rebels.

At the time of beginning my fieldwork I had been riding British-made motorcycles for three years and had talked briefly to members of the King's Crew MC in Calgary. But this was not enough to comprehend the outlaw-biker community or to study it. My impression of outlaw bikers was narrow and incomplete and, in that sense, almost as misleading as the stereotype held by most "citizens." I was physically close to the scene, but far removed from a balanced understanding; that understanding would only come from "being there."

I customized my Norton, donned some biker clothing, and set off to do some fieldwork. My first attempts at contacting an outlaw club were near disasters. In Calgary, I met several members of the King's Crew MC in a motorcycle shop and expressed an interest in "hanging around." But I lacked patience and pushed the situation by asking too many questions. A deviant society, especially one that walks on the wild side of illegal activities, will have its own information network for checking out strangers. I found out quickly that outsiders, even bikers, do not rush into a club, and that anyone who doesn't show the proper restraint will be shut out. That was mistake number one. Days later, I carelessly got into an argument with a club "striker," a probationary member, that led to blows in a bar-room skirmish. He flattened my nose and began choking me. Unable to get air down my throat and breathing only blood through my nostrils, I managed a body punch that luckily found his solar plexus and loosened his grip. I then grabbed one of his hands and pulled back on the thumb till I heard the joint break. Mistake number two. It was time to move on. I packed my sleeping-bag on my Norton and headed west for Vancouver with some vague and ridiculous notion of meeting up with the Satan's Angels, now a chapter of the Hell's Angels.

Riding into Burnaby (Greater Vancouver) I discovered that an outlaw biker has to learn a whole new set of rules for dealing with the law. I had decided to modify my public identity in order to facilitate participant observation of a deviant group; I could not expect any favours from legal authorities and I would have to learn how to cope with what might be termed differential treatment—bikers use the term "harassment"—on the part of police officers. I saw the flashing red light in my rear-view mirror moments before I heard the siren. I had been looking for the Admiral Hotel, a bar where the Satan's Angels hung out. I started to gear down when I noticed that the RCMP (Royal Canadian Mounted Police) cruiser was only three feet from my rear tire. I continued to slow down and hoped that he knew what he was doing. I pulled into the parking lot behind the Admiral bar, got off my bike, and turned around to approach the officer. As I reached for my wallet he immediately ordered me to turn around

and put my hands behind my head. I froze in what was probably 90 per cent uncertainty and 10 per cent defiance. When I didn't move he unlatched the holster that held his pistol; he gripped the weapon and then reached inside his car and grabbed the radio mike to call for a backup. Within moments a second cruiser was on the scene. He lined me up with the car's headlights, turned on the high beams, and then began the standard shakedown. Upon request I produced my operator's licence, vehicle registration, and insurance, and was then asked where I was from, what club I rode with, if I had a criminal record, and if I had ever been in trouble with the law before. As I answered the questions, wondering what kind of trouble I was in now, a third cruiser pulled up, turned on its bright lights, and two more officers joined in. At that time some of my identification read "Daniel" and some read "Danny," which prompted a series of questions about aliases and a radio check about outstanding arrest warrants and vehicle registration. When this failed to produce any evidence against me, I was asked if I was carrying any weapons or drugs. The answer to both questions was "no" and the whole situation began to seem absurd. I was being put on stage under the spotlights of three police cruisers in a back alley drama directed by five RCMP officers. Meanwhile, the Satan's Angels that I'd come to meet were relaxing and having some cool beers in the bar across the alley. I began to laugh at the irony, which was mistake number three. "Put your hands up against that wall!" yelled a constable who was angered by my apparent disdain for the law. One officer searched through the pockets of my leathers and jeans while another rummaged through the leather saddle-bags on my bike. After the bike and body search, I asked the officers if motorcycle clubs were a major problem in their area. I was told they weren't, "but some guys figure they're king shit when you pull them over, and you've got to remember that no matter how tough you are, there's always someone tougher!" I was then asked how long I was staying, and

I replied that it depended on my financial situation. I answered straightforwardly and stated that I was carrying credit cards and a little more than three hundred dollars, as the police already knew—having counted it. Only then did one of the officers explain: "When he asked you how long you're staying, what he's saying is that this road leads to Harvey Avenue, which leads to the highway out of town!"

I had sewn a secret pocket into the sleeve of my leather jacket. It contained a letter from the [Social Sciences and Humanities Research Council] . . . (SSHRC) addressed to the RCMP that identified myself and my research. The officers failed to find it, and I wasn't about to reveal it. My research goal was to find out and experience what happens within the outlaw-biker scene, not be told what happens from the outside. Three days earlier I had talked to a Vancouver city police officer who knew me as a researcher: "I'll save you a whole lot of trouble, maybe even your neck, and explain this whole biker thing to you," he said. "They're all just psychologically unstable. That's all you have to know; otherwise none of it makes any sense."

"Those cops [at the Admiral Hotel] were setting you up," Steve, the Rebels MC sergeant at arms, would explain some months later. "They were just waiting for you to make a stupid move and they've got you by the balls. They could have beaten the shit outta you, and you'd have five cops as witnesses. Well, it would've been tough shit for you!" I learned that one does not play the role of Jesse James when being pulled over by "the man," especially on a "club run," or motorcycle tour, where police can make a shakedown last up to two hours. One learns to avoid all eye contact and restrict all verbal responses to a monosyllabic "no" or "yes." Over the next few years I got lots of practice; that first summer I was pulled over and interrogated fifteen times—on only one of these occasions was I actually charged with an offence, a speeding violation.

While touring through the British Columbia interior I joined up with three members of the Tribesmen MC from Squamish, BC, whom I met at a Penticton hamburger stand. From the Tribesmen I learned that gaining entry into a club would take time. The time factor meant that my best chance of success lay in studying the Rebels in the familiar confines of my own back yard in Edmonton. "You don't make friends with members of a club," cautioned Lance of the Tribesmen. "You let them make friends with you." Lance pointed out that in order to ride with a club I would have to be accepted by all the members, get to know some of the members personally, and at least one member well enough that he would be willing to sponsor me and take responsibility for my actions. A critical suggestion emphatically made by all three Tribesmen was "Get yourself a hog [Harley-Davidson]!"

These first experiences "in the field" made it clear that I couldn't study any club I wanted, at any time that suited me. There was a good reason for this, as I discovered later. Restricting contacts with non-club members was a key to club survival. With time I realized that maintaining strict boundaries is a central theme that underlies all aspects of club life. This fact presented a major ethical dilemma. I could not do a study if I explained my research goal at the outset. However, an "undercover" strategy contravened a fundamental ethical tenet in which I believed, that no research should be carried out without the informants' full awareness. I devised an alternative strategy that satisfied myself, my thesis committee, and the guidelines that the University of Alberta had set down for ethical research. The plan was that initially I would attempt to establish contact with the Rebels as a biker who also happened to be a university—anthropology—student. If I were successful in achieving sufficient rapport and mutual trust with club members, I would officially ask the Rebels MC for permission to conduct a study. The bottom line was that it would be the Rebel club members I rode with who would make the final decision as to whether or not the study would go beyond my personal files.

This strategy was not without risks. Outlaw clubs are aware that they are under constant police surveillance, often by special police units, such as the RCMP's E-squad in Vancouver or the City of Calgary's Strike Force. I learned that the Edmonton Rebels suspected that a biker who had recently attempted to gain entry into their club as a "striker" was an agent of the RCMP. After repeated attempts, the police have long since discovered that infiltrating an outlaw club is a long, arduous, and risky process when it is being done for "professional" reasons. "Infiltration of the gangs is difficult. 'They have an internal discipline that makes it dangerous,' said a police officer. 'It's an area we have trouble infiltrating. The conditions of initiation make it almost impossible. . . . ' 'They are scary,' said one police intelligence officer, who asked not to be identified. 'We've had two or three informants killed, found tied to trees up north with bullet holes in them'" (Canadian Press release, *Edmonton Journal*, 29 September 1979).

In the United States the FBI had gone so far as to have several agents start up their own club in order to bypass the striker (probation) period that screens out bogus bikers. The Edmonton police play a wide variety of angles in order to update their information on the Rebels. On one occasion, two plain-clothes officers wore media badges at a biker rally protesting mandatory helmet legislation in order to move freely among the club members and take pictures. If the Rebels discovered my research motive before I was ready to tell them, it would have been difficult to communicate any good intentions, scientific or otherwise. There existed the distinct possibility that more than just the study would have been terminated prematurely. I lived with that possibility for three years.

I fine-tuned my image before I approached the Rebels. This was going to be my final make-it-or-forget-it attempt. I purchased an old 1955 Harley-Davidson FL, a "panhead," which I customized but later sold in favour of a mechanically more reliable 1972 Electraglide, a "shovelhead."

I had grown shoulder-length hair and a heavy beard. I bought a Harley-Davidson leather jacket and vest, wore studded leather wristbands and a shark's-tooth pendant, and sported a cut-off denim jacket with assorted Harley-Davidson pins and patches, all symbolic of the outlaw-biker world-view. While I was still very nervous about approaching the Rebels, I had become more comfortable with myself. My public image expressed what I now felt was my personal character. There was no pretension. As far as I was concerned, I was a genuine biker who was intrigued with the notion of riding with an outlaw club.

I discovered that I was a lot more apprehensive than I thought as I sat at the opposite end of the Kingsway Motor Inn and watched the Rebels down their drinks. The loud thunder of heavy-metal rock music would make initiating a delicate introduction difficult if not impossible; and there were no individual faces or features to be made out in the smoky haze, only a series of Rebel skull patches draped over leather jackets in a corner of the bar that outsiders seemed to warily avoid. It was like a scene out of a western movie: hard-faced outlaws in the bar, downing doubles while waiting for the stagecoach to arrive. I decided to go outside and devise an approach strategy, including how I would react if one of the Rebels turned to me and simply said, "Who invited you?" I had thought through five different approaches when Wee Albert of the Rebels MC came out of the bar to do a security check on the "Rebel iron" in the parking lot. He saw me leaning on my bike and came over to check me out. For some time Wee Albert and I stood in the parking lot and talked about motorcycles, riding in the wind, and the Harley tradition. He showed me some of the more impressive Rebel choppers and detailed the jobs of customizing that members of the club had done to their machines. He then checked out my "hog," gave a grunt of approval, and invited me to come in and join the Rebels at their tables. Drinking at the club bar on a regular basis gave me the opportunity to get to know the Rebels and gave them an opportunity to size me up and check me out on neutral ground. I had made the first of a long sequence of border crossings that all bikers go through if they hope to get close to a club.

Wee Albert became a good buddy of mine, and he sponsored my participation in club runs and at club parties. In addition to my having a Sponsor, my presence had to be voted on by the membership as a whole at their weekly Wednesday meeting, if two of the twenty-five members voted "no," then I wasn't around. The number of close friends that I had in the club increased and I was gradually drawn into the Rebel brotherhood. Measured in terms of social networking, brotherhood meant being part of a high frequency of interpersonal contacts that were activated over a wide range of social situations. Among the activities that I took part in were drinking and carousing in the club bar, assisting members in the chopping (customizing) and repair of motorcycles, loaning and borrowing money, shooting pool and "bullshitting" at the clubhouse, exchanging motorcycle parts along with technical information and gossip at a motorcycle shop owned by two club members, going on a duck hunt and on fishing trips, making casual visits and receiving dinner invitations to members' homes, general partying and riding together, providing emotional support, and, when necessary, standing shoulder-to-shoulder in the face of physical threat. Brotherhood, I came to learn, is the foundation of the outlaw-club community. It establishes among members a sense of moral, emotional, and material interdependence; feelings of commitment arise out of a sense of sharing a common fate. The enduring emotion of brotherhood is comradeship. To a "patch holder" (club member) brotherhood means being there when needed; its most dramatic expression occurs when brothers defend each other from outside threats. I vividly remember sitting with the Rebels in the Kingsway Motor Inn bar, trying to sober up quickly while I mentally acted out what I thought would be my best martial-arts moves. I looked down at my hand: I had sprained my thumb the night before while sparring in karate. My right hand was black, blue, swollen, and useless. I watched nervously as sixty-five members of the Canadian Airborne Regiment strutted into the bar. Their walk said that they were looking for us and a brawl. I came to view brotherhood as both a privilege and a tremendous personal responsibility.

I watched my own identity change as the result of experiences I had on my own as a biker and those I shared with club members. These often involved the process of public identification, or labelling, and other reactions by outsiders. I learned that a lone biker on the highway is vulnerable. I was run off the road three times over a four-year period. On one of those occasions I was forced off a mountain road into the side of a cliff and nearly catapulted into oblivion. Another lesson was that an outlaw biker has to be ready for "the heat to come down" at the most unexpected times. For instance, while I was washing my bike at a car wash, the owner phoned the police about a suspicious-looking biker. The police came, searched my bike, and I was arrested and charged with carrying a concealed and illegal weapon—a switch-blade. I felt sure that I would have a criminal record long before, and maybe instead of, a PhD. Fortunately, I discovered that a good lawyer, who is "owed a favour" by the crown prosecutor, can get the charges dropped—in this case, three minutes prior to the start of the trial. I learned that a police officer will follow an outlaw biker for five miles to give him a ticket for doing 35 mph in a 30-mph zone. A biker could be given a ticket for a balding tire or because his custom handlebars were one-half of an inch too high above the motorcycle's seat. I recall being turned down by insurance companies for vehicle coverage, refused admittance to private campgrounds, and kicked off a public beach by Penticton police who thought we intended to incite a riot. I found that associating with outlaw patch holders could be an invitation to danger. While riding with the club, I and some patch holders were pulled over by a cruiser and warned that members of the Highway Kings MC were out gunning for Rebels with shotguns. None of these situations could have been acted out in a detached manner. My involvement demanded the intensity of a highly emotional reaction. Each encounter was an escalation towards an outlaw-biker identity. My record of personal encounters with citizens and the police, especially those that were threatening, enabled me to understand and articulate the biker's perspective on drifting away from the Establishment and being drawn into the club. Sometimes, as I watched the faces of the Rebels, I could see the hardening of an attitude—"us-against-the-world."

Gradually my status changed from being a "biker" with a familiar face to being a "friend of the club." There were no formal announcements. Tiny just yelled across at me one afternoon while we were starting up our bikes, "Hey! 'Coyote!' No way I'm riding beside you. Some farmer is going to shoot our asses off and then say he was shooting at varmints." This was a reference to the coyote skin I had taken to wearing over my helmet. Wee Albert looked at me, grinned, and said "That's it, 'Coyote.' From now on that'll be your club name." Most of the patch holders had club names, such as Spider or Greaser. These names are reminders of club association. More important, they separate the individual from his past, giving him the opportunity to build a new persona in terms of group-valued traits. Pseudonyms give members an aura; they draw upon a collective power. They are no longer just Rick, Allan, or Bill; they are Blues, Terrible Tom, and Caveman; they are outlaw bikers!

As a "friend of the club" I took part informally in political rhetoric concerning the club's future, such as debates concerning the hot issue of club expansion. This position of trust with the Rebels brought me into contact with other outlaw clubs such as the King's Crew of Calgary, the Spokesmen of Saskatoon, the Bounty Hunters of Victoria, the Gypsy Wheelers of White Rock, and the Warlords of Edmonton. Through these inter-club contacts I became familiar with the political

relationships of conflict and alliance that exist among outlaw clubs. Meeting members of different clubs also provided me with the comparative data I needed to isolate those aspects of behaviour and organization that were shared by all clubs, and helped to explain how some clubs were different and why. My long-term association with the Rebels gave me a valuable historical perspective that included insights into the developmental sequence of clubs. I was able to describe how new clubs form, why few emergent clubs beat the odds and survive, and how a chosen few clubs achieved long-term success and expansion while all that remains of other clubs is their colours hanging upside down as trophies on the wall of a rival's clubhouse.

If the Rebels had at any time refused permission for the study, I would have destroyed all the data I had collected and closed the investigation. The fact that I had established myself as a friend of the club was no reason for the members to agree to become scientific units of analysis. Rejection of the study appeared more and more imminent as I grew to sense and share members' distrust of outsiders. I had come to appreciate some of the multifaceted advantages of having a negative public stereotype—however unrealistic. When outsiders look at an outlaw biker, they do not see an individual, all they see is the club patch that he wears on the back of his leathers. The negative image that comes with the Rebel skull patch discourages unnecessary intrusions by outsiders. "That way I'm not bothered," explained Steve of the Rebels, "and I don't have to tell the guy 'Fuck off, cunt!'" The patch becomes part of the biker's threat display: it effectively keeps violence to a minimum by warding off those outsiders who might otherwise choose to test the mettle of the bikers. For the majority of outsiders, the prospect of having to initiate even the briefest of encounters with an outlaw biker brings forth emotions ranging from uneasiness to sheer dread. Ironically, the more I got to know the members and the greater the bonds of trust and brotherhood, the less I expected that they would approve of the study. "The best public relations for us," according to Indian of the Rebels, "is no public relations!" I found it increasingly difficult to live with the fact that the closer I came to my destination of knowing the Rebels, the further distant became my goal of doing an ethnographic study.

One night, during a three-week Rebel run to the west coast, I was sharing a beer with Tiny while sitting on the porch of the Bounty Hunters' clubhouse. We were watching officers of the Victoria police force who were watching us from their cruisers in the street and from a nearby hotel—binoculars between closed curtains. "You know, Coyote," grumbled a 6-foot, 275-pound Tiny in a very personable tone, "I've talked with some of the guys and we think that you should strike [enter probationary membership] for the club. The way I see it, it shouldn't take you more than a year to earn your colours [club patch]." The pressure was now on and building for me to make a move that would bring me even closer to the club. I had made a commitment to myself that under no circumstances would I attempt to become a full-fledged member without first revealing my desire to do a study on the club. It was time to disengage. It was time for me to sell my study to the Rebels, but I was at a loss as to what to say. I had been a brother through good times and bad, thick and thin; but to distance myself from the Rebels by announcing a study done for outsiders of a way of life I had shared with them against the world seemed nothing short of a betrayal. Entering the field as a biker and maintaining relations of trust and friendship during the course of fieldwork prevented my leaving the field with my notes. I had accomplished what I had hoped to during my fieldwork, but at this point there was no way out. There was no formula for disengagement of the field project. As far as I was concerned, I had lost a three-year gamble.

Weeks of personal frustration and near-depression later, I had an incredible stroke of luck. Wee Albert, who took great pleasure in talking about "what it means to be a Rebel and a brother," approached me and said, "Being an anthropologist you study people, right? Well, have you ever thought of maybe doing a study on the club? Chances are it probably wouldn't carry [club approval], but maybe. I'd like to see it happen." I told Wee Albert that I'd consider it and approach the executive members with the proposal. The door of disengagement was open; Wee Albert had provided me with an honourable way out. Whether or not it would be a successful disengagement—the approval of an ethnography—remained to be seen.

I first talked to Ken and Steve about the prospect of "doing an anthropological study." Ken, president, and Steve, sergeant at arms, were both friends of mine and well-respected club officers, but their most positive response was a shrug of the shoulders and "We'll see." Ken decided to bring up the proposed study at a meeting of the club executive. The officers of the club discussed the proposal among themselves and determined that no harm would be done if they presented it one week later to the general membership at a club meeting. For me it was the longest night of the year as I waited for the decision. The issue was hotly debated, a vote was held, and the study approved. Why? Granting me permission for the study was done as a "personal favour": "You have come into favour with a lot of the members and been nothing but good to the club. All in all you've been a pretty righteous friend of the club. But there was a lot of opposition to your study, especially from guys like T.T. [Terrible Tom] and Blues. The way I see it the vote went the way it did because you were asking us a favour. You didn't come in promising us the moon, you know, money from books and that sort of thing. You promised us nothing so we did it as a personal favour" (Wee Albert). Any offers of economic remuneration on my part would have been interpreted as an insult; the Rebels were doing me a favour. I strongly suspect that any researcher who buys his or her way into a closed society—with promises of money or royalties—will garner information that is at best forced, at worst fabricated. However, I did give the "victims" of the four-and-one-half-hour questionnaire a twenty-six-ounce bottle of Alberta Springs (Old Time Sipping Whisky) and a Harley-Davidson beer mug. "Fair return" for the club as a whole was a bound copy of my thesis, which found a home in the Rebels' clubhouse.

I continued to ride with the Rebels for another year and a half, during which time I carried out formal data-gathering procedures. These included extensive open-ended interviews with a number of Rebel patch holders and ended with the administration of a four-hour-long structured questionnaire to six members. Interestingly enough, Blues, a Rebel who was both a friend and a staunch opponent of the study, was one of the six. "The club is all I have. It means everything to me. It's with me all the time. I feel leery about talking to anybody about it. If I wasn't 100 per cent for you I wouldn't be here. If you'd been asking these questions three years ago [when I initially made contact with the Rebels MC], well no fucking way. We've been burned before, but never again!" Blues's trust and vote of confidence brought me a tremendous degree of personal satisfaction.

The theoretical framework and methodological approach that I use in [my] book are based on a cognitive definition of culture. Culture is here defined as the rules and categories of meaning and action that are used by individuals to both interpret and generate appropriate behaviour. I therefore view the outlaw-biker subculture as a human experience. It is a system of meaning in which I, as an anthropologist, had to involve myself in order to develop an adequate explanation of what was being observed. That is, in order to understand the biker subculture, or any culture for that matter, one must first try to understand it as it is experienced by the bikers themselves. Only then can one comprehend both the meaning of being an outlaw and how that meaning is constructed and comes to be shared by bikers. Only

by first seeing the world through the eyes of the outlaws can we then go on to render intelligible the decisions that they make and the behaviours they engage in. Those meanings, decisions, and behaviours may lead you to applaud outlaw bikers as heroes. Alternatively, they may lead you to condemn them as villains. Labelling them as heroes or villains is a subsequent value judgment that the reader has the option of making. That value judgment is quite separate from first knowing outlaw bikers—my job as an ethnographer.

In order to operationalize this theoretical position of capturing an insider's perspective, I adopted a research methodology that closely resembles that of a symbolic interactionist. That is, within the overall framework of participant observation I emphasize analysis that is proximate—events are described in terms of variables that are close to the immediate situation in which the actors find themselves; processual—events are viewed as an emerging step-by-step reality whose completion requires actors to meet a series of contingencies; and phenomenological—events are explained in a manner that pays serious attention to how the actors experience them (Lofland, 1969: 296–97). By blending the methodological strategy of participant observation with the perspective of symbolic interactionism (Visano, 1989: 3, 29), I hope to replicate for the reader the experienced natural world as it unfolds for the outlaw biker.

CRITICAL THINKING QUESTIONS

1. Discuss the significance of the "one per-center" label for bikers.

2. Do you think that the image of the "biker" has changed since the Hollister incident in 1947? If so, in what ways? If not, why do you feel that the image has remained stable over time?

3. Has Wolf's presentation of the Rebels changed how you look at bike gangs? If so, how? If not, why not?

REFERENCES

Agar, M. 1986. *Speaking of ethnography.* Beverly Hills, CA: Sage.

Ayoob, M. 1982. Outlaw bikers. *Police Product News*, 6(5).

Forkner, W. 1986. "Wino" Willie Forkner: All the old romance retold. *Easyriders* 16(159).

Kapuscinski, B. A. 1988. Application for warrant to search and seize. Attorney-General of the Province of Alberta: 2.

Keiser, L. R. 1979. *The Vice Lords: Warriors of the streets.* Toronto: Holt, Rinehart and Winston.

Lofland, J. 1969. *Deviance and identity.* Englewood Cliffs. NJ: Prentice-Hall.

Maanen, J. van. 1988. *Tales of the field: On writing ethnography.* Chicago: University of Chicago Press.

Visano, L. 1989. Researching deviance: An interactionist account. Paper presented at the Canadian Sociology and Anthropology Association annual conference, Quebec City.

27

Deviance

CLASSIC

CONTEMPORARY

CROSS-CULTURAL

Canadian Cannabis: Marijuana as an Irritant/Problem in Canada–U.S. Relations

PAUL GECELOVSKY

What is considered deviant changes in terms of time and place. Alcohol and marijuana are both good examples in that countries around the world have different attitudes toward the two substances (e.g., alcohol is illegal in some Muslim countries).

Canada has a more open attitude toward marijuana, and Gecelovsky provides some detail of how important this crop is to the British Columbian economy. But the Americans are not happy about this type of entrepreneurial activity.

In a recent survey of the Canada–U.S. relationship, Munroe Eagles noted that the "popular impression" for many Americans was that Canadians were "out of step with their more conservative neighbor to the south" (Eagles 2006, 821). John Herd Thompson made a similar claim in his review of the bilateral relationship over the 1994–2003 period, writing that Canadians are perceived by some Americans as being "left wing wimps" (Thompson 2003, 17). One area in which Canada may be regarded as out of step with the United States, and Canadians as left wing wimps, is the issue of marijuana. There are real and noticeable differences between Canada and the U.S. in the way each side deals with the issue of marijuana. The following pages examine the marijuana issue in terms of the growing volume of the drug being smuggled into the United States

Source: American Review of Canadian Studies, Summer 2008; 38(2): CBCA Reference p. 207.

from Canada, the increased potency of the strains of marijuana grown in Canada, and the differences in judicial deterrents adopted to penalize possession and cultivation. This is followed by a look at a couple of possibilities that have the potential to transform the marijuana irritant into the marijuana problem in Canada–U.S. relations.

The amount of marijuana being produced in Canada and then illegally exported to the United States is of increasing concern to all levels of American law enforcement. While British Columbia (B.C.), Ontario, and Quebec are all of concern to U.S. officials, British Columbia presents the largest source of Canadian marijuana for the U.S. market, so the discussion will focus primarily upon that province. The marijuana cultivation industry in B.C. is thriving, as demonstrated by the fact that the province accounted for almost 40 percent of all growing operations found by law enforcement officials in Canada in 2003, the last year for which full data are available

(CCJS 2004). During that year, the province also had the highest rate of cultivation "incidents" in Canada, at 79 per 100,000 people. What this means is that 79 marijuana cultivation operations were found for every 100,000 people in the province. This is nearly triple the national rate of 27 per 100,000 people, and 33 higher than second-place New Brunswick, at 46. More marijuana cultivation facilities were uncovered by Canadian law enforcement officials in B.C. (3274) than in all of the other provinces combined (2564), except Quebec (2939), in 2003 (CCJS 2004). In their study of the B.C. marijuana growing industry over the 1997–2003 period, Darryl Plecas, Aili Malm, and Bryan Kinney identified over 25,000 cultivation operations uncovered by police officers in the province (Plecas, Malm, and Kinney 2005). In terms of the monetary value of marijuana, it is estimated that the annual wholesale value of the provincial industry is approximately C$6 billion, or what is equivalent to about 5 percent of the annual provincial gross domestic product. To provide some perspective, the B.C. marijuana industry is relatively equal in dollar value to the province's public sector, and bigger than the legal exports of sawmill products (C$4.6 billion) and oil and gas (C$2.5 billion). In terms of employment, it is estimated that the provincial marijuana industry employs roughly 150,000 people (Mulgrew 2006, 109).

The size of the B.C. marijuana industry is of concern to U.S. law officials, because upwards of 90 percent of the crop is exported to the American market (Hamilton et al. 2004, 36). More disconcerting to American law enforcement is that there has been a "sharp rise" in the smuggling of marijuana into the United States from Canada and that this has resulted in a near tripling in both the *number* of seizures and the *volume* of marijuana seized over the 2001–2004 period, the last period for which data are available (U.S. Department of Justice 2006). The 2006 International Narcotics Control Strategy Report (INCSR) prepared by the U.S. Department of State indicated that marijuana cultivation is a

"thriving industry in Canada" and that "large scale cross-border trafficking" is "a serious concern" of the American government (U.S. Department of State 2006).

It is not just the volume of marijuana being smuggled from Canada to the United States that is of concern to Americans; it is also the potency of the marijuana. Of particular interest is the marijuana cultivated in British Columbia: the so-called B.C. Bud. The U.S. Drug Enforcement Agency assessed B.C. Bud for its tetrahydrocannabinol (THC) content—the psychoactive drug in marijuana—and found that its THC content was 25 percent. In comparison, the average THC content is 7 percent for marijuana consumed in the United States today and only 2 percent for marijuana smoked in the 1970s (Hamilton et al. 2004, 36). The result of this is that, as Ian Mulgrew has noted, British Columbia "is a marijuana Mecca" and B.C. Bud is "a globally recognized brand name" that stands "in a pantheon of pot beside such legends as Acapulco Gold or California Sinsemilla" and "is sought by cannabis cognoscenti and commands the highest price" (Mulgrew 2006, 21). The INCSR, in 2006, listed Canada as "a principal drug concern" due to the "continuing large-scale production of high-potency, indoor grown marijuana for export to the United States" (U.S. Department of State 2006). Moreover John Walters, Director of the White House Office of National Drug Control Policy (the U.S. drug czar), critically remarked that "Canada is exporting to [the United States] the crack of marijuana" (Hamilton et al. 2004, 36).

While the increasing volume of marijuana being smuggled into the United States from Canada and the high potency of the drug are of importance to Americans, the source of gravest concern is what is perceived by Americans to be lax Canadian laws regarding marijuana possession and cultivation. The reasoning goes that if Canada adopted more stern measures and penalties concerning marijuana, the flow to the United States would be abated somewhat. The first area in which Canada is seen as being out of step with the United States is in penalties for marijuana possession. This was demonstrated in the 2003–2006 period, wherein the Chrétien and Martin governments in Canada proposed, wrote, and introduced legislation to decriminalize possession of marijuana of 15 grams or less. The American response to this was immediate and forceful. The U.S. drug czar, John Walters, pledged to "respond to the threat" that this posed to the United States (Klein 2003, 12). One of the means proposed to deal with the threat was the "re-criminalizing" of marijuana possession at the American border. Christopher Sands has noted that some members of Congress and the media in the United States "advanced the notion that such possession could be 're-criminalized' by U.S. border officials if it appeared on the criminal record of a Canadian requesting entry into the United States, even as a misdemeanor" (Sands 2006, 130). The American concerns over decriminalization of marijuana were allayed with the election, in January 2006, of the Conservative government led by Stephen Harper. The Harper government had campaigned on a promise to end the decriminalization initiative of the Martin government and, therefore, did not reintroduce the marijuana legislation after it died in committee at the end of the 38th Parliament.

While the decriminalization issue has been resolved for the duration of the present Conservative government, the laxity of Canadian laws pertaining to the production of marijuana is still troubling to many Americans. Of the 25,000 growing operations identified by B.C. law enforcement between 1997 and 2003 mentioned previously, less than 17,000 were investigated and less than one-half of those were prosecuted (Plecas, Malm, and Kinney 2005). Plecas, Malm, and Kinney found that charges were entered in less than one-half of all raids conducted on marijuana operations in British Columbia over the last seven years. Moreover, they noted that only about one in ten of those convicted were sentenced to a jail term, with the average sentence being five months (Plecas, Malm, and Kinney 2005, 50).

The authors compared the sentences handed out in B.C. with what would have happened had these cases come to trial in Washington state, just south of the border. Under sentencing guidelines found in Washington state, one-half of the convictions would have resulted in mandatory jail sentences of at least five years and over two-thirds of those convicted would have served some time in prison (Plecas, Malm, and Kinney 2005, 56). In comparison, the sentences received in Canada appear lenient. Mulgrew has noted that marijuana cultivators in Canada view judicial punishments not as a deterrent but rather as "an operating cost" (Mulgrew 2006, 5). Marijuana cultivation "has been a relatively minimum-risk activity due to low sentences meted out by Canadian courts," as noted in the 2006 INCSR. The report further "encourage[d] Canada to take steps to improve its ability to expedite investigations and prosecutions" and to "strengthen judicial deterrents" (U.S. Department of State 2006).

The result of all this is that Canada is regarded as being soft on marijuana use and cultivation. Evidence of this is provided by Canada being consistently mentioned in the annual Presidential Determination on Major Drug Transit or Major Illicit Drug Producing Countries. While Canada has thus far escaped being placed on the Majors List (i.e., those states listed as major drug transit or producing countries), it is the only state not on the list to have been mentioned in the reports over the last five years. For 2007, Canada and North Korea are the only two states not on the list but noted in the Presidential Determination (U.S. Office of the President 2006).

The Canadian and American governments cooperate on a wide range of policy issues, and the bilateral relationship is mostly without major controversy or difficulty. The differences in the Canadian and American approaches to marijuana are regarded primarily as an irritant in the relationship, but one of a number of policy areas on which Canada and the United States differ. There are, however, two ways in which the marijuana irritant could become the marijuana *problem* in the bilateral relationship. The first would be if the marijuana irritant were to become more directly linked with homeland security in the United States. Marijuana is still largely regarded as a law enforcement issue, not a national security problem. It is perceived more as a state-level concern than a national policy issue. This may change, however. For instance, if it is determined that groups in Canada on the U.S. list of foreign terrorist organizations maintained by the State Department are using marijuana to generate revenue for their operations, including purchasing weaponry and planning attacks in the U.S., this could result in the marijuana issue being redefined as part of the war on terror and, therefore, a homeland security problem. A second, and related, manner in which the marijuana irritant could become more problematic for Canada is if the Bush administration, or the U.S. Congress, began to link more closely the export to the U.S. of marijuana from Canada with cocaine and other drugs from Mexico in the current American war on drugs. Thus far, Canadian officials have been relatively successful in persuading American government officials of the differences in the scale and nature of the drug threats emanating from Canada and from Mexico. The result of this has been to differentiate the northern border with Canada from the southern border with Mexico (Sokolsky and Legassé 2006).

If either of the two scenarios outlined above were to occur, and the marijuana irritant were to become the marijuana problem, this would have significant implications for Canada. Two main lines of potential American response may be outlined briefly. The first would entail a further intensification and militarization of the Canada–U.S. border, or movement toward what Peter Andreas has referred to as a "Mexicanization of the Canadian border" (Andreas 2005). This, in turn, would cause a significant reduction in and delay of human and commercial cross-border traffic, thereby negatively impacting the bilateral commercial relationship for

both countries. A second manner in which the United States might respond should marijuana become a problem in the Canada–U.S. relationship is to increase pressure on Canada to more closely align Canadian marijuana policy with that of the United States.

CRITICAL THINKING QUESTIONS

1. What is your attitude toward marijuana? Should smoking it be considered a criminal activity? Do you think smoking marijuana constitutes deviant behaviour? Why or why not?

2. Why do you think alcohol is legal in both Canada and the United States and marijuana is not? Do you think the two substances are that much different?

3. What do you think would happen if marijuana was made legal in Canada? Would the United States object? Why do Americans take such a hard line on marijuana and drugs in general?

REFERENCES

Andreas, Peter. 2005. The Mexicanization of the US–Canada border: Asymmetric interdependence in a changing security context. *International Journal*, 60: 449–62.

Canadian Centre for Justice Statistics. 2004. Canadian crime statistics 2003. Available: **http://statscan.ca/english/freepub/85-205XIE/0000385-205-XIE.pdf**. Accessed April 17, 2007.

Eagles, Munroe. 2006. Canadian-American relations in a turbulent era. *PS: Political Science and Politics*, 39: 821–24.

Hamilton, Anita, Ben Bergman, Laura Blue, Chris Daniels, Deborah Jones, and Elaine Shannon. 2004. This Bud's for the U.S. *Time*, 164: 36–7.

Klein, Naomi. 2003. Canada: Hippie nation? *The Nation* (July 21/28): 12.

Mulgrew, Ian. 2006. *Bud Inc.: Inside Canada's marijuana industry.* Toronto: Vintage.

Pleces, Darryl, Aili Malm, and Bryan Kinney. 2005. Marihuana growing operations in British Columbia revisited, 1997–2003. Available: **http://www.ucfv.ca/pages/Special/Marihuana_Grow_Ops_in_BC_Study.pdf**. Accessed April 17, 2007.

28

Understanding Sexual Orientation

ALFRED C. KINSEY, WARDELL B. POMEROY, AND CLYDE E. MARTIN

Sexuality
CLASSIC
CONTEMPORARY
CROSS-CULTURAL

In 1948, Alfred Kinsey and his colleagues published the first modern study of sexuality in the United States—and raised plenty of eyebrows. For the first time, people began talking openly about sex, questioning many common stereotypes. Here Kinsey reports his finding that sexual orientation is not a matter of clear-cut differences between heterosexuals and homosexuals, but is better described as a continuum by which most people combine elements of both.

THE HETEROSEXUAL–HOMOSEXUAL BALANCE

Concerning patterns of sexual behavior, a great deal of the thinking done by scientists and laymen alike stems from the assumption that there are persons who are "heterosexual" and persons who are "homosexual," that these two types represent antitheses in the sexual world, and that there is only an insignificant class of "bisexuals" who occupy an intermediate position between the other groups. It is implied that every individual is innately—inherently—either heterosexual or homosexual. It is further implied that from the time of birth one is fated to be one thing or the other, and that there is little chance for one to change his pattern in the course of a lifetime.

Source: From *Sexual Behavior in the Human Male* by Alfred C. Kinsey, Wardell B. Pomeroy, and Clyde E. Martin. (Philadelphia: W. B. Saunders Company, 1948), pp. 636–39. Reprinted by permission of The Kinsey Institute.

It is quite generally believed that one's preference for a sexual partner of one or the other sex is correlated with various physical and mental qualities, and with the total personality which makes a homosexual male or female physically, psychically, and perhaps spiritually distinct from a heterosexual individual. It is generally thought that these qualities make a homosexual person obvious and recognizable to anyone who has a sufficient understanding of such matters. Even psychiatrists discuss "the homosexual personality" and many of them believe that preferences for sexual partners of a particular sex are merely secondary manifestations of something that lies much deeper in the totality of that intangible which they call the personality.

It is commonly believed, for instance, that homosexual males are rarely robust physically, are uncoordinated or delicate in their movements, or perhaps graceful enough but not strong and vigorous in their physical expression. Fine skins, high-pitched voices, obvious hand movements, a feminine carriage of the hips, and peculiarities of walking gaits are supposed accompaniments of a preference for a male as a sexual partner. It is commonly believed that the homosexual male is artistically sensitive, emotionally unbalanced, temperamental to the point of being unpredictable, difficult to get along with, and undependable in meeting specific obligations. In physical characters there have been attempts to show that the homosexual male has a considerable crop of hair and less often becomes bald, has teeth which are more like those of the female, a broader pelvis, larger genitalia, and a tendency toward being fat, and that he lacks a linea alba. The homosexual male is supposed to be less interested in athletics, more often interested in music and the arts, more often engaged in such occupations as bookkeeping, dress design, window display, hairdressing, acting, radio work, nursing, religious service, and social work. The converse to all of these is supposed to represent the typical heterosexual male. Many a clinician attaches considerable weight to these things in diagnosing the basic heterosexuality or homosexuality of his patients. The characterizations are so distinct that they seem to leave little room for doubt that homosexual and heterosexual represent two very distinct types of males. . . .

It should be pointed out that scientific judgments on this point have been based on little more than the same sorts of impressions which the general public has had concerning homosexual persons. But before any sufficient study can be made of such possible correlations between patterns of sexual behavior and other qualities in the individual, it is necessary to understand the incidences and frequencies of the homosexual in the population as a whole, and the relation of the homosexual activity to the rest of the sexual pattern in each individual's history.

The histories which have been available in the present study make it apparent that the heterosexuality or homosexuality of many individuals

Figure 28.1   Heterosexual–homosexual rating scale

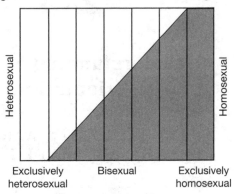

is not an all-or-none proposition. It is true that there are persons in the population whose histories are exclusively heterosexual, both in regard to their overt experience and in regard to their psychic reactions. And there are individuals in the population whose histories are exclusively homosexual, both in experience and in psychic reactions. But the record also shows that there is a considerable portion of the population whose members have combined, within their individual histories, both homosexual and heterosexual experience and/or psychic responses. There are some whose heterosexual experiences predominate, there are some whose homosexual experiences predominate, there are some who have had quite equal amounts of both types of experience (see Figure 28.1).

Some of the males who are involved in one type of relation at one period in their lives may have only the other type of relation at some later period. There may be considerable fluctuation of patterns from time to time. Some males may be involved in both heterosexual and homosexual activities within the same period of time. For instance, there are some who engage in both heterosexual and homosexual activities in the same year, or in the same month or week, or even in the same day. There are not a few individuals who engage in group activities in which they may make simultaneous contact with partners of both sexes.

Males do not represent two discrete populations, heterosexual and homosexual. The world is not to be divided into sheep and goats. Not all things are black nor all things white. It is a fundamental of taxonomy that nature rarely deals with discrete categories. Only the human mind invents categories and tries to force facts into separated pigeon-holes. The living world is a continuum in each and every one of its aspects. The sooner we learn this concerning human sexual behavior the sooner we shall reach a sound understanding of the realities of sex.

CRITICAL THINKING QUESTIONS

1. Why do you think people have long thought of heterosexuality and homosexuality as opposite and mutually exclusive (that is, only in terms of "exclusively heterosexual" or "exclusively homosexual," as in Figure 28.1)?

2. Kinsey suggests that anyone's sexual orientation may well change over time. Do you agree? Why or why not?

3. Why do people tend to label someone with any degree of homosexual experience as a "homosexual"? (After all, we don't do the same in the case of any heterosexual experience.)

29

"I'll Scratch Your Back If You'll Scratch Mine": The Role of Reciprocity, Power and Autonomy in the Strip Club[*]

JACQUELINE LEWIS

This study is an example of how qualitative methods, in this case face-to-face personal interviews, are employed to gather sociological data. This research depicts how work in strip clubs is organized along gender and occupational lines (bartender, server, etc). It also compares stripping to other service jobs and illustrates how sex work is not all that different from other kinds of work in that it is stratified and governed by both competition and cooperation.

The Canadian economy has increasingly become more service-based (Little, 1999), resulting in changing labour relations (Sallaz, 2002). In an effort to reduce labour costs, the service industry relies on the "tipping system." Although this emphasis results in a loss of worker commitment to the business (Sallaz, 2002), it motivates the worker to work hard to please customers and push the products that result in the accrual of earnings/tips and business revenue. In addition to reducing labour costs, one of the main benefits of the tipping system for the business owner is "that it keeps the . . . staff firmly at the front line in the battle to turn a profit" (Citron, 1989: 9). Workers in the service sector, however, "must be granted a much wider degree of autonomy to customize their service offerings" (Sallaz, 2002: 406). This

organizational feature provides workers with further incentive and freedom "to pursue their own interests at the expense of the company" (Paules, 1991: 55).

Although strip clubs are part of the service industry, they differ in terms of the way staff members earn their money. In most strip clubs in Southern Ontario, the majority of workers do not receive a salary from the club and some actually pay a fee to work there. As a result, they tend to operate as private entrepreneurs. These structural elements of the strip club create a work environment that inspires little in the way of worker commitment. Instead, workers focus on themselves, providing client services and engaging in co-operative activities that increase earnings and/or provide some sort of resource (e.g., support, security, friendship). The workplace structure also encourages the use of resistance strategies as a way to deal with the

Source: The Canadian Journal of Sociology and Anthropology, August 2006: 43(3), 297–298, 300–305, 309–310.

lack of security tied to jobs in the industry (Paules, 1991).

Various staff members play an integral role in the daily operations of the strip club: dancers, waitresses, shooter girls, bartenders, disc jockeys (DJs), doorpersons/bouncers and hostesses. Although strip clubs, like other sectors of the service industry, are highly gendered and sexualized establishments (Paules, 1991), there is a complex interplay of power dynamics among workers as each strives to enhance her/his autonomy, security and income. The result is a variety of mutually interdependent relationships between the various staff members.

The focus of this article is the social organization of the strip club. It examines the interplay of power relations in the club and how workers in this environment are able to enhance autonomy and use the resources at their disposal to decrease the inherent uncertainties of their job. Interconnections between and co-operative activities engaged in by workers as a means to deal with exploitive labour practices, as well as to create a socially and/or economically supportive work environment, are also explored.

METHODOLOGY

The findings reported in this paper are based on a study that explored the work and careers of exotic dancers. There were two primary means of data collection: participant observation and interviewing. Field observations were conducted at ten strip clubs in four cities in southern Ontario.

In-depth interviews were conducted with thirty female exotic dancers and eight strip club staff members (disc jockeys, waitresses, shooter girls, bartenders, hostesses and doormen). The positions held by all except one of the staff members were gender-specific (i.e., women were waitresses, shooter girls and hostesses, while men were bartenders, doormen and disc jockeys). The exception was a woman who

was working as a bartender at the time of her interview.

Although a semi-structured interview guide was used for each interview, interviews were conducted in an informal manner in order to allow participants to freely express themselves and [permit] the exploration of new lines of questioning that arose during the interview. When new questions appeared relevant to future interviews, they were incorporated into the interview guide. Interviews questions were designed to explore: entry into the strip club work environment; work history and future plans; the nature of the work and work environment, including relationships with customers and co-workers; strategies used to maintain personal power and manage the work situation; and significant other and reference group relationships.

THE SOCIAL ORGANIZATION OF THE STRIP CLUB

Strip clubs are highly gendered establishments where jobs tend to be gender-stratified and women outnumber men. In them, women predominately do "the grunt work" or stereotypical "women's work." They fill the roles of dancer, waitress and shooter girl, all of which require extended time on the floor of the strip club, interacting directly with customers (men) and servicing customers' needs. In contrast, men fill the roles of manager, bartender, doorman/bouncer and disc jockey (see Price, 2000), which require smaller degrees of direct customer service.

Gender and managerial power, however, are not the only forms of power relevant to the social organization of the strip club. Economic power also plays a role. It is determined by opportunities to earn money and, ultimately, by money earned. Dancers' economic power in the strip clubs is tied to their direct or indirect involvement with the way the club and most of its workers earn money.

In the strip club, dancing serves as "the pivot around which much of the social and economic life . . . revolves" (Prus and Irini, 1980: 4). In the interviews we conducted, it was obvious that many of the staff recognized the economic power of dancers and the importance of their relationships with dancers to their own incomes.

You've got to treat these girls with respect because without them you wouldn't have a job. That's why these customers are coming here, to see naked women, not to drink, because you can drink anywhere. (Doorman)

In the following section, the relationships between dancers, disc jockeys, waitresses and doormen are used to explore the complex interplay between the various forms of power found in the strip club, including the modes of resistance and adaptation available to strip club workers as a result of the clubs' social organization. The focus is on the individual and collective adaptations employed by strip club workers to deal with their work environment.

Disc Jockeys and Dancers

The power associated with the job of disc jockey is tied to it being a male-dominated position that carries some managerial power in a gendered industry. Disc jockeys are responsible for "keeping an eye on the girls [the dancers]," part of which involves determining whose turn it is to do a stage show and how long shows will last. Although all dancers are supposed to appear on stage in a specified order and dance for three songs, disc jockeys have the power to make alterations if they so desire. They also are able to choose who will do special performances, such as "shower shows."

For a $75 club fee bachelors can get a shower show . . . They bring the bachelor right onstage . . . and we [the disc jockeys] get one of the girls to join the bachelor in the shower . . . The DJ chooses the dancer. Usually we go from the top of the list down, but if there is a girl I'm mad at then she's going to do showers all night. They can't refuse. (Disc jockey)

The disc jockey's power is also directly related to the nature of the service they provide dancers during stage shows. There are two elements involved: stage show maintenance and security assistance. When dancers are on stage, disc jockeys can put on light shows and "talk up the girls" to "try to get guys interested in the show." Such promotional activities increase the potential for tipping during and table dance requests at the end of a stage show.

The DJ can get the crowd going for you and get them to pay attention. And you get more tips if the crowd's happy and they're excited. (Dancer)

In addition, disc jockeys assist dancers with their stage shows by paying attention to "how the show is going" and attending to their needs.

Sometimes you are up there and it isn't going well . . . You look at the DJ and make little signals . . . The DJs are pretty cool about that, they'll shorten your songs. (Dancer)

Due to their close proximity to the stage, disc jockeys are also the dancers' closest source of security and protection during stage performances. Disc jockeys usually watch dancers during their shows to make sure that men do not touch them when they are offering tips.[1] If the disc jockey observes any type of aggressive or inappropriate movement on a man's part he lets the customer know he is in violation of club rules and directs him how to behave.

When the girls are onstage I keep an eye on the guys tipping them. They are supposed to lie still and are not allowed to touch them [the dancers]. If they start to move I remind them "Don't touch." I do this to stop them, but also to alert the dancer that something is up. (Disc jockey)

Dancers know how important it is to be able to rely on the disc jockey during their performances, whether it is because they want the audience "pumped up," want relief from "a bad set" or are in a vulnerable position while accepting tips. Having a good working relationship with a disc jockey is one way to ensure that he stays alert. Both dancers and disc jockeys report feeling that tipping helps maintain good work relations and serves as an incentive or reward for disc jockeys to provide quality services to dancers.

Most of the dancers tip. A lot will give me two or three bucks . . . and some of them don't. And the ones that usually don't we don't do nothing for. (Disc jockey)

If you don't tip them [disc jockeys] and you're not nice to them, they don't do as much for you on stage. Whether it's your light shows, or just saying stuff about you, or promoting tips. (Dancer)

In addition, both dancers and disc jockeys acknowledge that due to their role in the club, disc jockeys "have the power" to impact on the quality of dancers' work lives. As one disc jockey noted:

If we [disc jockeys and dancers] don't have a good relationship we basically won't be doing anything for them . . . we won't play their music . . . or we screw something up on purpose, which we do a lot. If they're not nice to us then basically we're not gonna be nice to them . . . and they'll find it a little rougher.

Knowledge of this provides dancers with a further incentive to "kiss up" to disc jockeys and "tip them extra" in order to "stay in their good books." During interviews dancers talked about how the disc jockey is someone who has the ability to "make their job easier or tougher," someone who "can either be your best friend or your worst enemy" and therefore "someone you want on your side."

Although the disc jockey appears to have a lot of power vis-à-vis the dancers, it is mostly in the form of managerial power. Their economic power is restricted by their limited opportunities to earn money. They are typically not paid a wage by clubs and instead rely on income generated by a club-mandated "DJ fee" that all dancers are required to pay the club daily if they want to work. In the clubs we studied, the amount that disc jockeys received from the DJ fee ranged from five to ten dollars per dancer. Their only other real income-generating opportunities involve "encouraging" dancers to tip them for their services. In either case, the disc jockeys' earnings come primarily from dancers.

Since it is the dancers who provide the services that customers come to the club for, and are typically the major recipients of customer money, they are in an advantageous economic position. Their economic power helps balance out some of the power differential between them and the disc jockeys. Dancers use their economic power when they tip the disc jockey beyond the club-mandated fee and disc jockeys use their power to help dancers "drum up tips." Tips between workers are used to maintain good working relations and ensure service provision. When dancers use tips to "bribe" disc jockeys so they can violate club policies (e.g., leave their shift early; not go on stage during a particular shift), it provides dancers with a mechanism to ensure autonomy in the work place.

I mean you kiss up to the DJ so that you can get out of going on stage, or you bribe them. "Here's twenty bucks, I don't want to go on stage"-type thing. (Dancer)

CONCLUSION

The structural elements of the strip club create a work environment that motivates workers to engage in income-generating activities. Work structures that use the tipping system encourage workers to "push" business products that increase business revenues, but they do so at a cost. The workers in such an environment are less likely to feel a sense of loyalty, commitment, or lasting ties to their workplace than workers who receive a liveable wage or salary from an employer (see Paules, 1991; Sallaz, 2002).

The informal economic system that was found to develop among strip club staff works as a feedback loop, feeding back into and reinforcing itself. Staff members learn that it is easier to do one's job with a supporting cast (Prus and Sharpe, 1977). Those who work co-operatively are rewarded both socially (in terms of social support, future opportunities to earn money and violate club polices unnoticed) and economically (in terms of financial gain). In addition, it is likely that, in working together, the staff may experience a greater sense of autonomy, personal empowerment and enhanced economic security in an ever more exploitive work environment.

CRITICAL THINKING QUESTIONS

1. How are the tasks in a strip club divided according to gender? And along what lines is a strip club stratified? Who has economic power and why?

2. How does the reciprocal relationship between disc jockeys and strippers play out? How are disc jockeys paid and how does this influence their relationship with strippers?

3. Many service workers directly interact with the public. In terms of behaviour and expectations, what makes service-sector jobs different from industrial ones? What are the similarities between stripping and other service jobs? Are there pronounced differences in terms of organization between a restaurant and a strip club? Do you think that putting them both in the category of service work amounts to a fair comparison?

NOTE

1. In southern Ontario, when men offer tips to dancers performing on stage, they lie on the stage and put their "tip" between their teeth or lips. The dancer then kneels on the stage and slowly crawls over top of the customer (without touching him), until her face is above his genital area and her genital area is above his face. As she slowly crawls back she removes the money with her teeth, lips, hand, or breasts.

REFERENCES

Citron, Z. 1989. "Waiting for nodough: The case against tipping." *The New Republic* (January 2): 9–10.

Little, D. 1999. "Employment and remuneration in the service industries since 1984." Ottawa: Statistics Canada. Available at: **http://www.statcan.ca/bsolc/english/bsolc?catno'63F0002X1999024**.

Paules, G. F. 1991. *Dishing it out: Power and resistance among waitresses in a New Jersey restaurant.* Philadelphia: Temple University Press.

Prus, R. C. and S. Irini. 1980. *Hookers, rounders, and desk clerks: The social organization of the hotel community.* Toronto: Gage Publishing Limited.

Prus, R. C. and C. R. D. Sharpe. 1977. *Road hustler: The career contingencies of professional card and dice hustlers.* Toronto: Lexington Books.

Sallaz, J. J. 2002. "House rules: Autonomy and interests among service workers in the contemporary casino service industry." *Work and Occupation*, 29(4): 394–427.

30

Homosexual Behavior in Cross-Cultural Perspective

J. M. CARRIER[*]

Sexuality	
CLASSIC	
CONTEMPORARY	
CROSS-CULTURAL	

Although sexuality is a biological process, the meaning of sexuality is culturally variable. Carrier shows that attitudes toward homosexuality are far from uniform around the world. Some societies are quite accommodating about sexual practices that other societies punish harshly.

The available cross-cultural data clearly show that the ways in which individuals organize their sexual behavior vary considerably between societies (Westermarck, 1908; Ford & Beach, 1951; Broude & Greene, 1976). Although biological and psychological factors help explain variations of sexual behavior between individuals within a given society, intercultural variations in patterns of human sexual behavior are mainly related to social and cultural differences occurring between societies around the world. The purpose of this chapter is to consider what kinds of variations in homosexual behavior occur between societies, and to determine which sociocultural factors appear to account for the variance of the behavior cross-culturally.[1]

THE CROSS-CULTURAL DATA

Data available on homosexual behavior in most of the world's societies, past or present, are meager. Much is known about the dominant middle-class white populations of the United States, England, and northern European countries where most scientific research on human sexual behavior has been done, but very little is known about homosexual behavior in the rest of the world. The lack of knowledge stems from the irrational fear and prejudice surrounding the study of human sexual behavior and from the difficulties associated with the collection of information on a topic that is so personal and highly regulated in most societies.

Most of the cross-cultural information on sexual behavior has been gathered by Western

*The author is particularly indebted to Evelyn Hooker for her invaluable comments and criticism; and to the Gender Identity Research Group at UCLA for an early critique of the ideas presented in this paper.

Source: From *Homosexual Behavior: A Modern Reappraisal,* ed. Judd Marmor, copyright © 1980, by Basic Books, Inc. Reprinted with permission.

anthropologists. The quality of the information collected and published, however, varies considerably. Based on a survey of the literature, Marshall and Suggs (1971) report that: "Sexual behavior is occasionally touched upon in anthropological publications but is seldom the topic of either articles or monographs by anthropologists." Broude and Greene (1976), after coding the sexual attitudes and practices in 186 societies using the Human Relations Area Files, note:[2]

... information of any sort on sexual habits and beliefs is hard to come by . . . . when data do exist concerning sexual attitudes and practices, they are often sketchy and vague; what is more, such information is usually suspect in terms of its reliability, either because of distortions on the part of the subjects or because of biases introduced by the ethnographer. . . .

Cross-cultural data on homosexual behavior is further complicated by the prejudice of many observers who consider the behavior unnatural, dysfunctional, or associated with mental illness, and by the fact that in many of the societies studied the behavior is stigmatized and thus not usually carried out openly. Under these circumstances, the behavior is not easily talked about. At the turn of the twentieth century such adjectives as disgusting, vile, and detestable were still being used to describe homosexual behavior; and even in the mid-1930s some anthropologists continued to view the behavior as unnatural. In discussing sodomy with some of his New Guinea informants, Williams (1936), for example, asked them if they "had ever been subjected to an unnatural practice." With the acceptance of the view in the mid-1930s that homosexual behavior should be classified as a mental illness (or at best dysfunctional), many anthropologists replaced "unnatural" with the medical model. This model still finds adherents among researchers at present, especially those in the branch of anthropology referred to as psychological anthropology.

Because of the prejudice with which many researchers and observers approached the subject, statements about the reported absence of homosexual behavior, or the limited extent of the behavior where reported, should be viewed with some skepticism. Mead (1961) suggests that statements of this kind "can only be accepted with the greatest caution and with very careful analysis of the personality and training of the investigator." She further notes that "denials of a practice cannot be regarded as meaningful if that practice is verbally recognized among a given people, even though a strong taboo exists against it."

This chapter will mainly utilize the published research findings of empirical studies which have considered homosexual behavior in some detail. It will examine homosexual behavior in preliterate, peasant, and complex modern societies in all the major geographical regions of the world.[3] Where necessary, these findings will be supplemented with information found in accounts given by travelers, missionaries, and novelists.

SOCIOCULTURAL FACTORS

A number of sociocultural factors help explain variations of homosexual behavior between societies. Two of the most important are cultural attitudes and proscriptions related to cross-gender behavior, and availability of sexual partners.[4] The latter is in turn related to such variables as segregation of sexes prior to marriage, expectations with respect to virginity, age at marriage, and available economic resources and/or distribution of income.

Cross-Gender and Homosexual Behavior

Different expectations for male persons as opposed to female persons are culturally elaborated from birth onward in every known society. Although behavioral boundaries between the sexes may vary culturally, male persons are clearly differentiated from female persons; and progeny is assured by normative societal rules which correlate male and female gender roles with sexual behavior, marriage, and the family. There is a general expectation in every society that a majority of adult men and women will cohabit and produce the next generation. Social pressure is thus applied in the direction of marriage. The general rule is that one should not remain single.

The cross-cultural data on human sexual behavior suggest that a significant relationship exists between much of the homosexual behavior reported cross culturally and the continuing need of societies to deal with cross-gender behavior. Feminine male behavior, and the set of anxieties associated with its occurrence in the male part of the population, appears to have brought about more elaborate cultural responses temporally and spatially than has masculine female behavior. There are no doubt many reasons why this is so, but it appears to be related in general to the higher status accorded men than women in most societies; and, in particular, to the defense role that men have historically played in protecting women and children from outsiders.

Societies in which homosexual behavior can be linked to cultural responses to cross-gender behavior may be categorized according to the type of response made. Three major cultural types have been identified: those societies which make a basic accommodation to cross-gender behavior, those societies which outlaw the behavior as scandalous and/or criminal, and those societies which neither make an accommodation to such behavior nor outlaw it but instead have a cultural formulation which tries to ensure that cross-gender behavior does not occur.

Accommodating Societies

Societies making an accommodation to cross-gender behavior in one form or another have been reported in many different parts of the world. Munroe et al. (1969), for example, put together a list of societies having what they call "institutionalized male transvestism . . . the permanent adoption by males of aspects of female dress and/or behavior in accordance with customary expectations within a given society." Their list includes

Indian societies in North and South America, island societies in Polynesia and Southeast Asia, and preliterate and peasant societies in mainland Asia and Africa. Although reported for both sexes, male cross-gender behavior appears in the literature more often than female.

A folk belief exists in some of these societies that in every generation a certain number of individuals will play the gender role of the opposite sex, usually beginning at or prior to puberty and often identified at a very early age. The Mohave Indians of the American Southwest, for example, used to hold the following belief—typical of many Indian societies in North America—about cross-gender behavior of both sexes:

Ever since the world began at the magic mountain . . . it was said that there would be transvestites. In the beginning, if they were to become transvestites, the process started during their intrauterine life. When they grew up they were given toys according to their sex. They did not like these toys however. (Devereux, 1937)

In southern Mexico one group of Zapotec Indians believes that "effeminate males" are born, not made: "Typical comments include, But what can we do; he was born that way; he is like God made him. A related belief also exists that . . . it is a thing of the blood" (Royce, 1973). In Tahiti, the belief exists that there is at least one cross-gender behaving male, called a *māhū* in all villages: "When one dies then another substitutes . . . God arranges it like this. It isn't allowed (that there should be) two *māhū* in one place" (Levy, 1973).

Cross-gender behavior is accepted in other societies because it is believed that some supernatural event makes people that way prior to birth, or that the behavior is acquired through some mystical force or dream after birth. In India, for example, the following belief exists about the *Hijadās*, cross-gender behaving males thought to be impotent at birth who later have their genitals removed:

When we ask a *Hijadā* or an ordinary man in Gujarat "Why does a man become a *Hijadā*?" the usual reply is "One does not become a *Hijadā* by one's own will; it is only by the command of the *mātā* that one becomes a *Hijadā*." The same idea is found in a myth about the origin of the *Hijadās*. It is said that one receives the *mātā's* command either in dreams or when one sits in meditation before her image. (Shah, 1961)

Among the Chukchee of northeastern Asia, a role reversal was accepted because of an unusual dream or vision:

Transformation takes place by the command of the *ka'let* (spirits) usually at the critical age of early youth when shamanistic inspiration first manifests itself. (Bogores, 1904)

Among the Lango in Africa:

A number of Lango men dress as women, simulate menstruation, and become one of the wives of other males. They are believed to be impotent and to have been afflicted by some supernatural agency. (Ford & Beach, 1951)

Although not necessarily accepted gladly, the various folk beliefs make the behavior acceptable, and a certain number of cross-gender behaving individuals are to be expected in every generation. Expectations about the extent to which the opposite gender role is to be played, however, appear to have changed over time with acculturation. Affected individuals in the past often were required to make a public ritualized change of gender and cross-dress and behave in accordance with their new identity. Among the Mohave, for example, there was an initiation ceremony and it was important for the initiate "to duplicate the behavior pattern of his adopted sex and make 'normal' individuals of his anatomic sex feel toward him as though he truly belonged to his adopted sex" (Devereux, 1937). The *mahū* in Tahiti were described in the latter part of the eighteenth century as follows:

These men are in some respects like the Eunichs [*sic*] in India but are not castrated. They never cohabit with women but live as they do. They pick their beard out and dress as women, dance and sing with them and are as effeminate in their voice. (Morrison, 1935)

Affected individuals in most societies at present are allowed a choice as to the extent they want

to play the role; e.g., how far they want to identify with the opposite sex, whether they want to cross-dress or not, etc. Levy (1973) notes, for example, that in Tahiti: "Being a *mahū* does not now usually entail actually dressing as a woman." The North American Indian societies who used to have initiation ceremonies discontinued them long ago; and, although expectations about cross-gender behaving individuals persist, only remnants of the original belief system are remembered currently. They continue, however, to be tolerant and "there apparently is no body of role behavior aimed at humiliating boys who are feminine or men who prefer men sexually" (Stoller, 1976).

The link between cross-gender behavior and homosexual behavior is the belief that there should be concordance between gender role and sexual object choice. When a male behaves like a female, he should be expected therefore to want a male sexual partner and to play the female sex role—that is, to play the insertee role in anal intercourse or fellatio. The same concordance should be expected when a female behaves like a male. As a result of beliefs about concordance, it is important to note that a society may not conceptualize the sexual behavior or its participants as "homosexual."

There is some evidence in support of this linking of gender role and homosexual behavior in societies making an accommodation and providing a social role for cross-gender behaving individuals. Kroeber (1940), for example, concluded from his investigations that: "In most of primitive northern Asia and North America, men of homosexual trends adopted women's dress, work, and status, and were accepted as nonphysiological but institutionalized women." Devereux's Mohave informants said that the males who changed their gender role to female had male husbands and that both anal intercourse and fellatio were practiced, with the participants playing the appropriate gender sex role. The informants noted the same concordance for females who behaved like males.

Unfortunately, the anthropological data do not always make clear whether cultural expectations in a given society were for concordance between gender role and erotic object; or, in terms of actual behavior, how many cross-gender behaving individuals chose same sex, opposite sex, or both sexes as erotic objects. In the paper I just quoted, Kroeber also concluded: "How far invert erotic practices accompanied the status is not always clear from the data, and it probably varied. At any rate, the North American attitude toward the berdache stresses not his erotic life but his social status; born a male, he became accepted as a woman socially."

Many anthropologists and other observers confounded their findings by assuming an equivalence between "transvestite" and "homosexual."[5] Thus, when an informant described cross-gender behavior, they may have concluded without foundation that a same-sex erotic object choice was part of the behavior being described, and that they were eliciting information on "homosexuals." Angelino and Shedd (1955) provide supporting evidence. They reviewed the literature on an often used anthropological concept, berdache, and concluded that the "term has been used in an exceedingly ambiguous way, being used as a synonym for homosexualism, hermaphroditism, transvestism, and effeminism." They also note that the meaning of berdache changed over time, going from kept boy/male prostitute, to individuals who played a passive role in sodomy, to males who played a passive sex role and cross-dressed.

In spite of the confusion between "transvestite" and "homosexual," the available data suggest that in many of the societies providing a social role for cross-gender behavior, the selection of sexual partners was based on the adopted gender role; and, though they might be subjected to ridicule, neither partner in the sexual relationship was penalized for the role played.

The *māhū* role in Tahiti provides a contemporary look at how one Polynesian society continues to provide a social role for cross-gender behavior. According to Levy (1973), villagers in

his area of study do not agree on the sexual behavior of the *māhū*—some "believe that *māhū* do not generally engage in homosexual intercourse." Information from both *māhū* and non-*māhū* informants, however, leads to the conclusion that probably a majority of the *māhūs* prefer adolescent males with whom they perform "ote moa" (literally, "penis sucking"). The following are some aspects of the role and the community response to it:

It is said to be exclusive. Its essential defining characteristic is "doing woman's work," that is, a role reversal which is publicly demonstrated—either through clothes or through other public aspects of women's role playing. Most villagers approve of, and are pleased by, the role reversal. But homosexual behavior is a covert part of the role, and it is disapproved by many villagers. Men who have sexual relations with the *māhū* . . . do not consider themselves abnormal. Villagers who know of such activities may disapprove, but they do not label the partners as unmanly. The *māhū* is considered as a substitute woman for the partner. A new word, raerae, which reportedly originated in Papeete, is used by some to designate nontraditional types of homosexual behavior. (Levy, 1973)

It should also be noted that in Levy's village of study *māhū*s were the only adult men reported to be engaging in homosexual intercourse.

Another contemporary example of a social role for cross-gender behavior is the *Hijadā* role provided cross-gender behaving males in northwestern India. Given slightly different names by different observers (*Hijarās*, *Hinjrās*, and *Hijirās*), these males appear to be playing the same role. There is general agreement on the fact that they cross-dress, beg alms, and collect dues at special ceremonies where they dance and sing as women. There is a considerable difference of opinion, however, as to whether they engage in homosexual intercourse or in any sexual activity for that matter. From the available data, it appears that they live mostly in towns in communes, with each commune having a definite jurisdiction of villages and towns "where its members can beg alms and collect dues" (Shah, 1961). They are also reported to live separately by themselves. From the findings of Carstairs (1956) and Shah (1961), one can at least conclude that the *Hijadās* living alone are sexually active:

> Carstairs is wrong in considering all the Hijadās as homosexual, but there seems to be some truth in his information about the homosexuality of the Deoli Hijadā (Note: Deoli is the village of Carstairs' study.) Faridi and Mehta also note that some Hijadās practice "sodomy." This, however, is not institutionalized homosexuality. (Shah, 1961)

The finding by Opler (1960) that "they cannot carry on sexual activities and do not marry" may apply to the majority of *Hijadās* living in communes. The question of what kind of sexual behavior the *Hijadās* practice, if any, cannot be answered definitively with the data available. That they are still a viable group in India is confirmed by a recent Associated Press release:

> About 2000 eunuchs dressed in brightly colored saris and other female garb were converging on this northern town from all over India this weekend for a private convention of song, dance and prayer.

> Local reaction to the gathering was mixed. "They're perverts," commented a local peanut vendor. "We should have nothing to do with them. They should be run out of town."

> A New Delhi social worker . . . said they sometimes supplement their income as paid lovers of homosexuals. (Excerpts from AP, February 6, 1979)

Disapproving Societies

Societies in which cross-gender behavior produces strong emotional negative reactions in large segments of the population tend to have the following commonalities: (1) negative reactions produced by the behavior are essentially limited to the male part of the population and relate mainly to effeminate males; (2) cross-gender behavior is controlled by laws which prohibit cross-dressing, and by laws and public opinion which consider other attributes associated with the behavior as scandalous; (3) gender roles are sharply dichotomized; and (4) a general belief exists that

anyone demonstrating cross-gender behavior is homosexual.

A number of complex modern and peasant societies in the Middle East, North Africa, southern Europe, and Central and South America have the commonalities listed. The author's research in Mexico (Carrier, 1976 and 1977) illustrates how homosexual behavior in these societies appears to be linked to social responses to cross-gender behavior. The comments that follow are limited to male homosexual behavior. Female homosexuality is known to exist in these societies, but too little is known about the behavior to be included in the discussion.

Mexican Homosexual Behavior. The Mexican mestizo culture places a high value on manliness. One of the salient features of the society is thus a sharp delimitation between the roles played by males and females. Role expectations in general are for the male to be dominant and independent and for the female to be submissive and dependent. The continued sharp boundary between male and female roles in Mexico appears to be due in part to a culturally defined hypermasculine ideal model of manliness, referred to under the label *machismo*. The ideal female role is generally believed to be the reciprocal of the macho (male) role.[6]

As a consequence of the high status given manliness, Mexican males from birth onward are expected to behave in as manly a way as possible. Peñalosa (1968) sums it up as follows: "Any signs of feminization are severely repressed in the boy." McGinn (1966) concludes: "The young Mexican boy may be severely scolded for engaging in feminine activities, such as playing with dolls or jacks. Parents verbally and physically punish feminine traits in their male children." The importance of manly behavior continues throughout the life span of Mexican males.

One result of the sharp dichotomization of male and female gender roles is the widely held belief that effeminate males basically prefer to play the female role rather than the male. The link between male effeminacy and homosexuality is the additional belief that as a result of this role preference effeminate males are sexually interested only in masculine males with whom they play the passive sex role. Although the motivations of males participating in homosexual encounters are without question diverse and complex, the fact remains that in Mexico cultural pressure is brought to bear on effeminate males to play the passive insertee role in sexual intercourse, and a kind of de facto cultural approval is given (that is, no particular stigma is attached to) masculine males who want to play the active insertor role in homosexual intercourse.

The beliefs linking effeminate males with homosexuality are culturally transmitted by a vocabulary which provides the appropriate labels, by homosexually oriented jokes and word games (*albures*), and by the mass media. The links are established at a very early age. From early childhood on, Mexican males are made aware of the labels used to denote male homosexuals and the connection is always clearly made that these homosexual males are guilty of unmanly effeminate behavior.

The author's data also support the notion that prior to puberty effeminate males in Mexico are targeted as sexual objects for adolescent and adult males, and are expected to play the passive insertee sex role in anal intercourse. Following the onset of puberty, they continue to be sexual targets for other males because of their effeminacy. The consensus of my effeminate respondents in Mexico is that regardless of whether they are at school, in a movie theater, on the downtown streets, in a park, or in their own neighborhood, they are sought out and expected to play the anal passive sex role by more masculine males. As one fourteen-year-old respondent put it, in response to the question of where he had looked for sexual contacts during the year prior to the interview: "I didn't have to search for them . . . they looked for me."

The other side of the coin is represented by masculine male participants in homosexual encounters. Given the fact that effeminate males

in Mexico are assumed homosexual and thus considered available as sexual outlets, how do the cultural factors contribute to the willingness of masculine males to play the active insertor sex role? The available data suggest that, insofar as the social variables are concerned, their willingness to participate in homosexual encounters is due to the relatively high level of sexual awareness that exists among males in the society, to the lack of stigmatization of the insertor sex role, and to the restraints that may be placed on alternative sexual outlets by available income and/or by marital status. The only cultural proscriptions are that "masculine" males should not play the passive sex role and should not be exclusively involved with homosexual intercourse.

The passive sex role is by inference—through the cultural equivalence of effeminacy with homosexuality—prescribed for "effeminate" males. It becomes a self-fulfilling prophecy of the society that effeminate males (a majority?) are eventually, if not from the beginning, pushed toward exclusively homosexual behavior. Some do engage in heterosexual intercourse, and some marry and set up households; but these probably are a minority of the identifiably effeminate males among the mestizos of the Mexican population.

Brazilian Homosexual Behavior. Both Young (1973) and Fry (1974) note the relationship between cross-gender behavior and homosexuality in Brazil:

Brazilians are still pretty hung-up about sexual roles. Many Brazilians believe in the *bicha/bofe* (femme/butch) dichotomy and try to live by it. In Brazil, the average person doesn't even recognize the existence of the masculine homosexual. For example, among working-class men, it is considered all right to fuck a *bicha*, an accomplishment of sorts, just like fucking a woman. (Young, 1973)

In the simplest of terms, a male is a man until he is assumed or proved to have "given" in which case he becomes a *bicha*. With very few exceptions, males who "eat" *bichas* are not classified as anything other than "real men." Under this classificatory scheme they differ in no way from males who restrict themselves to "eating" females. (Note: the male who gives is an insertee, the one who eats is an insertor.) (Fry, 1974)

Southern European Homosexual Behavior. Contemporary patterns of male homosexual behavior in Greece appear similar to those observed by the author in Mexico. An American anthropologist who collected data on homosexual behavior in Greece while working there on an archaeological project (Bialor, 1975) found, for example, that preferences for playing one sex role or the other (anal insertor or anal insertee) appear to be highly developed among Greek males. Little or no stigma is attached to the masculine male who plays the active insertor role. The social setting in modern Greece also appears to be strikingly similar to that in modern Mexico. Karlen (1971) describes it as follows:

The father spends his spare time with other men in cafes; society is a male club, and there all true companionship lies. Women live separate, sequestered lives. Girls' virginity is carefully protected, and the majority of homicides are committed over the "honor" of daughters and sisters. In some Greek villages a woman does not leave her home unaccompanied by a relative between puberty and old age. Women walk the street, even in Athens, with their eyes down; a woman who looks up when a man speaks to her is, quite simply, a whore. The young male goes to prostitutes and may carry on homosexual connections; it is not unusual for him to marry at thirty having had no sexual experience save with prostitutes and male friends. (p. 16)

In an evaluation of the strategy of Turkish boys' verbal dueling rhymes, Dundes, Leach, and Ozkok (1972) make the following observations about homosexual behavior in Turkey:

It is extremely important to note that the insult refers to passive homosexuality, not to homosexuality in general. In this context there is nothing insulting about being the active homosexual. In a homosexual relationship, the active phallic aggressor gains status; the passive victim of such aggression loses status. It is important to play the active role in a homosexual relationship; it is shameful and demeaning to be forced to take the passive role.

Moroccan Homosexual Behavior. The author does not know of any formal studies of homosexual behavior in Morocco. The available information suggests, however, that contemporary patterns of homosexual behavior in Morocco are similar to those in Mexico; that is, as long as Moroccan males play the active, insertor sex role in the relationship, there is never any question of their being considered homosexual. Based on his field work in Morocco shortly after the turn of the century, Westermarck (1908) believed that "a very large proportion of the men" in some parts of the country were involved in homosexual activity. He also noted that "in Morocco active pederasty is regarded with almost complete indifference, whilst the passive sodomite, if a grown-up individual, is spoken of with scorn. Dr. Polak says the same of the Persians." Contemporary patterns of homosexual behavior in the Islamic Arab countries of North Africa are probably similar to those in Morocco. . . .

DISCUSSION

Heterosexual intercourse, marriage, and the creation of a family are culturally established as primary objectives for adults living in all of the societies discussed above. Ford and Beach (1951) concluded from their cross-cultural survey that "all known cultures are strongly biased in favor of copulation between males and females as contrasted with alternative avenues of sexual expression." They further note that this viewpoint is biologically adaptive in that it favors perpetuation of the species and social group, and that societies favoring other nonreproductive forms of sexual expression for adults would not be likely to survive for many generations.

Homosexual intercourse appears to be the most important alternative form of sexual expression utilized by people living around the world. All cultures have established rules and regulations that govern the selection of a sexual partner or partners. With respect to homosexual behavior, however, there appear to be greater variations of the rules and regulations. And male homosexual behavior generally appears to be more regulated by cultures than female homosexual behavior. This difference may be the result of females being less likely than males to engage in homosexual activity; but it may also just be the result of a lack of data on female as compared with male homosexual behavior cross-culturally.

Exclusive homosexuality, however, because of the cultural dictums concerning marriage and the family, appears to be generally excluded as a sexual option even in those societies where homosexual behavior is generally approved. For example, the two societies where all male individuals are free to participate in homosexual activity if they choose, Siwan and East Bay, do not sanction exclusive homosexuality.[7] Although nearly all male members of these two societies are reported to engage in extensive homosexual activities, they are not permitted to do so exclusively over their adult life span. Davenport (1965) reports that "East Bay is a society which permits men to be either heterosexual or bisexual in their behavior, but denies the possibility of the exclusively homosexual man." He notes that "they have no concept and therefore no word for the exclusive homosexual." There are not much data available on the Siwans, but it has been reported that whether single or married, Siwan males "are expected to have both homosexual and heterosexual affairs" (Ford & Beach, 1951).

In East Bay there are two categories of homosexual relationships. One category appears similar to that found in a number of Melanesian societies; an older man plays the active (insertor) sex role in anal intercourse with younger boys "from seven to perhaps eleven years of age." Davenport notes:

The man always plays the active role, and it is considered obligatory for him to give the boy presents in return for accommodating him. A man would not engage his own son in such a relationship, but fathers do not object when friends use their young sons in this way, provided the adult is kind and generous. (p. 200)

The other category is between young single men of the same age group who play both sex roles in anal intercourse. The young men, however, "are not regarded as homosexual lovers. They are simply friends or relatives, who, understanding each other's needs and desires, accommodate one another thus fulfilling some of the obligations of kinship and friendship." This category may be related to several social factors which limit heterosexual contacts of young single men. First, the population is highly masculine with a male/female ratio of 120:100 in the fifteen- to twenty-five-year-old age group. Second, females have historically been brought in as wives for those who could afford the bride price. Third, sexual relations between unmarried individuals and adultery are forbidden. Both relationships are classed as larcenies and "only murder carries a more severe punishment." At first marriage a bride is expected to be a virgin. Chastity is highly valued in that it indicates adultery is less likely to occur after marriage. And fourth, there is "an extensive system for separating the sexes by what amounts to a general social avoidance between men and women in all but a few situations." From early adolescence on, unmarried men and boys sleep and eat in the men's house; and married men spend much of their time there during the day. Davenport notes that both masturbation and anal copulation are socially approved and regarded as substitutes for heterosexual intercourse by members of the society. Female homosexual activity is not reported in East Bay.

Among Siwan males the accepted homosexual relationship is "between a man and a boy but not between adult men or between two young boys" (Bullough, 1976). They are reported to practice anal intercourse with the adult man always playing the active (insertor) sex role. In this society, boys are more valued than girls. Allah (1917) reports that

. . . bringing up of a boy costs very little whereas the girl needs ornaments, clothing, and stains. Moreover the boy is a very fruitful source of profit for the father, not for the work he does, but because he is hired by his father to another man to be used as a catamite. Sometimes two men exchange their sons. If they are asked about this, they are not ashamed to mention it.

Homosexual activity is not reported for Siwan females.

The way in which cross-gender behavior is linked to homosexual behavior, and the meaning ascribed to the "homosexual" behavior by participants and significant others, differ between the three categories of societies identified in this study. What is considered homosexuality in one culture may be considered appropriate behavior within prescribed gender roles in another, a homosexual act only on the part of one participant in another, or a ritual act involving growth and masculinity in still another. Care must therefore be taken when judging sexual behavior cross-culturally with such culture-bound labels as "homosexual" and "homosexuality."

From a cultural point of view, deviations from sexual mores in a given society appear most likely to occur as a result of the lack of appropriate sexual partners and/or a result of conditioning in approved sexual behavior which is limited by age or ritual (for example, where homosexual intercourse is only appropriate for a certain age group and/or ritual time period and inappropriate thereafter). Homosexual activity initiated by sociocultural variables may over time through interaction with personality variables, produce an outcome not in accordance with the sexual mores of the society.

The findings presented in this chapter illustrate the profound influence of culture on the structuring of individual patterns of sexual behavior. Whether from biological or psychological causation, cross-gender behaving individuals in many societies must cope with a cultural formulation which equates their behavior with homosexual activity and thus makes it a self-fulfilling prophecy that they become homosexually involved. There are also individuals in many societies who might prefer to be exclusively homosexual but are prevented from doing so by cultural edicts. From whatever causes that homosexual impulses originate, whether they be biological or psychological, culture provides an additional dimension that cannot be ignored.

CRITICAL THINKING QUESTIONS

1. What type of society tends to be accepting of homosexuality? What kind of society is disapproving of this sexual orientation? Why?

2. What insights can be drawn from this article that help to explain violence and discrimination directed toward gay people in Canadian society?

3. Are data about sexuality easily available to researchers? Why not?

NOTES

1. Homosexual behavior or activity will be used here to describe sexual behavior between individuals of the same sex; it may have nothing to do with sexual object choice or sexual orientation of the individual involved. Additionally, the terms "sex role" and "gender role" will be used to describe different behavioral phenomena. As Hooker (1965) points out, they "are often used interchangeably, and with resulting confusion." Following her suggestion the term "sex role," when homosexual practices are described, will refer to typical sexual performance only. "The gender connotations (M-F) of these performances need not then be implicitly assumed." The term "gender role" will refer to the expected attitudes and behavior that distinguish males from females.

2. The Human Relations Area Files (HRAF) contain information on the habits, practices, customs, and behavior of populations in hundreds of societies around the world. These files utilize accounts given not only by anthropologists but also by travelers, writers, missionaries, and explorers. Most cross-cultural surveys of sexual behavior, like those of Ford and Beach and Broude and Greene, have been based on HRAF information. A major criticism of the HRAF information on sexual behavior relates to the difficulty of assessing the reliability of the data collected in different time periods by different people with varying amounts of scientific training as observers.

3. "Preliterate" refers to essentially tribal societies that do not have a written language; "peasant" refers to essentially agrarian literate societies; and "complex modern" refers to highly industrialized societies.

4. In one of the first scholarly surveys of homosexual behavior done by an anthropologist, Westermarck (1908) concluded that: "A very important cause of homosexual practices is absence of the other sex."

5. The confounding of transvestism with homosexuality still occurs. For example, Minturn, Grosse, and Haider (1969) coded male homosexuality with transvestism in a recent study of the patterning of sexual beliefs and behavior, "because it is often difficult to distinguish

Homosexual Behavior in Cross-Cultural Perspective **167**

between the two practices, and because they are assumed to be manifestations of the same psychological processes and to have similar causes."

6. The roles described represent the normative cultural ideals of the mestizoized national culture. Mestizos are Mexican nationals of mixed Indian and Spanish ancestry. They make up a large majority of the population, and their culture is the dominant one.

7. Both societies are small, each totaling less than 1,000 inhabitants. The Siwans live in an oasis in the Libyan desert. The people of East Bay (a pseudonym) live in a number of small coastal villages in an island in Melanesia.

REFERENCES

Allah, M. 1917. Siwan customs. *Harvard African Studies*, 1: 7.

Angelino, A., and C. Shedd. 1955. A note on berdache. *American Anthropologist*, 57: 121–25.

Associated Press. 1979. Eunuchs gather for convention in India. *Panipat*, February 6, 1979.

Bialor, P. 1975. Personal communication.

Bogores, W. 1904. The Chukchee. *Memoirs of American Museum of Natural History*, 2: 449–51.

Broude, G., and S. Greene. 1976. Cross-cultural codes on twenty sexual attitudes and practices. *Ethnology*, 15(4): 410–11.

Bullough, V. 1976. *Sexual variance in society and history*, 22–49. New York: John Wiley.

Carrier, J. 1976. Cultural factors affecting urban Mexican male homosexual behavior. *Archives of Sexual Behavior*, 5(2): 103–24.

———. 1977. Sex-role preference as an explanatory variable in homosexual behavior. *Archives of Sexual Behavior*, 6(1): 53–65.

Carstairs, G. 1956. Hinjra and Jiryan: Two derivatives of Hindu attitudes to sexuality. *British Journal of Medical Psychology*, 2: 129–32.

Davenport, W. 1965. Sexual patterns and their regulation in a society of the southwest Pacific. In *Sex and behavior*, 164–207. New York: John Wiley.

Devereux, G. 1937. Institutionalized homosexuality of the Mohave Indians. In *The problem of homosexuality in modern society*, 183–226. New York: E. P. Dutton.

Dundes, A., J. Leach, and B. Ozkok. 1972. The strategy of Turkish boys' verbal dueling. In *Directions in sociolinguistics: The ethnography of communication*. New York: Holt.

Ford, C. S., and F. A. Beach. 1951. *Patterns of sexual behavior*. New York: Harper & Row.

Fry, P. 1974. Male homosexuality and Afro-Brazilian possession cults. Unpublished paper presented to Symposium on Homosexuality in Crosscultural Perspective, 73rd Annual Meeting of the American Anthropological Association, Mexico City.

Hooker, E. 1965. An empirical study of some relations between sexual patterns and gender identity in male homosexuals. In *Sex research: New developments*, 24–25. New York: Holt.

Karlen, A. 1971. *Sexuality and homosexuality: A new view*. New York: W. W. Norton.

Kroeber, A. 1940. Psychosis or social sanction. *Character and Personality*, 8: 204–15. Reprinted in *The nature of culture*, 313. Chicago: University of Chicago Press, 1952.

Levy, R. 1973. *Tahitians*. Chicago: University of Chicago Press.

Marshall, D., and R. Suggs. 1971. *Human sexual behavior*, 220–21. New York: Basic Books.

McGinn, N. 1966. Marriage and family in middle-class Mexico. *Journal of Marriage and Family Counseling*, 28: 305–13.

Mead, M. 1961. Cultural determinants of sexual behavior. In *Sex and internal secretions*, 1433–79. Baltimore: Williams & Wilkins.

Minturn, L., M. Grosse, and S. Haider. 1969. Cultural patterning of sexual beliefs and behavior. *Ethnology*, 8(3): 3.

Morrison, J. 1935. *The journal of James Morrison*. London: Golden Cockeral Press.

Munroe, R., J. Whiting, and D. Hally. 1969. Institutionalized male transvestism and sex distinctions. *American Anthropologist*, 71: 87–91.

Opler, M. 1960. The Hijarā (hermaphrodites) of India and Indian national character: A rejoinder. *American Anthropologist*, 62(3): 505–11.

Peñalosa, F. 1968. Mexican family roles. *Journal of Marriage and Family Counseling*, 30: 680–89.

Royce, A. 1973. Personal communication.

Shah, A. 1961. A note on the Hijadās of Gujarat. *American Anthropologist*, 63(6): 1325–30.

Stoller, R. 1976. Two feminized male American Indians. *Archives of Sexual Behavior*, 5(6): 536.

Westermarck, E. 1908. On homosexual love. In *The origin and development of the moral ideas*. London: Macmillan.

Williams, F. 1936. *Papuans of the trans-fly*. London: Oxford University Press.

Young, A. 1973. Gay gringo in Brazil. In *The gay liberation book*, eds. L. Richmond and G. Noguera, 60–7. San Francisco: Ramparts Press.

Social
Stratification

CLASSIC

CONTEMPORARY

CROSS-CULTURAL

31

The Vertical Mosaic: An Analysis of Social Class and Power in Canada

JOHN PORTER

In this chapter from the highly regarded book The Vertical Mosaic, *Porter highlights the importance of studying Canadian social class structures. Porter traces the Canadian belief that there are no clearly defined classes in Canada back to the frontier environment and the settlement of Canada.*

THE CANADIAN MIDDLE CLASS IMAGE

One of the most persistent images that Canadians have of their society is that it has no classes. This image becomes translated into the assertion that Canadians are all relatively equal in their possessions, in the amount of money they earn, and in the opportunities which they and their children have to get on in the world. An important element in this image of classlessness is that, with the absence of formal aristocracy and aristocratic institutions, Canada is a society in which equalitarian values have asserted themselves over authoritarian values. Canada, it is thought, shares not only a continent with the United States, but also a democratic ideology which rejects the historical class and power structures of Europe.

Source: From *The Vertical Mosaic* by John Porter. Toronto: University of Toronto Press, 1965, pp. 3–6. Reprinted with the permission of the publisher.

Social images are one thing and social realities another. Yet the two are not completely separate. Social images are not entirely fictional characters with only a coincidental likeness to a real society, living or dead. Often the images can be traced to an earlier historical period of the society, its golden age perhaps, which, thanks to the historians, is held up, long after it has been transformed into something else, as a model way of life. As well as their historical sources, images can be traced to their contemporary creators, particularly in the world of the mass media and popular culture. When a society's writers, journalists, editors, and other image-creators are a relatively small and closely linked group, and have more or less the same social background, the images they produce can, because they are consistent, appear to be much more true to life than if their group were larger, less cohesive, and more heterogeneous in composition.

The historical source of the image of a classless Canada is the equality among pioneers in the frontier environment of the last century. In the early part of the [twentieth] century there was a similar equality of status among those who were settlers in the west, although, as we shall see, these settlers were by no means treated equally. A rural, agricultural, primary producing society is a much less differentiated society than one which has highly concentrated industries in large cities. Equality in the rural society may be much more apparent than real, but the rural environment has been for Canada an important source of the image of equality. Later we shall examine more closely how the historical image has become out of date with the transformation of Canadian society from the rural to the urban type.

Although the historical image of rural equality lingers, it has gradually given way in the urban industrial setting to an image of a middle level classlessness in which there is a general uniformity of possessions. For families these possessions include a separate dwelling with an array of electrical equipment, a car, and perhaps a summer cottage. Family members, together or as individuals, engage in a certain amount of ritualistic behaviour in churches and service clubs. Modern advertising has done much to standardize the image of middle class consumption levels and middle class behaviour. Consumers' magazines are devoted to the task of constructing the ideal way of life through articles on child-rearing, homemaking, sexual behaviour, health, sports, and hobbies. Often, too, corporations which do not produce family commodities directly will have large advertisements to demonstrate how general social well-being at this middle level is an outcome of their own operations.

That there is neither very rich nor very poor in Canada is an important part of the image. There are no barriers to opportunity. Education is free. Therefore, making use of it is largely a question of personal ambition. Even university education is available to all, except that it may require for some a little more summer work and thrift.

There is a view widely held by many university graduates that they, and most other graduates, have worked their way through college. Consequently it is felt anyone else can do the same.

In some superficial respects the image of middle class uniformity may appear plausible. The main values of the society are concerned with the consumption of commodities, and in the so-called affluence that has followed World War II there seem to have been commodities for everybody, except, perhaps, a small group of the permanently poor at the bottom. Credit facilities are available for large numbers of low-income families, enabling them, too, to be consumers of commodities over and above the basic necessities of life. The vast array of credit facilities, some of them extraordinarily ingenious, have inequalities built into them, in that the cost of borrowing money varies with the amount already possessed. There are vast differences in the quality of goods bought by the middle income levels and the lower income levels. One commodity, for instance, which low-income families can rarely purchase is privacy, particularly the privacy of a house to themselves. It is perhaps the value of privacy and the capacity to afford it which has become the dividing line between the real and the apparent middle class.

If low-income families achieve high consumption levels it is usually through having more than one income earner in the household. Often this is the wife and mother, but it may be an older child who has left school, and who is expected to contribute to the family budget. Alternatively, high consumption levels may be achieved at a cost in leisure. Many low-income family heads have two jobs, a possibility which has arisen with the shorter working day and the five-day week. This "moonlighting," as it is called in labour circles, tends to offset the progress which has been made in raising the level of wages and reducing the hours of work. There is no way of knowing how extensive "moonlighting" is, except that we know that trade unions denounce it as a practice which tends to take away the gains which have been obtained for workers. For large segments of the population, therefore, a high level of consumption is obtained by means which are alien to a true middle class standard. [When] . . . we . . . examine closely the distribution of income, we . . . see what a small proportion of Canadian families were able to live a middle class style of life in the middle 1950s, the high tide of post-war affluence.

At the high end of the social class spectrum, also in contrast to the middle level image, are the families of great wealth and influence. They are not perhaps as ostentatious as the very wealthy of other societies, and Canada has no "celebrity world" with which these families must compete for prestige in the way Mills has suggested is important for the very rich in American society.[1]

Almost every large Canadian city has its wealthy and prominent families of several generations. They have their own social life, their children go to private schools, they have their clubs and associations, and they take on the charitable and philanthropic roles which have so long been the "duty" of those of high status. Although this upper class is always being joined by the new rich, it still contributes, as we shall see later, far more than its proportionate share to the elite of big business.

The concentration of wealth in the upper classes is indicated by the fact that in Canada in 1955 the top one per cent of income recipients received about 40 per cent of all income from dividends.

Images which conflict with the one of middle class equality rarely find expression, partly because the literate middle class is both the producer and the consumer of the image. Even at times in what purports to be serious social analysis, middle class intellectuals project the image of their own class onto the social classes above and below them. There is scarcely any critical analysis of Canadian social life upon which a conflicting image could be based. The idea of class differences has scarcely entered into the stream of Canadian academic writing despite the fact that class differences stand in the way of implementing one of the most important values of western society, that is equality.[2] The fact, which we shall see later, that Canada draws its intellectuals either from abroad or from its own middle class, means that there is almost no one producing a view of the world which reflects the experience of the poor or the underprivileged. It was as though they did not exist. It is the nature of these class differences and their consequences for Canadian society that [we] . . . seek to explore.

Closely related to differences in class levels are differences in the exercising of power and decision-making in the society: Often it is thought that once a society becomes an electoral democracy based on universal suffrage, power becomes diffused throughout the general population so that everyone participates somehow in the selection of social goals. There is, however, a whole range of institutional resistances to the transfer of power to a democratic political system.[3] . . .

CRITICAL THINKING QUESTIONS

1. Is Porter's assertion that Canadians believe they exist within a classless society still valid today? Why or why not?

2. Porter's work was published in 1965. Do any of his observations continue to be revealing in a contemporary analysis of Canadian society?

3. According to Porter, does democracy ensure the equal allocation of power and influence within society? Why or why not?

NOTES

1. C. W. Mills, *The Power Elite* (New York, 1956), chap. 4.
2. Nor does class appear as a theme in Canadian literature. See R. L. McDougall, "The Dodo and the Cruising Auk," *Canadian Literature*, no. 18 (Autumn 1963).
3. For a comparative study of social mobility see S. M. Lipset and R. Bendix, *Social Mobility in Industrial Society* (Berkeley, 1959).

32

Does the Vertical Mosaic Still Exist in Canada? Ethnicity and Income in Canada, 1991

JASON Z. LIAN AND
DAVID RALPH MATTHEWS

Social
Stratification

CLASSIC

CONTEMPORARY

CROSS-CULTURAL

Lian and Matthews review Porter's work and explore it using contemporary data. The authors find that race (particularly visible minorities) has become the fundamental basis for income inequality in Canada.

This paper updates our knowledge about the relationship between ethnicity and social class in Canada using *The Public Use Microdata File for Individuals* drawn from the 1991 Census of Canada. We provide three levels of analysis. First, we examine the relationship between ethnicity and education by ethnic group. Second, we examine the "return to education" in terms of income for those of various ethnic groups. Third, we use log-linear regression to examine the relationship between ethnicity, education, and income while controlling for the effects of a variety of other social variables. We find that, at most educational levels, Canadians of French

Source: Jason Z. Lian and David Matthews. 1998. "Does the Vertical Mosaic Still Exist? Ethnicity and Income in Canada, 1991." *Canadian Review of Sociology and Anthropology*, 35(4), 461–81. Reprinted by permission of the Canadian Sociology and Anthropology Association.

ethnicity now earn significantly more than those of British ethnicity when other variables are controlled. With this exception, for those of European ethnic backgrounds there are now virtually no significant differences in income within educational levels when other social variables are controlled. However, those who belong to visible minorities have significantly lower incomes than other Canadians at all educational levels. Race is now the fundamental basis of income inequality in Canada.

In 1965, John Porter described Canadian society as a "vertical mosaic" stratified along ethnic lines (1965: pp. 60–103). Porter argued that the British and French, as the first ethnic groups to come into Canada, became the "charter groups" and to a considerable extent dictated the circumstances under which other ethnic groups were subsequently permitted to enter. He argued that "entrance status" was generally granted to those of other ethnic groups who were willing to accept lower level occupational roles (pp. 63–73) and that, as a result, "immigration and ethnic affiliation . . . have been important factors in the formation of social classes in Canada" (p. 73). Porter used census data from the 1931 to 1961 period to demonstrate that the British dominated the French in all of the most prestigious occupational categories, and that other ethnic groups were generally distributed in a hierarchy below them.

Since then, considerable effort has been expended by researchers to support or refute Porter's thesis and to examine the extent to which ethnic social class mobility has occurred as previous immigrants overcame their "entrance status" and moved up the social class hierarchy. Proponents of the vertical mosaic thesis have argued that differences in occupational status among Canadian ethnic groups remain substantial. Over the past thirty years, they have demonstrated that, for the two charter groups, the occupational status of the British has remained significantly higher than that of the French (Royal Commission, 1969: 34–45; Breton & Roseborough, 1971; Boyd et al., 1981). They have argued that among other groups, Jews and those from the north and west of Europe are generally in favourable positions, South Europeans and visible minorities are generally in disadvantaged positions, and Aboriginal Peoples are at the bottom of the Canadian occupational hierarchy (Reitz, 1980; Porter, 1985; Jabbra & Cosper, 1988; Li, 1988; Lautard & Guppy, 1990). Thus, in 1984, Lautard and Loree could still claim that "occupational inequality is still substantial enough to justify the use of the concept 'vertical mosaic' to characterize this aspect of ethnic relations in Canada" (p. 343).

In contrast, a number of other researchers have argued that the influence of ethnicity in the process of social mobility was and/or is minimal in Canada, and that ethnic affiliation did not operate as a significant block to social mobility as Porter had suggested. Most such works have examined the relationship between ethnicity and occupation, while controlling for a range of other variables. Using such methods, they have argued that the association between ethnicity and occupational status was minimal and declining (Pineo, 1976; Darroch, 1979; Ornstein, 1981) and that the contention of the vertical mosaic thesis that the status of immigrants groups has been rigidly preserved is "patently false" (Tepperman, 1975: 156). Other researchers have suggested that a convergence process in occupational status among ethnic groups in Canada has become more apparent since Porter's original analysis (Reitz, 1980: 150–53), the relationship between ethnic origin and class position has been in flux (Nakhaie, 1951), and that gains by non-charter groups have been significantly greater than those of the charter groups (Boyd et al., 1981; Pineo & Porter, 1985: 382–83). Porter, himself, has argued that the situation he described in 1965 may have been in existence only for a relatively short period in Canadian history (Pineo & Porter, 1985: 390). It is also argued that, to the extent that any ethnic status hierarchy remains, Porter's status hierarchy of ethnic groups has changed dramatically with the British dropping from the top to the middle and the Asians moving to the top with the Jews (Herberg, 1990). As a result, it has been stated recently that ethnicity is no longer a drawback for social mobility in Canada (Isajiw, Sev'er & Driedger, 1993).

In many such works, the relation of education and ethnicity has come under considerable scrutiny. Thus, proponents of the ethnic inequality thesis have argued that the Canadian education system has been a mechanism to reproduce social inequality (Shamai, 1992: 44–5) and that educational opportunity was not equally accessible to all groups (Li, 1988: 77–96). Alternatively, those who have been critical of the ethnic inequality thesis have argued that there is little evidence of ethnic inequality in education in Canada and that a *"contest-achieved"* system of status attainment is operating (Herberg, 1990). Indeed, Porter was himself involved in work which argued that non-charter groups have gained significantly in educational achievement compared to the British (Pineo & Porter, 1985: 384) and that the educational system has worked to help minority Canadians overcome the disadvantages of their background (p. 391).

The general conclusion of this body of work would seem to be that there is a collapsing of the vertical mosaic. However, there is growing evidence (see Li, 1988; Reitz, 1980; Agocs & Boyd, 1993) that Canada has retained what Geschwender and Guppy have called a "colour-coded vertical mosaic" (1995: 2). Such works suggest that, whereas ethnic stratification has lessened among white European groups, differences between racial groups have persisted and that, in effect, Canada's mosaic has been reduced to a division based principally on skin colour (1995: 2).

This paper will examine the evidence for and against ethnic inequality in Canada with respect to income distribution, using *The Public Use Microdata Files for Individuals* (PUMFI) provided by Statistics Canada, which constitutes a 3% sample of the 1991 Census. Such files have been made available since 1971, but the 1991 PUMFI provides both a more extensive list of ethnic groups and a more detailed categorization of other variables that may be employed as controls than were available in previous issues. Thus, the present paper is able to provide more current information on the relationship between ethnicity and income than most previous studies, and also is able to identify ethnicity more precisely and use more stringent control variables in the analysis.

To carry out the analysis we have used those respondents in the PUMFI who were in the "working population," and from this group have eliminated those respondents for whom data were not available or who had zero or negative earnings.[1] These latter reductions reduce the number of respondents in the working population sample by 4.78%, nearly half of whom had zero or negative earnings in 1990. As a result of these adjustments, the average earnings of the sample increased by approximately 4%, but the ethnic composition changed very

little. . . . Thus, for purposes of the present study[,] which focuses on ethnicity, our sample was not affected significantly.

ETHNICITY AND EDUCATION

In any study of ethnic stratification and mobility, education is seen as a critically important intervening variable between ethnicity and income. A fundamental question in such studies is whether educational achievement is distributed equally among ethnic groups. Earlier we noted the diverging positions on this subject in Canada— some argued that the educational system has functioned to reproduce the existing socio-economic hierarchy in favour of the dominant groups (Li, 1988: 73–7; Shamai, 1992: 53–5), and others argued that the educational system has functioned as a source of upward mobility for Canadian minority groups since the early decades of this century (Herberg, 1990).

It is not possible to test this issue fully using data from a single time period. However, data from the 1991 PUMFI show a considerable variation in education among ethnic groups when compared with the Canadian average and this variation remains even when one separates out the Canadian born from the foreign born. This indicates that, among native-born Canadians, educational achievement is unevenly distributed by ethnicity. . . .

In 1991, approximately 30% of the employed labour force in Canada had less than secondary education, just over 54% had secondary or non-university post-secondary education, and almost 17% had post-secondary education. About two-thirds of the European groups and half of the visible minority groups were close to this Canadian average. However, several Southern European groups (Italians, Greeks, Portuguese), Vietnamese, and Aboriginal Peoples had proportionally more persons with this lower educational level while Arabs, West Asians, Jews and Filipinos were under-represented in the lower educational groups.

At the other extreme, in terms of post-secondary (university) education most European groups were around the national average, Poles were moderately above and Jews were nearly three times [more] likely to have a university degree than were those of European origin *per se*. With the exception of the Black/Caribbean and Aboriginal groups who ranked substantially below the national level, the remaining visible minority groups had high rates of university education. This was particularly the case for those of Arab, West Asian, South Asian, Chinese, Filipino and Other East and Southeast Asian ethnic backgrounds.

To some considerable degree this latter finding is a reflection of Canadian immigration policy since the 1970s, which has favoured those with high levels of education and training. Thus, Arab, West Asian, South Asian, Filipino, and Vietnamese foreign born were generally better educated than their Canadian-born counterparts. This relationship held for most other groups with the notable exception of the Greek, Italian, and Balkan ethnic groups among whom the native born were generally better educated than recent immigrants.

EDUCATION AND INCOME DIFFERENCES AMONG ETHNIC GROUPS

While differences in education by ethnic group, particularly among the Canadian-born, are an indication of possible ethnic discrimination, the more significant indication is whether the "returns for education" are also unequal among ethnic groups. That is, does similar education (at whatever level) generate significantly different incomes among the ethnic groups? . . .

At the national level, those with secondary education earned about 50% more than those without secondary education and those with university education earned about 150% more than those without secondary education. . . . However, there are extreme ethnic differences at all three educational levels.

The following analyses are all based on comparisons with the national average for each of the educational categories. Looking first at the two "charter groups," workers of British origin with non-secondary education earned 3% more than the national average for this educational level, those with secondary education earned 7% more, while those with university education earned 8% more. In comparison, workers of French ethnicity with non-secondary education earned 12% more than the national average, those with secondary education earned 1% less and those with university education earned 4% more. Thus, in contrast to Porter's finding that the French were rewarded significantly less than the British for their educational achievement, at the lower educational level they now have a significant edge over the British, and are above the national average in income at the higher educational levels.

Those of Western European ethnic background earned considerably higher incomes than the Canadian average in each of the education categories, the exception being university educated persons of Dutch and German ethnic backgrounds who earned only marginally more. Eastern Europeans also tended to earn more than the Canadian average, with Hungarians and Ukrainians earning substantially more at all levels. Persons of Polish ethnicity with lower as well as middle levels of education earned more than average, but better educated persons of Polish ethnicity earned less.

For those whose Jewish ethnic background was recorded, those with the lowest level of education earned 9% more than the Canadian average income for that level, while those with university education earned 19% more than the Canadian university educated average income. However, those with secondary education earned 4% less than the average Canadians at their educational level.

The pattern for Southern Europeans is mixed. At the lowest educational level, most of these ethnic groups earned above the Canadian average income[,] with those of Italian, Portuguese, Greek, and Balkan origin earning considerably higher than that average. However, at higher educational levels Southern Europeans were generally disadvantaged.

However, it is when we consider visible minorities that the largest discrepancies between education and income are apparent. At the lower education levels all 10 visible minority groups earned less than an average Canadian with similar education, ranging from 5% less for those of Arab ethnicity to 33% less for those of Filipino ethnic background and 42% less for Aboriginal Peoples. Likewise, among those with secondary education, all 10 visible minority groups earned substantially less than the comparable Canadian average. Similarly, amongst those with post-secondary education, while those of Black and Chinese ethnicity earned only somewhat less than the Canadian average, those in the other eight visible minority groups received earning[s] substantially below that level.

The overall conclusion to be drawn from these two tables is that persons of European background generally receive above average income for their educational level with the exception of persons with higher education from some Eastern and Southern European ethnic groups. Indeed, persons from many such ethnic backgrounds now receive incomes relative to education that are higher than for either of the two "charter groups." *However, for visible minorities a very different picture emerges. For all visible ethnic groups and at all educational levels, the rewards for education are substantially below the Canadian average.*

ETHNICITY AND INCOME DIFFERENCES WITHIN EDUCATIONAL CATEGORIES, TAKING INTO ACCOUNT OTHER VARIABLES

Although the preceding analysis has provided strong indications that the rewards for education vary by ethnic group and particularly that workers of visible minorities receive comparatively less than other workers with similar education, it is possible that these results are not due to

ethnicity *per se* but to a range of other factors such as the age composition, marital status, or period of immigration of workers from various ethnic groups. Thus, if one wants to measure directly the effect of ethnicity on earnings within educational categories, it is necessary to take into account the effect of these other earnings-related variables.

To do this, we developed a semi-logarithmic regression model of earnings determination with interaction terms constructed of ethnicity and education, controlling for gender; age and age squared; marital status; province of residence; metropolitan versus non-metropolitan area of residence; geographic mobility in the past five years; period of immigration; knowledge of official languages; occupational level; industrial sector; weeks worked and weeks worked squared; and full versus part-time weeks worked. Controlling for these factors in a semi-logarithmic regression yields an adjusted R square of 0.58007, indicating that 58% of the variations in log earnings have been accounted for by the variables included in the model.

Because of the dominant position of the British in Canadian society both numerically and socio-economically, we have used them as the base line category in the regression for an estimation of the net log earnings of the other ethnic groups at each educational level. While persons of British ethnicity with "no degree, certificate, or diploma" were used as the reference category for all other interactive categories of ethnicity and education in the regression, for easy interpretation, we have converted the partial coefficients for the other ethnic groups as deviations from those of their category of "no degree, certificate, or diploma" for the British. The coefficients derived in this manner have been converted into percentages and displayed in Table 32.1.

As an example of how to interpret the table, we would note that the 3.1% in the cell for French with "no degree, certificate, or diploma" indicates that workers of French ethnic origin earned 3.1% more than their British counterparts with comparable education when all the dimensions in

TABLE 32.1 Adjusted Earnings[a] of Persons of Different Ethnic Origins[b] as Percentage Differences from Those of Persons of British Origin by Educational Level, Canada, 1990

Ethnic Origin	No Degree, Certificate, or Diploma	High School Graduation Certificate	Trades Certificate	Other Non-University Certificate	University Certificate below Bachelor Level	Bachelor's Degree(s)	University Certificate above Bachelor Level	Master's Degree(s)	Earned Doctorate	Degree in Medicine[c]
British[d]	3.1**	13.2**	16.8**	21.3**	27.3**	39.6**	47.4**	58.3**	76.6**	141.7**
French	0.5	1.7*	3.0**	5.3**	8.1**	2.3*	2.8	1.2	5.4	4.2
Dutch	2.8	2.8	1.6	-2.0	-18.4**	-3.9	-3.9	-12.4*	1.9	-40.6**
German	3.7**	-0.5	-2.1	0.7	3.7	-2.6	-3.4	-7.0	-3.4	-14.7
Other W European	14.0**	5.2	1.0	14.3**	16.2	0.9	-7.4	2.4	6.1	-24.4
Hungarian	-2.4	-2.1	-1.3	-11.3**	-18.7	-2.0	4.4	11.4	-17.0	8.3
Polish	-3.6	-1.1	1.8	1.1	-19.2**	0.6	-3.0	-14.4**	-6.1	-12.5
Ukrainian	2.7	3.1	2.7	4.0**	-14.4**	5.6*	-2.2	-3.4	-13.8	6.3
Balkan	2.4	-3.6	-2.0	5.3	4.6	-2.1	-5.6	-5.8	-8.6	-3.4
Greek	-6.3**	-6.6**	0.4	-1.7	-32.5**	-9.3	-15.7	-2.4	-25.9	-50.1**
Italian	-0.6	2.7*	-0.0	7.1**	8.3	-1.1	-2.1	3.6	-1.8	-26.4*
Portuguese	11.0**	3.1	4.8	2.8	-22.5*	-4.9	5.3	0.6	–	41.7
Spanish	4.1	-14.4**	0.7	-6.0	-13.1	-14.7	0.5	-20.2	48.5	14.6
Jewish	21.9**	8.0**	3.3	3.1	3.2	4.4	6.7	0.7	6.7	-2.2
Arab	1.4	-6.2*	-12.6**	1.6	-22.7**	-17.8**	-22.3**	-18.1**	1.6	-27.7**
West Asian	-5.4	-10.4**	-5.3	-0.6	-10.2	-7.5	-15.6	-18.2**	-25.7	-30.5*
South Asian	2.9	-3.9*	-8.6*	-4.1	-0.7	-17.7**	-12.8*	-18.9**	-6.8	-15.9*
Chinese	-4.4**	5.3*	-3.3	-5.6*	-6.6	-7.3*	-14.1	-10.3*	-26.3**	-15.2*
Filipino	-6.4	-2.1	-12.5**	-8.2*	-7.5	-12.4**	-12.5	-20.9*	13.0	13.0
Vietnamese	0.8	-11.9**	-19.7**	3.2	-19.3*	-12.7*	-39.2**	-6.9	-7.0	-42.7**
Other E & SE Asian	-4.2	-10.2*	-3.7	-6.8	20.2*	-14.6**	-10.1	-12.1	-27.5	-35.1**
Latin American	3.7	-11.7**	-2.3	-29.8**	-7.8	-24.4**	-31.1**	-18.7	-30.4	-40.6
Black	-8.1**	-3.1	-3.3	-10.4**	-3.7	-10.0**	10.6	-12.4	-10.3	-10.2
Aboriginal	-18.8**	-16.0**	-20.0**	-24.7**	-1.9	-8.0	-24.2	-20.2	-49.4	-76.7**
Others	-2.7*	-0.3	-1.7*	-0.9	0.3	-3.7*	-2.5	-6.7*	-2.6	-7.2

Highest Degree Obtained

Source: Public Use Microdata File for Individuals, 1991 Census of Canada.

[a]Controlling for gender, age, marital status, province of residence, metropolitan/non-metropolitan area, geographic mobility, period of immigration, knowledge of official languages, occupation, industrial sector, weeks worked, and part-time/full-time weeks worked.

[b]The earnings of workers of various ethnic origins are expressed as percentage differences from the earnings of workers of British origin in the same educational category. . . . .

[c]Including degrees in medicine, dentistry, veterinary medicine, and optometry.

[d]The category of "no degree, certificate, or diploma" for the British is the base category for other categories for the British. . . . .

*Significant at 0.10

**Significant at 0.05

our model have been taken into account. Similarly, persons of British origin with "no degree, certificate, or diploma" are used as the base category for their British counterparts at other levels of education. Thus, for example, workers of British origin with "high school graduate certificates" earned 13.2% more than their counterparts of British origin, who had "no degree, certificate, or diploma," when all the other factors in our [regression] were taken into account. As also noted, this difference is significant at the 0.05 level.

Looking first at the two "charter groups," it is obvious that the net economic returns to education for workers of British origin is significant, with each advancing educational category providing progressively higher returns. It is clear that the economic value of education for persons of British origin in the Canadian labour market is beyond doubt.

However, of more significance is the somewhat surprising finding that, after the other factors are controlled, persons of French origin at *all* educational levels had earnings above that for persons of British origin. Moreover, at the Bachelor's degree level and below, these differences of income between the French and the British are statistically significant. Hence, whatever may have been the situation in the past, it is clear that any suggestion that today the French are discriminated against in terms of the returns they receive for their education, is clearly not the case. Indeed, especially at lower levels, the French are significantly favoured over the British in terms of this relationship.

Among Europeans, whether from the north, east, or south of Europe, most ethnic groups had approximately the same income levels as their British counterparts with similar education. Notable exceptions were the Dutch and Poles who, in several of the upper educational levels earned significantly less, and those of Jewish ethnicity in the lowest educational categories who earned significantly more. The most significant discrepancies occurred, not in relation to any ethnicity, but in terms of certain educational categories. Thus,

where respondents held either a "university certificate below the bachelor's level" or a "degree in medicine," persons from continental Europe were quite likely to have incomes significantly below that of the British when other factors were taken into account. The frequency of such discrepancies in these two categories suggests that this may have to do with the evaluation of educational qualification at these levels rather than just ethnicity.

In sharp contrast to the situation for Europeans, adjusted earnings of visible minorities were much lower than for the British at most educational levels. Compared to their British counterparts, out of the 10 educational categories, most visible minority groups earned less than their British counterparts in the majority of categories. Moreover, in many of the educational categories, visible minorities earned *significantly* less than their British counterparts.

Given this obvious evidence of discrimination against all visible minority groups, it is difficult to single out any one or two groups as being more hard done by than others. Perhaps persons of Chinese background might fit this category as they earned less than those of British ethnicity in all 10 educational categories and significantly less than the British in 8 of the 10 educational categories. However, Aboriginal Peoples and West Asians also earned less in 10 categories, and most other visible minority groups earned less in nine of them. While the Arabs might seem better off amongst visible minorities in that they earned lower in only 7 categories, they were significantly less in all 7, a level of earnings discrimination surpassed only by those of Chinese ethnicity.

Whereas one might have thought that increased level of education would lead to lower levels of discrimination, there is little in Table 32.1 to support such a position. From high school to doctorate there is clear evidence of lower earnings amongst visible minorities compared to their British counterparts at the same educational level. Thus, all visible minorities earned less than the British at the high school graduate level, at the level of bachelor's degree holder, master's degree holder and, with the exception of Arabs, at the level of doctorate degree holder. Likewise, all visible minorities who held degrees in medicine earned less than their British counterparts, as did all but the Blacks among those who held a university certificate above bachelor's but below master's level. Moreover, in the majority of cases *these differences were either significant or highly significant. In sum, it is clear from these findings that educational achievement at any level fails to protect persons of visible minority background from being disadvantaged in terms of the income they receive.*

SUMMARY AND DISCUSSION

We began this paper with the question, "Does the 'vertical mosaic' still exist?" It has been our assumption that the most appropriate place to look for evidence to either support or refute the vision of Canadian society as a "vertical mosaic" is through an examination of the relationship between ethnicity and income, first controlling for educational level, and then controlling for other key social variables so that this relationship can be measured more directly and precisely.

Our conclusion is that, by 1991, for the majority of ethnic groups in Canada there is no evidence that the traditionally accepted image of a vertical mosaic still remains. Among the two charter groups, the French now earn more for comparable education than their British counterparts when other factors are controlled. Likewise, many ethnic groups from all parts of Europe who had entered Canada with generally little education and hence occupied lower income positions, have now moved up the educational and income hierarchies and there is very little evidence of discrimination against any such ethnic groups.

On the other hand, there is also clear evidence that visible minorities have not fared well. When education and a range of other social variables are controlled, Aboriginal Peoples still remain mired at the bottom of Canadian society. Almost all Asian groups and most of those of Latin American and Middle Eastern ethnicity were also similarly disadvantaged.

In sum, the evidence indicates that similar educational qualifications carried different economic values in the Canadian labour market for individuals of different "racial" origins. All visible minority groups had below-average earnings in each of the categories, while most of those of European ethnicity had above-average earnings.

It is possible that there are some other variables than "race" which systematically operate to discriminate against people of colour in Canadian society. However, the 1991 *Public Use Microdata File for Individuals* permits more "controls" for other possible variables than has ever previously been possible in such a large data set based on Canadian society. Thus, we have controlled for most of the other competing factors and their interaction effects which might conceivably affect the fundamental relationship between education and income that lies at the centre of our analysis. If there are other factors which might affect this relationship, we cannot easily discern what these might be. More importantly, the large literature on the relationship between education, income, and ethnicity in Canada which we have reviewed provides no clue of any other factor or factors which might have such a significant influence.

Consequently, whereas we began this paper with the question, "Does the vertical mosaic still exist?," we must end it with an even more serious question, namely, "Is Canada a racist society?" Canadians have long prided themselves on their policy of ethnic pluralism in contrast to the "melting pot" of the United States. We have also generally seen ourselves as a more racially tolerant society than the American one. However, our data suggest that there are limits to our tolerance of cultural and racial divisions. While we are apparently willing to accept cultural differences (particularly from a wide range of European cultures) in terms of the income received relative to level of education, we show no such tolerance for those who are racially "visible" from the white majority in Canadian society. All our evidence suggests that, while our traditional "vertical mosaic" of ethnic differences may be disappearing, it has been replaced by a strong "coloured mosaic" of racial differences in terms of income rewards and income benefits. While this does not necessarily mean that we have racial discrimination when it comes to other social benefits such as location of residence, access to public facilities, and the extreme forms of discrimination that have characterized some other societies, our evidence leads us to conclude that there *is* some considerable level of racial discrimination in Canada in terms of financial rewards for educational achievement. In this respect at least, yes, we are a racist society.

CRITICAL THINKING QUESTIONS

1. Do contemporary data support Porter's original work in *The Vertical Mosaic*? If so, how? If not, why not?

2. Given the evidence presented in the article, do you feel that Canada is a racist society? What evidence from your own community supports your position?

3. What role, if any, does a person's level of education have on income in Canada?

NOTE

1. The analysis is based on 425,107 cases. The 1991 PUMFI contains 809,654 cases. Respondents who did not work in 1990 (nearly half of whom were under age 15) have been excluded, thereby dropping the sample to 446,478 cases representing the working population of Canada in 1990. A small number of persons were on employment authorizations or Minister's permits or were refugee claimants. As the income of such persons could have been significantly affected by factors atypical of the Canadian labour market, they have been excluded, thereby reducing the sample to 443,161 cases. Also eliminated were a small number of cases with missing information on education, age, marital status, geographic mobility, and period of immigration (i.e., the factors of earning determination used in this study), thereby reducing the sample to 439,959 cases. Finally, to estimate the net effect of ethnicity on earnings with educational categories, we employed linear least-squares regression with logarithms of earnings as the dependent variable . . . , and this meant persons with zero or negative earnings had to be eliminated. This further reduced the sample to 425,107 persons.

REFERENCES

Agocs, C., and M. Boyd. 1993. The Canadian ethnic mosaic recast for the 1990s. In *Social inequality in Canada: Patterns, problems, policies,* eds. J. Curtis, E. Grabb, and N. Guppy, 330–60. Scarborough, ON: Prentice-Hall Canada Inc.

Barringer, H., and G. Kassebaum. 1989. Asian Indians as a minority in the United States: The effects of education, occupations and gender on income. *Sociological Perspectives,* 32(4): 501–20.

Beggs, J. J. 1995. The institutional environment: Implications for race and gender inequality in the U.S. labour market. *American Sociological Review,* 60 (August): 612–33.

Boyd, M., J. Goyder, F. E. Jones, H. A. McRoberts, P. C. Pineo, and J. Porter. 1981. Status attainment in Canada: Findings of the Canadian mobility study. *Canadian Review of Sociology and Anthropology,* 18(5): 657–73.

Breton, R., and H. Roseborough. 1971. Ethnic differences in status. In *Canadian society: Sociological perspectives,* eds. B. R. Blishen, F. E. Jones, K. D. Naegele, and J. Porter, 450–68. Toronto: Macmillan of Canada Ltd.

Darroch, A. G. 1979. Another look at ethnicity, stratification and social mobility in Canada. *Canadian Journal of Sociology,* 4(1): 1–24.

Featherman, D. L., and R. M. Hauser. 1978. *Opportunity and change.* New York: Academic Press.

Fox, B. J. and J. Fox. 1986. Women in the labour market, 1931–81: Exclusion and competition. *The Canadian Review of Sociology and Anthropology,* 23(1): 1–21.

Geschwender, J. A., and N. Guppy. 1995. Ethnicity, educational attainment and earned income among Canadian-born men and women. *Canadian Ethnic Studies,* 27(1): 67–84.

Halvorsen, R., and R. Palmquist. 1980. The interpretation of dummy variables in semilogarithmic equations. *American Economic Review,* 70(3): 474–75.

Herberg, E. N. 1990. The ethno-racial socioeconomic hierarchy in Canada: Theory and analysis of the new vertical mosaic. *International Journal of Comparative Sociology,* 31(3–4): 206–20.

Isajiw, W. W., A. Sev'er, and L. Dreidger. 1993. Ethnic identity and social mobility: A test of the "drawback model." *Canadian Journal of Sociology,* 18(2): 177–96.

Jabbra, N. W., and R. L. Cosper. 1988. Ethnicity in Atlantic Canada: A survey. *Canadian Ethnic Studies,* 20(3): 6–27.

Lautard, E. H., and N. Guppy. 1990. The vertical mosaic revisited: Occupational differentials among Canadian ethnic groups. In *Race and ethnic relations in Canada,* ed. P. S. Li, 189–208. Toronto: Oxford University Press.

Lautard, E. H., and D. J. Loree. 1984. Ethnic stratification in Canada, 1931–1971. *Canadian Journal of Sociology,* 9: 333–43.

Li, P. S. 1988. *Ethnic inequality in a class society.* Toronto: Thompson Educational Publishing Inc.

Nakhaie, M. R. 1995. Ownership and management position of Canadian ethnic groups in 1973 and 1989. *Canadian Journal of Sociology,* 20(2): 167–92.

Ornstein, M. D. 1981. The occupational mobility of men in Ontario. *The Canadian Review of Sociology and Anthropology,* 18(2): 181–215.

Pineo, P. C. 1976. Social mobility in Canada: The current picture. *Sociological Focus,* 9(2): 109–23.

Pineo, P. C., and J. Porter. 1985. Ethnic origin and occupational attainment. In *Ascription and achievement: Studies in mobility and status attainment in Canada,* eds. M. Boyd, J. Goyder, F. E. Jones, H. A. McRoberts, P. C. Pineo, and J. Porter, 357–92. Ottawa: Carleton University Press.

Porter, J. 1965. *The vertical mosaic.* Toronto: University of Toronto Press.

Reitz, J. G. 1980. *The survival of ethnic groups.* Toronto: McGraw-Hill Ryerson, Ltd.

Royal Commission on Bilingualism and Biculturalism, Canada. 1969. *Report of the Royal Commission on Bilingualism and Biculturalism,* Vol. 3A. Ottawa: Queen's Printer.

Sandefur, G. D., and W. J. Scott. 1983. Minority group status and the wages of Indian and Black males. *Social Science Research,* 12(1): 44–68.

Shamai, S. 1992. Ethnicity and educational achievement in Canada: 1941–1981. *Canadian Ethnic Studies,* 24(1): 41–57.

Statistics Canada. 1993. *Standard occupational classification, 1991.* Ottawa: Ministry of Industry, Science and Technology.

———. 1994. User documentation for public use microdata file for individuals, 1991 Census. Catalogue No.: 48-030E. Ottawa: Statistics Canada.

Tepperman, L. 1975. *Social mobility in Canada.* Toronto: McGraw-Hill Ryerson.

Winn, C. 1988. The socio-economic attainment of visible minorities: Facts and policy implications. In *Social inequality in Canada: Patterns, problems, policies,* eds. J. Curtis, E. Grabb, N. Guppy, and S. Gilbert, 195–213. Scarborough, ON: Prentice-Hall Canada.

33

Introduction to *The Canadian Fact Book on Poverty*

DAVID P. ROSS, KATHERINE J. SCOTT, PETER J. SMITH

Social
Stratification

CLASSIC

CONTEMPORARY

CROSS-CULTURAL

This classic statement summarizes what it means to be poor in Canada and introduces students to politically contentious issues such as the definition and measurement of poverty. This book is published by the Canadian Council on Social Development, an organization that conducts research on poverty and economic inequality in Canada. The CCSD maintains a website that features some of the most recent poverty statistics available.

When most Canadians think of poverty, the image is of sickly children on the edge of starvation. In highly industrialized societies, however, this scene is not typical. What prevails instead is deprivation and need. In Canada, people suffer deeply not because the necessities of life barely exist for the population at large—the state of affairs in many Third World countries—but because an unequal distribution of income blocks access to Canada's abundance. Poverty in this country is a matter not of starving but rather of begging for food at food banks and shelters, and of being shunted from one substandard shelter arrangement to another. For an increasing number of people, it even means living on the street and panhandling. This dreary picture is the result of an unequal distribution of riches rather than a lack of riches.

Poverty of the type typically found in industrial countries is a serious matter, and pockets of Third World poverty do exist in Canada, in some of our inner cities and on the reserves of Aboriginal peoples. There is no shortage of statistics documenting a link between poverty in Canada and various debilitating behaviours and conditions. For the sake of the many sceptics, let it be stressed that the authors do not claim that lack of income itself causes these human conditions—one cannot demonstrate causation with statistics—but only that these conditions are strongly associated with low income. The question of causation is left to the reader's own judgement.

The statistics are especially striking for children—a segment of the population that is unequipped to overcome poverty by any efforts of its own. Income levels and the well-being of Canadian children are undeniably linked, as a

Source: David P. Ross, Katherine J. Scott, and Peter J. Smith. 2000. In *The Canadian Fact Book on Poverty*, pp. 1–7. Ottawa: The Canadian Council on Social Development.

pioneering study by the Canadian Council on Social Development (CCSD) has documented. Some of these links are:

- Poor children (family income less than $20,000) are 1.3 times more likely to be growing up in substandard housing as are children from middle-income families (family income $45,000), and 2.4 times as likely as are children from high-income families (income above $80,000).

- Poor children are 1.9 times more likely to be living in neighbourhoods with lots of problems such as fighting, drug dealing and vandalism, than are children in middle-income families, and 2.4 times more likely than are children in high-income families.

- Poor children are 1.4 times more likely to engage in aggressive behaviour than are children in middle-income families or higher-income families.

- Poor children are 1.5 and 1.7 times as likely to be hyperactive than are children from middle- and high-income families, respectively.

- Poor children are more likely to exhibit delinquent behaviours compared to middle- and high-income families: 1.8 and 2.6 times respectively.

- Serious health problems that affect a child's functioning such as vision, hearing, speech, mobility and cognition are 1.7 and 2.6 times more likely to be found in poor children than in children from middle- and high-income families, respectively.

- Four- and five-year-old children from poor families are 2.2 and 4.5 times more likely to exhibit delayed development on vocabulary tests than are the children from middle- and high-income families. In fact, over one-third (36 per cent) of poor children are judged to have delayed language development.

- Children from poor families are 1.8 times as likely to be registered in special education classes than are children from middle- and high-income families. Children enrolled in special education classes are at higher risk for falling behind in school and dropping out before high school completion.

- Poor children are 1.3 times less likely to participate in organized sports than are children from middle-income families and 2.8 times less likely than are children from high-income families. Almost three-quarters (72 per cent) of poor children do not participate compared to only one-quarter of children from high-income families.

- Older teens aged 16 to 19 years are normally expected to be either in school or in a job. However, poor children are 2.5 and 4.4 times more likely to be engaged in neither activity (in a sense, they are "idle") compared to teens from middle- and higher-income families.

This partial catalogue of misfortune makes clear that children who grow up in low-income families stand out in a variety of ways from their better-off peers. They are less healthy, have less access to skill-building activities, have more destructive habits and behaviours, live more stressful lives, and are subject to more humiliation. In short, they have less stable and less secure existences, and as a result are less likely to be secure as adults.

In a day and age when education, emotional maturity, leadership, and social and communication skills are prized as essential for prospering in an increasingly knowledge-based society, it is not promising that so many Canadian children are starting off with such disadvantage. The days of just making sure that children had enough to eat and a roof over their heads in order to produce strong arms and backs is long gone. The skills and attributes valued today require more than a start in life at a minimum subsistence level. In fact, the CCSD study (from which the above findings are taken) shows that after studying 27 living conditions and outcomes, the likelihood of a poor outcome dramatically diminishes up to a family income level of $30,000 in 80 per cent of the cases. Further, in 50 per cent of the cases, risk rapidly diminishes up to the $40,000 family income level. If a high level of child well-being is an important objective of a society, these are the income levels that need to be discussed in terms of setting a floor on income inequality in Canada.

The cataloguing of misfortune is not restricted to children. Adults with low incomes also suffer debilitating conditions according to a Statistics Canada study:

- Adults in low-income households (less than $30,000 income) are 4.6 times more likely to report being in poor or only fair health compared to high-income adults (over $60,000), and 2.2 times more likely than middle-income adults ($30,000 to $60,000). In fact, one-fifth of poor adults report being in poor or only fair health.

- Serious health problems that affect an adult's functioning such as vision, hearing, speech, mobility and cognition are 1.3 and 2.0 times more likely to be found in poor adults than in middle- and high-income adults respectively. Two-fifths of low-income adults have these health problems.

- Suffering from chronic health conditions such as asthma, high blood pressure, stomach ulcers and the effects of stroke is more prevalent in low-income adults. Whereas 55 per cent of low-income adults had two or more of these conditions, this was true for only 32 per cent of middle-income adults and 13 per cent of those with high incomes.

- The mental state of adults who responded to the Statistics Canada survey has been summed up in a mental health distress index. The results show that low-income adults are 2.4 times more likely to have a high distress score than are high-income adults, and 1.8 times more likely than are middle-income adults.

- Low-income adults are 1.3 times more likely to express low self-esteem compared to high-income adults. Esteem relates to whether a person feels they have a number of good qualities, are worth as much as others, have a positive attitude towards self, and whether they believe they are failures or not.

These results for adults cannot confirm that the debilitating conditions in each case are caused by low income. In some cases, it may be that the conditions are the cause of low incomes. However, this brief portrait does confirm that low income is associated with a disproportionate number of special problems. Thus, to integrate these people into society requires a special effort. To facilitate a permanent escape from poverty, such an effort must include special services to assist people in overcoming or adapting to some of the problems as well as income transfers to address their current poverty.

While noting the links between income and many child and adult outcomes, it would be gratifying to report that the inequality between rich and poor is narrowing and as a consequence, some of the riskier outcomes are being ameliorated. Unfortunately, the opposite is true—inequality is widening. For example, between 1973 and 1997, the share of total earnings in Canada going to the bottom 20 per cent of families with children fell steeply from a paltry 5.3 per cent to 2.6 per cent, which represents several billion dollars in total. In contrast, the share of earnings going to the top 20 per cent increased from an already generous 38.4 per cent to 42.8 per cent. This is income redistribution in reverse. Fortunately, after government transfers and income taxes, the picture improves: the bottom 20 per cent received 7.7 per cent of all income in 1973, but even this small amount had deteriorated to 7.0 per cent in 1997, while the top 20 per cent increased their share from 35.5 per cent to 37.2 per cent. So, over time, both labour market earnings and government assistance have let down the poor.

A DAY IN A LIFE OF POVERTY

Aside from the negative links between low income and child well-being, what does it mean in real-life terms to be raised in poverty in a well-off industrialized country such as Canada? Although some individuals raised in poor families turn out to be happy and successful adults, such exceptions do not disprove the rule. Most poor Canadian individuals or families suffer the effects of continual deprivation: a relentless feeling of being boxed in; a feeling that life is dictated by the requirements simply of surviving each day. In this way of life there is no choice, there is no flexibility, and if something unexpected happens—such as sickness, accident, family death, fire or theft, rent increase—there is no buffer to deal with the emergency. Life is just today, because tomorrow offers no hope.

Perhaps the easiest way to comprehend what a day in a life of poverty is like is to describe a family's left-over income after it pays for basic shelter, food and clothing. How much money does a typical poor family consisting of two adults and two children, and living in a large urban area, have at its disposal? In 1997, while the traditional Statistics Canada low income cut-off line for such a family was set at $28,100, the average two-parent family with two children was in fact below this line by an amount equal to $10,050, leaving it with $18,050 annually on which to live.

Compare this to the family's basic expenditures on shelter, food and clothing. Using the Canadian Mortgage and Housing Corporation (CMHC) survey of shelter costs across the country, the median rent for a three-bedroom apartment amounted to $8,495 per year (weekly equivalent of $40.84 per person). To adhere to Agriculture Canada's Nutritious Food Basket as a guide to basic food costs, the family required $6,885 (weekly equivalent of $33.10 per person). Using the Montreal Diet Dispensary guidelines for basic living, estimated clothing costs totalled $2,208 (weekly equivalent of $10.61 per person). This amounts to $17,588 per year for the typical poor four-member family. Deducting this from its gross income of $18,050 leaves a surplus of only $462 for the year, or $2.22 per person per week.

This $2.22 per week must be used to meet all other needs such as personal care, household needs, furniture, telephone, transportation, school supplies, health care and so on. There is

no money for entertainment, recreation, reading material, insurance, and charitable or religious donations.

It is easy to understand why poor families:

- cut into their budget for essentials;
- rent substandard housing;
- move often in attempts to save rent;
- purchase poor-quality food that lacks freshness or variety;
- supplement their food budget with trips to food banks;
- own a minimum selection of mainly used clothing.

DEFINING AND MEASURING POVERTY

There are two basic approaches to defining and measuring poverty in Canada. When taken to their respective extremes, they establish the possible income bounds of poverty. Numerous intermediate measures fall between these extremes.

- ***Absolute measure:*** The first approach is based on the belief that one can determine an *absolute* measure of poverty by examining an essential basket of goods and services deemed necessary for physical survival. The cost of this basket represents an objective dollar measure of poverty. The strictest application of this approach results in a standard of living sufficient only to keep the human body together. This purely physical approach stipulates a budget whose components are food provided by a charitable group or food bank, shelter provided by a community hostel, second-hand clothing, and access to basic remedial health care. The poverty line implied by such a budget would be very low; an annual income in the order of $2,000 per person would probably cover it.

    The consequence of the absolute approach, if rigorously applied, is an utter absence of choice and flexibility in how one lives. The shape of one's life is determined rigidly by the requirements of a fixed and rock-bottom physical existence.

- ***Relative approach:*** At the other definitional extreme is the *relative* approach, which is based on the belief that any definition of poverty must take into account social and psychological as well as physical well-being. The relative approach is based on social inclusion and equity, that is, on some notion of the extent to which society should tolerate inequality in the distribution of income. It argues that someone who has so little that he or she stands out in relation to the surrounding community will feel marginalized. Marginalized people, whether children or adults, affect the social cohesion of a community because they no longer feel part of what they see as an indifferent or hostile society.

In the rich countries of the industrialized world, the income level associated with a relative definition of poverty will be many times the level required to assure physical survival. In fact, an argument frequently voiced against relative definitions of poverty is that a typical poor family in Canada would be wealthy if the family lived in the Third World. But poor Canadians do not live in the Third World; they live in communities that have First World living costs and in which wealth surrounds them daily. Hence the justification for a relative measure.

Not surprisingly, there is no consensus on the question of which basic approach should be adopted. Most approaches compromise between the two, that is, they attempt to define a basket of goods and services that assures a minimum standard of living which is acceptable in social as well as purely physical terms. The difference in these approaches is their judgement of what constitutes a minimum that respects the need to function with dignity in society. The difference between the lower guidelines based on absolute or physical definitions of poverty, and the higher ones based on relative or social definitions, is considerable.

To a great extent, the enduring debate about the proper definition of poverty is academic. Although poverty standards have been loosely used as a guide to the level of payments under the federal government's elderly benefit programs, and to determine eligibility for school lunch programs and the like, they have not been used to set the level of the income safety net. The income of poor households falls well below the recommended incomes of the most widely accepted definitions of poverty. For example, the income of the average Canadian poor family in 1997 was $8,559 below the widely recognized low-income line established by Statistics Canada (and $8,942 below in the case of a lone-parent mother). It is accurate to conclude, therefore, that basic assistance to Canada's poor population is guided mainly by the absolute approach to the definition of poverty. The growth and persistence of food banks and the homeless underscore this conclusion.

CRITICAL THINKING QUESTIONS

1. What is the difference between a relative and absolute poverty line? Do you think that poverty should be measured on a relative or absolute basis?

2. Why do you think there is so much debate about where the poverty line should be drawn? Where do you think it should be placed? The Statistics Canada low-income cut-off for a family of four living in a large urban area is $39,399 (before taxes). Is this too generous or too stingy? Prepare an approximate budget (rent, food, clothing, transportation, etc.).

3. What is the government's role in combating poverty? Do you think that market forces are capable of dealing with poverty on their own? Can you think of countries where there are no welfare state programs? What is the likely result of not having any welfare programs?

34

Free Trade and the Third World

PETER URMETZER

The debate about the relationship between the First and Third World is a seemingly unending one. Are First World countries wealthy because they exploit poor countries or because they are more productive? This reading examines the role of international institutions, including the World Bank, World Trade Organization, and the International Monetary Fund, and how they govern economic interaction between rich and poor countries.

True individual freedom cannot exist without economic security and independence. People who are hungry and out of a job are the stuff of which dictatorships are made.

—Franklin D. Roosevelt

FREE TRADE AND THE THIRD WORLD

Based on the lottery that is life, or at least so the story goes, some countries are naturally better endowed with resources than others. Some, like Canada, find themselves with vast tracts of timber, whereas others, like Brazil, may have perfect conditions for growing coffee. One country's workforce may be skilled at manufacturing automobiles, another's at producing shirts, and if all engage in trade, according to the theory, all will

Source: Peter Urmetzer. 2003. In *From Free Trade to Forced Trade: Canada in the Global Economy*, pp. 165–169, 170–178, 179–183. Toronto: Penguin Canada.

be better off. This makes one wonder, why do poor countries, at least for the most part, continue to be poor? Not only that, why, as we shall soon see, is this gap widening? The answer may, ironically, have less to do with free trade than with too much interference by the West. By trying their best to ensure that the market system rules supreme in the Third World, the World Bank and the International Monetary Fund (IMF), and to some degree the World Trade Organization (WTO), might well have made things worse.

The World Bank and the IMF

The two institutions just mentioned, the World Bank and the IMF, are frequently mentioned in the same breath as the WTO, and for good reason: They share a common history. The World Bank and the IMF, and to a lesser degree the WTO, are all part of a monetary framework designed by Britain and the United States around the end of the Second World War.

The World Bank and the IMF are often referred to as the Bretton Woods Twins, and are considered sister institutions in that they fulfill similar roles. Both are located in Washington, DC, which should give some indication of who dominates these institutions. Another clue that hints at the cozy relationship between the US administration and these organizations is that some commentators have come to include the World Bank and the IMF when they refer to Washington (or the Washington Consensus). The World Bank and the IMF are a direct result of the Bretton Woods negotiations, which took place in New Hampshire in 1944. Given the geopolitical climate at the end of the Second World War, it should come as no surprise that only two countries mattered in these negotiations: Great Britain (represented by John Maynard Keynes) and the United States (represented by Harry Dexter White). After nearly six decades, these institutions are now well integrated into the American world order. With a few exceptions, such as Cuba and North Korea, this vision has been adopted around the world. By default, the free market system has replaced much of the socialist system in what used to be referred to as the Second World, the erstwhile Soviet Union.

The World Bank and the IMF epitomize the relationship between the First and the Third Worlds, a system in which political power directly corresponds to economic strength. Being the world's wealthiest nation in such a system, the United States reigns. This hierarchy is explicit within the World Bank and the IMF, as voting strength is directly related to the size of a country's economy. On this basis, the United States effectively has veto power over any decisions these institutions make. Although the IMF has provided assistance to countries in the First World, all World Bank loans (with the exception of a small number in its early days) and the majority of IMF interventions have been in the Third World. And as is often the case in these

situations, these monies come with strings attached. It is not altogether surprising that these strings can be traced to Anglo-Saxon ideas about the free market: no social programs, no deficit, low inflation, privatization, and no subsidies, with few allowances for labour or environmental standards. Not only are these policies an integral part of these institutions' ideologies, but they are explicitly practised in what are called the Structural Adjustment Programs (SAP).

World Bank

There is no such institution as the World Bank. It is merely a term of convenience used to describe two related institutions: the IBRD (International Bank for Reconstruction and Development) and the IDA (International Development Association). Both institutions, as well as the IMF and the WTO, are also part of the UN. The World Bank's headquarters is located, as already mentioned, in Washington, DC, with offices in New York, Paris, Geneva, London, and Tokyo.[1]

The majority of loans by the World Bank are from the IBRD. In 1999, for example, of the US $29 billion lent out by the World Bank, $22 billion, or around three-quarters of the total, originated with the IBRD. The other 25 percent of loans were associated with the IDA. Together these institutions have lent an amount fast approaching half a trillion dollars since their inception, a tidy sum, but one that still greatly underestimates the power of the World Bank. When the World Bank first lends money to a Third World country, the loan serves as a signal to private investors that the country is a safe haven for investment. In 1998, of the long-term debt owed by the Third World (in contrast with the short-term debt that is the bailiwick of the IMF), only 16 percent was owed to the World Bank. The other 84 percent was owed to private banks (57 percent) and other governments (27 percent). These figures do not include investments such as foreign direct investment, or FDI (the establishment of branch plants, buying of real estate, etc.). This private/public mix tends to favour public debt as risk increases. For example, 72 percent of South American debt is held in private hands, compared with only 24 percent in equatorial Africa.

There is considerable evidence that the bank was instrumental in the proliferation of Third World debt. In no way was this due to malice, but rather to two unfortunate and unanticipated developments. One, as part of its mandate, the World Bank attempted to help countries industrialize, which included sponsoring megaprojects such as dams, bridges, and other infrastructure. In order to finance these projects, Third World countries were encouraged to borrow. At first this did not present much of a problem, as in the 1960s and 1970s interest rates were low. But this would soon change. Central banks around the world—including the Federal Reserve in the United States, the Bundesbank in West Germany, and the Bank of Canada in Canada—declared war on inflation in the mid-1970s. Their primary policy instrument in this war was high interest rates. This meant that both debts and interest payments everywhere, including those of the Third World, skyrocketed. Put simply, when the Third World was first seduced into going on a borrowing spree money was cheap; when it was time to pay, it was dear.

The second reason for the Third World debt crisis is less well recognized. The West reasoned that if countries wanted to get on the right track towards modernization, they needed to trade more. More trade required that poor countries produce things that could be sold in foreign markets. As it was, these countries were primarily engaged in subsistence agriculture, and Western consumers were not all that interested in buying more rice or corn. Change, for the most part, meant the exploitation of natural resources and a shift from food to cash crops (crops like coffee, which could be sold on the international market rather than consumed locally). An increased

reliance on cash crops and natural resources, encouraged by the World Bank throughout the Third World, soon resulted in world markets being flooded with commodities like coffee, cocoa, rubber, and copper. And as any student of economics knows, when there are too many products on the market, prices drop. Things even got worse. In the push to modernize, Third World countries were also encouraged to export so they could acquire foreign exchange (US dollars, German marks) needed to buy products like machinery and oil, essential ingredients for industrialization. But this little plan soon backfired. Growing cash crops instead of food for local consumption led to increased reliance on food imports, which became relatively more expensive as commodity prices fell and local currencies lost value.

In short, the increase in interest rates coincided with falling commodity prices. Through no fault of its own, the Third World was suddenly faced with higher expenditures (in terms of increased debt maintenance) and lower income (due to falling commodity prices). Rather than going towards the purchase of products to modernize Third World economies as originally intended, foreign exchange went to pay foreign debts. It is important to keep in mind that these developments were not the result of the natural workings of the market but were initially orchestrated by the First World. In direct contradiction of free market doctrines, these programs were forced onto poor countries, illustrating once again that laissez-faire is planned. And badly planned at that.

Consequently, Third World debt soared, resulting in the 1980s debt crisis. At least from the perspective of the Third World, this crisis has yet to be resolved. Rather than take the blame and eliminate Third World debt, or at least substantially alleviate it, the World Bank used this opportunity to provide the Third World with another dose of First World medicine. When a country is in danger of defaulting on its debt, the World Bank and the IMF step in with emergency measures. The logic behind these programs is that the only remedy that will work is strict adherence to free market principles. These programs, commonly referred to as austerity programs, are officially known as Structural Adjustment Programs (SAP). These include privatization and downsizing of government; the promotion of exports and liberalization of imports; reduction or even elimination of subsidies to agriculture, food, health care, and education; and programs to curb inflation (including higher interest rates and reduction in wages).

Not surprisingly, these programs have failed to meet their objectives. Third World debt has continued to increase and its economies have faltered. The IMF and the World Bank have come under increasing scrutiny for their policies, both from the inside (including Joseph Stiglitz, the 2001 Nobel Prize winner in economics and former chief economist of the World Bank, who shared the prize with George Akerlof and Michael Spence) and the outside (the most prominent of their many critics being Paul David Hewson; a.k.a. the short guy with the funny glasses; a.k.a. Bono, the lead singer of the pop group U2).

The IMF (International Monetary Fund)

Like the World Bank, the IMF is part of the UN and a direct result of the Bretton Woods negotiations. The IMF, in particular, has been criticized for being overly secretive, and has historically been much less open to criticism than the World Bank. The IMF's major concern is international monetary co-operation and stability. When an emergency situation arises, such as balance of payment problems, currency instability, or inability to meet financial obligations, the IMF steps in and provides emergency loans. As of 2001, the IMF had approximately US $65 billion of loans outstanding. As with World Bank loans, monies are tied to SAPs, which gives the IMF considerable sway over how a country's economy

is managed. In comparison with the World Bank, details of what the IMF does are less clear. This can partly be blamed on the already mentioned lack of transparency. The World Bank also has the advantage of sharing similarities with regular banks, in that it lends money, which is easy to understand. Besides having no domestic counterpart, the responsibilities of the IMF are a little more technical. Furthermore, the IMF's mandate has changed considerably since its inception.

The primary role of the IMF following the Second World War was to supervise exchange rates. This was known as the Bretton Woods exchange system, whereby each country's currency was pegged to the American dollar, which, in turn, was pegged to the price of gold at US $35 per ounce. Some Canadians may remember that the price of foreign currencies, including that of the American dollar, fluctuated little between the war and the mid-1970s. For a variety of reasons, former US president Richard Nixon abandoned that system in 1971, and currencies were allowed to float. Suddenly, the price of currencies around the world became much more volatile (and as Canadians know too well, seemed only to drop). With the closing of the gold window, as it is sometimes referred to, one of the major responsibilities of the IMF had evaporated. But other commitments soon presented themselves. With the rapid rise in oil prices throughout the 1970s (which hurt importing countries) and the increase in interest rates (which hurt indebted countries), the IMF began to concentrate on short-term loans to countries that encountered balance of payment difficulties. Its role was further expanded when a series of Third World countries, starting with Mexico in 1982, came perilously close to defaulting on their debts.

The IMF also played a prominent role in the 1998 Asian crisis, but this debacle differed significantly from the 1980s debt crisis. The latter was largely caused by the increase in interest rates and affected mostly governments and big private banks. In contrast, in the Asian crisis the majority of investments were speculative in nature and involved private investors. Much of the foreign financing that had gone into Indonesia, South Korea, and Thailand went into risky ventures such as real estate speculation, and critics have pointed out that IMF loans did more for American, Japanese, and European investors than for the governments directly affected by the crisis. While the IMF guaranteed the investments of Westerners, austerity measures imposed on Indonesia, including the prohibition of subsidies for rice and cooking fuel, almost certainly contributed to the social unrest that the country underwent in 1999. According to the rules of the market, investors who greedily bankrolled foreign undertakings they knew little about should have suffered their own losses. But as it turned out, this was just another example of how institutions like the IMF are unable to stand by and do nothing when the judgment of the market fails to meet their expectations.

The Theory Behind Development

Essentially, the World Bank, the IMF, and the WTO are attempting to universalize the doctrines of laissez-faire, an ideology that originated in Great Britain in the eighteenth and nineteenth centuries. From there, mirroring colonization, it travelled to North America, Australia, and New Zealand, where the ideology still dominates. These ideas were also exported to other British colonies, including India and South Africa, and leaped the English Channel to the Continent, but there laissez-faire found a less welcoming environment and was tempered by the moderating influences of the host countries. In the twentieth century, dissemination of the free market ideology has continued unabated. It has now become the mission of institutions like the WTO and the World Bank to disseminate and enforce these ideas in the Third World.

Another important ideology that underlies institutions like the World Bank, the WTO, and

the IMF is the old saw, promulgated by early social theorists, that societies must go through an evolution of stages on their way to industrial status. It is worthwhile noting that this thesis, usually referred to as modernization theory, has, in a variety of incarnations, been around for centuries, and yet its more optimistic prophecies have never come to fruition. This theory became fashionable in eighteenth- and nineteenth-century Europe, and attempted to explain the transition from an agricultural to an urban society. This change was accompanied by much tumult, and social theorists shared a desire to make sense of it all. Whereas some, like Adam Smith, saw order, others, like Karl Marx, saw chaos. Based on their observations, these theorists sought to establish principles from which they could generalize; that is, to apply their theories to all times and places. Not surprisingly, these theorists all observed a society that was slowly evolving from agrarian to industrial status. This evolutionary element provided an integral component for many theories, including those of French theorist Emile Durkheim, the Englishman Herbert Spencer, and the German Ferdinand Tonnies. All contrasted a decaying feudal, traditional, or agricultural order with a burgeoning industrial, urban, or modern one. Marx's theory stood apart only in that it had more stages—primitive communism, slavery, feudalism, capitalism, socialism, and communism—but the underlying evolutionary impetus was the same. Many academics have judged these theories as perspicacious for their time, but are reluctant to vouch for their universal application. This hesitancy is understandable for, given the benefit of hindsight, we know that not all societies have gone through these same stages of evolution. As a matter of fact, to this day there are still more people on this planet toiling away in agrarian than industrial societies.

The fact that theories of evolution have been discredited by more than two hundred years of history has not discouraged twentieth-century pundits from continuing with this train of thought. Today these theories comfortably fit under the rubric of modernization theory. Its proponents point to countries like Taiwan and South Korea as evidence of what is in store for the rest of the world. Beyond that, they forecast the eventual industrialization, and eventually post-industrialization, of all countries. In essence, these theories are no different than those espoused by theorists in the eighteenth century. The only difference is that today this thesis has left the theoretical realm and found practical applications through institutions like the World Bank and the WTO.

Suffering under the delusion that the West's economic success is rooted in laissez-faire, organizations like the WTO and the World Bank have put their faith in the market to solve the problem of global inequality. These institutions, as well as free traders in general, allege that open markets will eventually increase the wealth of all those who choose to participate in the global economy. Advocates of free trade have used this line of reasoning in a roundabout way to attack anti–free traders, accusing them of being anti-poor. They argue that by denying poor countries the opportunity to trade, anti-globalists also deny them a chance to become wealthy. But this road to wealth, we are forewarned, is a long one, and we cannot expect results to happen overnight.

In 1950, the GDP per capita of industrialized countries (excluding Japan) was approximately double that of Third World countries. By 1998, this gap had widened considerably, as the industrial countries' GDP per capita had increased to approximately five times that of the Third World. Whereas that of Asia and Latin America increased marginally (approximately doubling), GDP per capita failed to increase in Africa and dropped to 1950s levels after the fall of communism in the erstwhile Soviet countries.

And the further one goes back, the more apparent becomes the growing disparity in wealth between the First and Third Worlds. Angus Maddison, an economic historian with the OECD (Organisation for Economic Co-operation and Development), has examined the incomes of six regions over a 172-year period (Western Europe,

North America, and Australia make up one region; Eastern Europe, Southern Europe, Latin America, Asia, and Africa are the other five).[2] In 1820, the ratio of economic output between the richest and poorest of these regions was 3:1. From that date on, the world economy grew at a monumental rate, although this growth affected each region differently. This should not be unexpected, given colonization as well as huge gaps in technology. Trade throughout that period also increased, particularly in the post-war era. At any rate, between 1820 and 1992 the ratio between the richest and poorest regions had grown from the original 3:1 to 16:1. When countries are considered instead of regions, this disparity becomes even more dramatic, growing from 3:1 in 1820 to 72:1 in 1992. At no time throughout this period did this process of polarization let up, let alone reverse. This even applies to the very prosperous post-war era, a period throughout which trade increased dramatically. The World Bank, despite claims that globalization is supposed to provide opportunities for less-developed countries, has published similar data. In terms of wealth, then, the world was a much more egalitarian place in the 1820s than in the 1990s, casting a shadow of doubt on theories that project a better future for the Third World on the basis of free trade or industrialization. Such promises have failed to materialize in the past 180 years and there is no reason to believe that they will bear fruit any time soon.

These theories, as advocated by the World Bank, and the WTO, have failed to produce the predicted results because they ignore the inter-relationships between countries, particularly that of the First and Third Worlds. Sociologists are keenly aware of how power imbalances affect relationships, whether between individuals or groups. From that perspective, it becomes clear that not all countries are equal. Suriname cannot boast the same influence on the world stage as the United States, for example. The reason, as Andre Gunder Frank has pointed out, is a history of colonialism. While that era has largely come to an end, First World countries continue to exert considerable power over the Third World in other, primarily economic, ways.

One reason that this disparity of wealth endures is precisely because of organizations like the World Bank and the WTO. Third World debt in 1998 was US $2.4 trillion (that's twelve zeros and approximately three and a half times Canada's yearly GDP). That same year, in order to service that debt, Third World countries paid US $296 billion in interest payments. This is more money than travelled the other direction in terms of aid. In other words, the industrialized world continues to be a net benefactor in this relationship. In the process, Third World economies are slowly being enslaved on account of their debts. For example, in Zambia 30 percent of government spending goes to paying off foreign debt, with only 10 percent going to social services, including health and education.

Ironically, despite their allegiance to free markets, these institutions are unable to keep their hands off them. First, they feel the inevitable evolutionary process towards modernization has to be nudged along, which does not necessarily have to be a bad thing. The transference of technology, knowledge, or capital investment can be of utmost value to poor countries. But even if modernization theory were correct in its fundamental premise that societies evolve, it does not necessarily follow that this process can be hurried along. There is good reason to believe that too quick a transition can ruin, rather than benefit, an economy. Witness, for example, the devastation that followed the sudden collapse of the Soviet economy a little over a decade ago. The transition from socialism to free market meant the economy went into free fall. When change is too rapid, or imposed from the outside as is often the case in the Third World, the effect may not always be that favourable. Second, the World Bank has always worked on the assumption that what is good for the First World must be equally good for the Third. But taken out of their Western context, free trade, privatization, and strict monetary policies have caused more ill to Third World

economies than good. Not that free trade, privatization, and strict monetary policies have been all that successful in the First World either, but such policies make even less sense in economies that are still primarily agricultural.

And last, but not least, the evidence showing that First World countries are wealthy because of their strict adherence to free market principles is far from conclusive. First, the benefits of free trade, as we have discussed, are dubious to begin with. Second, First World countries all have generous education and health programs, which they sometimes deny to Third World countries. (Even in the United States, often considered a welfare-state laggard, 45 percent of health care is publicly funded, which amounted to US $522 billion in 1998. Publicly funded education cost another US $498 billion in the 1998–1999 school year, which adds up to over $1 trillion in government expenditures on a yearly basis for these two programs alone.) Industrialized countries also have huge civil services that provide many well-paying jobs. Third, there is consideration neither of differences in culture, nor of the power relationship, between the First and Third Worlds. When intervention is neutral (that is, money comes with no strings attached), it may not be altogether bad. But as we have seen, in its eagerness to pull the Third World out of poverty, First World policies have only succeeded in making the Third World go into more debt.

This is not to say that debt should be avoided at all costs. In order for economies to grow, they require capital, and borrowing funds can play an invaluable role in this process. The expansion of the British Empire was expedited by the availability of easy money, and many governments today borrow money to invest in their future. But there is a crucial difference between First and Third World debt, in that the former is usually owed internally and the latter externally. The biggest shortcoming associated with foreign debt is the control that the lender is able to exert over the indebted. It is precisely for this reason that many religions have proscribed debt. The Bible counsels that "the borrower is a servant to the lender." In that sense, large debts have enslaved Third World countries, making it difficult for them to become independent. Programs that have attempted to alleviate debts through rescheduling, such as the notorious SAP, have only succeeded in imposing more Western control over the Third World.

CRITICAL THINKING QUESTIONS

1. Why do you think that some countries are rich and others are poor? It is often believed that people in Third World countries are less motivated than people in industrialized countries. Do you agree? Do you think the root cause for global economic inequality is structural (e.g., a history of colonialism) or behavioural (e.g., poor economic management)?

2. Why are the World Bank and the International Monetary Fund often referred to as sister institutions? Do you think that the poorest countries should repay their debts or (as Bono from U2 has championed) their debts should be forgiven?

3. Many cultures in the past have made it illegal to charge interest on loans. Is debt necessarily a bad thing? What is the power relationship between those who lend money and those who owe? Discuss the advantages and disadvantages of borrowing money for various institutions, including governments and corporations. What about the role of debt in your own life (e.g., purchasing a car or an education)?

NOTES

1. The factual information about the World Bank is from its website, as well as from Susan George and Fabrizio Sabelli. *Faith and Credit: The World Bank's Secular Empire*. Toronto: Penguin Books, 1994.

2. Angus Maddison. 1995. *Monitoring the World Economy, 1820–1992*. Paris: OECD.

Gender

CLASSIC

CONTEMPORARY

CROSS-CULTURAL

35

Sex and Temperament in Three Primitive Societies

MARGARET MEAD

The work of anthropologist Margaret Mead laid the foundation for much of our contemporary sociological research and debate on gender. Are "masculine" and "feminine" traits innate or learned? Do men and women differ because of nature (heredity) or nurture (socialization)? Based on her studies of three "primitive peoples" in New Guinea, Margaret Mead argues that cultural conditioning is more important than biology in shaping women's and men's behaviour.

We have now considered in detail the approved personalities of each sex among three primitive peoples. We found the Arapesh—both men and women—displaying a personality that, out of our historically limited preoccupations, we would call maternal in its parental aspects, and feminine in its sexual aspects. We found men, as well as women, trained to be cooperative, unaggressive, responsive to the needs and demands of others. We found no idea that sex was a powerful driving force either for men or for women. In marked contrast to these attitudes, we

Source: From *Sex and Temperament in Three Primitive Societies*, pp. 279–88, by Margaret Mead, Copyright © 1935, 1950, 1963, by Margaret Mead. Reprinted by permission of HarperCollins Publishers, Inc./William Morrow.

found among the Mundugumor that both men and women developed as ruthless, aggressive, positively sexed individuals, with the maternal cherishing aspects of personality at a minimum. Both men and women approximated to a personality type that we in our culture would find only in an undisciplined and very violent male. Neither the Arapesh nor the Mundugumor profit by a contrast between the sexes; the Arapesh ideal is the mild, responsive man married to the mild, responsive woman; the Mundugumor ideal is the violent aggressive man married to the violent aggressive woman. In the third tribe, the Tchambuli, we found a genuine reversal of the sex attitudes of our own culture, with the woman the dominant, impersonal, managing partner, the man the less responsible and the emotionally dependent person. These three situations suggest, then, a very definite conclusion. If those temperamental attitudes which we have traditionally regarded as feminine—such as passivity, responsiveness, and a willingness to cherish children—can so easily be set up as the masculine pattern in one tribe, and in another be outlawed for the majority of women as well as for the majority of men, we no longer have any basis for regarding such aspects of behaviour as sex-linked. And this conclusion becomes even stronger when we consider the actual reversal in Tchambuli of the position of dominance of the two sexes, in spite of the existence of formal patrilineal institutions.

The material suggests that we may say that many, if not all, of the personality traits which we have called masculine or feminine are as lightly linked to sex as are the clothing, the manners, and the form of head-dress that a society at a given period assigns to either sex. When we consider the behaviour of the typical Arapesh man or woman as contrasted with the behaviour of the typical Mundugumor man or woman, the evidence is overwhelmingly in favour of the strength of social conditioning. In no other way can we account for the almost complete uniformity with which Arapesh children develop into contented, passive, secure persons, while Mundugumor children develop as characteristically into violent, aggressive, insecure persons. Only to the impact of the whole of the integrated culture upon the growing child can we lay the formation of the contrasting types. There is no other explanation of race, or diet, or selection that can be adduced to explain them. We are forced to conclude that human nature is almost unbelievably malleable, responding accurately and contrastingly to contrasting cultural conditions. The differences between individuals who are members of different cultures, like the differences between individuals within a culture, are almost entirely to be laid to differences in conditioning, especially during early childhood, and the form of this conditioning is culturally determined. Standardized personality differences between the sexes are of this order, cultural creations to which each generation, male and female, is trained to conform. There remains, however, the problem of the origin of these socially standardized differences.

While the basic importance of social conditioning is still imperfectly recognized—not only in lay thought, but even by the scientist specifically concerned with such matters—to go beyond it and consider the possible influence of variations in hereditary equipment is a hazardous matter. The following pages will read very differently to one who has made a part of his thinking a recognition of the whole amazing mechanism of cultural conditioning—who has really accepted the fact that the same infant could be developed into a full participant in any one of these three cultures—than they will read to one who still believes that the minutiae of cultural behaviour are carried in the individual germ-plasm. If it is said, therefore, that when we have grasped the full significance of the malleability of the human organism and the preponderant importance of cultural conditioning, there are still further problems to solve, it must be remembered that these problems come after such a comprehension of the force of conditioning; they cannot precede it. The forces that make children born among the Arapesh grow up into typical Arapesh personalities are entirely social, and any discussion of the variations which do occur must be looked at against this social background.

With this warning firmly in mind, we can ask a further question. Granting the malleability of human nature, whence arise the differences between the standardized personalities that different cultures decree for all of their members, or which one culture decrees for the members of one sex as contrasted with the members of the opposite sex? If such differences are culturally created, as this material would most strongly suggest that they are, if the newborn child can be shaped with equal ease into an unaggressive Arapesh or an aggressive Mundugumor, why do these striking contrasts occur at all? If the clues to the different personalities decreed for men and women in Tchambuli do not lie in the physical constitution of the two sexes—an assumption that we must reject both for the Tchambuli and for our own society—where can we find the clues upon which the Tchambuli, the Arapesh, the Mundugumor, have built? Cultures are manmade, they are built of human materials; they are diverse but comparable structures within which human beings can attain full human stature. Upon what have they built their diversities?

We recognize that a homogeneous culture committed in all of its gravest institutions and slightest usages to a cooperative, unaggressive course can bend every child to that emphasis, some to a perfect accord with it, the majority to an easy acceptance, while only a few deviants fail to receive the cultural imprint. To consider such traits as aggressiveness or passivity to be sex-linked is not possible in the light of the facts. Have such traits, then, as aggressiveness or passivity, pride or humility, objectivity or a preoccupation with personal relationships, an easy response to the needs of the young and the weak or a hostility to the young and the weak, a tendency to initiate sex-relations or merely to respond to the dictates of a situation or another person's advances—have these traits any basis in temperament at all? Are they potentialities of all human temperaments that can be developed by different kinds of social conditioning and which will not appear if the necessary conditioning is absent?

When we ask this question we shift our emphasis. If we ask why an Arapesh man or an Arapesh woman shows the kind of personality that we have considered in the first section of this book, the answer is: Because of the Arapesh culture, because of the intricate, elaborate, and unfailing fashion in which a culture is able to shape each new-born child to the cultural image. And if we ask the same question about a Mundugumor man or woman, or about a Tchambuli man as compared with a Tchambuli woman, the answer is of the same kind. They display the personalities that are peculiar to the cultures in which they were born and educated. Our attention has been on the differences between Arapesh men and women as a group and Mundugumor men and women as a group. It is as if we had represented the Arapesh personality by a soft yellow, the Mundugumor by a deep red, while the Tchambuli female personality was deep orange, and that of the Tchambuli male, pale green. But if we now ask whence came the original direction in each culture, so that one now shows yellow, another red, the third orange and green by sex, then we must peer more closely. And leaning closer to the picture, it is as if behind the bright consistent yellow of the Arapesh, and the deep equally consistent red of the Mundugumor, behind the orange and green that are Tchambuli, we found in each case the delicate, just discernible outlines of the whole spectrum, differently overlaid in each case by the monotone which covers it. This spectrum is the range of individual differences which lie back of the so much more conspicuous cultural emphases, and it is to this that we must turn to find the explanation of cultural inspiration, of the source from which each culture has drawn.

There appears to be about the same range of basic temperamental variation among the Arapesh and among the Mundugumor, although the violent man is a misfit in the first society and a leader in the second. If human nature were completely homogeneous raw material, lacking specific drives and characterized by no important constitutional differences between individuals, then individuals who display personality traits so antithetical to the social pressure should not reappear in societies of such differing emphases. If the variations between individuals were to be set down to accidents in the genetic process, the same accidents should not be repeated with similar frequency in strikingly different cultures, with strongly contrasting methods of education.

But because this same relative distribution of individual differences does appear in culture after culture, in spite of the divergence between the cultures, it seems pertinent to offer a hypothesis to explain upon what basis the personalities of men and women have been differently standardized so often in the history of the human race. This hypothesis is an extension of that advanced by Ruth Benedict in her *Patterns of Culture*. Let us assume that there are definite temperamental differences between human beings which if not entirely hereditary at least are established on a hereditary base very soon after birth. (Further than this we cannot at present narrow the matter.) These differences finally embodied in the character structure of adults, then, are the clues from which culture works, selecting one temperament, or a combination of related and congruent types, as desirable, and embodying this choice in every thread of the social fabric—in the care of the young child, the games the children play, the songs the people sing, the structure of political organization, the religious observance, the art and the philosophy.

Some primitive societies have had the time and the robustness to revamp all of their institutions to fit one extreme type, and to develop educational techniques which will ensure that the majority of each generation will show a personality congruent with this extreme emphasis. Other societies have pursued a less definitive course, selecting their models not from the most extreme, most highly differentiated individuals, but from the less marked types. In such societies the approved personality is less pronounced, and the culture often contains the types of inconsistencies that many human beings display also; one institution may be adjusted to the uses of pride, another to a casual humility that is congruent neither with pride nor with inverted pride. Such societies, which have taken the more usual and less sharply defined types as models, often show also a less definitely patterned social structure. The culture of such societies may be likened to a house the decoration of which has been informed by no definite and precise taste, no exclusive emphasis upon dignity or comfort or pretentiousness or beauty, but in which a little of each effect has been included.

Alternatively, a culture may take its clues not from one temperament, but from several temperaments. But instead of mixing together into an inconsistent hotchpotch the choices and emphases of different temperaments, or blending them together into a smooth but not particularly distinguished whole, it may isolate each type by making it the basis for the approved social personality for an age-group, a sex-group, a caste-group, or an occupational group. In this way society becomes not a monotone with a few discrepant patches of an intrusive colour, but a mosaic, with different groups displaying different personality traits. Such specializations as these may be based upon any facet of human endowment—different intellectual abilities, different artistic abilities, different emotional traits. So the Samoans decree that all young people must show the personality trait of unaggressiveness and punish with opprobrium the aggressive child who displays traits regarded as appropriate only in titled middle-aged men. In societies based upon elaborate ideas of rank, members of the aristocracy will be permitted, even compelled, to display a pride, a sensitivity to insult, that would be deprecated as inappropriate in members of the plebeian class. So also in professional groups or in religious sects some temperamental traits are selected and institutionalized, and taught to each new member who enters the profession or sect. Thus the physician learns the bedside manner, which is the natural behaviour of some temperaments and the standard behaviour of the general practitioner in the medical profession; the Quaker learns at least the outward behaviour and the rudiments of meditation, the capacity for which is not necessarily an innate characteristic of many of the members of the Society of Friends.

So it is with the social personalities of the two sexes. The traits that occur in some members of each sex are specially assigned to one sex, and disallowed in the other. The history of the social definition of sex-differences is filled with such arbitrary arrangements in the intellectual and artistic field, but because of the assumed congruence between physiological sex and emotional endowment we have been less able to recognize that a similar arbitrary selection is being made among emotional traits also. We have assumed that because it is convenient for a mother to wish to care for her child, this is a trait with which women have been more generously endowed by a carefully teleological process of evolution. We have assumed that because men have hunted, an activity requiring enterprise, bravery, and initiative, they have been endowed with these useful attitudes as part of their sex-temperament.

Societies have made these assumptions both overtly and implicitly. If a society insists that warfare is the major occupation for the male sex, it is therefore insisting that all male children display bravery and pugnacity. Even if the insistence upon the differential bravery of men and women is not made articulate, the difference in occupation makes this point implicitly. When, however, a society goes further and defines men as brave and women as timorous, when men are forbidden to show fear and women are indulged in the most flagrant display of fear, a more explicit element enters in. Bravery, hatred of any weakness, of flinching before pain or danger—this attitude which is so strong a component of some human temperaments has been selected as the key to masculine behaviour. The easy unashamed display of fear or suffering that is congenial to a different temperament has been made the key to feminine behaviour.

Originally two variations of human temperament, a hatred of fear or willingness to display fear, they have been socially translated into inalienable aspects of the personalities of the two sexes. And to that defined sex-personality every child will be educated, if a boy, to suppress fear, if a girl, to show it. If there has been no social selection in regard to this trait, the proud temperament that is repelled by any betrayal of feeling will display itself, regardless of sex, by keeping a stiff upper lip. Without an express prohibition of such behaviour the expressive unashamed man or woman will weep, or comment upon fear or suffering. Such attitudes, strongly marked in certain temperaments, may by social selection be standardized for everyone, or outlawed for everyone, or ignored by society, or made the exclusive and approved behaviour of one sex only.

Neither the Arapesh nor the Mundugumor have made any attitude specific for one sex. All of the energies of the culture have gone towards the creation of a single human type, regardless of class, age, or sex. There is no division into age-classes for which different motives or different moral attitudes are regarded as suitable. There is no class of seers or mediums who stand apart drawing inspiration from psychological sources not available to the majority of the people. The Mundugumor have, it is true, made one arbitrary selection, in that they recognize artistic ability only among individuals born with the cord about their necks, and firmly deny the happy exercise of artistic ability to those less unusually born. The Arapesh boy with a tinea infection has been socially selected to be a disgruntled, antisocial individual, and the society forces upon sunny cooperative children cursed with this affliction a final approximation to the behaviour appropriate to a pariah. With these two exceptions no emotional role is forced upon an individual because of birth or accident. As there is no idea of rank which declares that some are of high estate and some of low, so there is no idea of sex-difference which declares that one sex must feel differently from the other. One possible imaginative social construct, the attribution of different personalities to different members of the community classified into sex-, age-, or caste-groups, is lacking.

When we turn however to the Tchambuli, we find a situation that while bizarre in one respect, seems nevertheless more intelligible in another. The Tchambuli have at least made the point of sex-difference; they have used the obvious fact of sex as an organizing point for the formation of social personality, even though they seem to us to have reversed the normal picture. While there is reason to believe that not every Tchambuli woman is born with a dominating, organizing, administrative temperament, actively sexed and willing to initiate sex-relations, possessive, definite, robust, practical and impersonal in outlook, still most Tchambuli girls grow up to display these traits. And while there is definite evidence to show that all Tchambuli men are not, by native endowment, the delicate responsive actors of a play staged for the women's benefit, still most Tchambuli boys manifest this coquettish play-acting personality most of the time. Because the Tchambuli formulation of sex-attitudes contradicts our usual premises, we can see clearly that Tchambuli culture has arbitrarily permitted certain human traits to women, and allotted others, equally arbitrarily, to men.

CRITICAL THINKING QUESTIONS

1. How do female and male personality traits differ among the Arapesh, the Mundugumor, and the Tchambuli?
2. How does Mead explain these differences? What does she mean, for example, when she states that "human nature is unbelievably malleable to cultural conditions"?
3. Most people in North America still describe men as aggressive, strong, confident, and ambitious while characterizing women as emotional, talkative, romantic, and nurturing. Does this mean that biology is more important than environment in shaping our personality and behaviour?

36

Sk8er Girls: Skateboarders, Girlhood and Feminism in Motion

SHAUNA POMERANTZ, DAWN H. CURRIE, AND DEIDRE M. KELLY

Gender plays an important role in all social situations, even in subcultures that generally reject the values and norms of mainstream society. This reading discusses the importance of gender at a local skate park in Vancouver B.C. in order to illustrate the obstacles that young women face when participating in what is generally a male-dominated sport.

Most skaters are young teenage boys who think they are kings and the world sits below them. Trying to tell them that women should be able to skate without being harassed may be an impossible task, but it must be done.[1]

—Jigsaw Youth

Skate parks are generally awash in a grey, graffiti-ridden concrete that is the necessary landscape for practicing tricks. Vancouver has several good places for skateboarding, but most are burdened with a reputation for drugs and vandalism. The largest indoor park in the city was recently shut down for its high level of drug trafficking and defacement of property. Underground skaters who detest anything remotely mainstream avoid the parks, confining their practice to the streets,

the parking lots of local establishments, and the (now monitored by security) area surrounding the art gallery downtown. For those skaters who do not mind mainstream skateboarding, the parks are the best place to practice, learn tricks, and participate in skate culture. But no matter which skate park or street location you choose to frequent, one thing is abundantly clear—there are very few girl skateboarders.

As Sandy, a self-proclaimed skateboarding "coach" for her friends announced in no uncertain terms, "Like, a lot of girls don't skateboard!"[1] Skateboarding is not a common activity for girls and finding a girl on a skateboard is rare. Despite the recent media frenzy around teen pop singer Avril Lavigne, who has been dubbed a "skate punk" for her style and loose connections to skateboarding, girls are often relegated to the sidelines while the boys "do their thing." Further evidence can be found by visiting skate parks, where girls hang off the railing as watchers, fans,

Source: Shauna Pomerantz, Dawn H. Currie and Deidre M. Kelly. 2004. "Sk8er Girls: Skateboarders, Girlhood, and Feminism in Motion." *Women's Studies International Forum*, 27: 547–557.

and girlfriends. Evidence of this can also be found on numerous Internet skater zines dedicated to girls.[2] One girl skater writes, "Every time I venture out to skate, either alone or with friends, I am in some way harassed, threatened, or opposition to my skating is voiced in some manner." And there is this testimonial of frustration by Morgan:

Once upon a time, I was a lonely girl skater in a big city. I went to the indoor park a few times a week, but there were never any other girls there and the guys seemed to want little to do with the girl in the corner teaching herself kickturns. As much as I loved skating, it was necessary to give myself a serious pep talk to get motivated to go back to the park each day.

These accounts of life at the skate park indicate the gendered nature of skater culture, where girls have to work much harder and overcome many more obstacles than boys to gain legitimate skater status. The subordination and delegitimation of girls to boys is a common theme in youth sub/cultures. Paul Willis (1981) represents girls in working class "lad" culture as sexual objects for the more powerful boys. In Dick Hebdige's (1979) analysis of punk culture, girls are represented as accoutrement and secondary figures. McRobbie and Garber (1997 [1976]) first pointed out that youth cultural studies theorists saw girls as backdrop characters in male dominated subcultures, whose lives revolved around finding a boyfriend, looking attractive, and being promiscuous. But in their own analysis of girls in male subcultures, they concluded that traditional sex roles were also dominant in biker culture, mod culture, and hippy culture. Girls were given very little status and almost no legitimation. In skater culture, girls are assigned a similar kind of derogatory positioning. Yet despite the sexism of the skate park and of skateboarding in general, there are still some girls who choose to take up the label of "skater."

The members of the Park Gang were 14 and 15 years old at the time of the study. They all lived in an area of Vancouver known for its family orientation, professional demographic, and urban chic. Four were Canadian-born Chinese girls, two were White, one was a Canadian-born Latina, and one was half First Nations, half White. This racial mix is representative of the city of Vancouver itself, which is ethnically and racially highly diverse. With the exception of one girl, who attended a Catholic school, the girls all attended a large urban high school known for its Asian population and academic achievement. Skateboarding was a passion for four of the girls; two of the girls called themselves "coaches" in the sense that they skated but preferred to "just help"; and two of the girls were skaters by association, meaning that they were involved in skate culture, music, and style—like all of the Park Gang—but without the desire to actually skate. They all hung out at a skate park that would be considered amateurish compared to the larger and more daunting parks downtown. This particular park was connected to a community centre in an affluent neighbourhood. It was relatively clean and safe.

Given their occupation of a subject position that held the possibility for a feminist politics, we found it interesting that some of the Park Gang espoused a postfeminist ethos. Sara, for example, did not see the relevance of feminism today because she had never encountered a situation where "I wanted to, like, do something because, like, it wasn't how I wanted it to be." And Emily did not think being a girl carried any stigma whatsoever: "I think it's pretty much even with guys now." To some of the Park Gang, feminism had become a form of reverse discrimination. Emily noted that feminists were not trying to make things equal, but rather "boost" the women above the men: "Like, it's constantly, like, a fight, instead of just being equal. They [feminists] just want to be better than men." Pete also expressed the idea that feminism was a form of discrimination. "I think sometimes feminism is brought a bit too far," she said. "Um, like, there is, 'Yeah, I want to be equal to the men, get paid the same wage for doing the same job.' And then there is, 'I'm going to go out and be a fire fighter just for the sake of having women in the force.'" Although some of the Park Gang expressed post-feminist sentiments, their desire to "do" skate-boarding told a different story.

Members of the Park Gang were relatively new skaters when we met them. They came to the sport through older brothers or boys at school. Grover noted that she got started because a friend did not want to learn alone:

There are not too many girl skateboarders so it is kind of better—she felt more comfortable if there was, like, you know, another person that, you know, could be with her. And so she asked if I wanted to try it, so I said sure, and, um, her brothers started teaching us and I found it was something that, it was a lot of fun, so I just stayed with it, so I'm still learning.

When more of the Park Gang decided to try skateboarding, they ventured into the skate park with their boards for the first time, hoping to gain acceptance and practice. But the park proved to be a location of struggle that was dominated by skater boys, who put the girls under surveillance. The skater boys were always asking members of the Park Gang to show them what they could do and Zoey spoke of the constant questioning of the girls' abilities. They often asked her, "Why don't you skate *more*?" She admitted that, "Sometimes we don't want to skate around them 'cause, like, they do really good stuff and we're just kind of learning."

The Park Gang quickly realized that being the only girl skaters at the park singled them out for some harassment. To the skater boys who domi-nated the park and acted as its gatekeepers, the park was their space—a space that left very little room for girls, unless they were occupying the traditionally feminine subject positions of watcher, fan, or girlfriend. Gracie theorized that girls skate less than boys due to this kind of terri-torial attitude: "Some [girls] are kind of, like, scared, because, um, of what people might think of them." When asked what she meant, Gracie

noted that the lack of girls who skated at the park might make the boys question girls' right to belong. Onyx added that the skater boys viewed the Park Gang as "invading their space." Grover felt that the Park Gang threatened the skater boys "just because, you know, girls are doing their sport." She went on to explain the attitudes of some of the boys at the park.

Sometimes, they'll be kind of, like, rude, like, I don't know if it's on purpose, but they just, you know, have this kind of attitude . . . I guess they think they're so good and one of them or two of them—I'm not sure if all of them are, like, sponsored by skateboarding companies—so they always feel, like, you know, they're kind of superior and so, you know, we're only a year younger, so it's kind of, like, we're obviously not as good as them, but they kind of forget that they had to start somewhere too, so, and it would be harder for us because we're girls.

The territory of the park became a contested space. The boys saw it as theirs. The girls wanted access. Grover, Gracie, and Onyx understood that the boys were threatened by their presence, but wished the boys could appreciate how hard it was for girls to get started. They wanted the boys to see them as equals who deserved the same kind of camaraderie that they gave each other. But in-stead, the boys saw them as interlopers with little legitimate claim to the space. Some of the boys accused some of the Park Gang of being "posers." Often, girls who try to gain skater status are seen as posers. A poser wears the right clothes, such as wide sneakers with fat laces, brand-name pants and hoodies, and, of course, carries a skateboard. But posers do not really skate. Although boys can be posers too, girls who attempt access to the label "skater" are singled out for this derogatory title. It is assumed that girls hang around the skate park as a way to meet skater boys, to flirt.

When this accusation was levelled at some of the Park Gang, they immediately took action to prove the skater boys wrong. Zoey recounted the story.

There's this one time where a couple of the guys thought we were just—they said it out loud that we're just there for the guys and we're like, "No!" And they're like, "But you're here all the time, like almost every day, skateboarding, and so are we." So we did this whole thing where we didn't come there for quite awhile just to show them; and then we came back and they stopped bugging us about it.

The girls involved in the park boycott practiced at an elementary school for two weeks and went to the park only when they knew the boys would not be around. When asked what they had gained by boycotting the park, Zoey responded, "That we're not there just for the guys and we're not there to watch them and be around them." Suddenly, the girls received more respect and experienced less harassment from the skater boys. Zoey noted a distinct change in their attitude. "I guess to some level, they treated us like an equal to them, kind of." Instead of placing the girls under surveillance, the skater boys watched the Park Gang in order to see "how they were doing." They suddenly became curious about the girls' progress. When asked if they thought they had successfully changed the opinions of the skater boys, Zoey enthusiastically replied, "Well yes!"

The girls involved in the boycott retreated to a safe space where they were not being monitored. When they re-emerged, they were ready to fully occupy the subject position of "skater." In so doing, the girls challenged who a "skater" could be by challenging the skater boys' power over who had legitimate claim to the park. This discursive struggle for naming and authorization necessitated an understanding of the discourse of the park. The boys were interfering in the girls' desire to occupy the subject position of "skater." By blocking the subject position of "skater," the boys retained some control over the girls' sense of who they were. Recognizing how unfair this was, the girls responded by gaining control over their own subjectivity. They retreated to a space where they were free to think of themselves as "skaters." When they returned to the park, they were armed with both a sense of confidence about their skating abilities and a sense of entitlement to the "skater" label. They took authorizing power away from the boys and legitimated themselves.

Before the boycott, the skater girls were thought of in a very specific way: as posers, flirts, or interlopers. But through the boycott, the girls believed they altered how the boys thought of them and, more significantly, how they thought of themselves. In their efforts to change the meaning of "skater," the Park Gang acknowledged how they had been subordinated at the park and successfully resignified the commonly accepted process of belonging. They carved out a space for girls where none used to exist. In this way, the Park Gang legitimated the subject position of "skater" for girls at the park and expanded the possibilities for subjectivity within girlhood. As Pete pointed out, "Lots of girls have actually started [skating] because my group started and then they kind of feel in power. I think they kind of feel empowered that they can start now, that it's okay for girls to skate."

CRITICAL THINKING QUESTIONS

1. Do you agree with one of the interview subjects when she says that women are "pretty much even with guys now"? Do you think this is true in general? Do you think this is true in the skate park?

2. What other sports are divided along gender lines? Can you name a sport in which men and women compete side by side? Why do you think the gender divide persists? Do you think women should be able to play on the same teams as men, in the National Hockey League, for example?

3. The authors observe that the skate park was a contested space. What do they mean by this? Can you think of other spaces, past and present, that are contested? Do you think the behaviour of the boys is sexist?

NOTES

1. All names are pseudonyms chosen by the girls in the study.
2. Examples of online skater girl zines include: frontsidebetty.com, withitgirl.com, sk8girl.com. girlskateboarding.com, girlsskatebetter.com, and gurlzonboards.com.

REFERENCES

Hebdige, Dick. 1979. *Subculture: The meaning of style*. London: Metheun.

McRobbie, Angela, and Jenny Garber. 1997 [1976]. Girls and subcultures. In *The subcultures reader*, eds. Ken Gelder and Sarah Thornton, 112–120. London: Routledge.

Willis, Paul E. 1981. In *Learning to labor: How working class kids get working class jobs*, ed. Morningside, 51–70. New York: Columbia University Press.

37

Domestic Violence: A Cross-Cultural View

ELAINE LEEDER

Domestic violence is a global problem and occurs in both industrialized and developing countries. Elaine Leeder discusses why women and children, especially girls, experience physical abuse in nations as diverse as India, Japan, Vietnam, and Africa. This dark side of family life reflects structural inequality and cultural attitudes about gender.

FAMILY VIOLENCE IN INDIA

The Indian government and feminist organizations are concerned about wife battering, child abuse and neglect, and infanticide, which occur quite regularly there. [Earlier] I mentioned bride burnings in India, called "dowry deaths," which occur as a result of rising demands for the dowry given from the bride's side to the groom's family. I also briefly mentioned female infanticide. Those are extreme forms of gender violence. However, in this [reading] we focus on the regular and daily patterns of domestic violence that take place in India.

Many forms of domestic violence in India occur as a result of rising industrialization and modernization. Families have rising economic

Source: The Family in Global Perspective: A Gendered Journey by Elaine Leeder. Thousand Oaks, CA: Sage, 2004, pp. 244–48, 251–54.

expectations, and the problems are acted out at home. Wife battering is a fairly common occurrence (Rao, 1997). Mild forms of wife beating are commonplace, and many men and women admit freely in interviews that it is justified if the woman does not "behave herself." Interestingly, though, in one study only 22 percent of the women admitted on surveys to having been beaten; it is unacceptable to admit abuse, yet it seems to be such a common practice that it is not considered worthy of mention. Only women for whom abuse is a serious or chronic problem are willing to admit it. Otherwise it is such an everyday affair that it is not considered a problem.

In rural India, women believe that alcohol and inadequate dowries provoke the abuse. Some drunken husbands beat their wives without provocation, and women who are beaten complain that the problem is exacerbated by the drunken fits of their husbands. Alcohol is widely available, as it is in the United States, and many

205

of the men say that their drinking is due to a feeling of hopelessness caused by poverty. Their lack of options for breaking out of poverty leads them to drink to "forget their troubles."

Also, as dowry demands have escalated in the past 20 years, many parents have been unable to keep up with the inflation. Some girls are kept hostage by their in-laws in an attempt to extract larger amounts of money from the girls' parents. When those demands are not met, the young bride is beaten, often living in terror of what might become of her. Her power is also diminished in the home after she has been beaten. Sometimes "family resources are transferred away from the wife and her children to other members of the household . . . and the husband and wife are unable to construct a strong marital bond."

It appears that if women have male children they are less likely to be beaten. Having fulfilled societal expectations seems to provide a deterrent to abuse. A rural woman is more likely to be beaten if she has been sterilized. Sterilization is a major form of birth control in rural India; after bearing enough children, a woman often chooses it as contraception. It appears that a man feels freer to beat a woman who has been sterilized, perhaps out of fear of her infidelity.

In rural India, abuse is tolerated under certain circumstances, which include dowry problems, a wife's infidelity, her neglect of household duties, or her disobedience to her husband's dictates. Abuse is also tolerated if a husband beats his wife when he is drunk but is otherwise a good husband. But if a man batters his wife beyond levels considered tolerable for the village, or if he beats her for reasons not considered legitimate by the village, then a village elder or a local monk will intervene to stop the violence.

Finally, we should mention that living outside of marriage is not an option for an Indian woman. There are no alternatives to marriage for Indian women at this time. Although many women work outside of the home, the types of jobs available are limited, pay is quite low, and marriage is considered the norm.

Clearly, wife battering is a prevalent and "normal" family dynamic in India. It is part of the social fabric, so much so that it is not even commented on unless it is extreme. So too is child abuse.

Child abuse has occurred since time immemorial and exists across cultures. Usually it is the poorer classes who get the attention of public health and welfare services. But middle-class practices are more reflective of whether or not abuse is common in a society. In India middle-class families have experienced a greater amount of stress as the country modernizes and industrializes. India is becoming more urban, and this points to a rise in child abuse among Indian families (Segal, 1995). There is intense competition and effort at upward mobility. This also puts stress on the family. In addition, there is a well-established pattern of corporal punishment in raising children. Children are socialized to obey their parents, and there is strict discipline, even though infants are highly indulged. The family is highly hierarchical, and now that families are moving away from the joint family, there is less support for raising children and sharing household tasks. All these factors create an environment that's ripe for an increase in child abuse rates.

The use of corporal punishment is so well entrenched in Indian society that even the middle and upper classes admit to using it. In one study of 319 highly educated, college-graduate parents in three cities in India, a full 56.9 percent reported having used "acceptable" forms of violence, while 41.9 percent engaged in "abusive" violence, and 2.9 percent admitted using "extreme" violence on their children. Unfortunately we have no specific studies of middle- and upper-class parents in the United States with which to compare this data. Suffice it to say that in the United States we have comparably high rates of child abuse, too (Gelles & Straus, 1986). Remember that in the United States *at least* a million children are abused a year.

Female infanticide and child neglect are also major child abuse issues in India, particularly in rural villages. Barbara Miller (1987) has spent years studying abuse in rural north India and has found significant discrimination against girl children there. There is a strong preference for sons. Boys are needed as economic assets, for farming, and for the money they send home if they move away. They are more likely to stay with their families after marriage and maintain their parents in old age. Girls move away when they marry and cannot contribute to the family upkeep. Sons bring dowries and perform rituals among the Hindus when the father dies; therefore boys are important to the maintenance of family life, while girls are seen as a drain economically. This strong preference for sons has led to disappointment when a girl is born, withholding of medical care for girls, and preferential feeding of boy children.

Infanticide is the killing of a child under one year old, and is the most extreme form of child abuse. *Neonaticide* is the killing of an infant up to 24 hours old, and *feticide* is the abortion of a baby in utero, particularly when it is done as sex selection. After a child is 12 months old, the killing is considered a homicide. In north India, the killing of female infants is quite an old phenomenon. The British discovered it as early as 1789 and outlawed it by 1870. In some parts of India during that time, the sex ratio was 118 men to 100 women. Nowadays, systematic, indirect female infanticide still exists. Girls are not actively killed; they are just neglected so badly that they die from lack of care. The numbers seem to cross class and caste, with even wealthier families preferring sons. This is also true for well-educated families.

In India there is also sex-selective abortion. Although there is a lack of definitive data, anecdotal evidence indicates that it is quite widespread. One study found that in one hospital, of the 700 amniocenteses done, 250 were male and 450 were female. A full 430 of the 450 females were aborted, while all the male fetuses were brought to full term.

Now that I have presented this data, I urge a suspension of any ethnocentric value judgments.

It is true that these figures are disturbing and certainly are contrary to Western-based humanistic values. Let's try to keep a view that is culturally relative, to understand why people would engage in such behavior. Understanding why it is done, and being aware of one's own bias, might lead us to think of what can be done about it. There are groups working in India and through the United Nations who have declared this problem a public health issue and are trying to prevent or reduce the incidence of these practices.

WIFE BATTERING IN JAPAN

Now let's focus our lens on another part of Asia, this time Japan. In previous chapters we talked about the way the Japanese family is organized, and how unlike it is to families in the United States, even though both countries are highly industrialized. In Japan the incidence of wife battering is quite high. In one study (Yoshihama & Sorenson, 1994), a survey was done of 796 married women, in which more than three-fourths reported at least one type of violence perpetrated by a male intimate partner. This ranged from a slap to an assault with a deadly weapon, from verbal ridicule to restriction of social activities, and from incompliance with contraception to forced, violent sex. About two-thirds of the most serious physically violent incidents resulted in injury.

Unlike the United States, Japan has no specific laws against wife battering as a crime, and there is no governmental funding for services that address the problem. Often, if women get help, it is through services intended for other purposes, like homes established under child welfare laws. Fully one-third of the women who use other services, like shelters that protect prostitutes, were actually battered women seeking protection from their abusers. A husband's violence is one of the primary reasons women list when they are seeking divorce, and contrary to the myths of the quiet, passive Japanese man, violence is an integral part of family life in Japanese society.

Often, when a woman seeks to end a violent marriage, the violence does not end. This is true in the United States as well as Japan. Violence often escalates during the process of separation and divorce. It is as if the man does not want to let go of his property, holding tighter and becoming more abusive as he fears the loss. Male violence in Japan seems to cross all socioeconomic strata and can lead to serious consequences. Women report broken bones, lacerations requiring stitches, ruptured eardrums, and other injuries requiring medical care.

Domestic violence in Japan is still an unrecognized problem. There is not even a word for it in Japanese; language has been adapted from the English to refer to it. An increasing level of media attention is being focused on the problem at the time of the publication of this book, but the level is far below that with which we are familiar in the West. This is a problem that bears watching closely, to see how well Japan deals with a problem that many countries are starting to grapple with. . . .

DOMESTIC VIOLENCE IN VIETNAM

. . . The Socialist Republic of Vietnam is rich in culture, deep in religion, and ancient yet modern. It is beautiful, with pristine beaches, huge rivers, and rice paddies galore. Eighty percent of the population lives in the rural areas, and it has a 94 percent literacy rate. We in the United States think that Vietnam is a place of war, and it was, in fact, for most of the past century. In 1945 Vietnam became independent of France, fought for its freedom, and then fought against the Americans, who established their presence there after the French pulled out.

The war has had a significant impact on family life in Vietnam. With the revolution in 1945 came the first attempts to change the inferior position of women there. Laws were passed to equalize the rights, positions, and interests of women. Unfortunately, today the vestiges of Confucian ideology still linger. Men act as kings in their homes even

while the women in the workforce make more money than their husbands (Quy, 1996). Women are employed in the labor market in great numbers, but still do the "second shift" that's common in the United States. After work at the factory, Vietnamese women spend five to six hours a night on housework at home. This has been called the "invisible violence" of Vietnam, because while there may not be physical violence between men and women, intimidation and fear drive the relationships. This inequity occurs for both urban educated and rural poor women. Many women feel that their situation is predestined, in accordance with Confucian ideology.

Then there is the "visible violence" that recently has led to a large number of divorces in Vietnam. One report indicates that as many as 87.5 percent of the divorces in 1992 were a result of violence or violence-related causes. There are numerous injuries and deaths related to violence in the home, although exact numbers are not available. What is known is that 17.5 percent of the deaths in Vietnam in 1992 were caused by family violence.

One of the reasons given for this problem is low socioeconomic status. Poor men, in particular, feel that it is permissible to take out their frustration and anger on their wives and children. Another reason given is the "feudal attitude": the old Confucian ideas of "thinking highly of men and slightly of women" seem to inform beliefs about hitting one's wife. Sometimes men take lovers, or even concubines, who come to live in the home with the wife, against the wife's will.

Other reasons for violence are drinking, gambling, adultery, and jealousy. Although there are no numbers available on this, the researcher conducted interviews with battered wives who attributed the abusive behavior to a few of these factors. Another reason given was what we would call the "intra-individual theory": that there is "mad blood" in the perpetrator. In Vietnam this means that there are people who always feel anxious and angry and tend to shift the blame onto others, especially their next of kin.

In Vietnamese law, men and women are considered equal. Violence toward wives and children is specifically prohibited and is considered a violation of human rights, and the government has established a series of local and state programs for intervention. There are also laws against the preference for male children, although as we will see, these have certainly not had much of an impact. Interestingly, however, the incidence of rape in Vietnam seems to be low, specifically as compared with the United States (Goodstein, 1996). The Vietnamese Women's Union plays a role at the local level, watching out for the rights of women (Johnson, 1996).

As in many parts of the world, preference for a son remains strong in Vietnam, especially in light of the family planning policy there, which recommends only two children per family (Haughton & Haughton, 1995). Payments must be made to the government should a family have more than two children, although the sanctions are not as strict as they are in neighboring China. Following the Confucian model, in Vietnam there is still the belief that a son will care for you in old age and that a son is an investment, while a daughter will leave. Even though women in Vietnam are well educated (remember, the literacy rate is 94 percent) and well integrated into the workforce, the Vietnamese still prefer male children.

Another problem related to violence in Vietnam is the trafficking in women (Barry, 1996). Vietnam's traditional values, like fate and filial piety, shape the culture and make it ripe for exploitation by the "sex work" industry. Other countries in the region, like Japan, Thailand, and Australia, have well-established sex industries that have begun moving into Vietnam as the country moves toward economic development. Vietnam has a history of sexual exploitation of women, most notably during the Vietnam War, when more than 500,000 women served as prostitutes to the U.S. troops. Many were rape victims or war widows needing to earn a living. Now many women are being forced into prostitution as part of the growing sex trade industry. Because prostitution provides immediate cash incentives for the women when other work is not available, it is becoming an increasingly viable option as the country moves toward a more westernized model of economics.

Vietnam, although a socialist country with some new elements of capitalism, seems to have similar domestic violence problems as other parts of the world: violence against wives, son sex-preference, and a growing sex trade. It appears that not many places in the world are free of domestic violence.

DOMESTIC VIOLENCE IN AFRICA

. . . In Uganda, violence against one's wife is accepted as legitimate; when it is mentioned, most men just shrug and say, "It's our culture" (Doro, 1999). If a woman attacks her husband, the violence is considered criminal. The U.S. Department of State Uganda Report on Human Rights Practices for 1998 says that violence against women, including rape, is quite common. There are no specific laws against wife battering, although a law passed in 1997 provides protection for families, including wives and children. But it is hard to implement the law since law enforcement officials view the problem the way the public does, as not a problem.

Families in Uganda endure violence in silence, and violence is worse in the countryside than it is in the city. According to the Human Rights Report, the pattern is similar in other African countries, too. Women have few rights, neighbors don't want to get involved, and the women lie about their injuries if asked about them at medical facilities.

Several women's organizations in coalition are actively pursuing reform and holding public workshops to lobby for a revision of the Domestic Relations Act. Most of the trouble in getting anything done is related to lack of funding. Many of the countries in Africa do not have adequate funds to handle the many social problems they have, like AIDS, and they have put domestic violence issues on the back burner, because they think, after all, "It is our culture."

Other studies done in Africa are also not comprehensive. One study of domestic violence in Nigeria found that polygamy lends itself more to wife battering than do monogamous marriages (Efoghe, 1990). In this study, more polygamous marriages were violent than were monogamous marriages. Another study, of child sexual abuse in Zimbabwe, found that sexual abuse of children is not as prevalent there as it is internationally, with only about 10 percent of the population being victims of this kind of abuse (Khan, 1995). The authors of the study wonder whether this discrepancy reflects underreporting, or if sexual abuse of children is really not a big problem in Zimbabwe.

Finally, let's remember that Africa and parts of Southwest Asia perform ritual circumcision of girls. In Somalia, Kenya, the Sudan, Tanzania, Ethiopia, Egypt, Uganda, Chad, Mali, Senegal, Cameroon, Zaire, Nigeria, to name just a few, girls are cut and scraped to make their bodies more attractive and marriageable. This practice has been framed as a human rights abuse, as well as a form of child abuse that is being taken up as a problem by the United Nations and the World Health Organization.

CRITICAL THINKING QUESTIONS

1. How is domestic violence similar in India, Japan, Vietnam, and Africa? How does it differ? Also, Leeder notes that rising industrialization and modernization increase the likelihood of family violence. Why, then, is wife battering also common in industrialized countries such as Japan and the United States?

2. Why do most of the women in these countries never complain about domestic violence? What individual, legal, historical, and cultural factors help explain their silence?

3. Leeder urges the reader to suspend "any ethnocentric value judgments" about family violence. What does she mean? And, if we do so, does this mean that the global community shouldn't interfere with a country's violent practices against women and children?

REFERENCES

Barry, K. 1996. Industrialization and economic development: The costs to women. In *Vietnam women in transition*, ed. K. Barry. New York: St. Martin's Press.

Doro, M. 1999. August 4. Available: End Violence@edc-cit. org.

Efoghe, G. B. 1990. Nature and type of marriage as predictors of aggressiveness among married men in Ekpoma, Bendel State of Nigeria. *International Journal of Sociology of the Family*, 20 (Spring): 67–78.

Gelles, R., and M. Straus. 1986. Societal change and change in family violence from 1975–1985 as revealed in two national surveys. *Journal of Marriage and the Family*, 48 (3): 465–80.

Goodstein, L. 1996. Sexual assessment in the U.S. and Vietnam: Some thoughts and questions. In *Vietnam women in transition*, ed. K. Barry, 275–86. New York: St. Martin's Press.

Haughton, J., and D. Haughton. 1995. Son preference in Vietnam. *Studies in Family Planning*, 26, 6 (Nov/Dec): 325–38.

Johnson, M. 1996. Violence against women in the family: The U.S. and Vietnam. In *Vietnam women in transition*, ed. K. Barry. New York: St. Martin's Press.

Khan, N. 1995. Patterns of child sexual abuse in Zimbabwe: An overview. *Zimbabwe Journal of Educational Research*, 7, 2 (July): 181–208.

Miller, B. 1987. Female infanticide and child neglect in rural North India. In *Child survival*, ed. N. Scheper-Hughes, 95–112. Dordrecht: D. Reidel Publishing Co.

Quy, L. 1996. Domestic violence in Vietnam. In *Vietnam women in transition*, ed. K. Barry, 263–74. New York: St. Martin's Press.

Rao, V. 1997. Wife beating in rural south India: A qualitative and econometric analysis. *Social Science and Medicine*, 44 (8): 1169–80.

Segal, U. 1995. Child abuse by the middle class: A study of professionals in India. *Child Abuse and Neglect*, 19 (2): 217–31.

Yoshihama, M., and S. Sorenson. 1994. Physical, sexual and emotional abuse by male intimates: Experiences of women in Japan. *Violence and Victims*, 9 (1): 63–77.

38

The Souls of Black Folk

W. E. B. DU BOIS

W. E. B. Du Bois, a pioneering U.S. sociologist and the first African American to receive a doctorate from Harvard University, describes how a colour-conscious society casts black people as strangers in their own homes. One result, Du Bois explains, is that African Americans develop a "double-consciousness," seeing themselves as Americans but always gazing back at themselves through the eyes of the white majority, as people set below and apart by colour.

Between me and the other world there is ever an unasked question: unasked by some through feelings of delicacy; by others through the difficulty of rightly framing it. All, nevertheless, flutter round it. They approach me in a half-hesitant sort of way, eye me curiously or compassionately, and then, instead of saying directly, How does it feel to be a problem? they say, I know an excellent colored man in my town; or, I fought at Mechanicsville; or, Do not these Southern outrages make your blood boil? At these I smile, or am interested, or reduce the boiling to a simmer, as the occasion may require. To the real question, How

Source: From *The Souls of Black Folk* by W. E. B. Du Bois (New York: Penguin, 1982; orig. 1903), pp. 43–53.

does it feel to be a problem? I answer seldom a word.

And yet, being a problem is a strange experience—peculiar even for one who has never been anything else, save perhaps in babyhood and in Europe. It is in the early days of rollicking boyhood that the revelation first bursts upon one, all in a day, as it were. I remember well when the shadow swept across me. I was a little thing, away up in the hills of New England, where the dark Housatonic winds between Hoosac and Taghkanic to the sea. In a wee wooden schoolhouse, something put it into the boys' and girls' heads to buy gorgeous visiting-cards—ten cents a package—and exchange. The exchange was merry, till one girl, a tall

FOR COLORED ONLY

211

newcomer, refused my card—refused it peremptorily, with a glance. Then it dawned upon me with a certain suddenness that I was different from the others; or like, mayhap, in heart and life and longing, but shut out from their world by a vast veil. I had thereafter no desire to tear down that veil, to creep through; I held all beyond it in common contempt, and lived above it in a region of blue sky and great wandering shadows. That sky was bluest when I could beat my mates at examination-time, or beat them at a foot-race, or even beat their stringy heads. Alas, with the years all this fine contempt began to fade; for the words I longed for, and all their dazzling opportunities, were theirs, not mine. But they should not keep these prizes, I said; some, all, I would wrest from them. Just how I would do it I could never decide: by reading law, by healing the sick, by telling the wonderful tales that swam in my head—some way. With other black boys the strife was not so fiercely sunny: Their youth shrunk into tasteless sycophancy, or into silent hatred of the pale world about them and mocking distrust of everything white; or wasted itself in a bitter cry, Why did God make me an outcast and a stranger in mine own house? The shades of the prison-house closed round about us all: walls strait and stubborn to the whitest, but relentlessly narrow, tall, and unscalable to sons of night who must plod darkly on in resignation, or beat unavailing palms against the stone, or steadily, half hopelessly, watch the streak of blue above.

After the Egyptian and Indian, the Greek and Roman, the Teuton and Mongolian, the Negro is a sort of seventh son, born with a veil, and gifted with second-sight in this American world—a world which yields him no true self-consciousness, but only lets him see himself through the revelation of the other world. It is a peculiar sensation, this double-consciousness, this sense of always looking at one's self through the eyes of others, of measuring one's soul by the tape of a world that looks on in amused contempt and pity. One ever feels his twoness—an American, a Negro; two souls, two thoughts, two unreconciled strivings; two warring ideals in one dark body, whose

dogged strength alone keeps it from being torn asunder.

The history of the American Negro is the history of this strife, this longing to attain self-conscious manhood, to merge his double self into a better and truer self. In this merging he wishes neither of the older selves to be lost. He would not Africanize America, for America has too much to teach the world and Africa. He would not bleach his Negro soul in a flood of white Americanism, for he knows that Negro blood has a message for the world. He simply wishes to make it possible for a man to be both a Negro and an American, without being cursed and spit upon by his fellows, without having the doors of Opportunity closed roughly in his face.

This, then, is the end of his striving: to be a coworker in the kingdom of culture, to escape both death and isolation, to husband and use his best powers and his latent genius. These powers of body and mind have in the past been strangely wasted, dispersed, or forgotten. The shadow of a mighty Negro past flits through the tale of Ethiopia the Shadowy and of Egypt the Sphinx. Through history, the powers of single black men flash here and there like falling stars, and die sometimes before the world has rightly gauged their brightness. Here in America, in the few days since Emancipation, the black man's turning hither and thither in hesitant and doubtful striving has often made his very strength to lose effectiveness, to seem like absence of power, like weakness. And yet it is not weakness—it is the contradiction of double aims. The double-aimed struggle of the black artisan on the one hand to escape white contempt for a nation of mere hewers of wood and drawers of water, and on the other hand to plough and nail and dig for a poverty-stricken horde—could only result in making him a poor craftsman, for he had but half a heart in either cause. By the poverty and ignorance of his people, the Negro minister or doctor was tempted toward quackery and demagogy; and by the criticism of the other world, toward ideals that made him ashamed of his lowly tasks. The would-be black savant was confronted by the paradox that the knowledge his people needed was a twice-told tale to his white neighbors, while the knowledge which would teach the white world was Greek to his own flesh and blood. The innate love of harmony and beauty that set the ruder souls of his people a-dancing and a-singing raised but confusion and doubt in the soul of the black artist; for the beauty revealed to him was the soul-beauty of a race which his larger audience despised, and he could not articulate the message of another people. This waste of double aims, this seeking to satisfy two unreconciled ideals, has wrought sad havoc with the courage and faith and deeds of ten thousand thousand people, has sent them often wooing false gods and invoking false means of salvation, and at times has even seemed about to make them ashamed of themselves.

Away back in the days of bondage they thought to see in one divine event the end of all doubt and disappointment; few men ever worshipped Freedom with half such unquestioning faith as did the American Negro for two centuries. To him, so far as he thought and dreamed, slavery was indeed the sum of all villainies, the cause of all sorrow, the root of all prejudice; Emancipation was the key to a promised land of sweeter beauty than ever stretched before the eyes of wearied Israelites. In song and exhortation swelled one refrain—Liberty; in his tears and curses the God he implored had Freedom in his right hand. At last it came, suddenly, fearfully, like a dream. With one wild carnival of blood and passion came the message in his own plaintive cadences:

Shout, O children!
Shout, you're free!
For God has bought your liberty!

Years have passed away since then—ten, twenty, forty; forty years of national life, forty years of renewal and development, and yet the swarthy spectre sits in its accustomed seat at the Nation's feast. In vain do we cry to this our vastest social problem:

Take any shape but that, and my firm nerves
Shall never tremble!

The Nation has not yet found peace from its sins; the freedman has not yet found in freedom his promised land. Whatever of good may have come in these years of change, the shadow of a deep disappointment rests upon the Negro people—a disappointment all the more bitter because the unattained ideal was unbounded save by the simple ignorance of a lowly people.

The first decade was merely a prolongation of the vain search for freedom, the boon that seemed ever barely to elude their grasp, like a tantalizing will-o'-the-wisp, maddening and misleading the headless host. The holocaust of war, the terrors of the Ku Klux Klan, the lies of carpet-baggers, the disorganization of industry, and the contradictory advice of friends and foes, left the bewildered serf with no new watchword beyond the old cry for freedom. As the time flew, however, he began to grasp a new idea. The ideal of liberty demanded for its attainment powerful means, and these the Fifteenth Amendment gave him. The ballot, which before he had looked upon as a visible sign of freedom, he now regarded as the chief means of gaining and perfecting the liberty with which war had partially endowed him. And why not? Had not votes made war and emancipated millions? Had not votes enfranchised the freedmen? Was anything impossible to a power that had done all this? A million black men started with renewed zeal to vote themselves into the kingdom. So the decade flew away, the revolution of 1876 came, and left the half-free serf weary, wondering, but still inspired. Slowly but steadily, in the following years, a new vision began gradually to replace the dream of political power—a powerful movement, the rise of another ideal to guide the unguided, another pillar of fire by night after a clouded day. It was the ideal of "book-learning"; the curiosity, born of compulsory ignorance, to know and test the power of the cabalistic letters of the white man, the longing to know. Here at last seemed to have been discovered the mountain path to Canaan; longer than the highway of Emancipation and law, steep and rugged, but straight, leading to heights high enough to overlook life.

Up the new path the advance guard toiled, slowly, heavily, doggedly; only those who have watched and guided the faltering feet, the misty minds, the dull understandings, of the dark pupils of these schools know how faithfully, how piteously, this people strove to learn. It was weary work. The cold statistician wrote down the inches of progress here and there, noted also where here and there a foot had slipped or someone had fallen. To the tired climbers, the horizon was ever dark, the mists were often cold, the Canaan was always dim and far away. If, however, the vistas disclosed as yet no goal, no resting-place, little but flattery and criticism, the journey at least gave leisure for reflection and self-examination; it changed the child of Emancipation to the youth with dawning self-consciousness, self-realization, self-respect. In those sombre forests of his striving his own soul rose before him, and he saw himself, darkly, as through a veil; and yet he saw in himself some faint revelation of his power, of his mission. He began to have a dim feeling that, to attain his place in the world, he must be himself, and not another. For the first time he sought to analyze the burden he bore upon his back, that dead-weight of social degradation partially masked behind a half-named Negro problem. He felt his poverty; without a cent, without a home, without land, tools, or savings, he had entered into competition with rich, landed, skilled neighbors. To be a man is hard, but to be a poor race in a land of dollars is the very bottom of hardships. He felt the weight of his ignorance, not simply of letters, but of life, of business, of the humanities; the accumulated sloth and shirking and awkwardness of decades and centuries shackled his hands and feet. Nor was his burden all poverty and ignorance. The red stain of bastardy, which two centuries of systematic legal defilement of Negro women had stamped upon his race, meant not only the loss of ancient African chastity, but also the hereditary weight of a mass of corruption from white adulterers, threatening almost the obliteration of the Negro home.

A people thus handicapped ought not to be asked to race with the world, but rather allowed to give all its time and thought to its own social problems. But alas! while sociologists gleefully count his bastards and his prostitutes, the very soul of the toiling, sweating black man is darkened by the shadow of a vast despair. Men call the shadow prejudice, and learnedly explain it as the natural defence of culture against barbarism, learning against ignorance, purity against crime, the "higher" against the "lower" races. To which the Negro cries Amen! and swears that to so much of this strange prejudice as is founded on just homage to civilization, culture, righteousness, and progress, he humbly bows and meekly does obeisance. But before that nameless prejudice that leaps beyond all this he stands helpless, dismayed, and well-nigh speechless; before that personal disrespect and mockery, the ridicule and systematic humiliation, the distortion of fact and wanton license of fancy, the cynical ignoring of the better and the boisterous welcoming of the worse, the all-pervading desire to inculcate disdain for everything black, from Toussaint to the devil—before this there rises a sickening despair that would disarm and discourage any nation save that black host to whom "discouragement" is an unwritten word.

But the facing of so vast a prejudice could not but bring the inevitable self-questioning, self-disparagement, and lowering of ideals which ever accompany repression and breed in an atmosphere of contempt and hate. Whisperings and portents came borne upon the four winds: Lo! we are diseased and dying, cried the dark hosts; we cannot write, our voting is vain; what need of education, since we must always cook and serve? And the Nation echoed and enforced this self-criticism saying: Be content to be servants, and nothing more; what need of higher culture for half-men? Away with the black man's ballot, by force or fraud—and behold the suicide of a race! Nevertheless, out of the evil came something of good—the more careful adjustment of education to real life, the clearer perception of the Negroes' social responsibilities, and the sobering realization of the meaning of progress.

So dawned the time of *Sturm und Drang*: Storm and stress today rocks our little boat on the mad waters of the world-sea; there is within and without the sound of conflict, the burning of body and rending of soul; inspiration strives with doubt, and faith with vain questionings. The bright ideals of the past—physical freedom, political power, the training of brains and the training of hands—all these in turn have waxed and waned, until even the last grows dim and overcast. Are they all wrong, all false? No, not that, but each alone was over-simple and incomplete—the dreams of a credulous race-childhood, or the fond imaginings of the other world which does not know and does not want to know our power. To be really true, all these ideals must be melted and welded into one. The training of the schools we need today more than ever—the training of deft hands, quick eyes and ears, and above all the broader, deeper, higher culture of gifted minds and pure hearts. The power of the ballot we need in sheer self-defence—else what shall save us from a second slavery? Freedom, too, the long-sought, we still seek, the freedom of life and limb, the freedom to work and think, the freedom to love and aspire. Work, culture, liberty—all these we need, not singly but together, not successively but together, each growing and aiding each, and all striving toward that vaster ideal that swims before the Negro people, the ideal of human brotherhood, gained through the unifying ideal of Race; the ideal of fostering and developing the traits and talents of the Negro, not in opposition to or contempt for other races, but rather in large conformity to the greater ideals of the American Republic, in order that some day on American soil two world-races may give each to each those characteristics both so sadly lack. We the darker ones come even now not altogether empty-handed: There are today no truer exponents of the pure human spirit of the Declaration of Independence than the American Negroes; there is no true American music but the wild sweet melodies of the Negro slave, the American fairy tales and folklore are Indian and African; and, all in all, we black men seem the sole oasis of simple faith and reverence in a dusty desert of dollars and smartness. Will America be poorer if she replace her brutal dyspeptic blundering with light-hearted but determined Negro humility? or her coarse and cruel wit with loving jovial good-humor? or her vulgar music with the soul of the Sorrow Songs?

Merely a concrete test of the underlying principles of the great republic is the Negro Problem, and the spiritual striving of the freedmen's sons is in the travail of souls whose burden is almost beyond the measure of their strength, but who bear it in the name of an historic race, in the name of this land of their fathers' fathers, and in the name of human opportunity.

CRITICAL THINKING QUESTIONS

1. What does Du Bois mean by the "double-consciousness" of African Americans?

2. Du Bois writes that people of colour aspire to realizing a "better and truer self." What do you think he imagines such a self to be?

3. What are some of the reasons, according to Du Bois, that Emancipation (from slavery in 1863) brought disappointment to former slaves, at least in the short run?

4. Does this essay seem optimistic or pessimistic about the future of race relations? Why?

39

Aboriginal Identity: The Need for Historical and Contextual Perspectives

JEAN-PAUL RESTOULE

Restoule explores Canadian Aboriginal identities from legal and historical perspectives as well as the personal and subjective experiences of Aboriginal peoples.

Employing a perspective that distinguishes between "identity" and "identifying" demonstrates the limitations inherent in typical conceptions of cultural identity. Identifying is situational and historical, shaped by the time and place in which it occurs, whereas identity is thought to transcend history and social situations. Identity is represented in the Indian Act and its definition of "Indian." Métis efforts for recognition as an Aboriginal people in their own right is seen as identifying. The potential harm of identity is demonstrated by the Crown's arguments in the case for Gitksan-Wet'suwet'en Aboriginal title.

I recently attended a conference where a number of us were discussing issues concerning Aboriginal identity. We talked about how our

Source: Jean-Paul Restoule. 2000. "Aboriginal Identity: The Need for Historical and Contextual Perspectives." *Canadian Journal of Native Education*, 24(2), 102–12. Abridged with the permission of the *Canadian Journal of Native Education*, University of Alberta and University of British Columbia.

parents had tried to hide any semblance of their Aboriginal identity and how in our experience today it was not only acceptable, but indeed desirable to be Aboriginal. In our experience dreamcatchers were everywhere and Aboriginal plays and events in the city were sold out. "What happened?" we asked each other. Then someone pointed out that where she came from there was not the luxury to talk about identifying as Aboriginal as if it were a choice. Shame about being Aboriginal continued to exist in her community. Most of the people from her community would hide their Aboriginality if possible. For many of them it was not even an option. They were "known" as Aboriginal people. Also, in her experience the issues of drug abuse, AIDS, diabetes, unemployment, spousal abuse, and others were seen as more pressing concerns than identity.

Her words had quite an impact on me. How can some of us talk about the struggle for identity when on a daily basis so many of us struggle just to survive? Is writing about these matters really helping to change anything? I keep coming back to this idea that some of the people in her community would hide their Aboriginality if they could. Understanding what influences our pride or shame in identifying as Aboriginal people is important. How we feel about ourselves contributes to and arises from the issues my colleague felt were more urgent to discuss than identity. I have seen examples where pride in Aboriginal identity is the basis for fighting addiction and where shame in identity is a factor in developing a habit of substance abuse (Restoule, 1999). It is important to explore what identifying as Aboriginal means and what is gained and lost in attempting to erase that identity, as well as what it means to change the referents of what is meant by Aboriginal identity.

IDENTITY AND IDENTIFYING

The term *identity* expressed popularly, as well as in academic circles, implies a fixed nature over a given time period. In psychology, identity is often qualified as, for example, sex-role identity or racial identity (Sutherland, 1989). These qualities are assumed to have some continuity over time for the individual. In Piaget's work, identity refers to a state of awareness that something holds its value despite surface appearances to the contrary (Sutherland, 1989). In logic, identity refers to two words, properties, or statements that are so similar that they can substitute one for the other in an equation without altering the meaning (Sutherland, 1989). In sum, identity has been conceived to mean sameness. For social scientists discussing cultural identity, the sameness inherent in the definition of identity refers to the shared norms, traits, and habits of members of a cultural group at one historical moment. Unfortunately, there are educators, lawyers, and policymakers who make the error of assuming Aboriginal identity must hold over several generations.

To talk about Aboriginal identity assumes a sameness and continuity that belies the fluidity and change that Aboriginal people experience and demonstrate. When this assumed permanence of character is run through institutions like the education and court systems "Aboriginal identity" can be constrictive and colonizing. I return to this idea below with a discussion of the case for Gitksan-Wet'suwet'en Aboriginal title. If we change the focus from *identity* to *identifying*, we move from noun to verb and set off a potentially liberating way of conceiving and talking about self-definition. *Identity* implies fixedness; that the "things" that make one Indian remain the same and should be the same as those things associated with Indianness by the Europeans at the time of historical "first" contact. Identity places power in the observer who observes Aboriginal people from the outside and defines them, giving them an identity. *Identifying* shifts control to the self, and motivations come to the fore. This perspective favors a set of referents that are put into action at the historical time one identifies as an Aboriginal person and in the contextual place where one identifies. Identifying is a process of being and becoming what one is in the moment. The power is placed in the self, for the Aboriginal person who emphasizes his or her Indigenous roots at a particular place and time. This allows for the salient components of an Aboriginal identity to be expressed as the actor feels is expedient, allowing for cultural change and adaptation. Identifying is situational and historical, whereas identity is thought to transcend history and social situations.

In this article I use a number of examples to make clearer the distinction between identity and identifying. Dunn's (2001) research on the Métis of the Red River region shows that the tension between identity and identifying existed even in the 1800s. I provide a brief overview of Canadian legislation defining "Indians" as an example of identity as I characterize it above. As a point of contrast, Métis participation in the Constitutional Conferences of the 1980s and the Royal

Commission on Aboriginal Peoples (RCAP, 1996) demonstrate identifying.

Employing a perspective that distinguishes between identity and identifying might help us problematize typical conceptions of cultural identity limited in their ability to reflect the situational and contextual identifying that exists in contemporary Aboriginal life. To demonstrate the limitations of an identity perspective, I look at Fitzgerald's (1977) notion of cultural identity as an interplay between color, culture, and class. This conception of cultural identity, I feel, is fairly typical. I refer to work by Valentine (1995) and Pinneault and Patterson (1997) to demonstrate that identity/identifying is indeed contextual and is shaped by the time and place in which it occurs. . . .

LIMITATIONS OF IDENTITY IN ABORIGINAL NORTH AMERICA

Identity is a complicated concept. Cultural identity is often conceived as an interplay between biology, socioeconomic status, and cultural knowledge. Fitzgerald (1977), in his study of Maori students, refers to these three components as color, culture, and class. To Fitzgerald color represents a biological connection to the original peoples. In other words, it is the blood connection, the lineage that can be traced to Aboriginal communities and families. By culture Fitzgerald means knowledge of the traditions, language, and ceremonies or the "markers" of the race. Class stands for socioeconomic position in the greater society. Society is perceived as the greater economic and political entity where many cultures coexist. Each culture participates in the larger society where it is located, although the cultural norms of the group may be distinct from the rest of the society.

Race is often conflated with class, so that a racial group or cultural group is likely to be thought of as occupying a particular class position in relation to the greater society. Power is maintained by barriers that keep racial groups from advancing socioeconomically. Although certain individuals may succeed in being upwardly mobile, much of the group continues to experience difficulty. As Fitzgerald (1993) observed, "The central tensions between groups do not seem to be essentially cultural but originate in inequalities over power and participation in society. More and more, groups are trying to invent cultures through identity assertions" (p. 221). Identity tends to be more persistent and stable over time, whereas cultures are in a constant state of reinvention. This is because identity often has to do with how the out-group culture views the in-group. Fitzgerald (1977) found that some Maoris he studied validated their right of acceptance in the Maori group by overemphasizing their biological connections and/or class position, especially if they knew little about the culture. I suspect this to be the case among Aboriginal people in Canada. Those who know little about the Aboriginal culture to which they claim a connection probably will emphasize their blood ties to an Aboriginal culture. Claiming to be born "Ojibwe" or "Blackfoot" does not necessarily entail a familiarity with the music, ceremonies, or language. This is a reality of living in a dispersed culture where there have been generations of increased pressure not to exhibit these cultural knowledges.

The interplay of biology, culture, and class cannot maintain its integrity when applied to Aboriginal cultures in North America. Perhaps in the mid-nineteenth century most Aboriginal people could be slotted by class, culture, and biology such that the categories remained relatively stable. Aboriginal persons for the most part were not only able to demonstrate who they were related to (biology), but also could make their way in their culture and were probably lower-class citizens in relation to the class structure of British North America. Today these factors are not necessarily applicable to each Aboriginal person, and it is impossible to predict with any certainty one's placement in each of these categories. For example, today many Aboriginal people may be slotted into lower socioeconomic categories in relation to Canadian class structure, but individual Aboriginal people are not necessarily reducible to a particular class. Also, many people with Aboriginal cultural knowledge have no ties to their home communities or to an officially recognized community. Conversely, many Aboriginal people with blood ties to Aboriginal communities have little or no Aboriginal cultural knowledge. The instability of these categories is evident when one looks at contemporary Aboriginal people on Turtle Island today.

IDENTIFYING AS SITUATIONAL AND CONTEXTUAL

Fitzgerald's (1977) observation that "cultural identity has relevance only in a situation of cultural homogeneity" (p. 59) appears to be supported by the research of both Valentine (1995) and Pinneault and Patterson (1997). Valentine lived and worked among the Anishinabe of Lynx Lake, Ontario where the community is composed almost entirely of Aboriginal families. As Valentine explains,

In southern Ojibwe communities, where forced contact with the White matrix society has been long standing, Native people tend to define themselves vis-à-vis the "other." Thus, if something is "White" then it is necessarily "not-Indian" and vice versa. . . . In the north, where there has been relatively little and generally recent contact with Whites, the Native people define themselves internally. In a situation such as that in Lynx Lake, it is moot to ask if one element or another is "White" or even "borrowed." If the people are using it, the item is being used "Natively." The question asked by the people of Lynx Lake is "Will X be useful to us?" not "Will the use of X compromise our Nativeness?" (p. 164)

Here the question of what is Aboriginal is raised only in comparison with cultures outside the community.

Contrast the Lynx Lake community with Pinneault and Patterson's (1997) work in urban schools in the Niagara region of Ontario. Here Pinneault and Patterson counsel youth who

struggle with debunking myths and labels or with trying to find where they fit in. Pinneault and Patterson describe the situation thus.

Attempt to put yourself in the following story. You are living in a land which is the first and only foundation of your philosophy, spiritual beliefs, historical patterns, cultural distinction, and ancestral connections. At the same time, you never see a reflection of yourself within the philosophy of others, the educational system, popular culture, or day-to-day events within the community. Stereotyping remains entrenched in most societal situations and you are constantly in a position of needing to defend your rights and position. When you are able to visualize yourself, it is through the interpretation of others who have little understanding of who you are. You are constantly being defined and redefined from an outside system. (p. 27)

Many students in the south are struggling with the creation of safe places to increase self-esteem and build understanding and acceptance of some of the Aboriginal cultural traditions. Obviously identity issues come to the fore when there is sustained contact between culturally different groups, and especially when they are valued differently on the social scale.

Another way to understand the differences between the disparate groups in Niagara and Lynx Lake is to discuss identifying rather than identity. Identifying in Niagara has different meanings and consequences than it does in Lynx Lake. Aboriginal people in Lynx Lake do not identify as "Native" in Lynx Lake because the homogeneous nature of the population makes it redundant to do so. The identity of the people in the distant communities is not different necessarily. Rather the factors that influence an Aboriginal person's choice to identify change from one region to another are different. . . .

LEGISLATIVE DEFINITIONS AS IDENTITY

The Indian Act has been the source of many problems in the history of Aboriginal survival. It has been the legal support for violence enacted against Aboriginal peoples in the form of regulations imposed on personal mobility, language use, and participation in cultural activities. Relevant to this discussion is its peculiar claim of distinction as a rare piece of legislation that sets out in law a definition of a people. This definition has had a profound impact not only in how we are understood by non-Aboriginal people, but also in how we have come to understand ourselves. . . .

In early legislation designed to contain potential violence between Aboriginal people and newcomers, a broad definition of *Indian* was set into law. For example, the 1850 Indian Protection Act defined Indians broadly:

The following classes of persons are and shall be considered as Indians belonging to the Tribe or body of Indians interested in such lands: First—All persons of Indian blood, reputed to belong to the particular Body or Tribe of Indians interested in such lands, and their descendants. Secondly—All persons intermarried with any such Indians and residing amongst them, and the descendants of all such persons. Thirdly—All persons residing among such Indians, whose parents on either side were or are Indians of such Body or Tribe, or entitled to be considered as such: And Fourthly—All persons adopted in infancy by any such Indians, and residing in the Village or upon the lands of such Tribe or Body of Indians, and their descendants.

The only important distinction was between European and Indian. Interestingly enough, early definitions of Indian like this one allowed for men and women of European descent who lived with an Aboriginal community to be considered Indian before the law. What mattered more than blood (although this too was important) was the evidence that one lived as an Indian. One would have to assume this distinction was relatively simple to make in the nineteenth century. Otherwise the definition would have been drafted differently.

As laws governing Indian lands were consolidated, the definition of an Indian in law was redrafted to exclude more Aboriginal people and to encourage the assimilation of registered Indians into the Canadian body politic (RCAP, 1996). Assimilation is genocide according to the United Nations Genocide Convention, signed by Canada in 1949 and unanimously adopted in Parliament in 1952. Chrisjohn and Young with Maraun (1997) have argued that Canada could be tried in violation of the genocide convention for the operation of residential schools. The Canadian Civil Liberties Union, in debates held before Canada enabled legislation in 1952, recognized the potential for Canada's transfer of Indian children to residential schools to be seen as genocide (Churchill, 1997). Enfranchisement was also a key tool of assimilation or genocide.

Enfranchisement, along with definitions privileging patrilineal descent, reduced the number of Indians eligible for the Register. The children of interracial marriages were counted as Indians only when the father was Indian. Native women who married non-Native men were removed from the Register and often distanced from their communities. Over the years there were many ways Indians could lose their status. Some examples include earning a university degree, requesting the right to vote in a federal election, or requesting removal from the Indian Register for a share of the monies that would have gone to the band on their behalf. Most significantly, Indian women who married non-Indian men were enfranchised involuntarily, and the children of these marriages were ineligible for status. Clearly the goal of the Gradual Enfranchisement Act, and its subsequent absorption into the Indian Act, was assimilation (RCAP, 1996).

The Métis, as an Aboriginal people, found themselves caught in the middle of the changing legal definitions. The numbers of Métis who would have been entitled to receive the benefits of Indian status in 1850 were gradually reduced by arbitrary legislation. Great pains were taken to extinguish Métis claims to Aboriginal title, and they were not accorded any benefits in exchange for the land. This does not mean that only "full-blooded" Indians were entitled to be registered. What mattered was whether it was one's father or mother who was officially recognized as Indian. Often these non-status Indians would align themselves politically with the cultural Métis, who had for the most part been denied any rights as Aboriginal people. This denial occurred despite Métis treaties with Canada in the Manitoba Act and the Dominion Lands Act(s).

BEING AND BECOMING MÉTIS AS AN EXAMPLE OF IDENTIFYING

The Métis provide an interesting example of how colonial definitions are played out and affect self-definitions. Most people believe that Métis means simply "mixed" denoting the mixing of the blood of European and Indian parents in their child. The word has been used to designate various groups with a tie to Aboriginal peoples present on the continent before European settlement. How were the new populations that were a result of the new interrelationships between Indian and non-Indian characterized or written about in the earliest times? How did Métis, which originally meant simply mixed, come to mean specific kinds of mixes and in specific times and locations?

Dunn (2001), a descendant of the Red River Métis and consultant to the RCAP, has an excellent Web site (www.otherMétis.net) that catalogues the many terms and names that have been used to describe the intermixing of European and Aboriginal peoples. It is important to note that there is little evidence of what these groups of people under discussion preferred to be called in the nineteenth century, and few records of what they called themselves exist. Most of these terms were used by colonial bureaucrats and traders who thought it important enough and necessary to write about this growing and influential population in their particular region. . . . The diversity of names used indicates at least two important points. First, the groups now known as Métis were seen as a distinct social fact by most of the social groups sharing the same region. Second, the names accorded these groups of "mixed-race" people are ways for people external to the group to make an identity for them. Obviously some terms are meant to be

disparaging. Dunn's ancestors were called Half-breed by the government officials of the day. At the same time, Dunn's great-great-grandfather used the term *Natives of the country* when referring to his group. In any case, as Dunn points out, "the external application of terminology does not guarantee that the term accurately communicates the expression of an internal identity" (para. 22). Identity is a process of being and becoming, and nouns cannot adequately be used to describe identity; rather they merely serve to label and fix a group of persons (Peterson & Brown, 1985). The attributes of the group that make it identifiable as distinct from others are constantly changing, and the words that are used to fix the group also change their referents. The use of the word Métis was taken up by these groups of "mixed blood" or "ancestry" and applied in different ways and for different ends.

At the constitutional conferences in the mid-1980s the leader of the Métis National Council (1986) stated:

Surely it is more than racial characteristics that makes a people. What about a common history, culture, political consciousness? Our origins, like that of any people when traced back far enough, are mixed, but once we evolved into a distinct aboriginal people, the amount of this much or that much ancestry mattered less than being Métis.

Note that he stressed the acceptance of the community and identification with the community.

This distinction was promoted by the 1996 *Report of the Royal Commission on Aboriginal Peoples*, although it made some concessions for the Congress of Aboriginal Peoples definition of Métis, which is based solely on Aboriginal ancestry (blood). The RCAP (1996) recommendation is as follows:

. . . 4.5.2 Every person who (a) identifies himself or herself as Métis and (b) is accepted as such by the nation of Métis people with which that person wishes to be associated, on the basis of criteria and procedures determined by that nation be recognized as a member of that nation for purposes of nation-to-nation negotiations and as Métis for that purpose. (vol. 4: 203)

This definition, although leaving the choice of political affiliation to the individual claimant, is broad enough to include both Métis National Council and Native Council of Canada/Congress of Aboriginal Peoples members.

It should be noted that the Commission's recommendation above is made in respect to the sphere of political rights. The Commission (1996) recognizes that the identification of Aboriginal communities for legal purposes has taken a different approach. Essentially, after some analysis, the Commission laid out three elements that seemed to be acceptable to courts in determining membership in an Aboriginal community:

- some ancestral family connection (not necessarily genetic) with the particular Aboriginal people;
- self-identification of the individual with the particular Aboriginal people; and
- community acceptance of the individual by the particular Aboriginal people. (vol. 4: 297–98)

A fourth element was mentioned as also being of relevance in some cases: "a rational connection, consisting of sufficient objectively determinable points of contact between the individual and the particular Aboriginal people" (vol. 4: 298). Acceptable criteria include residence, family connections, cultural ties, language, and religion (vol. 4: 298).

In many ways it seems as if we have come full circle. Early attempts to legislate who is an Indian were broad and inclusive and allowed for anyone living in an Aboriginal community to qualify as Indian under the law. Definitions became increasingly exclusive, causing inequities and suffering and dissension among Aboriginal peoples. The RCAP (1996) recommended that all Aboriginal peoples be entitled to rights as members of an Aboriginal community. But history has seen individuals with Aboriginal "blood" migrate to urban areas where they may not live in Aboriginal communities that are located in a tight geographical configuration. As sound and fair as it may appear for legal reasoning to recognize only

Aboriginal communities and members of those communities, in practice it may again turn out to be a politically expedient way of reducing the numbers of Aboriginal people whom the government must recognize. In the end it really may be up to the individuals in communities of interest to decide what factors of their personality and culture make them distinctly Aboriginal and continue a process of being and becoming that cannot be legislated.

THE IMPACT OF IDENTITY

Once when I was talking to a friend and tenant at a native housing co-op where I worked, I told her that my lack of knowledge on a particular issue was because I was not a politically active person. She replied, "For an Indian, being born is political." I realize now that she meant that from the time we are born, as Indians we are in a particular relationship with the Canadian state by virtue of the treaties, the Indian Register, and the Indian Act. She also meant that because the state had been seeking our disappearance for centuries, each time one more of us is born we are directly in opposition to the goals of the state. Each of us through our birth proved we would not disappear. When we are born, we are defined by the state as a particular kind of Indian. Either we are eligible for the Indian Register and designated a Status Indian, or we are denied the rights that this heritage should lend itself to. There were times when not being registered was an advantage because the strict enforcement of the Indian Act imposed many measures on recognized Indians. The drawback, of course, was that many identifiable Indians were disallowed connections with their extended families and some of the treaty rights their ancestors had negotiated.

Using strictly the legal view of Indianness, in my family's experience, my father was born an Indian, later "earned the right not to be an Indian" through enfranchisement, and many years later was seen as a Status Indian once again. I was not born an Indian and was given Indian Status only after passage of the amended Indian Act of 1985. Receiving that card in the mail made me question a lot of things, and it caused me to look at my family in a new way. I was confused about how we had an identity decided for us. Why was it not a given that we could define for ourselves who we were?

The issue of Aboriginal identity is most often played out in Canadian law. Aboriginal "difference" from others is used to maintain inequities in power when it is convenient for those with power (Macklem, 1993). However, when our difference results in what is seen as privilege, arguments are made that treating Aboriginal people differently is "un-Canadian" because it is in opposition to the stated goal of equality among individuals before the law. There is a constructed image of what Indians are supposed to be that has to be played into or against in order to make advances in Canadian institutions, especially courts of law (Crosby, 1992; Razack, 1998). If we do not appear Indian enough or do not exhibit enough of the traits that are somewhat expected of Indians, then we will be judged to be no longer different enough from the Euro-Canadian assumption of the mainstream, and thus no longer Aboriginal. We will, in fact, be assumed to have assimilated into the assumed mainstream Canadian norm.

This line of logic has been argued by lawyers for the Crown in the case for Gitksan-Wet'suwet'en Aboriginal title (Crosby, 1992). The Crown argued that because the contemporary Gitksan eat pizza from microwaves and drive cars, they have essentially given up their Aboriginality. Indian rights flow only to those who meet the criteria for authenticity established by the Eurocentric courts (Crosby, 1992). Sustained colonization has caused many Aboriginal people to move away from a subsistence economy to a market economy, often without their choice. Many of the traditional ways of life seen from the Eurocentric position as "authentic Indian ways" have been altered by the imposition of colonial policies and laws, and then these very charges are used against us as arguments that we are no longer Aboriginal people.

The criteria accepted in the legal system, however, are often limited to material "stuff." What makes one Aboriginal is not the clothes one wears or the food one eats, but the values one holds. There is more to Aboriginal cultures than "fluff and feathers" (Doxtator, 1992). Johnston (1995), an Ojibwe ethnologist, recalls the time a young student in an elementary school, having spent five weeks learning about tipis, buckskin, canoes, and so much other stuff, asked him, "Is that all there is?" Johnston wanted people to know that there was more to Anishinabe culture than mere stuff, and this led him to write books like *Ojibway Heritage* (1976), *Ojibway Ceremonies* (1982), and *The Manitous* (1995). Unfortunately, in museums, movies, and courts of law it is the stuff that is exhibited. We are not Indian unless we prove that we still cling to the stuff that defined us in the eyes of others over 100 years ago. This conception will continue as long as we talk about identity and not identifying.

An interesting exercise is to turn these arguments around and apply them to the Eurocentric arguments for our assimilation. Does the lawyer who said the Gitksan-Wet'suwet'en drive cars realize that Europeans did not drive cars at the point of contact either? Was this lawyer wearing the same clothes his forefathers wore in 1763? Does this lawyer use the number zero? I think the use of zero may be a case of cultural adoption, not unlike the Aboriginal people who adopt the use of snowmobiles. The culture that made the law is privileged to adapt and change over time, whereas the Aboriginal cultures are denied this same privilege. Although it may not be the stated objective of the law, the result is often the maintenance of inequitable relations of power. Keeping Indians in the place they had at confederation is a goal of the consolidated Indian Act of 1876.

CONCLUSION

The Indian Act had as its goal nothing less than the assimilation of Aboriginal people in Canada (RCAP, 1996). A key strategy in achieving this goal was increasingly to limit who is an Indian by law and to change the status of those who were already on the list through enfranchisement. In this law "Indians" are identical to one another, but "different" from the Canadian power majority. The writers of legislation did not consider our cultures and histories important. Our identity as Indians was invented. Although at times we have used this identity to our own interests, forming coalitions across cultures to seek political gains (such as inclusion in the Constitution Act, 1982), we have also used these invented identities against one another, allowing these government categories to intrude on our social and cultural affairs (Coates, 1999). In our lives, in our work, in our efforts to educate others, let us identify as Aboriginal people from our inside place, from ourselves, our communities, our traditions. Let us not allow others to decide our identity for us.

ACKNOWLEDGMENTS

I would like to thank the anonymous reviewers of an earlier draft for their comments.

CRITICAL THINKING QUESTIONS

1. From a sociological perspective, why would possessing a positive self-identity influence how you lived your life?

2. With reference to the article, what role has the government played in the development of Aboriginal identity in Canada?

3. Review the similarities and differences between the concepts of *identity* and *identifying*. Why is the distinction important?

4. Review some of the recommendations for the *Report of the Royal Commission on Aboriginal Peoples* (1996) as described in the article. Can you find any examples from your own community where these recommendations have been implemented?

REFERENCES

Chrisjohn, R., S. Young, with M. Maraun. 1997. *The circle game: Shadows and substance in the Indian residential school experience in Canada.* Penticton, BC: Theytus.

Churchill, W. 1997. *A little matter of genocide: Holocaust and denial in the Americas 1492 to the present.* San Francisco, CA: City Lights Books.

Coates, K. 1999. Being Aboriginal. In *Futures and identities: Aboriginal peoples in Canada*, ed. M. Behiels, 23–41. Montreal: Association for Canadian Studies.

Crosby, M. 1992. Construction of the imaginary Indian. In *Vancouver anthology: The institutional politics of art*, ed. S. Douglas, 267–91. Burnaby, BC: Talonbooks.

Doxtator, D. 1992. *Fluff and feathers: An exhibit of the symbols of Indianness.* Brantford, ON: Woodland Cultural Centre.

Dunn, M. 2001, January. Métis identity—A source of rights? Paper presented at Trent University. [Online]. Available: **http://www.otherMétis.net/index.html/Papers/trent/trent1.html#Terminology**. Retrieved January 4, 2001.

Fitzgerald, T. K. 1977. *Education and identity: A study of the New Zealand Maori graduate.* Wellington: New Zealand Council for Educational Research.

Johnston, B. 1976. *Ojibway heritage.* Toronto: McClelland and Stewart.

———. 1982. *Ojibway ceremonies.* Toronto: McClelland and Stewart.

———. 1995. *The Manitous: The spiritual world of the Ojibway.* Toronto: Key Porter Books.

Macklem, P. 1993. Ethnonationalism, Aboriginal identities, and the law. In *Ethnicity and Aboriginality: Case studies in ethnonationalism*, ed. M. D. Levin, 9–28. Toronto: University of Toronto Press.

The Métis Nation. 1986. 2(1): Winter.

Peterson, J., and J. S. H. Brown (eds.). 1985. *The new peoples: Being and becoming Métis in North America.* Winnipeg: University of Manitoba Press.

Pinneault, A., and C. Patterson. 1997. Native support circles in urban schools. *Orbit*, 28(1): 27–9.

Razack, S. 1998. *Looking white people in the eye: Gender, race and culture in courtrooms and classrooms.* Toronto: University of Toronto Press.

Restoule, J. P. 1999. Making movies, changing lives. Aboriginal film and identity. In *Futures and identities: Aboriginal peoples in Canada*, ed. M. Behiels, 180–89. Montreal: Association for Canadian Studies.

Royal Commission on Aboriginal Peoples. 1996. *Report of the Royal Commission on Aboriginal Peoples.* Ottawa: Ministry of Supply and Services.

Sutherland, N. S. 1989. *The international dictionary of psychology.* New York: Continuum.

Valentine, L. P. 1995. *Making it their own: Severn Ojibwe communicative practices.* Toronto: University of Toronto Press.

40

Ethnically Heterogamous Marriages: The Case of Asian Canadians

JESSIE M. TZENG

Tzeng's research investigates Canadian trends in interracial marriages. Findings suggest that while many believe their decision regarding whom to marry to be completely autonomous, it is in fact influenced by many social factors—whether they realize it or not.

INTRODUCTION

In an ethnically diverse society, such as Canada, the increases in intersection of group affiliations may promote intermarriage. A person often belongs to several social groups; for example, people live in a neighborhood, have an occupation, belong to an ethnic group, are members of a religious group, and have a socioeconomic status. Thus, the increasing social interactions among individuals of different backgrounds in modem society promote intergroup relations which in turn foster intermarriage (Blau, Beeker, and Fitzpatrick, 1984). In addition, the apparent growth of cultural pluralism, which stresses the acceptance of various ethnicities within a society, also shortens the social distances among persons of different ethnic backgrounds and may encourage intermarriage.

Many recent empirical studies suggest that various kinds of intermarriage have become more common over the course of this century (Kitano, Yeung, Chai, and Hatanaka, 1984; Lieberson and Waters, 1988; Kalmijn, 1993). However, the question of who marries whom remains a complicated mate-selection process for intermarried couples. The traditional theory of homogamy (like attracts like) is insufficient to explain interracial assortative mating because individuals in interracial relationships face unconventional and unique challenges when compared to couples in intraracial relationships. To better understand the mechanism behind interracial marriage selection, one needs to further explore the forces of pull and push in the decision to intermarry and the role which achieved socioeconomic status plays in the process of interracial assortative mating.

Source: J. M. Tzeng. 2000. Ethnically Heterogamous Marriages: The Case of Asian Canadians. *Journal of Comparative Family Studies*, 31(3), 321–37. Published by permission.

Dynamics in Intermarriage: Forces of Pull and Push

In principle, there are two major forces, pull and push, operating simultaneously in the interracial assortative mating. Young people today may assume that their choice of mate is completely autonomous; however, many factors, in fact, do place limits on autonomy, whether we consciously recognize their impact or not. One of the major influences on marital autonomy is the principle of endogamy, which requires a person to choose a partner from his or her own group (Larson, Goltz, and Hobart, 1994). This is one of the major pull sources constraining individuals from marrying someone outside their own group. Historically both family and society strongly opposed intermarriage. Almost all racial and ethnic groups have resisted intermarriage to protect and maintain their ethnic identities. Though there was no law prohibiting marriages between individuals from different racial and ethnic groups in Canada, intermarriage taboo exists not only in the importance of maintaining purity of one's own race or consistency of socialization for the younger generations, but also in the prevention of creating incompatible norms between members of diverse ethnic groups (Tinker, 1973; Merton, 1941). In this vein, it is said to be extremely difficult for a child of an intermarriage when it comes to selecting a role model for his or her identity; thus, those who oppose intermarriage believe marriage across racial and ethnic boundaries inevitably leads to a loss of identity among minority groups and signifies that a group is disintegrating, both socially and culturally (Goldstein and Segall, 1991).

Looking back in history, despite the persistence of negative attitudes and reactions toward intermarriage, people continue to intermarry, which may be a result of the following favorable push factors. First, recent social, economic and political environment changes provide some evidence that the society has become more open and tolerant to racial and cultural heterogeneity (Spickard, 1989; Goldstein and Segall, 1991).

Namely, a higher rate of interracial marriage is possible because social proximity is common across many areas of social life, thereby providing evidence of shortening social distances between different racial and ethnic groups. Second, significant changes in the racial and ethnic distributions of the population will inevitably increase the probability of intermarriage. As the opportunities for individuals to come into contact with someone outside their own group increase, so does the likelihood of intermarriage. Third, research suggests that individuals from various racial and ethnic groups with higher socioeconomic status are more likely to enter intermarriage (Glick, 1970; Tinker, 1973; Fitzpatrick and Gurak, 1979; Sung, 1990). For example, the recent success in socioeconomic achievement obtained by Japanese, Chinese, and Jews in the United States is consistent with their higher out-marriage rates (Kitano, et al., 1984; Mayer, 1985). On the one hand, individuals with higher socioeconomic status are more appealing to potential partners in the marriage market, both within and outside their own ethnic group. Since everyone is searching for a "better half" as a marriage partner, individuals from racial and ethnic groups with favorable socioeconomic positions increase their chance of out-marrying. On the other hand, this may also suggest that individuals from various racial and ethnic groups with higher socioeconomic status have a more liberal attitude toward marriage and are less likely to be bounded by traditional family or cultural norms, and thus are more likely to select mates outside their own group. Overall, it is argued that the number of interracial marriages will continue to rise as physical and social barriers between peoples diminish and the traditional approaches to mate selection will be replaced by the individual's choice (Sung, 1990).

Given the expansion of education and of women's participation in the labor force in the past few decades, young adults of all races are increasingly more likely to meet their potential spouses in school or at work. As a result of the current social forces, we are tempted to argue that the push force will play a more significant role than the pull force in an individual's marital choice.

The Significance of Achieved Status and Mate Selection

Some empirical evidence supports the theory of homogamy (that persons marry others either with similar ascribed family background or, increasingly, with similar achieved socioeconomic status). Couples who share similar cultural resources, either from ascribed or from achieved status, are more likely to enjoy similar views or agree with each other on certain issues and behaviors. On the one hand, the ascribed cultural characteristics from one's family of origin, including social class, religion, and race/ethnicity, are believed to have a major impact on an individual's choice of a future partner (Hollingshead, 1950). Among the many ascribed cultural characteristics used to describe the process of assortative mating, race and ethnicity is one of the most significant characteristics to represent one's cultural heritage. In particular, persons who were born and raised in Asian families have very distinctive cultural traits, such as unique physical appearance, languages, subcultures, values, norms, lifestyles, attitude, customs, and beliefs, all of which contribute to the uniqueness of their personalities, attitudes, social activities, and social circles and eventually affect their preference or choice of future mates.

On the other hand, the achieved cultural characteristics associated with individuals' socioeconomic status, such as language capability of the host society, educational attainment, and labor-market experience, are obtained by individuals through external institutions outside the home over time. The role of one's socioeconomic resources is becoming more important than race and ethnicity in the process of mate selection, due to the great expansion of education in the second half of the twentieth century, the greater flexibility in social mobility, and the changing role of women in the labor force.

For Asian immigrants, language ability is an important achieved characteristic clearly related to the assimilation process (White, Biddlecom, and Guo, 1993), because most Asian countries from which immigrants come do not use English or French as their official languages. Not only is the ability to speak English and/or French in Canada necessary for survival and assimilation in the host society, it helps to shorten the distance and to increase contact between individuals from different racial and ethnic groups. If immigrants lack knowledge of the official language, then there are cumulative as well as social and cultural barriers between immigrant groups and the host society (Stevens and Schoen, 1988). According to Murstein's (1970) stimulus-value-role theory of marital choice, marital choice involves a series of sequential stages: stimulus, value, and role; and, at any given point of the relationship, its viability can be determined as a function of the equality of exchange subjectively experienced by its participants. Without language capability, one cannot effectively go through the three stages of marital choice: interacting with each other, sharing values, and defining roles. In addition, the most obvious channel for communication between spouses is language, and when there is no common language between the potential marital partners, the channels of communication are blocked; thus, the odds of intermarriage will be small (Sung, 1990). Accordingly, Asian immigrants' knowledge of English and/or French will facilitate their propensity to intermarry in Canada (Castonguay, 1982).

In addition, numerous studies show that an individual's educational attainment and labor-market experience have become influential predictors in the process of marriage selection (Mare, 1991; Kalmijn, 1991, 1993; Qian and Preston, 1993; Schmitt, 1971; Hout, 1982). Educational attainment probably is one of the most significant social influences on the marriage process in many ways (Qian and Preston, 1993). Since education is often looked upon as being a key determinant of long-term socioeconomic status, research shows that the level of schooling varies positively with the propensity to marry (South, 1991). Following the exchange theory of mate selection (Merton, 1941), the higher the educational attainment of individuals, the more desirable they are in the marriage market, thus increasing their chances to marry. In addition, there has been a high level of marriage homogamy by education in the U.S. as well as in Canada (Sweet and Bumpass, 1987; Schoen and Wooldredge, 1989; Mare, 1991; Ishwaran, 1992). Most people tend to many those with a similar level of education, due to their comparable values, goals, interests, and outlooks on life.

Among the most significant social changes in the recent decades has been the increasing participation of women in the labor force (Cherlin, 1992; Bianchi and Spain, 1986). The labor-market experience of women may have two opposite effects on the overall propensity to marry. On the one hand, the new economic independence gained by employed women reduces the comparative gains from marriage, thereby reducing the propensity to marry (Becker, 1981). On the other hand, women's full-time labor-force participation may be viewed as potential marital capital which will contribute to the total family income, thus increasing their desirability in the marriage market.

In view of people's general interest to marry up and/or marry homogamously, the high educational attainment and labor-force participation of Asians may affect their odds of marrying someone outside their own group. However, for many individuals of Asian origin, the newly learned cultural traits may be in great conflict or competition with traditional cultural characteristics. Individuals with Asian background have one of the strongest family traditions and kinship ties, and it is extremely important for the members in each group to preserve and pass their cultural heritage from one generation to the next. Marriage, for most Asian families, is important for its effect on family continuity and for maintaining the family line, not just for two individuals (Tinker, 1973). If, among Asian groups, the family tradition still plays an important role (even implicitly) in the individual's choice of spouse, then the increasing trend of interracial marriage expected for Asian groups due to their high socioeconomic achievement would have been offset or lessened to a certain degree.

How one balances or weighs the two cultural forces when it comes to the individual's choice of a marital partner may vary with different groups and change over time. Thus, in this paper, I investigate the association between socioeconomic achievement and intermarriage for Asians in Canada and examine the changes in the importance of an individual's achieved socioeconomic status on his or her propensity to intermarry.

INTERMARRIAGE IN CANADA

This paper is aimed toward a better understanding of recent unique patterns in interracial marriage for Asians in Canada. Canada is widely regarded as an ethnoracially complex but remarkably ordered society of immigrants and refugees, aboriginal peoples, and colonizing groups (Fleras and Elliott, 1992). The immigrant population represented 16% (4.3 million persons) of Canada's population in 1991, almost unchanged since 1951, when the immigration population was 15% (Badets and Chui, 1994). Although the proportion of immigrants living in Canada has remained stable for the past 50 years, the distribution of immigrant population has become much more diverse now than it was a few decades ago. For example, in 1961, 90% of immigrants in Canada were from Europe, partly because immigration policy had systematically excluded non-white people; however, the proportion of European immigrants dropped significantly to less than a quarter in 1991. Among the new immigrant population, people reporting Asian origins were the fastest-growing group between 1981 and 1991. In 1991, more than 40% of immigrants came from Asia and the Pacific, while only 21% were from Europe (Statistics Canada, 1993). The shift in the source of immigrants from European to non-European countries has altered Canada's ethnic and linguistic composition and has created a greater diversity in the new "Canadian mosaic."[1]

Given Canada's new multicultural mosaic, one might expect to observe an ever-increasing trend in marriages among various racial and ethnic groups if current migration flow remains unchanged. Migration, indeed, is a major factor leading to interracial unions (Sung, 1990). If Asians or other racial and ethnic groups had not migrated to Canada, intermarriage would be less likely to occur. In the late 1980s, about 14% of the total married couples in Canada involved one foreign-born spouse, and 9% of the marriages were made up of two foreign-born persons (Dumas, 1990). The rate of interracial marriage would, no doubt, be even higher if I included second and later immigrant generations, as many studies have shown that generational differences account for a great deal of out-marriages (Tinker, 1973; Pagnini and Morgan, 1990). Compared to its southern neighbor, Canada has a higher rate of intermarriage than the U.S.,[2] mainly due to the following reasons. First, in the United States, racial intermarriage was legally restricted until 1967, while in Canada, no legal sanction was imposed on interracial marriage. Despite the fact that the U.S. Supreme Court's decision declaring its law on racial intermarriage unconstitutional, the social mores and the disfavor placed on interracial marriage by all major racial, religious, and ethnic groups have had major impact on an individual's choice of marital partner (Eshleman and Wilson, 1995). Second, most studies in Canada employ place of birth or countries of origin as the main source of identification of interracial marriages. This source allows a broader definition for interracial marriage than the self-identified race and ethnicity variable used in the U.S. studies. Third, the higher rate of intermarriage in Canada may also be directly attributed to its increasingly diverse immigrant population in recent years. For example, one out of six Canadians is a first-generation immigrant who is usually single and thus eligible for marriage (Statistics Canada, 1988), which also increases the opportunity for interracial marriage.

As a result of increasing Asian immigration to Canada in the past two decades, those reporting single Asian origins represented about 5% of the total population in 1991, and this trend is likely to persist with current immigration policies. Nevertheless, not only has systematic empirical research

on intermarriage for individuals with Asian origins rarely been conducted in Canada, but also little attention has been paid to married couples' socioeconomic status in the study of interracial marriages. Among the limited empirical research on interracial marriage for Asians in North America (mostly in the U.S.), studies are predominately descriptive in nature (Burma, 1963; Tinker, 1973; Kitano et al., 1984; Romano, 1988; Sung, 1990) and lack multivariate analyses linking Asians' socioeconomic achievement and interracial marriage. Recent studies in marriages have described the tendency for persons to choose partners of similar educational attainment (Mare, 1991), occupation (Hout, 1982), and other social standings. In addition, in his recent research, Kalmijn (1991, 1993) suggests that educational homogamy has increased its importance over social origin homogamy, such as class and race, in marriage selection in the U.S. during recent decades. Thus, the focus of this paper is to examine the patterns and changes in intermarriage for Asians in Canada from 1981 to 1991, focusing on the effects of married couples' individual characteristics and socioeconomic status on intermarriage.

DATA AND METHOD

Sample

To examine intermarriage for various Asian Groups in Canada, it would have been more fruitful to use the individual file from recent Canadian censuses, which would provide detailed information on the respondent's ethnic origin[3], place of birth, and other individual characteristics. However, the individual identification codes in each census file were removed from public access and the data was randomly rearranged to ensure its total confidentiality. Thus, it is impossible to identify married couples from this data structure. As a result of this constraint in using individual census records, I have resorted to the family census file for this analysis.

FINDINGS

Changes and Temporal Patterns of In- and Out-marriages

Table 40.1 presents descriptive statistics on selective spouses' characteristics for Asian in- and out-marriages in Canada for 1981 and 1991. Contrary to the popular belief, in-marriage rates for Asians increased from 75.5% in 1981 to 80.1% in 1991. Accordingly, both male and female out-marriage rates were somewhat lower in 1991 than in 1981, with male out-marriage rates dropping twice as much as female out-marriage rates (3.1% vs 1.5%) during the 10-year period. As a result, Asian women have a slightly higher out-marriage rate than Asian men in 1991; however, the gaps in out-marriage rates between Asian men and women are small in both time periods. Thus, a significant gender difference in intermarriage found in other studies (Tinker, 1973; Kitano et. al., 1984) is not evident for Asian men and women in our data.

TABLE 40.1   Descriptive Statistics for Selective Variables

		1981			1991	
Variables	*In-mar.*	*Out-mar. Husband*	*Out-mar. Wife*	*In-mar.*	*Out-mar. Husband*	*Out-mar. Wife*
Marriage Rate	75.5	12.8	11.7	80.1	9.7	10.2
Husband's Age	42.0	42.2	42.8	45.3	42.2	43.6
Wife's Age	38.2	37.8	38.8	41.4	38.8	39.8
Years of Immigration (Husband)						
≤10	64.1	42.7	18.9	45.7	24.9	10.6
>10	35.9	56.4	30.1	49.9	70.8	32.7
n/a	.9	51.0	4.4	4.4	56.7	
Years of Immigration (Wife)						
≤10	71.6	30.8	45.1	48.7	12.1	30.4
>10	28.4	24.7	53.4	46.5	29.8	64.8
n/a	44.5	1.5	4.8	58.1	4.8	
Official Language (Husband)						
English and/or French	89.2	98.7	98.5	88.2	98.6	99.1
Neither	10.8	1.3	1.5	11.8	1.4	.9
Official Language (Wife)						
English and/or French	81.1	97.8	98.1	82.8	98.9	98.1
Neither	18.9	2.2	1.9	17.2	1.1	1.9
Education (Husband)						
<12	25.7	14.5	12.6	28.1	15.1	16.4
12–13	29.9	36.1	46.1	22.3	19.9	24.3
14+	44.4	49.3	41.3	49.6	65.0	59.3
Education (Wife)						
<12	36.1	23.3	12.1	35.8	16.0	15.1
12–13	33.4	48.0	52.4	27.1	30.8	26.3
14+	30.5	28.6	35.4	37.1	53.2	58.6
Employment Status (Husband)						
Not employed	13.4	9.7	3.9	18.7	10.8	10.9
Part-time	3.3	2.2	3.9	4.3	5.8	5.6
Full-time	83.3	88.1	92.2	77.0	83.3	83.4
Employment Status (Wife)						
Not employed	37.0	34.4	35.9	33.6	24.9	25.8
Part-time	13.2	15.4	21.4	11.1	20.0	17.5
Full-time	49.8	50.2	42.7	55.4	55.2	56.7

The average ages for husbands and wives in our sample are 42.3 and 38.27 in 1981; 43.7 and 40 in 1991. The respondents in our sample are in their middle age because the age composition of the immigrant population differs markedly from that of non-immigrants in Canada (Fleras and Elliott, 1992). The immigrant population in Canada is older than the native-born population because most people who immigrate to Canada do so when they are adults. More specifically, the in-married couples in 1981 were about 3 years younger than those couples in 1991. However, the changes in the age distributions are within 1 year for both male and female out-marriers from 1981 to 1991. The average differences between husbands and wives in all marriage types range from 3.3 to 4.4 years.

In both time periods, there are more out-married couples than in-married couples who have no children in their family, and the proportions are higher in 1991 than in 1981. In particular, female out-marriers have the highest proportion of being childless—32% and 38.2% in 1981 and 1991, respectively. In addition, male out-marriers in 1981 and female out-marriers in 1991 have the lowest proportions of having more than 3 children in their families. Nevertheless, the majority of couples have 1 or 2 children in their families regardless of marriage types. For all marriages, about one-third of the couples have children under the age of 6. This is consistent with the literature in that inter-married couples tend to have fewer children due to their concern about adjustment problems for their children or their lack of time to have children if both of them are highly devoted to the labor force (Eberhard and Waldron, 1977; Sung, 1990).

The majority of Asians who married within group had been in Canada less than 10 years by the time of survey in 1981. In 1981, more than 50% of male (56.4%) and female (53.4%) out-marriers had been in the country for more than 10 years. However, for those who married within group in 1991, about half of them had been in Canada for more than 10 years and the other half had been in the country for less than 10 years. In addition, among out-marriers, 70.8% of men and

64.8% of women had been living in Canada for more than 10 years by the time of survey in 1991.

As to language capability, those who were unable to speak either English or French were more likely to marry within the Asian group. About 10% of men and 20% of women who had no knowledge of English or French were in in-marriages. On the other hand, more than 98% of the out-marriers were able to speak English, French, or both English and French in 1981 and 1991.

The lower half of Table 40.1 describes couples' labor-force characteristics for both in- and out-marriages. The overall educational attainment increased for all Asians during the period of 1981–1991. For in-marriages, the proportion of husbands and wives with more than 14 years[4] of schooling increased more than 5% from 1981 to 1991. The upward shift in educational achievement was even more significant for Asian out-marriers. The proportions of male and female out-marriers who were in the highest educational category increased from 49.3% to 65% and from 35.4% to 58.6% in the 10-year period, respectively.

The changes in the labor-force participation for husbands and wives show somewhat different patterns during this period. There was about a 5–6% decrease in full-time employment for both in- and out-married Asian males. On the contrary, the proportions of full-time employment increased from 49.8% to 55.4% for wives in in-marriages and from 42.7% to 56.7% for female out-marriers. In addition, the proportions of housewives for Asian females in both types of marriages declined, especially for female out-marriers.

The Effects of Individual Characteristics and Socioeconomic Factors on Intermarriage

In other analysis not shown here I estimated models that only include the effects of married couples' ages, the difference in age, and the respondents' duration of immigration on the probability of interracial marriage (Model I). Then, I added the variables indicating spouses' socioeconomic characteristics, such as individual's knowledge of the official language (i.e., English and/or French) in Canada, educational attainment, employment status, and the symmetrical positions of both spouses on educational attainment and employment status (model II, i.e., models in Table 40.2). In both years, scale deviances[5] drop significantly from model I to model II (Scale deviance {(model I model II)} = -129.5 and -616.3 in 1981 and 1991, respectively), with 15 degrees of freedom, which indicates the significant effects of spouses' socioeconomic characteristics in predicting the propensity of interracial marriage for Asians in Canada.

Thus, the following discussion will be focused on model II (shown on Table 40.2) for both years. The multivariate analyses presented in Table 40.2 examine the effects of both Asian husbands' and wives' social demographic and socioeconomic characteristics on the log odds of interracial marriage in 1981 and 1991, respectively. For models in Table 40.2, I report the logit coefficients, beta, and their standard deviations, se (beta).

Age

The results show that the effect of husband's age on the odds of interracial marriage is much stronger in 1991 than in 1981 except for the oldest age group. Husbands who were 35–44 or 45–54 years old are about 66% ($100[\exp(-1.079)-1]$) or 65% ($10)[\exp(-1.050)-1]$) less likely to be intermarried than those who were 15–24 years of age in 1991. Wife's age consistently shows a negative effect on the probability of intermarriage in both years. Namely, older wives are less likely than those who were 15–24 years old to marry out, especially for those who were older than 65 years of age in 1981 and those who were 55–64 years of age in 1991. I also examine the effect of age homogamy on intermarriage. The results indicate that age-heterogamous Asian couples are more likely than

age-homogamous couples (i.e., wife's age is equal to or less than 3 years younger than her husband's) to intermarry in both years. Especially in 1991, older wife–younger husband couples are about 62% ($100[\exp(0.481)-1]$) more likely to intermarry than age-homogamous couples.

Years of Immigration

The results also indicate the durations of immigration for both husband and wife significantly predict whether they enter intermarriage or not. Couples in which either one of the spouses or both spouses had been in Canada for more than 10 years are much more likely to be intermarried than those couples who had been in the country for less than 10 years. For example, if both spouses had been in Canada for more than 10 years, they are at least 5 times (1981: $100[\exp(1.859)-1]$; 1991: $100[\exp(1.954)-1]$) more likely to marry out than those [who] had been in the country less than 10 years. The effects of durations of immigration on the log odds of entering intermarriage have remained quite stable during the 10-year period.

Official Language

Furthermore, the ability to speak either English and/or French increases one's probability to marry someone outside the Asian group. As shown from both years, when either one of the spouses or neither of the spouses speak the official languages, the chance of out-marrying is reduced. Although the negative effects on the probability of intermarriage have lessened from 1981 to 1991 for couples with only one of the spouses speaking the official languages, they are still highly significant. In addition, when neither spouse speaks one of the official languages, couples are about 87% less likely to intermarry than those couples who both have the ability to speak English or French in 1991. The ability to negotiate life in the host society using the official languages helps the immigrants to achieve social

TABLE 40.2   Logistic Models of Asian Interracial Marriages in Canada

	1981		1991	
	beta	*se(beta)*	*beta*	*se(beta)*
Husband's Age (15–24)				
25–34	0.057	0.452	−0.761	0.208
35–44	−0.446	0.503	−1.079	0.227
45–54	0.006	0.558	−1.050	0.252
55–64	−0.019	0.640	−0.592	0.281
65+	1.386	0.760	0.027	0331
Wife's Age (15–24)				
25–34	−0.363	0.272	−0.042	0.138
35–44	−0.556	0.349	−0.375	0.167
45–54	−0.428	0.440	−0.495	0.202
55–64	−0.308	0.555	−0.737	0.248
65+	−1.625	0.768	−0.390	0.301
Age Homogamy				
(Husband–Wife = 0–3)				
Husband–Wife >3	0.167	0.158	0.138	0.068
Husband–Wife <0	0.212	0.199	0.481	0.081
Years of Immigration				
(>10 Yrs) (Neither)				
Husband only	1.982	0.256	1.866	0.123
Wife only	1.234	0.196	1.854	0.110
Both	1.859	0.166	1.954	0.086
Official Language (Both)				
Husband only	−2.069	0.531	−1.795	0.260
Wife only	−1.311	1.134	−0.984	0.388
Neither	−1.715	0.492	−2.074	0.257
Husband's Education (≤11)				
12–13	0.704	0.233	0.231	0.097
14+	0.467	0.280	0.336	0.117
Wife's Education (≤11)				
12–13	0.448	0.193	0.475	0.090
14+	0.114	0.255	0.744	0.109
Educational Homogamy				
(H = W)				
H > W	0.098	0.180	0.135	0.071
H < W	0.755	0.194	0.550	0.085
H's Employment Status				
(Not employed)				
Part-time	−0.162	0.601	0.398	0.175
Full-time	−0.454	0.793	0.275	0.258
W's Employment Status				
(Not employed)				
Part-time	0.093	0.194	0.325	0.092
Full-time	0.513	0.774	−0.045	0.243
Employment Homogamy				
(H − W)				
H > W	0.751	0.756	0.155	0.228
II <- W	−0.858	0.655	0.429	0.222
Scaled Deviance	1586.2	8812	–	–
Degrees of Freedom	1	738	10	567

and economic assimilation, which in turn can facilitate intermarriage (White et al., 1993).

Education

The results from the lower panel of Table 40.2 show that the odds of interracial marriage vary positively with the educational attainment of husbands and wives for both years. In particular, the magnitude of the effects of wife's educational attainment is about twice that of husband's in 1991. The models also indicate that educational heterogamous couples are, in general, more likely than homogamous couples to experience interracial marriage, especially when the wife has more years of schooling. Apparently, the high levels of marriage homogamy by education found in recent years for married couples in North America are not witnessed in the intermarried Asian couples in Canada.

Employment Status

The odds of interracial marriage are not affected by husband's and wife's employment status in 1981. However, the odds of out-marriage vary positively with husband's and wife's employment status in 1991, except for wife's full-time employment. And employment-heterogamous couples are also more likely to be intermarried than employment-homogamous couples in 1991, especially when wives work more than their husbands. The effects of employment heterogamy are consistent with that of educational heterogamy on intermarriage. That is, couples in which wives work more than their husbands are about 54% more likely to be intermarried than employment-homogamous couples in 1991.

CONCLUSIONS

Our results indicate the increasingly significant roles which the achieved socioeconomic characteristics play in interracial assortative mating.

Our study first builds on previous work by examining the effect of social demographic variables such as husband's and wife's age, age heterogamy, and years of immigration on Asian intermarriage in Canada from 1981 to 1991. The results are, in large part, in agreement with prior research. I find older individuals and those without any knowledge of English or French are less likely to marry out. Whereas, the propensity to intermarry is higher for age-heterogamous couples and when either one or both spouses have been in Canada for more than 10 years.

I then examined the effects of couples' socioeconomic characteristics on the odds of intermarriage. Our results indicate that educational attainment positively affects one's probability of interracial marriage. In addition, couples in which wives have higher educational achievement are also more likely to intermarry than educational homogamous couples. As for the effect of labor-force experience, I did not observe the same main effects of husband's and wife's employment status on intermarriage for both 1981 and 1991. In particular, the employment effect is not significant in 1981. On the contrary, in 1991 employment-heterogamous couples are more likely to be intermarried than employment-homogamous couples, especially when wives work more than their husband.

Thus, the results suggest age-, educational-, and employment-heterogamous Asian couples vary positively with the odds of intermarriage. In particular, the most unconventional couples, in which the wife is older, more educated, and with a higher level of labor-force participation than the husband, are more likely to be intermarried. These results may suggest that Asian women do have more to gain by intermarriage (Tinker, 1973). In general, older ages of the wives in intermarriage are highly correlated with their higher educational attainment and labor-market experience. Also, highly educated or full-time employed Asian women are more likely to intermarry due to their quest for a more egalitarian marriage and their desire to avoid traditional constraints set upon an Asian wife if she were to marry within her cultural group.

However, to my surprise, the rates of Asian intermarriage did not increase from 1981 to 1991, as I originally thought. The reasons for these decreasing rates may be due to the following: First, there is a larger selection as well as a more balanced sex ratio within one's own ethnic group as more Asian-origin groups immigrate to Canada. Most prior research suggests that population size and a balanced sex ratio positively correlate with in-marriage (Besanceney, 1965; Alba and Golden, 1986: Sung, 1990). Second, with a growing consciousness of multiculturalism in the Canadian society, many racial and ethnic minorities, including Asians, are increasingly aware of their cultural and linguistic heritage as a positive component of personal identity and are anxious to remain culturally distinct, which may pose cultural constraints on intermarriage (Fleras and Elliott, 1992). Though I observe a declining trend in intermarriage over this 10-year period, it is premature to predict a downward trend in Asian intermarriage in Canada, because I only include the first generation, foreign-born Asians in this sample, which usually has much lower out-marriage rates than later generations of immigrants. In addition, there may exist a large variation in the patterns of intermarriage for various Asian ethnic groups, which was not captured in this study.

CRITICAL THINKING QUESTIONS

1. Judging from the married people that you know, do you believe that the principle of *endogamy* still prevails? Provide examples to support your answer.

2. One of the findings revealed in the article is that people of higher socioeconomic status are more likely to intermarry. As a sociologist, why do you think this is the case?

3. According to Tzeng, how has the increasing participation of women in the labour force influenced rates of intermarriage?

NOTES

1. Although people of British (Anglophones) and French (Francophones) backgrounds are still the largest ethnic groups in Canada, neither of them account for a majority of the population (Statistics Canada, 1993).

2. About 2.2% of all marriages were interracial in the 1990s (U.S. Bureau of the Census, 1993).

3. Respondent's race-ethnicity was not included in Canadian censuses.

4. The reason I did not use 12 years of schooling as the dividing criterion for different educational categories is that secondary school may include grade 13 in some provinces in Canada.

5. Scale deviance describes the lack of fit of a given unsaturated model versus saturated model, i.e., Scale Deviance = -2log (L2/L1), where L2 is the maximum likelihood of the model understudy, and L1 is the maximum likelihood of the saturated model. Under regularity conditions, the difference in scale deviances has approximately a chi-squared distribution, with degrees of freedom equal to the difference between the numbers of parameters in the two models (Agresti, 1990).

REFERENCES

Agresti, A. 1990. *Categorical data analysis*. New York: Wiley-Interscience.

Alba, R. & R. M. Golden. 1956. Patterns of ethnic marriage in the United States. *Social Forces*, 65: 202–23.

Badets, J., and T. W. Chui. 1994. Canada's changing immigrant population. Statistics Canada-Catalogue No. 96–311E. Scarborough, ON: Prentice Hall.

Becker, G. S. 1981. *A treatise on the family*. Cambridge: Harvard University Press.

Besanceney, P. H. 1965. On reporting rates of intermarriage. *American Journal of Sociology*, 70 (6): 717–21.

Bianchi, S. M. and D. Spain. 1986. *American women in transition*. New York: Russell Sage Foundation.

Blau, P. M., C. Beeker, and K. M. Fitzpatrick. 1984. Intersecting social affiliations and intermarriage. *Social Forces*, 62 (3): 585–605.

Burma J. H. 1963. Interethnic marriage in Los Angeles, 1948–1959. *Social Forces*, 42 (1): 156–65.

Castonguay, C. 1982. Intermarriage and language shift in Canada. 1971 and 1976. *Canadian Journal of Sociology*, 7 (3): 263–77.

Cherlin, A. J. 1992. *Marriage, divorce, remarriage*. Cambridge: Harvard University Press.

Dumas, J. 1990. Report on the demographic situation in Canada. 1988. Statistics Canada-Catalogue No. 91-209E. Ottawa: Statistics Canada.

Eberhard, M., and J. Waldron. 1977. Intercultural marriage and child rearing. In *Adjustment in intercultural marriage*, eds. W. S. Tseng et al. Honolulu: University of Hawaii Press.

Eshleman, R. J., and S. J. Wilson. 1995. *The family.* Canadian Edition. Scarborough, ON: Allyn & Bacon Canada.

Fitzpatrick, J. T., and D. T. Gurak. 1979. *Hispanic intermarriage in New York City.* 1975. New York: Fordham University Hispanic Research Center.

Fleras, A., and J. L. Elliott. 1992. *Multiculturalism in Canada: The challenge of diversity.* Scarborough. ON: Nelson Canada.

Glick, P. 1970. Intermarriage among ethnic groups in the United States. *Social Biology,* 17(4): 293–98.

Goldstein, J., and A. Segall. 1991. Ethnic intermarriage and ethnic identity. In *Continuity & change in marriage and family,* ed. Jean E. Veerers. Toronto: Holt, Rinehart and Winston.

Hollingshead, A. B. 1950. Cultural factors in the selection of marriage mates. *American Sociological Review,* 15: 619–27.

Hout, M. 1982. The association between husbands' and wives' occupations in two-earner families. *American Journal of Sociology,* 88: 397–409.

Ishwaran, K. 1992. *Family and marriage: Cross-cultural perspectives.* Toronto: Thompson Educational Publishing.

Kalmijn. M. 1991. Status homogamy in the United States. *American Journal of Sociology,* 97(2): 496–523.

—— 1993. Trends in Black/White intermarriage. *Social Forces,* 72(1): 119–46.

Kitano, H. H., Y. Wai-Tsang, L Chai, and H. Hatanaka. 1984. Asian-American interracial marriage. *Journal of Marriage and the Family,* 46(1): 179–90.

Larson, I. E., W. Goltz, and C. W. Hobart. 1994. *Families in Canada.* Scarborough, ON: Prentice Hall.

Lieberson, S. and M. C. Waters. 1985. *From many strands: Ethnic and racial groups in contemporary America.* New York: Russell Sage.

Mare, R. D. 1991. Five decades of educational assortative mating. *American Sociological Review,* 56, 15–32.

Mayer, E. 1985. *Love and tradition: Marriage between Jews and Christians.* New York: Plenum Press.

Merton, R. K. 1941. Intermarriage and social structure: Fact and theory. *Psychiatry,* 4: 361–74.

Murstein, B. 1970. Stimulus—Value—Role: A theory of marital choice. *Journal of Marriage and the Family,* 32: 465–81.

Pagnini, D. I., and S. P. Morgan. 1991. Intermarriage and social distance among U.S. immigrants at the turn of the century. *American Journal of Sociology,* 96 (2): 405–32.

Qian, Z., and S. H. Preston. 1993. Changes in American marriage, 1972 to 1987: Availability and forces of attraction by age and education. *American Sociological Review,* 58: 482–95.

Romano, D. 1988. *Intercultural marriage: Promises & pitfalls.* Yarmouth, ME: Intercultural Press.

Schoen, R., and J. Wooldredge. 1989. Marriage choices in North Carolina and Virginia, 1969–71 and 1979–81. *Journal of Marriage and the Family,* 51: 465–81.

Schmitt, R. C. 1971. Recent trends in Hawaiian interracial marriage rates by occupation. *Journal of Marriage and the Family,* 33: 373–74.

South, S. J. 1991. Sociodemographic differentials in mate selection preferences. *Journal of Marriage and the Family,* 53: 928–40.

Spickard, P. R. 1989. *Mixed blood: Intermarriage and ethnic identity in twentieth-century America.* Madison, WI: University of Wisconsin Press.

Statistics Canada. 1988. Marriage and conjugal life in Canada. Statistics Canada—Demography Division. Ottawa: Statistics Canada.

—— 1993. Ethnic origin and occupied private dwellings. *The Daily,* Statistics Canada—Catalogue No. 96-304E. Ottawa: Statistics Canada.

Stevens, G., and R. Schoen. 1988. Linguistic intermarriage in the United States. *Journal of Marriage and the Family,* 50: 267–79.

Sung, B. L. 1990. *Chinese American intermarriage.* New York: Center for Migration Studies.

Sweet, J. A., and L. L. Bumpass. 1987. *American families and households.* New York: Russell Sage Foundation.

Tinker, J. N. 1973. Intermarriage and ethnic boundaries: The Japanese American case. *Journal of Social Issues,* 29(2): 49–66.

Tucker, M. B., and C. Mitchell-Kernan. 1990. New trends in Black American interracial marriage: The social structural context. *Journal of Marriage and the Family,* 52(1): 209–18.

U.S. Bureau of the Census. 1993. Current population reports. Series P-25, no. 455. Population projections of the United States, by age, sex, race, and hispanic origin: 1993 to 2050. Washington, DC: U.S. Department of Commerce.

White, M, J., A. E. Biddlecom, and G. Shenyang. 1993. Immigration, naturalization, and residential assimilation among Asian Americans in 1980. *Social Forces,* 72 (1): 93–117.

41

Growing Old in Inuit Society

LEE GUEMPLE

Guemple's intention in "Growing Old in Inuit Society" is to investigate how, in precontact Inuit society, the elderly were loved and revered but were also killed or allowed to die by their family and friends. This apparent contradiction, at least to Westerners, allows a glimpse into the rich diversity of human adaptation.

The treatment the Inuit (Eskimo) traditionally accorded their old people during the precontact period has been a source of some consternation to members of the Euro–North American cultural tradition because of a seeming paradox. We know that Inuit lavished care and concern on their old people and invested considerable interest in them. But we also know that they sometimes abandoned them on the trail (Freuchen, 1961: 194–203) and that they stood ready at times even to help them to dispose of themselves by drowning or strangulation (Rasmussen, 1908: 127). Our own notion of what people are like makes it difficult for us to see how they could be so affectionate in one context and cold-hearted in another, when the chips were down.

Source: Reprinted with permission from Lee Guemple 1980. "Growing Old in Inuit Society." In Victor Marshall (ed.), *Aging in Canada: Social Perspectives* (pp. 95–101). Fitzhenry and Whiteside Ltd., Markham, ON.

The aim of this essay is to try to resolve the paradox; to show how the attitude of love and affection is not incompatible with the idea of killing one's own parents or helping them to kill themselves. To do so we must make a brief foray into the cognitive universe of the Inuit—into their own notion of how the world (of people and things) works. Only then can we fathom how they manage to mix sentiment with seeming cruelty without a sense of contradiction.

First, however, it will be useful to offer some background material on aging in Inuit society. Inuit have no generic term for "senior citizens." Instead, they use one term for an old man, *ituq*, and another for an old woman, *ningiuq*. These terms are used mainly while speaking about the old people, seldom when speaking to them.

It is difficult to establish the age in years at which people are consigned to old age. Like us, Inuit associate adulthood with work status, and old age constitutes a kind of "retirement" from full participation in community affairs. But Inuit do not keep vital statistics like we do. We cannot reckon an age of retirement for them. Besides, everyone is encouraged to continue working for as long as possible so that retirement comes not by convention, but by the gradual process of biological aging. While doing research in the Belcher Islands Inuit community, I was able to calculate the mean age at which men acquire the label of *ituq* at about fifty years of age (Guemple, 1969). Women seem to maintain the status of adult somewhat longer, but will ordinarily pass over into being classed as *ningiuq* at age sixty or so.

Men become old when they can no longer hunt on a year-round basis but pass on the task of routine hunting to younger members of the household—generally a mature son or son-in-law. Hunting in winter is very demanding and because of its importance to the maintenance of life it is the crucial determinate of male status. At somewhere around fifty years of age a man can no longer sustain the strength and stamina to perform this task on a regular basis and will "retire." His withdrawal can be gradual but is often dramatic.

Women's allocated tasks are both more varied and less strenuous with the result that advancing age does not limit their effectiveness nearly as much as it does men's. Women routinely share work among themselves and the heavy work is often passed along to mature girls even in early adulthood while the older women tend to younger children and infants. Loss of strength and agility will not quickly be noticed in a woman. She will simply spend more time at home, performing other routine tasks such as cooking or sewing. The transition to old age is thus more gradual and comes later in the lifecycle than it does for men.

The onset of old age is hastened by debilitating diseases and may be slowed by what I have elsewhere called "renewal" (Guemple, 1969). The major forms of physical impairment that affect premature entry into old age are arthritis and blindness. The cold, damp character of the traditional igloo and tent tend to promote arthritis; and the incidence of blindness due to

trachoma and glaucoma is relatively high. Men also suffer a relatively high incidence of corneal abrasion and snow blindness which can often lead to partial impairments of sight. In the recent past tuberculosis has also taken a considerable toll, particularly in those people who have been sent out to hospital to have portions of lungs or bones removed to rid them of infection.

Old age can also be delayed in some instances. Men often accomplish this by extraordinary effort in hunting during the spring and summer seasons when the demands of production are not so great; and they sometimes undergo symbolic renewal by taking younger women as wives in their maturity. Women cannot aspire to marry younger men in their later years; but they can and frequently do assert they are still able to perform their primary functions by seeking to adopt children. It is said that adopting a child makes an old woman feel young again; and while the primary aim of adoption is not stated to be renewal, it is the only reason given that makes very much sense.[1]

Old people are well cared for in Inuit society because they can draw upon two interlocking social institutions as sources of support: the household and the community at large. Members of a household share equitably; so long as there are younger workers in the household to work on behalf of their elders their interests are seen to with great care and devotion (Gubser, 1965: 122; Hawkes, 1916: 117). The rules of residence stipulate that young hunters stay home until they marry, and so an aging elder can expect to have his son do much of his hunting for him. When the daughters marry their husbands will come to live in the household, and they are answerable to their fathers-in-law, at least until after the first child is born. They may also remain in the household of an in-law if there is need and relations between the son-in-law and other household members are cordial.

Old people can expect some support from the community at large so long as they are able to contribute to the fund of resources from which others draw. Inuit rules of sharing enjoin that successful hunters share a portion of their catch with those who were less successful; and mature hunters are generally only too happy to be able to offer support to other community members, since it is the single source of prestige in the local hunting community. In return, the old people offer the produce of the hunting of their sons or sons-in-law or, as circumstances permit, they offer the help in sewing and gathering wood by their daughters, and they themselves will pitch in to help in any way they can to the general good. Men often offer work in repair jobs, executing technically difficult parts of various pieces of technology where knowledge and patience are particularly needed. They go for short hunting trips around camp, and often school young hunters on how to set snares, stalk land animals, etc. Women contribute their domestic labour for sewing, cooking, cleaning, baby tending, and so on. In the evenings, the old people, as keepers of the sacred and secular lore of this non-literate society, maintain a sense of tradition by telling stories and offering advice which experience shows to be particularly applicable to some predicament.

This system seems to work well so long as old people have someone to rely on to make their contribution to the community pool; and the institutional structure appears to break down only when the old people are left stranded by the departure of their children from the household and the community for one reason or another for an extended period of time. In that context, members of the community at large gradually come to view the old couple as parasitic and begin to complain about their dependency. So far as I am aware, community members would not flatly refuse to feed old people in such a situation; but they often receive a lesser share or the least desirable portion. And they may from time to time suffer the indignity of being gossiped about or verbally abused for their failure to contribute adequately.

As the couple grows into old age, one or the other will die leaving the survivor to move in with a son or daughter or with some more distant relative. The children generally accept the added burden gracefully; though more distant relatives may find it a bit inconvenient to be saddled with a sibling or cousin in old age. The Inuit of the Canadian North never collected material possessions as a form of wealth. The need to be continually on the move prevented the accumulation of luxuries. But men with ambition often collected people as a kind of "wealth"; and old men or women who were not too feeble were generally welcome in the household of an influential hunter if they had no children to care for them. Seldom were old people to be found in utterly desperate straits unless the entire community was impoverished.

If old people were well treated and cared for by their fellows in the traditional culture, they appear also to have been the objects of startling cruelties. Inuit are known to have abandoned their old people on the trail from time to time with very little ceremony; and there are even cases where the children stood ready to help them end their lives if asked to do so. Such behaviour strikes us as terribly inconsistent and begs for an explanation.

The well-documented facts are that Inuit sometimes abandon their old people. This was generally done either by leaving them behind while on the trail or by allowing them to go off on their own to make an end to themselves. When old people were abandoned, it was most often done out of necessity, seldom out of indifference to the old (Burch, 1975: 148–50; Gubser, 1965: 122; Jenness, 1922: 236; Low, 1906: 165; Spencer, 1959: 252), though cases of apparently cruel treatment are known (Stefánsson, 1914: 130).

Freuchen (1961: 200–03) describes a typical case with his usual dramatic flair: a couple is travelling from one community to another accompanied by their immature children and an old woman, the wife's mother. Sometime during the night, the old lady, having faced an arduous day on the trail, decides the burden of living is too heavy for her to carry any longer, that she should now end the struggle to survive, that she has become a millstone to her children and grandchildren. She tells the two adults that she can go on no longer. They try to dissuade her, but she persists. Finally they agree, and in the morning they pack their gear and depart with only a word or two of farewell, leaving the old lady behind in the igloo, alone with her thoughts and her few meagre possessions.

Other examples appear to be even more unfathomable. An old man, perhaps nettled over some incident which has led to a quarrel or an insult to his sense of dignity, calls his two sons to him and tells them that he is old and useless, the butt of community jokes. Because of this, he has decided that, with their help, he will do away with himself. The sons encourage him to think positively, to remember the joys of playing with his grandchildren, and so on, but he insists that he has seen enough of life and wishes to be rid of it. Eventually, they leave off pleading, and under his direction, fetch a seal skin line and, wrapping the middle around his neck a couple of turns, take the ends and strangle him.

The conventional explanation of these situations is that the old are stoic about death and embrace the notion of their dying fearlessly and with resignation, when they feel they are no longer useful. So the sons or daughters accept the old person's decision with very little coaxing.

There are a number of problems with this formulation of their reaction to the possibility of death. For one thing, it assumes that life in the Arctic is a continuous struggle for survival which people perceive and respond to by a sort of stoic resignation. While this notion is one of our favourite themes, it is certainly not part of the Inuit repertoire. They do not see their lives as endangered by their marginal situation. They know its hazards well and have what are to them adequate means for coping with them. It is strangeness that creates a sense of threat, not familiarity; so their situation strikes us as threatening. The Inuit do not perceive it to be so.

How then are we to explain their casual acceptance of the death of loved ones, particularly the old? The answer is that old people do not, in Inuit cosmology, really die. In order to understand this statement, it will be necessary to set aside momentarily our consideration of old age as such and examine briefly the Inuit conception of the underlying character of people, whether old or young. That inquiry will provide us with the basis for solving the riddle of their indifference to death.

Inuit believe that the essential ingredient of a human being is its name. The name embodies a mystical substance which includes the personality, special skills, and basic character which the individual will exhibit in life. Without that substance he will die; and should he exchange his name substance for another through a ritualized renaming process, he will become a different person.

The name substance is derived from other humans, but is not thought of as biological in character; and it bears little resemblance to units of heredity such as genes or of some more metaphorical analogue of biological inheritance such as "blood." The name substance is induced into the body within three or four days after birth; and the process of naming a child is viewed by Inuit as one in which a ritual specialist divines what particular name substance has entered its body. Often the name is that of some recently deceased community member, frequently a relative of the child. But it is never the substance of a parent or sibling of the child and the most frequent "choices" of names are those belonging to members of the grandparent generation. The names of children who are sickly are sometimes changed shortly after birth, and shamans and a few others change their names in adulthood and thus become different persons; but most people keep their given names throughout their lifetimes. At death, the name separates from the body but remains within the vicinity of the body or of the place of death for three or four days during which time it is thought to be dangerous to living humans. After that time, it is thought to return to the underworld to wait till it can enter the body of a newborn child. Names thus cycle as do the social identities which are attached to them.

Names are never exclusively held by individuals in Inuit society. Three or sometimes four individuals may bear the same name and thus be the same person in principle. We might express this idea in a different way and say that from the standpoint of the Inuit community at large, the society consists of a limited number of names each having its own social identity—personal history, personality, work skills, attributes, and attitudes, etc.—attached to it. The identities are shared out in the community among its members on roughly a one-for-four basis, and cycle. At birth, individuals step into one of these well-established identities and bear them in latent form until they come to full expression in adulthood. During their lifetimes, they may contribute to their shape; and at death, they pass their part of the identities on to the next generation fully formed. These identities are indestructible; they neither die nor dissipate, but instead go on endlessly cycling through one generation after another.

Since the name substance is not inherited from the parents and not passed on to one's own biological posterity, parents contribute little to the children's identities except body substance which, to Inuit, is of little significance. And, since the social identity comes to the individual fully formed, it is not something the individual or the community were believed to be able to change in any major way, though in special cases it was possible to actually change identities.

We are now in a position to see why Inuit are relatively casual about the death of old people even if they are bound tightly to them in life. Children permit their parents to do away with themselves because they are not attached to them as we are to our parents. Every individual shares a community of spirit with others, but in Inuit

society, that community is with those who bear the same name, not those who share the same blood or some metaphorical analogue. Sentiments link parents and children together, but these can never be binding because parents and children share nothing more vital than those sentiments.

A more compelling reason for the seeming indifference to the death of the parents is related to their understandings about the fate of the person concerned. In our cosmology, the death of an individual means at best his departure to another place, at worst the end of all being, the end of all subjective experience of self. In either case, it is a mystery that makes life precious, that makes us rather bear those ills we have than fly to others. In Inuit cosmology, the persona is the one enduring, immutable substance. Whatever else may happen, Inuit know that their persona live on, not in consciousness, but certainly as fully formed social entities. It is this fact of their existence, and not a resigned stoicism, that make[s] them indifferent to death when the body becomes infirm and the will to live weakens.

The treatment of the old we have described here and the cosmological order we have explored to explain what give[s] them confidence and courage in facing old age and death is part of a tradition that is now on the verge of extinction across the Arctic as conversion to Christianity and the transition to modern living conditions gradually replace the aboriginal customs and beliefs. Modern-day old people of the North live in pre-fab homes, draw old age and disability pensions, take their sustenance from the shelf at the store, and receive their medical care from the local nursing station or hospital. These benefits have done much to make old age comfortable materially; and old men and women alike are quick to express their gratitude for these amenities. That the cosmological explanations we offer serve them as well in death as the material comforts we lavish on them in life is a little more difficult to assert with confidence.

CRITICAL THINKING QUESTIONS

1. How do the definitions of old age differ for men and women in traditional Inuit society? Are there similar factors influencing our definitions of old age in contemporary Canadian society?

2. Discuss the significance of a name in Inuit society and how it helps explain their somewhat indifferent approach to death.

3. Guemple concludes by questioning how the transition of Inuit society into a more modern and materialist one may affect their cosmological understanding of death. What do you feel are some of the other costs associated with this transition? Elderly Inuit today benefit from greater material wealth, but do you feel that the benefits outweigh the costs?

NOTE

1. The principal reason given for adoption [of children] by older women is that the adoption will provide someone to take care of the adopter "when they are old." But this same reason is given when the prospective adopter is in her sixties and the child is but one or two years of age. Further, the same reason is given by older women who have numerous children of their own, in some cases children already grown to maturity, and ready to care for the parent.

REFERENCES

Burch, E. 1975. *Eskimo kinsmen: Changing family relationships in Northwest Alaska.* New York: West Publishing Company (American Ethnological Society Monograph No. 59).

Freuchen, P. 1961. *Peter Freuchen's book of the Eskimos.* Cleveland: World.

Gubser, N. J. 1965. *The Nunamiut Eskimo: Hunters of caribou.* New Haven: Yale University Press.

Guemple, L. 1969. Human resource management: The dilemma of the aging Eskimo. *Sociological Symposium,* 2: 59–74.

Hawkes, E. W. 1916. *The Labrador Eskimo: Canada Department of Mines, Geological Survey Memoir 91.* Anthropological Series No. 14. Ottawa: Government Printing Bureau.

Jenness, D. 1922. *The life of the Copper Eskimos. Report of the Canadian Arctic islands.* Ottawa: Government Printing Bureau.

Low, A. P. 1906. *Report on the Dominion Government expedition to Hudson Bay and the Arctic islands.* Ottawa: Government Printing Bureau.

Rasmussen, K. 1908. *People of the polar north.* London: Kegan Paul, Trench, Trubner.

Spencer, R. F. 1959. *The North Alaskan Eskimo.* Washington: Smithsonian Institute. Bureau of American Ethnology, Bulletin 171.

Stefánsson, B. W. A. 1914. *The Stefánsson-Anderson Arctic expedition of the American Museum.* Anthropological Papers of the American Museum of Natural History. Volume 14, Part I.

42

How the Grandparent
Role Is Changing

ROSEANN GIARRUSSO, MERRIL
SILVERSTEIN, AND VERN L. BENGSTON

Increasing numbers of adults—especially in Western nations—are now great-grandparents and even great-great-grandparents. Such unprecedented longevity suggests the growing importance of multigenerational family relations. In this reading, Roseann Giarrusso, Merril Silverstein, and Vern L. Bengston examine how our longevity has already affected intergenerational family structures and why grandparent–grandchild relationships will become more important.

Grandparenthood has changed over the past decades as demographic shifts have increased the complexity of family structures and roles. Increases in longevity, in divorce and remarriage rates, and in old-age migration have simultaneously produced new opportunities and new stresses for grandparents. The longevity revolution has increased the number of three-, four-, and five-generation families, thereby lengthening the time spent in the grandparent role and adding multiple roles of great- and great-great-grandparent. Increases in divorce and remarriage rates have resulted in a high proportion of blended families and step-grandparent relationships. Improved health, stable finances, and early retirement have made geographic mobility possible for retirees. How have these changes in family structure,

Source: Reprinted with permission from *Generations*, 20:1, (Spring, 1996), pp. 17–23. Copyright © The American Society on Aging (San Francisco, CA). www.asaging.org.

composition, and living arrangements influenced the role of grandparents? What are the implications of these changes for the psychological well-being and resources available to grandparents?

In this [reading] we first examine how population aging and the changing structure of the intergenerational family highlight the increasing diversity in grandparenting and great-grandparenting styles. Second, we examine how divorce and remarriage in the middle generation influence grandparents' ability to enact their role when custodial parents act as gatekeepers to their children, and we underscore the need for research on grandparents rearing grandchildren in order to determine the psychological costs and rewards to caregiving grandparents. Third, we discuss how household arrangements and geographic mobility of grandparents and grandchildren jointly influence their relationship. We conclude with an overview of some research and policy implications that result from these complex family arrangements and emphasize the need for greater conceptual and theoretical development in grand-parenting studies.

CHANGING INTERGENERATIONAL FAMILY STRUCTURES

Because of dramatic increases in average longevity over the past century, it has become more likely that grandparents, great-grandparents, and even great-great-grandparents will survive long enough to have relationships with grand-children, great-grandchildren, or great-great-grandchildren. Where fewer than 50 percent of adolescents in 1900 had two or more grandparents alive, by 1976 that figure had grown to almost 90 percent (Uhlenberg, 1980). Thus, there is an un-precedented number of grandparents in American society today; more than three-quarters of adults can expect to become a grandparent (Barranti, 1985; Hagestad, 1985; Kivnick, 1982).

While historical increases in life expectancy have resulted in families with more generations alive simultaneously, reductions in fertility have resulted in smaller average family size (Bengtson & Treas, 1980; Uhlenberg, 1980; Watkins, Menken, & Bongaarts, 1987). Consequently, the shape of American families has gone from that of a pyramid, with larger numbers of young people at the base, to that of a beanpole. Three, four, and five generations of family members are increas-ingly present, but with fewer numbers being born in each subsequent generation than in previous eras (Bengtson, Rosenthal, & Burton, 1990).

With fewer family members in each genera-tion, existing *intergenerational* family relations take on added significance. Since there may be more *between*-generation kin than *within*-generation kin available in such a family struc-ture, grandchildren may emerge as potentially more important sources of emotional meaning and practical support for grandparents than in the past. Thus, grandparenthood may be an increas-ingly significant social role for older people,

offering valuable rewards. At the same time, it is important to consider whether a more involved grandparenthood also results in social, economic, and psychological costs—especially for grand-parents who become "surrogate parents" for their grandchildren (Bengtson, Rosenthal, & Burton, 1995).

Elongation of multigenerational families also can occur from age-condensed family patterns: Teenage pregnancy can produce differences of less than twenty years between generations, lead-ing to grandparenthood in one's twenties or thir-ties, over four or five generations. This kind of intergenerational structure is more common among ethnic minorities than among the white majority. In addition, higher rates of fertility, along with the tendency to include fictive kin in definitions of family, have created a paradox for minority grandparents: Although they have a larger kin network from which they may draw potential support, they also have a larger number of kin to whom they must *provide* support (Bengtson, Rosenthal, & Burton, 1995). . . .

ADULT GRANDCHILDREN

Not only have relationships with grandparents, great-grandparents, and great-great-grandparents been a neglected topic of research, so too have relationships of grandparents with *adult* grand-children. Most previous research has tended to focus only on pre-adult grandchildren or those living with the grandparent (Jendrek, 1994; Robertson, 1995). Given the growth recently of studies examining adult parent-child relations, it is surprising that only scant attention has been devoted to studying relationships between grand-parents and adult grandchildren.

Because of increases in longevity over the past century, it has become more likely that a grandparent will not only survive, but live long enough to have *long-term* relationships with *adult* grandchildren. As the median age of first grandparenthood has remained relatively constant over the past century at forty-five years (Hagestad, 1985), gains in life expectancy imply that grandparents are spending many more years in the grandparent role: Among women, for example, this status can engage 50 percent of their lives, and the prevalence of grandparents who have adult grandchildren is historically unprecedented (Goldman, 1986). Farkas and Hogan (1994) examined intergenerational family structure in seven economically developed nations (including the United States) during the 1980s and found that more than half (50.6 percent) of people sixty-five years of age and older have a grandchild who is at least eighteen years old. Lawton, Silverstein, and Bengtson (1994) found a slightly higher percentage in a study of intergenerational relations in the United States conducted by the American Association of Retired Persons (AARP), with 56 percent of Americans sixty-five years of age and older having at least one adult grandchild.

In light of the recent expansion in adult grandchild–grandparent relations in the American population, it is unfortunate that little attention has been paid by large-scale survey researchers to these adult intergenerational relationships. For example, most of the major national surveys designed to study social aspects of aging ask no specific questions of older adults about their relationships with grandchildren (or great-grandchildren) or of younger adults about their relationships with grandparents.

Other scholarly analyses concerning the relationships of grandparents with pre-adult grandchildren suggest that grandparents are more involved with their younger grandchildren than ever before. Some researchers have speculated that the grandparent–grandchild bond may be even more significant in adult relations (Hagestad, 1981; Troll, 1980). As yet, however, the trajectory or life-course "career" of grandparent–grandchild relationships, and the contribution of "successful" grandparenting to quality of life of older adults, are issues that are unclear and remain unexamined. . . .

DIVERSITY IN THE STYLES OF GRANDPARENTING

Population aging has not only led to the long-term viability of grandparenthood; it has also led to an increasing diversity in the demographic characteristics of individuals holding the roles of grandparent and grandchild. Today grandparents may range in age from 30 to 110, and grandchildren range from newborns to retirees (Hagestad, 1985). With demographic diversity in grandparents has come a corresponding diversity in grandparenting styles (Bengtson, 1985). Consequently, some scholars have suggested that the role of grandparent is ill-defined, that it is a social status without clear normative expectations attached to it. Fischer and Silverman (1982) and Wood (1982) refer to the grandparent role as "tenuous" or "ambiguous," without clear prescriptions regarding the rights and duties of grandparents. In fact, there is no single "grandparent role," but there are multiple ways to be a grandparent. It is important not to confuse variance in styles of role enactment with lack of role definition. What is needed is a classification of the different types of grandparenting since there are a variety of reasons that grandparents do not perform the role in the same way.

Yet there has been little empirical research on the styles of grandparenting and the sources of diversity in those styles. In the only previous attempt to classify grandparent–grandchild relations, Cherlin and Furstenberg (1986) identified five types of grandparenting styles by cross-classifying grandparents on three relationship dimensions: exchange of services with grandchild, influence over grandchild, and frequency of contact with grandchild. They labeled these types as follows: (1) detached, (2) passive, (3) supportive, (4) authoritative, and (5) influential. Their analysis suggested that none of the five styles is dominant, and they conclude that grandparenting styles are quite diverse in contemporary American society.

However, Cherlin and Furstenberg's classification does not take into account several relevant dimensions of grandparent–grandchild relations. One of the most important issues related to grandparenting styles is the extent of bonds, solidarity, or connectedness in multigenerational relationships. The lives of grandparents or great-grandparents and their grandchildren and great-grandchildren are linked in a number of ways: through roles, through interactions, through sentiments, and through exchanges of support. Connectedness between grandparents and grandchildren can also be considered along more social-psychological dimensions. One approach is a typology of grandparenting styles based on six dimensions of intergenerational solidarity (Bengtson & Schrader, 1982) that are comprehensive in describing intergenerational relations and that have been widely used in empirical studies (Atkinson, Kivett, & Campbell, 1986; Roberts & Bengtson, 1990; Rossi & Rossi, 1990). These six dimensions are affection (emotional closeness), association (frequency of contact), consensus (agreement), normative quality (importance of familial obligations to members), structure (geographic proximity), and function (helping behavior).

Silverstein, Lawton, and Bengtson (1994) used data from the AARP national study of intergenerational linkages to create a typology of five categories of adult parent–child relations based on five of the six dimensions of intergenerational solidarity. They found five types of intergenerational relationships: (1) *tight-knit*—connected on all five dimensions of intergenerational solidarity; (2) *sociable*—connected only on associational, structural, affectional, and consensual dimensions of solidarity; (3) *cordial but distant*—connected only on affectional and consensual dimensions of solidarity; (4) *obligatory*—connected on associational, structural, and functional solidarity; and (5) *detached*—connected on none of the five dimensions of intergenerational solidarity. While these dimensions have been used to describe parent–child relations, the same five types of parenting styles may also characterize grandparenting styles and grandparent–grandchild relations—an issue awaiting future research development.

DIVORCE AND REMARRIAGE

The structure of American families has undergone profound changes as a result of increases in divorce and remarriage during the past decade. Such changes in family composition and living arrangements can interfere with grandparents' ability to perform their role. The parental generation mediates the grandparent–grandchild relationship, since they provide the opportunities for grandparents and grandchildren to socialize together (Barranti, 1985; Hagestad, 1985; Robertson, 1977). When the parents are divorced, the quality of the grandparent–grandchild relationship may suffer—or it may strengthen.

Divorce may weaken grandparent–grandchild relations on the noncustodial (usually paternal) side of the family but strengthen those relations on the custodial (usually maternal) side of the family (Clingempeel et al., 1992; Creasey, 1993; Matthews & Sprey, 1984). Custodial parents can effectively prevent the parents of an estranged spouse from seeing their grandchildren (Gladstone, 1989). Thus, divorce has a particularly harsh effect on the relationship between grandchildren and grandparents whose children have not been given custody. Even though all states now have grandparents' rights legislation, which gives grandparents the power to go to court to secure their right to visit their grandchildren (Wilson & DeShare, 1982), grandparent–grandchild association after divorce will probably become increasingly matrilineal. Further, if the divorced parent remarries, then stepgrandparents may enter with a new role that is fraught with ambiguous expectations (Cherlin, 1978; Henry, Ceglian, & Ostrander, 1993).

The greater their investment in the grandparent role, the more distress grandparents may feel when contact with grandchildren declines following the parental divorce (Myers & Perrin, 1993), and one would expect that reduced contact between grandparent and grandchild will have an enduring effect on the well-being of both generations. The long-term consequence of early parental divorce and remarriage for grandparents and adult grandchildren is a subject that requires further research investigation.

Future research should also examine possible positive outcomes of the increasing complexity of family arrangements; steprelationships, for example, may have taken on added importance. These changes in the family have led to the development of "latent kin networks" (Riley, Kahn, & Foner, 1994), which have the potential of being activated when needed. It is possible that such complex family arrangements have led to new definitions of family, making it necessary to test long-held assumptions about the primacy of biological relationships over other kinship forms. Stepchildren and stepgrandchildren may represent untapped resources for family members in later life.

Most past research on steprelations has focused on the difficulties that exist between pre-adult stepchildren and their stepparents (Pasley, Ihinger-Tillman, & Lofquist, 1994). We know of no research on how these steprelations develop over the life course, as stepchildren, siblings, parents, grandparents, or great-grandparents age. When stepgrandparents share many years of life with stepgrandchildren, especially during the grandchildren's formative years, the intergenerational bonds that develop may equal or surpass those of biological relations—particularly in cases where custody arrangements preclude contact with biological grandchildren.

GRANDPARENTS AS SURROGATE PARENTS

Increasing numbers of grandparents are rearing their grandchildren because of divorce and other problems such as drug and alcohol addiction, AIDS, incarceration, and unemployment within the parental generation (Chalfie, 1994). Census figures estimate the number of grandchildren living with their grandparents (many without a parent present) to be as high as 3.4 million, with African American grandchildren being slightly more than three times more likely than their white counterparts to be in this type of living arrangement (U.S. Bureau of the Census, 1993). Grandparents caring for grandchildren is such a rapidly growing problem that AARP established the Grandparent Information Center in 1993, which in its first four months of operation received over 2,100 calls and requests for information from grandparents who are rearing a grandchild.

Only recently has research begun to address the role of the grandparents who assume direct, full-time caregiving responsibilities for their grandchildren (Burton, 1995; Chalfie, 1994; Shore & Hayslip, 1994). These studies indicate that caregiving grandparents experience a variety of stresses and strains for which there is little institutional support. They encounter difficulties in such matters as obtaining financial assistance, health insurance coverage, and housing, as well as in gaining legal rights to make decisions regarding the child's education and medical care (Chalfie, 1994). Minority caregiving grandparents, because they tend to have low incomes and multiple caregiving roles, may experience greater stress than similar white grandparents, putting them in "double-jeopardy" of experiencing psychological distress (Dowd & Bengtson, 1978). Many questions on caregiving grandparents need to be addressed in future research: What are the consequences of becoming a parent again in midlife? Does this responsibility lead to lower levels of psychological well-being, or an increase in intergenerational conflict? When grandparents become parents to their grandchildren, who takes over their previous function as safety net in times of family emergencies? And, while providing full-time care for a grandchild may be stressful, grandparent caregivers are also likely to obtain certain rewards and informal support from their intergenerational family relations (Burton, 1995). Future research needs to examine these benefits. . . .

GEOGRAPHIC MOBILITY AND HOUSEHOLD ARRANGEMENTS

Grandparent–grandchild relationships are obviously influenced by how close geographically the generations are to each other, since this factor structures opportunities for interaction (Baranowski, 1987). There is evidence that movement of older people to retirement communities reduces in-person contact between older people and their adult children, and, it may be concluded, with their grandchildren. Developmental approaches to late-life migration have found that return of the elderly to their home community or to the household of an adult child often follows a decline in functioning and death of a spouse (Litwak & Longino, 1988; Silverstein, 1995). However, the role of grandchildren in caregiving to their grandparents following such a move is not known and needs further study.

The role of parent as "gatekeeper" to grandchildren remains a critical factor in regulating grandparent contact. Remarriage of a divorced parent influences the amount of contact between grandparents and their grandchildren when the parent relocates (Gladstone, 1991). The number of adult children moving to the parental home (following divorce or unemployment) with young children in tow has swelled the number of generationally complex households with the older—grandparent—generation as the head of household. At the same time, after leaving the parental nest, adult grandchildren renegotiate their relationships with their grandparents—most commonly reducing the frequency of contact with them (Field & Minkler, 1988). A recent trend may moderate this residential transition: A "boomerang" generation of young adults is moving back to or never leaving the parental nest, to take advantage of a lower cost of living. The result is an increase in the number of three-generational households that have two adult generations. Young-adult "boomerangers" might maintain or strengthen their relationships with grandparents by virtue of living with parents who facilitate extended intergenerational involvement.

In immigrant families, acculturation of adult grandchildren, especially those in ethnic groups with traditional values and orientations, may serve to distance grandparents from their grandchildren. Does assimilation and loss of native language among native-born grandchildren result in reduced intergenerational cohesion with traditional grandparents? There is some evidence that acculturation—the adoption of mainstream values, language, and practices—does create a cultural gulf between generations in the Hispanic family. Schmidt and Padilla (1983) find that Spanish-language compatibility between grandparents and grandchildren predicts the amount of contact between them, underscoring the importance of cultural affinity in structuring intergenerational relations. Research also shows that the better the grandchild speaks the native language of the grandparent, the greater the tendency of grandchildren to live with grandparents (Perez, 1994). Yet, we are unaware of research that formally links acculturation to the propensity of adult grandchildren to move away from grandparents or to leave their ethnic enclave in pursuit of educational or employment opportunities. . . .

POLICY IMPLICATIONS

The results reviewed above concerning increasing family complexity and grandparent–grandchild relations raise new questions not only for researchers but also for program planners and policy makers as well. Recently implemented cuts to government health programs such as Medicare make it clear that federal and state government can go only so far in providing support for old-age dependencies. It is more important than ever to look for alternative solutions to the support and care of the growing population of aging Americans.

The most cost-effective solution may be to develop new programs and policies to shore up or strengthen intergenerational family ties. But before developing such programs, policy makers need to consider the increasing complexity of family arrangements. Successful programs would accommodate the diversity that characterizes the role of grandparent, and also revise traditional definitions of caregiving to conform with changes in the shape of the intergenerational family from pyramid to beanpole. Legislators are familiar with the concept of the "sandwich generation," wherein the middle generation is faced with caring for aging parents while simultaneously raising minor children. However, changes in family structure, coupled with increases in divorce, have resulted in a situation, unparalleled in human history, of fifty-five-year-old children caring for seventy-five-year-old parents and ninety-five-year-old grandparents while rearing adolescent grandchildren—a "club sandwich generation." Policy makers need to develop more programs that provide financial support in such situations—"dependent" care tax credits, for example.

Finally, policy makers must anticipate intergenerational conflict that might result from certain types of geographic mobility or household arrangements and should develop programs that could help families prevent such intergenerational conflicts.

CONCLUSION

In this article we have highlighted three social changes that have increased structural complexity in the intergenerational family, consequently expanding the varieties and contingencies of grandparent–grandchild relationships. Because of the almost exponential rise in the heterogeneity of grandparenting experiences and styles over the last several decades, the investigation of these relationships represents one of the most fertile areas of inquiry in family studies. We predict that social scientists and policy makers will continue to be challenged in their efforts to keep pace with rapid societal changes affecting this everevolving and increasingly disparate population of middle-aged and older adults. In the future, intergenerational family structures might become even more diverse. Coupled with shifts in social, political, and economic conditions, such family complexities make even more pressing the need for fresh theoretical perspectives, informed research designs, and innovative intervention strategies to address the needs of grandparents.

CRITICAL THINKING QUESTIONS

1. What do Giarrusso and her colleagues mean when they say that the shape of U.S. families has gone from a "pyramid" to a "beanpole"? What are the rewards and costs for grandparents and grandchildren in terms of this changing family structure?

2. Some researchers speculate that grandparent–grandchild relationships in the future may be more significant than in the past. What are the reasons for such predictions? How do divorce, remarriage, and geographical mobility threaten the positive impact of such relationships?

3. Giarrusso and her colleagues propose several economic policies to strengthen intergenerational family ties. Do you think their suggestions are realistic? Also, what role, if any, can families play in addressing the needs of grandparents, adult children, and grandchildren that the authors address?

REFERENCES

Atkinson, M. P., V. R. Kivett, and R. T. Campbell. 1986. Intergenerational solidarity: An examination of a theoretical model. *Journal of Gerontology*, 41: 408–16.

Baranowski, M. D. 1987. The grandfather–grandchild relationship: Patterns and meaning. Paper presented at 40th Annual Scientific Meeting of the Gerontological Society of America, Washington, D.C., Nov. 18–22.

Barranti, C. C. R. 1985. The grandparent/grandchild relationship: Family resources in an era of voluntary bonds. *Family Relations*, 34: 43–52.

Bengtson, V. L. 1985. Symbolism and diversity in the grandparenthood role. In *Grandparenthood*, eds. V. L. Bengtson and J. F. Robertson. Beverly Hills, CA: Sage.

Bengtson, V. L., C. J. Rosenthal, and L. M. Burton. 1990. Families and aging: Diversity and heterogeneity. In *Handbook of aging and the social sciences*, 3rd ed., eds. R. H. Binstock and L. K. George. San Diego, CA: Academic Press.

———. 1995. Paradoxes of families and aging. In *Handbook of aging and the social sciences*, 4th ed., eds. R. H. Binstock and L. K. George. San Diego, CA: Academic Press.

Bengtson, V. L., and S. S. Schrader. 1982. Parent–child relations. In *Handbook of research instruments in social gerontology*, vol. 2, eds. D. Mangen and W. Peterson. Minneapolis: University of Minnesota Press.

Bengtson, V. L., and J. Treas. 1980. The changing family context of mental health and aging. In *Handbook of mental health and aging*, eds. J. E. Birren and B. Sloane. Englewood Cliffs, NJ: Prentice-Hall.

Burton, L. M. 1995. Early and on-time grandmotherhood in multigeneration Black families. Doctoral dissertation. University of Southern California.

Chalfie, D. 1994. *Going it alone: A closer look at grandparents parenting grandchildren*. Washington, DC: AARP Women's Initiative.

Cherlin, A. 1978. Remarriage as an incomplete institution. *American Journal of Sociology*, 84: 634–50.

Cherlin, A., and F. Furstenberg. 1986. *The new American grandparent: A place in the family*. New York: Basic Books.

Clingempeel, W. G., et al. 1992. Children's relationships with maternal grandparents: A longitudinal study of family structure and pubertal status effects. *Child Development*, 63: 1404–22.

Creasey, G. L. 1993. The association between divorce and late adolescent grandchildren's relations with grandparents. *Journal of Youth and Adolescence*, 22(5): 513–29.

Dowd, J. J., and V. L. Bengtson. 1978. Aging in minority populations: An examination of the double jeopardy hypothesis. *Journal of Gerontology*, 33(3): 427–36.

Farkas, J. I., and D. P. Hogan. 1994. The demography of changing intergenerational relationships. In *Adult intergenerational relations: Effects of societal change*, eds. V. L. Bengtson, K. W. Schaie, and L. M. Burton. New York: Springer.

Field, D., and M. Minkler. 1988. Continuity and change in social support between young-old and old-old or very-old age. *Journal of Gerontology*, 43(4): 100–06.

Fischer, L. R., and J. Silverman. 1982. Grandmothering as a tenuous role relationship. Paper presented at the Annual Meeting of the National Council on Family Relations, Detroit, MI.

Gladstone, J. W. 1989. Grandmother–grandchild contact: The mediating influence of the middle generation following marriage breakdown and remarriage. *Canadian Journal on Aging*, 8: 355–65.

———. 1991. An analysis of changes in grandparent–grandchild visitation following an adult child's remarriage. *Canadian Journal on Aging*, 10(2): 113–26.

Goldman, N. 1986. Effects of mortality levels on kinship. In *Consequences of mortality trends and differentials*. New York: United Nations.

Hagestad, G. O. 1981. Problems and promises in the social psychology of intergenerational relations. In *Stability and change in the family*, eds. R. Fogel et al. New York: Academic Press.

———. 1985. Continuity and connectedness. In *Grandparenthood*, eds. V. L. Bengtson and J. F. Robertson. Beverly Hills, CA: Sage.

Henry, C. S., C. P. Ceglian, and D. L. Ostrander. 1993. The transition to step-grandparenthood. *Journal of Divorce and Remarriages*, 19: 25–44.

Jendrek. M. P. 1994. Grandparents who parent their grandchildren. Circumstances and decisions. *Gerontologist*, 34(2): 206–16.

Kivnick, H. Q. 1982. Grandparenthood: An overview of meaning and mental health. *Gerontologist*, 22(1): 59–66.

Lawton, L., M. Silverstein, and V. L. Bengtson. 1994. Solidarity between generations in families. In *Hidden connections: Intergenerational linkages in American society*, eds. V. L. Bengtson and R. A. Harootyan. New York: Springer.

Litwak, E., and C. F. Longino. 1988. Migration patterns among the elderly: A developmental perspective. *Gerontologist*, 27: 266–72.

Matthews, S., and J. Sprey. 1984. The impact of divorce on grandparenthood: An exploratory study. *Gerontologist*, 24: 41–7.

Myers, J. E., and Perrin, N. 1993. Grandparents affected by parental divorce: A population at risk? *Journal of Counseling and Development*, 22: 62–6.

Pasley, K., M. Ihinger-Tallman, and A. Lofquist. 1994. Remarriage and step-families: Making progress in understanding. In *Stepparenting*, eds. K. Pasley and M. Ihinger-Tallman. Westport, CT: Greenwood Press.

Perez, L. 1994. The household structure of second-generation children: An exploratory study of extended family arrangements. *International Migration Review*, 28(4): 736–47.

Riley, M. W., R. L. Kahn, and A. Foner, eds. 1994. *Age and structural lag: Society's failure to provide meaningful opportunities in work, family and leisure*. New York: John Wiley.

Roberts, R. E. L., and V. L. Bengtson. 1990. Is intergenerational solidarity a unidimensional construct? A second test of a formal model. *Journal of Gerontology: Social Sciences*, 45: S12–20.

Robertson, J. F. 1977. Grandmotherhood: A study of role conceptions. *Journal of Marriage and the Family*, 39: 165–74.

———. 1995. Grandparenting in an era of rapid change. In *Handbook of aging and the family*, eds. R. Blieszner and V. H. Bedford. Westport, CT: Greenwood Press.

Rossi, A. S., and P. H. Rossi. 1990. *Of human bonding: Parent–child relationships across the life course.* New York: Aldine de Gruyter.

Schmidt, A., and A. M. Padilla. 1983. Grandparent–grandchild interaction in a Mexican American group. *Hispanic Journal of Behavioral Sciences*, 5(2): 181–98.

Shore, R. J., and B. Hayslip, Jr. 1994. Custodial grandparenting: Implications for children's development. In *Redefining families: Implications for children's development*, eds. A. E. Gottfried and A. W. Gottfried. New York: Plenum Press.

Silverstein, M. 1995. Stability and change in temporal distance between the elderly and their children. *Demography*, 32(1): 29–45.

Silverstein, M., L. Lawton, and V. L. Bengtson. 1994. Types of relations between parents and adult children. In *Hidden connections: Intergenerational linkages in American society*, eds. V. L. Bengtson and R. A. Harootyan. New York: Springer.

Troll, L. E. 1980. Grandparenting. In *Aging in the 1980s: Psychological issues*, ed. L. W. Poon. Washington, DC: American Psychological Association.

Uhlenberg, P. 1980. Death and the family. *Journal of Family History*, 5(3): 313–20.

U.S. Bureau of the Census. 1993. Marital status and living arrangements: March 1993. *Current Population Reports* (Series P-20, No. 478). Washington, DC: Government Printing Office.

Watkins, S. C., J. A. Menken, and J. Bongaarts. 1987. Demographic foundations of family change. *American Sociological Review*, 52: 346–58.

Wilson, K. B., and M. R. DeShare. 1982. The legal rights of grandparents: A preliminary discussion. *Gerontologist*, 22: 67–71.

Wood, V. 1982. Grandparenthood: An ambiguous role. *Generations*, 7(2): 18–24.

43

Our Aging World

FRANK B. HOBBS AND
BONNIE L. DAMON

The average age in societies around the world is rising. Even now, demographers report, the eighty-and-over age group is the fastest-growing portion of the elderly population. Frank B. Hobbs and Bonnie L. Damon describe the growing number of elderly persons worldwide, compare the growth of the elderly population in developed and developing countries, and raise important questions about the future implications of our aging world.

POPULATION AGING IS WORLDWIDE

To set the aging of the United States in context it is useful to look at aging in the rest of the world. Fertility rates and infant and maternal mortality have declined in most nations. Also, mortality from infectious and parasitic diseases has declined. The world's nations generally have improved other aspects of health and education. All of these factors have interacted so that every major region in the world shows an increased proportion of the population that will be sixty-five or older by 2020.

There were 357 million persons aged sixty-five and over in the world in 1994 [see Table 43.1]. They represent 6 percent of the world's population.

Source: From *65+ in the United States.* U.S. Bureau of the Census, Current Population Reports, Special Studies, P23–190 (Washington, D.C.: Government Printing Office, 1996), pp. 24–27.

By the year 2000, there would be about 418 million elderly. The annual growth rate for the elderly was 2.8 percent in 1993–94 (compared with an average annual rate for the total world population of 1.6 percent). Such growth is expected to continue far into the twenty-first century.

Numerical growth of the elderly population is worldwide. It is occurring in both developed and developing countries. The average annual growth rate in 1993–94 of persons sixty-five years and over was 3.2 percent in developing countries compared with 2.3 percent in the developed world. In absolute numbers, from 1993 to 1994, the net balance of the world's elderly population (sixty-five years and over) increased by over 1,000 persons every hour. Of this increase, 63 percent occurred in developing countries.

Over half (55 percent) of the world's elderly lived in developing nations in 1994. These developing regions could be home to nearly two-thirds (65 percent) of the world's elderly by the year

TABLE 43.1   World Population by Age and Sex, 1994 and 2000

	Population (millions)			Percentage of Total			
Year and Age	Both Sexes	Male	Female	Both Sexes	Male	Female	Males per 100 Females
1994							
All ages	5,640	2,841	2,798	100.0%	100.0%	100.0%	101.5
Under 15 years	1,790	917	873	31.7	32.3	31.2	105.1
15 to 64 years	3,492	1,771	1,722	61.9	62.3	61.5	102.9
65 years and over	357	153	204	6.3	5.4	7.3	75.2
2000							
All ages	6,161	3,103	3,057	100.0	100.0	100.0	101.5
Under 15 years	1,877	962	915	30.5	31.0	29.9	105.2
15 to 64 years	3,866	1,959	1,907	62.7	63.1	62.4	102.8
65 years and over	418	182	236	6.8	5.9	7.7	77.1

Source: U.S. Bureau of the Census, International Data Base.

2020. Thirty nations had elderly populations of at least 2 million in 1994. . . . Current population projections indicate there will be fifty-five such nations by 2020.

Among countries with more than 1 million population, Sweden has the highest proportion of people aged sixty-five and over, with 18 percent in 1994—about the same as the state of Florida. Sweden also has the highest proportion aged eighty and over with 5 percent. The Caribbean is the oldest of the major developing regions with 7 percent of its population sixty-five or older in 1994.

By 2020, the elderly will constitute from one-fifth to nearly one-fourth of the population of many European countries. For example, Census Bureau projections indicate that 23 percent of Germany's population would be elderly compared with 22 percent for Italy, Finland, Belgium, Croatia, Denmark, and Greece. The elderly population of twelve additional European countries with more than 1 million population will constitute at least one-fifth of the total country population. The United States would be 16 percent.

Japan's population age sixty-five and over is expected to grow dramatically in the coming decades. According to projections, the percentage of Japan's population that is elderly could grow from 14 percent (17.1 million) in 1994 to 17 percent (21.0 million) in 2000 and to

26 percent (32.2 million) by 2020. . . . This is a rapid rise in a short time. Japan's population eighty years and over also is projected to grow very rapidly, from 3 percent of their total population in 1994 to 7 percent by 2020. Already the Japanese are reducing retirement benefits and making other adjustments to prepare for the economic and social results of a rapidly aging society.

In 1994, the world had an estimated 61 million persons aged eighty or older. That number is expected to increase to 146 million by the year 2020. Persons eighty years and over constituted only 1 percent of the world's total population in 1994 and more than 20 percent of the world's elderly (28 percent in developed countries, 16 percent in developing nations).

DEVELOPED COUNTRIES NOW HAVE MOST OF THE WORLD'S OLDEST POPULATION

Although the developed countries of the world represented only 22 percent of the total world population in 1994, the majority of the world's population aged eighty and over live in developed countries. However, it is projected that by 2020, the majority will live in developing countries. For many nations, the eighty-and-over age group will be the fastest growing portion of the elderly

TABLE 43.2   Projected Population for Countries with More Than One Million Persons Aged 80 Years and Over, 1994 and 2020

Country/Area	Rank 1994	Rank 2020	Population Aged 80 Years and Over (in thousands, based on rank in 1994) 1994	Population Aged 80 Years and Over (in thousands, based on rank in 1994) 2020
China, Mainland	1	1	9,010	28,737
United States	2	2	7,760	13,007
India	3	3	4,021	12,639
Japan	4	4	3,597	9,362
Russia	5	5	3,317	7,191
Germany	6	6	3,313	5,889
France	7	8	2,563	3,754
United Kingdom	8	9	2,342	3,400
Italy	9	7	2,221	4,142
Ukraine	10	12	1,421	2,923
Spain	11	13	1,287	2,488
Brazil	*	10	*	3,132
Indonesia	*	11	*	3,034
Mexico	*	14	*	2,296
Poland	*	15	*	1,877
Turkey	*	16	*	1,751
Canada	*	**17**	*	**1,595**
Thailand	*	18	*	1,477
Pakistan	*	19	*	1,385
Romania	*	20	*	1,264
South Korea	*	21	*	1,221
Vietnam	*	22	*	1,199
Argentina	*	23	*	1,072
Iran	*	24	*	1,039

Source: U.S. Bureau of the Census, International Data Base.

*Indicates population 80 years and over in 1994 was less than 1 million.

population. In 2000, 26 percent of the elderly in the United States would be eighty or older, which, among countries with a population size of at least 5 million, would rank sixth, behind Sweden, Denmark, Switzerland, Cuba, and the United Kingdom.

In 1994, China had the largest number of persons aged eighty or older followed by the United States [see Table 43.2]. Nine additional countries had over 1 million persons eighty years and over in 1994. By 2020, this list is expected to include thirteen additional countries, ten of which are developing countries. In many developing countries, the population eighty and over in 2020 is likely to at least quadruple from 1994. This highlights the problems governments may have in planning support services for this burgeoning population group.

The rapid growth of the oldest old has various health and economic implications for individuals, families, and governments throughout the world. The oldest old often have severe chronic health problems which demand special attention. The nature and duration of their illnesses are likely to produce a substantial need for prolonged care. Developing nations already have diluted resources. They are the most limited in being able to provide preventive measures and, in future years, supportive services. The United States and other countries face enormous investments and payments to maintain current levels of services for the oldest old.

CRITICAL THINKING QUESTIONS

1. What are some of the reasons for the growth of aging populations worldwide?

2. In the 1990s, the majority of the world's population aged eighty and over lived in developed countries. How is this expected to change by 2020? As the average length of life continues to increase in both developed and developing countries, who, if anyone, is responsible for improving the quality of extended life?

3. Hobbs and Damon observe that "the United States and other countries face enormous investments and payments to maintain current levels of services for the old." What, specifically, are examples of such investments and payments? Who will pay for the necessary services for elderly populations—individuals? families? government? corporations? people in the labour force? others?

44

Alienated Labor

KARL MARX

The human species, argues Karl Marx, is social by nature and expresses that social nature in the act of production. But within the capitalist economic system, Marx claims, the process of production does not affirm human nature but denies it. The result is what he terms "alienated labor."

[We] have shown that the worker sinks to the level of a commodity, and to a most miserable commodity; that the misery of the worker increases with the power and volume of his production; that the necessary result of competition is the accumulation of capital in a few hands, and thus a restoration of monopoly in a more terrible form; and finally that the distinction between capitalist and landlord, and between agricultural laborer and industrial worker, must disappear, and the whole of society divide into the two classes of property *owners* and *property-less* workers. . . .

Source: "Alienated Labor," by Karl Marx from *Karl Marx: Early Writings*, trans. and ed. by T. B. Bottomore. Copyright © 1963, McGraw-Hill Companies. Reprinted with permission.

Thus we have now to grasp the real connexion between this whole system of alienation—private property, acquisitiveness, the separation of labor, capital and land, exchange and competition, value and the devaluation of man, monopoly and competition—and the system of *money*. . . .

We shall begin from a *contemporary* economic fact. The worker becomes poorer the more wealth he produces and the more his production increases in power and extent. The worker becomes an ever cheaper commodity the more goods he creates. The *devaluation* of the human world increases in direct relation with the *increase in value* of the world of things. Labor does not only create

255

goods; it also produces itself and the worker as a *commodity*, and indeed in the same proportion as it produces goods.

This fact simply implies that the object produced by labor, its product, now stands opposed to it as an *alien being*, as a *power independent* of the producer. The product of labor is labor which has been embodied in an object and turned into a physical thing; this product is an *objectification* of labor. The performance of work is at the same time its objectification. The performance of work appears in the sphere of political economy as a *vitiation*[1] of the worker, objectification as a *loss* and as *servitude to the object*, and appropriation as *alienation*.

So much does the performance of work appear as vitiation that the worker is vitiated to the point of starvation. So much does objectification appear as loss of the object that the worker is deprived of the most essential things not only of life but also of work. Labor itself becomes an object which he can acquire only by the greatest effort and with unpredictable interruptions. So much does the appropriation of the object appear as alienation that the more objects the worker produces the fewer he can possess and the more he falls under the domination of his product, of capital.

All these consequences follow from the fact that the worker is related to the *product of his labor* as to an *alien* object. For it is clear on this presupposition that the more the worker expends himself in work the more powerful becomes the world of objects which he creates in face of himself, the poorer he becomes in his inner life, and the less he belongs to himself. It is just the same as in religion. The more of himself man attributes to God the less he has left in himself. The worker puts his life into the object, and his life then belongs no longer to himself but to the object. The greater his activity, therefore, the less he possesses. What is embodied in the product of his labor is no longer his own. The greater this product is, therefore, the more he is diminished. The *alienation* of the worker in his product means not only that his labor becomes an object, assumes an *external* existence, but that it exists independently, *outside himself*, and alien to him, and that it stands opposed to him as an autonomous power. The life which he has given to the object sets itself against him as an alien and hostile force.

Let us now examine more closely the phenomenon of *objectification*; the worker's production and the *alienation* and *loss* of the object it produces, which is involved in it. The worker can create nothing without *nature*, without the *sensuous external world*. The latter is the material in which his labor is realized, in which it is active, out of which and through which it produces things.

But just as nature affords the *means of existence* of labor, in the sense that labor cannot *live* without objects upon which it can be exercised, so also it provides the *means of existence* in a narrower sense; namely the means of physical existence for the *worker* himself. Thus, the more the worker *appropriates* the external world of sensuous nature by his labor the more he deprives himself of *means of existence*, in two respects: First, that the sensuous external world becomes progressively less an object belonging to his labor or a means of existence of his labor, and secondly, that it becomes progressively less a means of existence in the direct sense, a means for the physical subsistence of the worker.

In both respects, therefore, the worker becomes a slave of the object; first, in that he receives an *object of work*, i.e., receives *work*, and secondly, in that he receives *means of subsistence*. Thus the object enables him to exist, first as a *worker* and secondly, as a *physical subject*. The culmination of this enslavement is that he can only maintain himself as a *physical subject* so far as he is a *worker*, and that it is only as a *physical subject* that he is a worker.

(The alienation of the worker in his object is expressed as follows in the laws of political economy: The more the worker produces the less he has to consume; the more value he creates the more worthless he becomes; the more refined his product the more crude and misshapen the worker; the more civilized the product the more barbarous the worker; the more powerful the work the more feeble the worker; the more the work manifests intelligence the more the worker declines in intelligence and becomes a slave of nature.)

Political economy conceals the alienation in the nature of labor insofar as it does not examine the direct relationship between the worker (work) and production. Labor certainly produces marvels for the rich but it produces privation for the worker. It produces palaces, but hovels for the worker. It produces beauty, but deformity for the worker. It replaces labor by machinery, but it casts some of the workers back into a barbarous kind of work and turns the others into machines. It produces intelligence, but also stupidity and cretinism for the workers.

The direct relationship of labor to its products is the relationship of the worker to the objects of his production. The relationship of property owners to the objects of production and to production itself is merely a *consequence* of this first relationship and confirms it. We shall consider this second aspect later.

Thus, when we ask what is the important relationship of labor, we are concerned with the relationship of the *worker* to production.

So far we have considered the alienation of the worker only from one aspect; namely, *his relationship with the products of his labor.* However, alienation appears not merely in the result but also in the *process of production*, within *productive activity* itself. How could the worker stand in an alien relationship to the product of his activity if he did not alienate himself in the act of production itself? The product is indeed only the *résumé* of activity, of production. Consequently, if the product of labor is alienation, production itself must be active alienation—the alienation of activity and the activity of alienation. The alienation of the object of labor merely summarizes the alienation in the work activity itself.

What constitutes the alienation of labor? First, that the work is *external* to the worker, that it is not part of his nature; and that, consequently, he does not fulfill himself in his work but denies himself, has a feeling of misery rather than well-being, does not develop freely his mental and physical energies but is physically exhausted and mentally debased. The worker, therefore, feels himself at home only during his leisure time, whereas at work he feels homeless. His work is not voluntary but imposed, *forced labor*. It is not the satisfaction of a need, but only a *means* for satisfying other needs. Its alien character is clearly shown by the fact that as soon as there is no physical or other compulsion it is avoided like the plague. External labor, labor in which man alienates himself, is a labor of self-sacrifice, of mortification. Finally, the external character of work for the worker is shown by the fact that it is not his own work but work for someone else, that in work he does not belong to himself but to another person. . . .

We arrive at the result that man (the worker) feels himself to be freely active only in his animal functions—eating, drinking, and procreating, or at most also in his dwelling and in personal adornment—while in his human functions he is reduced to an animal. The animal becomes human and the human becomes animal.

Eating, drinking, and procreating are of course also genuine human functions. But abstractly considered, apart from the environment of human activities, and turned into final and sole ends, they are animal functions.

We have now considered the act of alienation of practical human activity, labor, from two aspects: (1) the relationship of the worker to the *product of labor* as an alien object which dominates him. This relationship is at the same time the relationship to the sensuous external world, to natural objects, as an alien and hostile world; (2) the relationship of labor to the *act of production* within *labor*. This is the relationship of the worker to his own activity as something alien and not belonging to him, activity as suffering (passivity), strength as powerlessness, creation as emasculation, the *personal* physical and mental energy of the worker, his personal life (for what is life but activity?), as an activity which is directed against himself, independent of him and not belonging to him. This is *self-alienation* as against the [afore]mentioned alienation of the *thing*.

We have now to infer a third characteristic of *alienated labor* from the two we have considered.

Man is a species-being not only in the sense that he makes the community (his own as well as those of other things) his object both practically and theoretically, but also (and this is simply another expression for the same thing) in the sense that he treats himself as the present, living species, as a *universal* and consequently free being.

Species-life, for man as for animals, has its physical basis in the fact that man (like animals) lives from inorganic nature, and since man is more universal than an animal so the range of inorganic nature from which he lives is more universal. Plants, animals, minerals, air, light, etc. constitute, from the theoretical aspect, a part of human consciousness as objects of natural science and art; they are man's spiritual inorganic nature, his intellectual means of life, which he must first prepare for enjoyment and perpetuation. So also, from the practical aspect, they form a part of human life and activity. In practice man lives only from these natural products, whether in the form of food, heating, clothing, housing, etc. The universality of man appears in practice in the universality which makes the whole of nature into his inorganic body: (1) as a direct means of life; and equally (2) as the material object and instrument of his life activity. Nature is the inorganic body of man; that is to say nature, excluding the human body itself. To say that man *lives* from nature means that nature is his *body* with which he must remain in a continuous interchange in order not to die. The statement that the physical and mental life of man, and nature, are interdependent means simply that nature is interdependent with itself, for man is a part of nature.

Since alienated labor (1) alienates nature from man; and (2) alienates man from himself, from his own active function, his life activity; so it alienates him from the species. It makes *species-life* into a means of individual life. In the first place it alienates species-life and individual life, and secondly, it turns the latter, as an abstraction, into the purpose of the former, also in its abstract and alienated form.

For labor, *life activity, productive life*, now appear to man only as *means* for the satisfaction of a need, the need to maintain his physical existence. Productive life is, however, species-life. It is life creating life. In the type of life activity resides the whole character of a species, its species-character; and free, conscious activity is the species-character of human beings. Life itself appears only as a *means of life*.

The animal is one with its life activity. It does not distinguish the activity from itself. It is *its activity*. But man makes his life activity itself an object of his will and consciousness. He has a conscious life activity. It is not a determination with which he is completely identified. Conscious life activity distinguishes man from the life activity of animals. Only for this reason is he a species-being. Or rather, he is only a self-conscious being, i.e., his own life is an object for him, because he is a species-being. Only for this reason is his activity free activity. Alienated labor reverses the relationship, in that man because he is a self-conscious being makes his life activity, his *being*, only a means for his *existence*.

CRITICAL THINKING QUESTIONS

1. Does Marx argue that work is inevitably alienating? Why does work within a capitalist economy produce alienation?

2. In what different respects does labour within capitalism alienate the worker?

3. Based on this analysis, under what conditions do you think Marx would argue that labour is not alienating?

NOTE

1. Debasement.

45

Experiences of Social Class: Learning from Occupational Therapy Students

BRENDA L. BEAGAN

This reading brings to light some of the problems that people from working-class backgrounds experience when they enter middle-class jobs (in this case, occupational therapy). It discusses poverty and, above all, the impact of social class. This study also uses a somewhat novel method of data collection. Professor Beagan asked students to write about their experiences, which she then systematically analyzed and documented. Permission to be included in the research was given by the students involved in the study.

This paper analyses the personal accounts of occupational therapy students on the ways their own occupational lives have been affected by growing up in working-class or impoverished families and communities. The student accounts provide a unique blending of profession-specific understanding of occupation and experiential understanding of social class.

The working class includes about a third of the Canadian population, men and women usually working at manual (blue-collar), clerical (pink-collar) or retail jobs (MacIonis, Clarke, & Gerber, 1997). They generally have a high school education, but not post-secondary. The lower class, about 20 percent of Canadians, live in poverty; some rely on social assistance for their

Source: Brenda L. Beagan. 2007. "Experiences of Social Class: Learning from Occupational Therapy Students." *Canadian Journal of Occupational Therapy*, 74(2): 126–128, 129, 130–131.

only source of income, some work at low-prestige, minimum-wage jobs. They may or may not have a high school education (MacIonis, Clarke, & Gerber, 1997). With universal access to basic health care, the impact of poverty on health is not as dramatic as in the United States. Nevertheless, lower-income Canadians die earlier and suffer more illnesses than Canadians with higher incomes, regardless of age, sex, race and geographic location (Health Canada, 2004; Raphael et al., 2005).

METHODS

This paper is based on student assignments submitted for an undergraduate occupational therapy course in which the impact of social factors on occupational engagement and opportunities were explored. The class occurred in the second term of the first year of the program. In one exercise, students were asked to write an occupational autobiography in which they analysed the ways their own membership in particular social groups had shaped their occupational lives. In these essays, several students explored the ways growing up in working-class or impoverished families affected their occupations in profound and ongoing ways.

With written permission from these students, this paper drew on parts of their essays as qualitative data.

RESULTS

The participants

The 17 students (3 male and 14 female) whose essays were used as data all self-identified as coming from working-class, lower-class or impoverished family backgrounds, for at least part of their lives. Three were raised by single mothers; three students had parents with chronic illnesses or disabilities; four had at least one parent struggling with alcoholism. Five students experienced significant periods of time when social assistance or employment insurance was the main source of family income. In general, however, these students grew up in families that were considered among the working poor, where one or both parents were employed yet wages were insufficient to bring the family above the poverty line. Their parents worked in a range of positions including: childcare, homecare, manual labour, farming, fishing, factory work, manual trades, clerical work and retail.

Experiences of poverty differed among the students. None of the students described ever being homeless, but several remembered shortages of food when they were young: "I can remember a very empty fridge at times." All of the students described times when money was limited and they had to do without. Treats and luxuries were rare: "My mother couldn't even spare me a quarter when I asked her for money to buy penny candies at the store." Students described restricted or non-existent leisure opportunities, having no telephone, wearing hand-me-down clothing, using food banks, and living in substandard housing: "Our apartment was clean but always cold." The broad themes that emerged from their essays included shame and stigma, "passing" as middle class, leisure and responsibilities, experiences of family and schooling, and positive qualities.

The shame and stigma of poverty

Students identified marginalization and stigma as central to their experience of living in poverty. They argued that people who are not middle-class are "regularly discriminated against because these individuals are seen as lazy or intellectually inferior." Stigma attaches a powerful, negative social label that diminishes a person's self concept. Many students wrote about housing or neighbourhoods that were stigmatized, causing them tremendous shame and embarrassment.

I never invited friends over to my house . . . I did not want my friends to see how shabby and ugly my home was. I thought they would see that I was poor and not like me anymore.

Some students noted that the shame accompanying social stigma is not easily overcome. One student is still too embarrassed to bring his girlfriend to the house where he grew up. Another was not particularly ashamed of her home while she was growing up, but since entering occupational therapy school has made friends with people "from higher social classes":

People talk about coming and visiting in the summer time to my home town but I am embarrassed about the condition of my parents' house and that people will think my family is dirty or lazy based on what they see.

Students also described particular shame and stigma concerning clothing and physical appearance. Especially in junior high and high school they were teased, judged and ridiculed when they wore clothes identifiable as inexpensive or not brand-name.

I got picked on, stigmatized, labelled and left out due to the fact that we had little money and I wore second hand clothing. The worst was going to school in what was a new article of clothing for me, unaware that the same article was one a classmate of mine gave to the second hand store last week.

One student described a direct impact on her daily occupations. She could never afford to have the right sneakers to avoid ridicule, so she stopped participating in gym class: "I would bring 'dress' shoes and pretend I'd forgotten my sneakers."

The relentless mockery and derision had profound effects on some students' sense of self-worth. Several described learning to hate themselves, and learning to loathe going to school: "I was constantly made fun of and picked on because I did not have the latest style clothes, or the coolest sneakers . . . I felt like dirt." Not surprisingly, messages so hurtful can have lasting effects. A few students described a pervasive belief that they were not good enough. As one said, "I believe that it is a mistake that I was accepted into the [occupational therapy] program. I feel that I am not smart enough or good enough."

Occupied with "passing"

In response to shame and stigma, almost all of the students at some point engaged in activities that could be defined as attempts to "pass" as middle class. "Passing" occurs when members of social groups, who face discrimination, attempt to be identified as members of a higher-status social group. Students tried to pass as middle class to avoid or lessen the stigma attached to a lower-class status: "I put all my energy into having middle-class friends and 'appearing' to be of middle-class descent . . . I always felt that I was an impostor." One student described herself as extremely self-conscious: "I lived in fear that others would come to the realization that I was poor."

Students employed multiple strategies in their efforts to pass. Some found involvement in particular leisure occupations, such as teams or sports, that allowed them to fit in or pass, at least in that venue. For example, one student had a mentor who sponsored her involvement in figure skating. Many friends then assumed she belonged to the middle class because of her engagement in skating: "When I was at the arena I felt as though I could hide who I really was and pretend to be who I wished I was." More commonly, however, students described how they invested considerable energy in lying and hiding, and in devising strategies to avoid risky situations that might blow their cover and prevent them from passing as middle class.

One night after a party when a group of friends was driving me home, they saw the trailer court and began making redneck jokes. I then directed them to a house that was not mine and was dropped off there so I would not hear them make more jokes about where I lived.

One student had a simple strategy for hiding her lack of money from university friends: "When we went out to eat, I had water or tea and told them I had already eaten."

If an occupation can be understood as an activity invested with meaning, cultural significance, and power (Christiansen & Townsend, 2004), these students accurately point out that passing as middle class can become an occupation in and of itself. They invest time, energy, thought, care, skill, and effort into producing an appearance of middle-class membership.

It is an occupation to produce one's class identity, or in my case to mask or cover-up my class identity. In my youth I spent a lot of my time pretending that I was in a higher social class than I actually belonged to.

Finally, it is clear that the desire to pass, and the habits and strategies developed in the service of that goal, are not easily abandoned upon entry to university or to occupational therapy school. A few students described the direct impact on their self-care occupations with implications for time use.

My dress and self-care began to consume a large part of my daily routine. As I wrote this paper I came to realize why I cannot leave the house in old clothes and I have to shower every day, wear make up and feel good about the outfit I choose for the day. I worry about who will see me and what they will think, and this is a result of being paranoid as a child about how people felt about how I looked and whether they could tell I was poor.

Another student noted that she has to wash her hair daily, "even when it is not dirty."

Not only clothing, cleanliness and appearance are loaded with potential for revealing a student's true class status, but also manners and etiquette. One student described a particularly powerful way her childhood poverty, and her desire to pass as middle class, continue to affect her daily in the self-care occupation of eating.

In elementary school I would pretend that I had forgotten my lunch because I did not want to eat in front of people. I was sure my eating habits and etiquette were less than those of my friends. I was so hungry that I had difficulties retaining information and therefore learning. Even in university, I go to the library in another building to eat lunch because I am not comfortable eating in front of others.

This student, who already feels marginalized, further isolates herself everyday by eating on her own where no one she knows will see her, lest they detect lower-class manners.

Experiences of family

Family was often experienced as another site of shame or stigma, especially when students were younger. One student avoided having her friends interact with her family lest they figure out her mother's single-parent status. Another skipped her prom and graduation and noted, "I did not want my classmates to see my parents and make fun of them and judge me." Others simply did the best they could to hide their parents from view, and saw their jobs, their possessions, and their actions as embarrassing. Families had the potential to reveal the true class status of someone successfully passing as middle class. For example, one student passed through involvement in figure skating until her peers met her mother.

My social class started to become evident when my mother began to attend my practices. I was so embarrassed of her and ashamed to admit that she was my mother. She did not dress like the other mothers; she was a little unkempt and very outspoken. . . She was supposed to be well-kept, well-spoken, nice to look at and polite, like all the other kids' mothers. I was not right, nor was my family, for the sport I was in.

Shame concerning family seemed particularly deep-rooted and powerful in dating relationships. Several students were still unwilling to let romantic partners meet their families.

A few students also wrote about having what they perceived to be unusual adult responsibilities or concerns. Some wrote about pervasive awareness of family financial pressures and parental sacrifices to provide for the family: "A child's occupations should never be about money." Others felt they had to somehow take care of their parents.

I would go to bed crying, wishing there was some way I could help my parents out, feeling guilty because I had eaten too much that day and deprived another family member of having a full stomach.

Last, these students' experiences of family were complicated by the fact that university—especially entering a professional school—represented upward class mobility for them. Several students wrote about feeling pressure from family members proud of their admission to a health professional program. These pressures were often complicated by conflicting messages and emotions. While students were expected to "do better" than their parents had, the parents were often proud of their working-class heritage, and did not want their successful, upwardly mobile offspring to forget where they came from, or start thinking that they were better than anyone else. A few students struggled with how to act around friends and family "from home," not wanting to be seen as putting on airs.

Personal qualities from class background

All of the students emphasized that growing up in poverty or in a working-class family was not an entirely negative experience. They identified ways in which important learning, positive characteristics or qualities, and specific values derived from their social class status. Several students spoke of their own determination, drive, strength, independence, compassion and work ethic as class-related.

I can stretch a dollar further than anybody I know; I can find a deal where nobody else can; I have learned to balance my time between work, play and school without a second to waste; but most of all, I have learned that I am a much more resilient person than I would have ever imagined.

Some developed work skills, leadership skills and time management strategies from years of job experience. Several students wrote about a fierce sense of pride that can be both an asset and a drawback. Some felt that they were quick to spot pity—which they resented—and slow to accept help, assistance, or gifts. Some described a compelling need for respect: "I desire to be respected and treated as though I am worth more than how much money I have."

Lastly, many of the students detailed values, particularly relating to family, friends and possessions, which they attributed to their class backgrounds. They wrote about how their shame concerning family turned to admiration as they grew older, as they learned to recognize the strength, resourcefulness, skills and dependability their parents had displayed. A few students suggested that being raised with few material possessions allowed them to focus more on interpersonal relationships.

I learned to appreciate everything I have, especially the small things . . . I have learned that what makes life happy and worth living are the people who surround you everyday, not the material things that surround you or that you can buy.

Again, such values can be assets and drawbacks in occupational therapy school. If family and friends are priorities, why remove yourself from loved ones in the name of future success?

I often struggle with being away from friends and family to better myself. That is not how I was raised . . . I was raised to believe in the quality of time not the quantity of goods . . . Life was good for me as a kid, why don't I just go home and work the day to day and forget about putting myself in debt for the sake of school?

DISCUSSION

The student essays suggest that distinctive, class-based experiences shape people's ways of being in the world. The pervasive stigma and shame that accompany poverty caused them to restrict their own social occupations and avoid situations where friends would encounter their homes, their family members, or other aspects of their lives that might reveal class status. For some, mockery and ridicule of their clothing and appearance resulted in a lasting sense of low self-worth. For most, the clearest legacy of stigma was engagement in the occupation of passing. Numerous small strategies helped to conceal their own class backgrounds and accentuate attributes of the middle class. In the interest of passing, self-care occupations may become imbued with whole new levels of meaning.

Our experiences of the world lead to internalized predispositions to act in patterned ways that may become habits, or social roles with attached "scripts" and expectations (Kielhofner, 2002). At the same time, our sense of personal capacity and self-efficacy develop through experiencing the impact we are able to have on the world around us, in order to meet our goals or needs. Constant reminders that our efforts have little impact can result in a sense of powerlessness and reduced sense of capacity: "When shame or fear of failure governs a person's sense of capacity, there is disincentive to take risks, to learn new skills" (Kielhofner, p. 48).

Beyond the individual, whole social groups (e.g., social classes, cultural groups, racialized groups) can internalize a diminished sense of capacity and efficacy (Bourdieu, 1977). This might be expressed in the notion, 'That's not for the likes of us,' or 'Our people don't do that,' concerning, for example, higher education (Bellamy, 1994). Thus invisible processes of exclusion are implemented; members of marginalized groups, in effect, exclude themselves by perceiving occupations as beyond their reach, or not legitimately belonging to them.

This idea was profoundly expressed in student descriptions of education. One young man "felt like an outsider trespassing on someone else's land." Olson argues that educational institutions show "a systematic preference for middle-class values, language, and views of the world" (1995, p. 201). The culture of education is middle class; students are evaluated not only on their academic merits, but also on their ability to display expected behaviours. Working-class students arrive without the right values, norms, skills, and commonplace understandings to move easily through the system. Feeling out of place, some disengage through poor attendance, poor performance, or more direct rebellion. One student detailed a deep sense of not belonging at the occupational therapy school leading to behaviours she interpreted as self-sabotage—an externalization of the belief, 'That's not for the likes of us.'

In part, students from low-income backgrounds feel marginalized in higher education because they do not have the right social capital: social networks and relationships that include the right kinds of people with the right kinds of connections and knowledge (Bourdieu, 1986). As one student wrote, her middle-class friends seemed to have "some sort of invisible knowledge" concerning options for university that she "didn't know how to get." That knowledge, which came from growing up around "the sophisticated conversations of lawyers and doctors," is middle-class social capital.

The students may also lack middle-class cultural capital: knowing how to operate smoothly in the midst of middle-class norms (Bourdieu, 1986). These norms are the intangibles that make someone a competent member of a particular culture. The absence of middle-class occupations leaves some students with perceived gaps in cultural knowledge—they have not been to the right places, watched the right television shows, or experienced the right activities.

CRITICAL THINKING QUESTIONS

1. Have you ever been in a situation where you have felt uncomfortable because of your social or class background? Discuss the situation and how and why you felt different from the other people (clothing, speech, etc.).

2. What does the author mean by "passing"? Beagan writes about the norms and expectations of the middle class. Can you name some of these and describe how they might differ from those of the working class?

3. Beagan observes that Canadians with working-class backgrounds have a shorter life expectancy and are generally less healthy than their middle-class counterparts. How do you explain these differences?

REFERENCES

Bellamy, L.A. 1994. Capital, habitus, field, and practice: An introduction to the work of Pierre Bourdieu. In *Sociology of education in Canada: Critical perspectives on theory, research and practice*, eds. L. Erwin and L. MacLennan, 120–36. Toronto: Copp Clark Longman.

Bourdieu, P. 1972/1977. *Outline of a theory of practice* (trans. R. Nice). Cambridge, MA: Cambridge University Press.

Bourdieu, P. 1973/1986. The forms of capital. In *Handbook of theory and research for the sociology of education*, ed. J. C. Richardson (trans. R. Nice), 241–58. New York: Greenwood Press.

Christiansen, C. G., and E. A. Townsend. 2004. *Introduction to occupation: The art and science of living.* Upper Saddle River, NJ: Prentice Hall.

Ginsberg, E. ed. 1996. *Passing and the fictions of identity.* Durham, NC: Duke University Press.

Health Canada. 2004. *Population health.* Available: http://www.hcsc.gc.ca/hppb/phdd/determinants. Accessed July 13, 2004.

Kielhofner, G. 2002. *Model of human occupation: Theory and application*, 3rd ed. Baltimore, MD: Lippincott Williams & Wilkins.

MacIonis, J. J., J. N. Clarke, and L. M. Gerber. 1997. *Sociology: The Canadian edition*, 2nd ed. Scarborough, ON: Prentice-Hall Canada.

Olson, P. 1995. Poverty and education in Canada. In *Social change and education in Canada*, eds. R. Ghosh and D. Ray, 196–208. Toronto: Harcourt Brace.

Raphael, D., J. Macdonald, R. Colman, R. Labonte, K. Hayward, and R. Torgerson. 2005. Researching income and income distribution as determinants of health in Canada: Gaps between theoretical knowledge, research practice, and policy implementation. *Health Policy, 72*, 217–32.

46

A Fortunate Country

DAVID K. FOOT

Demography is an important area of research within sociology, both in terms of analysis and explanatory power. This article is written from the perspective of what the Canadian economy will be like in 2020 based on an aging population. This naturally includes a focus on the Baby Boomers. There has been a growing realization in the past few years that an aging population is going to translate into significant changes in the labour market. This article highlights the demographic trends that are involved and discusses some possible consequences.

The generation that was never going to grow old has discovered that nature had other plans, and its influence is finally starting to wane.

In 2020, annual economic growth in Canada is forecast to drop to an anemic 1 per cent. There is no recession. National economic growth has been declining for more than a decade.

There is much hand-wringing among the nation's economic elite about this lacklustre economic performance, especially since economic growth in the U.S. is expected to be higher. But there should be no surprise. This difference in economic performance reflects, in large part, the higher fertility of Americans 20 years earlier that has resulted in more consumers and workers.

Moreover, despite the continued claims from both business and government of widespread labour shortages, the unemployment rate in

Canada remains mired above 5 per cent as older workers and immigrants continue to languish in the changing labour market. It appears that little has been learned from the previous 20 years.

That is not to say that government has been inactive. In the mid-2010s, Canada championed new legislation that, despite strong opposition from employers, outlawed ageism in the workplace and required employers to "respect and recognize" foreign credentials. It also required employers to pay for skills upgrading necessary for new hires.

This legislation imposed costly evaluation and retraining on employers. It also exposed them to potentially expensive lawsuits from immigration lawyers and Boomers now in their 60s and early 70s. Unrelenting demands for lower taxes and reductions in the size of the public sector left federal and provincial governments with insufficient resources to respond to these educational challenges, especially since health-care

Source: David K. Foot. 2006. "A Fortunate Country." *Toronto Star*, December 27, p. A25.

spending had absorbed all discretionary spending. The electorate was angry and had demanded action.

The quid pro quo for final passage of the legislation was a commitment to employers to raise immigration to levels that had not been experienced for a century. Nearly 400,000 immigrants arrived the previous year. Intake rules had been changed years earlier to permit limited numbers of unskilled and semi-skilled workers who were not immediately subject to minimum wage laws. This caused much debate in the general population and especially in the immigrant community.

However, employers were still "negotiating" with the various unions, professional associations and government agencies over who would evaluate their credentials.

The debate created an unusual alliance as both unions and professional associations united with employers in their opposition to the legislation.

Yet it had become clear to many that employers wanted abundant cheap labour, while unions and professional associations were fighting to protect their incomes. No one appeared to be concerned about the increasing numbers of unemployed and the ever-widening disparities in income that had resulted from past policies. The public became increasingly disillusioned, so the new Egalitarian party used its balance of power in Ottawa to get the legislation enacted.

Much of the debate had focused on declining standards of living and Canada's role in the global economy. Despite a decade of tepid economic performance and a divisive national debate, Canadians wondered why they were still admired globally.

Faster economic growth in the U.S.—a Canadian benchmark—had not guaranteed the U.S. global domination or admiration. However, the Canadian economy had outperformed most other countries in the former developed world, including Europe, Japan and other former Asian powers. Canadians remained one of the better-educated populations and natural resources,

including open spaces, forests, diamonds, oil, gas, uranium and especially water, continued to provide Canada with potential that many other nations lacked. Canada was viewed as a fortunate country.

In addition, continued workforce growth was envied in many countries now dealing with shrinking workforces. This moderate growth reflected somewhat higher Canadian fertility in previous decades and a long, well-established commitment to immigration. The economy continued to grow, albeit at a slower pace and quality of life remained high in global comparisons.

How could this be? Quality of life is difficult to measure. It depends on many things—the air we breathe, the leisure time we enjoy, the security of our persons and possessions and, of course, our incomes. Choosing any one limits discussion, but understanding part of the picture contributes to an understanding of the whole. This is why economists often focus on an economic measure, namely income per person, which is sometimes referred to as the standard of living.

With slower economic growth, how could Canadians' standard of living be globally admired in 2020? A non-shrinking population helped, as did continued participation in the expanding global economy. The incomes generated by selling at home and abroad the myriad of products and services produced in Canada added to incomes.

It is important to remember that standards of living are measured in per person terms so the number of people who share in the income influences the outcome. For standards of living to rise, income growth must be faster than population growth. Alternatively, and perhaps of more relevance when populations decline, stagnant or even negative income growth can still result in rising standards of living, albeit for fewer people. Japan has become a prime example of this phenomenon over the 21st century.

Slower population growth became a reality for many countries of the world in the late 20th century. By the early 21st century, population decline had set in for some such as Russia and Japan. Not surprisingly stagnant economic growth also became a reality.

This did not automatically mean these peoples were worse off. In fact, reducing the growth and especially the size of the human footprint had environmental benefits, thereby improving the quality of life as well as the standard of living.

The age of declining population growth and, in some countries, declining population size reduced the pressures for rapid economic growth.

People came to understand that they could be better off with slower economic growth, even if business continued to pine for more rapid economic growth to sell their wares.

WHY HAD ECONOMIC GROWTH SLOWED?

Workforce growth was always the crucial determinant of a country's economic growth. The slower the workforce growth, the slower is potential economic growth. Whether the economy under- or over-performs relative to its potential depends on the share of the workforce that has jobs and the productivity of those who are employed.

This depends on the behaviour of both employees and employers. High unemployment rates sap economic growth, while productivity performance depends not only on work effort but also on the quantity and quality of equipment provided to workers.

In many formerly developed countries, the Baby Boom generation had determined their economic history. In Canada, which had one of the loudest Booms, the first Boomer born in 1947 turned 16 in 1963, while the last Boomer born in 1966 turned 16 in 1982. Consequently, Canadian workforce growth rose rapidly over the 1960s and, especially, the 1970s and then subsided in the 1980s. The impact of the birth control pill on births ensured slower workforce growth over the 1990s and into the new millennium.

Of course, not everyone enters the workforce at age 16. Increasing education reduced workforce participation among younger adults and increased it among middle working ages, especially for women. In the new millennium, workforce participation in the later working ages increased for both sexes. This increasing workforce participation contributed to faster workforce growth.

However, the inability of both the public and private sectors to enable the participation of aging Boomers reduced the potential for growth. This lost opportunity contributed to worker dissatisfaction and, ultimately, slower economic growth.

Nonetheless, history had already set the scene for 2020. By the 1990s, workforce growth was one-third of the 1970s, so slower economic growth in Canada was well entrenched by the beginning of the 21st century. The fact that average economic growth over the 1990s was two-thirds of the 1970s implied that the country's workforce became more productive. However, overall population growth did not slow as fast as workforce growth so the per person standard of living did not rise as fast. Increasing productivity had not automatically produced increased standards of living as many commentators had promised.

Recognition of the importance of population growth in determining workforce and economic growth led to receptivity in the general population for increased immigration providing the newcomers were integrated into the workplace. However, despite rising immigration levels, population growth continued to slow. The entrenched below-replacement fertility levels continued to dominate population growth.

More dramatic, however, was the slowing growth of the workforce. The first Boomer had reached 65 in 2012 and while many Boomers continued to seek work through their 60s, ageism and the pension inflexibilities frustrated their desires to keep working. Their search for flexible employment opportunities consistent with part-time retirement continued to meet resistance from employers.

This is what precipitated the demands for legislative solutions. By 2020, most of the first half of the Boomer population had left the workforce. Average workforce growth over the 2010s was one-eighth of the growth rate of the 1970s.

Slower economic growth mirrored workforce growth and fell to less than one-third of the economic growth rate of the 1960s. While alarm bells rang in the corridors of economic power, polling results showed Canadians happy with their standard of living. Why the inconsistency?

Slower economic growth certainly made management more challenging in the new millennium. There was less flexibility to reallocate resources in both the private and public sectors.

In the more rapid growth days of the past, management could reduce the relative importance of one area by freezing rather than reducing budgets elsewhere. That strategy became increasingly difficult when the pie was not growing as fast. As a result, pressure from shareholders and the press increased on management to be more accountable and more creative along the road to 2020.

Of course, any economic growth in excess of population growth increases the standard of living.

However, as workforce growth dropped below population growth, this became more difficult to achieve. Attention became focused on the causes of continuing high unemployment and ongoing concerns about discrimination in the workplace, as well as Boomer retirement and productivity performance. This attention sowed the seeds for the new legislation.

With increasing shares of new immigrant and older workers in the workforce, eliminating discrimination became an important part of the economic growth challenge.

For the immigrant worker it meant recognizing the skills that they brought from their homelands. For the older worker it became necessary to implement new policies to enable and encourage older workers to remain in the workforce. Policies that allowed workers to simultaneously add to and withdraw from pensions were discussed. But the reluctance of employers, unions and professional associations to voluntarily confront the challenges led to the legislative initiative.

Nonetheless, as challenging as this scenario was for Canada, it was even more challenging for many other countries in the world. Canada had at least experienced workforce growth rather than the decline that occurred elsewhere.

France, Germany, Italy, Japan, Korea, Scandinavia and much of East Europe (Czech Republic, Hungary, Poland, Slovakia) had faced declining workforces and many other countries such as Belgium, Greece, Netherlands, Norway, Portugal, Spain and Britain had faced even slower workforce growth than Canada.

This is a substantial list. Only Australia, the U.S. and a number of smaller countries (Iceland, Ireland, Luxembourg and New Zealand) had experienced faster workforce growth than Canada. And we had its natural resources. By comparison with these other developed countries Canada had performed remarkably well in the 21st century.

Not surprisingly, this comparatively poor economic performance in the former developed world had led to a precipitous decline in its economic power in the global economy. There was no surprise in the increasing role played by the demographic superpowers of India and China, but China's need for international workers had taken the world by surprise.

No pundit appeared to have anticipated the impact of the one-child policy on subsequent growth performance. New global superpowers were emerging from surprising places.

Turkey in Europe, Brazil in South America, Vietnam in South Asia and Iran in the Middle East were assuming leadership roles in their regions and in the global economy. The world was changing, and Canada was changing with it. Immigrants from these and similar countries were now business leaders in Canada and provided invaluable links that ensured Canada's continued presence in the global economy.

Slower workforce growth is inevitable in aging populations. The magnitude of the slow-down in many countries, including Canada, substantially reduced economic growth in the new millennium.

This should not have been a surprise or even a cause for concern. It is still possible to maintain continued rising standards of living if economic growth exceeds population growth.

A number of countries were relying on shrinking populations to maintain their standards of living, but Canada was not in this group. With the gradual retirement of the Boomers over the 2010s, immigration had played an ever-increasing role in population growth and the controversial legislation had laid the foundation for bolstering workforce growth.

The road to 2020 had been largely predictable through the demographic lens. Canada had performed admirably, especially by comparison with most other countries in the former developed world. The good fortune of abundant natural resources had helped. By 2020 the country's standard of living and quality of life was universally admired.

And Canada's role in the global economy was as strong as ever as it used its resources and immigrants to forge links with the emerging superpowers. Canada was indeed a fortunate country. And Canadians remained surprised!

CRITICAL THINKING QUESTIONS

1. What are some of the characteristics that Foot lists which can be incorporated when measuring a country's standard of living? Can you think of others? Do you think income is the most important variable?

2. What are the consequences of an aging population and decreasing fertility rates for industrial countries? What will the one-child policy in China mean for that country's future?

3. Do you think immigration is a solution to some of the problems caused by an aging population? Do you think it is fair to pay new immigrants (e.g., nannies or farm workers) less than minimum wage? Why or why not?

47

The Changing Colour of Poverty in Canada

ABDOLMOHAMMAD KAZEMIPUR AND SHIVA S. HALLI

Kazemipur and Halli investigate the issue of poor or low-income immigrants. They reveal that immigrants are consistently overrepresented among Canada's poor; moreover, immigrants belonging to visible-minority groups are the most likely to suffer poverty.

Using the 1991 and 1996 Canadian census data, the present study addresses the issue of poor or low-income immigrants, a topic largely overlooked in previous immigration research. The authors found that, compared to native-born Canadians, immigrants were consistently overrepresented among the poor, and that this overrepresentation had a clear ethnic and racial colour, with visible-minority immigrants experiencing the most severe conditions. For them, the logistic regression models show, the odds of poverty are noticeably higher, even after controlling for all other relevant variables. The poverty rates of different generations of immigrants also show an unexpected pattern, in which those who have migrated during their adolescent years experience unusually severe poverty conditions.

Source: A. Kazemipur and S. S. Halli. 2001. "The Changing Colour of Poverty in Canada." *Canadian Review of Sociology and Anthropology*, 38(2), 217–38.

A comparison of the situation in 1991 and 1996 shows that human capital endowments are becoming less rewarding for immigrants.

In the last two decades of the 20th century, like many other industrial nations, Canada went through some radical transformations, influenced by two major forces—one economic, the other political. The Canadian economy has been shifting away from a structure based on manufacturing to one dependent on information processing, and from one dependent on domestic resources to one increasingly operating in a global scene. This development has influenced many aspects of Canadian society, but particularly its occupational structure, income distribution, and regional inequality (Marchak, 1991; Rifkin, 1995). In the political arena, a new wave of conservatism, which some have called Neoliberalism (Abu-Laban, 1998) and others New Right (Marchak, 1991), has swept across the country, forcing major Canadian social institutions—such as education, health care, occupations, the social safety net and the taxation system—to depart from their postwar paths of development. Despite having dynamics of their own, these two trends—economic and political—have converged in at least one area, eroding the middle class and generating a bipolar structure in the economy, job market, and income distribution (Teeple, 1995). The essence of this development is well captured in a commonly expressed metaphor that the industrial societies are leaving a pyramid shape in favour of an hourglass one (Portes and Rumbaut, 1996).

One area in which the effects of the new economic and political circumstances have been more visible is in immigration policy and the social and economic experiences of immigrants. This has partly to do with the nature of the Neoliberal prescriptions that, according to Abu-Laban (1998: 194), "have a tendency to create discourses of enemies and scapegoats, transforming what were once seen as victims into victimizers (e.g., single mothers, the poor, immigrants and so on are blamed for stealing 'our' welfare, 'our' social and educational services, or 'our' jobs)." In many Western countries, she argues, "such discourses relating to immigrants have resulted in both a tightening of criteria for formal citizenship, and a tightening of immigration controls vis-à-vis certain groups and nationals—typically those from countries of the Third World" (Abu-Laban, 1998: 194). The clear implication of this proposition is that, in an era of Neoliberal politics, with its associated fiscal conservatism and priority of deficit reduction, the vulnerable groups such as immigrants are more likely to suffer disproportionately.

The present study tries to shed some light on the validity of the above proposition by empirically examining the experience of poverty by immigrants to Canada and the factors behind it. The choice of poverty as the topic is justified based on two facts. First, in an era marked by transition from a "pyramid"- to an "hourglass"-shaped social structure, a larger number of

people may find themselves at the lower level of social structure and income scale, as reflected in the constant rise of poverty levels in Canada since the late 1980s. A study of poverty, therefore, will address a social problem that more and more people will be struggling with. Second, in the particular case of immigrants, most of the previous research has treated them as one homogeneous sub-population, masking the enormous diversity that exists among them. The plight of low-income immigrants has gone largely unnoticed in serious academic research, though it has received some attention in the popular media.

The central questions with which we are concerned are: 1) What is the magnitude of poverty among immigrants, compared to non-immigrants? 2) What is the composition of poor immigrants, in terms of ethnic origin, location of residence, period of migration, and age at arrival? 3) What are the causes of poverty among immigrants, and are they different from those of non-immigrants? and finally, 4) How has immigrants' experience of poverty and its causative factors changed during the period of the Neoliberal swing in Canadian politics? In what follows, we first introduce an overarching conceptual framework for understanding the causes of poverty among immigrants. This framework has an eclectic nature; it includes conceptual elements taken from various theoretical approaches. This allows for an examination of the relative significance of the different factors emphasized by different perspectives. Then we address the methodological issues and describe the nature of the data used. The article concludes with a presentation of the findings, and the implications for future research.

THE CONCEPTUAL FRAMEWORK

The paucity of research on poverty among immigrants has hindered the development of theories specifically formulated to address this issue. This theoretical shortage is certainly, at least partly, a result of the paucity of research on poverty in

Canada. But it has also been reinforced by the long-held view that the problem of poverty among immigrants is not any more serious than among the native-born. Against this background, it is understandable why the poverty of immigrants has never come to the foreground, nor ever been high in the immigration-research agenda. To these factors of theoretical significance, one may add a possible third factor of a more practical nature: an unconscious reluctance among researchers to raise an issue that could be easily used against immigrants and in favour of more restrictive immigration policies. The result, whatever the causes, is the current lack of a well-developed theory of immigrant poverty.

The paucity of specific theories of poverty, however, does not mean that we are left in a theoretical vacuum. Indeed, there exists a rich literature on the general economic performance of immigrants that has useful implications for the study of poverty. Examining the validity of John Porter's thesis of the "vertical mosaic," Lautard and Loree (1984: 342), for instance, found that the occupational inequality among ethnic groups in Canada was substantial enough to justify the use of the notion of a "vertical mosaic," and that the differences observed "do not seem to be explainable by the effects of differences in regions and differences in education." In a search for factors that can explain these persisting patterns of inequality, Grant and Oertel (1998: 70) suggest three possibilities: "A slower rate of acquisition of unobservable skills (such as language proficiency and awareness of cultural norms specific to Canada); a higher degree of discrimination with the rising percentage of visible minorities among immigrants; or a change in the structure of employment in Canada in favour of lower-paid service occupations." This proposition, indeed, encompasses three major theoretical approaches employed in the previous research on the economic performance of immigrants: one that emphasizes the individual factors such as assimilation and human capital; another that stresses the economic environment of the host society at the time of immigrants' arrival; and a third that highlights the social environment in the receiving country, along with factors such as discrimination, as predictors of immigrants' performance. Over time, each of these theoretical approaches has branched out into various versions, with slight differences. Below, we introduce the variations of these perspectives in more detail, along with their implications for the issue of concern in this study, that is, poverty.

Assimilation Thesis

The *assimilation thesis* considers poverty of immigrants as a passing phenomenon due to immediate post-migration difficulties, a problem that eases up with longer stay in the new home. The assimilation theory would hypothesize that over time immigrants produce better economic records, as they become increasingly familiar with their new environments, develop better communication skills, and become more realistic in their expectations. In other words, in their early years after arrival immigrants face the harshest situation. This harshness, however, subsides as time allows for more assimilation to take place. It follows that the situation is even more favourable for the second generation of immigrants, as for them such a process starts from childhood and even from birth. As far as poverty is concerned, the most vulnerable immigrants—that is, those with a high risk of poverty—are to be found among those in their early years of arrival, those with little or no knowledge of the official languages, and those who migrated at an older age.

Entrance Status Thesis

While the early "assimilationists" paid more attention to cultural and ideational processes (see Park and Burgess, 1924; Gordon, 1964), the later ones put more emphasis on economic factors. Porter (1965) suggested "the entrance status thesis," in which immigrants start from the lowest jobs in the market and move their way up the occupational hierarchy, leaving the entrance status jobs for the newly arrived immigrants. In this perspective, immigrants' economic performance is a function of their occupational ranking, itself a function of their duration of stay in the host society and the existence of consecutive waves of immigrants. Those immigrants who are in the early years of their arrival, according to this view, are more likely to have higher poverty rates, but this likelihood diminishes with longer stays and movement to more rewarding jobs.

Human Capital Thesis

This perspective puts more emphasis on human capital endowments of immigrants as determinants of their economic performance. A low-income status, according to this thesis, can result from factors such as low education, low job skills, old age, poor health, and low geographical mobility. A low education, for example, can suppress one's chance of admission into well-paid jobs that demand a highly skilled labour force; old age can be detrimental when successful performance in a job requires mastery of modern technology; low geographical mobility, both nationally and internationally, tends to deprive one of the job opportunities available elsewhere. Borjas (1994), for instance, has attributed the lower level of economic achievement among recent immigrants in the United States to the fact that they have come mostly from developing countries, and with low levels of educational qualifications and occupational skills (Massey et al., 1994).

Discrimination Thesis

Despite the significance of human capital factors, many studies have shown that an explanation merely based on such factors runs the risk of being too static and fairly simplistic. Some have raised the possibility that the lower economic achievement of recent immigrants may be attributed not to their lower level of human capital endowment but to the diminishing returns for it. Gordon (1995: 530), for example, attributes the lower educational attainments of second generation immigrants to the diminishing returns for their education: "[against] a background of environmental disadvantages, institutional racism, and doubts about the likely rewards for qualifications, educational attainments have been uneven." Basran and Zong (1999), on the other hand, argue that even when the educational attainments are high for immigrants, they are not recognized accordingly. They show that large numbers of immigrants in Canada have occupations inferior, in terms of both prestige and financial gains, to those for which they are trained, due to the fact that their credentials are not recognized appropriately.

The studies cited above clearly imply that the positive impact of human capital factors can be intercepted by other factors such as discrimination, both at interpersonal and institutional levels. Among all possible types of discrimination, one based on race and ethnic characteristics is found to be most common and persistent, as well as more conducive to poverty. This relationship is well captured in an observation by Dunk (1999) that "it is no historical accident . . . that skin colour and poverty are related."

Empirical studies of the impact of discrimination on the economic performance of immigrants in Canada have yielded mixed results. A report by the Economic Council of Canada (1991), for instance, claimed that there was no substantial discrimination against immigrants, and in particular against visible minorities. This report was later criticized for its flawed statistical and measurement methods, two of which being the use of country of birth instead of ethnic and racial origins, and the smallness of the samples—as low as a dozen for some ethnic groups (Reitz and Breton, 1994). More rigorous treatment of the problem in later research resulted in an opposite finding. In a study to measure the "market value of race," for example, Li (1999: 126) found that "non-white origin creates a penalty for all visible minorities in the labour market." He attributed such a penalty to a range of mechanisms, from refusing to recognize the non-white immigrants' credentials, to their lower likelihood of being hired, higher chances of being screened out in the job-application process owing to their language characteristics, accent, and deviation from the language standard of the dominant group. Along this line, Reitz and Breton (1994: 122) found "consistent and substantial net earnings disadvantages" for both adult immigrants and immigrants raised in Canada. The expression of the opposing views in regard to whether immigrants face discrimination in Canada justifies their inclusion in our analysis. However, due to the fact that discrimination does not easily lend itself to direct observation, and that its impact is often confounded by other variables, the findings of this study on discrimination need to be approached cautiously. The variables included in census data are only indirect proxies for discrimination.

Period Effect Thesis

In addition to assimilation, human capital, and discrimination, the period in which one migrated can also affect one's economic performance. Commenting on the experiences of recent immigrants to the United States, Gans (1992: 181) remarked:

. . . the long-term periods of economic growth, the first that began after the Civil War and the second that started after World War II, are not likely to return soon. The first helped to spur the arrival of the new European immigrants and enabled them to find more or less steady jobs so that many of them or their children could escape poverty by the end of the 1920s. The second enabled the descendents of that immigration to move at least into the upper-working and lower-middle classes, and in many cases, firmly into the middle class. Even if periods of long-term economic growth return, they will probably not be equally labour-intensive. No-one expects a revival in physical labour, and even many low-level service jobs may be computerized, sent abroad, or left undone.

Such trends have special meaning for the new immigration and its second generation since, among other things, they could lead to what I have earlier called second-generation decline.

In Canada, likewise, the post–World War II decades were especially prosperous, providing newly arrived immigrants with plenty of opportunities. Shorter periods of waiting to get into a first job, the rarity of employment terminations, and the prevalence of full-time occupations enabled immigrants to have an early financial take-off and establish themselves more easily. Such an economic environment, however, is totally nonexistent for those immigrants who have landed in Canada since the mid-1970s. There is, therefore, a higher likelihood for these groups of immigrants to be poorer than their preceding peers.

The theoretical propositions discussed above guide the present study. While some of these propositions are derived from competing theoretical perspectives, as mentioned earlier, we have attempted to include all of them in our conceptual model to verify them empirically. Figure 47.1 encapsulates the conceptual synthesis that we use in the present study.

DATA AND METHODOLOGY

The data used in this study consist of the individual Public Use Micro Files (PUMFs) of Canada's 1991 and 1996 censuses.

A word is needed on the notion of poverty and the way it is defined. Like most discussions of poverty in Canada during the last 25 years, this study has employed Statistics Canada's "Low Income Cut-Offs" (LICOs), which are calculated for communities and for families of various sizes within those communities. Table 47.1 contains the poverty lines for the census year 1996. It is important to note that not all researchers agree upon the legitimacy of using LICOs as poverty status indicators. Whether LICOs should be used as

Figure 47.1 The Conceptual Model of the Causes of Poverty among Immigrants

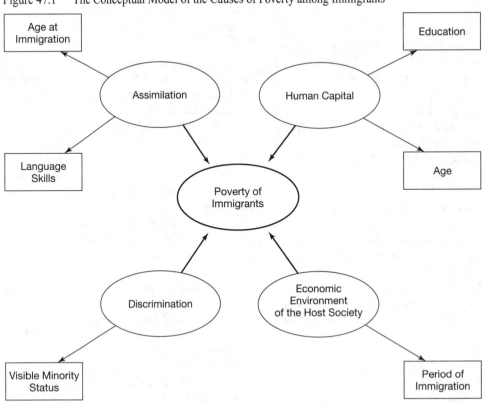

TABLE 47.1 Low-Income Cut-offs for Families and Unattached Individuals (1986-based), in Dollars, 1996

	Size of Area of Residence				
Family Size	*500,000 or More*	*100,000 to 499,999*	*30,000 to 99,999*	*Small Urban Areas*	*Rural Areas (Farm and Non-farm)*
1	15,819	13,895	13,574	12,374	10,769
2	21,442	18,835	18,399	16,771	14,600
3	27,256	23,941	23,387	21,318	18,556
4	31,383	27,561	26,927	24,547	21,364
5	34,287	30,114	29,419	26,818	23,343
6	37,219	32,686	31,932	29,109	25,337
7 or More	40,029	35,159	34,347	31,311	27,252

Source: Statistics Canada (1998).

indicators of poverty, or should simply be considered as indicators of low income, is still debated (see, for instance, Sarlo, 1992, 1994; Fellegi, 1997). Such a debate is not new, and is certainly not confined to Canada. It is a part of a larger and yet unsettled debate among academics and policy makers on the measure of poverty (see Ruggles, 1990; Kazemipur and Halli, 2000). An examination of the debate surrounding this issue, however, is beyond the scope of this study. Even if the reader does not consider low-income and poverty as equivalent, the trends and patterns found in this study will still remain pertinent to low-income, if not poor, immigrants.

FINDINGS

Table 47.2 shows the magnitude of poverty for immigrants in Canada in 1996. To provide a better view of the possible impacts of location and ethnicity, poverty rates are reported by city and ethnic origin. Poverty rates of non-immigrants are also included, to compare and to isolate the particular effect of immigrant status. The values that are highlighted specify those groups of immigrants who have poverty rates higher than their non-immigrant counterparts of the same ethnic origin and living in the same city. The table is also divided into three sections based on the geographical origins of the ethnic groups. The top section shows the rates for western and northwestern Europe, the middle section for southern and eastern Europe, and the bottom section for the developing countries.

The first thing to note is the overall magnitude of poverty rates in the three sections of Table 47.2, which reveal a number of consistent patterns. First, a cursory look at the distribution of the cases in the table shown in boldface—that is, the ethnic groups in which immigrants have higher poverty rates than non-immigrants of the same ethnic origin—shows that they occur with much higher frequencies in the middle and bottom sections. To be more specific, considering the three centres of concentration of immigrants, i.e., Montreal, Toronto and Vancouver, out of a total of fifteen groups in this category, seven groups (47%) show higher rates of poverty for immigrants as compared to non-immigrants of the European ethnic origin. The proportion is 26 out of 30 (or 87%) for the middle section, and 18 out of 33 (or 57%) for the bottom section. At face value, this may indicate that immigrants of

eastern and southern European origin are the most disadvantaged groups. This implication, however, is qualified when the magnitude of poverty is taken into consideration. The poverty rates for the eastern and southern European groups vary mostly in the range of 20s and 30s, while those of visible minorities in the bottom section vary in the range of 40s and 50s, with one higher than 60. Also, it should be noted that the poverty rates of the non-immigrants in the bottom section are so noticeably high that being an immigrant hardly aggravates the poverty level. Except for variations in the range of poverty rates, this pattern exists for all three cities.

Second, in addition to the differential rates of poverty for immigrants and non-immigrants, the severity of poverty for certain groups is particularly noticeable. A search for the groups with poverty rates of more than 50% in all CMAs yields an alarming result: one western/north western European group, 21 southern/eastern European (particularly Spanish), and 103 visible minorities, four of which show a 100% poverty rate (i.e., West Asian non-immigrants in Quebec City, West Asian immigrants in Sherbrooke–Trois-Rivières, Spanish non-immigrants in Hamilton, and Lebanese immigrants in Regina–Saskatoon).

It should be noted, however, that more than 60% of the Spanish reported a Latin American country as their place of birth. This is to say that the most disadvantaged group in the middle section of Table 47.2 is more closely associated with the developing world than with Europe.

The immigrant groups with the highest rates of poverty have another thing in common: the majority of them arrived in Canada since the late 1960s. This commonality can be related to their higher rates of poverty in two ways. First, they arrived after the postwar economic boom in Canada, hence their lower economic performance and higher poverty rates. Second, they are still new immigrants, with a low level of familiarity with Canada, and are still building up their careers. The former possibility alludes to what may be called the "period effect"; the latter, to the

TABLE 47.2 Poverty Rates by Ethnic Origin, CMA and Immigration Status, 1996

	Montreal		Toronto		Vancouver		All other CMAs	
	Non-immigrants	Immigrants	Non-immigrants	Immigrants	Non-immigrants	Immigrants	Non-immigrants	Immigrants
British	26.6	22.7	15.1	14.5	18.4	17	17.1	13.3
French	20.5	**27.3**	16.4	**18.6**	21.8	**28.6**	19.7	17.7
Dutch (Netherlands)	13.5	13.2	9.9	**12.9**	14.9	**21.3**	12.4	**12.5**
German	20.7	15.9	12.3	**15.9**	19.2	17.4	14.5	**16.2**
Other Western European	19.3	**21.3**	15.4	14.2	21.9	18.6	12.0	**14.2**
Hungarian (Magyar)	18	**27.2**	18.8	**27.8**	28.6	**36.6**	13.8	**19.9**
Polish	32.7	**37.1**	17.7	**30.2**	23.9	**31.1**	15.3	**22.0**
Ukrainian	25.6	**29.8**	14.5	**32**	20.9	**36.6**	15.7	**20.1**
Balkan	26.2	**37.1**	13.4	**25.8**	15	**41.7**	16.2	**33.2**
Greek	28.8	**31.7**	19.7	**21.5**	19.5	**24**	19.0	16.3
Italian	19.9	**23.2**	11.7	**17.2**	15.3	**18.8**	11.0	**15.3**
Portuguese	25.3	24	19.5	**19.7**	15.6	**18.3**	16.9	14.2
Spanish	53.5	52.8	49.3	43.8	45.2	36	67.1	48.6
Jewish	19.7	**29.5**	8.3	**20.5**	10.7	**13.5**	10.4	**22.3**
Other European	20.3	42.7	14.6	**23.4**	22.7	**27.8**	17.5	**20.5**
African	70.7	62.6	57.8	55.2	36.4	**45.5**	57.6	**65.6**
Lebanese	54.9	53	38.4	**45.6**	27.3	**30.8**	42.4	**46.6**
Other Arab	47.9	54.6	35.5	**46.1**	38.5	**46.4**	44.9	**50.1**
West Asian	38.8	**48.1**	45.8	**47.3**	61.8	50.4	50.8	**59.7**
South Asian	51.4	**54.9**	27.6	**32.6**	20.2	**23.9**	23.4	**25.9**
Chinese	37.7	**45.9**	22.1	**33.4**	19.5	**39.5**	19.2	**31.5**
Filipino	28.8	27.5	18.8	**23.3**	16.1	**22.2**	18.4	**22.4**
Vietnamese	41.1	40.5	47.5	38.7	72.2	52	43.3	41.2
Other East/Southeast Asian	56.9	49.8	15.5	**36.7**	22.4	**35.7**	28.7	**42.2**
Latin/Central/South American	69.2	58.7	40.7	35.7	52	44.8	49.2	45.3
Caribbean	58.4	53.4	44.7	32.5	25.9	17.6	41.2	32.6
Total	24	**39.6**	16	**27.7**	18.3	**29.9**	18.2	**23.9**

Note: Bold-faced figures indicate groups of immigrants with higher poverty rates than their non-immigrant counterparts from the same ethnic origin living in the same CMA.

"assimilation effect." By showing the poverty rates of different cohorts of immigrants, Table 47.3 allows an empirical examination of these possibilities.

Table 47.3 reports the poverty rate of immigrants by their period of immigration. The last row of the table contains the overall poverty rates for those who migrated in seven different periods. The poverty rate starts at 21.3% for those who arrived before 1946, and consistently declines in three subsequent categories, reaching its lowest level in the 1960s (14.2%). It then rises noticeably. This trend clearly supports the period effect, as it is perfectly synchronized with the postwar periods of economic boom and bust in Canada. This general confirmation should be qualified, however, with a reminder that the best way to isolate the period effect is through the use of longitudinal data. In the absence of such data, the period effect can be confounded by other variables, thus obscuring the findings.

When it comes to testing the assimilation effect, however, Table 47.3 is more reliable. One implication of assimilation theory was that immigrants who migrated at an earlier age would show better economic performance, owing to their familiarity with the social environment and market demands in their new homes, access to job-searching social networks, better language skills, less severe cultural conflict, and recognized education. It follows that the poverty rates of immigrants should increase as their age at migration increases. The average poverty rates of immigrants by their age at migration shown in the last two columns of Table 47.3 support this argument, though with some qualification. The poverty rates for all immigrants reported in the first column yields the surprising result that those who migrated at a younger age are as, or more, disadvantaged than their parents, as far as their poverty is concerned. The exclusion of those under 16, with the justification that they are not at the employment age and therefore do not yet earn income, improves the results to some extent. It clearly shows that those who migrated at age 0–4,

who can be considered analogous to second-generation immigrants, have the lowest rate of poverty. The poverty rate then rises as the age at migration increases. The only anomaly in this trend is the poverty rate of those who migrated at age 13–19, for whom the poverty rate exceeds those of the age groups immediately before and after them. This anomaly persists regardless of the period of immigration, and it clearly runs in contrast to the expectation derived from the assimilation theory. It therefore demands an explanation. In the absence of any previous study on this issue, one can only speculate about the possible reasons, as potential hypotheses for future research.

Rumbaut (1997) lays a theoretical foundation for treating various generations of immigrants, which may be of use here. To the conventional categories of first and second generations, Rumbaut (1997: 951) adds the intermediary categories of "1.25," "1.5," and "1.75" generations, in reference to those who migrated at ages 13–17 (adolescence and secondary school), 6–12 (after primary socialization and the beginning of elementary school), and 0–5 (preschool), respectively. Using this categorization, it is clear that the age group with an unusually high rate of poverty is the "1.25" generation. Adolescence is often a time of enormous psychological and emotional unrest. Adolescents have to deal with a range of difficulties, from generational conflict to peer pressures. Such pressures are confounded for immigrant adolescents, as they have also to deal with the burdens of learning a new language and functioning in a new cultural environment. Immigrant adolescents are also more likely to experience what Igoa (1995) calls "fragmented formal education" owing to their families' frequent mobility and high instability during the immediate years after arrival. Rumbaut points out that to overcome these difficulties, they need strong support by, and the collaboration of, parents and teachers. In most cases, however, immigrant parents are too busy securing their economic foothold, particularly in the early years of arrival, and have little time to spend with their children. The possibility of discrimination at

TABLE 47.3 Poverty Rates of Cohorts of Immigrants, 1996*

Age at Immigration	Period of Immigration							Average (All Immigrants)	Average*
	Before 1946*	1946–50*	1951–60*	1961–70*	1971–80*	1981–90*	1991–96*		
0–4	17.1	10.9	10.8	12.7	21.9	23.0	—	23.9	15.7
5–12	18.3	10.5	10.5	12.7	18.9	34.0	50.0	27.2	19.0
13–19	28.8	13.5	14.6	13.2	18.8	31.7	54.9	26.6	25.9
20–24	27.5	12.8	16.4	10.4	16.6	29.4	44.9	21.6	21.6
25–29	27.6	17.6	15.7	12.9	14.9	29.6	43.1	23.4	23.4
30–34	33.3	18.6	17.4	17.3	15.6	25.6	48.7	26.6	26.6
35–39	37.5	29.9	19.5	19.7	18.8	27.9	53.4	31.7	31.7
40–44	100.0	34.6	28.3	19.1	22.6	28.9	53.5	34.5	34.5
45–49	—	31.3	27.7	21.7	24.9	29.2	51.0	34.5	34.5
50–54	—	33.3	38.7	33.7	28.2	30.1	44.4	34.7	34.7
55–59	—	—	14.3	30.8	31.3	35.4	43.7	36.9	36.9
60 +	—	—	—	27.3	31.1	36.2	40.5	37.1	37.1
Average	21.3	15.1	15.2	14.2	18.8	30.1	48.3	26.6	24.9

*Only those aged 16 years and older in 1996 included.

school also deprives adolescent immigrants of the potential support of their teachers. The "1.25" generation immigrants find themselves alone in the face of these difficulties. Everything is left to their individual capacities and motivation. But, as Gordon (1995: 530) has remarked, the individual motivation for educational attainment and economic success may also be suppressed against "a background of environmental disadvantages, institutional racism, and doubts about the likely rewards for qualifications." The most likely outcome to which such circumstances are conducive is failure.

Another possible explanation of the poor economic performance of the "1.25" generation immigrants may be their lower level of social capital, as suggested by Portes (1995). The main thrust of Portes's thesis is that second-generation immigrants become assimilated, but not necessarily into the mainstream culture. Depending on factors such as their neighbourhoods, he argues, they may be assimilated into the underclass:

[the] overconcentration in the inner cities, which is a direct consequence of the lower economic resources of recent immigrants, has an unexpected consequence, namely to bring the offspring of these immigrants into close contact with downtrodden domestic minorities. . . . The confrontation with inner-city values places the second generation in a serious dilemma (Portes, 1995: 252).

Although this issue has not been systematically addressed in the Canadian context, the available studies allude to its relevance to Canada as well. In a study of neighbourhood poverty in Canada, Kazemipur and Halli (1997), for instance, have shown the overconcentration of certain ethnic groups, mostly visible minorities, in neighbourhoods with more than 40% poverty rates. In another attempt, Kazemipur and Halli (2000) have found that the visible minority immigrants, who are overrepresented in ghetto neighbourhoods, also tend to show a lower level of intergenerational mobility in terms of education and occupation. Further and more sophisticated research on this issue is seriously hampered by the lack of specific data sets combining the neighbourhood variables and individual characteristics.

CONCLUSION AND IMPLICATIONS

Some have argued that recent immigrants show a lower-than-expected economic performance, and have alluded to their lower "quality" (e.g., education, work experience) as the cause (Borjas, 1994). Our study of the experiences of low-income immigrants in Canada supports the first part of this argument—that is, that recent immigrants have a poorer economic record as compared to the previous cohorts—but it seriously questions the validity of the second part pertaining to the causes of such trends. Rather, we found that the odds of poverty among immigrants increased due to lower levels of returns to "quality" variables such as education, language skills, and type of employment, along with the penalizing effects of factors such as their racial origin and immigrant status.

Such findings, if sustained through more rigorous studies using more comprehensive data, have far-reaching implications for both public policy and future research. Over the past few years, Canadian studies have increasingly highlighted the significance of the lower returns to human capital endowments of immigrants, manifested in things such as the mismatch between their educational qualifications and occupations, or between their professional qualifications before and after migration (Basran and Zong, 1998); the lower returns to the educational investment of those immigrants with credentials earned abroad (Wanner, 1998); and the adoption of self-employment by immigrants as a result of their blocked mobility in salaried jobs typically dependent on education (Li, 2000). The problem is cited too frequently, and its existence and prevalence shown in too many different ways, to be disregarded as a passing phenomenon. It calls for a thorough revision of the procedures currently in effect for evaluation of the foreign credentials of immigrants.

Racial discrimination is another problem that deserves more attention. Although the findings of this study on the effect of racial discrimination are far from definitive (due to the inherent measurement limitations in the data used here), they are consistent with the findings of many previous studies and also with the trends observed in other immigrant-receiving countries. If left unchecked, the problem of race is only going to intensify. As Reitz (1998) has legitimately argued, the current flows of immigrants from Asia, Africa, and Latin America is going to make racial diversity a central feature of all industrial nations, and more so for immigrant-intensive countries such as Canada. Against this background, prevalence of racial discrimination in Canada would imply underutilization of human resources at present, and the potential for social conflicts in the future. None of these is a small enough problem to ignore.

The present study also implies two particular directions for future research, one more of a technical nature, the other conceptual. Despite their richness, the census data do not provide adequate information on language skills. Given the centrality of language acquisition in the later social and economic experiences of immigrants, this inadequacy renders census data of limited use for the study of immigrants. Ironically, there is enough emphasis on measuring language skills in procedures related to immigrants—including the processing of the applications for landed immigrant status, or the decisions regarding the costs of language training of family-class immigrants—but these emphases evaporate in the later data-collection practices.

The conceptual problem involves the gender aspect of the issue of poverty examined above. In the recent surge of poverty in Canada, women have suffered more severely compared to men, a notion captured in the use of the term "feminization of poverty" in recent sociological literature (see Duffy and Mandell, 1994; Duffy and Pupo, 1992; Kazemipur and Halli, 2000). So, a study of poverty in the general population without regard to gender runs the risk of masking the peculiar situation of low-income women. For immigrant women, the problem has an additional dimension, as their experiences are different from both native-born women and also immigrant men. At the heart of these differential experiences lies the fact that, according to Pendakur and Pendakur

(1998), the heads of prospective immigrant families are likely to be men, screened for occupational suitability and job readiness, and therefore more likely to enter Canada with recognized and rewarded credentials and jobs ready for them. As a result, female immigrants are more susceptible to losing their human capital or not getting its full return. Several studies have persuasively shown that the findings based on the study of male immigrants are not readily generalizable to female immigrants (Satzewich, 1995; Reitz, 1998; Pendakur and Pendakur, 1998), so much so that Ng (1986) has argued that "immigrant women" have come to be constituted as a distinct social category in the Canadian labour market. The findings of this study need to be furthered by including the gender dimension of poverty among immigrants.

CRITICAL THINKING QUESTIONS

1. With reference to the article, review your choice of three reasons why immigrants are more likely to suffer from poverty than non-immigrants. As a sociologist, do you think poverty among Canadian immigrant populations will get better or worse over the next twenty years? Defend your answer.

2. Compare and contrast two theories introduced by the authors that attempt to explain the economic performance of immigrants.

3. Review and discuss the unique challenges faced by the "1.25" generation.

REFERENCES

Abu-Laban, Y. 1998. Welcome/STAY OUT: The contradictions of Canadian integration and immigration policies at the millennium. *Canadian Ethnic Studies*, 30(3): 190–211.

Basran, G. S., and L. Zong. 1998. Devaluation of foreign credentials as perceived by nonwhite professional immigrants. *Canadian Ethnic Studies*, 30(3): 6–23.

Borjas, G. J. 1994. The economics of immigration. *Journal of Economic Literature*, 32: 1667–1717.

Duffy, A., and N. Mandell. 1994. Poverty in Canada. In *Society in question*, ed. R. Brym, 96–104. Toronto: Harcourt Brace & Company.

Duffy, A., and N. Pupo. 1992. *Part-time paradox: Connecting gender, work, and family.* Toronto: McClelland & Stewart.

Dunk, P. 1999. Racism, ethnic prejudice, whiteness and the working class. In *Racism and social inequality in Canada,* (ed.) V. Satzewich, 201–22. Toronto: Thompson Educational Publishing.

Economic Council of Canada. 1991. *New faces in the crowd: Economic and social impacts of immigration.* Ottawa: Minister of Supply and Services.

Fellegi, I. P. 1997. On poverty and low income. [Online]. Available: http:// www.statcan.ca/english/concepts/poverty/ pauv.htm. Accessed January 27, 1998.

Gans, H. J. 1992. Second-generation decline: Scenarios for the economic and ethnic futures of the post-1965 American immigrants. *Ethnic and Racial Studies,* 15(2): 173–92.

Gordon, I. 1995. The impact of economic change on minorities and migrants in western Europe. In *Poverty, inequality, and the future of social policy,* (eds.) K. McFate, R. Lawson, and W. Wilson, 521–42. New York: Russell Sage Foundation.

Gordon, M. M. 1964. *Assimilation in American life.* New York: Oxford UP.

Grant, H. M., and R. R. Oertel. 1998. Diminishing returns to immigration? Interpreting the economic experience of Canadian immigrants. *Canadian Ethnic Studies,* 30(3): 56–76.

Igoa, C. 1995. *The Inner world of the immigrant child.* New York: St. Martin's Press.

Kazemipur, A., and S. S. Halli. 1997. Plight of immigrants: The spatial concentration of poverty in Canada. *Canadian Journal of Regional Science,* 20(1–2): 11–28.

——2000. *The new poverty in Canada: Ethnic groups and ghetto neighbourhoods.* Toronto: Thompson Educational Publishing, Inc.

Lautard, E. H., and D. J. Loree. 1984. Ethnic stratification in Canada, 1931–1971. *Canadian Journal of Sociology,* 9(3): 333–44.

Li, P. 1999. The market value and social value of race. In *Racism and social inequality in Canada,* (ed.) V. Satzewich, 115–30. Toronto: Thompson Educational Publishing, Inc.

Li, P. 2000. Economic returns of immigrants' self-employment. *Canadian Journal of Sociology,* 25(1): 1–34.

Marchak, M. P. 1991. *The integrated circus.* Montreal and Kingston: McGill-Queen's University Press.

Massey et al., 1994. An evaluation of international migration theory: The North American case. *Population and development review,* 20(4): 699–751.

Ng, R. 1986. The social construction of immigrant women in Canada. In *The politics of diversity: Feminism, Marxism and nationalism,* (eds.) R. Hamilton and M. Barrett, 269–86. Montreal: Bookcentre.

Park, R. E., and E. W. Burgess. 1924. *Introduction to the science of sociology.* Chicago: U of Chicago P.

Pendakur, K., and R. Pendakur. 1998. The colour of money: Earnings differentials among ethnic groups in Canada. *Canadian Journal of Economics,* 31(3): 518–48.

Porter, J. 1965. *The vertical mosaic.* Toronto: U of Toronto P.

Portes, A. 1995. Children of immigrants: Segmented assimilation and its determinants. In *The economic sociology of immigration,* (ed.) A. Portes. New York: Russell Sage Foundation.

Portes, A., and R. G. Rumbaut. 1996. *Immigrant America: A portrait,* 2nd ed. Berkeley: U of California P.

Reitz, J. G. 1998. *Warmth of the welcome: The social causes of economic success for immigrants in different nations and cities.* Boulder, CO: Westview Press.

Reitz, J. G., and R. Breton. 1994. *The illusion of difference: Realities of ethnicity in Canada and the United States.* Toronto: C.D. Howe Institute.

Rifkin, J. 1995. *The end of work.* New York: G.E. Putnam's Sons.

Ruggles, P. 1990. Drawing the line: Alternative poverty measures and their implications for public policy. Washington, DC: The Urban Institute Press.

Rumbaut, R. G. 1997. Assimilation and its discontents: Between rhetoric and reality. *International Migration Review,* 31(4): 923–60.

Sarlo, C. A. 1992. *Poverty in Canada.* Vancouver: The Fraser Institute.

——1994. *Poverty in Canada,* 2nd ed. Vancouver: The Fraser Institute.

Satzewich, V. 1995. Social stratification: Class and racial inequality. In *Social issues and contradictions in Canadian society,* 2nd ed., (ed.) B. S. Bolaria, 98–121. Toronto: Harcourt Brace Canada.

Statistics Canada. 1998. Low Income Cut-offs. Cat. No. 13-551-X1B.

Teeple, G. 1995. *Globalization and the decline of social reform.* Toronto: Garamond Press.

Wanner, R. A. 1998. Prejudice, profit, or productivity: Explaining returns to human capital among male immigrants to Canada. *Canadian Ethnic Studies,* 30(3): 24–55.

Politics,
Government,
and the Military

CLASSIC

CONTEMPORARY

CROSS-CULTURAL

48

The Power Elite

C. WRIGHT MILLS

Conventional wisdom suggests that U.S. society operates as a democracy, guided by the "voice of the people." C. Wright Mills argues that above ordinary people—and even above many politicians—are "the higher circles," those who run the corporations, operate the military establishment, and manipulate the machinery of the state. It is this relatively small handful of people whom Mills calls "the power elite."

The powers of ordinary men are circumscribed by the everyday worlds in which they live, yet even in these rounds of job, family, and neighborhood they often seem driven by forces they can neither understand nor govern. "Great changes" are beyond their control, but affect their conduct and outlook nonetheless. The very framework of modern society confines them to projects not their own, but from every side, such changes now press upon the men and women of the mass society, who accordingly feel that they are without purpose in an epoch in which they are without power.

Source: From *The Power Elite*, New Edition, by C. Wright Mills. Copyright © 1956, 2000 by Oxford University Press, Inc.; renewed 1984 by Yaraslava Mills. Reprinted by permission of Oxford University Press, Inc.

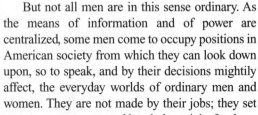

But not all men are in this sense ordinary. As the means of information and of power are centralized, some men come to occupy positions in American society from which they can look down upon, so to speak, and by their decisions mightily affect, the everyday worlds of ordinary men and women. They are not made by their jobs; they set up and break down jobs for thousands of others; they are not confined by simple family responsibilities; they can escape. They may live in many hotels and houses, but they are bound by no one community. They need not merely "meet the demands of the day and hour"; in some part, they create these demands, and cause others to meet them. Whether or not they profess their power, their technical and political experience of it far transcends that of the underlying population. What Jacob Burckhardt said of "great men," most Americans might well say of their elite: "They are all that we are not."

The power elite is composed of men whose positions enable them to transcend the ordinary environments of ordinary men and women; they are in positions to make decisions having major consequences. Whether they do or do not make such decisions is less important than the fact that they do occupy such pivotal positions: Their failure to act, their failure to make decisions, is itself an act that is often of greater consequence than the decisions they do make. For they are in command of the major hierarchies and organizations of modern society. They rule the big corporations. They run the machinery of the state and claim its prerogatives. They direct the military establishment. They occupy the strategic command posts of the social structure, in which are now centered the effective means of the power and the wealth and the celebrity which they enjoy.

The power elite are not solitary rulers. Advisers and consultants, spokesmen and opinion-makers are often the captains of their higher thought and decision. Immediately below the elite are the professional politicians of the middle levels of power, in the Congress and in the pressure groups, as well as among the new and old upper classes of town and city and region. Mingling with them, in curious ways which we shall explore, are those professional celebrities who live by being continually displayed but are never, so long as they remain celebrities, displayed enough. If such celebrities are not at the head of any dominating hierarchy, they do often have the power to distract the attention of the public or afford sensations to the masses, or, more directly, to gain the ear of those who do occupy positions of direct power. More or less unattached, as critics of morality and technicians of power, as spokesmen of God and creators of mass sensibility, such celebrities and consultants are part of the immediate scene in which the drama of the elite is enacted. But that drama itself is centered in the command posts of the major institutional hierarchies.

The truth about the nature and the power of the elite is not some secret which men of affairs know but will not tell. Such men hold quite various theories about their own roles in the sequence of event and decision. Often they are uncertain about their roles, and even more often they allow their fears and their hopes to affect their assessment of their own power. No matter how great their actual power, they tend to be less acutely aware of it than of the resistances of others to its use. Moreover, most American men of affairs have learned well the rhetoric of public relations, in some cases even to the point of using it when they are alone, and thus coming to believe it. The personal awareness of the actors is only one of the several sources one must examine in order to understand the higher circles. Yet many who believe that there is no elite, or at any rate none of any consequence, rest their argument upon what men of affairs believe about themselves, or at least assert in public.

There is, however, another view: Those who feel, even if vaguely, that a compact and powerful elite of great importance does now prevail in America often base that feeling upon the historical trend of our time. They have felt, for example, the domination of the military event, and from this they infer that generals and admirals, as well as other men of decision influenced by them, must be enormously powerful. They hear that the Congress has again abdicated to a handful of men decisions clearly related to the issue of war or peace. They know that the bomb was dropped over Japan in the name of the United States of America, although they were at no time consulted about the matter. They feel that they live in a time of big decisions; they know that they are not making any. Accordingly, as they consider the present as history, they infer that at its center, making decisions or failing to make them, there must be an elite of power.

On the one hand, those who share this feeling about big historical events assume that there is an elite and that its power is great. On the other hand, those who listen carefully to the reports of men apparently involved in the great decisions often do not believe that there is an elite whose powers are of decisive consequence.

Both views must be taken into account, but neither is adequate. The way to understand the power of the American elite lies neither solely in recognizing the historic scale of events nor in accepting the personal awareness reported by men of apparent decision. Behind such men and behind the events of history, linking the two, are the major institutions of modern society. These hierarchies of state and corporation and army constitute the means of power; as such they are now of a consequence not before equaled in human history—and at their summits, there are now those command posts of modern society which offer us the sociological key to an understanding of the role of the higher circles in America.

Within American society, major national power now resides in the economic, the political, and the military domains. Other institutions seem off to the side of modern history, and, on occasion, duly subordinated to these. No family is as directly powerful in national affairs as any major corporation; no church is as directly powerful in the external biographies of young men in America today as the military establishment; no college is as powerful in the shaping of momentous events as the National Security Council. Religious, educational, and family institutions are not autonomous centers of national power; on the contrary, these decentralized areas are increasingly shaped by the big three, in which developments of decisive and immediate consequence now occur.

Families and churches and schools adapt to modern life; governments and armies and corporations shape it; and, as they do so, they turn these lesser institutions into means for their ends. Religious institutions provide chaplains to the armed forces where they are used as a means of increasing the effectiveness of its morale to kill. Schools select and train men for their jobs in corporations and their specialized tasks in the armed forces. The extended family has, of course, long been broken up by the industrial revolution, and now the son and the father are removed from the family, by compulsion if need be, whenever the army of the state sends out the call. And the symbols of all these lesser institutions are used to legitimate the power and the decisions of the big three.

The life-fate of the modern individual depends not only upon the family into which he was born or which he enters by marriage, but increasingly upon the corporation in which he spends the most alert hours of his best years; not only upon the school where he is educated as a child and adolescent, but also upon the state which touches him throughout his life; not only upon the church in which on occasion he hears the word of God, but also upon the army in which he is disciplined.

If the centralized state could not rely upon the inculcation of nationalist loyalties in public and private schools, its leaders would promptly seek to modify the decentralized educational system. If the bankruptcy rate among the top 500 corporations were as high as the general divorce rate among the 37 million married couples, there would be economic catastrophe on an international scale. If members of armies gave to them no more of their lives than do believers to the churches to which they belong, there would be a military crisis.

Within each of the big three, the typical institutional unit has become enlarged, has become administrative, and, in the power of its decisions, has become centralized. Behind these developments there is a fabulous technology, for as institutions, they have incorporated this technology and guide it, even as it shapes and paces their developments.

The economy—once a great scatter of small productive units in autonomous balance—has become dominated by two or three hundred giant corporations, administratively and politically interrelated, which together hold the keys to economic decisions.

The political order, once a decentralized set of several dozen states with a weak spinal cord, has become a centralized, executive establishment which has taken up into itself many powers previously scattered, and now enters into each and every cranny of the social structure.

The military order, once a slim establishment in a context of distrust fed by state militia, has become the largest and most expensive feature of government, and, although well-versed in smiling public relations, now has all the grim and clumsy efficiency of a sprawling bureaucratic domain.

In each of these institutional areas, the means of power at the disposal of decision makers have increased enormously; their central executive powers have been enhanced; within each of them modern administrative routines have been elaborated and tightened up.

As each of these domains becomes enlarged and centralized, the consequences of its activities become greater, and its traffic with the others increases. The decisions of a handful of corporations bear upon military and political as well as upon economic developments around the world. The decisions of the military establishment rest upon and grievously affect political life as well as the very level of economic activity. The decisions made within the political domain determine economic activities and military programs. There is no longer, on the one hand, an economy, and, on the other hand, a political order containing a military establishment unimportant to politics and to money-making. There is a political economy linked, in a thousand ways, with military institutions and decisions. On each side of the world-split running through central Europe and around the Asiatic rimlands, there is an ever-increasing interlocking of economic, military, and political structures. If there is government intervention in the corporate economy, so is there corporate intervention in the governmental process. In the structural sense, this triangle of power is the source of the interlocking directorate that is most important for the historical structure of the present.

The fact of the interlocking is clearly revealed at each of the points of crisis of modern capitalist society—slump, war, and boom. In each, men of decision are led to an awareness of the interdependence of the major institutional orders. In the nineteenth century, when the scale of all institutions was smaller, their liberal integration was achieved in the automatic economy, by an autonomous play of market forces, and in the automatic political domain, by the bargain and the vote. It was then assumed that out of the imbalance and friction that followed the limited decisions then possible a new equilibrium would in due course emerge. That can no longer be assumed, and it is not assumed by the men at the top of each of the three dominant hierarchies.

For given the scope of their consequences, decisions—and indecisions—in any one of these ramify into the others, and hence top decisions tend either to become coordinated or to lead to a commanding indecision. It has not always been like this. When numerous small entrepreneurs made up the economy, for example, many of them could fail and the consequences still remain local; political and military authorities did not intervene. But now, given political expectations and military commitments, can they afford to allow key units of the private corporate economy to break down in slump? Increasingly, they do intervene in economic affairs, and as they do so, the controlling decisions in each order are inspected by agents of the other two, and economic, military, and political structures are interlocked.

At the pinnacle of each of the three enlarged and centralized domains, there have arisen those higher circles which make up the economic, the political, and the military elites. At the top of the economy, among the corporate rich, there are the chief executives; at the top of the political order, the members of the political directorate; at the top of the military establishment, the elite of soldier-statesmen clustered in and around the Joint Chiefs of Staff and the upper echelon. As each of these domains has coincided with the others, as decisions tend to become total in their consequence, the leading men in each of the three domains of power—the warlords, the corporation chieftains, the political directorate—tend to come together, to form the power elite of America.

The higher circles in and around these command posts are often thought of in terms of what their members possess: They have a greater share than other people of the things and experiences that are most highly valued. From this point of view, the elite are simply those who have the most of what there is to have, which is generally held to include money, power, and prestige—as well as all the ways of life to which these lead. But the elite are not simply those who have the most, for they could not "have the most" were it not for their positions in the great institutions. For such institutions are the necessary bases of power, of wealth, and of prestige, and at the same time, the chief means of exercising power, of acquiring and retaining wealth, and of cashing in the higher claims for prestige.

By the powerful we mean, of course, those who are able to realize their will, even if others resist it. No one, accordingly, can be truly powerful unless he has access to the command of major institutions, for it is over these institutional means of power that the truly powerful are, in the first instance, powerful. Higher politicians and key officials of government command such institutional power; so do admirals and generals, and so do the major owners and executives of the larger corporations. Not all power, it is true, is anchored in and exercised by means of such institutions, but only within and through them can power be more or less continuous and important.

Wealth also is acquired and held in and through institutions. The pyramid of wealth cannot be understood merely in terms of the very rich; for the great inheriting families, as we shall see, are now supplemented by the corporate institutions of modern society: Every one of the very rich families has been and is closely connected—always legally and frequently managerially as well—with one of the multimillion-dollar corporations.

The modern corporation is the prime source of wealth, but, in latter-day capitalism, the political apparatus also opens and closes many avenues to wealth. The amount as well as the source of income, the power over consumer's goods as well as over productive capital, are determined by position within the political economy. If our interest in the very rich goes beyond their lavish or their miserly consumption, we must examine their relations to modern forms of corporate property as well as to the state; for such relations now determine the chances of men to secure big property and to receive high income.

Great prestige increasingly follows the major institutional units of the social structure. It is obvious that prestige depends, often quite decisively, upon access to the publicity machines that are now a central and normal feature of all the big institutions of modern America. Moreover, one feature of the hierarchies of corporation, state, and military establishment is that their top positions are increasingly interchangeable. One result of this is the accumulative nature of prestige. Claims for prestige, for example, may be initially based on military roles, then expressed in and augmented by an educational institution run by corporate executives, and cashed in, finally, in the political order, where, for General Eisenhower and those he represents, power and prestige finally meet at the very peak. Like wealth and power, prestige tends to be cumulative: The more of it you have, the more you can get. These values also tend to be translatable into one another: The wealthy find it easier than the poor to gain power; those with status find it easier than those without it to control opportunities for wealth.

If we took the 100 most powerful men in America, the 100 wealthiest, and the 100 most celebrated away from the institutional positions they now occupy, away from their resources of men and women and money, away from the media of mass communication that are now focused upon them—then they would be powerless and poor and uncelebrated. For power is not of a man. Wealth does not center in the person of the wealthy. Celebrity is not inherent in any personality. To be celebrated, to be wealthy, to have power requires access to major institutions, for the institutional positions men occupy determine in large part their chances to have and to hold these valued experiences.

The people of the higher circles may also be conceived as members of a top social stratum, as a set of groups whose members know one another, see one another socially and at business, and so, in making decisions, take one another into account. The elite, according to this conception, feel themselves to be, and are felt by others to be, the inner circle of "the upper social classes." They form a more or less compact social and psychological entity; they have become self-conscious members of a social class. People are either accepted into this class or they are not, and there is a qualitative split, rather than merely a numerical scale, separating them from those who are not elite. They are more or less aware of themselves as a social class and they behave toward one another differently from the way they do toward members of other classes. They accept one another, understand one another, marry one another, tend to work and to think if not together at least alike.

Now, we do not want by our definition to prejudge whether the elite of the command posts are conscious members of such a socially recognized class, or whether considerable proportions of the elite derive from such a clear and distinct class. These are matters to be investigated. Yet in order to be able to recognize what we intend to investigate, we must note something that all biographies and memoirs of the wealthy and the powerful and the eminent make clear: No matter what else they may be, the people of these higher circles are involved in a set of overlapping "crowds" and intricately connected "cliques." There is a kind of mutual attraction among those who "sit on the same terrace"—although this often becomes clear to them, as well as to others, only at the point at which they feel the need to draw the line; only when, in their common defense, they come to understand what they have in common, and so close their ranks against outsiders.

The idea of such ruling stratum implies that most of its members have similar social origins, that throughout their lives they maintain a network of informal connections, and that to some degree there is an interchangeability of position between the various hierarchies of money and power and celebrity. We must, of course, note at once that if such an elite stratum does exist, its social visibility and its form, for very solid historical reasons, are quite different from those of the noble cousinhoods that once ruled various European nations.

That American society has never passed through a feudal epoch is of decisive importance to the nature of the American elite, as well as to Amer-

ican society as a historic whole. For it means that no nobility or aristocracy, established before the capitalist era, has stood in tense opposition to the higher bourgeoisie. It means that this bourgeoisie has monopolized not only wealth but prestige and power as well. It means that no set of noble families has commanded the top positions and monopolized the values that are generally held in high esteem; and certainly that no set has done so explicitly by inherited right. It means that no high church dignitaries or court nobilities, no entrenched landlords with honorific accouterments, no monopolists of high army posts have opposed the enriched bourgeoisie and in the name of birth and prerogative successfully resisted its self-making.

But this does not mean that there are no upper strata in the United States. That they emerged from a "middle class" that had no recognized aristocratic superiors does not mean they remained middle class when enormous increases in wealth made their own superiority possible. Their origins and their newness may have made the upper strata less visible in America than elsewhere. But in America today there are in fact tiers and ranges of wealth and power of which people in the middle and lower ranks know very little and may not even dream. There are families who, in their well-being, are quite insulated from the economic jolts and lurches felt by the merely prosperous and those farther down the scale. There are also men of power who in quite small groups make decisions of enormous consequence for the underlying population. . . .

CRITICAL THINKING QUESTIONS

1. What institutions form the "interlocking triangle" in Mills's analysis? Why does he think these are the most powerful social institutions?

2. Explain how Mills argues that the existence of a power elite is not a consequence of people per se but a result of the institutions of U.S. society.

3. Does the lack of an aristocratic history mean that power is dispersed throughout U.S. society?

Politics,
Government, and
the Military

CLASSIC

CONTEMPORARY

CROSS-CULTURAL

49

Who's Running America?

THOMAS R. DYE

In the previous reading, C. Wright Mills asserted that a small power elite run U.S. society. Was he right? Thomas Dye contends that some groups are far more powerful than others. He adds that the military establishment and Congress are much less influential than most people (and even Mills) believed.

If there ever was a time when the powers of government were limited—when government did no more than secure law and order, protect individual liberty and property, enforce contracts, and defend against foreign invasion—that time has long passed. Today it is commonplace to observe that governmental institutions intervene in every aspect of our lives—from the "cradle to the grave." Government in America has the primary responsibility for providing insurance against old age, death, dependency, disability, and unemployment; for organizing the nation's health-care system; for providing education at the elementary, secondary, collegiate, and postgraduate levels; for providing public highways and regulating water, rail, and air transportation; for providing police and fire protection; for providing sanitation services and

sewage disposal; for financing research in medicine, science, and technology; for delivering the mail; for exploring outer space; for maintaining parks and recreation; for providing housing and adequate food for the poor; for providing job training and manpower programs; for cleaning the air and water; for rebuilding central cities; for maintaining full employment and a stable money supply; for regulating business practices and labor relations; for eliminating racial and sexual discrimination. Indeed, the list of government responsibilities seems endless, yet each year we manage to find additional tasks for government to do.

THE CONCENTRATION OF GOVERNMENTAL POWER

Government in the United States grew enormously throughout most of the twentieth century, both in absolute terms and in relation to the

Source: Thomas R. Dye, *Who's Running America? The Bush Restoration,* 7th edition. Upper Saddle River, NJ: Prentice Hall, 2002, pp. 55–96.

size of the national economy. The size of the economy is usually measured by the gross domestic product (GDP), the dollar sum of all the goods and services produced in the United States in a year. Governments accounted for only about 8 percent of the GDP at the beginning of the century, and most governmental activities were carried out by state and local governments. Two world wars, the New Deal programs devised during the Great Depression of the 1930s, and the growth of the Great Society programs of the 1960s and 1970s all greatly expanded the size of government, particularly the federal government. The rise in government growth relative to the economy leveled off during the Reagan presidency (1981–89), and no large new programs were undertaken in the Bush and Clinton years. An economic boom in the 1990s caused the GDP to grow rapidly, while government spending grew only moderately. The result was a modest decline in governmental size in relation to the economy. Today, federal expenditures amount to about 20 percent of GDP, and total governmental expenditures are about 30 percent of GDP (see Figure 49.1).

Not everything that government does is reflected in governmental expenditures. *Regulatory activity*, for example, especially environmental regulations, imposes significant costs on individuals and businesses; these costs are not shown in government budgets.

We have defined our governmental elite as the top executive, congressional, and judicial officers of the *federal* government; the President and Vice-President; secretaries, undersecretaries, and assistant secretaries of executive departments; senior White House presidential advisers; congressional committee chairpersons and ranking minority members; congressional majority and minority party leaders in the House and Senate; Supreme Court Justices; and members of the Federal Reserve Board and the Council of Economic Advisers. And we add to this definition of political elites the "fat cat" contributors who keep them in power.

Figure 49.1   The Growth of Government

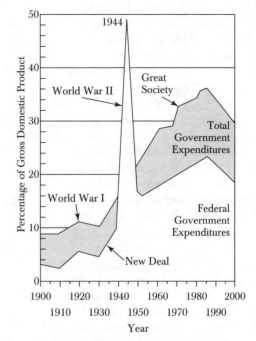

Source: Budget of the United States Government, 2000.

THE FAT CAT CONTRIBUTORS

More money was spent on political campaigning in 2000 than in any election year in American history. An estimated $3 *billion* was spent by all presidential and congressional candidates, Democratic and Republican parties, political action committees sponsored by interest groups, and independent political organizations in federal, state, and local elections combined. The costs of elections rise in each election cycle. The largest increases in campaign finance came not from regulated "hard money" contributions to candidates, but rather from large unregulated "soft money" contributions to the parties.

Virtually all of the top "fat cat" campaign contributors from the *corporate, banking, and investment* worlds have been previously listed among the nation's largest corporate and monied institutions. AT&T, Philip Morris, Citigroup, and Goldman Sachs regularly appear each election cycle among contributors of $2 to $3 million or more (see Table 49.1). One notable newcomer among top corporate "fat cat" contributors in 2000 is Bill Gates's Microsoft Corporation. In the past, Gates tried to avoid politics altogether; Microsoft was notably absent from previous lists of top campaign contributors. But Gates learned a hard lesson when Clinton's Justice Department under Attorney General Janet Reno launched its costly antitrust suit against Microsoft.

While contributions form the corporate, banking, and investment institutions are usually divided between the parties (albeit weighted toward Republicans), contributions from *unions* are almost exclusively directed toward Democrats. Indeed, union contributions are the single largest source of campaign money for the Democratic Party, followed by contributions from Hollywood's entertainment industry.

Contributions from wealthy individuals failed to match institutional contributions. While more than 100 institutions contributed $1 million or more in 2000, only two individuals contributed over this amount. (Peter Buttenwieser of Buttenwieser & Associates of Philadelphia and S. Daniel Abraham of Slim-Fast Foods both contributed over $1 million to Democrats.)

Expenditures for congressional campaigns also reached a new high. The U.S. Senate race in New York, featuring former First Lady Hillary Clinton against relative newcomer Republican Rick Lazio, set a new combined spending record for congressional elections at more than $85 million. A new individual congressional spending record of $65 million was set by multibillionaire investment banker (Goldman Sachs) Democrat Jon Corzine, who dug into his own fortune to win a U.S. Senate seat from New Jersey.

The *average* candidate for a U.S. Senate seat raised and spent over $5 million. And the *average* candidate for a U.S. House seat raised and spent about $800,000. This means that the average incumbent member of Congress must raise about

$8,000 *per week*, every week of their term in office.

THE POLITICIANS: AMBITION AND OFFICE SEEKING

Ambition is the driving force in politics. Politics attracts people for whom power and celebrity are more rewarding than money, leisure, or privacy. "Political office today flows to those who want it enough to spend the time and energy mastering its pursuit. It flows in the direction of ambition— and talent."[1]

Political ambition is the most distinguishing characteristic of elected officeholders. The people who run for and win public office are not necessarily the most intelligent, best informed, wealthiest, or most successful business or professional people. At all levels of the political system, from presidential candidates, members of Congress, governors and state legislators, to city councils and school board members, it is the most politically ambitious people who are willing to sacrifice time, family and private life, and energy and effort for the power and celebrity that comes with public office.

Politics is becoming increasingly professionalized. "Citizen-statesmen"—people with business or professional careers who get into politics part-time or for short periods of time—are being driven out of political life by career politicians— people who enter politics early in life as a full-time occupation and expect to make it their career. Politically ambitious young people seek out internships and staff positions with members of Congress, with congressional committees, in state legislators' or governors' offices, or mayors' or council chambers. Others volunteer to work in political campaigns. Many find political mentors, as they learn how to organize campaigns, contact financial contributors, and deal with the media. By their early thirties, they are ready to run for local office or the state legislature. Rather than challenge a strong incumbent, they may wait for

TABLE 49.1   The Top Fifty Fat Cat Campaign Contributors, 2000

Rank	Contributor	Total Contributions	To Dems.	To Repubs.
1	American Fedn. of St./Cnty./Munic. Employees	$6,935,989	98%	2%
2	Service Employees International Union	$4,961,010	95%	5%
3	AT&T	$4,667,844	38%	61%
4	Microsoft Corp	$4,309,856	46%	54%
5	Communications Workers of America	$3,871,185	99%	0%
6	National Assn. of Realtors	$3,834,600	41%	59%
7	Goldman Sachs Group	$3,646,382	68%	32%
8	United Food & Commercial Workers Union	$3,578,452	99%	1%
9	Intl. Brotherhood of Electrical Workers	$3,561,860	97%	3%
10	Citigroup Inc.	$3,559,566	53%	47%
11	Philip Morris	$3,460,200	18%	81%
12	SBC Communications	$3,418,466	46%	54%
13	Verizon Communications	$3,357,420	36%	64%
14	Carpenters & Joiners Union	$3,183,383	92%	8%
15	United Parcel Service	$3,133,119	26%	73%
16	American Federation of Teachers	$3,110,055	99%	1%
17	Assn. of Trial Lawyers of America	$3,030,750	88%	12%
18	Laborers Union	$2,929,275	93%	7%
19	National Rifle Assn.	$2,885,377	8%	92%
20	MBNA America Bank	$2,733,000	17%	83%
21	National Education Assn.	$2,584,478	92%	7%
22	Sheet Metal Workers Union	$2,551,584	99%	1%
23	Machinists/Aerospace Workers Union	$2,546,138	99%	1%
24	Teamsters Union	$2,517,240	93%	7%
25	Ernst & Young	$2,497,761	42%	58%
26	National Auto Dealers Assn.	$2,410,200	32%	68%
27	Federal Express Corp.	$2,388,428	34%	66%
28	Enron Corp.	$2,365,458	28%	72%
29	National Assn. of Home Builders	$2,336,799	37%	63%
30	Lockheed Martin	$2,333,794	39%	61%
31	Emily's List	$2,328,840	100%	0%
32	Credit Suisse First Boston	$2,325,705	29%	70%
33	Bristol-Myers Squibb	$2,300,792	14%	86%
34	United Auto Workers	$2,248,755	99%	0%
35	Morgan Stanley, Dean Witter & Co.	$2,225,823	39%	60%
36	BellSouth Corp.	$2,219,752	41%	59%
37	Freddie Mac	$2,198,839	48%	52%
38	AFL-CIO	$2,173,638	96%	4%
39	Global Crossing	$2,142,386	50%	50%
40	Pfizer Inc.	$2,136,647	14%	86%
41	Blue Cross/Blue Shield	$2,125,552	27%	73%
42	American Medical Assn.	$2,077,644	47%	52%
43	National Beer Wholesalers Assn.	$2,059,061	19%	80%
44	Bank of America	$1,889,318	59%	40%
45	Time Warner	$1,860,237	73%	27%
46	National Assn. of Letter Carriers	$1,830,700	86%	13%
47	Union Pacific Corp	$1,805,144	16%	84%
48	General Electric	$1,793,879	39%	61%
49	Joseph E Seagram & Sons	$1,791,060	62%	38%
50	Andersen Worldwide	$1,781,412	29%	70%

an open seat to be created by retirement, reapportionment, or its holder seeking another office. Or they may make an initial attempt against a strong incumbent of the opposition party in order to gain experience and win the appreciation of their own party's supporters for a good effort. Over time, running for and holding elective office becomes their career. They work harder at it than anyone else, in part because they have no real private sector career to return to in case of defeat.

The prevalence of lawyers in politics is an American tradition. Among the nation's Founders—the fifty-five delegates to the Constitutional Convention in 1787—some twenty-five were lawyers. The political dominance of lawyers is even greater today, with lawyers filling nearly two thirds of U.S. Senate seats and nearly half of the seats in the U.S. House of Representatives.

It is sometimes argued that lawyers dominate in politics because of the parallel skills required in law and politics. Lawyering is the representation of clients; a lawyer employs similar skills whether representing clients in private practice or representing constituents in Congress. Lawyers are trained to deal with statutory law, so they may at least know how to find United States Code (the codified laws of the United States government) in a law library when they arrive in Congress to make or amend these laws.

But it is more likely that the people attracted to politics decide to go to law school, fully aware of the tradition of lawyers in American politics. Moreover, political officeholding, at the state and local level as well as in the national government, can help a struggling lawyer's private practice through free public advertising and opportunities to make contacts with potential clients. Finally, there are many special opportunities for lawyers to acquire public office in "lawyers only" posts in federal, state, and local government as judges and prosecuting attorneys. The lawyer-politician is not usually a top professional lawyer. Instead, the typical lawyer-politician uses his or her law career as a

means of support—one that is compatible with political office seeking and officeholding.

A significant number of top politicians have inherited great wealth. The Roosevelts, Rockefellers, Kennedys, Bushes, and others have used their wealth and family connections to support their political careers. However, it is important to note that *a majority of the nation's top politicians have climbed the ladder from relative obscurity to political success*. Many have acquired some wealth in the process, but most political leaders started their climb from very middle-class circumstances. Thus, as in the corporate world, we find more "climbers" than "inheritors" at the top in the world of politics. . . .

EXECUTIVE DECISION-MAKERS: THE SERIOUS PEOPLE

The politician is a professional office-seeker. The politician knows how to run for office—but not necessarily how to run the government. After victory at the polls, the prudent politician turns to "serious" people to run the government. The corporate and governmental experience and educational credentials of these "serious" decision-makers greatly exceed those of most members of Congress or other elected officials. When presidents turn from the task of *running for office* to the task of *running a government*, they are obliged to recruit higher quality leadership than is typically found among political officeholders.

The responsibility for the initiation of national programs and policies falls primarily upon the top White House staff and the heads of executive departments. Generally, Congress merely responds to policy proposals initiated by the executive branch. The President and his key advisers and administration have a strong incentive to fulfill their responsibility for decision-making. In the eyes of the American public, they are responsible for everything that happens in the nation, regardless of whether they have the authority or capacity to do anything about it. There is a general expectation that every administration, even one committed to a "caretaker" role, will put forth some sort of policy program.

The President and Vice-President, White House presidential advisers and ambassadors-at-large, Cabinet secretaries, undersecretaries, and assistant secretaries constitute our executive elite. . . .

THE CONGRESSIONAL ESTABLISHMENT

Although policy initiatives are usually developed outside Congress, Congress is no mere "rubber stamp." Key members of Congress do play an independent role in national decision-making; thus, key congressional leaders must be included in any operational definition of a national elite.

Political scientists have commented extensively on the structure of power *within* the Congress. They generally describe a hierarchical structure in both houses of the Congress—a "congressional establishment"—which largely determines what the Congress will do. The congressional establishment has survived periodic efforts at decentralization. It is composed of the Speaker of the House and president *pro tempore* of the Senate; House and Senate majority and minority leaders and whips; and committee chairpersons and ranking minority members of House and Senate standing committees. Party leadership roles in the House and Senate are major sources of power in Washington. The Speaker of the House and the majority and minority leaders of the House and Senate direct the business of Congress. Although they share this task with the standing committee chairpersons, these leaders are generally "first among equals" in their relationships with committee chairpersons. But the committee system also creates powerful congressional figures, the chairpersons of the most powerful standing committees—particularly

the Senate Foreign Relations, Appropriations, Judiciary, Finance, Armed Services, and Budget committees, and the House Rules, Appropriations, International Relations, Judiciary, Armed Services, Budget, and Ways and Means committees.

Viewed within the broader context of a *national elite*, congressional leaders appear "folksy," parochial, and localistic. Because of the local constituency of members of Congress, they are predisposed to concern themselves with local interests. Members of Congress are part of local elite structures "back home"; they retain their local businesses and law practices, club memberships, and religious affiliations. Members of Congress represent many small segments of the nation rather than the nation as a whole. Even top congressional leaders from safe districts, with many years of seniority, cannot completely shed their local interests. Their claim to *national* leadership must be safely hedged by attention to their local constituents.

THE JUDGES

Nine people—none of whom is elected and all of whom serve for life—possess ultimate authority over all the other institutions of government. The Supreme Court of the United States has the authority to void the acts of popularly elected Presidents and Congresses. There is no appeal from their decision about what is the "supreme law of the land," except perhaps to undertake the difficult task of amending the Constitution itself. Only the good judgment of the Justices—their sense of "judicial self-restraint"—limits their power. It was the Supreme Court, rather than the President or Congress, that took the lead in important issues such as eliminating segregation from public life, ensuring voter equality in representation, limiting the powers of police, and declaring abortion to be a fundamental right of women.

Social scientists have commented frequently on the class bias of Supreme Court Justices: "White; generally Protestant . . . ; fifty to fifty-five years of age at the time of his appointment; Anglo-Saxon ethnic stock . . . ; high social status; reared in an urban environment; member of a civic[-]minded, politically active, economically comfortable family; legal training; some type of public office; generally well educated."[2] No blacks had served on the Supreme Court until the appointment of Associate Justice Thurgood Marshall in 1967. No women had served until the appointment of Sandra Day O'Connor in 1981. Of course, social background does not necessarily determine judicial philosophy. But as John R. Schmidhauser observes, "If . . . the Supreme Court is the keeper of the American conscience, it is essentially the conscience of the American upper-middle class sharpened by the imperative of individual social responsibility and political activism, and conditioned by the conservative impact of legal training and professional attitudes and associations."[3] . . .

THE MILITARY ESTABLISHMENT

In his farewell address to the nation in 1961, President Dwight D. Eisenhower warned of "an immense military establishment and a large arms industry." He observed: "In the councils of government, we must guard against the acquisition of unwarranted influence, whether sought or unsought, by the military-industrial complex."

The phrase the *military-industrial complex* caught on with many commentators over the years. It implied that a giant network of defense contractors—for example, Lockheed Aircraft, General Dynamics, Rockwell, McDonnell Douglas, Boeing, Litton, Hughes Tool, Grumman Aircraft—together with members of Congress in whose districts their plants were located, conspired with the generals in the Pentagon to create a powerful force in governmental and corporate circles. Indeed, radical social commentators held the military-industrial complex responsible for war and "imperialism."

But whatever the power of defense contractors and the military at the height of the Cold War, their influence today in governing circles is miniscule. Indeed, their goal today is to avoid complete dismantlement. Spending for national defense has declined precipitously from 10 percent of the GNP in the Eisenhower and Kennedy years to less than 3 percent today. Spending on Social Security, Medicare, and welfare, including Medicaid, exceeds 58 percent of the federal budget, compared to 16 percent for national defense.[4] There are 2 million civilian employees of the federal government, compared to only 1.4 million people in the armed forces. The long-term decline of U.S. defense spending suggests that the American military-industrial complex was *not* a very powerful conspiracy.

It seems clear in retrospect that C. Wright Mills placed too much importance on the military in his work, *The Power Elite*.[5] Mills was writing in the early 1950s when military prestige was high following victory in World War II. After the war, a few high-level military men were recruited to top corporate positions to add prestige to corporate boards. But this practice ended in the 1960s. The contrast between the political prestige of the military in the post–World War II years and in the post–Vietnam years is striking: The Supreme Allied Commander in Europe in World War II, Dwight D. Eisenhower, was elected President of the United States; the U.S. Commander in Vietnam, William Westmoreland, was defeated in his bid to become governor of South Carolina! Moreover, in contrast with corporate and governmental elites, military officers do *not* come from the upper or upper-middle class of society. Military officers are more likely to be recruited from lower- and lower-middle-class backgrounds, and more likely to have rural and southern roots than are corporate or governmental elites.[6]

CRITICAL THINKING QUESTIONS

1. Why does Dye argue that government has far more power today compared to 1900? Why does he include "fat cat" contributors in his definition of political elites?

2. "Politics attracts the best and brightest people." Would Dye agree with this statement? Do you? In addition, why do lawyers dominate U.S. politics?

3. Consider Congress, the military, and the Supreme Court. According to Dye, which group is the most powerful of all the governing circles? Do you agree with Dye's analysis? Explain why or why not.

NOTES

1. Alan Ehrenhalt, *The United States of Ambition: Politicians' Power and Pursuit of Office* (New York: Random House, 1991), p. 22.

2. Henry Abraham, *The Judicial Process* (New York: Oxford University Press, 1962), p. 58.

3. John R. Schmidhauser, *The Supreme Court* (New York: Holt Rinehart and Winston, 1960), p. 59.

4. Budget of the United States Government 2001 gives this breakdown by function: Social Security: 23.2%; Medicare: 12.0%; Income Security: 14.2%; Medicaid: 9.1%.

5. C. Wright Mills, *The Power Elite* (New York: Oxford, 1956).

6. Morris Janowitz, *The Professional Soldier* (New York: Free Press, 1960), p. 378.

Politics,
Government,
and the Military

CLASSIC

CONTEMPORARY

CROSS-CULTURAL

50

The Roots of Terrorism

THE 9/11 COMMISSION REPORT

September 11, 2001, was a day of unprecedented shock and suffering in the United States. Almost 3,000 people died in Manhattan, New York, a field in Pennsylvania, and the Pentagon after multiple terrorist attacks. In this selection, the 9/11 Commission Report provides some insights into the growth of a "new kind of war" that was responsible for the mass murders.

A DECLARATION OF WAR

In February 1998, the forty-year-old Saudi exile Usama Bin Ladin and a fugitive Egyptian physician, Ayman al Zawahiri, arranged from their Afghan headquarters for an Arabic newspaper in

Source: The 9/11 Commission Report: Final Report of the National Commission on Terrorist Attacks Upon the United States, 47–55. Washington, DC: U.S. Government Printing Office, 2004.

Note: Islamic names often do not follow the Western practice of the consistent use of surnames. Given the variety of names we mention, we chose to refer to individuals by the last word in the names by which they are known; Nawaf al Hazmi as Hazmi, for instance, omitting the article "al" that would be part of their name in their own societies. We generally make an exception for the more familiar English usage of "Bin" as part of a last name, as in Bin Ladin. Further, there is no universally accepted way to transliterate Arabic words and names into English. We have relied on a mix of common sense, the sound of the name in Arabic, and common usage in source materials, the press, or government documents. When we quote from a source document, we use its transliteration, e.g., "al Qida" instead of al Qaeda.

London to publish what they termed a fatwa issued in the name of a "World Islamic Front." A fatwa is normally an interpretation of Islamic law by a respected Islamic authority, but neither Bin Ladin, Zawahiri, nor the three others who signed this statement were scholars of Islamic law. Claiming that America had declared war against God and his messenger, they called for the murder of any American, anywhere on earth, as the "individual duty for every Muslim who can do it in any country in which it is possible to do it."[1]

Three months later, when interviewed in Afghanistan by ABC-TV, Bin Ladin enlarged on these themes.[2] He claimed it was more important for Muslims to kill Americans than to kill other infidels. "It is far better for anyone to kill a single American soldier than to squander his efforts on other activities," he said. Asked whether he approved of terrorism and of attacks on civilians, he replied: "We believe that the worst thieves in the world today and the worst terrorists are the Americans. Nothing could stop you except perhaps retaliation in kind. We do not have to differentiate between military or civilian. As far as we are concerned, they are all targets."

Though novel for its open endorsement of indiscriminate killing, Bin Ladin's 1998 declaration was only the latest in the long series of his public and private calls since 1992 that singled out the United States for attack.

In August 1996, Bin Ladin had issued his own self-styled fatwa calling on Muslims to drive American soldiers out of Saudi Arabia. The long, disjointed document condemned the Saudi monarchy for allowing the presence of an army of infidels in a land with the sites most sacred to Islam, and celebrated recent suicide bombings of American military facilities in the Kingdom. It praised the 1983 suicide bombing in Beirut that killed 241 U.S. Marines, the 1992 bombing in Aden, and especially the 1993 firefight in Somalia after which the United States "left the area carrying disappointment, humiliation, defeat and your dead with you."[3]

Bin Ladin said in his ABC interview that he and his followers had been preparing in Somalia for another long struggle, like that against the Soviets in Afghanistan, but "the United States rushed out of Somalia in shame and disgrace." Citing the Soviet army's withdrawal from Afghanistan as proof that a ragged army of dedicated Muslims could overcome a superpower, he told the interviewer: "We are certain that we shall—with the grace of Allah—prevail over the Americans." He went on to warn that "If the present injustice continues . . ., it will inevitably move the battle to American soil."[4]

Plans to attack the United States were developed with unwavering single-mindedness throughout the 1990s. Bin Ladin saw himself as called "to follow in the footsteps of the Messenger and to communicate his message to all nations,"[5] and to serve as the rallying point and organizer of a new kind of war to destroy America and bring the world to Islam.

BIN LADIN'S APPEAL IN THE ISLAMIC WORLD

It is the story of eccentric and violent ideas sprouting in the fertile ground of political and social turmoil. It is the story of an organization poised to seize its historical moment. How did Bin Ladin—with his call for the indiscriminate killing of Americans—win thousands of followers and some degree of approval from millions more?

The history, culture, and body of beliefs from which Bin Ladin has shaped and spread his message are largely unknown to many Americans. Seizing on symbols of Islam's past greatness, he promises to restore pride to people who consider themselves the victims of successive foreign masters. He uses cultural and religious allusions to the holy Qur'an and some of its interpreters. He appeals to people disoriented by cyclonic change as they confront modernity and globalization. His rhetoric selectively draws from multiple sources—Islam, history, and the region's political and economic malaise. He also stresses grievances against the United States widely shared in the Muslim world. He inveighed against the presence of U.S. troops in Saudi Arabia, the home of Islam's holiest sites. He spoke of the suffering of the Iraqi people as a result of sanctions imposed after the Gulf War, and he protested U.S. support of Israel.

Islam

Islam (a word that literally means "surrender to the will of God") arose in Arabia with what Muslims believe are a series of revelations to the Prophet Mohammed from the one and only God, the God of Abraham and of Jesus. These revelations, conveyed by the angel Gabriel, are recorded in the Qur'an. Muslims believe that these revelations, given to the greatest and last of a chain of prophets stretching from Abraham through Jesus, complete God's message to humanity. The Hadith, which recount Mohammed's sayings and deeds as recorded by his contemporaries, are another fundamental source. A third key element is the Sharia, the code of law derived from the Qur'an and the Hadith.

Islam is divided into two main branches, Sunni and Shia. Soon after the Prophet's death, the question of choosing a new leader, or caliph, for the Muslim community, or Ummah, arose. Initially, his successors could be drawn from the Prophet's contemporaries, but with time, this was no longer possible. Those who became the Shia held that any leader of the Ummah must be a direct descendant of the Prophet; those who became the Sunni argued that lineal descent was not required if the candidate met other standards of faith and knowledge. After bloody struggles, the Sunni became (and remain) the majority sect. (The Shia are dominant in Iran.) The Caliphate—the institutionalized leadership of the Ummah—thus was a Sunni institution that continued until 1924, first under Arab and eventually under Ottoman Turkish control.

Many Muslims look back at the century after the revelations to the Prophet Mohammed as a golden age. Its memory is strongest among the Arabs. What happened then—the spread of Islam from the Arabian Peninsula throughout the Middle East, North Africa, and even into Europe within less than a century—seemed, and seems, miraculous.[6] Nostalgia for Islam's past glory remains a powerful force.

Islam is both a faith and a code of conduct for all aspects of life. For many Muslims, a good government would be one guided by the moral principles of their faith. This does not necessarily translate into a desire for clerical rule and the abolition of a secular state. It does mean that some Muslims tend to be uncomfortable with distinctions between religion and state, though Muslim rulers throughout history have readily separated the two.

To extremists, however, such divisions, as well as the existence of parliaments and legislation, only prove these rulers to be false Muslims usurping God's authority over all aspects of life. Periodically, the Islamic world has seen surges of what, for want of a better term, is often labeled "fundamentalism."[7] Denouncing waywardness among the faithful, some clerics have appealed for a return to observance of the literal teachings of the Qur'an and Hadith. One scholar from the fourteenth century from whom Bin Ladin selectively quotes, Ibn Taimiyyah, condemned both corrupt rulers and the clerics who failed to criticize them. He urged Muslims to read the Qur'an and the Hadith for themselves, not to depend solely on learned interpreters like himself but to hold one another to account for the quality of their observance.[8]

The extreme Islamist version of history blames the decline from Islam's golden age on the rulers and people who turned away from the true path of their religion, thereby leaving Islam vulnerable to encroaching foreign powers eager to steal their land, wealth, and even their souls.

Bin Ladin's Worldview

Despite his claims to universal leadership, Bin Ladin offers an extreme view of Islamic history designed to appeal mainly to Arabs and Sunnis. He draws on fundamentalists who blame the eventual destruction of the Caliphate on leaders who abandoned the pure path of religious devotion.[9] He repeatedly calls on his followers to embrace martyrdom since "the walls of oppression and humiliation cannot be demolished except in a rain of bullets."[10] For those yearning for a lost sense of order in an older, more tranquil world, he offers his "Caliphate" as an imagined alternative to today's uncertainty. For others, he offers simplistic conspiracies to explain their world.

Bin Ladin also relies heavily on the Egyptian writer Sayyid Qutb. A member of the Muslim Brotherhood[11] executed in 1966 on charges of attempting to overthrow the government, Qutb mixed Islamic scholarship with a very superficial acquaintance with Western history and thought. Sent by the Egyptian government to study in the United States in the late 1940s, Qutb returned with an enormous loathing of Western society and history. He dismissed Western achievements as entirely material, arguing that Western society possesses "nothing that will satisfy its own conscience and justify its existence."[12]

Three basic themes emerge from Qutb's writings. First, he claimed that the world was beset with barbarism, licentiousness, and unbelief (a condition he called jahiliyya, the religious term for the period of ignorance prior to the revelations given to the Prophet Mohammed). Qutb argued that humans can choose only between Islam and jahiliyya. Second, he warned that more people, including Muslims, were attracted to jahiliyya and its material comforts than to his view of Islam; jahiliyya could therefore triumph over Islam. Third, no middle ground exists in what Qutb conceived as a struggle between God and Satan. All Muslims—as he defined them—therefore must take up arms in this fight. Any Muslim who rejects his ideas is just one more nonbeliever worthy of destruction.[13]

Bin Ladin shares Qutb's stark view, permitting him and his followers to rationalize even unprovoked mass murder as righteous defense of an embattled faith. Many Americans have wondered, "Why do 'they' hate us?" Some also ask, "What can we do to stop these attacks?"

Bin Ladin and al Qaeda have given answers to both these questions. To the first, they say that America had attacked Islam; America is responsible for all conflicts involving Muslims. Thus Americans are blamed when Israelis fight with Palestinians, when Russians fight with Chechens, when Indians fight with Kashmiri Muslims, and when the Philippine government fights ethnic Muslims in its southern islands. America is also held responsible for the governments of Muslim countries, derided by al Qaeda as "your agents." Bin Ladin has stated flatly, "Our fight against these governments is not separate from our fight against you."[14] These charges found a ready audience among millions of Arabs and Muslims angry at the United States because of issues ranging from Iraq to Palestine to America's support for their countries' repressive rulers.

Bin Ladin's grievance with the United States may have started in reaction to specific U.S. policies but it quickly became far deeper. To the second question, what America could do, al Qaeda's answer was that America should abandon the Middle East, convert to Islam, and end the immorality and godlessness of its society and culture: "It is saddening to tell you that you are the worst civilization witnessed by the history of mankind." If the United States did not comply, it would be at war with the Islamic nation, a nation that al Qaeda's leaders said "desires death more than you desire life."[15]

History and Political Context

Few fundamentalist movements in the Islamic world gained lasting political power. In the nineteenth and twentieth centuries, fundamentalists helped articulate anticolonial grievances but played little role in the overwhelmingly secular struggles for independence after World War I. Western-educated lawyers, soldiers, and officials led most independence movements, and clerical influence and traditional culture were seen as obstacles to national progress.

After gaining independence from Western powers following World War II, the Arab Middle East followed an arc from initial pride and optimism to today's mix of indifference, cynicism, and despair. In several countries, a dynastic state already existed or was quickly established under a paramount tribal family. Monarchies in countries such as Saudi Arabia, Morocco, and Jordan still survive today. Those in Egypt, Libya, Iraq, and Yemen were eventually overthrown by secular nationalist revolutionaries.

The secular regimes promised a glowing future, often tied to sweeping ideologies (such as those promoted by Egyptian President Gamal Abdel Nasser's Arab Socialism or the Ba'ath Party of Syria and Iraq) that called for a single, secular Arab state. However, what emerged were almost invariably autocratic regimes that were usually unwilling to tolerate any opposition—even in countries, such as Egypt, that had a parliamentary tradition. Over time, their policies—repression, rewards, emigration, and the displacement of popular anger onto scapegoats (generally foreign)—were shaped by the desire to cling to power.

The bankruptcy of secular, autocratic nationalism was evident across the Muslim world by the late 1970s. At the same time, these regimes had closed off nearly all paths for peaceful opposition, forcing their critics to choose silence, exile, or violent opposition. Iran's 1979 revolution swept a Shia theocracy into power. Its success encouraged Sunni fundamentalists elsewhere.

In the 1980s, awash in sudden oil wealth, Saudi Arabia competed with Shia Iran to promote its Sunni fundamentalist interpretation of Islam, Wahhabism. The Saudi government, always conscious of its duties as the custodian of Islam's holiest places, joined with wealthy Arabs from the Kingdom and other states bordering the Persian Gulf in donating money to build mosques and religious schools that could preach and teach their interpretation of Islamic doctrine.

In this competition for legitimacy, secular regimes had no alternative to offer. Instead, in a number of cases their rulers sought to buy off local Islamist movements by ceding control of many social and educational issues. Emboldened rather than satisfied, the Islamists continued to push for power—a trend especially clear in Egypt. Confronted with a violent Islamist movement that killed President Anwar Sadat in 1981, the Egyptian government combined harsh repression of Islamic militants with harassment of moderate Islamic scholars and authors, driving many into exile. In Pakistan, a military regime sought to justify its seizure of power by a pious public stance and an embrace of unprecedented Islamist influence on education and society.

These experiments in political Islam faltered during the 1990s: the Iranian revolution lost momentum, prestige, and public support, and Pakistan's rulers found that most of its population had little enthusiasm for fundamentalist Islam. Islamist revival movements gained followers across the Muslim world, but failed to secure political power except in Iran and Sudan. In Algeria, where in 1991 Islamists seemed almost certain to win power through the ballot box, the military preempted their victory, triggering a brutal civil war that continues today. Opponents of today's rulers have few, if any, ways to participate in the existing political system. They are thus a ready audience for calls to Muslims to purify their society, reject unwelcome modernization, and adhere strictly to the Sharia.

Social and Economic Malaise

In the 1970s and early 1980s, an unprecedented flood of wealth led the then largely unmodernized oil states to attempt to shortcut decades of development. They funded huge infrastructure projects, vastly expanded education, and created subsidized social welfare programs. These programs established a widespread feeling of entitlement without a corresponding sense of social obligations. By the late 1980s, diminishing oil revenues, the economic drain from many unprofitable development projects, and population growth made these entitlement programs unsustainable. The resulting cutbacks created enormous resentment among recipients who had come to see government largesse as their right. This resentment was further stoked by public understanding of how much oil income had gone straight into the pockets of the rulers, their friends, and their helpers.

Unlike the oil states (or Afghanistan, where real economic development has barely begun), the other Arab nations and Pakistan once had seemed headed toward balanced modernization.

The established commercial, financial, and industrial sectors in these states, supported by an entrepreneurial spirit and widespread understanding of free enterprise, augured well. But unprofitable heavy industry, state monopolies, and opaque bureaucracies slowly stifled growth. More importantly, these state-centered regimes placed their highest priority on preserving the elite's grip on national wealth. Unwilling to foster dynamic economies that could create jobs attractive to educated young men, the countries became economically stagnant and reliant on the safety valve of worker emigration either to the Arab oil states or to the West. Furthermore, the repression and isolation of women in many Muslim countries have not only seriously limited individual opportunity but also crippled overall economic productivity.[16]

By the 1990s, high birthrates and declining rates of infant mortality had produced a common problem throughout the Muslim world: a large, steadily increasing population of young men without any reasonable expectation of suitable or steady employment—a sure prescription for social turbulence. Many of these young men, such as the enormous number trained only in religious schools, lacked the skills needed by their societies. Far more acquired valuable skills but lived in stagnant economies that could not generate satisfying jobs.

Millions, pursuing secular as well as religious studies, were products of educational systems that generally devoted little if any attention to the rest of the world's thought, history, and culture. The secular education reflected a strong cultural preference for technical fields over the humanities and social sciences. Many of these young men, even if able to study abroad, lacked the perspective and skills needed to understand a different culture.

Frustrated in their search for a decent living, unable to benefit from an education often obtained at the cost of great family sacrifice, and blocked from starting families of their own, some of these young men were easy targets for radicalization.

Bin Ladin's Historical Opportunity

Most Muslims prefer a peaceful and inclusive vision of their faith, not the violent sectarianism of Bin Ladin. Among Arabs, Bin Ladin's followers are commonly nicknamed takfiri, or "those who define other Muslims as unbelievers," because of their readiness to demonize and murder those with whom they disagree. Beyond the theology lies the simple human fact that most Muslims, like most other human beings, are repelled by mass murder and barbarism whatever their justification.

"All Americans must recognize that the face of terror is not the true face of Islam," President Bush observed. "Islam is a faith that brings comfort to a billion people around the world. It's a faith that has made brothers and sisters of every race. It's a faith based upon love, not hate."[17] Yet as political, social, and economic problems created flammable societies, Bin Ladin used Islam's most extreme, fundamentalist traditions as his match. All these elements—including religion—combined in an explosive compound.

Other extremists had, and have, followings of their own. But in appealing to societies full of discontent, Bin Ladin remained credible as other leaders and symbols faded. He could stand as a symbol of resistance—above all, resistance to the West and to America. He could present himself and his allies as victorious warriors in the one great successful experience for Islamic militancy in the 1980s: the Afghan jihad against the Soviet occupation.

By 1998, Bin Ladin had a distinctive appeal, as he focused on attacking America. He argued that other extremists, who aimed at local rulers or Israel, did not go far enough. They had not taken on what he called "the head of the snake."[18]

Finally, Bin Ladin had another advantage: a substantial, worldwide organization. By the time he issued his February 1998 declaration of war, Bin Ladin had nurtured that organization for nearly ten years. He could attract, train, and use recruits for ever more ambitious attacks, rallying new adherents with each demonstration that his was the movement of the future.

CRITICAL THINKING QUESTIONS

1. How does Usama Bin Ladin's perspective differ from that found in Islamic teachings? Why does the 9/11 Commission describe Bin Ladin's worldview as an "extremist" position that promotes violence and terrorism?

2. After the 9/11 attacks, many people in the United States wondered, "Why do 'they' hate us?" How does the 9/11 Commission answer this question?

3. What are the historical, political, religious, educational, and economic factors that increase Bin Ladin's following?

NOTES

1. "Text of World Islamic Front's Statement Urging Jihad Against Jews and Crusaders," *Al Quds al Arabi*, Feb. 23, 1998 (trans. Foreign Broadcast Information Service), which was published for a large Arab world audience and signed by Usama Bin Ladin, Ayman al Zawahiri (emir of the Egyptian Islamic Jihad), Abu Yasir Rifa'i Ahmad Taha (leader of the Egyptian Islamic Group), Mir Hamzah (secretary of the Jamiat ul Ulema e Pakistan), and Fazlul Rahman (head of the Jihad Movement in Bangladesh).

2. "Hunting Bin Ladin," PBS *Frontline* broadcast, May 1998 (online at www.pbs.org/wgbh/pages/frontline/shows/binladen/who/interview.html).

3. Usama Bin Ladin, "Declaration of War Against the Americans Occupying the Land of the Two Holy Places," Aug. 23, 1996 (trans., online at www.terrorismfiles.org/individuals/declaration_of_jihad1.html).

4. "Hunting Bin Ladin," PBS *Frontline* broadcast, May 1998.

5. Ibid.

6. For a classic passage conveying the nostalgic view of Islam's spread, see Henri Pirenne, *A History of Europe*, trans. Bernard Miall (University Books, 1956), pp. 25–26.

7. See Martin Marty and R. Scott Appleby, eds., *Fundamentalism Observed*, vol. 1 (Univ. of Chicago Press, 1994).

8. See Emmanuel Sivan, *Radical Islam: Medieval Theology and Modern Politics*, enlarged ed. (Yale Univ. Press, 1990).

9. From the perspective of Islamic, not Arab, history, the Baghdad Caliphate's destruction by the Mongols in 1292 marks the end not of Islamic greatness but of Arab dominance of the Muslim world. Moghul India, Safavid Persia, and, above all, the Ottoman Empire were great Islamic powers that arose long after the Baghdad Caliphate fell.

10. Bin Ladin, "Declaration of War," Aug. 23, 1996.

11. The Muslim Brotherhood, which arose in Egypt in 1928 as a Sunni religious/nationalist opposition to the British-backed Egyptian monarchy, spread throughout the Arab world in the mid–twentieth century. In some countries, its oppositional role is nonviolent; in others, especially Egypt, it has alternated between violent and nonviolent struggle with the regime.

12. Sayyid Qutb, *Milestones* (American Trust Publications, 1990). Qutb found sin everywhere, even in rural mid-western churches. Qutb's views were best set out in Sayyid Qutb, "The America I Have Seen" (1949), reprinted in Kamal Abdel-Malek, ed., *America in an Arab Mirror: Images of America in Arabic Travel Literature: An Anthology* (Palgrave, 2000).

13. For a good introduction to Qutb, see National Public Radio broadcast, "Sayyid Qutb's America," May 6, 2003 (online at www.npr.org/display_pages/features/feature_1253796.html).

14. "Bin Laden's 'Letter to America,'" *Observer Worldview*, Nov. 24, 2002 (trans., online at http://observer.guardian.co.uk/worldview/story/0,11581,845725,00.html). The al Qaeda letter was released in conjunction with the release of an audio message from Bin Ladin himself.

15. Ibid.

16. See *Arab Human Development Report 2003* (United Nations, 2003), a report prepared by Arabs that examines not only standard statistical data but also more sensitive social indicators recently identified by the Nobel Prize–winning economist Amartya Sen. It says little, however, about the political dimensions of economic and social trends. See Mark LeVine, "The UN Arab Human Development Report: A Critique," *Middle East Report*, July 26, 2002 (online at www.merip.org/mero/mero072602.html).

17. President Bush, remarks at roundtable with Arab- and Muslim-American leaders, Sept. 10, 2002 (online at www.whitehouse.gov/news/releases/2002/09/20020910-7.html).

18. See, e.g., Intelligence report, interrogation of Zubaydah, Oct. 29, 2002, CIA analytic report, "Bin Ladin Terrorist Operations: Meticulous and Adaptable," CTC 00-40017CSH, Nov. 2, 2000.

51

"His" and "Her" Marriage

JESSIE BERNARD

Social scientists have found that men and women are not joined at the hip by a wedding ceremony. Rather, their subsequent lives differ in terms of gender roles, power, and ways of communicating. Bernard was among the first sociologists to point out that marriage has a different meaning for women and men. As this selection shows, spouses rarely define reality in the same way, even with regard to simple routines such as sweeping the floor or mowing the lawn.

. . . [T]here is by now a very considerable body of well-authenticated research to show that there really are two marriages in every marital union, and that they do not always coincide.

"HIS" AND "HER" MARRIAGES

. . . [T]he differences in the marriages of husbands and wives have come under the careful scrutiny of a score of researchers. They have found that when they ask husbands and wives identical questions about the

Source: From *The Future of Marriage* by Jessie Bernard. Copyright © by Jessie Bernard. Reprinted with permission.

union, they often get quite different replies. There is usually agreement on the number of children they have and a few other such verifiable items, although not, for example, on length of premarital acquaintance and of engagement, on age at marriage, and interval between marriage and birth of first child. Indeed, with respect to even such basic components of the marriage as frequency of sexual relations, social interaction, household tasks, and decision-making, they seem to be reporting on different marriages. As, I think, they are.

In the area of sexual relations, for example, Kinsey and his associates found different responses in from one- to two-thirds of the couples they studied. Kinsey interpreted these differences in terms of selective perception. In the generation he was studying, husbands wanted sexual relations oftener than the wives did, thus "the females may be overestimating the actual frequencies" and "the husbands . . . are probably underestimating the frequencies." The differences might also have been vestiges of the probable situation earlier in the marriage when the desired frequency of sexual relations was about six to seven times greater among husbands than among wives. This difference may have become so impressed on the spouses that it remained in their minds even after the difference itself had disappeared or even been reversed. In a sample of happily married, middle-class couples a generation later, Harold Feldman found that both spouses attributed to their mates more influence in the area of sex than they did to themselves.

Companionship, as reflected in talking together, he found, was another area where differences showed up. Replies differed on three-fourths of all the items studied, including the topics talked about, the amount of time spent talking with each other, and which partner initiated conversation. Both partners claimed that whereas they talked more about topics of interest to their mates, their mates initiated conversations about topics primarily of interest to themselves. Harold Feldman concluded that projection in terms of needs was distorting even simple, everyday events, and lack of communication was permitting the distortions to continue. It seemed to him that "if these sex differences can occur so often among these generally well-satisfied couples, it would not be surprising to find even less consensus and more distortion in other less satisfied couples."

Although, by and large, husbands and wives tend to become more alike with age, in this study of middle-class couples, differences increased with length of marriage rather than decreased, as one might logically have expected. More couples in the later than in the earlier years, for example, had differing pictures in their heads about how often they laughed together, discussed together,

exchanged ideas, or worked together on projects, and about how well things were going between them.

The special nature of sex and the amorphousness of social interaction help to explain why differences in response might occur. But household tasks? They are fairly objective and clear-cut and not all that emotion-laden. Yet even here there are his-and-her versions. Since the division of labor in the household is becoming increasingly an issue in marriage, the uncovering of differing replies in this area is especially relevant. Hard as it is to believe, Granbois and Willett tell us that more than half of the partners in one sample disagreed on who kept track of money and bills. On the question, who mows the lawn? more than a fourth disagreed. Even family income was not universally agreed on.

These differences about sexual relations, companionship, and domestic duties tell us a great deal about the two marriages. But power or decision making can cover all aspects of a relationship. The question of who makes decisions or who exercises power has therefore attracted a great deal of research attention. If we were interested in who really had the power or who really made the decisions, the research would be hopeless. Would it be possible to draw any conclusion from a situation in which both partners agree that the husband ordered the wife to make all the decisions? Still, an enormous literature documents the quest of researchers for answers to the question of marital power. The major contribution it has made has been to reveal the existence of differences in replies between husbands and wives.

The presence of such inconsistent replies did not at first cause much concern. The researchers apologized for them but interpreted them as due to methodological inadequacies; if only they could find a better way to approach the problem, the differences would disappear. Alternatively, the use of only the wife's responses, which were more easily available, was justified on the grounds that differences in one direction between the partners in one marriage compensated for differences in another direction between the partners in another marriage and thus canceled them out. As, indeed, they did. For when Granbois and Willett, two market researchers, analyzed the replies of husbands and wives separately, the overall picture was in fact the same for both wives and husbands. Such canceling out of differences in the total sample, however, concealed almost as much as it revealed about the individual couples who composed it. Granbois and Willett concluded, as Kinsey had earlier, that the "discrepancies . . . reflect differing perceptions on the part of responding partners." And this was the heart of the matter.

Differing reactions to common situations, it should be noted, are not at all uncommon. They are recognized in the folk wisdom embedded in the story of the blind men all giving different replies to questions on the nature of the elephant. One of the oldest experiments in juridical psychology demonstrates how different the statements of witnesses of the same act can be. Even in laboratory studies, it takes intensive training of raters to make it possible for them to arrive at agreement on the behavior they observe.

It has long been known that people with different backgrounds see things differently. We know, for example, that poor children perceive coins as larger than do children from more affluent homes. Boys and girls perceive differently. A good deal of the foundation for projective tests rests on the different ways in which individuals see identical stimuli. And this perception—or, as the sociologists put it, definition of the situation—is reality for them. In this sense, the realities of the husband's marriage are different from those of the wife's.

Finally, one of the most perceptive of the researchers, Constantina Safilios-Rothschild, asked the crucial question: Was what they were getting, even with the best research techniques, family sociology or wives' family sociology? She answered her own question: What the researchers who relied on wives' replies exclusively were reporting on was the wife's marriage. The husband's

was not necessarily the same. There were, in fact, two marriages present:

One explanation of discrepancies between the responses of husbands and wives may be the possibility of two "realities," the husband's subjective reality and the wife's subjective reality—two perspectives which do not always coincide. Each spouse perceives "facts" and situations differently according to his own needs, values, attitudes, and beliefs. An "objective" reality could possibly exist only in the trained observer's evaluation, if it does exist at all.

Interpreting the different replies of husbands and wives in terms of selective perception, projection of needs, values, attitudes, and beliefs, or different definitions of the situation, by no means renders them trivial or incidental or justifies dismissing or ignoring them. They are, rather, fundamental for an understanding of the two marriages, his and hers, and we ignore them at the peril of serious misunderstanding of marriage, present as well as future.

IS THERE AN OBJECTIVE REALITY IN MARRIAGE?

Whether or not husbands and wives perceive differently or define situations differently, still sexual relations are taking place, companionship is or is not occurring, tasks about the house are being performed, and decisions are being made every day by someone. In this sense, some sort of "reality" does exist. David Olson went to the laboratory to see if he could uncover it.

He first asked young couples expecting babies such questions as these: Which one of them would decide whether to buy insurance for the newborn child? Which one would decide the husband's part in diaper changing? Which one would decide whether the new mother would return to work or to school? When there were differences in the answers each gave individually on the questionnaire, he set up a situation in which together they had to arrive at a decision in his laboratory. He could then compare the results of the questionnaire with the results in the simulated situation. He found neither spouse's question-naire response any more accurate than the other's; that is, neither conformed better to the behavioral "reality" of the laboratory than the other did.

The most interesting thing, however, was that husbands, as shown on their questionnaire response, perceived themselves as having more power than they actually did have in the labora-tory "reality," and wives perceived that they had less. Thus, whereas three-fourths (73 percent) of the husbands overestimated their power in decision-making, 70 percent of the wives under-estimated theirs. Turk and Bell found similar results in Canada. Both spouses tend to attribute decision-making power to the one who has the "right" to make the decision. Their replies, that is, conform to the model of marriage that has characterized civilized mankind for millennia. It is this model rather than their own actual behav-ior that husbands and wives tend to perceive.

We are now zeroing in on the basic reality. We can remove the quotation marks. For there is, in fact, an objective reality in marriage. It is a reality that resides in the cultural—legal, moral, and conventional—prescriptions and proscrip-tions and, hence, expectations that constitute marriage. It is the reality that is reflected in the minds of the spouses themselves. The differences between the marriages of husbands and of wives are structural realities, and it is these structural differences that constitute the basis for the differ-ent psychological realities.

THE AUTHORITY STRUCTURE OF MARRIAGE

Authority is an institutional phenomenon; it is strongly bound up with faith. It must be believed in; it cannot be enforced unless it also has power. Authority resides not in the person on whom it is conferred by the group or society, but in the recognition and acceptance it elicits in others. Power, on the other hand, may dispense with the prop of authority. It may take the form of the ability to coerce or to veto; it is often personal,

charismatic, not institutional. This kind of per-sonal power is self-enforcing. It does not require shoring up by access to force. In fact, it may even operate subversively. A woman with this kind of power may or may not know that she possesses it. If she does know she has it, she will probably dis-guise her exercise of it.

In the West, the institutional structure of mar-riage has invested the husband with authority and backed it by the power of church and state. The marriages of wives have thus been officially dominated by the husband. Hebrew, Christian, and Islamic versions of deity were in complete accord on this matter. The laws, written or un-written, religious or civil, which have defined the marital union have been based on male concep-tions, and they have undergirded male authority.

Adam came first. Eve was created to supply him with companionship, not vice versa. And God himself had told her that Adam would rule over her; her wishes had to conform to his. The New Testament authors agreed. Women were cre-ated for men, not men for women; women were therefore commanded to be obedient. If they wanted to learn anything, let them ask their hus-bands in private, for it was shameful for them to talk in the church. They should submit them-selves to their husbands, because husbands were superior to wives; and wives should be as subject to their husbands as the church was to Christ. Timothy wrapped it all up: "Let the woman learn in silence with all subjection. But I suffer not a woman to teach, nor to usurp authority over the man, but to be in silence." Male Jews continued for millennia to thank God three times a day that they were not women. And the Koran teaches women that men are naturally their superiors because God made them that way; naturally, their own status is one of subordination.

The state as well as the church had the same conception of marriage, assigning to the husband and father control over his dependents, including his wife. Sometimes this power was well-nigh absolute, as in the case of the Roman *patria potestas*—or the English common law, which flatly said, "The husband and wife are as one and that one is the husband." There are rules still lingering today with the same, though less extreme, slant. Diane B. Schulder has summarized the legal framework of the wife's marriage as laid down in the common law:

The legal responsibilities of a wife are to live in the home established by her husband; to perform the domestic chores (cleaning, cooking, washing, etc.) necessary to help maintain that home; to care for her husband and children. . . . A husband may force his wife to have sexual relations as long as his demands are reasonable and her health is not endangered. . . . The law allows a wife to take a job if she wishes. However, she must see that her domestic chores are completed, and, if there are children, that they receive proper care during her absence.

A wife is not entitled to payment for household work; and some jurisdictions in the United States expressly deny payment for it. In some states, the wife's earnings are under the control of her husband, and in four, special court approval and in some cases husband's consent are required if a wife wishes to start a business of her own.

The male counterpart to these obligations includes that of supporting his wife. He may not disinherit her. She has a third interest in property owned by him, even if it is held in his name only. Her name is required when he sells property.

Not only divine and civil law but also rules of etiquette have defined authority as a husband's prerogative. One of the first books published in England was a *Boke of Good Manners*, translated from the French of Jacques Le Grand in 1487, which included a chapter on "How Wymmen Ought to Be Gouerned." The thirty-third rule of Plutarch's *Rules for Husbands and Wives* was that women should obey their husbands; if they "try to rule over their husbands they make a worse mistake than the husbands do who let themselves be ruled." The husband's rule should not, of course, be brutal; he should not rule his wife "as a master does his chattel, but as the soul governs the body, by feeling with her and being linked to her by affection." Wives, according to Richard Baxter, a seventeenth-century English divine, had to obey even a wicked husband, the only exception being that a wife need not obey a husband if he ordered

her to change her religion. But, again, like Plutarch, Baxter warned that the husband should love his wife; his authority should not be so coercive or so harsh as to destroy love. Among his twelve rules for carrying out the duties of conjugal love, however, was one to the effect that love must not be so imprudent as to destroy authority.

As late as the nineteenth century, Tocqueville noted that in the United States the ideals of democracy did not apply between husbands and wives:

Nor have the Americans ever supposed that one consequence of democratic principles is the subversion of marital power, or the confusion of the natural authorities in families. They hold that every association must have a head in order to accomplish its objective, and that the natural head of the conjugal association is man. They do not therefore deny him the right of directing his partner; and they maintain, that in the smaller association of husband and wife, as well as in the great social community, the object of democracy is to regulate and legalize the powers which are necessary, not to subvert all power.

This opinion is not peculiar to men and contested by women; I never observed that the women of America consider conjugal authority as an unfortunate usurpation [by men] of their rights, nor that they thought themselves degraded by submitting to it. It appears to me, on the contrary, that they attach a sort of pride to the voluntary surrender of their own will, and make it their boast to bend themselves to the yoke, not to shake it off.

The point here is not to document once more the specific ways (religious, legal, moral, traditional) in which male authority has been built into the marital union—that has been done a great many times—but merely to illustrate how different (structurally or "objectively" as well as perceptually or "subjectively") the wife's marriage has actually been from the husband's throughout history.

THE SUBVERSIVENESS OF NATURE

The rationale for male authority rested not only on biblical grounds but also on nature or natural law, on the generally accepted natural superiority of men. For nothing could be more self-evident than that the patriarchal conception of marriage, in which the husband was unequivocally the boss, was natural, resting as it did on the unchallenged superiority of males.

Actually, nature, if not deity, is subversive. Power, or the ability to coerce or to veto, is widely distributed in both sexes, among women as well as among men. And whatever the theoretical or conceptual picture may have been, the actual, day-by-day relationships between husbands and wives have been determined by the men and women themselves. All that the institutional machinery could do was to confer authority; it could not create personal power, for such power cannot be conferred, and women can generate it as well as men. . . . Thus, keeping women in their place has been a universal problem, in spite of the fact that almost without exception institutional patterns give men positions of superiority over them.

If the sexes were, in fact, categorically distinct, with no overlapping, so that no man was inferior to any woman or any woman superior to any man, or vice versa, marriage would have been a great deal simpler. But there is no such sharp cleavage between the sexes except with respect to the presence or absence of certain organs. With all the other characteristics of each sex, there is greater or less overlapping, some men being more "feminine" than the average woman and some women more "masculine" than the average man. The structure of families and societies reflects the positions assigned to men and women. The bottom stratum includes children, slaves, servants, and outcasts of all kinds, males as well as females. As one ascends the structural hierarchy, the proportion of males increases, so that at the apex there are only males.

When societies fall back on the lazy expedient—as all societies everywhere have done—of allocating the rewards and punishments of life on the basis of sex, they are bound to create a host of anomalies, square pegs in round holes, societal misfits. Roles have been allocated on the basis of sex which did not fit a sizable number of both sexes—women, for example, who chafed at

subordinate status and men who could not master superordinate status. The history of the relations of the sexes is replete with examples of such misfits. Unless a modus vivendi is arrived at, unhappy marriages are the result.

There is, though, a difference between the exercise of power by husbands and by wives. When women exert power, they are not rewarded; they may even be punished. They are "deviant." Turk and Bell note that "wives who . . . have the greater influence in decision making may experience guilt over this fact." They must therefore dissemble to maintain the illusion, even to themselves, that they are subservient. They tend to feel less powerful than they are because they ought to be.

When men exert power, on the other hand, they are rewarded; it is the natural expression of authority. They feel no guilt about it. The prestige of authority goes to the husband whether or not he is actually the one who exercises it. It is not often even noticed when the wife does so. She sees to it that it is not.

There are two marriages, then, in every marital union, his and hers. And his . . . is better than hers. The questions, therefore, are these: In what direction will they change in the future? Will one change more than the other? Will they tend to converge or to diverge? Will the future continue to favor the husband's marriage? And if the wife's marriage is improved, will it cost the husband's anything, or will his benefit along with hers?

CRITICAL THINKING QUESTIONS

1. What evidence does Bernard offer to support her conclusion that there are "his" and "her" marriages rather than "our" marriage?

2. Does the traditional inequality of men and women support or undermine marital roles? How?

3. What are the consequences for marriage of the gradual process by which the two sexes are becoming more socially equal?

52

Housework in Canada: The National Picture*

M. R. NAKHAIE

Researchers generally agree that women perform the majority of domestic work. Nakhaie looks at this assertion from a Canadian perspective and attempts to address the lack of research on domestic labour in Canada.

Recent survey research indicates that women are still overwhelmingly responsible for, and primarily carry out, the chief household chores (Coverman & Sheley, 1986; Berardo et al., 1987; Michelson, 1988). Most importantly, there appears to be little significant increase in the amount of domestic labour performed by men when their wives take on a second job (i.e., full-time paid work outside the home). Canadian local studies in Vancouver (Meissner et al., 1975), Halifax (Harvey Clarke,

1975), Toronto (Michelson, 1985), Quebec (Bourdais et al., 1987), and Flin Flon (Luxton, 1980; Luxton & Rosenberg, 1986) support these conclusions.

There is, however, no national Canadian research to substantiate these findings. This is a surprising shortcoming, given the persistent conclusion among contributors to the domestic labour debate that there is a great need for empirical research (Fox, 1986: 188; Seccombe, 1986: 207; Armstrong & Armstrong, 1990: 33). In an attempt to contribute to the ongoing debate, this paper provides a multivariate analysis of housework and evaluates its major determinant in the Canadian national setting.

*I gratefully acknowledge that the data presented here were drawn from Class Structure and Class Consciousness: Merged Multi-Nation File, the Canadian portion of which was conducted by Professor John Myles of Carleton University with funding from the Social Sciences and Humanities Research Council of Canada. I am indebted to Professors Robert Arnold, James Curtis and Roberta Hamilton, and anonymous reviewers for their helpful and critical comments.

Source: M. R. Nakhaie. (1995). "Housework in Canada." *Journal of Comparative Family Studies,* 26(3), 409–25. Reprinted with the permission of the *Journal of Comparative Family Studies.*

HYPOTHESES

Aside from the importance of capitalism and patriarchy in the institutionalization of gender specific task allocations (see Molyneux, 1979; Fox, 1980; Hamilton & Barrett, 1986; Armstrong & Armstrong, 1990), most theorists agree that the organization of domestic life is a negotiated process between household occupants. . . . There is, however, little agreement as to whether this process is power-based or a free choice.

The best-known sociological theory which is concerned with the conjugal power as an explanation of housework performance is that of Wolfe (1959), Blood and Wolfe (1960: 48, 73–4) and Spitze (1986: 691). This theory views power and resources such as income as instrumental in the family structure whereby those members with more income or power are better able to exercise their wills, or to achieve desired goals or outcomes. Davidoff (1976: 124), likewise, argues that the performance of housekeeping and housework are a means of maintaining order and predictability in the immediate environment thus making meaningful patterns of activity, people and material. Cleaning, for example, entails the separation of wanted from unwanted, desirable from undesirable, and is therefore a way of making the environment conform to cultural standards. Those who are powerful, however, can enforce and maintain this order by delegating it to the less powerful. Thus, the resource/power theory suggests that housework is generally undesirable and those with more resources confer power and negotiate or impose household tasks on the powerless. Empirical research has supported this hypothesis (see Bane, 1976; Clark et al., 1978; Nicols and Metzen, 1978; Ericksen et al., 1979; Vanek, 1980; Model, 1982; Bird et al., 1984; Spitze, 1986; Bourdais et al., 1987; but see, Farkas, 1976; Robinson, 1977; Herdesty & Bokemeir, 1989: 263). For example, Ericksen et al. (1979) show a negative relationship between men's income and their hours of housework performance. Similarly, Nicols and Metzen (1978) show that as wives' incomes increase, the number of hours they spend on housework decrease, and that the husbands' housework increases.

The New Home Economics, or Chicago School, builds on the resource/power theory but sees the household operation as based on free choice. It suggests that the household unit seeks to maximize the aggregate utility of the occupants' labour power in the house and in the market by deciding which commodities to produce in the house and which to purchase from the market. Since women often earn less for the same work as men, this thesis argues that households can maximize utility by adopting a gendered division of labour. This places wives at home doing domestic work while their husbands are involved in the paid work force (Becker, 1974). The traditional sexual division of labour is thus seen as a rational decision made by households which wish to maximize utility (see also Becker, 1976, 1981).

More precisely, this theory is concerned with the "husband-wife earning ratio" as the determinant of home responsibility (Becker, 1974: 303). It suggests that the relative income contribution of spouses to the family signifies the worth of each partner's work in the market and thus is used as the determinant of housework performance. The earliest test of this thesis by Farkas (1976), based on the national U.S. Income Dynamic data, shows that the strength of the net effect of wage-ratio does not appear to warrant the conclusion that the value of human time is the main explanation for spousal contribution to housework. Model (1982), however, revealed that the level of contribution to housework is determined by income differentials between spouses. The latter, in fact, proves to be a better predictor of housework responsibilities than individual income. Similarly, Maret and Finlay's (1984) findings support the hypothesis that the wife's relative economic contribution to the household determines her domestic responsibilities (1984: 362; but see [the] Hardesty and Bokemeir study of rural Kentucky, 1989: 263).

Finally, the time availability hypothesis also sees housework allocation as a negotiated process but not so much based on power or utility maximization. This thesis suggests that husbands and wives perform housework in response to the availability of time after involvement in paid work. Blood and Wolfe (1960: 74), for example, argue that "more household tasks are humdrum and menial in nature," and the most important factor contributing to their performance is available time. Usually the person with the most time is the wife who is not working outside the home. But if she works for pay, the husband incurs a moral obligation to contribute to the housework. Thus, this thesis suggests that as more women work for pay, they have less time to perform housework. Consequently, their husbands have to contribute more to the housework because "the work must be done." Or, alternatively, the more husbands have available free time, because their jobs require fewer hours, the more they will contribute to domestic work.

Several studies point to women's participation in the labour force as the reason for a decrease in their housework and an increase in the home responsibilities of their partners. (Walker, 1970; Epstein, 1971; Holmstrom, 1973; Elliott et al., 1973; Vanek, 1974; Nicols and Metzen, 1978; Pleck, 1979; Sanik, 1981; Berk, 1985; Bourdais et al., 1987; Michelson, 1988; Luxton, 1980). For example, Spitze (1986) uses data from the National Longitudinal Surveys of Young and Mature Women and finds that, as women's hours of employment increases, their share of housework decreases slightly. Similarly, Barnett and Baruch (1987) reveal that women's employment outside the home prompts increased male acceptance of housework.

Despite the positive relationship in the above studies, the impact of wives' employment on husband's housework is also shown to be insignificant (Vanek, 1974; Sanik, 1981), quite small (Walker & Woods, 1976), or at best modest (Nicols & Metzen, 1978). Most importantly, there appears to be little significant increase in men's domestic labour as women take on paid work outside the home. For example, Meissner et al. (1975) studied a random sample of Vancouver couples on a week day and weekend day. They show that women's total workload, involving work both inside and outside the home, increases

as they take on paid work, but husbands' does not. While men are reported to spend only a fraction of the time that women spend doing housework, it is women who are found to adjust their schedules to the changing family situation. Based on a similar study in 1971–72 in Halifax, Harvey and Clarke (1975) also conclude that women, and not men, adjust their work efforts to changing family needs. Michelson's (1985) 1980 survey of Toronto families, based on time-budget data, also shows that full-time paid working women still do far more housework than men. Finally, another local study by Bourdais et al. (1987) in Quebec, reveals that women, on average, contribute three times as many hours as men to household chores. This proportion decreases to twice as much as men's when both partners have a paid job. However, even though a woman's employment decreases her work around the house by nine hours, it increases men's housework by only one hour (Bourdais et al., 1987).

In sum, American and Canadian local studies reveal that women who work for pay outside the home do not necessarily decrease and their husbands increase their share of housework. Moreover, while homemaking is the largest occupational category in this country (Luxton & Rosenberg, 1986), housework ranks as the most systematically under-researched (Hale, 1990). There have been several very informative studies of local samples, referred to above. The present study will show the generalizability to national data of several results from these earlier local studies. Furthermore, due, perhaps, to differences in research procedures (measures, samples, and the extent of controls), the previous American literature is inconsistent enough in its findings to require further tests. Most American studies rely on an ordinal level of measurement for housework—mostly husband, mostly wife, jointly (Stafford et al., 1977; Clarke et al., 1978; Ericksen et al., 1979; Marret and Finlay, 1984; Bird et al., 1984; Hardesty and Bokemeir, 1989). Other researchers ask respondents to estimate their contribution to housework in terms of the percentage of time or number of hours (Coverman, 1985; Barnett & Baruch, 1987; Berardo et al., 1987). Still other researchers obtain time-use data by a diary of activities kept by each respondent for about 24 hours or a week (Walker, 1970; Walker & Woods, 1976; Robinson et al., 1972; Robinson, 1977; Juster and Stafford, 1985; Coverman and Sheley, 1986). These American studies have also been limited in population coverage to white middle class families (Berardo et al., 1987; Barnet & Baruch, 1987), to women aged 30–44 (Marret & Finlay, 1984), to college students (Stafford et al., 1977), to college and university administrators (Bird et al., 1984), or to local samples (Clarke et al., 1978; Ericksen et al., 1979), although national samples have also been used, as discussed above.[1]

DATA SOURCE

Our data source is the Canadian portion of "The Class Structure and Class Consciousness: Merged Multi-Nation File" (CSCC) which involved in-home personal interviews with a national multi-stage stratified sample of Canadians. The interviews were conducted between November 1982 and April 1983. There were 2576 respondents, 1,810 of whom were married and/or cohabiting and 480 of which both partners worked more than 30 hours per week for pay. The latter subsample is selected to evaluate the findings by Maret and Finlay (1984) that women in dual-earner families continue to bear full responsibility for housework. The sample is weighted to make it representative of the population in terms of gender, age, household size, and community size within provinces.

Dependent Variables

Housework refers to all types of activities which are undertaken to maintain the household, both physically and socially, as well as the maintenance of the physical structure of the house (Clark &

Stephenson, 1986: 75). The CSCC survey asked respondents to report how they handle various routine household chores by indicating what percentage of particular tasks is done by them.[2] These tasks, however, were limited to eight, including: looking after children and doing things with them, cooking meals, cleaning after meals, doing laundry, general housecleaning, grocery shopping, yardwork, and house maintenance.

Independent Variables

The measures of personal resource and power include two variables: (1) income scaled from 1 = none to 12 = over $100,000; and (2) perceived power. Blood and Wolfe (1960), in their study of Detroit and Michigan, measured power in terms of an individual's ability to make decisions in critical areas of life (including income and expenditures) and showed that this measure was strongly related to various measures of inequality such as income and prestige. Likewise, the CSCC contained three questions which could measure conjugal power: (1) "who has the most say in making major financial decisions in [the respondent's] household, like a decision to take out a loan or buy a car"; (2) "who has most say about the overall family budget; that is, about how much of the family income goes for different general purposes such as running the house, recreation, new clothes, and so forth"; and (3) "who has the most say in deciding the specific neighborhood where you live now." If the respondents make the decision in any of these areas they receive a score of +1; if their partners make this decision the respondents receive a score of –1 and if both equally decide the respondents receive a score of zero (0). The power variable is created by summing the scores for these questions. Scores range from –3 to +3.

Relative income represents the respondent's relative contribution to the family income. Respondents are asked to report the percentage of annual family income resulting from their spouses' jobs. A score of zero (0) is assigned to those respondents who reported that their spouse does not have a paying job.

There are two measures of time availability. First, the survey asked the respondents to report the number of hours they work per week. This variable ranges from 8 to 97. The second measure evaluates the time availability of spouses. The survey asked the respondents to report their partner's number of hours of paid work per week. This variable ranges from 8 to 87.

In addition to the predictors of homework discussed above we were concerned about the extent to which the presence of children increases women's and men's share of housework (Berk & Berk, 1979; Meissner et al., 1975; Hamilton, 1981). We included the number of children and their ages (under 5, 6–12, 13 plus) to control for children's effect.

RESULTS

Among the total sample, male respondents have a higher mean level of income (about $20K) than females (about $7K) and work more per week (37.4 hours) than females (18.6 hours). Spouses of the male respondents spend 15.44 hours per week in the paid force and contribute 17.3% to the family income, while spouses of the female respondents spend 35.28 hours per week in the paid force and contribute 66.9% to the family income. On average, males score higher in the power construct (.45) than females (–.20). As expected, the magnitude of these gaps declines, though not substantially, among full-time respondents when compared to the total sample. The main differences between males and females in the total and full-time paid working sample are in the income and time availability areas. Among full-time paid working respondents, men's total income does not differ much from that reported by males in the full sample but females' total income increases from about $7K to $13K and their contribution to the family income increases

from 17.2 percent to 40.6 percent. The total hours of paid employment for males does increase slightly (from 37.4 to 45.7), but that of females increases substantially (from 18.6 to 40.2). Similarly, when comparing the two groups, males report that their partners' total hours of paid work increase from 15.4 to 40.3 while females report that their partners' total hours of paid work increases from 35.3 to 44.2.

Another expected difference between the two sub-samples is in the numbers of children. Although there is little difference in the number of children reported by either males or females in the total sample, full-time paid working females report fewer children than their male counterparts.

Finally, male respondents reported performing about 33% of the housework, compared to 62% for the female respondents. A similarly large gap in performing housework emerged among full-time paid working respondents. Men increased their housework by about 4% and females decreased theirs by about 3% when compared to the total sample (see Table 52.1). Consistent with previous research, full-time paid work by women does not relieve them from most of the housework (Maret and Finlay, 1984; Meissner et al., 1975; Luxton, 1980). . . . .

DISCUSSION AND CONCLUSIONS

The results of this study support previous findings that relative income, personal resources and time availability as well as the presence of children affect the division of housework. Among these, power, as measured by the ability to make decisions regarding the affairs of the house, receives the least support when compared to the time availability (Meissner et al., 1975: 425; Blood & Wolfe, 1960; Spitze, 1986; Walker, 1970; Epstein, 1971; Holmstrom, 1973; Pleck, 1979; Sanik, 1981; Berk, 1985; Bourdais et al., 1987), relative income (Farkas, 1976: 482; Model, 1982; Maret & Finlay, 1984), presence of children (Hamilton, 1981; Berk & Berk, 1979;

TABLE 52.1   Mean Scores for the Dependent and Independent Variables by Gender: Total Sample and Full-Time Paid Working Respondents (Canada, 1983)

	Total Sample		Full-time	
	Males	*Females*	*Males*	*Females*
Power	.45	−.20	−.37	−.08
Income	6.93	3.90	6.81	5.54
Relative income	17.28	66.95	40.46	60.98
# Hours of paid work by spouse	15.44	35.28	40.39	44.23
# Hours of paid work by Resp.	37.40	18.62	45.74	40.24
# Children	1.24	1.25	1.13	1.02
Age of children	10.72	10.82	10.90	9.82
Share of Housework	33.30	62.30	37.50	59.30

Bourdais et al., 1987; Meissner, 1975) and income (Bane, 1976; Nicols & Metzen, 1978; Bourdais et al., 1987) variables. The power measure failed to show the expected effect, probably because it is measured by asking respondents who makes what decisions and therefore indicates perceived authority rather than actual power (McDonald, 1980).

Although the New Home Economic model is supported in our study, the impact of the husband-wife earning ratio on doing housework is stronger for males than females. This finding suggests that the economic model, by assuming that people make decisions based on free choice, has ignored power relationships involved in the household. As Coverman (1989) argued, the allocation of household chores is subject to difficult negotiation and conflict among household members. The outcome of these negotiations often depends, however, on the ability and power of the household occupants. Husbands seem to have a structural advantage in this process. Wives, however, have to develop a variety of tactics and strategies to increase their spouses' contributions to housework (Luxton, 1980; see also Hartmann, 1981; Hamilton, 1981).

The suggestion that housework is power-based is also borne out by findings on the relationships between the time availability measures and doing housework. As males increase their hours of paid work per week, they do less housework (particularly among double earner couples),

while women do *more* of the housework as they increase their hours of paid work. Moreover, women are more responsive to the increases in their partners' hours of paid work than are men.

Two conclusions can be reached by these findings. First, among the total sample, females do more housework because gender stands as a proxy of a relatively fewer paid hours of work by women compared to men. Thus, among the full-time paid respondents, gender in itself does not have a significant impact on doing housework. Second, there are indications of a "superwomen" (Steinem, 1987: 57; Luxton, 1980) ethic among women who work for long hours in the paid work force and do an even larger share of housework than before. These findings, thus, support the studies in Vancouver (Meissner, 1975), Halifax (Harvey & Clarke, 1975), Flin Flon (Luxton, 1980) and in Quebec (Bourdais et al., 1987) which show that full-time paid working women still do most of the housework, perhaps at the expense of their own leisure and personal care. As these local studies conclude, women's involvement in the paid labour force simply adds to their housework in the family (Anderson, 1988: 165).

The differential impact of the hours of paid work for males and females, particularly among the full-time two income earners, may thus point to Eichler's (1990) argument that the value of time differs systematically in relation to one's power position. Since women as a group are less powerful than men, time spent performing paid work becomes less valuable and cannot easily help reduce their share of housework. This power seems to have been derived from husbands' economic advantage in the labour force, their greater cognitive power in the public domain and from women's cultural mandate, which places priority on the family (Mackie, 1991: 234–235; Luxton & Rosenberg, 1986: 11; Gaskell, 1988).

Finally, one of the persistent findings in this study (and of the previous research) is that gender/sex is the most significant force in accounting for the performance of housework, net of other variables. These consistent findings point to the structural and historical forces which have gradually helped institutionalize a "gender factory" in the house so that each generation of sons learned to do less housework and each generation of daughters continued to be trained in domestic activities. This gendered socialization of housework seems to have been sealed in the best social cement of all: the patterns of daily life and the relationship between parents and children (Cowan, 1983: 86; England & Farkas, 1986; Finley, 1989; Molyneux, 1979; Fox, 1980; Zaretsky, 1982; Hamilton & Barrett, 1986; Armstrong & Armstrong, 1990).

Moreover, the gendered division of labour is passed down to children in the family and schools and through media and religions which portray women as engaged in a narrow range of "female" occupations and household-related tasks (see Russell, 1986; Mackie, 1991). These forces have constructed sex-specific images and stereotypes and have enforced a "tendency for many women to accept as truth the social constraints and mental images which society has prescribed for them" (Pike & Zureik, 1975: 3). Thus, boys' and girls' involvement in housework in their early teens becomes readily distinguishable along gender lines (Benin & Edwards, 1990; White and Brinkerhoff, 1981). Not surprisingly, Gaskell's (1988) study of young girls in their last years of high school in a Vancouver working-class neighborhood revealed that they all

assumed that eventually they would care for their children and do the housework. Young girls seem to have learned that "[c]ooking a nice meal, providing clean sheets or eliminating dull, yellow floor wax" are ways of expressing love (Luxton, 1980: 159). Boys, on the other hand, internalize the male breadwinner ideology as their fundamental gender consciousness (Livingstone & Luxton, 1989).

There are some indications of a shift in Canadian attitudes toward sharing housework. Canadians' support for husbands sharing housework has increased from 57% in 1976 to 81% in 1986 (Wilson, 1991: 56). However, these attitude changes are very slowly translated into changes in behaviour. Although the men of Flin Flon seem to have increased their contribution to housework by 8.3 hours per week between 1976–81, women of this town decreased their contribution to housework by only 4.3 hours per week (Luxton, 1986). Perhaps an equal contribution to housework is possible only if the power relationship between men and women in the wider society and in the house is altered. Simultaneously, gender consciousness should be transcended so that an ideology of breadwinning for males and family priority for females loses its gendered-significance. These, however, may not be easy tasks, given the powerful forces which have split the labour market and have segregated the household as a private domain.

CRITICAL THINKING QUESTIONS

1. Review the *conjugal power* explanation for who performs the majority of housework. Given your own experiences, does this explanation seem accurate?

2. Why do you think there has not been more research into domestic labour in Canada?

3. Do you believe that the gender factory continues to reinforce traditional male and female roles as they relate to domestic labour? If yes, how? If not, why?

NOTES

1. There are substantial differences among the American studies. It is difficult to know to what extent these differences in findings are due to small sample areas, measurement differences and/or differing interpretations of the results. It is plausible that since there is little variation in the amount of housework performed by men, every different analysis will likely conclude with the explanatory importance of different variables.

2. The exact question is: "Now we would like to ask you some questions about how you handle various routine household chores. For each of the following tasks, please tell me roughly what percentage of this task is done by you."

REFERENCES

Armstrong, P., and H. Armstrong. 1990. *Theorizing women's work.* Toronto: Network Basics Series.

Bane, M. J. 1976. *Here to stay: American families in the twentieth century.* New York: Basic Books.

Benin, M. H., and D. A. Edwards. 1990. Adolescents' chores: The difference between dual and single-earner families." *Journal of Marriage and the Family,* 52: 361–73.

Barnett, R. C., and G. K. Baruch. 1987. Determinants of father's participation in family work. *Journal of Marriage and the Family,* 49: 29–40.

Becker, G. S. 1974. A theory of marriage. In *Economics of the family,* ed. T. W. Schultz. Chicago: University of Chicago Press.

———. 1976. *The economic approach to human behavior.* Chicago: University of Chicago Press.

———. 1981. *A treatise on the family.* Harvard, MA: Harvard University Press.

Berk, R. 1980. The new home economics: An agenda for sociological research. In *Women and household labor,* ed. S. F. Berk, 113–48. Beverly Hills, CA: Sage.

Berk, R., and S. Berk. 1979. *Labour and leisure at home.* Beverly Hills, CA: Sage.

Berk, S. 1985. *The gender factory: The apportionment of work in the American household.* New York: Plenum Press.

Berardo, D. H., C. L. Shehah, and G. R. Leslie. 1987. A residue of tradition: Jobs, careers, and spouses' time in house work. *Journal of Marriage and the Family,* 49: 381–90.

Bird, G. W., G. A. Bird, and M. Scruggs. 1984. Determinants of family task sharing: A study of husbands and wives. *Journal of Marriage and the Family,* 46(2): 345–55.

Blood, R. O., and D. M. Wolfe. 1960. *Husbands and wives: The dynamics of married living.* Glencoe, IL: Free Press.

Bourdais, C., P. J. Hamel, and R. Bernard. 1987. Le travail et l'ouvrage: Charge et portage des tâches domestiques chez les couples québécois. *Sociologie et Societés,* XIX(1: Avril): 37–55.

Clark, R. A., F. I. Nye, and V. Gecas. 1978. Work involvement and marital role performance. *Journal of Marriage and the Family,* 40: 9–22.

Clark, S., and M. Stephenson. 1986. Housework as real work. In *Work in the Canadian context,* eds. K. L. P. Lundy, and B. Warme, 211–31. Markham, ON: Butterworths.

Coverman, S., and J. E. Sheley. 1986. Change in men's housework and child care time 1965–1975. *Journal of Marriage and the Family,* 48: 413–22.

Cowan, R. S. 1983. *More work for mothers: The ironies of household technology from the open hearth to the microwave.* New York: Basic Books.

Davidoff, L. 1976. The rationalization of housework. In *Dependence and exploitation in work and marriage,* eds. D. L. Barker, & S. Allen. London: Longman.

Eichler, M. 1991. Gender and the value of time. In *Images of Canada: The sociological tradition,* eds. J. Curtis and L. Tepperman. Scarborough, ON: Prentice-Hall Canada Inc.

Elliott, D., A. S. Harvey, and D. Procos. 1973. *An overview of Halifax time-budget.* Halifax/Institute of Public Affairs, Dalhousie University.

England, P., and G. Farkas. 1986. *Households, employment, and gender: A social, economic, and demographic view.* New York: Aldine de Gruyter.

Ericksen, J., W. Yancey, and E. Ericksen. 1979. The division of family roles. *Journal of Marriage and the Family,* 41: 301–14.

Epstein, C. 1971. Law partners and marital partners: Strains and solutions in the dual-career family enterprise. *Human Relations,* 24 (December): 549–64.

Farkas, G. 1976. Education, wage rate and the division of labour between husband and wife. *Journal of Marriage and the Family,* 38: 473–84.

Finley, N. J. 1989. Theories of family labour as applied to gender differences in caregiving for elderly parents. *Journal of Marriage and the Family,* 51: 79–86.

Fox, B. 1980. *Hidden in the household: Women's domestic labour under capitalism.* Oshawa, ON: Women's Press.

Gaskell, J. 1988. The reproduction of family life: Perspectives of male and female adolescents. In *Gender and society: Creating a Canadian women's sociology,* ed. A. T. McLaren, 146–68. Toronto: Copp Clark Pitman.

Hale, S. M. 1990. *Controversies in sociology: A Canadian introduction.* Toronto: Copp Clark Pitman Ltd.

Hamilton, R. 1981. Working at home. *Atlantis,* 7(1): 114–26.

Hamilton, R., and M. Barrett. 1986. Introduction. In *The politics of diversity: Feminism, Marxism and nationalism,* eds. R. Hamilton and M. Barrett, 1–35. London: Verso.

Hardesty, C., and J. Bokemeir. 1989. Finding time and making do: Distribution of household labour in non-metropolitan marriages. *Journal of Marriage and the Family,* 51: 253–67.

Hartmann, H. I. 1981. The family as the locus of gender, class, and political struggle: The example of housework. *Signs,* 6(3): 366–94.

Harvey, A. S., and S. Clarke. 1975. *Descriptive analysis of Halifax time-budget data.* Halifax: Institute of Public Affairs, Dalhousie University.

Holmstrom, L. L. 1973. *The two-career family.* Cambridge, MA: Schenkman.

Juster, F. T., and F. J. Stafford. 1985. *Time, goods and well-being.* Ann Arbor, MI: Survey Research Center, Institute for Social Research, University of Michigan.

Livingstone, D. W., and M. Luxton. 1988. Gender consciousness at work: Modification of the male breadwinner norm among steelworkers and their spouses. *Canadian Review of Sociology and Anthropology*, 26(2): 240–74.

Luxton, M. 1980. *More than a labour of love: Three generations of women's work at home.* Toronto: Women's Press.

Luxton, M., and H. Rosenberg. 1986. *Through the kitchen windows: The politics of home and family.* Toronto: Garamond Press.

Mackie, M. 1991. *Gender relations in Canada: Further explorations.* Markham, ON: Butterworths Canada Ltd.

Maret, E., and B. Finlay. 1984. The distribution of household labour among women in dual-earner families. *Journal of Marriage and the Family*, 46: 357–64.

McDonald, G. W. 1980. Family power: The assessment of a decade of theory and research, 1970–1979. *Journal of Marriage and the Family*, 42: 841–54.

Meissner, M., E. W. Humphrey, S. M. Meis, and W. J. Scheu. 1975. No exit for wives: Sexual division of labour and cumulation of household demands. *Canadian Review of Sociology and Anthropology*, 12: 424–39.

Michelson, W. 1985. *From sun to sun: Daily obligations and community structure in the lives of employed women and their families.* Tomwa, NJ: Rowman & Allanheld Publishers.

———. 1988. The daily routines of employed spouses as a public affairs agenda. In *Readings in sociology: An introduction*, eds. L. Tepperman and J. Curtis, 400–09. Toronto: McGraw-Hill Ryerson Limited.

Model, S. 1982. Housework by husbands: Determinants and implications. In *Two paychecks: Life in dual earner families*, ed. J. Aldous, 193, 206. Beverly Hills, CA: Sage Publications.

Molyneux, M. 1979. Beyond the domestic labour debate. *New Left Review*, 116: 3–27.

Nicols, S., and E. Metzen. 1978. Housework time of husband and wife. *Home Economics Research Journal*, 17: 85–97.

Pike, R., and E. Zuriek. 1975. *Socialization and values in Canadian society.* Toronto: McClelland and Stewart Limited.

Pleck, J. H. 1979. Men's family work: Three perspectives and some new data. *Family Coordinator*, 28: 481–88.

Robinson, J. 1977. *How Americans use time.* New York: Praeger.

Robinson, J., P. Converse, and A. Szali. 1972. Everyday life in the twelve countries. In *The use of time*, ed. A. Szalai. The Hague: Mouton.

Sanik, M. 1981. Division of household work: A decade of comparison, 1967–1977. *Home Economic Research Journal*, 10: 175–80.

Seccombe, W. 1986. Patriarchy stabilized: The construction of male breadwinner wage norm in nineteenth-century Britain. *Social History*, II (1).

Spitze, G. D. 1986. Division of home responsibilities. *Social Forces*, 64: 689–701.

Stafford, R., E. Backman, and R Dibona. 1977. The division of labour among cohabiting and married couples. *Journal of Marriage and the Family*, 39: 43–57.

Steinem, G. 1987. Looking to the future. *Ms.* (July/August): 55–7.

Vanek, J. 1974. Time spent in housework. *Scientific American* (November): 116–21.

Vanek, J. 1980. Household work, wage work and sexual equality. In *Women and household labor*, ed. S. F. Berk, 275–95. Beverly Hills, CA: Sage.

Walker, K. E. 1970. *Time-use patterns for household work related to homemaker's employment.* Washington, DC: U.S. Department of Agriculture.

Walker, K. E., and M. E. Woods. 1976. *Time use: A measure of household production of family goods and services.* Washington, DC: Center for the Family of the American Home Economic Association.

White, L. K., and D. B. Brinkerhoff. 1981. Children's work in the family: Its significance and meaning. *Journal of Marriage and the Family*, 81: 789–98.

Wilson, S. J. 1991. *Women, families, and work*, 3rd ed. Toronto: McGraw-Hill Ryerson Limited.

Wolfe, D. 1959. Power and authority in the family. In *Studies in social power*, ed. D. Cartwright. Ann Arbor, MI: University of Michigan Press.

Zaretsky, E. 1982. *Capitalism, the family and personal life.* London: Pluto Press.

53

Mate Selection and Marriage around the World

BRON B. INGOLDSBY

The institution of marriage is very popular throughout the world. Yet, how mates are chosen varies considerably from one culture to another. As Bron B. Ingoldsby shows, free-choice mate selection—which is common in Western countries—is not how couples have been paired with their prospective spouses in most other societies.

MATE SELECTION PROCEDURES

Historically, there have been three general approaches to choosing one's mate: marriage by capture, marriage by arrangement, and free-choice mate selection. I examine each of them in turn.

Marriage by Capture

Although it has probably never been the usual method of obtaining a wife, men have taken women by force in many times and places. This typically occurred in patriarchal societies in which women were often considered property. Often women were seized as part of the spoils of

war, and other times a specific woman was forced into marriage because the man wanted her and could not afford the brideprice or obtain the permission of her parents. The capture and marriage of a woman was legal in England until the reign of Henry VII, who made it a crime to abduct an heiress (Fielding, 1942).

The ancient Hebrews would seize wives under certain circumstances. A dramatic example is recounted in the Old Testament (Judges, chapter 21), where it was arranged for young women to be kidnapped from two different areas to serve as wives so that the tribe of Benjamin would not die out after a war that they had lost.

There was also a formal procedure for dealing with wives captured in warfare (Deuteronomy 21: 10–14):

When thou goest forth to war against thine enemies, and the Lord thy God hath delivered them into thine hands, and thou has taken them captive, And seest among the captives a beautiful woman, and hast a

Source: "Mate Selection and Marriage," by Bron B. Ingoldsby in *Families in Multicultural Perspective*, eds. by Bron B. Ingoldsby and Suzanna Smith, pp. 143–5. Copyright © 1995 Guilford Press, NY. Reprinted by permission of Guilford Press.

desire unto her, that thou wouldest have her to thy wife; Then thou shalt bring her home to thine house; and she shall shave her head, and pare her nails; And she shall put the raiment of her captivity from off her, and shall remain in thine house, and bewail her father and her mother a full month: and after that thou shalt go in unto her, and be her husband, and she shall be thy wife. And it shall be, if thou have no delight in her, then thou shalt let her go whither she will; but thou shalt not sell her at all for money, thou shalt not make merchandise of her, because thou has humbled her.

At least she was given time to get used to the idea and never sold into slavery! Fielding (1942) cites a number of different cultures, including the Australian aborigines, who frequently resorted to marriage by capture in the recent past. The Yanomamö of Venezuela (an Amazonian tribe) are reported (Peters, 1987) to use capture as one of their mate selection options. One village is often raided by another for the specific purpose of finding wives. If a man captures a young, attractive female, he must be careful as other men from his own village will try to steal her from him.

In the popular musical *Seven Brides for Seven Brothers*, the concept of marriage by capture is acted out, and one of the songs is based on the historical incident of the rape of the Sabine women. There are many cultures that still have remnants of the old practice of marriage by capture in their wedding ceremonies. In each of them, the match is prearranged, but the husband pretends to take his bride by force, and she feigns resistance.

One example is the Roro of New Guinea. On the wedding day, the groom's party surrounds the bride's home and acts out an assault on it. The bride attempts to run away but is caught. Then a sham battle ensues, with the bride's mother leading the way and crying at the loss of her daughter when she is taken off to the groom (Fielding, 1942).

Marriage by Arrangement

It appears that the most common method of mate selection has been by arrangement. Typically, the parents, often with the aid of certain relatives or professional matchmakers, have chosen the spouse for their child. This form of mate choice is more common when extended kin groups are strong and important. Essentially, marriage is seen as of group, rather than individual, importance, and economics is often the driving force rather than love between the principals.

Arranged marriages have been considered especially important for the rulers of kingdoms and other nobility. Care had to be taken to preserve bloodlines, enhance wealth, and resolve political issues. It is believed, for instance, that the majority of King Solomon's 700 wives and 300 concubines were acquired for the purpose of political alliances.

Stephens (1963) identifies four major reasons that determine mate choice in societies in which marriages are arranged. The first is *price*. The groom's family may need to pay for the bride, with either money or labor. In some cultures, the situation is reversed, with the bride's family paying a dowry to the husband. In other cases, there is a direct exchange, where both families make payments to each other or simply trade women for each other's sons.

The second consideration is *social status*. That is, the reputation of the family from which the spouse for one's child will come is very important. A third determinant is any *continuous marriage arrangement*. This refers to a set pattern for mate selection, which is carried on from generation to generation. For instance, cousin marriages are preferred in many societies.

The final criteria for mate choice are *sororate* and *levirate* arrangements, which refer to second marriages and tend to be based on brideprice obligations. These terms are more fully explained later in the [reading]. Stephens also notes nineteen societies (including, for example, some large ones such as China and Renaissance Europe) that have practiced child betrothals or child marriages. This means that the marriage is arranged before puberty and can even be worked out before the child is born.

In addition to marriage by capture, the Yanomamö also practice variety within arranged marriages. The ideal match is between cross-cousins, and the majority of unions fall into this category. Most betrothals are made before the girl is three years of age. Men initiate these arrangements at about the time they become hunters, which is shortly after they turn fifteen. Another acceptable form of mate selection is sister exchange. Two unrelated single males wish to acquire wives and have sisters who are not promised to anyone, so they simply trade sisters (Peters, 1987).

Some societies have provided an "out" for couples who have strong personal preferences that go against the arrangement of their families. This is to permit elopement. Stephens (1963: 200) gives this account of the Iban of Borneo:

When a young woman is in love with a man who is not acceptable to her parents, there is an old custom called *nunghop bui*, which permits him to carry her off to his own village. She will meet him by arrangement at the waterside, and step into his boat with a paddle in her hand, and both will pull away as fast as they can. If pursued he will stop every now and then to deposit some article of value on the bank, such as a gun, a jar, or a favor for the acceptance of her family, and when he has exhausted his resources he will leave his own sword. When the pursuers observe this they cease to follow, knowing he is cleared out. As soon as he reaches his own village he tidies up the house and spreads the mats, and when his pursuers arrive he gives them food to eat and toddy to drink, and sends them home satisfied. In the meanwhile he is left in possession of his wife.

Following is a detailed look at some of the specific mechanisms of arranged marriages.

Brideprice Throughout much of human history, marriage has been seen as chiefly an economic transaction. As an old German saying goes, "It is not man that marries maid, but field marries field, vineyard marries vineyard, cattle marry cattle" (Tober, 1984: p. 12). The purpose of a bride-price is to compensate the family of the bride for the loss of her services. It is extremely common

and is indicative of the value of women in those societies. Stephens (1963) reports that Murdock's World Ethnographic Sample yields the following breakdown on marriage payments:

Brideprice—260 societies
Bride service—75 societies
Dowry—24 societies
Gift or woman exchange—31 societies
No marriage payment—152 societies

This means that in 62 percent of the world's societies, a man must pay in order to marry a woman. The price is usually paid in animals, shell money, or other valuable commodities and often exceeds one's annual income. Some cultures prefer payment in service, often many years of labor to the bride's parents, or at least permit it for suitors who cannot afford to pay in goods. One famous example from the Old Testament is that of Jacob, who labored seven years for each of Laban's two daughters, Leah and Rachel.

Dowry The dowry appears to be an inducement for a man to marry a particular woman and therefore relieve her family of the financial burden of caring for her. Although relatively rare, it is a sign of a culture that places a low value on women. Actually, the key purpose of a dowry is probably to stabilize a marriage, because it is not given to the husband but is something that the bride brings with her into the marriage. For example, in Cyprus before the time of English influence, the expected dowry was often a house. If the husband divorced his wife or mistreated her and she left him, the dowry went with her. Like modern-day wedding gifts, or the bride's trousseau, it was an investment in the marriage and intended to reduce the chances of a breakup (Balswick, 1975).

The dowry has been around for a long time. The Babylonian code of Hammurabi (1955 B.C.E.) clearly stated that the wife's property stayed with her if her husband divorced her and passed on to her children when she died. Ancient Greece and

Rome also considered the dowry to be essential in any honorable marriage (Fielding, 1942).

. . . [R]esearch in the southern Indian state of Kerala (Billig, 1992) differentiates between the traditional dowry and an actual "groomprice." Groomprice is money paid by the bride's family directly to the husband to use as he sees fit. In the 1950s and 1960s, rapid population growth resulted in more younger women looking for husbands a few (average of seven) years older than themselves. This surplus of potential brides increased the value of husbands. Popular revulsion for the groomprice has resulted in a decrease in the age difference (now five years), women lowering their social status expectations for their husband or increasing their own education, and a government outlawing of the practice.

Sororate and Levirate These terms refer to marriage practices designed to control remarriages after the death of the first spouse. In cultures that practice the sororate, a sister replaces a deceased wife. Assume that a man has paid a good brideprice for his wife but some time later she becomes ill and dies. He has lost his wife and the brideprice. Therefore, to make good on the original bargain, the parents who received the brideprice provide the man with a new wife. This new wife is an unmarried sister or other close relative of the first wife. Here we see how marriage is often more of an economic transaction than it is a personal relationship.

Much more widely practiced has been the levirate. Under this system, it is the husband who dies, and his wife must be married to a brother of the deceased man. There are various reasons for this practice. One is that the wife belonged to her husband as part of his property and as such would be inherited along with the other possessions by a near relative. Another is that it is presumed that women need someone to take care of them, and brothers-in-law (which is the meaning of the Latin word *levir*) should assume that responsibility. It has been reported that the levirate has been practiced by the New Caledonians, the Mongols,

the Afghans, the Abyssinians, the Hebrews, and the Hindus, as well as certain Native American and African tribes (Fielding, 1942).

The chief reason that the Hindus and Hebrews practiced the levirate was religious and had to do with the importance of having a son in the family. Hindu men needed a son to perform certain sacrifices, so if a man died before having one, a boy born to his former wife and brother would carry out those ceremonies in his name (Fielding, 1942).

For the Hebrews, it was also important that every man have a son, so that his name would not die out. There was a ritualized penalty for men who refused to marry their brother's widow and rear a son in his name (Deuteronomy 25: 7–9):

And if the man like not to take his brother's wife, then let his brother's wife go up to the gate unto the elders, and say, My husband's brother refuseth to raise up unto his brother a name in Israel, he will not perform the duty of my husband's brother. Then the elders of his city shall call him, and speak unto him: and if he stand to it, and say, I like not to take her; Then shall his brother's wife come in to him in the presence of the elders, and loose his shoe from his foot, and spit in his face, and shall answer and say, So shall it be done unto that man that will not build up his brother's house.

The punishment for refusing to practice the levirate used to be more severe than the above-quoted ritual. In Genesis, chapter 38, we read of Judah's son Onan and how he was killed by the Lord for refusing to impregnate his dead older brother's wife. The book of Ruth in the Old Testament is also an excellent example of how the levirate worked. It is an account of how Naomi has no more sons for her daughter-in-law Ruth to marry, so she arranges for another male relative, Boaz, to take on the responsibility.

Matchmaking There are various ways in which two young people can be brought together. Typically, the parents of both boys and girls will work out the details among themselves and then announce it to their children. The initial go-between in Turkey has been the boy's mother, who would inspect possibilities at the public baths and then give reports to her son (Tober, 1984). The popular musical *Fiddler on the Roof* is about father-arranged marriages. Often, hired go-betweens, or matchmakers, assist in making the arrangement. They might act as intermediaries between the families or suggest potential spouses. Checking for astrological or other religious signs and requirements could also be part of their job.

In the 1800s, bachelor pioneers in the American West would sometimes find a wife by ordering one from a mail-order catalog. Even today, many Asian families publish matrimonial want ads in search of a respectable spouse for their child (Tober, 1984). I recently found the following in the classified section of a Philippine newspaper:

Foreigner: video match a decent friendship marriage consultant office introducing a beautiful single educated Filipina view friendship to marriage.

Ladies: Australian European businessmen newly arrive[d] in town sincerely willing to meet decent Filipina view friendship to marriage. Ambassador Hotel suite 216.

Computer dating services in the United States, Japan, and elsewhere manifest the continued utility of professional matchmaking, even in societies in which the individuals involved make the final decisions themselves. There are also magazines designed for singles that include matrimonial or relationship want ads.

There are immigrants to Western societies who are not comfortable with love-based unions and prefer to have their marriages arranged by their parents or through a mediator. It is estimated, for instance, that up to 90 percent of the marriages in the East Indian community in Edmonton, Alberta, are to some degree arranged (Jimenez, 1992). Some ethnic Indians return to the Indian subcontinent to find a spouse, whereas others allow their parents to find a match locally for them. Some place ads in newspapers such as *India Today* or *India Abroad*, which focus on desired background characteristics such as education, religion, and age. In deference to Western customs, the young people can veto any match that does not appeal to them, and a dowry is rarely accepted.

Free-Choice Mate Selection

. . . [L]ove gradually became the principal criterion for marriage in the Western world after the Renaissance. The shift from kinship and economic motives to personal ones in mate selection led to the conclusion that the individuals themselves, rather than their parents or others, were best qualified to make the decision. In societies in which the basic family unit is nuclear, both romantic love and free mate choice are more common. This is because extended kin groups are not important enough to see marriage as needing to be group controlled.

Even though free choice is the mate selection method of the modern United States, one should not conclude that it is the most common approach in the world. In a survey of forty societies, Stephens (1963) found only five in which completely free mate choice is permitted. An additional six allowed the young people to choose their spouse, but subject to parental approval. Twelve other cultures had a mix of arranged marriages and free-choice (usually subject to approval) unions, and the final sixteen allowed only arranged marriages.

Moreover, even free choice does not mean that one can marry anyone. All societies have marital regulations. The rule of *exogamy* declares that a person must marry outside his/her group. Typically, this means that certain relatives are unavailable as marriage partners. Exogamous rules are generally the same as the incest taboos of the society, which prohibit sexual intercourse between close blood relatives. Others go beyond that, however. In classical China, two people with the same surname could not marry even if there was no kinship relation (Hutter, 1981).

The rule of *endogamy* declares that a person must marry someone who is similar to oneself in important ways, including religion, race, or ethnic group; social class; and age. These factors have been found to be related to marital compatibility and are precisely the kinds of things considered by parents in arranged marriages. One reason why the divorce rate seems to be higher in free-choice societies may be that many couples ignore endogamy issues and allow romantic love to be practically the sole consideration in mate selection. There is a tendency for marriages to be fairly homogamous, however, even in free-mate-choice societies.

A final factor is *propinquity* (geographical nearness). It is, of course, impossible to marry someone who lives so far away from you that you never meet. At another level, however, this principle refers to a human tendency to be friends with people with whom it is convenient to interact. Let us say that you leave your hometown to attend college elsewhere. You left a boyfriend or girlfriend back at home and you also meet someone new at college. All other things being equal, which one will you marry? Generally, it will be the one at school simply because it is easier.

Some Examples Free mate choice is on the rise in China today. However, it is very different from the courtship pattern in North America. Young people gather information about each other first and check for mutual suitability before going public with their relationship. In fact, dating follows, rather than precedes, the decision to marry. Typically, the couple knows each other for well over two years before marrying. This cautious approach is paying off, as the quality of these marriages seems to be higher than that of arranged unions (Liao & Heaton, 1992).

The Igbo are a people living in present-day Nigeria (Okonjo, 1992). About 55 percent of the Igbo have their marriages arranged, while the remaining 45 percent are in free-choice unions. Most of the latter are younger, indicating a move from arranged to free choice, which we see occurring throughout much of the world today. Regardless of type, premarital chastity is very highly valued among the Igbo.

As the Igbo move to free mate choice based on love, their various arranged practices are falling into disfavor. Customs that are quickly disappearing include woman-to-woman marriage. In this situation, an older childless woman pays the brideprice to marry a younger female, usually a cousin. A male mate is chosen for the "wife" to have children with, but they belong to the older female spouse, who has the legal role of "husband."

Another way of securing an heir is father-to-daughter marriage. If a man has no sons, he may prohibit a daughter from marrying. She has children from a male mate (not the father) but her sons are considered her father's. Women whose husbands turn out to be impotent are allowed to have a lover from whom to have children, who are considered to be the legal husband's. Other arranged practices seldom practiced anymore are the levirate and child marriages.

CRITICAL THINKING QUESTIONS

1. What four major issues influence mate choice in societies where marriages are arranged? What societal functions do the specific mechanisms of arranged marriages (such as brideprice, dowry, sororate, levirate, and matchmaking) fulfill?

2. Does marriage by free choice mean that a person can really marry *anyone*? What factors (or rules) considerably narrow the field of eligible mates in societies with free-choice mate selection?

3. What are the advantages and disadvantages of marrying for love (in free-choice societies) rather than economic or political considerations (in societies with arranged marriages)? Would marriages in North America be less likely to end in divorce if marriages were arranged?

REFERENCES

Balswick, J. 1975. The function of the dowry system in a rapidly modernizing society: The case of Cyprus. *International Journal of Sociology and the Family*, 5(2): 158–67.

Billig, M. 1992. The marriage squeeze and the rise of groomprice in India's Karala state. *Journal of Comparative Family Studies*, 23(2): 197–216.

Fielding, W. 1942. *Strange customs of courtship and marriage*. New York: New Home Library.

The Holy Bible. King James Version.

Hutter, M. 1981. *The changing family: Comparative perspectives*. New York: Wiley.

Jimenez, M. 1992. Many Indo-Canadians follow age-old custom. *Edmonton Journal* (July 26): B3.

Liao, C., and T. Heaton. 1992. Divorce trends and differentials in China. *Journal of Comparative Family Studies*, 23(3): 413–29.

Okonjo, K. 1992. Aspects of continuity and change in mate selection among the Igbo west of the river Niger. *Journal of Comparative Family Studies*, 23(3): 339–60.

Peters, J. 1987. Yanomamö mate selection and marriage. *Journal of Comparative Family Studies*, 18(1): 79–98.

Stephens, W. 1963. *The family in cross-cultural perspective*. New York: Holt, Rinehart & Winston.

Tober, B. 1984. *The bride: A celebration*. New York: Harry N. Abrams.

54

The Protestant Ethic and the Spirit of Capitalism

MAX WEBER

Religion

CLASSIC

CONTEMPORARY

CROSS-CULTURAL

In perhaps his most well-known treatise, Max Weber argues that a major factor in the development of the capitalist economic system was the distinctive world view of early, ascetic Protestantism, especially Calvinism and Puritanism. In this excerpt from his classic analysis, Weber explains that religious ideas about work and materials initially fostered capitalism's growth; ultimately, he concludes, capitalism was able to stand on its own without religious supports.

A product of modern European civilization, studying any problem of universal history, is bound to ask himself to what combination of circumstances the fact should be attributed that in Western civilization, and in Western civilization only, cultural phenomena have appeared which (as we like to think) lie in a line of development having *universal* significance and value. . . . All over the world there have been merchants, wholesale and retail, local and engaged in foreign trade. . . .

But in modern times the Occident has developed, in addition to this, a very different

Source: From *The Protestant Ethic and the Spirit of Capitalism* by Max Weber, copyright © 1988, Prentice-Hall, Inc. Reprinted by permission.

form of capitalism which has appeared nowhere else: the rational capitalistic organization of (formally) free labour. Only suggestions of it are found elsewhere. Even the organization of unfree labour reached a considerable degree of rationality only on plantations and to a very limited extent in the *Ergasteria* of antiquity. In the manors, manorial workshops, and domestic industries on estates with serf labour it was probably somewhat less developed. Even real domestic industries with free labour have definitely been proved to have existed in only a few isolated cases outside the Occident. . . .

Rational industrial organization, attuned to a regular market, and neither to political nor irrationally speculative opportunities for profit, is not, however, the only peculiarity of Western capitalism. The modern rational organization of the capitalistic enterprise would not have been possible without two other important factors in its development: the separation of business from the household, which completely dominates modern economic life, and closely connected with it, rational bookkeeping. . . .

Hence in a universal history of culture the central problem for us is not, in the last analysis, even from a purely economic viewpoint, the development of capitalistic activity as such, differing in different cultures only in form: the adventurer type, or capitalism in trade, war, politics, or administration as sources of gain. It is rather the origin of this sober bourgeois capitalism with its rational organization of free labour. Or in terms of cultural history, the problem is that of the origin of the Western bourgeois class and of its peculiarities, a problem which is certainly closely connected with that of the origin of the capitalistic organization of labour, but is not quite the same thing. For the bourgeois as a class existed prior to the development of the peculiar modern form of capitalism, though, it is true, only in the Western Hemisphere.

Now the peculiar modern Western form of capitalism has been, at first sight, strongly influenced by the development of technical possibilities. Its rationality is today essentially dependent on the calculability of the most important technical factors. But this means fundamentally that it is dependent on the peculiarities of modern science, especially the natural sciences based on mathematics and exact and rational experiment. On the other hand, the development of these sciences and of the technique resting upon them now receives important stimulation from these capitalistic interests in its practical economic application. It is true that the origin of Western science cannot be attributed to such interests. Calculation, even with decimals, and algebra have been carried on in India, where the decimal system was invented. But it was only made use of by developing capitalism in the West, while in

India it led to no modern arithmetic or bookkeeping. Neither was the origin of mathematics and mechanics determined by capitalistic interests. But the *technical* utilization of scientific knowledge, so important for the living conditions of the mass of people, was certainly encouraged by economic considerations, which were extremely favourable to it in the Occident. But this encouragement was derived from the peculiarities of the social structure of the Occident. We must hence ask, from *what* parts of that structure was it derived, since not all of them have been of equal importance?

Among those of undoubted importance are the rational structures of law and of administration. For modern rational capitalism has need, not only of the technical means of production, but of a calculable legal system and of administration in terms of formal rules. Without it adventurous and speculative trading capitalism and all sorts of politically determined capitalisms are possible, but no rational enterprise under individual initiative, with fixed capital and certainty of calculations. Such a legal system and such administration have been available for economic activity in a comparative state of legal and formalistic perfection only in the Occident. We must hence inquire where that law came from. Among other circumstances, capitalistic interests have in turn undoubtedly also helped, but by no means alone nor even principally, to prepare the way for the predominance in law and administration of a class of jurists specially trained in rational law. But these interests did not themselves create that law. Quite different forces were at work in this development. And why did not the capitalistic interests do the same in China or India? Why did not the scientific, the artistic, the political, or the economic development there enter upon that path of rationalization which is peculiar to the Occident?

For in all the above cases it is a question of the specific and peculiar rationalism of Western culture. . . . It is hence our first concern to work out and to explain genetically the special peculiarity of Occidental rationalism, and within this field that of the modern Occidental form. Every such attempt at explanation must, recognizing the fundamental importance of the economic factor, above all take account of the economic conditions. But at the same time the opposite correlation must not be left out of consideration. For though the development of economic rationalism is partly dependent on rational technique and law, it is at the same time determined by the ability and disposition of men to adopt certain types of practical rational conduct. When these types have been obstructed by spiritual obstacles, the development of rational economic conduct has also met serious inner resistance. The magical and religious forces, and the ethical ideas of duty based upon them, have in the past always been among the most important formative influences on conduct. In the studies collected here we shall be concerned with these forces.

Two older essays have been placed at the beginning which attempt, at one important point, to approach the side of the problem which is generally most difficult to grasp: the influence of certain religious ideas on the development of an economic spirit, or the *ethos* of an economic system. In this case we are dealing with the connection of the spirit of modern economic life with the rational ethics of ascetic Protestantism. Thus we treat here only one side of the causal chain. . . .

. . . [T]hat side of English Puritanism which was derived from Calvinism gives the most consistent religious basis for the idea of the calling. . . . For the saints' everlasting rest is in the next world; on earth man must, to be certain of his state of grace, "do the works of him who sent him, as long as it is yet day." Not leisure and enjoyment, but only activity serves to increase the glory of God according to the definite manifestations of His will.

Waste of time is thus the first and in principle the deadliest of sins. The span of human life is infinitely short and precious to make sure of one's own election. Loss of time through sociability, idle talk, luxury, even more sleep than is necessary for health, six to at most eight hours, is worthy of absolute moral condemnation. It does not yet hold, with Franklin, that time is money, but the proposition is true in a certain spiritual sense. It is infinitely valuable because every hour lost is lost to labour for the glory of God. Thus inactive contemplation is also valueless, or even directly reprehensible if it is at the expense of one's daily work. . . .

[T]he same prescription is given for all sexual temptation as is used against religious doubts and a sense of moral unworthiness: "Work hard in your calling." But the most important thing was that even beyond that labour came to be considered in itself the end of life, ordained as such by God. St. Paul's "He who will not work shall not eat" holds unconditionally for everyone. Unwillingness to work is symptomatic of the lack of grace.

Here the difference from the mediæval viewpoint becomes quite evident. Thomas Aquinas also gave an interpretation of that statement of St. Paul. But for him labour is only necessary *naturali ratione* for the maintenance of individual and community. Where this end is achieved, the precept ceases to have any meaning. Moreover, it holds only for the race, not for every individual. It does not apply to anyone who can live without labour on his possessions, and of course contemplation, as a spiritual form of action in the Kingdom of God, takes precedence over the commandment in its literal sense. Moreover, for the popular theology of the time, the highest form of monastic productivity lay in the increase of the *Thesaurus eccleslæ* through prayer and chant.

. . . For everyone without exception God's Providence has prepared a calling, which he should profess and in which he should labour. And this calling is not, as it was for the Lutheran, a fate to which he must submit and which he must make the best of, but God's commandment to the individual to work for the divine glory. This seemingly subtle difference had far-reaching psychological consequences, and became connected with a further development of the providential interpretation of the economic order which had begun in scholasticism.

It is true that the usefulness of a calling, and thus its favour in the sight of God, is measured primarily in moral terms, and thus in terms of the importance of the goods produced in it for the community. But a further, and, above all, in practice the most important, criterion is found in private profitableness. For if that God, whose hand the Puritan sees in all the occurrences of life, shows one of His elect a chance of profit, he must do it with a purpose. Hence the faithful Christian must follow the call by taking advantage of the opportunity. "If God show you a way in which you may lawfully get more than in another way (without wrong to your soul or to any other), if you refuse this, and choose the less gainful way, you cross one of the ends of your calling, and you refuse to be God's steward, and to accept His gifts and use them for Him when He requireth it: you may labour to be rich for God, though not for the flesh and sin.". . .

The superior indulgence of the *seigneur* and the parvenu ostentation of the *nouveau riche* are equally detestable to asceticism. But, on the other hand, it has the highest ethical appreciation of the sober, middle-class, self-made man. "God blesseth His trade" is a stock remark about those good men who had successfully followed the divine hints. The whole power of the God of the Old Testament, who rewards His people for their obedience in this life, necessarily exercised a similar influence on the Puritan who . . . compared his own state of grace with that of the heroes of the Bible. . . .

Although we cannot here enter upon a discussion of the influence of Puritanism in all . . . directions, we should call attention to the fact that the toleration of pleasure in cultural goods, which contributed to purely aesthetic or athletic enjoyment, certainly always ran up against one characteristic limitation: They must not cost anything. Man is only a trustee of the goods which have come to him through God's grace. He must, like the servant in the parable, give an account of every penny entrusted to him, and it is at least hazardous to spend any of it for a purpose which does not serve the glory of God but only one's own enjoyment. What person, who keeps his eyes open, has not met representatives of this viewpoint even in the present? The idea of a man's duty to his possessions, to which he subordinates himself as an obedient steward, or even as an acquisitive machine, bears with chilling weight on his life. The greater the possessions the heavier, if the ascetic attitude toward life stands the test, the feeling of responsibility for them, for holding them undiminished for the glory of God and increasing them by restless effort. The origin of this type of life also extends in certain roots, like so many aspects of the spirit of capitalism, back into the Middle Ages. But it was in the ethic of ascetic Protestantism that it first found a consistent ethical foundation. Its significance for the development of capitalism is obvious.

This worldly Protestant asceticism, as we may recapitulate up to this point, acted powerfully against the spontaneous enjoyment of possessions; it restricted consumption, especially of luxuries. On the other hand, it had the psychological effect of freeing the acquisition of goods from the inhibitions of traditionalistic ethics. It broke the bonds of the impulse of acquisition in that it not only legalized it, but (in the sense discussed) looked upon it as directly willed by God. . . .

As far as the influence of the Puritan outlook extended, under all circumstances—and this is, of course, much more important than the mere encouragement of capital accumulation—it favoured the development of a rational bourgeois economic life; it was the most important, and above all the only consistent influence in the development of that life. It stood at the cradle of the modern economic man.

To be sure, these Puritanical ideals tended to give way under excessive pressure from the temptations of wealth, as the Puritans themselves knew very well. With great regularity we find the most genuine adherents of Puritanism among the classes which were rising from a lowly status, the small bourgeois and farmers while the *beati possidentes*, even among Quakers, are often found tending to repudiate the old ideals. It was the same fate which again and again befell the predecessor of this worldly asceticism, the monastic asceticism of the Middle Ages. In the latter case, when rational economic activity had worked out its full effects by strict regulation of conduct and limitation of consumption, the wealth accumulated either succumbed directly to the nobility, as in the time before the Reformation, or monastic discipline threatened to break down, and one of the numerous reformations became necessary.

In fact the whole history of monasticism is in a certain sense the history of a continual struggle with the problem of the secularizing influence of wealth. The same is true on a grand scale of the worldly asceticism of Puritanism. The great revival of Methodism, which preceded the expansion of English industry toward the end of the eighteenth century, may well be compared with such a monastic reform. We may hence quote here a passage from John Wesley himself which might well serve as a motto for everything which has been said above. For it shows that the leaders of these ascetic movements understood the seemingly paradoxical relationships which we have here analysed perfectly well, and in the same sense that we have given them. He wrote:

I fear, wherever riches have increased, the essence of religion has decreased in the same proportion. Therefore I do not see how it is possible, in the nature of things, for any revival of true religion to continue long. For religion must necessarily produce both industry and frugality, and these cannot but produce riches. But as riches increase, so will pride, anger, and love of the world in all its branches. How then is it possible that Methodism, that is, a religion of the heart, though it flourishes now as a green bay tree, should continue in this state? For the Methodists in every place grow diligent and frugal; consequently they increase in goods. Hence they proportionately increase in pride, in anger, in the desire of the flesh, the desire of the eyes, and the pride of life. So, although the form of religion remains, the spirit is swiftly vanishing away. Is there no way to prevent this—this continual decay of pure religion? We ought not to prevent people from being diligent and frugal; *we must exhort all Christians to gain all they can, and to save all they can; that is, in effect, to grow rich.*

As Wesley here says, the full economic effect of those great religious movements, whose significance for economic development lay above all in their ascetic educative influence, generally came only after the peak of the purely religious enthusiasm was past. Then the intensity of the search for the Kingdom of God commenced gradually to pass over into sober economic virtue; the religious roots died out slowly, giving way to utilitarian worldliness. Then, as Dowden puts it, as in *Robinson Crusoe*, the isolated economic man who carries on missionary activities on the side takes the place of the lonely spiritual search for the Kingdom of Heaven of Bunyan's pilgrim, hurrying through the marketplace of Vanity. . . .

A specifically bourgeois economic ethic had grown up. With the consciousness of standing in the fullness of God's grace and being visibly blessed by Him, the bourgeois business man, as long as he remained within the bounds of formal correctness, as long as his moral conduct was spotless and the use to which he put his wealth was not objectionable, could follow his pecuniary interests as he would and feel that he was fulfilling a duty in doing so. The power of religious asceticism provided him in addition with sober, conscientious, and unusually industrious workmen, who clung to their work as to a life purpose willed by God.

Finally, it gave him the comforting assurance that the unequal distribution of the goods of this world was a special dispensation of Divine Providence, which in these differences, as in particular grace, pursued secret ends unknown to men. . . .

One of the fundamental elements of the spirit of modern capitalism, and not only of that but of all modern culture: Rational conduct on the basis of the idea of the calling, was born—that is what this discussion has sought to demonstrate—from the spirit of Christian asceticism. One has only to reread the passage from Franklin, quoted at the beginning of this essay, in order to see that the essential elements of the attitude which was there called the spirit of capitalism are the same as what we have just shown to be the content of the Puritan worldly asceticism, only without the religious basis, which by Franklin's time had died away. . . .

Since asceticism undertook to remodel the world and to work out its ideals in the world, material goods have gained an increasing and finally an inexorable power over the lives of men as at no previous period in history. Today the spirit of religious asceticism—whether finally, who knows?—has escaped from the cage. But victorious capitalism, since it rests on mechanical foundations, needs its support no longer. The rosy blush of its laughing heir, the Enlightenment, seems also to be irretrievably fading, and the idea of duty in one's calling prowls about in our lives like the ghost of dead religious beliefs. Where the fulfilment of the calling cannot directly be related to the highest spiritual and cultural values, or when, on the other hand, it need not be felt simply as economic compulsion, the individual generally abandons the attempt to justify it at all. In the field of its highest development, in the United States, the pursuit of wealth, stripped of its religious and ethical meaning, tends to become associated with purely mundane passions, which often actually give it the character of sport.

No one knows who will live in this cage in the future, or whether at the end of this tremendous development entirely new prophets will arise, or there will be a great rebirth of old ideas and ideals, or, if neither, mechanized petrification, embellished with a sort of convulsive self-importance. For of the last stage of this cultural development, it might well be truly said: "Specialists without spirit, sensualists without heart; this nullity imagines that it has attained a level of civilization never before achieved."

But this brings us to the world of judgments of value and of faith, with which this purely historical discussion need not be burdened. . . .

Here we have only attempted to trace the fact and the direction of its influence to their motives in one, though a very important point. But it would also further be necessary to investigate how Protestant Asceticism was in turn influenced in its development and its character by the totality of social conditions, especially economic. The modern man is in general, even with the best will, unable to give religious ideas a significance for culture and national character which they deserve. But it is, of course, not my aim to substitute for a one-sided materialistic an equally one-sided spiritualistic causal interpretation of culture and of history. Each is equally possible, but each, if it does not serve as the preparation, but as the conclusion of an investigation, accomplishes equally little in the interest of historical truth.

CRITICAL THINKING QUESTIONS

1. What are the distinctive characteristics of the religious orientation that Weber called the "Protestant ethic"? In what ways did they promote the development of the capitalist economic system?

2. In what respects do early Calvinists with a sense of "calling" differ from today's "workaholics"?

3. In what sense does Weber's analysis differ from the materialist orientation of Karl Marx (Reading 44), who suggested that productive forces shape the world of ideas?

55

Canada's Mythical Religious Mosaic: Some Census Findings

REGINALD W. BIBBY

Religion

CLASSIC

CONTEMPORARY

CROSS-CULTURAL

Bibby finds that many Canadians believe that since Canada is a multicultural society it must also feature considerable religious diversity. However, national census data suggest that Canada's "religious mosaic" is largely a myth. Bibby's research reveals that Christianity continues to enjoy a significant numerical majority in Canada and that new religions are finding it difficult to attract new members. In fact, the author suggests that Canada is characterized by an extremely narrow spectrum of religious diversity and that it is dominated by Catholic and Protestant "companies."

Canada historically has been a country of immigrants. Similar to the United States, much of its early population growth from the seventeenth century onward was due to the arrival of people from France and England, and increasingly from around the world. Since the 1960s, there has been a shift in the dominant origins of immigrants, with a majority now coming from Asia and other Third World countries, rather than Europe.

In the face of such cultural group diversity, Canada has taken pride in defining itself as a mosaic, a "community of communities." Such a self-definition is more than mere rhetoric. In 1971, the federal government unveiled its official policy of multiculturalism, complete with an array of programs aimed at enabling citizens of all backgrounds to participate fully in Canadian

life, and to perpetuate their national cultures to the extent they so desired. In 1988, these twin ideals were enshrined in the *Multiculturalism Act* that states the Canadian government is committed to a policy "designed to preserve and enhance the multicultural heritage of Canadians while working to achieve the equality of all Canadians."

A widely held assumption is that the cultural diversity of Canadians is translating into increasing religious diversity, as people arriving from other countries bring with them an array of different religions. Data from Canada's latest national census calls such an assumption into question.

The statistical gathering body of the Canadian government, known as *Statistics Canada*, carries out a major national census in the second year of each new decade that includes the item "What is your religion?" The question has been asked dating back to the first national census in 1871. Select runs of the 1991 census data that

Source: R. W. Bibby. 2000. "Canada's Mythical Religious Mosaic: Some Census Findings." *Journal for the Scientific Study of Religion*, 39(2), 235–39.

shed some important light on religious identification patterns among culturally diverse Canadians were made available to the author in 1996. What follows is a brief summary of key findings relating to religious identification and some of its key family- and cultural-group correlates.

RELIGIOUS IDENTIFICATION

The 1991 census found that 88% of Canadians continue to "think" that they are Catholic (46%), Protestant (36%), or adherents of Other Faiths (6%). An examination of religious identification over time shows that the proportion of the population who regard themselves as Catholics has remained fairly constant over time, while the proportion who identify themselves as Protestants has declined. The overall "Christian" total, including Eastern Orthodox, was 98% in 1871, 96% in 1931, and 84% in 1991. The remaining 16% of the populace consists primarily of those who report they have no religion (12%); this category only became a methodological possibility in 1971 through the introduction of self-enumeration. Over time, the Jewish total has remained a constant 1%, while those identifying with Other Faiths (including, in Statistics Canada's classification scheme, atheists and agnostics) has increased only marginally, from 2% to 3%.

THE ROLE OF THE FAMILY IN TRANSMITTING RELIGIOUS IDENTIFICATION

The key source of religious identification continues to be parents. People who marry partners of the same faith are inclined to pass that faith on to their children—reporting in the census that their children have the same religious identification as they do. This intergenerational pattern also holds in the case of cohabitation, as well as for the offspring of both female and male lone parents. It also is equally true in situations where parents do not identify with any religion.

Where there are exceptions to the rule, parents usually indicate that their children see themselves as having no religion. However, in the Other Faith and No Religion parental instances, some "switching" of offspring to Catholicism or Protestantism is acknowledged—2% to 4% by Other Faith and No Religion couples and, among lone parent "nones," 6% by females and 12% by males.

To the extent that identification changes, a key variable appears to be intermarriage and "intercohabitation." Catholics in particular, along with Protestants, tend to be the big winners numerically when relationships cross religious lines, while the "No Religion" category and other religious groups tend to experience significant net losses. The reasons are fairly straightforward. When people of different religions marry or cohabit, the religion of women predominates, even in the case of women who have no religious preference. Women in such relationships tend to raise their children in their own tradition, and are matched only by men when Catholic men marry Protestant women. A very important singular exception to this pattern is when women with Other Faith preferences intermarry: in such cases, they—along with Other Faith men—are inclined to raise their children in *their partner's* tradition.

The most numerous intermarriage and "intercohabitation" arrangements involve Catholic and Protestant women, who in effect "recruit" large numbers of offspring at the expense of the "No Religion" and Other Faith categories. These gains offset the frequent losses that occur when Catholic and Protestant men become involved with women who have no religious preference. Yet Catholic and Protestant men typically "add" offspring when they marry or cohabit with women who identify with other world faiths.

CULTURAL GROUP AFFINITIES

As a result of such intermarriage patterns, Christianity continues to be overwhelmingly dominant in Canada. Despite the stimulus of immigration,

TABLE 55.1 Religious Identification of Canadians, 1871–1991

	1871	1901	1931	1961	1991
Identification					
Catholic	42%	42	41	47	46
Protestant	56	56	54	49	36
Eastern Orthodox	<1	<1	1	1	2
Jewish	<1	<1	1	1	1
Other Faiths	2	2	2	1	3
No Religion	<1	<1	<1	<1	12

other major world religions are having considerable difficulty making significant numerical inroads in Canada.

The 1991 census reveals that some 65 to 75% of the affiliates of Islam, Buddhism, Hinduism, and Sikhism are immigrants, compared to about 13% in the case of both Catholics and Protestants. The census further shows that less than 2% of Canadians of British, French, German, and Italian origins *combined* are identifying with religions other than Christianity. Individuals who are identifying with Islam, Buddhism, Hinduism, and Sikhism are primarily people with Middle East and Asian cultural roots. Affiliates with European backgrounds do not exceed 3% in any of these faith instances.

In order to sustain their numbers and grow, faith groups such as these have to be able to replace their aging immigrants with offspring (birth) and resident Canadians (proselytism). To date there is little indication that such demographic developments are occurring in the numbers required.

Asian includes Middle East, South Asian, East Asian; European includes British, French, and other Western European.

For a complete listing of affiliation figures for all religious groups, broken down by province, gender, age, education, ethnicity, and language, see Statistics Canada, *Religions in Canada,* Ottawa: Science and Technology Canada, 1993. 1991 Census of Canada, Catalogue Number 93-319.

Smaller religions in the "Other Faith" category are faring even worse. For all the media hype about disenchanted and disaffiliated Canadians turning to a wide range of religious options in the last half of this century—what sociologists dub "new religions" or "para-religious groups"—the census reveals that relatively few people are actually identifying with the available alternatives. In a nation of close to 30 million people, less than 5,000 individuals are identifying with religions including New Age, Scientology, and Theosophy. Such data suggest that Canada has an extremely tight "religious market" dominated by Catholic

TABLE 55.2 Religious Identification of Children* by Parental Identification and Marital Status

Parental Identification	Married Partner Same	Common-Law Partner Same	Female Lone Parent	Male Lone Parent
Catholic	99%	95	93	94
Protestant	95	87	87	85
Eastern Orthodox	98	98	82	85
Jewish	99	97	95	88
Other Faiths	94	89	86	57
No Religion	98	97	94	88

*As reported by parents for children living at home.

TABLE 55.3 Religious Identification of Children by Religious Identification of Mothers and Fathers

Religion of Mother/Father	No. of Couples	Religion of Children						
		Catholic	Protestant	Eastern Orthodox	Jewish	Other Faiths	No Religion	Totals**
Catholic/Protestant	259,130	70%	11	*	*	*	9	100
Protestant/Catholic	254,105	42	44	*	*	*	14	100
Catholic/East Orthodox	12,735	54	1	39	*	*	6	100
East Orthodox/Catholic	8,625	62	4	28	*	*	7	101
Catholic/Jewish	3,070	38	2	*	25	*	35	100
Jewish/Catholic	2,055	28	1	1	45	*	25	100
Catholic/Other Faiths	7,600	57	1	*	*	21	20	99
Other Faiths/Catholic	3,195	58	4	*	*	12	26	100
Catholic/No Religion	82,745	67	3	*	*	*	30	100
No Religion/Catholic	35,050	40	3	*	*	*	57	100
Protestant/East Orthodox	10,300	2	55	29	*	*	14	100
East Orthodox/Protestant	6,595	4	47	36	*	*	13	101
Protestant/Jewish	3,555	2	38	*	26	*	34	100
Jewish/Protestant	2,520	1	23	*	52	*	24	100
Protestant/Other Faiths	5,735	1	45	*	*	26	28	100
Other Faiths/Protestant	3,220	2	42	*	*	26	29	99
Protestant/No Religion	126,935	1	58	*	*	*	41	100
No Religion/Protestant	35,115	2	27	*	*	*	71	100
Other Faiths/No Religion	4,415	3	5	*	*	22	70	100
No Religion/Jewish	1,225	2	6	*	29	*	62	99
No Religion/Other faiths	2,365	5	4	*	*	22	70	101

*Less than 1%.
**Because of rounding on the part of Statistics Canada, some totals do not equal 100.

and Protestant "companies." New entries find the going extremely tough.

DISCUSSION

The net result of these patterns of socialization and switching is that the vast majority of Canadians are continuing to identify with the numerically dominant Christian groups. Demographically at 82% strong, Catholics and Protestants have a large numerical advantage over other religious groups when it comes to issues of cultural maintenance and intermarriage. Even with a national policy of multiculturalism, smaller cultural and religious groups find themselves absorbing many parts of the dominant ways of life in this country. In the case of socialization and marriage, groups whose members typically comprise less than 1% of the national population usually find that their children befriend, date, and frequently marry people from

other cultural and religious groups. Apparent gains through increased immigration are neutralized by assimilation.

Numerically dominant Catholics and Protestants who marry and live with people of other religious persuasions tend to experience net gains when it comes to the religious identification of offspring. It needs to be emphasized that the key issue is not whether or not the partner "converts" to the other's faith; what is more important, numerically speaking, is how the children are raised. And here the patterns are fairly clear: the religion of the woman dominates. Given the large Catholic and Protestant numbers, the end result is that the population tends to gravitate toward Catholic and Protestant identifications.

This pattern is particularly evident when Catholics and Protestants marry people of Other Faiths, excluding Judaism. Regardless of whether the Other Faith partner is female or male, the inclination is for the ensuing offspring to be raised

TABLE 55.4   Cultural Group Origins of Affiliates of Select World Religions

Cultural Group Origin*	World Religions				
	Islam	*Buddhist*	*Hindu*	*Sikh*	*Totals*
Total - Single Origin	90%	93	90	94	91
Asian Regions	75	89	77	91	81
European	3	3	2	2	3
Other Countries	12	1	11	1	7
Total - Multiple Origins	10	7	10	6	9
Grand Total	100	100	100	100	100

*The census differentiates between "single origin" where only one national group heritage is cited, versus more than one.

as Catholics or Protestants—or No Religion. Put bluntly, most smaller groups are losing many of their children and grandchildren to the Catholic and Protestant traditions. Alternately, they do not affiliate with any group.

It's true that there has been an increase in recent decades in the number of people arriving from countries where other world faiths are dominant. It also is true that widespread secularization has led to a decline in individual participation and organizational influence. Nonetheless, the vast majority of Canadians in the 90s continue to "think" they are Catholic or Protestant, and "think" that they are raising "Catholic" and "Protestant" children. Other world religions are having difficulty growing, due to both the tendency of their children to "defect" to Christian groups and their inability to recruit "outsiders." Even the Religion Nones are showing a net loss to the "somethings" when intermarriage and intercohabitation occur—if not immediately, then intergenerationally.

Secularization may have drastically reduced the influence that Catholic and Protestant groups have in Canada. But tradition and assimilation appear to function to keep identification with Christianity at a very high level. From the standpoint of numbers, the heralded emerging religious mosaic, so far at least, is largely a myth.

CRITICAL THINKING QUESTIONS

1. Given that Canadian law, as embodied in the *Multiculturalism Act* (1988), confirms the national support for cultural diversity, were you surprised to find out that Christian faiths continue to enjoy such a monopoly? As a sociologist, how would you explain such stability in religious faith over time?

2. With reference to the article, what influences do *intermarriage* and *intercohabitation* have on parents' decisions regarding the religious tradition in which to raise their children?

3. Bibby suggests that although secularization is diminishing the influence of religion in people's lives, religion is still identified as an important element by many of today's families. Do you see the influence of religion increasing or decreasing over the next hundred years? Why?

56

Women and Islam

JANE I. SMITH

Many Westerners have a vague notion that women in Iran, Saudi Arabia, and other Islamic societies are subject to relentless control by men. Although there is some truth to this stereotype, a more realistic account of the relationship between Islam and gender must begin with a basic understanding of this unfamiliar religion. In this article, Jane Smith provides an overview of Islamic tenets, explores some of the variations that divide the vast Islamic world, and assesses the relative social standing of the sexes—as Muslims themselves understand it.

To attempt to talk about women in Islam is of course to venture into an area fraught with the perils of overgeneralization, oversimplification, and the almost unavoidable limitations of a Western bias. The first problem is simply one of raw numbers. There are perhaps close to half a billion Muslim women inhabiting all major areas of the world today. Is it possible to say anything that holds true for all of them, let alone for their sisters over the past fourteen centuries of Islam?

Then one must consider all the various elements that comprise the picture of Islamic womanhood. Many of these elements are directly related to the religion of Islam itself, such as past and present legal realities, roles permitted and enforced as a result of Muslim images of women, and the variety of Islamic and hetero-Islamic rites

Source: Reprinted by permission from *Women in World Religions* by Arvind Sharma (ed.), the State University of New York Press © 1987, State University of New York. All rights reserved.

and practices in which Islamic women have traditionally participated. Other elements contributing to the full picture of women in Islam—such as education, political rights, professional employment opportunities, and the like—have less to do with the religion per se but are still influenced by it.

The Holy Qur'ān (sometimes transliterated as "Koran") still forms the basis of prevailing family law in most areas of the Muslim world. It has always been and still is considered to be the last in a series of divine revelations from God given in the seventh century C.E. to humanity through the vehicle of his final prophet Muhammad. The Qur'ān is therefore the literal and unmitigated word of God, collected and ordered by the young Muslim community but untainted with the thoughts and interpretations of any persons, including Muhammad himself. It is obvious, then, why the regulations formulated by the Qur'ān in regard to women have been adhered to with strictness and why changes in Muslim family law are coming about only very slowly in the Islamic world.

The circumstances of women in pre-Islamic Arabia are subject to a variety of interpretations. On the one hand, certain women—soothsayers, priestesses, queens, and even singular individuals—did play powerful roles in society. On the other hand, whatever the earlier realities for women in terms of marriage, divorce, and inheritance of property, it is clear that the Qur'ān did introduce very significant changes that were advantageous for women. Contemporary Muslims are fond of pointing out, quite correctly, that Islam brought legal advantages for women quite unknown in corresponding areas of the Western Christian world. What, then, does the Qur'ān say about women?

The earliest messages of the Qur'ān, and the twin themes that run through all the chapters, are of the realities of the oneness of God and the inevitability of the day of judgment. All persons, men and women, are called upon to testify to those realities. . . . Religiously speaking, then, men and women are fully equal in the eyes of God according to the Qur'ān.

Before looking at the specifics of the legal injunctions for women, it is necessary to consider two verses that have caused a great deal of consternation to Westerners. One is 2:228, which says literally that men are a step above women, and the other is 4:34, clarifying that men are the protectors of women (or are in charge of women) because God has given preference to one over the other and because men provide support for women. Perhaps because these verses have been so troublesome for non-Muslims (especially feminists), they have been subject to an enormous amount of explanation and interpretation by contemporary Muslim apologists eager to present a defense of their religion. These writers, men and women, affirm that it is precisely because men are invested with the responsibility of taking care of women, financially and otherwise, that they are given authority over the females of their families. And that, affirm many Muslim women today, is exactly the way it should be. We will return to this perspective later, particularly in light of what a desire for liberation means—and does not mean—for many Muslim women. . . .

According to the Qur'ān, a man may marry up to four wives, so long as he is able to provide for each equally. He may marry a Muslim woman or a member of the Jewish or Christian faith, or a slave woman. A Muslim woman, however, may marry only one husband, and he must be a Muslim. Contemporary Muslim apologists are quick to point out that these restrictions are for the benefit of women, ensuring that they will not be left unprotected. In Islam, marriage is not a sacrament but a legal contract, and according to the Qur'ān a woman has clearly defined legal rights in negotiating this contract. She can dictate the terms and can receive the dowry herself. This dowry (*mahr*) she is permitted to keep and maintain as a source of personal pride and comfort.

Polygamy (or more strictly polygyny, plurality of wives) is practiced by only a small percentage of the contemporary Muslim population, and a man with more than two wives is extremely rare. Many countries are now taking steps to modify the circumstances in which a husband may take more than one wife, although only in two countries, Turkey and Tunisia, are multiple marriages actually illegal. Other countries have made such moves as requiring the husband to have the permission of the court (as in Iraq and Syria) or to get the permission of the first wife (as in Egypt), or permitting the wife to write into her marriage contract that she will not allow a cowife (as in Morocco and Lebanon). It seems reasonable to expect that other countries will make changes and modifications. It is interesting to note that while for some finances have dictated monogamy—most husbands have simply not been able to afford more than one wife—changing economic realities may again dictate that a man contemplate the possibility of having several wives to work and supply income for the family.

Muslim women traditionally have been married at an extremely young age, sometimes even before puberty. This practice is related, of course, to the historical fact that fathers and other male relatives generally have chosen the grooms themselves, despite the guarantee of the Qur'ān that marriage is a contract into which male and female enter equally. While it is true that technically a girl cannot be forced into a marriage she does not want, pressures from family and the youth of the bride often have made this prerogative difficult to exercise. Today, the right of a male member of the family to contract an engagement for a girl against her wishes has been legally revoked in most places, although it is still a common practice, especially in rural areas. . . .

In the contemporary Islamic world, divorce rates vary considerably from one country to the next. Muslim apologists insist that divorce is not nearly as common in Islamic countries as it is, for example, in the United States. This statement is generally true, although in some countries, such as Morocco, the rate is high and continues to grow. Often what is really only the breaking of the engagement contract is included in divorce statistics, skewing the measure. Many countries are now considering serious changes in divorce procedures. The simultaneous triple repudiation generally has been declared illegal, and in many countries divorce initiated by either party, the man or the woman, must take place in the court of law. Other countries add special stipulations generally favorable to the woman. It remains true, however, that men can divorce for less cause than women, and often divorces hung up in courts with male judges can prove enormously difficult for women to gain.

In accordance with Islamic law, custody of the children traditionally has gone to the father at some time between the age of seven and nine for boys and between seven and puberty for girls, depending on the legal school. This practice too is slowly changing, and in most areas women who have been divorced by their husbands are allowed to keep their sons until puberty and their daughters until they are of an age to be married.

It is considered one of the great innovations of the Qur'ān over earlier practices that women are permitted to inherit and own property. Non-Muslims have generally found great difficulty with the Qur'ānic stipulation that a woman is allowed to inherit property but that the inheritance should be only half that of a male. According to the Islamic understanding, however, the rationale is precisely that which applies to the verse saying that men are in charge of women. Because women are permitted to keep and maintain their own property without responsibility for taking care of their families financially, it is only reasonable that the male, who must spend his own earning and inheritance for the maintenance of women, should receive twice as much. . . .

According to the Qur'ān, women should not expose themselves to public view with lack of modesty. It does not say that they should be covered specifically from head to toe, nor that they should wear face veils or masks or other of the paraphernalia that has adorned many Islamic women through the ages. The Qur'ān also suggests that the wives of the Prophet Muhammad, when speaking to other men, should do so from behind a partition, again for purposes of propriety. It has been open to question whether this statement is meant to apply to all women. In the early Islamic community, these verses were exaggerated and their underlying ideas elaborated and defined in ways that led fairly quickly to a seclusion of women which seems quite at odds with what the Qur'ān intended or the Prophet wanted. When the community in Medina was established, women participated fully with men in all activities of worship and prayer. Soon they became segregated, however, to the point where an often-quoted *hadith* (no doubt spurious) attributed to Muhammad has him saying that women pray better at home than in the mosque, and best of all in their own closets. Today a number of contemporary Muslim writers are urging a return to the practices of the young Muslim community, with women no longer segregated from the mosque or relegated to certain rear or side portions as they generally have been, but participating fully in worship with men. . . .

What is popularly known as "veiling" is part of the general phenomenon of the segregation of women and yet is also distinctly apart from it. The two are increasingly seen as separate by contemporary Islamic women seeking to affirm a new identity in relation to their religion. Veils traditionally have taken a number of forms: a veil covering the face from just below the eyes down; a *chador* or *burka* covering the entire body, including the face, often with a woven screen in front through which women can see but not be seen; and a full face mask with small slits through the eyes, still worn in some areas of the Arabian Gulf. These costumes, so seemingly oppressive to Western eyes, at least have allowed women to observe without being observed, thus affording their wearers a degree of anonymity that on some occasions has proven useful.

The general movement toward unveiling had its ostensible beginning in the mid-1920s, when the Egyptian feminist Huda Sha'rawi cast off her veil after arriving in Egypt from an international meeting of women. She was followed literally and symbolically by masses of women in the succeeding years, and Egyptian women as well as those in other Middle Eastern countries made great strides in adopting Western dress. At the present time in the history of Islam, however, one finds a quite different phenomenon. Partly in reaction against Western liberation and Western ideals in general, women in many parts of the Islamic world are self-consciously adopting forms of dress by which they can identify with Islam rather than with what they now see as the imperialist West. Islamic dress, generally chosen by Muslim women themselves rather than forced upon them by males, signals for many an identification with a way of life that they are increasingly convinced represents a more viable alternative than that offered by the West. . . .

We see, then, that while legal circumstances for women have undergone some significant changes in the past half-century, the dictates of the Qur'ān continue to be enormously influential in the molding of new laws as well as in the personal choices of Muslim men and women. . . .

I have stressed here the insistence of the Qur'ān on the religious and spiritual equality of men and women. And aside from some unfortunate *hadith* with very weak chains of authority suggesting that the majority of women will be in the Fire on the Day of Judgment because of their mental and physical inferiority, religious literature in general, when talking about human responsibility and concomitant judgment, makes women full partners with men under the divine command to live lives of integrity and righteousness. . . .

Of course, women do participate in many of the activities and duties considered incumbent on all good Muslims, but generally these practices have a somewhat different function for them than for men. Prayer for women, as we have said, is usually in the home rather than in the mosque, and does not necessarily follow the pattern of the regularized five times a day. Participation in the fast itself is normally the same as for the men (except when women are pregnant, nursing, or menstruating), but the particular joys of preparing the fast-breaking meals are for the women alone. While the husband determines the amount of money or goods to be distributed for almsgiving, another responsibility of all Muslims, it is often the wife who takes charge of the actual distribution.

The last duty incumbent on Muslims after the testimony to the oneness of God and prophethood of his apostle Muhammad, the prayer, the fast, and paying the almstax is the pilgrimage once in a lifetime to the holy city of Mecca. Women do participate in this journey, and as transportation becomes easier and the care provided for pilgrims in Saudi Arabia becomes more regularized with modernization, increasing numbers of females join the throngs which gather to circumambulate the Xaaba at Mecca each year. . . .

Saints in Islam are both male and female. One is normally recognized as a saint not by any process of canonization but because of some miraculous deed(s) performed or through a dream communication after death with a living person requesting that a shrine be erected over his or her tomb. Often a woman is favored with these dreams and after the construction of the shrine she becomes the carekeeper of the tomb, a position of some honor and responsibility. . . .

While women in the Islamic world have been segregated and secluded, and historically have been considered second-class citizens by the vast majority of males in the community, they have not been totally without power. They have been able to maintain a degree of control over their own lives and over the men with whom they live through many of the religious practices described above. The fact that they alone have the ability to bear children, the influence they continue to play in the lives of their sons, and the power they have over their sons' wives are subtle indications that there are certain checks and balances on the obvious authority invested by the Qur'ān in men. From sexuality to control of the network of communications in the family to manipulation of such external agencies as spirits and supernatural beings, women have had at their control a variety of means to exert their will over the men in their families and over their own circumstances. The subtle means of control available to women throughout the world have of course been exploited: withholding sexual favors (a questionable but often-quoted *hadith* says that if a woman refuses to sleep with her husband, the angels will curse her until the morning), doing small things to undermine a husband's honor such as embarrassing him in front of guests, indulging in various forms of gossip and social control, and the like. . . .

Until fairly recently, education for women in the Muslim world has been minimal. Girls were given the rudiments of an Islamic education, mainly a little instruction in the Qur'ān and the traditions so as to be able to recite their prayers properly. Beyond that their training was not academic but domestic. In the late nineteenth and early twentieth centuries, Islamic leaders awoke with a start to the reality that Muslims were significantly behind the West in a variety of ways, including technology and the education necessary to understand and develop it. Many of these leaders recognized that if Islamic nations were to compete successfully in the contemporary world, it had to be with the aid of a well-educated and responsible female sector. Thus, this century has seen a number of educational advances for women, and in some countries, such as Egypt, Iraq, and Kuwait, women constitute very significant numbers of the university population. Nonetheless, illiteracy in many Muslim nations continues to be high, and the gap between male and female literacy rates is even increasing in some areas. In Saudi Arabia, where at present the economic resources are certainly available, large numbers of Saudi girls are receiving a full education, though separated from boys, and are taught either by men through television transmission or by women.

In education as in most areas of life, the male understanding of women as encouraged by certain parts of the Islamic tradition continues to play an important role. The Qur'ān does state, along with the stipulation that women can inherit only half of what men inherit, that the witness (in the court of law) of one man is equal to that of two women. This unfortunately has been interpreted by some in the history of Islam to mean that women are intellectually inferior to men, unstable in their judgment, and too easily swayed by emotion. Such perspectives are certainly not shared by all but nonetheless have been influential (and in some places are increasingly so today) in making it difficult for a woman to have access to the same kinds of educational opportunities that are available to men. Certain subjects are deemed "appropriate" for a woman to study, particularly those geared to make her the best and most productive wife, mother, and female participant in the family structure.

The prevalent view, confirmed by the Qur'ān, is that women should be modest and should neither expose themselves to men nor be too much in public places, where they will be subject to men's observation or forced to interact with males not in their immediate families. This view obviously has contributed to the difficulties of receiving a full education and of securing employment outside the home. More employment opportunities are open to women today than in the past, however, and in many countries women hold high-level positions in business, government, civil service, education, and other sectors. Statistics differ greatly across the Islamic world and are difficult to assess because they often fail to take into account the rural woman who may work full time in the fields or other occupation outside the house but does not earn an independent salary. . . .

Saudi Arabia presents an interesting case study of the confrontation of Islamic ideas with contemporary reality. Women are greatly inhibited in the labor arena; because of conservative religious attitudes they must be veiled and covered, are not permitted to drive or even ride in a taxi with a strange man, and in general are unable to participate on the social and professional level with males. However, in a country in which production is both necessary and economically possible and which suffers from a lack of manpower, the use of women in the workforce or increased importation of foreign labor seem the only two (both undesirable) alternatives. Thus more Saudi women are working, and because of their right to inherit, are accumulating very substantial amounts of money. It is interesting to note the rapid rate of construction of new banks exclusively for women in places like Jiddah and Riyadh.

The aforementioned Qur'ān verse about the witness of two women being equal to that of one man and the supporting literature attesting to female intellectual, physical (and in fact sometimes moral) inferiority have made it difficult for Muslim women to achieve equal political rights. In most Arab countries (except Saudi Arabia and certain of the Gulf States), as well as in most other parts of the Islamic world, women have now been given the vote. Centuries of passivity in the political realm, however, have made it difficult for women to take advantage of the opportunities now available to them. In some countries, such as Egypt, women are playing major political roles, but generally women politicians find little support from men or even from other women for their aspirations. This is not to underestimate the strong current in Islamic thinking which encourages the full participation of women in politics, as well as in the educational and professional fields.

Like an intricate and complex geometric pattern on a Persian rug or a frieze decorating a mosque, the practices, roles, opportunities, prescriptions, hopes, and frustrations of Islamic women are woven together in a whole. The colors are sometimes bold and striking, at other times muted and subtle. Some contemporary Muslim women are progressive and aggressive, no longer content to fit the traditionally prescribed patterns. Others are passive and accepting, not yet able to discern what new possibilities may be open to them, let alone whether or not they might want to take advantage of such opportunities. Some are Westernized as their mothers and grandmothers were and have every intention of staying that way, while others are increasingly clear in their feelings that the West does not have the answers and that Islam, particularly the Islam of the Qur'ān and the community of the Prophet Muhammad, is God's chosen way for humankind. For the latter, their dress, their relationships with their husbands and families, and their verbal assent to Islamic priorities reflect this conviction that the time has come to cease a fruitless preoccupation with things Western and to reaffirm their identity as Muslim women.

It is difficult for Western feminists to grasp exactly what the Muslim woman may mean by "liberation." For many Islamic women, the fruits of liberation in the West are too many broken marriages, women left without the security of men who will provide for them, deteriorating relations between men and women, and sexual license that appears as rank immorality. They see the Islamic system as affirmed by the Qur'ān as one in which male authority over them ensures their care and protection and provides a structure in which the family is solid, children are inculcated with lasting values, and the balance of responsibility between man and woman is one in which absolute equality is less highly prized than cooperation and complementarity.

The new Islamic woman, then, is morally and religiously conservative and affirms the absolute value of the true Islamic system for human relationships. She is intolerant of the kind of Islam in which women are subjugated and relegated to roles insignificant to the full functioning of society, and she wants to take full advantage of educational and professional opportunities. She may agree, however, that certain fields of education are more appropriate for women than others, and that certain professions are more natural to males than to females. She participates as a contributor to and decisionmaker for the family, yet recognizes that in any complex relationship final authority must rest with one person. And she is content to delegate that authority to her husband, father, or other male relative in return for the solidarity of the family structure and the support and protection that it gives her and her children.

That not all, or even most, Muslim women subscribe to this point of view is clear. And yet, at the time of this writing, it seems equally clear that if Western observers are to understand women in the contemporary Islamic world, they must appreciate a point of view that is more and more prevalent. The West is increasingly identified with imperialism, and solutions viable for women in the Islamic community are necessarily different from the kinds of solutions that many Western women seem to have chosen for themselves. For the Muslim the words of the Qur'ān are divine, and the prescriptions for the roles and rights of females, like the other messages of the holy book, are seen as part of God's divinely ordered plan for all humanity. Change will come slowly, and whatever kinds of liberation ultimately prevail will be cloaked in a garb that is—in one or another of its various aspects—essentially Islamic.

CRITICAL THINKING QUESTIONS

1. In what formal ways does Islam confer on men authority over women?

2. In what formal and informal ways does Islam give power to women to affect their own lives and those of men?

3. From a Muslim perspective, what are some of the problems with Western living and, particularly, Western feminism?

57

Education and Inequality

SAMUEL BOWLES AND HERBERT GINTIS

Education

CLASSIC

CONTEMPORARY

CROSS-CULTURAL

Education has long been held to be a means to realizing U.S. ideals of equal opportunity. As Lester Ward notes at the beginning of this selection, the promise of education is to allow "natural" abilities to win out over the "artificial" inequalities of class, race, and sex. Samuel Bowles and Herbert Gintis claim that this has happened very little in the United States. Rather, they argue, schooling has more to do with maintaining existing social hierarchy.

Universal education is the power, which is destined to overthrow every species of hierarchy. It is destined to remove all artificial inequality and leave the natural inequalities to find their true level. With the artificial inequalities of caste, rank, title, blood, birth, race, color, sex, etc., will fall nearly all the oppression, abuse, prejudice, enmity, and injustice, that humanity is now subject to.

—Lester Frank Ward, *Education*, 1872

A review of educational history hardly supports the optimistic pronouncements of liberal educational theory. The politics of education are better understood

Source: From *Schooling in Capitalist America: Educational Reform and the Contradictions of Economic Life* by Samuel Bowles and Herbert Gintis. Copyright © 1976 by Basic Books, Inc. (Includes Fig. 1, p. 436). Reprinted with permission.

in terms of the need for social control in an unequal and rapidly changing economic order. The founders of the modern U.S. school system understood that the capitalist economy produces great extremes of wealth and poverty, of social elevation and degradation. Horace Mann and other school reformers of the antebellum period knew well the seamy side of the burgeoning industrial and urban centers. "Here," wrote Henry Barnard, the first state superintendent of education in both Connecticut and Rhode Island, and later to become the first U.S. Commissioner of Education, "the wealth, enterprise and professional talent of the state are concentrated ... but here also are poverty, ignorance, profligacy and irreligion, and the classification of society as broad and deep as ever divided the plebeian and patrician of ancient Rome."[1] They lived in a world in which, to use de Tocqueville's words, ". . . small aristocratic societies . . . are formed by some manufacturers in the midst of the immense democracy of our age [in which] . . . some men are opulent and a multitude . . . are wretchedly poor."[2] The rapid rise of the factory system, particularly in New England, was celebrated by the early school reformers; yet, the alarming transition from a relatively simple rural society to a highly stratified industrial economy could not be ignored. They shared the fears that de Tocqueville had expressed following his visit to the United States in 1831:

When a workman is unceasingly and exclusively engaged in the fabrication of one thing, he ultimately does his work with singular dexterity; but at the same time he loses the general faculty of applying his mind to the direction of the work. . . . [While] the science of manufacture lowers the class of workmen, it raises the class of masters. . . . [If] ever a permanent inequality of conditions . . . again penetrates into the world, it may be predicted that this is the gate by which they will enter.[3]

While deeply committed to the emerging industrial order, the farsighted school reformers of the mid-nineteenth century understood the explosive potential of the glaring inequalities of factory life. Deploring the widening of social divisions and fearing increasing unrest, Mann, Barnard, and others proposed educational expansion and reform. In his Fifth Report as Secretary of the Massachusetts Board of Education, Horace Mann wrote:

Education, then[,] beyond all other devices of human origin, is the great equalizer of the conditions of men—the balance wheel of the social machinery. . . . It does better than to disarm the poor of their hostility toward the rich; it prevents being poor.[4]

Mann and his followers appeared to be at least as interested in disarming the poor as in preventing poverty. They saw in the spread of universal and free education a means of alleviating social distress without redistributing wealth and power or altering the broad outlines of the economic system. Education, it seems, had almost magical powers:

The main idea set forth in the creeds of some political reformers, or revolutionizers, is that some people are poor because others are rich. This idea supposed a fixed amount of property in the community . . . and the problem presented for solution is how to transfer a portion of this property from those who are supposed to have too much to those who feel and know that they have too little. At this point, both their theory and their expectation of reform stop. But the beneficent power of education would not be exhausted, even though it should peaceably abolish all the miseries that spring from the coexistence, side by side, of enormous wealth and squalid want. It has a higher function. Beyond the power of diffusing old wealth, it has the prerogative of creating new.[5]

The early educators viewed the poor as the foreign element that they were. Mill hands were recruited throughout New England, often disrupting the small towns in which textile and other rapidly growing industries had located. Following the Irish potato famine of the 1840s, thousands of Irish workers settled in the cities and towns of the northeastern United States. Schooling was seen as a means of integrating this "uncouth and dangerous" element into the social fabric of American life. The inferiority of the foreigner was taken for granted. The editors of the influential *Massachusetts Teacher*, a leader in the educational reform movement, writing in 1851, saw ". . . the increasing influx of foreigners . . ." as a moral and social problem:

Will it, like the muddy Missouri, as it pours its waters into the clear Mississippi and contaminates the whole united mass, spread ignorance and vice, crime and disease, through our native population?

If . . . we can by any means purify this foreign people, enlighten their ignorance and bring them up to our level, we shall perform a work of true and perfect charity, blessing the giver and receiver in equal measure. . . .

With the old not much can be done; but with their children, the great remedy is *education*. The rising generation must be taught as our own children are taught. We say *must be* because in many cases this can only be accomplished by coercion.[6]

Since the mid-nineteenth century the dual objectives of educational reformers—equality of opportunity and social control—have been intermingled, the merger of these two threads sometimes so nearly complete that it becomes impossible to distinguish between the two. Schooling has been at once something done for the poor and to the poor.

The basic assumptions which underlay this commingling help explain the educational reform movement's social legacy. First, educational reformers did not question the fundamental economic institutions of capitalism: Capitalist ownership and control of the means of production and dependent wage labor were taken for granted. In fact, education was to help preserve and extend the capitalist order. The function of the school system was to accommodate workers to its most rapid possible development. Second, it was assumed that people (often classes of people or "races") are differentially equipped by nature or social origins to occupy the varied economic and social levels in the class structure. By providing equal opportunity, the school system was to elevate the masses, guiding them sensibly and fairly to the manifold political, social, and economic roles of adult life.

Jefferson's educational thought strikingly illustrates this perspective. In 1779, he proposed a two-track educational system which would prepare individuals for adulthood in one of the two classes of society: the "laboring and the learned."[7] Even children of the laboring class would qualify for leadership. Scholarships would allow ". . . those persons whom nature hath endowed with genius and virtue . . ." to ". . . be rendered by liberal education worthy to receive and able to guard the sacred deposit of the rights and liberties of their fellow citizens."[8] Such a system, Jefferson asserted, would succeed in ". . . raking a few geniuses from the rubbish."[9] Jefferson's two-tiered educational plan presents in stark relief the outlines and motivation for the stratified structure of U.S. education which has endured up to the present. At the top, there is the highly selective aristocratic tradition, the elite university training future leaders. At the base is mass education for all, dedicated to uplift and control. The two traditions have always coexisted although their meeting point has drifted upward over the years, as mass education has spread upward from elementary school through high school, and now up to the post-high-school level.

Though schooling was consciously molded to reflect the class structure, education was seen as a means of enhancing wealth and morality, which would work to the advantage of all. Horace Mann, in his 1842 report to the State Board of Education, reproduced this comment by a Massachusetts industrialist:

The great majority always have been and probably always will be comparatively poor, while a few will possess the greatest share of this world's goods. And it is a wise provision of Providence which connects so intimately, and as I think so indissolubly, the greatest good of the many with the highest interests in the few.[10]

Much of the content of education over the past century and a half can only be construed as an unvarnished attempt to persuade the "many" to make the best of the inevitable.

The unequal contest between social control and social justice is evident in the total functioning of U.S. education. The system as it stands today provides eloquent testimony to the ability of the well-to-do to perpetuate in the name of equality of opportunity an arrangement which consistently yields to themselves the aspirations and advantages, while thwarting the aspirations and needs of the working people of the United States. However grating this judgment may sound to the ears of the undaunted optimist, it is by no means excessive in light of the massive statistical data on inequality in the United States. Let us look at the contemporary evidence.

We may begin with the basic issue of inequalities in the years of schooling. As can be seen in Figure 57.1, the number of years of schooling attained by an individual is strongly associated with parental socioeconomic status. This figure presents the estimated distribution of years of schooling attained by individuals of varying

Figure 57.1 Educational Attainments Are Strongly Dependent on Social Background Even for People of Similar Childhood IQs

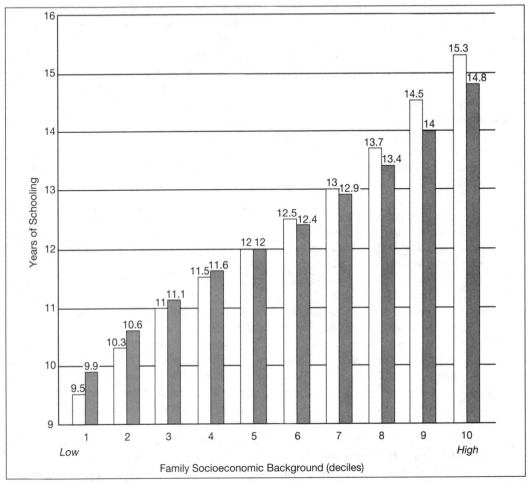

Notes: For each socioeconomic group, the left-hand bar indicates the estimated average number of years of schooling attained by all men from that group. The right-hand bar indicates the estimated average number of years of schooling attained by men with IQ scores equal to the average for the entire sample. The sample refers to "non-Negro" men of "nonfarm" backgrounds, aged 35–44 years in 1962.

Source: Samuel Bowles and Valerie Nelson, "The 'Inheritance of IQ' and the Intergenerational Transmission of Economic Inequality," *The Review of Economics and Statistics,* vol. LVI, no. 1 (Feb. 1974).

socioeconomic backgrounds. If we define socio-economic background by a weighted sum of income, occupation, and educational level of the parents, a child from the ninetieth percentile may expect, on the average, five more years of school-ing than a child in the tenth percentile.[11]

. . . We have chosen a sample of white males because the most complete statistics are available for this group. Moreover, if inequality for white males can be documented, the proposition is merely strengthened when sexual and racial differences are taken into account.

Additional census data dramatize one aspect of educational inequalities: the relationship between family income and college attendance. Even among those who had graduated from high school in the early 1960s, children of families earning less than $3,000 per year were over six times as likely *not* to attend college as were the children of families earning over $15,000.[12] Moreover, children from less well-off families are *both* less likely to have graduated from high school and more likely to attend inexpensive, two-year community colleges rather than a four-year B.A. program if they do make it to college.[13]

Not surprisingly, the results of schooling differ greatly for children of different social backgrounds. Most easily measured, but of limited importance, are differences in scholastic achievement. If we measure the output of schooling by scores on nationally standardized achievement tests, children whose parents were themselves highly educated outperform the children of parents with less education by a wide margin. Data collected for the U.S. Office of Education Survey of Educational Opportunity reveal, for example, that among white high-school seniors, those whose parents were in the top education decile were, on the average, well over three grade levels in measured scholastic achievement ahead of those whose parents were in the bottom decile.[14]

Given these differences in scholastic achievement, inequalities in years of schooling among individuals of different social backgrounds are to be expected. Thus one might be tempted to argue that the close dependence of years of schooling attained on background displayed in the left-hand bars of Figure 57.1 is simply a reflection of unequal intellectual abilities, or that inequalities in college attendance are the consequences of differing levels of scholastic achievement in high school and do not reflect any additional social class inequalities peculiar to the process of college admission.

This view, so comforting to the admissions personnel in our elite universities, is unsupported by the data, some of which is presented in the figure. The right-hand bars of Figure 57.1 indicate that even among children with identical IQ test scores at ages six and eight, those with rich, well-educated, high-status parents could expect a much higher level of schooling than those with less-favored origins. Indeed, the closeness of the left-hand and right-hand bars in the figure shows that only a small portion of the observed social class differences in educational attainment is related to IQ differences across social classes.[15] The dependence of education attained on background is almost as strong for individuals with the same IQ as for all individuals. Thus, while Figure 57.1 indicates that an individual in the ninetieth percentile in social class background is likely to receive five more years of education than an individual in the tenth percentile, it also indicates that he is likely to receive 4.25 more years schooling than an individual from the tenth percentile with the same IQ. Similar results are obtained when we look specifically at access to college education for students with the same measured IQ. Project Talent data indicates that for "high ability" students (top 25 percent as measured by a composite of tests of "general aptitude"), those of high socioeconomic background (top 25 percent as measured by a composite of family income, parents' education, and occupation) are nearly twice as likely to attend college than students of low socioeconomic background (bottom 25 percent). For "low ability" students (bottom 25 percent), those of high-social background are more than four times as likely to attend college as are their low-social background counterparts.[16]

Inequality in years of schooling is, of course, only symptomatic of broader inequalities in the educational system. Not only do less well-off children go to school for fewer years, they are treated with less attention (or more precisely, less benevolent attention) when they are there. These broader inequalities are not easily measured. Some show up in statistics on the different levels of expenditure for the education of children of different socioeconomic backgrounds. Taking account of the inequality in financial resources for each year in school and the inequality in years of schooling obtained, Jencks estimated that a child whose parents were in the top fifth of the income distribution receives roughly twice the educational resources in dollar terms as does a child whose parents are in the bottom fifth.[17]

The social class inequalities in our school system, then, are too evident to be denied. Defenders of the educational system are forced back on the assertion that things are getting better; the inequalities of the past were far worse. And, indeed, there can be no doubt that some of the inequalities of the past have been mitigated. Yet new inequalities have apparently developed to take their place, for the available historical evidence lends little support to the idea that our schools are on the road to equality of educational opportunity. For example, data from a recent U.S. Census survey reported in Spady indicate that graduation from college has become no less dependent on one's social background. This is true despite the fact that high-school graduation is becoming increasingly equal across social classes.[18] Additional data confirm this impression. The statistical association (coefficient of correlation) between parents' social status and years of education attained by individuals who completed their schooling three or four decades ago is virtually identical to the same correlation for individuals who terminated their schooling in recent years.[19] On balance, the available data suggests that the number of years of school attained by a child depends upon family background as much in the recent period as it did fifty years ago.

Thus, we have empirical reasons for doubting the egalitarian impact of schooling. . . . We conclude that U.S. education is highly unequal, the chances of attaining much or little schooling being substantially dependent on one's race and parents' economic level. Moreover, where there is a discernible trend toward a more equal educational system—as in the narrowing of the black education deficit, for example—the impact on the structure of economic opportunity is minimal at best.

CRITICAL THINKING QUESTIONS

1. Does Bowles and Gintis's description of the American education system apply to the Canadian system? How are the two systems similar? How are they different?

2. In what respects, according to Bowles and Gintis, has schooling supported the capitalist economic system? How have such supports shaped the content of the educational system?

3. What are Bowles and Gintis's conclusions about the relationship between schooling and natural ability? Between schooling and social background?

NOTES

1. H. Barnard, *Papers for the Teacher: 2nd Series* (New York: F. C. Brownell, 1866), pp. 293–310.

2. A. de Tocqueville, as quoted in Jeremy Brecher, *Strike!* (San Francisco: Straight Arrow Books, 1972), pp. xi, xii.

3. Ibid., p. 172.

4. Horace Mann as quoted in Michael Katz, ed., *School Reform Past and Present* (Boston: Little, Brown, 1971), p. 141.

5. Ibid., p. 145.

6. *The Massachusetts Teacher* (Oct., 1851), quoted in Katz, pp. 169–70.

7. D. Tyack, *Turning Points in American Educational History* (Waltham, MA: Blaisdell, 1967), p. 89.

8. Ibid., p. 10.

9. Ibid., p. 89.

10. Mann, quoted in Katz, p. 147.

11. This calculation is based on data reported in full in Samuel Bowles and Valerie Nelson, "The 'Inheritance of IQ' and the Intergenerational Transmission of Economic Inequality," *The Review of Economics and Statistics*, 56, 1 (Feb., 1974). It refers to non-Negro males from nonfarm backgrounds, aged 35–44 years. The zero-order correlation coefficient between socioeconomic background and years of schooling was estimated at 0.646. The estimated standard deviation of years of schooling was 3.02. The results for other age groups are similar.

12. These figures refer to individuals who were high-school seniors in October 1965, and who subsequently graduated from high school. College attendance refers to both two- and four-year institutions. Family income is for the twelve months preceding October 1965. Data is drawn from U.S. Bureau of the Census, *Current Population Reports*, Series P-60, No. 183 (May, 1969).

13. For further evidence, see ibid.; and Jerome Karabel, "Community Colleges and Social Stratification," *Harvard Educational Review*, 424, 42 (Nov., 1972).

14. Calculation based on data in James S. Coleman et al., *Equality of Educational Opportunity* (Washington, D.C.: U.S. Government Printing Office, 1966), and the authors.

15. The data relating to IQ is from a 1966 survey of veterans by the National Opinion Research Center; and from N. Bayley and E. S. Schaefer, "Correlations of Maternal and Child Behaviors with the Development of Mental Ability: Data from the Berkeley Growth Study," *Monographs of Social Research in Child Development*, 29, 6 (1964).

16. Based on a large sample of U.S. high-school students as reported in John C. Flannagan and William W. Cooley, *Project Talent, One Year Follow-up Study*, Cooperative Research Project, No. 2333 (Pittsburgh: University of Pittsburgh, School of Education, 1966).

17. C. Jencks et al., *Inequality: A Reassessment of the Effects of Family and Schooling in America* (New York: Basic Books, 1972), p. 48.

18. W. L. Spady, "Educational Mobility and Access: Growth and Paradoxes," in *American Journal of Sociology*, 73, 3 (Nov. 1967); and Peter Blau and Otis D. Duncan, *The American Occupational Structure* (New York: John Wiley, 1967). More recent data support the evidence of no trend toward equality. See U.S. Bureau of Census, op. cit.

19. Ibid., Blau and Duncan.

58

Stubborn Disparities: Explaining Class Inequalities in Schooling

SCOTT DAVIES

One of the most important concepts in sociology is that of social class, in that one's background plays a major role in determining one's life chances, tastes, and even life expectancy. Many people believe that all Canadians have equal opportunities regardless of their class background. But this is not always the case. This article details that this process starts early in life and how the educational system is used to stream students according to their socio-economic background.

Canada has been transformed over this century from a predominantly rural, agricultural society to an urban, post-industrial nation. Whereas one hundred years ago most people were self-employed in family-owned farms and small businesses, today the vast majority earn their livelihood by competing in the labour market. Coinciding with these changes, the school system has expanded enormously, greatly increasing the educational attainments of Canadians. Most Canadians, regardless of social origin, earn more school credentials than did their ancestors. Indeed, Canada has more citizens attending school at its various levels—elementary, secondary, and post-secondary—than almost any other country (see Guppy and Davies 1998).

Schooling has become an increasingly important determinant of one's chances of securing a good job and a stable income, and by extension, education has become a prime arena for social competition. Schools sift and sort people into highly stratified career paths.

This raises a key question: Have all Canadians benefited equally from the expansion of the school system? Recent studies have examined trends in educational outcomes by race, gender, and social class.[1] As for race, most visible minorities, whether immigrant or Canadian-born, fare better in school than Whites, except for Aboriginal Canadians (Geschwender and Guppy 1995; Davies and Guppy 1998). Non-Aboriginal minorities, taken as a group, are less likely to drop out of high school, and are more likely to attend university. With the exception of Aboriginals, race or ethnic heritage is not a strong predictor of Canadians' educational attainment.

Source: Scott Davies. 2004. "Stubborn Disparities: Explaining Class Inequalities in Schooling." In James Curtis, Edward Grabb, and Neil Guppy, eds., *Social Inequality in Canada: Patterns, Problems, and Policies,* 4th ed., pp. 173–186. Toronto: Pearson Education Canada Inc.

In terms of gender, Canadian educational trends resemble those of most other nations: an overall movement toward male-female parity (Bradley and Ramirez 1996). Whereas males still earn more advanced degrees (masters, doctorates) and continue to dominate lucrative fields of study such as computer science and engineering, females are catching up in these and other areas. Females now attend and graduate from university at higher rates than males, and are less likely to drop out of high school. Despite some lingering female disadvantages, the main trend in Canadian education, as elsewhere, is toward gender equality.

However, a very different story emerges for social class. Whether measured by high school dropout rates, standardized test scores, or university attendance rates, youth from working-class and underclass backgrounds do not fare as well as their middle- and upper-class peers. Students' class origin markedly influences their school success regardless of their race, gender, or ethnicity. Certainly, the relation between class and educational outcomes is not a perfect fit. Within every socio-economic status (SES) category a wide range of outcomes exists, and some working-class students are very successful in school. Nevertheless, SES is the strongest and most enduring social determinant of educational attainment. Indeed, in Canada, as in most nations, socio-economic disparities in educational attainment have persisted despite decades of educational expansion and reform (see Shavit and Blossfeld 1993; Deng and Treiman 1997).

This chapter presents and evaluates sociological explanations for the persistence of these SES inequalities. While acknowledging the variation in education achievements within any SES category, I dwell on explanations of the unequal average attainments of working-class versus middle-class youth. I focus on Canada, though drawing heavily on American and British research, since socio-economic patterns of educational inequality in Canada and the United States are remarkably similar, and because much

British research on the topic has influenced Canadian sociologists.[2]

HOW INEQUALITIES EMERGE: SELECTION AND CUMULATIVE DISADVANTAGE

Educational inequality is best understood as a series of dissimilar transition and survival rates between groups (see Mare 1993 for an elaboration). Schooling is laddered, with student pools becoming smaller and smaller with successive transitions. For instance, most students now finish elementary schooling and enter high school. But since approximately 20% of Canadians who enter high school fail to graduate by age 24 (Frank 1996), the pool of high school graduates is selective relative to the entering high school cohort. Since SES is an important predictor of dropping out (Gilbert et al. 1993), high school graduates have a smaller proportion of working-class students than high school entrants. In turn, another selection takes place when only some high school graduates pursue post-secondary schooling. The "survivors" of this transition are again relatively select, as the proportion of students from lower SES origins again shrinks (for Canada, see Guppy and Davies 1998; for other countries, see Shavit and Blossfeld 1993). And there is still more. In the U.S., lower SES students are less likely to attend prestigious universities, even controlling for academic ability (Davies and Guppy 1997). What causes these class disparities in educational attainment?

ECONOMIC ARGUMENTS: MONEY MATTERS

Perhaps the most elemental explanation for working-class underachievement in school focuses on how working-class families face economic constraints that impede their educational progress. Although publicly funded, school attendance and performance requires money to pay for optional field trips, learning materials, and private tutors (e.g., piano, reading). Research shows that class background affects students' decisions about attending university, even controlling for their academic ability. This is usually interpreted as an effect of the increasingly prohibitive costs of tuition (Porter et al. 1979, Gambetta 1996, Steelman and Powell 1991). Private schools, which send the vast majority of their graduates to universities, are largely unaffordable to lower-income families. Wealthier parents are more likely to pay for additional private tutoring outside school hours (though lower-income parents would hire tutors "if they had the time and/or money" [Environics 1997]). Another economic factor is the quality of public schooling. Public schools in more affluent neighbourhoods enjoy superior resources and attract better teachers.[3] Though resource level itself does not directly produce better educational outcomes, better-funded schools produce an environment that is more conducive to educational success.

Nevertheless, economic resources—whether used for tuition, transportation, private tutors, or to avoid the need for part-time work—are not the sole factor that affects school outcomes. Countries that largely eliminated university tuition fees, such as Great Britain, France, and Australia, have class inequalities in university attendance similar to those in Canada and the U.S. This suggests that pure economic factors, while palpable, are not all-determining. There is an explanatory gap, something unexplained by economic factors. To complement economic explanations, sociologists have turned to the realm of culture.

CLASS AND FRAMES OF REFERENCE

People's economic conditions affect their sense of life options. SES origins influence their perceptions of the kinds of jobs they are likely to obtain, and the lives they are likely to lead. Judgments about school are thus influenced by these surrounding economic conditions. In particular, this context shapes the various "push" factors providing disincentives for remaining in school, and the "pull" factors providing incentives to leave school. Working-class students confront two obvious push factors: economic constraints (as elaborated above), and their underachievement relative to middle-class children (as elaborated below). Other factors give push and pull forces extra strength and efficacy.

When explaining socio-economic disparities in education, the key factor is the gap between people's abstract values and their concrete aspirations and expectations (see Mickelson 1990). Everyone "values" education in an abstract sense. Whether through surveys, interviews, or policy statements, virtually all Canadians stress the importance they place on education. Our consumer-driven, success-striving society encourages people to pursue the "North American dream" of a prestigious, well-paying job. As a result, the number of young people wanting professional careers greatly exceeds the number of such positions that exist. Hopes for professional jobs are unrealistically high (Jacobs, Karen, and McClelland 1991).

Expressing an appreciation for education is one thing, but converting desires into reality is another. Part of this gap between expressed values and reality can be traced to factors beyond the economic realm.

"Frames of reference" refer to people's sense of desirable yet possible life options, their mental horizons that influence what they expect they can realistically attain. Immediate family and friends influence these frames greatly. We develop expectations by comparing ourselves to similar people, aligning our aspirations and efforts accordingly. These frames of reference shape our ideas of what kinds of jobs and lifestyle we want, and the role school plays in our desires.

Social class strongly influences people's frames of reference. Middle-class students have higher expectations for jobs and education than do working-class students, even controlling for differences in measured academic ability. Their higher aspirations can be attributed largely to the influence of their family and friends (Sewell and Hauser 1980; McClelland 1990).[4] These differences in frames of reference explain part of the socio-economic gap in educational success (Sewell and Hauser 1980; Jacobs, Karen, and McClelland 1991).

How does class shape these frames? In some instances, people's past experience and current social position cause them to "come to terms" with their circumstances and adjust their expectations to what is "realistic." When asked what they would like to be when they grow up, very young children often reply "police officer," "nanny," or "teacher." As they grow older, learning about the jobs of their parents' friends, these choices change. The choices change again as young people hear others encouraging or remaining mute about their occupational dreams. When confronting barriers, economic or otherwise, they often lower their original goals. Additionally, "pull factors" disproportionately entice working-class youth out of school. Especially for youth not faring well in school, domestic and employment roles act as school-leaving incentives. Relatively secure blue-collar jobs requiring few educational credentials appear as viable alternatives to schooling (Brown 1987), as do marriage plans. Even among the previously ambitious, and among the talented, early marriage reduces aspirations (Jacobs, Karen, and McClelland 1991).

PUSH FACTORS: THE STRUCTURE OF SCHOOLING

Working-class students in most countries, including Canada, are more likely than their middle-class counterparts to be streamed into less challenging, terminal programs in high school (Davies 1992; Curtis, Livingstone, and Smaller 1992). The very existence of these streaming systems, critics contend, disadvantages working-class students. These youth would fare better in a non-streamed high school environment that offered them the same curricula and expectations as other students. Being stuck in lower tracks offers these students less challenging work, and lowers their expectations and aspirations for the future. Once in different tracks, fatalistic frames of reference are reinforced, as opportunities to rise in school and learn are limited. The incentives of available jobs and/or impending domestic roles, when combined with streaming, lead these youth to perceive school as irrelevant to their future. School becomes a pointless dress rehearsal that is irrelevant to their upcoming roles.

American Catholic schools place far fewer students in lower streams, and as a result greater proportions of working-class students in these schools score well on standardized tests, graduate from high school, and attend post-secondary institutions (Lee, Bryk, and Smith 1993). Such research findings encourage the "de-streaming" movement, which seeks to abolish differential grouping and to mix students of all abilities. In the early 1990s, Ontario removed streams in grade 9, and planned eventually to phase out all streaming. However, for a variety of reasons—but largely due to teacher complaints about the practical difficulties imposed by heterogeneous ability groups—the government ended the experiment. Nevertheless, American research suggests that de-streaming could be a valid tool for easing class disparities in schooling if practical problems associated with student heterogeneity can be overcome.

Another factor shaping frames of reference, and their relation to class, is knowledge about education. Even when students from humble origins have lofty aspirations, and are academically gifted, other factors mitigate against their success. The daunting variety of choices available in modern post-secondary education, such as the distinctions between community colleges and universities, different types of degrees, the informal ranking of institutions, and the wide variety of programs available within any institution, creates an elaborate system of selection with many ports of entry. To make wise choices and maximize one's benefit, one must understand how the system operates; for example, what are the efficacious strategies for success or the informal rankings of programs and institutions? Such navigational savvy is held disproportionately by students from middle-class origins. These youth have superior information about the academic marketplace, and they are more likely to know which fields offer lucrative rewards and how to find competitive advantages. As a result, students from disadvantaged origins have a lower probability of survival in advanced stages of the education system (Davies and Guppy 1997).

MORE PUSH FACTORS: THE CULTURE OF SCHOOLING

A notable characteristic of class inequality in education is that disparities in skills, such as the ability to read, write, and reason, can be detected from the earliest days in school (Alexander, Entwisle, and Horsey 1997). Why does this occur? As has been well documented, some parents can pass on to their children non-material resources that facilitate school success. Because parental education attainment better predicts student success than parental income or class position, many sociologists have looked to the role of non-material resources in facilitating class differences in educational attainment.

More educated parents pass on to their children "human capital"—basic reading, writing, and vocabulary skills, disciplined work habits—giving their children a distinct advantage in school. More highly educated parents spend more time helping their children with school-related activities (Environics 1997), a finding that is likely a consequence of their more flexible work schedules and greater familiarity with academic matters (Lareau 1989).

Another cultural approach places less emphasis on particular skills and focuses instead on cultural tastes and aesthetics. "Cultural capital," the signature concept of French sociologist Pierre

Bourdieu (Bourdieu and Passeron 1990) refers to the advantage enjoyed by students who possess sophisticated (as opposed to merely competent) conversational abilities and who have acquired a taste for literature and the arts.

In addition to the culture of the home, the culture of the classroom is also important. Many sociologists focus less on working-class culture and more on possible school cultures in order to understand class disparities. For instance, Bourdieu contends that since schools reward children who possess a certain type of cultural sophistication that is less likely to be found among the working class, schools in essence are rewarding middle-class culture. The way school is conducted—expected styles of speech, dress, and the content of the curriculum—are deemed to be largely foreign to working-class youth.

For instance, Basil Bernstein's (1973) research in East London (England) led him to postulate that middle-class children and working-class children come to school speaking different "codes"—that is, different styles of language with different grammatical rules and themes that lead to different ways of communicating. Schooling, Bernstein argued, is conducted in the more elaborate code of the middle class, putting working-class students at a distinct linguistic disadvantage. Other cultural idioms used in schools also may be class-biased. For instance, critics of standardized testing have long contended that such tests are more tests of "culture" than of cognitive ability, in that success in these tests is dependent upon having a certain cultural exposure (Contenta 1993).

Another longstanding charge of systematic bias in North American schools is that teachers, themselves middle class, hold higher expectations for middle-class students than for working-class students (see Wineburg 1987). Teachers are said to generalize, perhaps unconsciously, from the physical and social attributes of students (e.g., dress, demeanour, and speech style) to their abilities. According to this argument, teachers subtly expect well-dressed, presentable, and articulate children to be good students, and expect those with the opposite traits to be poorer students. This typecasting is also said to create a self-fulfilling prophecy. Whether via body language or the attention they give to students, teachers are said to express their expectations by treating students differently, and students are said to internalize these subtle messages. Thus, students for whom teachers have low expectations are said to eventually develop poor self-images, which in turn lead to poor academic performance.

Creating bold theories of working-class underachievement is one thing; providing convincing empirical evidence to support such theories is another. How have these theories fared over decades of sociological research?

Results are mixed, offering only qualified support. Beginning with cultural capital theory, sociologists have tested whether school outcomes are statistically correlated with various indicators of cultural capital, such as whether students have attended art galleries or museums, or whether their household provides reading material such as newspapers, magazines, and books. Findings suggest that students who regularly visit art galleries and museums achieve superior test scores (DiMaggio 1982). High school students exposed to household reading material are more likely to complete high school, attend selective universities, and enter lucrative post-secondary programs (Davies and Guppy 1997; Tanner, Davies, and O'Grady 1997). However, the link between cultural capital and class background is not exactly as Bourdieu imagines. Class background affects school success independently of cultural capital, and conversely, students with cultural capital enjoy advantages in school, independently of SES (Aschaffenburg and Maas 1997). Not all middle-class youth participate in high-status culture—far from it—and not all lower SES children are excluded from this culture.

Bernstein's theory of language codes is less successful. His theory, while popular in the 1970s, lacks any large-scale empirical confirmation, and many researchers are highly skeptical as

to whether it is applicable beyond the setting of East London in the 1960s and 1970s. Similarly, sweeping claims that working-class students are culturally alienated in schools appear to be based more on assertion than argument and detailed evidence. Examples of successful "working-class schools," where such students thrive in a culturally proletarian environment, would aid the case for these theories, but, to my knowledge, no such schools exist. In fact, research suggests that working-class student performance is raised in schools that have a more middle-class composition.

As with studies of cultural capital, research on teacher biases offers mixed findings. Proof for the famous "self-fulfilling prophecy" thesis was originally said to be provided by the famous "Pygmalion in the classroom" experiment (Rosenthal and Jacobson 1968). Rosenthal and Jacobson tested whether labelling a group of elementary students as "gifted" (when in reality they were chosen at random) would cause those children to markedly improve not only their grades but their IQ scores as well. Any improvement, the researchers reasoned, would be strong evidence of the self-fulfilling prophecy. One year later, the researchers claimed they had evidence of a strong labelling effect. The study quickly became famous and remains one of the best known in the history of educational research. Other studies quickly followed that argued that teacher typecasting was a root cause of working-class and minority underachievement in schools.

But is there clear evidence to support this claim? Few observers at the time noticed that the actual Pygmalion results were weak and uneven, and that the conclusions drawn from the data far overshot the content of the actual study, which did not directly test whether teachers negatively stereotyped working-class students. Subsequent attempts at replication have produced mixed results. Teacher expectations do not appear to consistently influence student ability.

Other types of research on teacher expectations find nuanced effects. While some conclude that teacher expectations are largely the consequence of the academic actions of students, and not vice versa (see Wineburg 1987; Farkas et al. 1990; Hurn 1993: 170–176), some suggest working-class students do endure biased treatment. Teachers from high-status origins appear to have lower expectations and give lower grades to low SES students (Alexander, Entwisle, and Thompson 1987). These students, even controlling for academic ability, are less likely to be assigned to upper tracks (Hurn 1993: 165–170). Thus, while sweeping claims that schools are culturally biased and directly "push out" able working-class students may be overstated, evidence suggests that those youth encounter some unequal treatment in schools.

SOCIAL CAPITAL AND ACTIVE CAPITAL

What might account for the complex and somewhat inconsistent effects found in research on resources and school biases? Research frequently underplays agency. The concept of cultural capital points to a potential. Parental endowments in human capital and cultural capital aid educational success, but their influence is contingent upon whether those resources are acted upon in those families. Families with impressive resources "on paper" may not spend time helping their children. Exposure to music, art galleries, and world travel may offer advantages, but only if this potential is actualized through strategic action.

Family advantages can be reinforced in different ways. Having a sizable income, for instance, can boost one's cultural capital in the form of tutoring services, attending cultural events, or travelling to exotic locales. Money allows one to take advantage of one's knowledge of the school system. Knowledge that a high LSAT score is crucial to one's chances of acceptance into law school, for example, is especially helpful if one can afford the books and study courses that can improve such scores. Conversely, families that lack advantages in some areas can compensate by

excelling in other areas. For instance, many Asian immigrant parents possess little of the dominant cultural capital, few English skills, and have relatively little direct contact with teachers, yet compensate by enrolling their children in private tutoring and monitoring their children's homework at higher-than-average rates (Schneider and Coleman 1993).

"Active capital" (Looker 1994) refers to the conversion of potential resources—economic or cultural—into real educational advantage. Research shows that academic advantages are enjoyed by children whose parents more actively monitor their children's homework, spend more time with their children, and intervene positively if their children run into difficulties at school (Schneider and Coleman 1993; Lareau 1989).

What activates capital? At one level, motivation is an individual, idiosyncratic matter. Yet, sociologists know that individual effort does not occur in a social vacuum, but is embedded in broader social contexts. Relationships among students, parents, neighbouring communities, and educators can influence and channel an individual's actions. In conceptualizing these broader social effects, Coleman has referred to "social capital" as the set of collective expectations within a community that affects the goal-seeking behaviour of its members (see Coleman 1988). Communities create social capital by forging reciprocal norms of obligation among parents, youth, and schools. Such norms breed strong bonds of trust, cooperation, and mutual respect, and can channel motivation and effort. Conversely, communities with weak obligations and expectations may be less committed to their educational goals.

Differences in social capital can reinforce socio-economic disparities. Studies show that parents from lower SES categories are less active in their children's schooling (Schneider and Coleman 1993). Working-class parents are disadvantaged vis-à-vis middle-class parents by their relatively inflexible work schedules, less detailed knowledge of the school system, lesser familiarity with the social culture of teaching, and by schools that do not actively encourage parental participation (Lareau 1989; Epstein 1995).

However, these effects can be counteracted. Working-class students appear better motivated in more academically oriented schools. Researchers have found that schools with strong expectations of success raise the attainment of all children, particularly lower SES students (Willms 1986; Shouse 1996). Schools of mixed socio-economic composition benefit working-class children by exposing them to an enriched academic environment, high-status role models, and peers with high aspirations (see Hurn 1993: 168).

THEORIES OF DEEP CULTURAL DIVISIONS: DEPRIVATION AND RESISTANCE

Notions of frames of reference and forms of capital, described above, portray middle-class versus working-class families as having different outlooks and unequal resources regarding school. These cultural differences are not seen to be "deep," in the sense of reflecting profoundly dissimilar values or norms, but rather stem from their adjustments to their respective socio-economic conditions. Yet, some sociologists see much deeper cultural differences. A controversial idea that has haunted sociologists for over forty years is that working-class children are outperformed by their middle-class counterparts because of a fundamental mismatch between the cultural orientations required for school success and the culture of lower socio-economic groups. There are two versions of this thesis.

The first version, called "cultural deprivation" or "cultural deficit" theory, was popular in the 1950s and 1960s (see Hyman 1953). In this view, modern schools, as part of the societal contest for economic status and social climbing, require of the populace a set of "middle class" orientations aimed at achievement, competition, and aspiration for upward social mobility. Families from lower socio-economic strata, these theorists reasoned, desire the same material goals of income and wealth as their middle-class counterparts, but fail to embrace the attitudes or orientations needed to reach those goals. Working-class families were seen to be behind the times, mired in a pre-modern value set.

Cultural deficit theory met a barrage of criticism in the late 1960s and early 1970s. Much of this criticism consisted of moralistic charges of elitism and "blaming the victim," but there were substantive sociological criticisms as well. Perhaps the most powerful was a challenge to the claim of deep cultural divisions rooted in class. Writers such as William Ryan (1971), drawing on notions of frames of reference, passionately argued that virtually everyone in North America shares common aspirations for material wealth, but the working class adjust their expectations in response to their lower objective chances of realizing their aspirations.

The idea of deep cultural division did not vanish, however, but resurfaced in a new guise. Many sociologists in the 1970s and 1980s, influenced by Marxism, offered a novel account of deep cultural differences to explain why working-class students underperformed. In what became known as *Resistance theory* (see Davies 1995 for a review), Marxists such as Paul Willis (1977) argued that class disparities in school stem less from a working-class inability to compete, but more from their *unwillingness* to compete. This unwillingness, they argued, is rooted in a profound culture clash. Rather than sharing an orientation of status striving, Willis and his followers argued, the working class has its own defiant mores, which it forged through historic struggles with its capitalist employers. These values are said to include a preference for solidarity over competitiveness, pride in manual labour, and an antagonism to institutional authority.

Resistance theorists make two crucial inferential leaps. First, they argue that many, if not most, working-class youth are generally indifferent to school, exert little effort in classes, and participate in school deviance. Second, they argue that these anti-school subcultures have a proletarian character that, in essence, is a youthful version of factory culture. The solidarity of the shop floor is said to be mimicked by close peer relationships among teens. The pride in heavy, manual labour is said to be expressed by their disparaging of the "pencil-pushing" that pervades school work, and resentment toward the second-class status that is accorded to manual labour in schools. The antagonism to authority, as visibly expressed in workers' conflicts with factory supervisors and bosses, is transferred to student-teacher relations.

These subcultural values, in this account, lead these youth to reject school and eagerly anticipate the "real world" of employment. Simply put, working-class kids get working-class jobs by developing rebellious subcultures, thereby condemning themselves to educational failure. While acknowledging that not all working-class students engage in deviance, resistance theorists view working-class resistance to school as a prime cause of their educational underachievement.

Resistance theory has had a huge impact in sociology, but has sparked much criticism. Willis and his followers stand accused of greatly exaggerating the extent to which working-class students actually oppose school, and of offering overly romantic interpretations of school deviance. Indeed most concrete instances of "resistance"—often amounting to little more than expressions of boredom—are simply unconvincing as evidence of a deep and ideologically charged cultural division.

CONCLUSION: CHANGING SOCIETY, PERSISTING INEQUALITIES?

Class disparities in education stem from a variety of factors—unequal economic constraints, different frames of reference and endowments in various forms of capital, and some forms of bias in school. Each of these interacting factors has multiple levels of influence, from the individual, to the family, to the surrounding community, to the school. Documenting class inequalities is relatively easy, but the complexity of how class affects schooling makes convincing explanations backed by solid evidence much harder to find. Part of this difficulty stems from the fact that society and its educational institutions are constantly changing.

Schools have changed. One possible reason why recent research on school bias finds such uneven effects is that teachers and their methods have been continually altered over recent decades. While the notion of the self-fulfilling prophecy perhaps had a stronger reality thirty years ago, educators today are generally far more sensitive and alert to issues of equity and bias. Teacher colleges focus much of their training on issues of "diversity." Curricula and tests have been modified constantly in an effort to better suit a diverse student body.

Cultural configurations are shifting as well. Sociologists, more than before, doubt that social class is a primary source of cultural division in our society. Before the mid-1980s, many commonly referred to a "working-class culture" as a recognizable and coherent entity. These ideas led Resistance theorists, like the Functionalists before them, to depict a deep culture clash between working-class youth and schools. But this notion of such a distinct culture, in semi-opposition to the middle class, seems less and less plausible in North America. Most sociologists now stress instead race, ethnicity, religion, or region as more potent sources of social attachments, self-conceptions, group loyalties, and cultural conflict. Class may continue to shape frames of reference and senses of people's life options, but it is not a source of deep cultural attachment. An essential irony is that while working-class culture may have faded, class remains the key objective barrier to school success.

These culture shifts can be linked to changing economic conditions. De-industrialization is transforming the job structure that helped forge class-differentiated frames of reference. Until the mid-1980s, blue-collar jobs in resources and manufacturing that required few educational credentials attracted many working-class youth, particularly males, out of school. But the stock of such jobs is now smaller. More school leavers now encounter service-sector jobs (often requiring educational credentials, even if not high levels of skill) or the spectre of unemployment. Further, on average, women are marrying and bearing children at later ages and, perhaps as a result, female educational attainments among all classes have shot upwards. Thus, two viable alternatives that previously attracted many working-class students out of school have been recently undercut.

What impact will this change have on frames of reference and aspirations? One might expect that the weakening of these pull factors will strengthen most youth's attachments to schooling. As our society transforms itself into a "knowledge economy," lifetime learning is being hailed as the next source of educational expansion. People of all descriptions, so the argument goes, will return to school numerous times over their employment lifetimes to upgrade their skills. Will this alter the frames of reference of those who would not otherwise consider post-secondary schooling? It might, but we need to remember that educational inequality is a relational concept, not an absolute measure of attainment. Often overlooked is the fact that over the past four decades, working-class families have substantially boosted their attainments, but inequalities have remained largely stable because the middle class has boosted equally its attainments. An understanding of inequality requires not only recognition of the barriers faced by working-class youth, but the advantages and strategies of middle-class youth. Even if working-class frames of reference change and school biases are removed—which would render working-class students more competitive—middle-class families will likely develop new strategies to keep ahead. The sharp increases in recent years in the number of families seeking private schooling and private tutoring is a likely indication of a new middle-class strategy aimed at maintaining a competitive edge in education.

CRITICAL THINKING QUESTIONS

1. What is your class background? How would you measure that? What social classes does Davies discuss? Which variables besides social class determine success in school?

2. Why do students from the middle class perform better in school than those with a working-class background? What resources are needed in order to succeed in school? How does socio-economic background affect one's career options?

3. What are the basic elements of deprivation and resistance theory? Do you think either theory (or both) provides substantial insights into why fewer people from working-class backgrounds pursue higher education? What are some shortcomings associated with these theories?

NOTES

1. Although the terms "class" and "socio-economic status" (SES) have different theoretical and empirical meanings in sociology, I use them interchangeably to refer to one's relative economic standing. Canadian trends are taken from data cited in Guppy and Davies (1998).

2. Two very important and related topics—group differences in "equity"—that is, the power to shape and influence the content and form of education, and the question of how class interacts with region, race, ethnicity, or gender—cannot be pursued here for reasons of space.

3. This tends to be a much starker phenomenon in the U.S. than in Canada. In fact, schools in neighbourhoods populated by racial minorities in urban areas like Toronto and Vancouver receive greater funds than the average.

4. The relation between frames of reference and class, like the relation between educational outcomes and class, is far from a perfect fit. Research needs to be further developed to understand why there is wide range within any class. One possibility is that low-income communities that are less tight-knit and bonded allow their members to develop expectations that are atypical of those communities (see Portes and Sensenbrenner 1993). Some low-income communities may have resources that can compensate for their class position (see Kao, Tienda, and Schneider 1996).

REFERENCES

Alexander, Karl L., Doris R. Entwisle, and Maxine S. Thompson. 1987. School performance, status relations, and the structure of sentiment: Bringing the teacher back in. *American Sociological Review*, 52(5): 665–82.

Alexander, Karl L., Doris R. Entwisle, and Carrie S. Horsey. 1997. From first grade forward: Early foundations of high school dropout. *Sociology of Education*, 70(2): 87–107.

Aschaffenburg, Karen, and Ineke Maas. 1997. Cultural and educational careers: The dynamics of social reproduction. *American Sociological Review*, 62(4): 573–87.

Bernstein, Basil (ed.). 1973. *Class, codes and control, vol. 2: Theoretical studies towards a sociology of language.* London, Boston: Routledge & Kegan Paul.

Blossfeld, Hans-Peter, and Yossi Shavit. 1993. Persisting barriers: Changes in educational opportunities in thirteen countries. In *Perpetual inequality: Changing educational attainment in thirteen countries*, eds. Yossi Shavit and Hans-Peter Blossfeld, 1–24. Boulder, CO: Westview Press.

Bourdieu, Pierre, and Jean-Claude Passeron. 1990. *Reproduction in education, society and culture*, 2nd ed. London: Sage.

Bradley, Karen, and Francisco O. Ramirez. 1996. World polity and gender parity: Women's share of higher education, 1965–1985. *Research in Sociology of Education and Socialization*, 11: 63–92.

Brown, P. 1987. *Schooling ordinary kids: Inequality, unemployment and the new vocationalism.* London: Tavistock.

Coleman, James S. 1988. Social capital in the creation of human capital. *American Journal of Sociology*, 94: s95–s120.

Contenta, Sandro. 1993. *Rituals of failure: What schools really teach.* Toronto: Between the Lines.

Curtis, Bruce, David W. Livingstone, and Harry Smaller. 1992. *Stacking the deck: The streaming of working class kids in Ontario schools.* Toronto: Our Schools/Our Selves.

Davies, Scott. 1992. In search of the culture clash: Evaluating a sociological theory of social class inequalities in education. Doctoral dissertation. Department of Sociology, University of Toronto.

———. 1995. Reproduction and resistance in Canadian high schools. An empirical examination of the Willis thesis. *British Journal of Sociology*, 46(4): 662–87.

Davies, Scott, and Neil Guppy. 1997. Fields of study, college selectivity, and student inequalities in higher education. *Social Forces*, 75(4): 1417–1138 [*sic*].

Davies, Scott, and Neil Guppy. 1998. Race and Canadian education. In *The racist imagination: The sociology of racism in Canada*, ed. Vic Satzewich. Toronto: Thompson Educational Publishing.

Deng, Zhong, and Donald J. Treiman. 1997. The impact of the cultural revolution on trends in educational attainment in People's Republic of China. *American Journal of Sociology*, 103(2): 391–428.

DiMaggio, Paul. 1982. Cultural capital and school success: The impact of status culture participation on the grades of U.S. high school students. *American Sociological Review*, 47(2): 189–201.

Environics. 1997. *Focus Canada report 1997-2.* Toronto: Environics.

Epstein, Joyce L. 1995. School/family/community partnerships. *Phi Delta Kappan,* 72(5): 701–12.

Farkas, George, P. Grobe, D. Sheehan, and Y. Shuan. 1990. Cultural resources and school success: Gender, ethnicity and poverty groups within an urban school district. *American Sociological Review*, 55(1): 127–42.

Frank, Jeffrey. 1996. *After high school: The first report of the School Leavers Following-up Survey, 1995.* Ottawa: Minister of Public Works and Government Services Canada.

Gambetta, Diego. 1996. *Were they pushed or did they jump? Individual decision mechanisms in education.* Boulder, CO: Westview Press.

Geschwender, Jim, and Neil Guppy. 1995. Ethnicity, educational attainment, and earned income among Canadian-born men and women. *Canadian Ethnic Studies*, XXVII(1): 67–84.

Gilbert, Sid, Lynn Barr, Warren Clark, Matthew Blue, and Deborah Sunter. 1993. *Leaving school: Results from a national survey comparing school leavers and high school graduates 18 to 20 years of age.* Ottawa: Statistics Canada.

Guppy, Neil, and Scott Davies. 1998. *Education in Canada: Recent trends and future challenges.* Ottawa: Statistics Canada and Nelson Canada.

Hurn, Christopher J. 1993. *The limits and possibilities of schooling*, 3rd ed. Boston: Allyn and Bacon.

Hyman, Herbert H. 1953. The value systems of different classes: A social psychological contribution to the analysis of stratification. In *Class, status and power: A reader in social stratification*, eds. Reinhard Bendix and Seymour Martin Lipset, 426–42. Glencoe, IL: Free Press.

Jacobs, Jerry A., David Karen, and Katherine McClelland. 1991. The dynamics of young men's career aspirations. *Sociological Forum*, 6(4): 609–39.

Kao, Grace, Marta Tienda, and Barbara Schneider. 1996. Racial and ethnic variation in academic performance. *Research in Sociology of Education and Socialization*, 11: 263–97.

Lareau, Annette. 1989. *Home advantage: Social class and parental intervention in elementary education.* London: Falmer.

Lee, Valerie E., Anthony S. Bryk, and J. B. Smith. 1993. The organization of effective secondary schools. *Review of Research in Education*, 19:171–268.

Looker, E. Dianne. 1994. Active capital: The impact of parents on youths' educational performance and plans. *Sociology of education in Canada: Critical perspective on theory, research and practice.* Toronto: Copp Clark Longman.

Mare, Robert D. 1993. Educational stratification on observed and unobserved components of family background. In *Persistent inequality: Changing educational attainment in thirteen countries*, eds. Y. Shavit and H.P. Blossfeld, 351–76. Boulder, CO: Westview Press.

McClelland, Katherine. 1990. Cumulative disadvantage among the highly ambitious. *Sociology of Education*, 63(2): 102–21.

Mickelson, Rosalyn A. 1990. The attitude-achievement paradox among black adolescents. *Sociology of Education*, 63: 44–61.

Porter, Marion, John Porter, and Bernard Blishen. 1979. *Does money matter?* Downsview, ON: Institute for Behavioural Research.

Portes, Alejandro, and Julia Sensenbrenner. 1993. Embeddedness and immigration: Notes on the social determinants of economic action. *American Journal of Sociology*, 98(6): 1320–50.

Rosenthal, R., and L. Jacobson. 1968. *Pygmalion in the classroom*. New York: Rinehart and Winston.

Ryan, William. 1971. *Blaming the victim*. New York: Vintage.

Schneider, Barbara, and James S. Coleman. 1993. *Parents, their children, and schools*. Boulder, CO: Westview Press.

Sewell, William, and Robert Hauser. 1980. The Wisconsin longitudinal study of social and psychological factors in aspirations and achievements. *Research in Sociology of Education and Socialization*, 1: 59–99.

Shavit, Yossi, and Hans-Peter Blossfeld (eds.). 1993. *Persistent inequality: Changing educational attainment in thirteen countries*. Boulder, CO: Westview Press.

Shouse, Roger C. 1996. Academic press and sense of community: Conflict and congruence in American high schools. *Research in Sociology of Education and Socialization*, 11: 173–202.

Steelman, Lala Carr, and Brian Powell. 1991. Sponsoring the next generation: Parental willingness to pay for higher education. *American Journal of Sociology*, 96(6): 1505–29.

Tanner, Julian, Scott Davies, and Bill O'Grady. 1997. Whatever happened to yesterday's rebels? Longitudinal effects of teenage delinquency on educational and occupational attainment. Unpublished manuscript, University of Toronto.

Teachman, Jay D. 1987. Family background, educational resources, and educational attainment. *American Sociological Review*, 52: 548–57.

Willis, P. 1977. *Learning to labour:* Farnborough: Saxon House, Teakfield.

Willms, J. Douglas. 1986. Social class segregation and its relationship to pupils' examination results in Scotland. *American Sociological Review*, 51(2): 224–41.

Wineburg, Samuel S. 1987. The self-fulfillment of the self-fulfilling prophecy: A critical appraisal. *Educational Researcher*, 16(9): 28–37.

CLASSIC

CONTEMPORARY

CROSS-CULTURAL

59

Japanese Mothers as the Best Teachers

KEIKO HIRAO

The Japanese government has tried to encourage fathers to share in their children's upbringing, including placing advertisements in major newspapers that read "We don't call a man a father if he doesn't participate in childcare." Nonetheless, employed mothers rather than employed fathers are the ones who leave the labour force to devote a major part of their lives to their young children's education.

. . . The intensity and the depth of involvement of many Japanese mothers in their children's education has received considerable attention (Boocock 1991; Ellington 1992; Uno 1993; White 1987). The phenomenon of the *kyōiku mama* (education mother), in which a woman devotes a major part of her life to her child's academic career, is both praised as the source of Japanese students' impressive academic success and criticized for depriving children of their free time. The description of the *kyōiku mama* phenomenon, however, has been limited by a lack of attention to how Japanese education has been privatized in the past twenty years and how the role of *kyōiku mama* has been shaped and influenced by the reality of the educational system in Japan.

According to a survey by the Ministry of Education, over 35 percent of schoolchildren attend *juku* (private educational institutions) that provide supplemental academic training (Ministry of Education 1994). The rate of attendance is highest among older children: in 1993, an amazing 67 percent of Japanese ninth graders were enrolled. Between 1985 and 1993 *juku* attendance increased from 17 to 24 percent for elementary school children. These *juku* statistics, however, tell only a small part of the story, which includes correspondence courses, tutoring services, and various private lessons available to children. When these services are included, 82 percent of all Japanese schoolchildren are enrolled in one or a combination of private educational programs (Ministry of Education 1994).

. . . A recent notable development in educational competition and the *kyōiku mama* phenomenon in Japan is that ever-younger children are becoming involved in educational activities

Source: Keiko Hirao, "Mothers as the Best Teachers: Japanese Motherhood and Early Childhood Education." In Mary C. Brinton (Ed.), *Women's Working Lives in East Asia*. Stanford, CA: Stanford University Press, 2001, pp. 180–203.

outside of school. Approximately 42 percent of Japanese preschool children are enrolled in some kind of educational program outside of kindergarten and day nurseries (Ministry of Health and Welfare 1991). As Norma Field notes, childhood in contemporary Japan has become streamlined as a series of preparatory steps to productive adulthood (Field 1995), and parents—especially mothers—play a vital role as the agents of human capital investment. . . .

DATA

This [reading] is based on interviews conducted on the parenting behaviors of mothers in the Tokyo area during 1991–1992 and in Nagoya (Aichi Prefecture) in 1994–1995. The samples for the Tokyo interviews were recruited through three parenting classes sponsored by local governments and playgroup networks. The parenting classes involved approximately eighty participants in total. As I served as the coordinator/instructor, I was able to request the names of participants who were willing to cooperate in the interviews. I then added to the samples through snowball sampling methods. Twenty women from the classes were contacted for the in-depth interviews. I also utilized the discussions in the classes as a means of participant observation. Because the parenting classes were offered in the daytime, the participants were limited to full-time housewives and part-time workers. The format of the interview was mostly open-ended, with some structured questions about personal background. . . .

DEVELOPMENT OF EARLY EDUCATION PROGRAMS: AN OBSESSION WITH PRODIGIES

The educational role played by Japanese mothers starts when children are very young. Kindergartens and nursery schools expect mothers to incorporate an educational agenda into the routine of daily life (Allison 1996). The intensity of this responsibility is illustrated by the recent development of *sōki-kyōiku*, early educational programs that are given either at home or at private, extra-school institutions. These are geared explicitly toward the development of cognitive skills in preschool children.

These programs are "extra-school" in the sense that they are independent from formal kindergartens and accredited day nurseries. Kindergartens and day nurseries operate under the auspices of the Ministry of Education and the Ministry of Health and Welfare, respectively. Because more than 93 percent of preschool children are enrolled in one or the other of these institutions, kindergartens and day nursery programs have now become comparable to formal schools. Private enterprises that provide educational services for preschoolers can be compared to the preschool version of *juku* for school-aged children. *Juku* is distinguished from extracurricular activities as it is administered outside the school system. In the same manner, early education programs function externally to the formal system of kindergarten and nursery schools.

. . . The course content offered in the extra-preschool curriculums varies widely, ranging from music lessons to reading and writing, simple mathematics to foreign languages. Some courses are purely academically oriented, some specialize in preparatory training for entrance examinations for prestigious elementary schools, and others emphasize artistic skills and music lessons. Many boast a combination of some or all of these benefits.

Kumon, a prominent *juku*, for example, invites preschoolers to work on mathematics, English, and Japanese. Founded by Toru Kumon in 1958 in Osaka as a small neighborhood *juku* for school-children, Kumon is now one of the largest *juku* establishments in Japan, with more than 18,000 branch classroom locations all over the country and a total enrollment of 1.5 million (Kumon Kyōiku Kenkyūkai 1998). . . .

During the late 1980s, Kumon expanded its programs to include the enrollment of preschoolers. In 1990, they started a correspondence course through which they delivered monthly educational kits such as videos, flash cards, and workbooks to children between the ages of two and five. In the mid-1980s, Kumon began to commend their high achievers. Among them were preschool children who could work out differential and integral calculus. These youngsters had already finished the high school level mathematics curriculum, and some of their mothers were reported to have started the program while they were pregnant.

The Association of Early Childhood Development, founded by Masaru Ibuka, the founder of Sony, states its mission as assisting in the sound development of the mother–child relationship. Its operation includes developing teaching materials, such as electronically prerecorded flash cards called "talking cards." Courses are offered to children aged 12 to 24 months old. Courses are also available to pregnant women on how to enhance the potential abilities of their unborn children. . . .

The Child Academy, founded by Makoto Shichida, offers comprehensive programs such as storytelling, flash-card learning, haiku, arts and crafts, and music. The Ishii School of Kanji Education focuses on the teaching of reading and writing Chinese characters for preschoolers, offering correspondence courses as well as instruction in classrooms. . . .

The spur for early education began in 1976 when Ibuka published a sensational book titled *Yōchien de wa Ososugiru* ("Kindergarten Is Too Late"). This book became a best-seller and was followed by a flood of publications that advocated early intervention in order to develop the cognitive and verbal skills of infants. Such publications include Shichida's *Miraculous Education for the Zero-Year-Old* (1983) and *Tips on Raising an Intelligent Baby* (1985), Mitsuishi's *Creating Prodigies* (1988), and Oshima's *Prenatal Education* (1988). The acceleration of early education can be seen through the titles of Ibuka's successive books: *Kindergarten Is Too Late* (1976), followed by *Zero-Year-Old* (1991) and *From Embryo* (1992). We can see the shift in the

messages. Kindergarten was too late in the 1970s. But in the 1990s mothers were instructed to be concerned about their children's academic achievements *from conception.*

The accelerated education in Japan parallels, to some extent, the proliferation of educational programs for preschool children in the United States. Programs with heavy educational components for prekindergarten children are also on the increase in the United States. The well-publicized "superkid" practice by Glenn Doman, *How to Teach Your Baby to Read* (1964) and *How to Multiply Your Baby's Intelligence* (1984), for example, resonates with many of the publications by Ibuka, Shichida, and Ishii. They share the common premises that children's IQ is not fixed at birth but is determined by environment and intellectual stimulation, that children's potential for learning has long been underestimated, and that intellectual growth is very rapid during early childhood. In other words, the cognitive potential of children, according to both Doman and Ishii, can be significantly boosted by early intervention programs. . . .

Once education for preschoolers proved to be a profitable business for *juku* industries, other sectors began to enter the market. For example, a company that sells underwear and other home-related products through direct-mail catalogs decided to go into the extra-preschool education business in 1992. They converted their customer list into a mailing list through which they delivered educational materials each month for children under the age of six. It is not unusual, especially in urban areas, for mothers of newborn babies to receive a direct-mail advertisement of courses offered to "enhance the academic ability" of their offspring. The early education "boom" was thus driven by the supply of these services.

Ironically, this development took place outside the public school system just as the Ministry of Education was trying to relax school schedules to remedy the excessive competition for entrance examinations. The public schools have taken to heart the criticism that excessive academic competition causes poor health among children, school violence, and bullying. Contrary to the common belief that Japanese schools are driving their students with relentless pressure for academic success, they are now shifting their emphasis to "creativity," "sociability," and "whole development" and away from rote learning. Approximately one-fourth of the time spent at Japanese schools is now devoted to nonacademic activities, such as recess and club activities (Stevenson 1992). Moreover, the Ministry of Education decided to reduce the time spent in school by seventy hours per year for elementary school students and thirty-five hours for junior high school students. The ministry also stipulates in the new curriculum guidelines that the content be cut by 30 percent, beginning in 2002.

In spite of the ministry's attempt to give children more free time and develop their creativity, the reforms have not extended to broad changes in the entrance examination system for colleges. As a result, many parents feel that school classrooms have become a place to confirm what children already know instead of a center for learning and mastering new subjects. This concern has prompted them to plan ahead out of the fear of having their children fall behind.

For example, Natsuko, who is age 36 and has three school-aged children, comments that

I was too naive when I was raising my first child. You can't believe how smart today's children are. Most first graders already know several *kanji* [Chinese characters], not to mention being able to read and write *hiragana* [the Japanese phonetic syllabary]. My daughter was the only one in the class who could not write her name. Although we are told that teachers don't expect children to have mastered these things by the time they enter school, the fact that all the other children already know them makes the slow starters fall behind.

Another problem with the educational reforms is that all schools must meet minimum standards, but private schools are not bound by the curriculum guidelines stipulated by the Ministry of Education. That is, private schools can use more advanced materials than those used in public schools. They can also allocate more hours to important subjects, such as English, which carries more weight in the college entrance exams.

Given that a sizable portion of students admitted to the University of Tokyo, the most prestigious university in the Japanese educational hierarchy, come from private high schools with admission tracks tied to their own attached junior high schools, parents are reminded that educational competition starts at a very young age. Many of these schools push their curricula forward so that students can devote their entire senior year in high school to preparing for college entrance examinations. Private elementary schools are also attractive to parents who worry that their children will not fare well in the intense competition for junior high schools: many of these private institutions provide an admission track all the way up to high school. Consequently, the age for competition has been lowered, and the competition for a better school career has involved young preschool children.

Chisato is married to a computer engineer and has a three-year-old son. She is planning to send him to a private elementary school. He is attending a weekly preparatory program for the screening test. He also has to do workbook exercises at home with his mother. Chisato comments on their decision as follows:

I know it is a pity that a small boy like him has to work so hard, but it is for his own good. It is much easier to push him now than it will be later. If he can avoid the pressure of the entrance examination for junior high and high school, he can devote more time to developing his talents during the twelve years [he is in school full-time].

Kumiko, who is married to a physician, had a son just three weeks before I interviewed her. When I asked her how she felt about having a baby, she said,

I am glad Satoshi was born in April. Of course it's the best time for having a baby! The weather is nice, and I can take him outside and let him breathe fresh air. You know, oxygen is very important for brain development. Also, he will be one of the oldest in his class [the school year starts in April in Japan], and that will make him ahead of most children. Kids born in spring have better school records. I think that's why children born in April and May are overrepresented among students in the University of Tokyo.

I wish I had asked her where she got this idea about the birth month and the chance of being accepted to the University of Tokyo. When I met her a year later, she had put Satoshi in an enrichment class for infants run by one of the large *juku* establishments. She escorted Satoshi every week and joined an hour-long class with him. She commented bashfully,

Well, I don't mean to raise him as a "super kid." It's just a play group sort of program where children play with toys and listen to songs and so on. I just think it is important to let him play with other babies, because he has to know how to cooperate and socialize with his peers by the time he goes to kindergarten.

Although Kumiko's example may be an extreme case, there are three points that represent the ideas shared by many *kyōiku mama* today. First, a child has to go through keen academic competition in order to obtain a decent educational background. Second, a child's educational success depends on how much the parent puts into it. Third, the younger the child, the better the time for preparation. It is almost always the mother who is responsible for seeing to the provision of these opportunities and who is expected to be closely involved in the process. . . .

JAPANESE WOMEN IN THE COMMUNITY

While the publication trends in popular books set the tenor of public discourse on "good parenting," they also mirror what the public wants to read. The increased demands for parenting advice reflect the social context in which adult socialization takes place for young Japanese mothers.

Adult Socialization and the Role of the Mass Media

Assuming the parental role is a totally fresh endeavor for most Japanese women, who generally become mothers without any firsthand experience of taking care of small children (given that Japanese families typically now have few children). Unlike in the United States, baby-sitting is not a socially accepted way for teenagers to earn money. So it is not unusual for a mother to start parenting with no experience in changing diapers or bathing babies. Parenting, or mothering specifically, is a performance without rehearsal.

Japanese women learn parenting from several socializing agents: parents and in-laws, friends, neighbors, older siblings, books, magazines, television programs, parenting courses sponsored by local governments, and kindergartens and daycare centers. Among these sources, the mass media is of increasing importance as a socializing agent. When asked where they obtained information on infant care, 35 percent of mothers surveyed in Tokyo named the mass media (books, magazines, and television) as the primary source of information, 34 percent named friends, and 17 percent answered kindergartens and daycare centers (Shirasa 1990). Parents and kin networks still play a major role in providing emotional support, but apparently they are somewhat secondary in the transmission of parenting knowledge.

Given the rapid pace at which childrearing practices have changed over the past decades, it is understandable that what grandmothers did thirty years ago is not often applicable to today's childrearing. For example, women in their 60s raised children when bottle-feeding was predominant; it was regarded as superior and as the "modern" way of feeding. Now the trend has reversed. Today more mothers opt for breast-feeding if it is possible (Katsuura-Cook 1991).

The arrival of parenting magazines is a rational consequence of this "information gap." They began to be published in the early 1980s and now provide detailed, up-to-date information on childrearing practices based on children's ages. Opposite to the decline in the birth rate, the circulation of parenting magazines has steadily increased. The total circulation of the major twelve parenting magazines is estimated to be as high as 2,710,000 (Shiomi 1996). Almost all of these parenting magazines contain advertisements and paid publications by companies that provide extra-preschool curricula and educational materials. No single issue appears without their advertisements and their sponsored articles on early intervention programs.

The effect of the mass media on the early education boom can be seen in a survey that showed a positive relationship between mothers' reliance on published materials for parenting know-how and their attitudes toward extra-preschool curricula. The more they are exposed to parenting information through the mass media, the more they are likely to be influenced to provide enrichment "stimulus" through extra-preschool curricula (Shirasa 1990). These mothers are also more likely to feel uneasy about their child's development if other children of the same age are more advanced in writing Chinese characters and in computations. Thus reliance on the mass media for parenting information seems to go hand in hand with the popularization of early education.

Isolation and Anxiety: Childrearing Behind Closed Doors

Another prominent aspect in the lives of Japanese mothers who stay at home full-time is their isolation with their children. Because the social spheres of Japanese men and women tend to be so distinctly separated, there are very few opportunities for full-time housewives of salaried workers to socialize. The husband is busy with long working hours and rarely has spare time to help around the home with chores and childcare. Baby-sitters are not readily available in the neighborhood, and commercialized services are often too expensive. A mother is not qualified to have her baby enrolled in an accredited daycare center if she is not working or does not have another "legitimate" reason, such as illness. Commenting on her days with her baby, Toshiko, a full-time housewife married to a "salaryman," says: "A day, a week, and a month could easily pass without talking to any adult except for people in

the market or with a salesperson who comes to our door to sell educational toys and *futon*."

In spite of the great emphasis placed on close mother-child relationships in Japanese families, literature in psychology and sociology has long ignored the situation of young mothers. The focus of attention has always been on children and on how the mother-child relationship affects the development of a child's personality, well-being, and so on. Little has been written or known about how the mother-child relationship affects mothers.

The isolation of mothers from other adult interaction is another precondition for the development of the early education boom. Ironically, extra-preschool courses provide lonely mothers with a place to meet people. Toshiko said that she decided to put her son in an enrichment program because she wanted to meet people and make friends. The "friends" she was talking about were not for her son, but for herself. Kumiko, mentioned earlier in this chapter, also said that chatting with other mothers in the waiting room while their children took classes provided a nice change of pace.

Many mothers are aware of the suffocation of lonely childrearing and many of them do try to get out of the isolation. Ochiai (1989) argues that a new type of network among mothers is emerging in urban areas in response to the lack of support from husbands and kin. They are of a spontaneous nature, usually composed of mothers who meet each other in neighborhood parks or parenting classes sponsored by the local government. These neighborhood networks provide mutual support in parenting and supplement kin networks. However, my observation is that much of what Ochiai calls "networks" tend to be exclusive, rarely involve fathers, and limit concerns to matters revolving around children.

Yoshiko used to work as a secretary at a trading company until she became pregnant. She decided to leave her job and take care of her son at home. The change in her lifestyle and the routines of a full-time housewife were "a kind of culture shock" to her. She described her days as follows:

I usually take my son to a neighborhood park in the morning so that he can play with other children. Mothers chat while children play in the sandbox. If the kids move to the swings, we move with them and chat around the swing, or slides, or whatever. Then we usually go to one of the mothers' houses, order pizza or noodles for lunch, and then chat in the afternoon while the children play in the house. When daddies are on business trips, we sometimes eat supper together. The members are the same and the topic of our conversation is the same. At first I enjoyed being with these people, but I am getting tired of it. It's so suffocating!

After several months, she decided to have her son enroll in Suzuki violin and Kumon so that she could avoid this situation.

I was getting tired of this, but did not want to be ostracized and to be left alone with my kid. Having a private lesson for him gave me a good excuse for keeping some distance from other mothers. They won't feel bad about me if I just say, "I can't join you today because I have to take my kid to a violin lesson."

Again, extra-preschool courses are meeting the demands of their patrons. They provide a place to meet other mothers—and to avoid them.

"A GOOD MOTHER" AS A STATUS: THE CULTURAL CONTRADICTIONS IN WOMEN'S ROLES

Mothers receive mixed and conflicting messages [about] labor force participation: you have to be a good mother, but childrearing will not occupy you for your entire life. On the one hand, mothers are pressed to stay home at least until their children reach the age of three. On the other hand, mothers are aware that they have to be prepared to pursue their "own lives," for their children will grow up and leave the nest. Men and women, especially those who have pursued higher education, have been exposed to contemporary cultural values that emphasize the significance of achievement. . . .

Over 80 percent of Japanese women join the labor force upon graduating from school, but more than 80 percent of these women have withdrawn from the labor force for one year or longer by the time they reach the age of 34. The probability of leaving one's job is not necessarily lower for women with higher education (Brinton 1993; Hirao 1997). That is, highly educated women are as likely to be out of the labor force as their less-educated counterparts during the prime parenting years. Moreover, the probability of coming back to the labor force after initial "retirement" is not necessarily higher for four-year university graduates (Hirao 1998). In other words, Japanese women's human capital is very much under-utilized in the labor force.

The most striking thing that I noticed throughout my interviews was the frustration shared by many young mothers. "What depresses me is the social trend that gives praise to career women," said Yuko, a graduate from a prestigious four-year university. She used to work at a large department store as a sales assistant and resigned from her job when she had her second daughter.

They say it's good to be "at the top," pursue your career, and earn money. Super moms who can handle both work and family appear as attractive figures in TV dramas. I used to have self-confidence. I was always at the top both in school and work. My grades were higher than those of my male classmates. I thought I was in a career track until I left it to take care of my kids. Now, I ask myself, "What am I doing here?" I feel trapped and left behind by the rest of the world.

Emiko, who also has two children, expresses her frustration more clearly.

I used to have everything except kids: study, work, travel, and love. I was imbued with the pleasure of achieving what I deserved. But now, I am doing nothing but raising children, feeding them, bathing them, chasing them around, and yelling at them. My speculation is that, in spite of the primacy given to mothering by childcare experts, the perceived value of childrearing is declining.

These women, particularly those with higher education, have experienced an egalitarian school environment and have internalized, to some extent, the idea that it is crucial even for women to have status in society. Upon becoming mothers, however, the role of mother becomes their primary social identity.

Ōhinata (1982) reports changes in mothers' attitudes toward the value of childcare. She compared the attitude of two cohorts of highly educated mothers, one in their 60s and the other in their 30s. Both cohorts shared the idea that child-rearing is physically and emotionally demanding. A significant difference was observed, however, in how they viewed the value of childrearing. A majority (74 percent) of the older cohort agreed that childrearing is a worthwhile and wonderful job, while only 40 percent of the younger cohort shared this view. The majority (61 percent) of the younger cohort asserted that their reasons to live exist outside childrearing, while only 20 percent of the older cohort expressed this view.

The ambivalence toward parenting among young mothers is a natural consequence of changing lifestyles. Being a mother no longer necessarily provides a sense of achievement. Becoming a "good mother," however, is a different story. The ideology of the good mother has exerted a strong normative force on Japanese women during the last two decades. This is because mother and child have been seen as an inseparable pair, the mother and child relationship has been conceptualized as an extension of a mother's "self," a substantial proportion of a child's achievement is believed to result from his or her "effort" rather than from innate individual capabilities, and a child's outcomes have become more easily measurable at an early stage of childhood (e.g., school records and results in entrance examinations to prestigious elementary schools).

Mothers can learn where their child stands relative to other children at quite an early stage through various assessments. The results are thought to reflect how hard the child—and the mother—worked. When we take into account the presumably close psychological proximity between mother and

child in Japan and the beliefs related to the causal link between maternal care and child outcomes, it is logical to see being a good mother as a status, one that is achievable depending on how much effort one makes.

Natsumi works part-time as a shop clerk in a confectionery store. She feels that her parenting is constantly being assessed. In her view, "'a good child' is necessary for becoming 'a good mother.'"

When I talk with other mothers, I often feel that they are evaluating each other's "worth" by the "quality" of the child. A good child is what makes you proud. It isn't your career, your achievement, or what you do as an individual. These things don't count in the world of mothers!

Tomoe, a physician's wife and the full-time mother of one daughter, described early intervention programs as "addictive."

I wasn't serious when I started sending my daughter to a *yōji kyōshitsu*. I was just curious about the program when I saw their flyer in the newspaper. After I enrolled her, however, I soon learned that such a program has an addictive power. She liked going there, and it was exciting to see how quickly and how much a child can learn. This excitement makes you feel as if it was you who took the test and scored so well. Once you feel this excitement, it is very hard to stop; you don't want to feel that you have failed in something.

The *kyōiku mama* syndrome is not an irreversible process: Tomoe began to notice that she was seeking a vicarious sense of achievement.

One day, I was telling my daughter to do her homework. She must have thought I was nagging her too much. She stared at me and said, "Mom, it's my homework, not yours. Don't talk to me like that." I realized that I was pushing her too hard and that being an extreme *kyōiku mama* can be its own form of child abuse.

CRITICAL THINKING QUESTIONS

1. The Japanese government has tried to reduce the extreme competition to enter college. Why have these efforts been largely unsuccessful?

2. How are Japanese mothers, but not fathers, socialized to be active participants in their children's early education? Also, how is the isolation of mothers one of the reasons for their involvement in the early education boom?

3. What is the cultural contradiction about gender roles that educated mothers encounter in Japanese society? Do you think that Canadian mothers experience the same contradictions? Why or why not?

REFERENCES

Allison, Anne. 1996. *Permitted and prohibited desires: Mothers, comics, and censorship in Japan*. Boulder, CO: Westview Press.

Boocock, Sarane Spence. 1991. The Japanese preschool system. In *Windows on Japanese Education*, ed. Edward R. Beauchamp, 97–126. New York: Greenwood Press.

Brinton, Mary C. 1993. *Women and the economic miracle: Gender and work in postwar Japan*. Berkeley: University of California Press.

Doman, Glenn. 1964. *How to teach your baby to read*. New York: Random House.

———. 1984. *How to multiply your baby's intelligence*. New York: Doubleday.

Ellington, Lucien. 1992. *Education in the Japanese life-cycle*. Lewiston, NY: E. Mellen Press.

Field, Norma. 1995. The child as laborer and consumer: The disappearance of childhood in contemporary Japan. In *Children and the politics of culture*, ed. Sharon Stephens, 51–78. Princeton, NJ: Princeton University Press.

Hirao, Keiko. 1997. Work histories and home investment of married Japanese women. Doctoral dissertation. University of Notre Dame, Department of Sociology.

———. 1998. Saishushoku no taiming: Kekkon/shussan taishokugo no rōdōshijō saisanyū katei no hasādo bunseki (Hazard analyses on the timing of re-entry to the labor force). Paper presented at the annual meeting of the Japanese Sociological Society, Kwansei Gakuin University, Nishinomiya, Japan.

Ibuka, Masaru. 1976. *Yōchien dewa ososugiru* (Kindergarten is too late). Tokyo: Goma Shobo.

———. 1991. *Zerosai* (Zero-year-old). Tokyo: Gomashobo.

———. 1992. *Taijikara* (From embryo). Tokyo: Tokumashobo.

Katsuura-Cook, Noriko. 1991. *Nihon no kosodate, Amerika no kosodate* (Child-rearing in Japan and the United States). Tokyo: Saiensu.

Kumon Kyōiku Kenkyūkai. 1998. *Company profiles*. Tokyo: Kumon Kyōiku Kenkyūkai.

Ministry of Education, Japan. 1994. *Survey report on Juku and other extra-school programs*. Tokyo: Author.

Ministry of Health and Welfare, Japan. 1991. *Survey on children's environment*. Tokyo: Government Printing Office.

Mitsuishi, Yukiko. 1988. *Tensaiji o tsukuru!* (Creating prodigies). Tokyo: Foyu.

Ochiai, Emiko. 1989. *Kindai kazoku to feminizumu* (Modern families and feminism). Tokyo: Keisōshobō.

Ōhinata, Masami. 1982. Hahaoya no shinriteki antei to jūsoku o motomete (For the mental stability and fulfillment of mothers). In *Ikuji noirōze* (Childrearing depression). Tokyo: Yūhikaku.

Ōshima, Kiyoshi. 1988. *Taikyō* (Prenatal education). Tokyo: Gomashobō.

Shichida, Makoto. 1983. *Kiseki ga okiru shichidashiki zerosai kyōiku* (Miraculous education for zero-year-olds). Tokyo: Homeidō.

———. 1985. *Akachan wo kashikoku sodateru himitsu* (Tips on raising an intelligent baby). Tokyo: Nihon Keizai Shimbunsha.

Shiomi, Toshiyuki. 1996. *Yōji kyōiku sangyō to kosodate* (Education industry and childrearing). Tokyo: Iwanami Shoten.

Shirasa, Izumi. 1990. *Sōki kyōiku ni kansuru kahaoya no taidō* (Attitude of mothers on early education). Master's paper, University of Tokyo.

Stevenson, Harold W. 1992. Learning from Asian schools. *Scientific American*, 267 (December): 70–6.

Uno, Kathleen S. 1993. The death of "good wife, wise mother"? In *Postwar Japan as history*, ed. Andrew Gordon. Berkeley: University of California Press.

White, Merry. 1987. *The Japanese educational challenge: A commitment to children*. New York: Free Press.

60

The Social Structure of Medicine

TALCOTT PARSONS

CLASSIC

CONTEMPORARY

CROSS-CULTURAL

Talcott Parsons, one of the most influential U.S. sociologists during the twentieth century, contributed greatly to the development of structural-functional analysis. In this selection, he examines the significance of health and illness within a social system, with particular attention to the social roles of physicians and patients.

A little reflection will show immediately that the problem of health is intimately involved in the functional prerequisites of the social system. . . . Certainly by almost any definition health is included in the functional needs of the individual member of the society so that from the point of view of functioning of the social system, too low a general level of health, too high an incidence of illness, is dysfunctional. This is in the first instance because illness incapacitates for the effective performance of social roles. It could of course be that this incidence was completely uncontrollable by social action, an inde-

Source: Reprinted with the permission of The Free Press, a Division of Simon & Schuster Adult Publishing Group, from *The Social System* by Talcott Parsons. Copyright © 1951, copyright renewed 1979 by Talcott Parsons.

pendently given condition of social life. But insofar as it is controllable, through rational action or otherwise, it is clear that there is a functional interest of the society in its control, broadly in the minimization of illness. As one special aspect of this, attention may be called to premature death. From a variety of points of view, the birth and rearing of a child constitute a "cost" to the society, through pregnancy, child care, socialization, formal training, and many other channels. Premature death, before the individual has had the opportunity to play out his full quota of social roles, means that only a partial "return" for this cost has been received.

All this would be true were illness purely a "natural phenomenon" in the sense that, like the vagaries of the weather, it

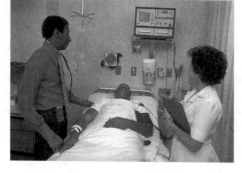

was not, to our knowledge, reciprocally involved in the motivated interactions of human beings. In this case illness would be something which merely "happened to" people, which involved consequences which had to be dealt with and conditions which might or might not be controllable but was in no way an expression of motivated behavior.

This is in fact the case for a very important part of illness, but it has become increasingly clear, by no means for all. In a variety of ways motivational factors accessible to analysis in action terms are involved in the etiology of many illnesses, and conversely, though without exact correspondence, many conditions are open to therapeutic influence through motivational channels. To take the simplest kind of case, differential exposure, to injuries or to infection, is certainly motivated, and the role of unconscious wishes to be injured or to fall ill in such cases has been clearly demonstrated. Then there is the whole range of "psychosomatic" illness about which knowledge has been rapidly accumulating in recent years. Finally, there is the field of "mental disease," the symptoms of which occur mainly on the behavioral level. . . .

Summing up, we may say that illness is a state of disturbance in the "normal" functioning of the total human individual, including both the state of the organism as a biological system and of his personal and social adjustments. It is thus partly biologically and partly socially defined. . . .

Medical practice . . . is a "mechanism" in the social system for coping with the illnesses of its members. It involves a set of institutionalized roles. . . . The immediately relevant social structures consist in the patterning of the role of the medical practitioner himself and, though to common sense it may seem superfluous to analyze it, that of the "sick person" himself. . . .

The role of the medical practitioner belongs to the general class of "professional" roles, a subclass of the larger group of occupational roles. Caring for the sick is thus not an incidental activity of other roles though, for example, mothers do a good deal of it—but has become functionally specialized as a full-time "job." This, of course, is by

no means true of all societies. As an occupational role it is institutionalized about the technical content of the function which is given a high degree of primacy relative to other status-determinants. It is thus inevitable both that incumbency of the role should be achieved and that performance criteria by standards of technical competence should be prominent. Selection for it and the context of its performance are to a high degree segregated from other bases of social status and solidarities. . . . Unlike the role of the businessman, however, it is collectivity-oriented not self-oriented.

The importance of this patterning is, in one context, strongly emphasized by its relation to the cultural tradition. One basis for the division of labor is the specialization of technical competence. The role of physician is far along the continuum of increasingly high levels of technical competence required for performance. Because of the complexity and subtlety of the knowledge and skill required and the consequent length and intensity of training, it is difficult to see how the functions could, under modern conditions, be ascribed to people occupying a prior status as one of their activities in that status, following the pattern by which, to a degree, responsibility for the health of her children is ascribed to the mother-status. There is an intrinsic connection between achieved statuses and the requirements of high technical competence. . . .

High technical competence also implies specificity of function. Such intensive devotion to expertness in matters of health and disease precludes comparable expertness in other fields. The physician is not, by virtue of his modern role, a generalized "wise man" or sage—though there is considerable folklore to that effect—but a specialist whose superiority to his fellows is confined to the specific sphere of his technical training and experience. For example, one does not expect the physician as such to have better judgment about foreign policy or tax legislation than any other comparably intelligent and well-educated citizen. There are of course elaborate subdivisions of specialization within the profession. . . . The physician is [also] expected to treat an objective problem in objective, scientifically justifiable terms. For example, whether he likes or dislikes the particular patient as a person is supposed to be irrelevant, as indeed it is to most purely objective problems of how to handle a particular disease.

. . . The "ideology" of the profession lays great emphasis on the obligation of the physician to put the "welfare of the patient" above his personal interests, and regards "commercialism" as the most serious and insidious evil with which it has to contend. The line, therefore, is drawn primarily vis-à-vis "business." The "profit motive" is supposed to be drastically excluded from the medical world. This attitude is, of course, shared with the other professions, but it is perhaps more pronounced in the medical case than in any single one except perhaps the clergy. . . .

An increasing proportion of medical practice is now taking place in the context of organization. To a large extent this is necessitated by the technological development of medicine itself, above all the need for technical facilities beyond the reach of the individual practitioner, and the fact that treating the same case often involves the complex cooperation of several different kinds of physicians as well as of auxiliary personnel. This greatly alters the relation of the physician to the rest of the instrumental complex. He tends to be relieved of much responsibility and hence necessarily of freedom, in relation to his patients other than in his technical role. Even if a hospital executive is a physician himself, he is not in the usual sense engaged in the "practice of medicine" in performing his functions any more than the president of the Miners' Union is engaged in mining coal.

As was noted, for common sense there may be some question of whether "being sick" constitutes a social role at all—isn't it simply a state of fact, a "condition"? Things are not quite so simple as this. The test is the existence of a set of institutionalized expectations and the corresponding sentiments and sanctions.

There seem to be four aspects of the institutionalized expectation system relative to the sick role. First is the exemption from normal social role responsibilities, which of course is relative to the nature and severity of the illness. This exemption requires legitimation by and to the various alter involved and the physician often serves as a court of appeal as well as a direct legitimating agent. It is noteworthy that, like all institutionalized patterns, the legitimation of being sick enough to avoid obligations can not only be a right of the sick person but an obligation upon him. People are often resistant to admitting they are sick and it is not uncommon for others to tell them that they *ought* to stay in bed. The word generally has a moral connotation. It goes almost without saying that this legitimation has the social function of protection against "malingering."

The second closely related aspect is the institutionalized definition that the sick person cannot be expected by "pulling himself together" to get well by an act of decision or will. In this sense also he is exempted from responsibility—he is in a condition that must "be taken care of." His "condition" must be changed, not merely his "attitude." Of course the process of recovery may be spontaneous but while the illness lasts he can't "help it." This element in the definition of the state of illness is obviously crucial as a bridge to the acceptance of "help."

The third element is the definition of the state of being ill as itself undesirable with its obligation to want to "get well." The first two elements of legitimation of the sick role thus are conditional in a highly important sense. It is a relative legitimation so long as he is in this unfortunate state which both he and alter hope he can get out of as expeditiously as possible.

Finally, the fourth closely related element is the obligation—in proportion to the severity of the condition, of course—to seek *technically competent* help, namely, in the most usual case, that of a physician and to cooperate with him in the process of trying to get well. It is here, of course, that the role of the sick person as patient becomes articulated with that of the physician in a complementary role structure.

It is evident from the above that the role of motivational factors in illness immensely broadens the scope and increases the importance of the institutionalized role aspect of being sick. For then the problem of social control becomes much more than one of ascertaining facts and drawing lines. The privileges and exemptions of the sick role may become objects of a "secondary gain" which the patient is positively motivated, usually unconsciously, to secure or to retain. The problem, therefore, of the balance of motivations to recover becomes of first importance. In general motivational balances of great functional significance to the social system are institutionally controlled, and it should, therefore, not be surprising that this is no exception.

A few further points may be made about the specific patterning of the sick role and its relation to social structure. It is, in the first place, a "contingent" role into which anyone, regardless of his status in other respects, may come. It is, furthermore, in the type case temporary. One may say that it is in a certain sense a "negatively achieved" role, through failure to "keep well," though, of course, positive motivations also operate, which by that very token must be motivations to deviance. . . .

The orientation of the sick role vis-à-vis the physician is also defined as collectively-oriented. It is true that the patient has a very obvious self-interest in getting well in most cases, though this point may not always be so simple. But once he has called in a physician the attitude is clearly marked, that he has assumed the obligation to co-operate with that physician in what is regarded as a common task. The obverse of the physician's obligation to be guided by the welfare of the patient is the latter's obligation to "do his part" to the best of his ability. This point is clearly brought out, for example, in the attitudes of the profession toward what is called "shopping around." By that is meant the practice of a patient "checking" the advice of one physician against that of another without telling physician A that he intends to consult physician B, or if he comes back to A that he has done so or who B is. The medical view is that if the patient is not satisfied with the advice his physician gives him he may properly do one of two things. First he may request a consultation, even naming the physician he wishes called in, but in that case it is physician A not the patient who must call B in, the patient may not see B independently, and above all not without A's knowledge. The other proper recourse is to terminate the relation with A and become "B's patient." The notable fact here is that a pattern of behavior on the part not only of the physician but also of the patient, is expected which is in sharp contrast to perfectly legitimate behavior in a commercial relationship. If he is buying a car there is no objection to the customer going to a number of dealers before making up his mind, and there is no obligation for him to inform any one dealer what others he is consulting, to say nothing of approaching the Chevrolet dealer only through the Ford dealer.

The doctor-patient relationship is thus focused on these pattern elements. The patient has a need for technical services because he doesn't—nor do his lay associates, family members, etc.—"know" what is the matter or what to do about it, nor does he control the necessary facilities. The physician is a technical expert who by special training and experience, and by an institutionally validated status, is qualified to "help" the patient in a situation institutionally defined as legitimate in a relative sense but as needing help. . . .

CRITICAL THINKING QUESTIONS

1. Does Parsons understand illness as a biological condition, that is, "something that happens to people"? What are the social elements in health and illness?

2. According to Parsons, what are the distinctive characteristics of the social role of the physician?

3. What are the major elements of "the sick role"? In what respects does Parsons view the social roles of physicians and patients as complementary? Can you see ways in which they may be in conflict?

61

Getting What We Pay For: Myths and Realities About Financing Canada's Health Care System

RAISA B. DEBER

This research illustrates how the concept of privatization is often misunderstood by conflating private delivery with private insurance. It also argues that public insurance is more equitable because it provides care for everybody regardless of health status. In contrast, private insurers prefer healthy clients and are likely to turn down potential customers who need health care the most—people who have a high risk of becoming ill or suffer from chronic conditions such as AIDS.

Canadian Medicare is, once again, under attack. Despite being wildly popular among Canadians, and internationally admired, our system of universal insurance for "medically necessary" hospital and physician services is being dismissed by critics as old-fashioned, unsustainable, economically unfeasible, and otherwise out of step with our new global times. The newspapers are full of announcements of "privatization" of hospital care in Alberta, accusations that "we already have two tier medicine" and might as well finish the job, and seemingly erudite pronouncements that we must choose between "maintaining equity" and economic good sense. Too often, however, these criticisms result from some fundamental

confusions about both concepts and evidence. In consequence, they often misinterpret the actual problems with Medicare. Just as physicians cannot treat without an accurate diagnosis, healing Medicare requires that we be clear in defining our terms.

DEFINING OUR TERMS: ELEMENTS OF HEALTH CARE SYSTEMS AND THE PUBLIC-PRIVATE MIX

Although we commonly speak of a "health care system," it is important to recognize that we are usually focused more narrowly upon care for people who are (or are at risk of becoming) ill. Clearly, medical care is only one small part of what makes us healthy. As individuals, we are faced with an endless stream of admonitions to watch our diet, stop smoking, exercise more, practice safe sex, avoid recreational drug use,

Source: Raisa B. Deber. 2000. "Getting What We Pay For: Myths and Realities about Financing Canada's Health Care System," pp. 1–6, 8–10. Paper prepared for the Dialogue on Health Reform: Sustaining Confidence in Canada's Health Care System.

and, by the way, avoid stress, even when thinking about all of our unhealthy habits. As a society, we are well aware of the importance of clean air, clean water, safe foods, and being immunized against infectious diseases. We know that poverty is strongly correlated to ill health, and that an individual who must sleep on the street is unlikely to be healthy. Although we recognize the critical importance of public health or other policies outside the "health care system" toward maintaining and improving the health of the general population, and note that present-day Canadians appear to be among the healthiest and longest-lived populations in human history, this paper will deal more narrowly with medical care. There is still a need for health care services when we are sick or injured. The question this paper will focus on is how best to pay for these services.

What we will concentrate upon are the payment questions involved when an individual seeks care from hospitals, doctors, nurses, rehabilitation specialists, pharmacists, and other health care workers. We will begin by speaking of these in the language of economics. In effect, economists often view obtaining such care as a series of transactions, in which a "consumer" (often known as a "patient") "demands" services from a "provider" who in turn is paid (by someone) for the services which they provide. As we will note below, there are some conceptual differences between being a "patient" and being a "consumer," but for the time being, let us stick with the language of economics.

Using this sort of language, we can separate health care systems into three dimensions:

We will use the term *financing* to refer to the methods by which money is collected from all of those consumers, and potential consumers, of health care. Financing thus includes an array of taxes and premiums, collected from individuals and corporations, and collected by governments, insurers, and providers. Financing also includes consideration of who will be covered, and for what services.

We will use the term *delivery* to refer to all the ways in which those health care services are actually organized and delivered.

Finally, we will use the term *allocation* to refer to the variety of ways in which financing is linked to delivery. In other words, allocation refers to the way in which we choose to pay providers, and includes such topics as what incentives are inherent in the ways providers of care are paid for delivering services.

As we will see, many of the problems we have had in diagnosing the problems in our health care system have arisen from the failure to distinguish between financing and delivery. Other confusions have arisen when pathologies are diagnosed in allocation, but the suggested therapies instead deal with financing or delivery, which are working relatively well. To shift metaphors, one doesn't fix a malfunctioning appliance by breaking the parts which are already working!

Public and Private

Another set of confusions has arisen over the meaning of the terms *public* and *private*. Here, we are using the term "public" to denote "government." As we recognize, Canada has many levels of government. By "public," we can accordingly be speaking of the *federal* government in Ottawa, of the various *provincial* governments, of the series of *regional* governments and authorities within most provinces, or of *local* governments. Indeed, there has been a series of noisy battles occurring within the public sector, as provinces battle with Ottawa for more funds, and as provincial governments download some responsibilities to regions and local governments.

The term "private" is even more confusing. When we hear "private," we usually think about large *for-profit corporations,* responsible for providing a good return on investment to their shareholders. But private also encompasses *small businessmen*/entrepreneurs who do not issue stock; indeed, most Canadian physicians are private providers, running their own small businesses and making their living from the "profit." (Physicians are understandably annoyed to have their billings misrepresented as "salary"—the billings are instead their revenues, from which they must run their practices and pay their staff.) Private also includes a large *not-for-profit* sector. Some of these not-for-profit organizations, such as the Canadian Cancer Society or a local agency which delivers Meals on Wheels, rely heavily upon volunteer labour. But other not-for-profits are sizeable organizations, with paid employees. Finally, private includes *individuals* and their families. As any parent knows, most care for minor conditions is delivered privately, and never even comes in contact with the formal care delivery system.

Within the Canadian health care system, it is important to realize that almost all delivery of care is already private. Canada is not England. Under the system of "socialized medicine" found in such countries as the UK or Scandinavia, providers of health care work for some level of government and are therefore categorized as public employees. In contrast, most Canadian providers work in the private sector. This fact is often obscured because Canada has long used the rather confusing term "public hospital" to refer to private, not-for-profit institutions. To clarify the distinction, employees of "public hospitals" do not work for government, and are not civil servants. Ontario's provincial psychiatric hospitals would accordingly be classified as public delivery, because their employees are indeed part of the Ontario public service, and their management must follow civil service guidelines. In contrast, employees of the North York General Hospital report to an independent hospital board and management, and would therefore be classified as working for a private sector, not-for-profit organization. Even in the provinces which have moved toward regional authorities, the employees of these regional boards are not civil servants, and the regional management is not bound by civil service requirements.

One reason for the confusion is that our "public hospitals" do receive most of their funding from government; in 1997, just over 90% of the spending for hospital care came from public sources. However, this reliance upon public financing does not eliminate their formal organizational independence. Indeed, in that same year, physicians received 99% of their funding from the public sector, but are certainly not government employees (much as they may feel so if the paper work gets sufficiently aggravating). Political scientists are fond of attaching labels to this sort of private organization which nonetheless often acts on behalf of the public interest, and may be regulated by and funded from government. Some refer to them as "mediating structures"; others refer to them as the "third sector." Under any label, they are a critical component of Canada's health care system.

As we will see, this distinction between types of private is important in clarifying whether Ralph Klein's initiative in Alberta really represents "privatizing" hospitals. Premier Klein has introduced legislation which would permit for-profit clinics to be paid by the government for delivering insured health care services, as an alternative to giving the money to existing not-for-profit hospitals. This initiative does not represent a shift from public delivery to private delivery; instead, it is a shift from not-for-profit private to for-profit private delivery. The distinction also clarifies that privatization of funding has little to do with the need "to allow innovation in a stultified public delivery system," since, as we have just noted, most Canadian providers are already private. Instead, these debates are really about three things. First, we are often arguing about the total amount of money allocated—whether it is sufficient, and whether it is being used appropriately. Second, we may concentrate upon the nature of the incentives built into the funding allocation approach, and whether these are effective in ensuring that the services we want are being provided. Third, and critical to the debate about the Alberta initiative, we are debating the role of for-profit corporations, as opposed to not-for-profit organizations, in delivering health care in Canada.

BASIC ECONOMICS AND THE CONCEPT OF MEDICAL NECESSITY

Consider the following two scenarios:

1. You hail a taxi and ask the driver to take you to a destination across the city. You do not have enough money for the trip. Should you be taken there anyhow?
2. You have won a free all-expenses-paid week for two in a vacation spot of your choice, with the only catch being that the trip had to be taken sometime within the next twelve months. Do you accept?

In its simplest form, microeconomics deals with three components: supply, demand, and price. Price acts as the signalling factor that links supply and demand. Any self-respecting economist can plot supply and demand curves and look for their intersection. For example, if the price drops, the quantity demanded should increase; there should be a near infinite demand for free goods. Conversely, if supply is fixed and demand increases, price should rise until enough people get priced out of the market to balance the quantity supplied and this new (lower) quantity demanded at the new equilibrium price. Most people agree with the predictions which economic theory would make. For scenario 1, most would agree that the taxi driver is under no obligation to take you. If you cannot pay the cost the taxi driver wishes for the trip, you are priced out of the market for taxicabs. In turn, if you are priced out of the taxicab market, you can walk. If taxi fares get so high that there are insufficient customers, either some providers will leave the market, or prices will fall to a level with a more satisfactory balance of quantity supplied and quantity demanded.

For scenario 2, most people would be delighted to accept the free vacation.

Now consider two similar scenarios relating to health matters:

1. You come into a hospital emergency room with a ruptured appendix. You do not have enough money for the surgery. Should you be treated anyhow?
2. You have won free open heart surgery in the hospital of your choice, with the only catch being that the surgery must be performed within the next twelve months. Do you accept?

Suddenly, economic theory does not seem to apply. Most people would agree that your appendix should be treated, and would be horrified were you turned away for financial reasons. In economic terms, however, this means that we will not allow you to be priced out of the market for appendix care, or other sorts of services which you "need." Under those circumstances, we have set up a rather peculiar economic model, in which there is a "floor price" (whatever charity or the public system agrees to pay for that service) but no ceiling price. The private tier is thus free to jack up their prices as high as they wish, because anyone priced out of their market has the option of falling back into the publicly-funded tier. Indeed, providers working simultaneously within both tiers are assured that they will get at least the price which would be paid by the public tier, with the ability to collect whatever additional private charges they can as a bonus. Two disquieting consequences follow. First, under these circumstances, market forces can no longer achieve cost control; the refusal to allow people to be priced out of the market means that markets can't set a ceiling price. Second, unless the publicly-funded tier is inadequate (or at least, perceived to be inadequate), there would be no reason for "consumers" to pay extra for care. As we will note below, the myth that a privately-funded tier could strengthen the public system by "freeing up" time and resources accordingly makes no economic sense, precisely because a viable private tier depends upon eroding the publicly funded system to create a market for privately funded care.

But need has a flip side, as can be seen in considering our likely responses to scenario 2. Most people would be eager to take that free trip. However, whenever I have tested this hypothetical offer of free surgery, the main response is laughter, and then the statement, "only if I needed it." Microeconomics speaks of "demand." However, much of health care instead speaks the language of "need."

There is a category of good, often referred to as "merit goods," which most societies believe should not operate according to the laws of the market. Instead, these goods are allocated on some basis of need and merit. Need is a complex concept, and notoriously difficult to define. However, we tend to know it when we see it, at least in extreme situations. Market models are not designed to assist us in allocating resources on the basis of need. Indeed, the concept is inherently paternalistic, since "need" must be validated by some outside authority. I can tell you what I want, but we allow health professionals (or "society") to determine what I need. The term "consumer" is accordingly inappropriate when we are talking about these sorts of services. Consumers purchase what they want and can afford. Patients receive what they need. And, just as we are unwilling to deny people with a ruptured appendix care they "need," we consider it inappropriate, or even unethical, to provide most medical services if they are not needed. If a shoe store has an excess supply, they may hold a sale, and no one worries if I already have twelve pairs of similar shoes, if the shoes are unattractive, or even whether or not they fit. However, if my local hospital had surplus operating room time, it could not advertise Half-price Surgery, Today Only. We can speak of unnecessary surgery, in a way we cannot speak about unnecessary shoes. And in turn, this implies that the issue of finding the resources to pay for things that we "need" is fundamentally different from paying for things which we merely "want" or "demand."

THE NATURE OF INSURANCE

Insurance is a way to distribute risks by pooling expected costs both across time, and across a wider population. To take an arbitrary example, imagine 10,000 homes, distributed across many communities and each valued at $300,000. Now assume that, on average, one will be destroyed every year by lightning. Without insurance, most people would not be struck by lightning, and therefore would not have to replace their house, but one unlucky individual would incur a bill of $300,000. Most people would find that cost prohibitive. However, if each household paid a $40 premium, we could create a pool of $400,000. That should be enough to reimburse the unlucky individual, cover the costs of collecting the premiums, and still allow a profit for the group willing to act as the insurer. Each individual would be trading a sure loss of $40 to avoid a potential loss of $300,000. However, "on average" is not the same as "exactly." Some years, no houses would be struck. In other years, lightning might hit two or even three. If only $400,000 were collected, the pool would not be large enough to cover the losses in such years. Precisely because the number of unlucky individuals is unpredictable, the logic of insurance encourages large risk pools, so that peaks and valleys are more likely to average out to a predictable value.

However, not all houses are at equal risk. In insurance markets, this difference in risk links to two important concepts—"moral hazard," which pertains to the behaviour of those insured, and "risk selection," which pertains to the behaviour of those who are doing the insuring.

Economists use the term "moral hazard" to refer to the fact that rational individuals are more likely to buy insurance if they think they are more likely to use services. Indeed, people may even engage in risky behaviour precisely because they are insured (*e.g.*, building on a flood plain if they have flood insurance). Moral hazard in turn suggests that rational insurers are not willing to extend unlimited coverage to a population which can voluntarily decide whether they wish to purchase insurance. Some obvious examples suggest themselves. Those people wishing cosmetic surgery would be far more likely to purchase insurance which would cover such services than would the general population. Women in their 70s would not purchase additional coverage for childbirth. Similarly, those who are young and healthy may be more willing to forego health insurance than those who already know they have a chronic disease. However, moral hazard in health care does not work in quite the same way that it does for other insurance markets. People are unlikely to abuse their health solely because they will not have to pay for the resulting care, because poor health has too many other unpleasant consequences.

The flip side of "moral hazard" is referred to as "risk selection." In this case, the rational insurer seeks to avoid those customers most likely to cost them money. Sometimes, they refuse a policy outright. Other times, they charge higher premiums. If they can, they will also seek to limit their "exposure" to claims. Just as the insurer can cap the amount payable for the destroyed house at $300,000, sellers of health insurance also try to limit the amount they must pay for claims. As one example, most dental policies sold limit the total amount that they will pay for dental work.

As Deborah Stone has noted,[1] there are two basic ways to determine insurance premiums. One approach is to charge everyone the same rate; she refers to this as employing solidarity principles. Under this type of system, often known as "community rating," those at high risk are subsidized by those at lower risk. The alternative is to employ actuarial principles, also known as risk-rating or medical underwriting. Under this model, premiums are based on expected claims. Automobile insurance works on this principle; the teenager with the sports car will pay far higher premiums than the proverbial little old lady who only drives to church on Sundays.

In general, we consider this fair. If the teenager finds insurance too expensive, she can walk or find a part-time job. Neither are we concerned if the person with a history of traffic accidents finds he cannot afford to keep driving. However, when we are talking about health care, things become a bit trickier. We are no longer as comfortable to find people priced out of the market. We are not sure whether the person with a history of cancer should pay higher premiums for health insurance. Unfortunately, any altruistic insurer who agrees to give lower rates to these high risk individuals is likely to lose their lower risk customers to less magnanimous competitors who can offer bargain rates to the healthy. As Fein has noted, the resulting spiral means that those companies willing to cover such high-risk cases usually become less and less competitive, precisely because they find themselves left with the costliest cases.[2] Solidarity-based markets are inherently unstable if competition among insurers is allowed; therefore, because competitors have an incentive to woo those at lower risk by offering them lower premiums and/or enhanced benefits (*e.g.*, wellness programs). Without government regulation, competing insurers will employ actuarial rating, which means that high risks will eventually be priced out of the market. For example, a General Accounting Office (GAO) study of the US private insurance market found that they "virtually always denied coverage" to individuals with AIDS or heart disease; for individuals with other serious conditions, such as chronic back pain, anemia, knee injury, glaucoma, and asthma, the coverage excluded costs arising from these "pre-existing conditions." Similarly, almost all travel health insurance policies will tend to exclude pre-existing conditions and carefully examine the medical history of their prospective clients. Very few travel health insurers are willing to cover your 85-year-old mother with a cardiac condition, even though she really wants to visit Florida. In the US, insurers are increasingly seeking to avoid having to cover individuals at high risk of needing health care services; paradoxically, of course, these are precisely those who need such insurance the most. You can easily buy health insurance, as long as you are healthy and seen as likely to remain that way.

In summary, competitive insurance principles give economic incentives for insurers to limit their risk, both through defining whom they will cover, and through ensuring that liability will not be open ended. Any company not abiding by these incentives will be uncompetitive. In a competitive model, those most in need of insurance coverage are least likely to find anyone willing to insure them; if coverage is available, it is likely to be at a very high (often unaffordable) cost. Overall costs also tend to be higher, in part because fragmented payers have a diminished ability to control the costs they must pay to providers, and in part because of the additional administrative overhead introduced. (As one of many examples, providers have to deal with a myriad of insurance companies, each with different forms, rules, and regulations.) Many of these added costs fall upon employers, decreasing their economic competitiveness. For these reasons, health economists are virtually unanimous in agreeing that introducing competition in financing medically necessary care—as opposed to competition in how this care is delivered—is a bad idea. Indeed, the international evidence is clear that, when dealing with this sort of necessary care, single payer systems tend to be more economically efficient than more pluralistic approaches to financing medically necessary services. Canadian insurers and employers agree.[3-4]

CRITICAL THINKING QUESTIONS

1. What is the difference between private insurance and private delivery, and why is this important? In your opinion, will for-profit delivery of health services solve Canada's health care woes?

2. What are some of the determinants of health that the author enumerates? Can you name some additional factors? What role do these determinants play in your own life? That is, what activities do you engage in (or reject) in order to stay healthy?

3. Explain how a private insurance system works in terms of risk (who pays the highest premiums, for example). Does such a system work for health insurance? Why or why not?

NOTES

1. Stone, D. A. 1993. The struggle for the soul of health insurance. *J. Health Polit. Policy Law*, 18(2): 287–317.

2. Fein R. 1986. *Medical care, medical costs: The search for a health insurance policy*. Cambridge, MA: Harvard University Press.

3. Deber, R. B., A. Gildiner, and P. Baranek. 1999. Why not private health insurance? Part I. Insurance made easy. *C.M.A.J.*, 161(5): 539–44.

4. Deber, R. B., A. Gildiner and P. Baranek. 1999. Why not private health insurance? Part II. Actuarial principles meet provider dreams. *C.M.A.J.*, 161(5): 545–50.

62

Crack and Prostitution: Gender, Myths, and Experiences

PATRICIA G. ERICKSON, JENNIFER BUTTERS, PATTI MCGILLICUDDY, AND ASE HALLGREN

In this article, Erickson et al. report on their research into crack-using women who work in the sex trade to support their drug use. Their findings reveal the harsh realities of the streets and how socially marginalized these women are. The authors conclude that the increasing availability and use of crack have particularly serious consequences for poor women who are, or become, sex-trade workers.

Who wants to be a crack head when you think about it? Who wants to fucking stand on the corner in the fucking –18C and sell their body for a piece of rock that's going to be gone in fucking 10 minutes?

—"Jenny," age 25

The woman who sells her body for drugs is the most dependent person in the world.

—Germaine Greer, *The Whole Woman*, p. 6

This paper presents the results from in-depth interviews with 30 crack-using women also working in the sex trade to support their drug use. The gender roles perspective highlights traditional beliefs from past decades about the appeal of cocaine to women, its effects on their sexuality, and the reasons they become prostitutes.

Source: P. G. Erickson, J. Butters, P. McGillicuddy, and A. Hallgren, 2000. "Crack and Prostitution: Gender, Myths, and Experiences." *Journal of Drug Issues,* 30(4), 767–88.

INTRODUCTION

The image of the crack-using prostitute has come to epitomize the ultimate shame and sexual degradation of women, but this portrayal is merely the latest in a long series of linkages between "fallen women" and substance use (Carstairs, 1998). The drug use experience of women has long been interpreted through the lens of ingrained cultural assumptions about their "remarkable vulnerability" to addiction and their inevitable downfall once they succumb to intoxicating temptations (Fillmore, 1984). In the early decades of the past century, indulgence in alcohol, tobacco, marijuana, and heroin for pleasure or "highs" was subject to severe social disapproval, while consuming the same substances in medicinal form was acceptable (Gomberg, 1982).

In the early 1980s, the gender roles perspective articulated a broader view on substance use within the framework of women's normative role as nurturer and caregiver (Colten & Marsh, 1984). Concern about women who use alcohol or other drugs is seen as rooted in the perception that such behavior impairs the performance of their primary role; thus, they are viewed as more sick and deviant than male substance users (Marsh, 1982). Women who engage in illicit drug use are doubly deviant because they are not only breaking the law but also engaging in a predominantly male activity (Erickson & Watson, 1990). The negative sanctions applied to women who depart from mainstream standards serve as a form of social control and warning to all women to stay in their place (Rosenbaum, 1981). Like women who reject the housewife role for less traditional pursuits, women who use cocaine pose a particular threat to the gender role expectations of society.

The primary focus of this paper is the impact of crack addiction on poor women who were in, or became involved in, the sex trade. Building on the tradition of studies linking drug-using women with prostitution (Erickson & Watson, 1990), recent research has examined this latest manifestation in the crack era (Inciardi, Lockwood, & Pottieger, 1993; Maher, 1997). Maher and Daly (1996, pp. 483–484) describe how women in the street-level sex trade were affected by increased crack consumption in a New York neighborhood: "The market became flooded with novice sex workers, the going rate for sexual transactions decreased, and 'deviant' sexual expectations by dates increased, as did the levels of violence and victimization." Studies in several U.S. locales made similar observations; common practices include women repeatedly turning tricks for $5 or $10, just enough for another "rock" of crack, accepting dangerous dates, engaging in a variety of sexual practices beyond oral sex and intercourse, and servicing multiple partners in crack houses for a hit of crack (Bourgois & Dunlap, 1993; Inciardi, 1993; Pottieger & Tressell, 1999a). Like Fagan (1994), Sterk, Dolan, and Hatch (1999) contend that many of these acts go beyond conventional understandings of prostitution and constitute abusive sexual encounters.

This paper will present the results of an intensive interview study with 30 women who are heavily involved in crack use and obtain it primarily by selling or trading sex. We examine experiences in the effects of crack and the meanings of addiction for these women.

Sample and Method

Locating respondents who are engaged in activities that are both illegal and highly deviant is challenging. While studies of treatment samples have been the primary source of generalizations about illicit drug users in the past, their failure to reflect the much larger pool of unidentified users has led to more emphasis on community-based recruitment (Erickson & Alexander, 1989). Drug researchers have developed methods of locating low-profile subjects through an adaptation of qualitative and ethnographic techniques pioneered in the broader study of deviant populations (Douglas, 1972). Along with the time required to gain trust, a large element of self-selection is involved in such recruitment; cocaine use and prostitution have been studied this way (e.g. Goldstein, 1979; Erickson, Adlaf, Smart, & Murray, 1987). Since crack use is even more rare than cocaine use and lodged in groups that are quite inaccessible to random-sample household surveys, more targeted fieldwork is required.

While hidden populations of crack users have most often been studied in treatment or street samples, both approaches have strengths and limitations (Pottieger, Tressell, Surrall, Inciardi, & Chitwood, 1995). Treatment programs provide more ready access in safer settings, and their participants may be more ready to allow researchers access to their histories and experiences. They will not, however, be representative of those crack users at large on the street where ongoing use and income-generating activities are still paramount. A number of street studies of female crack users have been conducted, some utilizing large samples of several hundred women (Fagan,

1994; Pottieger & Tressler, forthcoming), others focusing on in-depth and sometimes repeated interviews with smaller samples (Maher & Daley, 1996; Sterk et al., 1999). It is clear that with empathy and persistence, researchers are able to locate women who use crack and gain the trust necessary for them to tell their stories honestly.

The site of this study was an inner-city neighborhood of Toronto known as "East Downtown," which had become notable for its street market in crack cocaine in the early 1990s. One author [Erickson] had gained some field presence and credibility in the area by undertaking some earlier collaborative research with local service-agency staff on violence in the crack trade (Erickson et al., 1996; Erickson, Butters, & German, 2000). These ongoing connections with health care providers in the area, combined with a growing concern for the impact of crack on residents and, in particular, the use of crack by some women living and working on these streets, led to this collaborative study.

Between November 1996 and February 1997, 30 women were recruited on the basis of being known heavy crack users for some years. The approach was made by a trusted local street worker who knew the women well [co-author Hallgren]. A trained person, also known and respected in the community, conducted the interviews in a local drop-in centre. The women were paid $20 and provided with food, soft drinks, and cigarettes. No names were recorded, and the identity of the women remained unknown to the research team. Most of the interviews, which took about one hour to complete, were tape recorded and transcribed, but in a few cases, at the participant's request, verbatim responses were recorded by hand. The women divulged information about many aspects of their lives related to drug use, experience with violence, and the sex trade, and appeared to be honest and open in their responses. While this particular group of women cannot be said to represent female crack users in general, it does reflect the range of characteristics and backgrounds of such women in this area of Toronto. While a

contrast to more conventional, middle-class users (Erickson, Adlaf, Smart, & Murray, 1994; Murphy & Rosenbaum, 1997), such a sample may be considered quite appropriate for providing insights into the world of the poor, female crack user.

The demographic and drug-use profile of the 30 women in our study is the following. The average age of the Toronto East Downtown sample was 31, ranging from 22 to 52 years. The majority (17) of participants were White; seven were Native Canadian, five were Black, and one was East Indian. While 27 had been pregnant and 25 had given birth, all of their children were living with relatives, had been taken into care, or were grown up. All the women interviewed lived in the area, some most of their lives, with an average time spent of seven years. While 17 women had some form of relatively stable housing such as an apartment or room, the rest were homeless, living either on the street or transiently in neighborhood shelters. Although we did not probe their educational or occupational histories in depth, very few mentioned any previous conventional jobs other than housewife, and all but one had a criminal arrest record that would have further limited employment options. All of the participants acknowledged past as well as recent or current involvement in prostitution, identifying it as their major source of income. For less than half of the women, other forms of petty crime, drug selling, and panhandling, as well as some form of welfare benefit, were additional sources of income. While we did not ask the question directly, most of the women volunteered a history of childhood or adolescent physical and/or sexual abuse.

While all the women were current crack users at the time of the interview, using it for an average of eight and one-half years (the range of time these women had been using crack was between two and 13 years), they also had a poly-drug use history. All had used cannabis, 28 had also used powder cocaine, and 27 had used numerous prescription drugs; 25 had used LSD, 14 had used speed, and 11 had used heroin. Age of first drug use was 14 years on average and ranged from eight to 26 years. Most also continued to use alcohol, marijuana, and prescription drugs in the past year and past month, with very few exclusively using crack. This profile is similar to the street samples described by Fagan (1994), Maher and Daley (1996), Sterk et al. (1999), and Pottieger and Tressler (forthcoming), with the primary demographic distinction being the higher proportion of White participants in our Canadian sample. The social disadvantage of the women in all these studies is evident, regardless of location.

In the next sections, we shall present the women's introduction to crack, their perceptions of its effects, and what they like and dislike about it.

Experience of Crack Use

The women were asked what was going on in their lives when they first were exposed to crack and what had led them to try it. Responses fell mainly in two categories. About half—16 women—identified some particularly traumatic or difficult chronic personal situations. These included the death of family members, serious illness, divorce, miscarriage, losing their children, experiencing a rape or other form of abuse, and suffering from stress, depression, or other serious mental instability. Sometimes it was a combination of things:

Three things in a row—I got raped; I came home and found my partner of 11 years in bed with my best friend; then I lost my child.

Crack's "bad press" could be an incentive to someone who was looking for escape:

I was just out of a bad, an abusive relationship. I tried to kill myself . . . I was lonely and depressed. I was watching TV one day, *COPS* or something, and saw it (crack) being done. I actually drove my car to _____ and asked for a rock. And so I started on my own.

A second set of responses referred to crack coming along when the women were already quite drug-involved; for example:

Me and my husband were both (methamphetamine) addicts. We had got arrested for dealing speed and then when I came out of jail all of a sudden this new drug was around, crack cocaine. And I went off the speed immediately and started smoking the crack.

Other women who switched their drug of choice to crack had previously been doing powder cocaine or injecting heroin. Its ready availability in their circles made crack easy to try. Finally, a third and smaller group of other responses were offered by women who simply tried it because it was around, others were doing it, or they described themselves as young and naïve.

They liked the rush, the relaxation, and the numbing effects on their emotions while still keeping them mentally alert. They could articulate many positive aspects of crack, but they also recognized its down side. Their more negative comments included that "crack wears you out," and that it made them sick, led to weight loss, and destroyed their lungs. Feelings of paranoia, depression, and memory loss were also mentioned. The worst aspect identified was coming down from a crack high, or "jonesing" as they termed it, when their supply ran out.

Are these women addicted to crack? From their own perspective, 27 of the 30 women answered that they were. Their expressions of craving and what they will do to get crack appear to substantiate their personal assessment. The question, "do you *get* all the crack you want?" produced these typical replies:

There's never enough.

The thing about crack cocaine is you never get enough.

One [hit] is too many and a thousand is never enough.

You never get all the drugs you need or want.

When asked what they do if they can't get crack, responses varied, with many women pointing out that "there's always some way to get it" if you are desperate enough:

You'll do anything to get it, that one hit on the pipe.

You want the crack so bad you'd do anything.

EXPERIENCE OF PROSTITUTION

For some women, life on the street started quite late, often after leaving an abusive relationship and having no money. "Cynthia," a 45-year-old woman with three grown children who has spent four years on the streets in Toronto East Downtown, provided this account:

Since I started crack it's been a whole different life for me. I didn't live on the street before, until I was 40 years old. I didn't start hooking until I was 40 years old. After being a wife and a mother for so many years, then all of a sudden you're into hooking and you are doing that to pay for your crack.

For others, getting involved in drug use and prostitution started at an early age. "Marlene," a 25-year-old woman who had been working in the area for the past two years, described this sequence:

I've been doing it (prostitution) since I was 16 years old, that's like what I know best. I started prostitution to support my habit for alcohol and marijuana . . . when you have so many people touching your body, I did the drugs first. I got addicted (to crack) when I was 18 and I've never stopped since that.

While some had started prostitution to support themselves, as a way to survive on the streets, or to pay for other drugs, at this stage all of these women acknowledged spending most of what they earned now on crack. These are some responses to a question asking, why do you work in the sex trade?

To support my habit . . . that's not initially why I started.

Because I don't have any other way of getting money.

I'm addicted to crack cocaine and I have no other source of income.

Central to an understanding of the sex–crack dynamic is that stopping crack use was not considered a serious option by these women. Only a minority (nine) even identified their drug use as a problem. To most, it is the solution—they continue to use because it's what makes their lives bearable or interesting. Selling sex is the means to this end.

The sexual marketability of these women may have been reinforced by the effect of cocaine on body image and body weight. By keeping thin and subject to sexual objectification, crack-using women reflect the historical assertion that "women's social value has been inseparable from their bodies" (Brown & Jasper, 1993, p. 18). However, their subordination extended beyond simply selling sex. Some of the women recounted sexual deviations beyond what they considered normal heterosexual services for the trade (i.e., genital and oral sex), with which, nevertheless, they had complied, or been forced to perform:

I've done a lot of things for crack. Sure I've sucked a dick for crack. Sure I've been with four men one time. I had to.

In the context of street prostitution in an area with a high volume of crack consumption going on, many of the customers will also be using crack. Some of the women did sex-for-crack exchanges, what they called "freaking," in crack houses. Others serviced well-off male professionals who paid for crack and expected to get high and have sex as part of the overall transaction. This gave the women ample opportunity to observe the differential effect of crack on women and men. The Swiss psychiatrist, Hans Maier, in his 1926 treatise on cocaine addiction, believed that cocaine reduced the sexual potency of men but had this effect on women: "In women there is, without exception, an increase in both the physical and psychological components of sexual drive. There is an exaggerated sensitivity to sexual stimuli . . . [she] often makes direct sexual advance to any man who happens to be present" (Maier, 1926: tr. Kalant, 1987, p. 82). While the women in our study universally and emphatically denied that crack stimulated their own sexual arousal, they saw it affecting men quite differently:

Men get extremely horny where a lot of women don't.

Men want sex when they're on it and I can't stand it.

The women also thought that men tended to get violent on crack and that this added additional risk when sex was being traded for crack or money to male crack users, a major segment of their clientele.

Crack markets are characterized by a high degree of systemic violence (Goldstein, 1985), and prostitution is an occupation that also entails a high degree of personal risk of violence (Erickson & Watson, 1990); the combination of the two is dangerous and can be lethal. Maher and Daly (1996) noted that three of the 45 women in their study were murdered. "Sally," a 34-year-old respondent who had worked in the Toronto East Downtown for 10 years, said, "I risk my life every day," and provided some examples:

There have been fights with knives over crack, over 20 pieces in a crack house, I was almost raped because I did not want to give this guy a blowjob after he gave me a toke . . . I had my jaw broken (by my boyfriend) when I was partying with this girl. [Why?] Because I smoked without him.

Three quarters of the women in our study reported being hurt as a result of their involvement with crack, most of them experiencing multiple incidents of violence. Nevertheless, these women acknowledge their feelings of vulnerability in their responses to the question "What is the most pressing issue to women on the street?":

There is always the fear of being beaten, robbed or killed.

Rape. It's happened to me twice this year, when I've been intoxicated.

The effects of a form of post-traumatic stress related to a history of assault and abuse may indeed contribute to the need to continue to use crack (Ledray, 1994), and the effects of abuse may become compounded for women of color (McGillicuddy, 1993). That these women survive on the street and cope as well they do after many years of crack and other drug use reflects their ability to be streetwise and handle numerous threatening situations. Some take a certain pride or satisfaction in the various ways

their lives have evolved. "Cynthia," who came to crack later in life than most, described herself this way:

I've always been someone who liked to live dangerously, sort of on the edge . . . I know it sounds strange for you to hear me say this, but I wouldn't change the experience that I've had, on the whole. I've learned so much.

"Rosa" described crack as a kind of catalyst:

My daughter's father was very abusive, and for some strange reason, cocaine gave me the courage to tell him to get the fuck out of my life.

Despite these assets of interpersonal skills and the excitement of the street life that clearly appeals to many of the women, their awareness of the dangers is realistic. [Two women working in the area were murdered soon after we did this study, and another was shot in a back alley in May, 2000.]

EXPERIENCE OF MOTHERHOOD

Virtually all of the women (25 of the 30) in this study are mothers. The number of children these women have had ranges from one to eight, with the majority giving birth to between one and three children; about five of them have more. In each case, none of the children are currently living with their mother but are instead being cared for by other relatives (including grandparents, aunts, fathers, sisters), have been adopted, or have been placed in foster care. In addition, some are already adults, and one woman said her daughter was on the streets.

Why are these children not with their mothers? A variety of reasons were given in response to this question. Some revolved quite clearly around issues of substance abuse:

I gave her up for adoption. She's not with me because I couldn't stop using crack. Best thing for her. I didn't want to do to her what my mother did to me, so I just figured I would just, you know, give her to Children's Aid. Then the youngest one, I went back to using and my mom took the babies and I'm still using.

My 12-year-old was taken away because I was only 14 [when she was born], my 10-year-old I sent down to my mother when she was 5, my son was born with crack in his system so the Children's Aid were involved but his grandmother took him.

[My] other daughter and son are with my little sister because of my addiction.

Many of these women recognized on their own that active mothering and cocaine use were incompatible. They were not in the position of being able to provide adequate care for their children because of their substance use—crack use in particular—and the lifestyle that went with it. They were often fortunate in having other family members available to take on the care of their children.

While these women have not given up cocaine use for the sake of their children, they have been able to make, or at least accept, the choice not to be the primary caregiver.

IMAGES OF SELF

Cooley's (1902) discussion of the "looking-glass self" suggests that self-concepts are the reflection of others' perceptions of us; in essence we are, or become, what we think others think we are. More contemporary formulations have extended this notion to a consideration of stigma (Goffman, 1963) and shame (Fossum & Mason, 1986). Since crack users and prostitutes are typically regarded with much disdain, the combination of the two identities places individuals at the extreme of stigmatization. Sometimes, external perceptions translate into self-concepts and may aid in the understanding of deviant subgroups such as the women in this study. While we did not explore this relationship in depth, we are concerned with the extent to which perceptions of others become internalized and contribute to a self-fulfilling prophecy or act as barriers to seeking help.

When the respondents in this study were asked how they felt others in their neighborhood perceived them, their vulnerability to derogatory and demeaning self-images was quite evident. Some perceptions were tied closely to crack use:

They see me as a crack-head and like a nobody. And that is true, they do, they look at me like a nobody and it really pees me off. You see me sometimes, how angry I get in that church when they start talkin' about me and putting me down 'cause they're no better than me.

Other responses identify images that revolve as much or more so around prostitution:

. . . as a drug addict, prostitute drug addict, basically that's what they think.

As a tramp. But I don't care, though, because I'm addicted to crack. I'm addicted to it, eh? I can't help myself, what they think of me 'cause whatever they think about me, I don't have time to think because my mind is just busy on the next toke.

The ability to resist such ingrained and widespread perceptions held by others poses a significant challenge to these women, and accepting the labels is perhaps the path of least resistance. However, it may also be a contributing factor to the downward spiral in which these women find themselves. If these images are internalized, then the doors to treatment and life-changing options may also be perceived as pointless. And this may in fact be one of the greatest dangers these women face.

OPTIONS FOR CHANGE?

What might make a difference in these women's lives? We asked them about their prior experience with treatment, their views on different forms of drug access, and what sorts of services they thought would be helpful to women like them. While seeking treatment had been part of the drug-use history of 22 of the women, their reasons were predominantly either to "get some rest and rehab," or to respond to some external threat, such as the loss of their children or their housing, or to reduce jail time. The short-term nature of most of these interventions and the return to life on the streets did not present a successful picture of treatment outcome.

When asked what a free supply of drugs would do to their current way of life, 23 said they would stop other illegal activities and leave the street:

Absolutely. I'm not a law breaker by choice. I much prefer not to be putting my ass on the line, so to speak.

Definitely. I wouldn't have time to do it. I'd be too busy getting high.

Not surprisingly, given that any form of co-caine maintenance has almost never been discussed even in drug-treatment or drug-policy circles, most women had not thought about such an alternative (Erickson & Cheung, 1999). For poor women, there would still be the issue of where they would get money to live. Therefore, prostitution and other illegal acts may not necessarily subside. We also asked them if they would take a "crack substitute" if one were available: 18 said they would, seven said they wouldn't, and three were undecided. The negative responses were geared mainly to not wanting to stop crack or not wishing to substitute one addictive drug for another.

The women were more expansive when offered the chance to suggest the kinds of services they would like to see offered in the community. They enumerated a number of simple needs like places to shower, do laundry, and sleep safely when they were exhausted. Most of the women, 24 of 30, also would like to see more health services geared to their needs, and many also mentioned counseling—often defined as just someone to talk to—on a 24-hour basis. These are some of the examples they elaborated:

A hotline for women, someone to offer support
Counseling to get back on track
A roof over my head 3 to 4 nights a week
A year's treatment out of the city
Somewhere to call your own
An understanding, good ear
Somewhere to go and be safe

In other words, being treated like human beings with the same needs as everyone else.

SUMMARY AND CONCLUSION

Our study of 30 crack-using prostitutes refutes the view that cocaine makes these women "sexually licentious," as was believed in earlier eras (Carstairs, 1998; Maier, 1926, in tr. Kalant, 1987). It is clear that they work in the sex trade to get money and/or crack to support their own usage when few other sources of income are available to them. Far from enjoying sex while intoxicated, they describe it as aversive. Nor was their use of crack the main impetus to a career on the streets—most were involved in both the drug and sex trades previously, but crack intensified that life and led to more dangerous and perverse sexual activities. This is similar to the conclusions of Maher and Daly (1996) and others. Nor has research on women who use crack and lead otherwise conventional lives indicated any particularly positive effect of cocaine on their sexual activities (Erickson et al., 1994). Nevertheless, it is possible that women in the lower echelon of the sex trade, many of whom have histories of early childhood and adolescent sexual and physical abuse, may be less inclined to take pleasure in sex, irrespective of cocaine use.

The other prevailing stereotype, that crack-using women are unfit mothers, was in a sense upheld by the women themselves. Most had given up their children or had them taken away, but none disputed the appropriateness of this decision. This did not mean that they had no feelings for their children—quite the opposite. We would argue that they were acting, insofar as they were able, in the best interests of their children.

The policy of legal and social suppression of crack has helped it to find ready markets in vulnerable portions of the population. Nevertheless, there is no simple answer to these women's problems, such as legalizing the supply of the drug. As they say, "you can never have enough." Unlike methadone maintenance for heroin users, there is no "cocadone" that alleviates withdrawal symptoms or provides a longer-acting substitute (Erickson & Cheung, 1999). Effective intervention strategies for problem cocaine use depend, in part, on motivation for change—noticeably absent in most of this population, who lack the stakes in conformity that provide self- and informal controls over the most excessive use-patterns (Waldorf, Reinarman, & Murphy, 1991). Moreover, these women are characterized by the poverty and lack of social support that predicts poor compliance and relapse in the management of chronic conditions generally (McLellan, Lewis, O'Brien, & Kleber, 2000). Strategies that would provide a safer environment for use of drugs, along with community outreach of health and social services, might have more individual and social benefit for such women than drug-focused policy options.

The pervasive violence and fear of violence that these women experience speaks to the importance of improving the working conditions on the street and providing safe shelters and support for these women. While they are unlikely to choose a life without crack in their present situation, some of the riskier aspects of their existence might be ameliorated by nonjudgmental approaches to meeting their basic needs. As the above discussion indicated, abstinence-oriented treatment is not a particularly appealing or an effective approach for these women. Whether a longer-term investment, geared to their lifestyle, and treating crack addiction as a chronic medical condition might produce a more favorable result remains to be tried (McLellan et al., 2000). Our participants are positively inclined to more services and support in their immediate community. These types of broad harm-reduction measures, such as housing, medical attention, and safer work conditions, might realistically focus on keeping the women alive and HIV negative rather than ending their crack addiction.

ACKNOWLEDGMENTS

This project was funded by the Drug Abuse Prevention Program of the Department of Public Health, Toronto, and facilitated by Teresa Damaso.

CRITICAL THINKING QUESTIONS

1. Review the authors' discussion of how traditional gender-role behaviours influence the public's perception of female crack-using prostitutes.

2. In the article the authors describe some of the challenges researchers face when investigating illegal-drug users. Speculate on some of the challenges researchers might confront when investigating prescription-drug use among the middle class.

3. Of the 30 women interviewed as part of this research, only 9 felt that their drug use was a *problem;* to most of the women, it was in fact a *solution.* Explain this apparent contradiction from the sociological perspective.

REFERENCES

Bourgois, P., and E. Dunlap. 1993. Exorcising sex-for-crack: An ethnographic perspective from Harlem. In *Crack pipe as pimp: An ethnographic investigation of sex-for-crack exchanges,* ed. M. Rather. New York: Lexington Books.

Brown, Catrina, and Karin Jasper. 1993. *Consuming passions: Feminist approach to weight preoccupation and eating disorders.* Toronto: Second Story Press.

Butters, J., A. Hallgren, and P. McGillicuddy. 1997. *Poor women and crack use in downtown Toronto.* Research Report.

Carstairs, C. 1998. Innocent addicts, dope fiends and nefarious traffickers: Illegal drug use in 1920s English Canada. *Journal of Canadian Studies, 33,* 145–62.

Colten, M., and J. Marsh. 1984. A sex-roles perspective on drug and alcohol use by women. In *Sex roles and psychopathology,* ed. C. Widom. New York: Plenum.

Cooley, Charles. 1902. *Human nature and the social order.* New York: Scribner.

Douglas, J. 1972. *Research on deviance.* New York: Random House.

Erickson. P., E. Adlaf, R. Smart, and G. Murray. 1994. *The steel drug: Cocaine and crack in perspective,* 2nd ed. New York: Lexington Books.

Erickson, P., and B. Alexander. 1989. Cocaine and addictive liability. *Social Pharmacology*, 3, 249–70.

Erickson, P., J. Butters, B. Fischer, E. Fehrman, D. Haans, and B. Poland. 1996. Exploring drug market violence in a more peaceable society. Appendix G in the Draft Report of the Drugs–Violence Task Force, U.S. Sentencing Commission, Washington, DC.

Erickson, P., J. Butters, and B. German. 2000. Flexing crack in Toronto: A deviant pathway for poor, homeless drug users. Paper presented at the International Conference on Deviant Pathways, Porto, Portugal, January.

Erickson. P., and Y. Cheung. 1999. Harm reduction among cocaine users: Reflections on individual intervention and community social capital. *International Journal of Drug Policy*, 10, 235–46.

Erickson, P., and V. Watson. 1990. Women, illicit drugs and crime. *Research Advances in Alcohol and Drug Problems*, 10, 859–77.

Fagan, J. 1994. Women and drugs revisited: Female participation in the cocaine economy. *Journal of Drug Issues*, 24, 179–225.

Fillmore, K. 1984. When angels fall: Women's drinking as cultural preoccupation and as reality. In *Alcohol problems in women*, eds. S. Wilsnack and L. Beckman. New York: Guilford Press.

Fossum, Merle, and Marilyn Mason. 1986. *Facing shame*. New York: Norton.

Goffman, Erving. 1963. *Stigma: Notes on the management of spoiled identity*. Englewood Cliffs, NJ: Prentice-Hall.

Goldstein, P. 1979. *Prostitution and drugs*. Lexington, MA: Lexington Books.

——. 1985. The drugs/violence nexus: A tripartite conceptual framework. *Journal of Drug Issues*, 21, 345–67.

Gomberg, E. 1982. Historical and political perspectives: Women and drug use. *Journal of Social Issues*, 38, 9–23.

Humphries, D. 1999. *Crack mothers: Pregnancy, drugs and the media*. Columbus, OH: The Ohio State University.

Inciardi, J. 1993. King rats, chicken heads, slow necks, freaks and blood suckers: A glimpse of Miami sex-for-crack market. In *Crack pipe as pimp: An ethnographic investigation of sex-for-crack exchanges*, ed. M. Ratner. New York: Lexington Books.

Kalant, O. [tr.] 1987. *Maier's cocaine addiction [Der Kokainismus 1926]*. Toronto: Addiction Research Foundation.

Ledray, Linda. 1994. *Recovery from rape*. Holt and Company, New York.

McGillicuddy, Patricia. 1993. Embodied and emboldened: Dealing with sexual violence. In *Consuming passions: Feminist approach to weight preoccupation and eating disorders*, ed. C. Brown and K. Jasper. Toronto: Second Story Press.

McLennan. A., D. Lewis, C. O'Brien, and H. Kleber. 2000. Drug dependence, a chronic mental illness: Implications for treatment, insurance and outcome evaluation. *Journal of the American Medical Association*, 284, 1689–95.

Maher, L. 1997. *Sexed work: Gender, race and resistance in a Brooklyn drug market*. Oxford: Clarendon Press.

Maher, L., and K. Daly. 1996. Women in the street-level drug economy: Continuity or change? *Criminology*, 34, 465–91.

Marsh, J. 1982. Public issues and private problems: Women and drug use. *Journal of Social Issues*, 38, 153–65.

Murphy, S., and M. Rosenbaum. 1997. Two women who used cocaine too much: Class, race, gender, crack and coke. In *Crack in America: Demon drugs and social justice*, eds. C. Reinarman and H. Levine. California: University of California Press.

Pottieger. A., and P. Tressell. Social relationships of crime-involved women cocaine users. *Journal of Psychoactive Drugs*.

——. 1999a. Dimensions of sex trading among women cocaine users. Paper presented at the Annual Meeting of the American Society of Criminology, Washington, DC, November 1998.

——. 1999b. Barriers to treatment for crime-involved cocaine-dependent women. Paper presented at the Annual Meeting of the American Sociological Association, New York, August 1996.

Pottieger, A., P. Tressell, H. Surrall, J. Inciardi, and D. Chitwood. 1995. Drug use patterns of adult crack users in street and residential treatment samples. *Journal of Psychoactive Drugs*, 27, 27–38.

Rosenbaum, M. 1981. Sex roles among deviants: The woman addict. *International Journal of the Addictions*, 16, 859–77.

Sterk, C., K. Dolan, and S. Hatch. 1999. Epidemiological indicators and ethnographic realities of female cocaine use. *Substance Use and Misuse*, 34, 2057–72.

Waldorf, D., C. Reinarman, and S. Murphy. 1991. *Cocaine changes: The experience of using and quitting*. Philadelphia: Temple University Press.

63

Disability and Genetics: Affirming the Bare Life

JAMES OVERBOE

Along with advances in medical technology come novel and challenging ethical considerations. Sociologist James Overboe writes about his experiences with cerebral palsy and raises concern about prenatal genetic testing for this and other diseases. He is afraid that this technology will result in a kind of "genetic fundamentalism." He further expresses concern about the immense power that this type of technology gives to the medical community. Armed with this new science, medical practitioners can effectively make life-and-death decisions based on genes.

DISABLING OF THE DISABLED

Today many members of society argue for genetic testing for disabilities because they believe that the "quality of life" for both the "afflicted" individuals and their "caregivers" is diminished. Will good parenting be measured by the extent of compliance to genetic technology? If so, what are the underlying pressures for women to submit their bodies to genetic testing, and genetic diagnostics?

I would argue the disabled subject is produced in an ableist matrix. One must ask . . . does the disabled person emerge as having a "bare life," where his or her ability to achieve a "political life" is in doubt? Or perhaps more correctly

how does an ableist matrix prohibit a disabled existence from coming to fruition? By "naming" the infant "disabled," he or she is abjectified. Making the infant the "state of exception" to varying degrees paints the future not only of the infant but also of the family and the community at large as a series of problems and catastrophes that derive from the unfortunate circumstance of disability. Yet as Elliot (2001) and Skidmore (1994) argue, it is impossible to accurately predict the future "quality of life" of a disabled person. If the disabled baby is born, then the marker "disability" looms over the child's life, and is reiterated by various authorities and throughout various intervals of time to reinforce or contest this unnatural state. The naming of the disabled demarcates or places them outside normality and, in doing so, repeatedly reaffirms the norm. Thus, the binary of disability and non-disability serves to reinforce normality within our society.

Source: James Overboe. 2007. "Disability and Genetics: Affirming the Bare Life (the State of Exception)." *Canadian Journal of Sociology and Anthropology*, 44(2): 219–35. The original article was extensively reorganized and edited for this book.

Jean Bethke Elshtain (1995: 35) claims that supporters of the primacy of the "right to choice" for women have seemingly contradictory positions. On one hand, they advocate genetic testing for disabilities, while on the other they are appalled at any suggestion of testing for the sex of the foetus. Sophia Isako Wong (2002: 97) writes, "Feminists have spent ample time clarifying the distinction between biological sex (having chromosome XX or XY) and the social construction of gender." Moreover, Wong (2002: 97) asks, "Might there be an analogous distinction between trisomy 21 (having three twenty-first chromosomes instead of two) and the social construction of people with Down syndrome as disabled?" Wong (2002: 114–15) concludes:

I see no sharp line between the difficulties of being a woman in a patriarchal society and those engendered by having Down syndrome in a society focused on cognitive capacity. My intuition is that the possibilities for people with Down syndrome will increase as our society dismantles the deeply entrenched institutionalization of sexual difference. If we can move toward overcoming the Enlightenment fetishization of cognitive ability and dislodge the institutional barriers enforcing cognitive difference, perhaps we can build a society in which everyone is at home with Down syndrome.

As Wong argues, it is not simply a matter of women taking these contradictory positions in regards to genetic testing. Rather, women who are bestowed this right are being pressured into making the "correct" choice. The discourse concerning disability as it applies to the proliferation of reproductive technologies, in particular prenatal testing for detectable foetal anomalies, is not inclusive. Tremain (2006), Rapp and Ginsburg (2001), and Ettore (2001) agree that the offices of genetic counsellors, along with the overall environment, weigh the decision in favour of genetic testing. Rayna Rapp and Faye Ginsburg (2001: 538) assert, "[G]enetic counsellors are trained to express neutrality about the choice a pregnant woman and her partner may make around amniocentesis testing, the very essence of such technology and the offer of such tests under the terms of consumer choice are premised on the desire for normalcy and fear of unknown abnormalities."

In the following passages from the article "Miracle Kid" by Lucinda Franks, a family with a child with Fraser syndrome relate how they risk going against both normative assumptions and expert advice in order to affirm the (bare) life of their son, Max, who is living as a "state of exception."

"I don't know what this is, I just don't know," a doctor said as he put the baby into her [Max's mother's] arms. Beneath the lush head of hair, the baby's face was like a child's unfinished drawing. He had only one, unnaturally small eye, on the right side of his face. On the other side, there was a concave blankness beneath the brow. His nostrils were separated by a deep cleft, and his nasal ridge was squashed. Penelope took his curled fist and felt for fingers, but none were there [later Bernard discovered Max had fingers and toes] (Franks, 1999: 68).

Penelope and Bernard had to overcome the medical staff's negative attitude towards Max. As Penelope kept watch over Max, she noticed clusters of interns and residents came to look, and heard some of them referring to him as "it." Finally, Penelope had enough. "This 'it' is my son, and he wants to be left alone," she said. Penelope persuaded a reluctant nurse to put the child to her breast, and he began to suck vigorously. The nurse said firmly, "It's only instinct. *Any* baby will nurse [original emphasis]." Then she pointed out another nurse who was unhooking a plump baby from a ventilator and rushing out the door with him. "That baby has been on life support for months," the first nurse said, "It has been unending agony for the mother, and she's decided to end it. She's waiting in a private room so the baby can die in her arms" (Franks, 1999: 69). In comparing Max to the other baby, the nurse was placing Max in the realm of the "state of exception"—a "bare life" that was "not worth living."

This interpellation of the "bare life" that is the "state of exception" was reinforced by other medical practitioners outside the hospital. Max required various health professionals for his ongoing home-care. "The original day nurse was fired after Lulu, the babysitter, caught her washing Max's bottles in dirty dishwater. 'What's the difference? He is going to be a vegetable,' the nurse said with a shrug" (Franks, 1999: 69).

The predominant attitude towards Max epitomizes the belief that some disabled infants' existence is "not worth living." Franks (1999: 71) reports,

At a meeting to discuss Max's future, with the support of out-dated information a hospital official advised, Max's parents might be better off warehousing him for his sake and theirs. Armed with positive research on Fraser Syndrome, Penelope jumped in. "We do not intend to warehouse our son," she said icily, "There's only one option we'd like to discuss, and that is aggressive medical intervention."

Franks (1999: 77) asserts,

Max has had a profound positive effect on his mother: "The truth is that Max has made me more deeply happy than I have ever been," she explained. "He changes everyone who meets him. He changes their ideas about beauty, about worth. He has made every member of our family—immediate as well as extended—grow up and change their life view in some essential way." Max also changed the attitude of many members of the hospital staff. "We think everyone has to be perfect, physically, mentally," Dr. Flaum said, "It's easy to write people off, say, this one's so abnormal forget it. Max has reaffirmed that you cannot look at a person and know for sure he has no ability to learn and be a good member of our society."

DISABILITY AS A "BARE LIFE," WHICH IS A "STATE OF EXCEPTION"

On September 28, 1997, I was forced to look back on my own genetic makeup (as some other people perceive it) to critique the future.

Listening to the Canadian Broadcasting Corporation radio program *Cross Country Checkup* (Murphy, 1997), I heard a geneticist claim that he had "discovered" the genetic cause for cerebral palsy. Over the years, my physicians have concluded that my cerebral palsy was caused by a lack of oxygen to the brain. This new genetic explanation is a pre-cursor, and reduces

the "lack of oxygen to the brain" to a complication resulting from genetic mutations. Consequently, my body and my life are now being read through the lens of genetic fundamentalism.

Provoked, I felt compelled to respond and called the program. In my interview, I explained that the question "When should we screen for genetic defects?" devalues the experience of disability by presuming that genetic intervention is not only permissible but preferable in certain cases. In terms of so-called genetic abnormalities that may cause illness and disability, "common sense" would suggest that some intervention is not only desirable but is a societal goal. I spoke about the positive aspects of my cerebral palsy, stating, "not in the sense of a 'gift' from which other people learn, or as God's chosen 'crippled angels,' but rather how my spasms give me great joy and how they inform my life. Any success I have is not despite my cerebral palsy but because of it!"

I also argued that these positive aspects of cerebral palsy cannot be "measured," because the ways and means of measurement are developed from the perspective that devalues cerebral palsy as an "expression of life." I spoke about the similarities between myself and Tracy Latimer, who was murdered, to forestall the invocation of a continuum of cerebral palsy with myself at the pinnacle (the poster-child for overcoming) and Tracy Latimer (symbolizing victims) shackled to the lowest rung in life and memory.

As my segment concluded, the host, Rex Murphy, thanked me for educating him as well as others. I corrected him, stating, "My intention is not to educate others but to give cerebral palsy a life-affirming presence. I explained that my life is not, and should not be, dependent upon able-bodied people understanding me or giving me their blessing." Often people who privilege an able-bodied life have demanded an explanation for my being alive. Today, by having a presence, I conveyed to the audience that no longer did I have to explain, justify, apologize for, or educate others about my cerebral palsy. The radio segment offered me another opportunity to expose the vivaciousness of cerebral palsy as a life affirming force. Consequently, I am moving beyond the dichotomous pairing of disability and ability which restricts my vivacity.

Since I was a disembodied voice over the radio, ableist rhetoric and anger could be vented. One caller screamed, "How dare you question normality!" Others said that I should be thankful they allowed me into a regular school and I repay their generosity by making such outlandish statements. No matter what I said, the ableism was pervasive. Believing that I was too intelligent, some callers questioned my ability to comment on the lives of severely disabled people. Others maligned me for being outrageous and lacking rational thought. Paradoxically, I was either too intelligent or too stupid. Either way, the status quo which favours the body and lives of nondisabled people remains intact.

Following my segment on the radio program *Cross Country Checkup,* a mother of a disabled baby called the program. She explained how strangers would call her a "bad mother" for giving birth to a disabled child. Respondents to her segment accused her of being an irresponsible member of society for giving birth to a future "burden" on society. Like me, she was called irrational, especially after reiterating she loved her child. For the most part, respondents pathologized her decision-making abilities as well as her refusal to see the error of her ways.

The coercive nature of both public opinion and genetic counselling create an environment where the eradication of disability becomes "matter-of-fact" and "common sense," and creates a guilt-free atmosphere where the initiative to get rid of a pathology is deemed necessary. The mother who chooses to carry the defective foetus to term (by either refusing genetic testing or ignoring a positive outcome) has her status of being worthy of a "political life" questioned, especially if she does not acknowledge the error of her ways. Cautioning us about our reliance on the promise genomics, bioethicist Dr. Robert

Klitzman (2006) warns, "As we enter the new genetic age, more education is needed to help doctors, nurses, genetics counselors, patients and their families face these quandaries. We have much to learn from the Greeks: to be cautious in interpreting prognostications, to beware that genetic information, like oracles, may offer an illusion of certainty."

Researching the extermination of psychiatric patients and disabled children during the Nazi Regime, Proctor (1995: 172) writes, "Euthanasia took on less the character of a single Reich-wide 'operation' and more the character of normal hospital routine. Equally disturbing is the fact that doctors were never *ordered* (emphasis in original) to murder psychiatric patients and handicapped children they were *empowered* (emphasis in original) to do so, and fulfilled their task without protest, often on their own initiative." In this genetic age, David Le Breton (2004: 5) asserts, "The identification of a genetic illness which is currently untreatable leads potentially to the decision to carry out a therapeutic abortion, and in this way a drift occurs, whereby medicine moves away from a therapeutic role to the project of eliminating that which it cannot treat." The Critical Art Ensemble (1998: 125) add, "To be sure, once eugenics is perceived as a means to empower the child and the parent, it loses its monstrous overtones, and becomes another part of everyday life medical procedure. Capitalism will achieve its goals of genetic ideological inscription, while at the same time realizing tremendous profits for providing the service."

(RE)AFFIRMING A DISABLED "BARE LIFE" AS AN EXPRESSION OF LIFE

Since 1997, I have become further embedded in the academic culture and my life is further read as being greatly removed from my previous existence as a cripple, as a "bare life." It is assumed that I have evolved from my earlier existence as a baby who could not communicate, sit or control any aspect of either my body or my life (what many people believe is "a life not worth living" and the epitome of "the state of exception"). I feel tremendous pressure to put on a charade and try to present myself as human and subsume my spasms. Throughout my life I have had to work to maintain my status as living a political life. Moreover, I have had to take great care not to slip back to a "bare life" (or to be perceived by others to be slipping) and returning to the "state of exception."

I am restricted by what I call "normative shadows." To varying degrees most people are restricted by "normative shadows"—a somewhat enigmatic and elusive concept—that lead to the suppression of desires that do not conform to accepted norms. Like most shadows, normative shadows cannot be grasped in a material way. They remain a feeling, a sense that one is constantly being judged according to differing criteria of normality. Like all shadows, normative shadows are elusive yet always present, simultaneously everywhere and nowhere. Yet, for those of us deemed as possible "states of exception," adhering to "normative shadows" is a necessary precondition to maintaining a "political life." A similar feeling is expressed by Neil Marcus who states, "People are always watching me . . . [ellipses in original] they're watching to see how well I do this thing . . . [ellipses in original] this thing called 'human'" (Brueggemann, 2002: 322).

Following my appearance on *Cross Country Checkup,* many people congratulated me on my strong resistance to ableism. However, I question whether resistance could create a positive space for the vivaciousness of disabled existences. Addressing the question of resistance, Linda Martin Alcoff (1999: 67) writes, "There is a kind of quest purity in the attempt to maintain only a resistance which is itself defined as a reaction to power rather than a fight for power. Resistance so circumscribed suggests a desire to inhabit a space free from criticism, responsibility, and accountability, to be always a critic never the advocate."

Simply put, I believe my disabled "expressions of life" should not defer to able-bodiedness. However, even resisting the privileging of able-bodiedness is a manner of "deference." Always "reacting against" ableism rather than "fighting for" the affirmation of my spasms left me feeling empty. When articulating positions from the dichotomy of ability and disability, I feel restricted by the incessant need to respond to the normative shadows of able-embodiment that are omnipresent in discussions and influence the parameters for the "rules of engagement" as well as the means of articulation.

CRITICAL THINKING QUESTIONS

1. What does Overboe mean by "genetic fundamentalism"? What are the dangers associated with this kind of thinking?

2. Why the comparison between abortion and genetic disease? Do you think this comparison is a fair one?

3. What point is the author meaning to make by comparing the contemporary use of genetic testing with that of eugenics in the Nazi regime? Do you agree that this is a valid point? Why or why not?

REFERENCES

Brueggemann, B. 2002. An enabling pedagogy. In *Disability studies: Enabling the humanities*, eds. S. L. Snyder, B. A. Brueggemann, and R. Garland Thompson, 317–36. New York: Modern Language Association.

Critical Art Ensemble. 1998. *Flesh machine: Cyborgs, designer babies, and new eugenic consciousness.* New York: Autonomedia.

Elliott, C. 2001. Attitudes, souls, and persons: Children with severe neurological impairments. In *Slow cures and bad philosophers: Essays on Wittgenstein, medicine and bioethics*, ed. C. Elliott, 89–102. Durham, NC: Duke University Press.

Elshtain, J. B. 1995. The new eugenics and feminist quandaries. In *Politics and the human body: Assault on dignity*, eds. J. B. Elshtain and T. Cloyd, 24–40. Nashville, TN: Vanderbilt University Press.

Ettore, B. 2000. Reproductive genetics, gender and the body: "Please Doctor, may I have a normal baby?" *Sociology*, 36(3), 403–20.

Franks, L. 1999. Miracle kid. *The New Yorker*, (May): 68–77.

Klitzman, B. 2006. Genetic testing creates new versions of ancient dilemmas. *New York Times*, (Jan. 17): http://www.nytimes.com/2006/0l/17/health/17case.html.

Le Breton, D. 2004. Genetic fundamentalism or the cult of the gene. *Body & Society*, 10(4): 1–20.

Martin, Alcoff, L. 1999. Becoming an epistemologist. In *Becomings: Explorations in time, memory, and futures*, ed. B. Gross, 55–75. Ithaca, NY: Cornell University Press.

Murphy, R. 1997. Should we screen embryos for genetic defects? *Cross Country Checkup*. Canadian Broadcasting Corporation, Radio One, (Sep. 28).

Proctor, R. N. 1995. The destruction of lives not worth living. In *Deviant bodies: Critical perspectives on difference in science and popular culture*, eds. J. Terry and J. Urla, 170–96. Indianapolis: Indiana University Press.

Rapp, R. and P. Ginsberg. 2001. Enabling disability: Rewriting kinship, reimagining citizenship. *Public Culture*, 13(3): 553–56.

Skidmore, M. 1994. Interview with Peter Gzowski. *Morningside*. CBC Radio. (Nov. 29).

Tremain, S. 2006. Reproduction freedom, self-regulation, and the government of impairment in utero. *Hypatia*, 21(1): 35–53.

Wong, S. I. 2002. At home with down syndrome and gender. *Hypatia*, 11(3): 89–117.

64

Female Genital Mutilation

EFUA DORKENOO AND SCILLA ELWORTHY

In recent decades, numerous women's organizations around the world have focused on a variety of health-related issues and problems, including domestic violence, rape, sexual harassment, and poverty. In this selection, Efua Dorkenoo and Scilla Elworthy examine the complex cultural issues surrounding female genital mutilation, a practice that has received international attention since the early 1990s.

THE FACTS

. . . [F]emale genital mutilation covers four types of operation:

1. *Circumcision*, or cutting of the prepuce or hood of the clitoris, known in Muslim countries as Sunna (tradition). This, the mildest type, affects only a small proportion of the millions of women concerned. It is the only type of mutilation that can correctly be called circumcision, though there has been a tendency to group all kinds of mutilations under the misleading term "female circumcision."

2. *Excision*, meaning the cutting of the clitoris and of all or part of the labia minora.

3. *Infibulation*, the cutting of the clitoris, labia minora, and at least part of the labia majora.

Source: "Female Genital Mutilation," by Efua Dorkenoo and Scilla Elworthy from *Female Genital Mutilation: Proposals for Change*, an MRG Report, 92/3. Reprinted with permission.

The two sides of the vulva are then pinned together by silk or catgut sutures, or with thorns, thus obliterating the vaginal introitus except for a very small opening, preserved by the insertion of a tiny piece of wood or a reed for the passage of urine or menstrual blood. These operations are done with special knives, with razor blades or pieces of glass. The girl's legs are then bound together from hip to ankle and she is kept immobile for up to forty days to permit the formation of scar tissue.

4. *Intermediate*, meaning the removal of the clitoris and some parts of the labia minora or the whole of it. Various degrees are done according to the demands of the girl's relatives. . . .

Most frequently these operations are performed by an old woman of the village or by a traditional birth attendant and only rarely by qualified nurses or doctors. The age at which the mutilations are carried out varies from area to

Figure 64.1 Female Genital Mutilation in Africa.

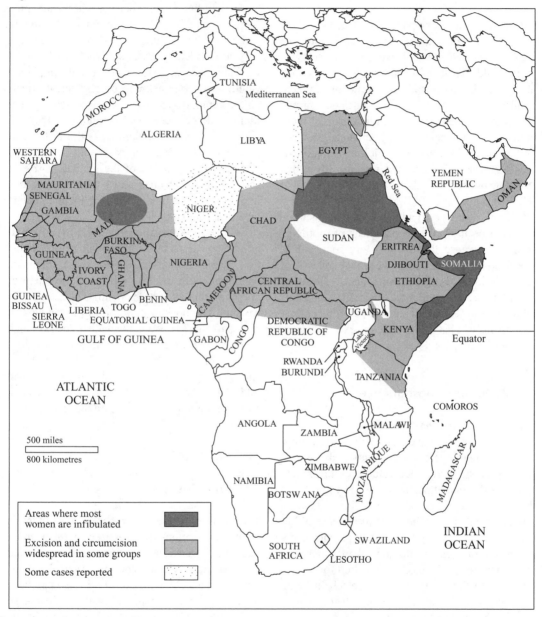

area, and according to whether legislation against the practice is foreseen or not. It varies from a few days old (for example, the Jewish Falashas in Ethiopia, and the nomads of the Sudan) to about seven years (as in Egypt and many countries of Central Africa) or—more rarely—adolescence, as among the Ibo of Nigeria. Most experts are agreed that the age of mutilation is becoming younger, and has less and less to do with initiation into adulthood.[1]

Physical Consequences

Health risks and complications depend on the gravity of the mutilation, hygienic conditions, the skill and eyesight of the operator, and the struggles of the child. Whether immediate or long term, they are grave.[2] Death from bleeding is not uncommon, while long-term complications include chronic infections of the uterus and vagina, painful menstruation, severe pain during intercourse, sterility, and complications during childbirth. Though evidence has yet to be collected, it is also likely that bleeding or open wounds increase the likelihood of HIV transmission and AIDS.

There is great difficulty in obtaining accurate research on the sexual experiences of mutilated women, because the majority are reluctant to speak on the subject and are generally ambivalent on questions of sexual enjoyment.[3] However, in all types of mutilation, even the "mildest" clitoridectomy, a part of a woman's body containing nerves of vital importance to sexual pleasure is amputated.

Psychological Consequences

Even less research has been done to date on the psychological consequences of these traditions. However, many personal accounts and research findings contain repeated references to anxiety prior to the operation, terror at the moment of being seized by an aunt or village matron, unbearable pain, and the subsequent sense of humiliation and of being betrayed by parents, especially the mother. On the other hand, there are references to special clothes and good food associated with the event, to the pride felt in being like everyone else, in being "made clean," in having suffered without screaming.

To be different clearly produces anxiety and mental conflict. An unexcised, non-infibulated girl is despised and made the target of ridicule, and no one in her community will marry her. Thus what is clearly understood to be her life's work,

namely marriage and childbearing, is denied her. So, in tight-knit village societies where mutilation is the rule, it will be the exceptional girl who will suffer psychologically, unless she has another very strong identity which she has lost.[4]

There is no doubt that genital mutilation would have overwhelming psychological effects on an unmotivated girl, unsupported by her family, village, peers, and community. To those from other cultures unfamiliar with the force of this particular community identity, the very concept of amputation of the genitals carries a shock value which does not exist for most women in the areas concerned. For them, not to amputate would be shocking.

These observations concern social-psychological factors rather than central question, namely, what effects do these traumatic operations have on little girls at the moment of operation and as they grow up? The fact is that we simply don't know. We do not know what it means to a girl or woman when her central organ of sensory pleasure is cut off, when her life-giving canal is stitched up amid blood and fear and secrecy, while she is forcibly held down and told that if she screams she will cause the death of her mother or bring shame on the family.

THE PRACTICE

The Area Covered

The countries where one or more forms of female genital mutilation are practised number more than twenty in Africa from the Atlantic to the Red Sea, the Indian Ocean, and the eastern Mediterranean. Outside Africa, excision is also practised in Oman, South Yemen, and in the United Arab Emirates (UAE). Circumcision is practised by the Muslim populations of Indonesia and Malaysia and by Bohra Muslims in India, Pakistan and East Africa.[5]

On the map of Africa, an uninterrupted belt is formed across the centre of the continent, which then expands up the length of the Nile. This belt, with the exception of the Egyptian buckle, corresponds strikingly with the pattern of countries that have the highest child mortality rates (more than 30 percent for children from one to four years of age).[6] These levels reflect deficiencies of medical care, of clean drinking water, of sanitary infrastructure, and of adequate nutrition in most of the countries.

The gravity of the mutilations varies from country to country. Infibulation is reported to affect nearly all the female population of Somalia, Djibouti, and the Sudan (except the non-Muslim population of southern Sudan), southern Egypt, the Red Sea coast of Ethiopia, northern Kenya, northern Nigeria, and some parts of Mali. The most recent estimate of women mutilated is 74 million.[7]

Ethnic groups closely situated geographically are by no means affected in the same way: For example, in Kenya, the Kikuyu practise excision and the Luo do not; in Nigeria, the Yoruba, the Ibo, and the Hausa do, but not the Nupes or the Fulanis; in Senegal, the Woloff have no practice of mutilation. There are many other examples.

As the subject of female genital mutilation began to be eligible at least for discussion, reports of genital operations on non-consenting females have appeared from many unexpected parts of the world. During the 1980s, women in Sweden were shocked by accounts of mutilations performed in Swedish hospitals on daughters of immigrants. In France, women from Mali and Senegal have been reported to bring an *exciseuse* to France once a year to operate on their daughters in their apartments.[8] In July 1982 a Malian infant died of an excision performed by a professional circumciser, who then fled to Mali. In the same year, reports appeared in the British press that excision for nonmedical reasons had been performed in a London private clinic.

Legislation

In Africa Formal legislation forbidding genital mutilation, or more precisely infibulation, exists in the Sudan. A law first enacted in 1946 allows for a term of imprisonment up to five years and/or a fine. However, it is not an offence (under Article 284 of the Sudan Penal Code for 1974) "merely to remove the free and projecting part of the clitoris."

Many references have been made to legislation in Egypt, but after researching the available materials, all that has been traced is a resolution signed by the Minister of Health in 1959, recommending only partial clitoridectomy for those who want an operation, to be performed only by doctors.[9]

In late 1978, largely due to the efforts of the Somali Women's Democratic Organization (SWDO), Somalia set up a commission to abolish infibulation. In 1988 at a seminar held in Mogadishu, it was recommended that SWDO should propose a bill to the competent authorities to eradicate all forms of female genital mutilation.

In September 1982, President Arap Moi took steps to ban the practices in Kenya, following reports of the deaths of fourteen children after excision. A traditional practitioner found to be carrying out this operation can be arrested under the Chiefs Act and brought before the law.

Official declarations against female genital mutilation were made by the late Captain Thomas Sankara and Abdou Diouf, the heads of state in Burkina Faso and Senegal respectively.

In Western Countries A law prohibiting female excision, whether consent has been given or not, came into force in Sweden in July 1982, carrying a two-year sentence. In Norway, in 1985, all hospitals were alerted to the practice. Belgium has incorporated a ban on the practice. Several states in the U.S.A. have incorporated female genital mutilation into their criminal code.

In the U.K., specific legislation prohibiting female circumcision came into force at the end of 1985. A person found guilty of an offence is liable to up to five years' imprisonment or to a fine. Female genital mutilation has been incorporated in the child protection procedures at local authority levels. As yet no person has been committed in the English courts for female circumcision, but since 1989 there have been at least seven local authority legal interventions which prevented parents from sexually mutilating their daughters or wards.

France does not have specific legislation on female sexual mutilation but under Article 312–3 of the French Penal Code, female genital mutilation can be considered as a criminal offence. Under this code, anybody who exercises violence or seriously assaults a child less than fifteen years old can be punished with imprisonment from ten to twenty years, if the act of violence results in a mutilation, amputation of a limb, the loss of an eye or other parts of the body, or has unintentionally caused the death of the child.

In 1989, a mother who had paid a traditional woman exciser to excise her week-old daughter, in 1984, was convicted and given a three-year suspended jail sentence. In 1991 a traditional exciser was jailed for five years in France.

Contemporary Practices

Opinions are very divided as to whether the practice is disappearing because of legislation or social and economic changes. Esther Ogunmodede, for instance, believes that in Nigeria, Africa's most populous country, the tradition is disappearing but extremely slowly, with millions of excisions still taking place. She reports that in areas where the operations are done on girls of marriageable age, they are "running away from home to avoid the razor." This confirms Fran Hosken's assertion that operations are being done at earlier and earlier ages, in order that the children should be "too young to resist." Fran Hosken does not think that the custom is dying out, and she indisputably has the best published range of information concerning all the countries where the practice is known.

An interesting development took place in Ethiopia during the years of civil warfare which only ended in 1991. When the Eritrean People's Liberation Front (EPLF) occupied large areas from January 1977 to December 1978, among many other reforms they categorically and successfully forbade genital mutilation and forced marriage. In fact, the reason given for the large numbers of young women in the EPLF army was that they were running away from home in other parts of Ethiopia to avoid forced marriage and the knife.[10] Although it appears the practice continues in remote areas, because the consciousness of Eritrean women has changed dramatically during the war years, it is easier to persuade men and women to let go of this practice.

Since 1983, the number of educational programmes initiated to raise public awareness of the health risk associated with female genital mutilation at local, national, and international levels have increased. The media have played a major role in bringing this issue from the domestic to the public domain. As a result of these efforts it can be said that the taboo surrounding even public mention of the practice has at last been broken. There is an increase in public awareness of the harmful effects of female genital mutilation.

It has been noted that female genital mutilation is becoming unpopular amongst the urban elite in some African countries. In Sierra Leone, for example, Koso-Thomas claims that urban men are willing to marry uncircumcised women, in particular when the marriage is not pre-arranged.[11]

In general, among urban educated women, reasons often cited against female genital mutilation include the pointlessness of mutilation, health risks, and reduction of sexual sensitivity. The last reason points to a changing attitude towards women's fundamental human rights amongst urban Africans.

In the main, the practice continues to be widespread among large sectors and groups within Africa. Those in favour of the practice are noted in the 1986 U.N. study to be a passive majority who refer back to traditional society, without necessarily sharing that society's values.[12] In some cases, the practice appears to be spreading to population groups who traditionally never practised female genital mutilation, as observed with city women in Wau, Sudan, who regard it as fashionable, and among converted Muslim women in southern Sudan who marry northern Sudanese men.[13] Furthermore, even in areas where some groups are turning against the practice, the absolute numbers affected may be increasing. Rapid population growth in Africa means greater numbers of female children are born, who in turn are exposed to the risk of mutilation.

THE ISSUES

Female genital mutilation is a complex issue, for it involves deep-seated cultural practices which affect millions of people. However, it can be divided into (at least) four distinct issues.

Rights of Women

Female genital mutilation is an extreme example of the general subjugation of women, sufficiently extreme and horrifying to make women and men question the basis of what is done to women, what women have accepted and why, in the name of society and tradition.

The burning of Indian widows and the binding of the feet of Chinese girl children are other striking examples, sharp enough and strange enough to throw a spotlight on other less obvious ways in which women the world over submit to oppression. It is important to remember that all these practices are, or were, preserved under centuries of tradition, and that foot-binding was only definitively stopped by a massive social and political revolution (replacing the many traditions which it swept away by offering an entirely new social system, revolutionary in many aspects: land ownership, class system, education, sex equality, etc.) which had been preceded by years of patient work by reformers.

Thus, to be successful, campaigns on female genital mutilation should consider carefully not only eliminating but also replacing the custom. (The example of Eritrea, previously quoted, is

illuminating here.) Furthermore, such success may be predicated on long-term changes in attitudes and ideologies by both men and women.

A major international expression of the goal of equal rights for women was taken in December 1979, when the U.N. General Assembly adopted the Convention on the Elimination of All Forms of Discrimination Against Women. This came into force in September 1981. The comprehensive convention calls for equal rights for women, regardless of their marital status, in all fields: political, economic, social, cultural, and civil. Article 5(a) obliges states' parties to take:

. . . all appropriate measures to modify the social and cultural patterns of conduct of men and women, with a view to achieving the elimination of prejudices and customary and all other practices which are based on the idea of the inferiority or superiority of either of the sexes or on stereotyped roles for men and women.

To succeed in abolishing such practices will demand fundamental attitudinal shifts in the way that society perceives the human rights of women. The starting point for change should be educational programmes that assist women to recognize their fundamental human rights. This is where UNESCO, the U.N. Centre for Human Rights, and international agencies could help by supporting awareness-building programmes.

Rights of Children

An adult is free to submit her or himself to a ritual or tradition, but a child, having no formed judgement, does not consent but simply undergoes the operation (which in this case is irrevocable) while she is totally vulnerable. The descriptions available of the reactions of children—panic and shock from the extreme pain, biting through the tongue, convulsions, necessity for six adults to hold down an eight-year-old, and death—indicate a practice comparable to torture.

Many countries signatory to Article 5 of the Universal Declaration of Human Rights (which provides that no one shall be subjected to torture, or to cruel, inhuman, or degrading treatment) violate that clause. Those violations are discussed and sometimes condemned by various U.N. commissions. Female genital mutilation, however, is a question of torture inflicted not on adults but on girl children, and the reasons given are not concerned with either political conviction or military necessity but are solely in the name of tradition.

The Declaration of the Rights of Children, adopted in 1959 by the General Assembly, asserts that children should have the possibility to develop physically in a healthy and normal way in conditions of liberty and dignity. They should have adequate medical attention and be protected from all forms of cruelty.

It is the opinion of Renée Bridel, of the Fédération Internationale des Femmes de Carrières Juridiques, that "One cannot but consider Member States which tolerate these practices as infringing their obligations as assumed under the terms of the Charter [of the U.N.]."[14]

In September 1990, the United Nations Convention on the Rights of the Child went into force. It became part of international human rights law. Under Article 24(3) it states that "States Parties shall take all effective and appropriate measures with a view to abolishing traditional practices prejudicial to the health of children." This crucial article should not merely remain a paper provision, to be given lip service by those entrusted to implement it. Members of the U.N. should work at translating its provisions into specific implementation programmes at [the] grassroots level. Much could be learned (by African states in particular) from countries with established child protection systems.

The Right to Good Health

No reputable medical practitioner insists that mutilation is good for the physical or mental health of girls and women, and a growing number offer research indicating its grave permanent damage to health and underlining the risks of death. Medical facts, carefully explained, may be the way to discourage the practice, since these facts are almost always the contrary of what is believed, and can be shown and demonstrated.

Those U.N. agencies and government departments specifically entrusted with the health needs of women and children must realize that it is their responsibility to support positive and specific preventative programmes against female genital mutilation, for while the practice continues the quality of life and health will inevitably suffer. However, this approach, if presented out of context, ignores the force of societal pressures which drive women to perform these operations, regardless of risk, in order to guarantee marriage for their daughters and to conform to severe codes of female behaviour laid down by male-dominated societies.

The Right to Development

The practice of female genital mutilation must be seen in the context of underdevelopment,[15] and the realities of life for the most vulnerable and exploited sectors—women and children. International political and economic forces have frequently prevented development programmes from meeting the basic needs of rural populations. With no access to education or resources, and with no effective power base, the rural and urban poor cling to traditions as a survival mechanism in time of socioeconomic change.

In societies where marriage for a woman is her only means of survival, and where some form of excision is a prerequisite for marriage, persuading her to relinquish the practice for herself or for her children is an extraordinarily difficult task. Female (and some male) African analysts of development strategies are today constantly urging that the overall deteriorating conditions in which poor women live be made a major focus for change, for unless development affects their lives for the better, traditional practices are unlikely to change.

DIRECTIONS FOR THE FUTURE

The mutilation of female genitals has been practised in many areas for centuries. The greatest determination, combined with sensitivity and understanding of local conditions, will be needed if it is to be abolished. In every country and region where operations are carried out, the situation is different, as is the political will, whether at local or national levels. In Western countries the way forward is relatively clear. In Africa the problem is more profound and the economic and political conditions vastly more difficult, while international agencies have hardly begun to explore their potential role.

What all three have in common is that, to date, nearly all programmes have been individual or *ad hoc* efforts, with little integration into other structures, with minimal evaluation or monitoring, and lacking in long-term goals and strategies. To achieve real change will require more resources, more detailed planning, and more real, sustained commitment from governments and international organizations.

CRITICAL THINKING QUESTIONS

1. What are the four types of female genital mutilation? How widespread are these practices?

2. What do Dorkenoo and Elworthy mean when they describe female genital mutilation as a "complex" issue? Do they feel that this practice can be abolished or not?

3. Many Western countries have denounced female genital mutilation as barbaric. But what about comparable practices in Canada and other Western nations? Even though they are voluntary, are silicone breast transplants, facelifts, or liposuction more "civilized" in making women's bodies more acceptable to men?

NOTES

1. Fran Hosken, *The Hosken Report—Genital and Sexual Mutilation of Females* (third enlarged/revised edition,

Autumn, 1982, published by Women's International Network News, 187 Grant St., Lexington, Mass. 02173, USA). This is the most detailed and comprehensive collection of information available.

2. The consequences of sexual mutilations on the health of women have been studied by Dr. Ahmed Abu-el-Futuh Shandall, Lecturer in the Department of Obstetrics and Gynaecology at the University of Khartoum, in a paper entitled, "Circumcision and Infibulation of Females" (*Sudanese Medical Journal*, Vol. 5, No. 4, 1967); and by Dr. J.A. Verzin, in an article entitled "The Sequelae of Female Circumcision," (*Tropical Doctor*, October, 1975). A bibliography on the subject has been prepared by Dr. R. Cook for the World Health Organization.

3. Readers interested to read more about research on the sexual experience of circumcised women may want to read Hanny Lightfoot-Klein, *Prisoners of Ritual: An Odyssey into Female Genital Mutilation in Africa* (New York: The Haworth Press, 1989).

4. These feelings of rejection are clearly articulated by Kenyan girls in "The Silence over Female Circumcision in Kenya," in *Viva*, August, 1978.

5. Q.R. Ghadially, "Ali for 'Izzat': The Practice of Female Circumcision among Bohra Muslims," *Manushi*, No. 66, New Delhi, India, 1991.

6. See map of Childhood Mortality in the World, 1977 (Health Sector Policy Paper, World Bank, Washington, DC, 1980).

7. See Hosken for details and estimates of ethnic groups involved.

8. *F Magazine*, No. 4, March, 1979, and No. 31, October, 1980.

9. Marie Assaad, *Female Circumcision in Egypt—Current Research and Social Implications* (American University in Cairo, 1979), p. 12.

10. "Social Transformation of Eritrean Society," paper presented to the People's Tribunal, Milan, 24–26 May 1980, by Mary Dines of Rights and Justice.

11. Koso-Thomas, *The Circumcision of Women: A Strategy for Elimination* (London: Zed Books, 1987).

12. UN Commission on Human Rights, Report of the Working Group on Traditional Practices Affecting Women and Children, 1986.

13. Ellen Ismail et al., *Women of the Sudan* (Bendestorf, Germany: EIS, 1990).

14. *L'enfant mutilé* by Renée Bridel, delegate of the FIFCJ to the UN, Geneva, 1978. See also Raqiya Haji Dualeh Abdalla, *Sisters in Affliction* (London: Zed Press, 1982) and Asma El Dareer, *Woman, Why Do You Weep?* (London: Zed Press, 1982).

15. Belkis Woldes Giorgis, *Female Circumcision in Africa*, ST/ECA/ATRCW 81/02.

65

The Metropolis and Mental Life

GEORG SIMMEL

*In this, one of his best-known essays, Simmel examines what might be called the "spiritual
condition" of the modern world. His focus is the city, in which forces of modernity—
including anonymity, a detached sophistication, and a preoccupation with commercial
matters—are most clearly evident. Note that Simmel finds reason both to praise this new
world and to warn of its ability to destroy our humanity.*

The deepest problems of modern life derive from the claim of the individual to preserve the autonomy and individuality of his existence in the face of overwhelming social forces, of historical heritage, of external culture, and of the technique of life. The fight with nature which primitive man has to wage for his *bodily* existence attains in this modern form its latest transformation. The eighteenth century called upon man to free himself of all the historical bonds in the state and in religion, in morals and in economics.

Source: Reprinted and abridged with the permission of The Free Press, a Division of Simon & Schuster from *The Sociology of Georg Simmel*, translated and edited by Kurt H. Wolff. Copyright © 1950, copyright renewed 1978 by The Free Press.

Man's nature, originally good and common to all, should develop unhampered. In addition to more liberty, the nineteenth century demanded the functional specialization of man and his work; this specialization makes one individual incomparable to another, and each of them indispensable to the highest possible extent. However, this specialization makes each man the more directly dependent upon the supplementary activities of all others. Nietzsche sees the full development of the individual conditioned by the most ruthless struggle of individuals; socialism believes in the suppression of all competition for the same reason. Be that as it may, in all these positions the same basic motive is at work: The person resists ... being leveled down and worn out by a social-technological mechanism. An inquiry into the inner meaning of specifically modern life and its products, into the soul of the cultural body, so to speak, must seek to solve the equation which structures like the metropolis set up between the individual and the superindividual contents of life. Such an inquiry must answer the question of how the personality accommodates itself in the adjustments to external forces. This will be my task today.

The psychological basis of the metropolitan type of individuality consists in the *intensification of nervous stimulation* which results from the swift and uninterrupted change of outer and inner stimuli. Man is a differentiating creature. His mind is stimulated by the difference between a momentary impression and the one which preceded it. Lasting impressions, impressions which differ only slightly from one another, impressions which take a regular and habitual course and show regular and habitual contrasts—all these use up, so to speak, less consciousness than does the rapid crowding of changing images, the sharp discontinuity in the grasp of a single glance, and the unexpectedness of onrushing impressions. These are the psychological conditions which the metropolis creates. With each crossing of the street, with the tempo and multiplicity of economic, occupational and social life, the city sets up a deep contrast with small town and rural life with reference to the sensory foundations of psychic life. The metropolis exacts from man as a discriminating creature a different amount of consciousness than does rural life. Here the rhythm of life and sensory mental imagery flows more slowly, more habitually, and more evenly. Precisely in this connection the sophisticated character of metropolitan psychic life becomes understandable—as over against small town life, which rests more upon deeply felt and emotional relationships. These latter are rooted in the more unconscious layers of the psyche and grow most readily in the steady rhythm of uninterrupted habituations. The intellect, however, has its locus in the transparent, conscious, higher layers of the psyche; it is the most adaptable of our inner forces. In order to accommodate to change and to the contrast of phenomena, the intellect does not require any shocks and inner upheavals; it is only through such upheavals that the more conservative mind could accommodate to the metropolitan rhythm of events. Thus the metropolitan type of man—which, of course, exists in a thousand individual variants—develops an organ protecting him against the threatening currents and discrepancies of his external environment which would uproot him. He reacts with his head instead of his heart. In this an increased awareness assumes the psychic prerogative. Metropolitan life, thus, underlies a heightened awareness and a predominance of intelligence in metropolitan man. The reaction to metropolitan phenomena is shifted to that organ which is least sensitive and quite remote from the depth of the personality. Intellectuality is thus seen to preserve subjective life against the overwhelming power of metropolitan life, and intellectuality branches out in many directions and is integrated with numerous discrete phenomena.

The metropolis has always been the seat of the money economy. Here the multiplicity and concentration of economic exchange give an importance to the means of exchange which the scantiness of rural commerce would not have allowed. Money economy and the dominance of the intellect are intrinsically connected. They share a matter-of-fact attitude in dealing with men and with things; and, in this attitude, a formal justice is often coupled with an inconsiderate hardness. The intellectually sophisticated person is indifferent to all genuine individuality, because relationships and reactions result from it which cannot be exhausted with logical operations. In the same manner, the individuality of phenomena is not commensurate with the pecuniary principle. Money is concerned only with what is common to all: It asks for the exchange value, it reduces all quality and individuality to the question: How much? All intimate emotional relations between persons are founded in their individuality, whereas in rational relations man is reckoned with like a number, like an element which is in itself indifferent. Only the objective measurable achievement is of interest. Thus metropolitan man reckons with his merchants and customers, his domestic servants and often even with persons with whom he is obliged to have social intercourse. These features of intellectuality contrast with the nature of the small circle in which the inevitable knowledge of individuality as inevitably produces a warmer tone of behavior, a behavior which is beyond a mere objective balancing of service and return. In the sphere of the economic psychology of the small group it is of importance that under primitive conditions production serves the customer who orders the goods, so that the producer and the consumer are acquainted. The modern metropolis, however, is supplied almost entirely by production for the market, that is, for entirely unknown purchasers who never personally enter the producer's actual field of vision. Through this anonymity the interests of each party acquire an unmerciful matter-of-factness; and the intellectually calculating economic egoisms of both parties need not fear any deflection because of the imponderables of personal relationships. The money economy dominates the metropolis; it has displaced the last survivals of domestic production and the direct barter of goods; it minimizes, from day to day, the amount of work ordered by customers. The matter-of-fact attitude is obviously so intimately interrelated with the money economy, which is dominant in the metropolis, that nobody can say whether the intellectualistic mentality first promoted the money economy or whether the latter determined the former. The metropolitan way of life is certainly the most fertile soil for this reciprocity, a point which I shall document merely by citing the dictum of the most eminent English constitutional historian: Throughout the whole course of English history, London has never acted as England's heart but often as England's intellect and always as her moneybag!

In certain seemingly insignificant traits, which lie upon the surface of life, the same psychic currents characteristically unite. Modern mind has become more and more calculating. The calculative exactness of practical life which the money economy has brought about corresponds to the ideal of natural science: to transform the world into an arithmetic problem, to fix every part of the world by mathematical formulas. Only money economy has filled the days of so many people with weighing, calculating, with numerical determinations, with a reduction of qualitative values to quantitative ones. Through the calculative nature of money a new precision, a certainty in the definition of identities and differences, an unambiguousness in agreements and arrangements has been brought about in the relations of life-elements—just as externally this precision has been effected by the universal diffusion of pocket watches. However, the conditions of metropolitan life are at once cause and effect of this trait. The relationships and affairs of the typical metropolitan usually are so varied and complex that without the strictest punctuality in promises and services the whole structure would break down into an inextricable chaos. Above all, this necessity is brought about by the aggregation of so many people with such differentiated interests, who must integrate their relations and activities into a highly complex organism. If all clocks and watches in Berlin would suddenly go wrong in different ways, even if only by one hour, all economic life and communication of the city would be disrupted for a long time. In addition an apparently mere external factor, long distances, would make all waiting and broken appointments result in an ill-afforded waste of time. Thus, the technique of metropolitan life is unimaginable without the most punctual integration of all activities and mutual relations into a stable and impersonal time schedule. Here again the general conclusions of this entire task of reflection become obvious, namely, that from each point on the surface of existence—however closely attached to the surface alone—one may drop a sounding into the depth of the psyche so that all the most banal externalities of life finally are connected with the ultimate decisions concerning the meaning and style of life. Punctuality, calculability, exactness are forced upon life by the complexity and extension of metropolitan existence and are not only most intimately connected with its money economy and intellectualistic character. These traits must also color the contents of life and favor the exclusion of those irrational, instinctive, sovereign traits and impulses which aim at determining the mode of life from within, instead of receiving the general and precisely schematized form of life from without. . . .

The same factors which have thus coalesced into the exactness and minute precision of the form of life have coalesced into a structure of the highest impersonality; on the other hand, they have promoted a highly personal subjectivity. There is perhaps no psychic phenomenon which has been so unconditionally reserved to the metropolis as has the blasé attitude. The blasé attitude results first from the rapidly changing and closely compressed contrasting stimulations of the nerves. From this, the enhancement of metropolitan intellectuality, also, seems originally to stem. Therefore, stupid people who are not intellectually alive in the first place usually are not exactly blasé. A life in boundless pursuit of pleasure makes one blasé because it agitates the nerves to their strongest reactivity for such a long time that they finally cease to react at all. In the same way, through the rapidity and contradictoriness of their changes, more harmless impressions force such violent responses, tearing the nerves so brutally hither and thither that their last reserves of strength are spent; and if one remains in the same milieu they have no time to gather new strength. An incapacity thus emerges to react to new sensations with the appropriate energy. This constitutes that blasé attitude which, in fact, every metropolitan child shows when compared with children of quieter and less changeable milieus.

This physiological source of the metropolitan blasé attitude is joined by another source which flows from the money economy. The essence of the blasé attitude consists in the blunting of discrimination. This does not mean that the objects are not perceived, as is the case with the half-wit, but rather that the meaning and differing values of things, and thereby the things themselves, are experienced as insubstantial. They appear to the blasé person in an evenly flat and gray tone; no one object deserves preference over any other. This mood is the faithful subjective reflection of the completely internalized money economy. By being the equivalent to all the manifold things in one and the same way, money becomes the most frightful leveler. For money expresses all qualitative differences of things in terms of "how much?" Money, with all its colorlessness and indifference, becomes the common denominator of all values; irreparably it hollows out the core of things, their individuality, their specific value, and their incomparability. All things float with equal specific gravity in the constantly moving stream of money. All things lie on the same level and differ from one another only in the size of the area which they cover. In the individual case this coloration, or rather discoloration, of things through their money equivalence may be unnoticeably minute. However, through the relations of the rich to the objects to be had for money, perhaps even through the total character which the mentality of the contemporary public everywhere imparts to these objects, the exclusively pecuniary evaluation of objects has become quite considerable. The large cities, the main seats of the money exchange, bring the purchasability of things to the fore much more impressively than do smaller localities. That is why cities are also the genuine locale of the blasé attitude. In the blasé attitude the concentration of men and things stimulate the nervous system of the individual to its highest achievement so that it attains its peak. Through the mere quantitative intensification of the same conditioning factors this achievement is transformed into its opposite and appears in the peculiar adjustment of the blasé attitude. In this phenomenon the nerves find in the refusal to react to their stimulation the last possibility of accommodating to the contents and forms of metropolitan life. The self-preservation of certain personalities is brought at the price of devaluating the whole objective world, a devaluation which in the end unavoidably drags one's own personality down into a feeling of the same worthlessness.

Whereas the subject of this form of existence has to come to terms with it entirely for himself, his self-preservation in the face of the large city demands from him a no less negative behavior of a social nature. This mental attitude of metropolitans toward one another we may designate, from a formal point of view, as reserve. If so many inner reactions were responses to the continuous external contacts with innumerable people as are those in the small town, where one knows almost everybody one meets and where one has a positive relation to almost everyone, one would be completely atomized internally and come to an unimaginable psychic state. Partly this psychological fact, partly the right to distrust which men have in the face of the touch-and-go elements of metropolitan life, necessitates our reserve. As a result of this reserve we frequently do not even know by sight those who have been our neighbors for years. And it is this reserve which in the eyes of the small-town people makes us appear to be cold and heartless. Indeed, if I do not deceive myself, the inner aspect of this outer reserve is not only indifference but, more often than we are aware, it is a slight aversion, a mutual strangeness and repulsion, which will break into hatred and fight at the moment of a closer contact, however caused. The whole inner organization of such an extensive communicative life rests upon an extremely varied hierarchy of sympathies, indifferences, and aversions of the briefest as well as of the most permanent nature. The sphere of indifference in this hierarchy is not as large as might appear on the surface. Our psychic activity still responds to almost every impression of somebody else with a somewhat distinct feeling. The unconscious, fluid, and changing character

of this impression seems to result in a state of indifference. Actually this indifference would be just as unnatural as the diffusion of indiscriminate mutual suggestion would be unbearable. From both these typical dangers of the metropolis, indifference and indiscriminate suggestibility, antipathy protects us. A latent antipathy and the preparatory stage of practical antagonism affect the distances and aversions without which this mode of life could not at all be led. The extent and the mixture of this style of life, the rhythm of its emergence and disappearance, the forms in which it is satisfied—all these, with the unifying motives in the narrower sense, form the inseparable whole of the metropolitan style of life. What appears in the metropolitan style of life directly as dissociation is in reality only one of its elemental forms of socialization.

This reserve with its overtone of hidden aversion appears in turn as the form or the cloak of a more general mental phenomenon of the metropolis: It grants to the individual a kind and an amount of personal freedom which has no analogy whatsoever under other conditions. The metropolis goes back to one of the large developmental tendencies of social life as such, to one of the few tendencies for which an approximately universal formula can be discovered. The earliest phase of social formations found in historical as well as in contemporary social structures is this: a relatively small circle firmly closed against neighboring, strange, or in some way antagonistic circles. However, this circle is closely coherent and allows its individual members only a narrow field for the development of unique qualities and free, self-responsible movements. Political and kinship groups, parties and religious associations begin in this way. The self-preservation of very young associations requires the establishment of strict boundaries and a centripetal unity. Therefore they cannot allow the individual freedom and unique inner and outer development. From this stage social development proceeds at once in two different, yet corresponding, directions. To the extent to which the group grows—numerically, spatially, in significance and in content of life—to the same degree the group's direct, inner unity loosens, and the rigidity of the original demarcation against others is softened through mutual relations and connections. At the same time, the individual gains freedom of movement, far beyond the first jealous delimitation. The individual also gains a specific individuality to which the division of labor in the enlarged group gives both occasion and necessity. . . .

It is not only the immediate size of the area and the number of persons which, because of the universal historical correlation between the enlargement of the circle and the personal inner and outer freedom, has made the metropolis the locale of freedom. It is rather in transcending this visible expanse that any given city becomes the seat of cosmopolitanism. The horizon of the city expands in a manner comparable to the way in which wealth develops; a certain amount of property increases in a quasi-automatical way in ever more rapid progression. As soon as a certain limit has been passed, the economic, personal, and intellectual relations of the citizenry, the sphere of intellectual predominance of the city over its hinterland, grow as in geometrical progression. Every gain in dynamic extension becomes a step, not for an equal, but for a new and larger extension. From every thread spinning out of the city, ever new threads grow as if by themselves, just as within the city the unearned increment of ground rent, through the mere increase in communication, brings the owner automatically increasing profits. At this point, the quantitative aspect of life is transformed directly into qualitative traits of character. The sphere of life of the small town is, in the main, self-contained and autarchic. For it is the decisive nature of the metropolis that its inner life overflows by waves into a far-flung national or international area. . . .

The most profound reason, however, why the metropolis conduces to the urge for the most individual personal existence—no matter whether justified and successful—appears to me to be the following: The development of modern culture is characterized by the preponderance of what one may call the "objective spirit" over the "subjective spirit." This is to say, in language as well as in law, in the technique of production as well as in art, in science as well as in the objects of the domestic environment, there is embodied a sum of spirit. The individual in his intellectual development follows the growth of this spirit very imperfectly and at an ever increasing distance. If, for instance, we view the immense culture which for the last hundred years has been embodied in things and in knowledge, in institutions and in comforts, and if we compare all this with the cultural progress of the individual during the same period—at least in high status groups—a frightful disproportion in growth between the two becomes evident. Indeed, at some points we notice a retrogression in the culture of the individual with reference to spirituality, delicacy, and idealism. This discrepancy results essentially from the growing division of labor. For the division of labor demands from the individual an ever more one-sided accomplishment, and the greatest advance in a one-sided pursuit only too frequently means dearth to the personality of the individual. In any case, he can cope less and less with the overgrowth of objective culture. The individual is reduced to a negligible quantity, perhaps less in his consciousness than in his practice and in the totality of his obscure emotional states that are derived from this practice. The individual has become a mere cog in an enormous organization of things and powers which tear from his hands all progress, spirituality, and value in order to transform them from their subjective form into the form of a purely objective life. It needs merely to be pointed out that the metropolis is the genuine arena of this culture which outgrows all personal life. Here in buildings and educational institutions, in the wonders and comforts of space-conquering technology, in the formations of community life, and in the visible institutions of the state, is offered such an overwhelming fullness of crystallized and impersonalized spirit that the personality, so to speak, cannot maintain itself under its impact. On the one hand, life is made infinitely easy for the personality in that stimulations, interests, uses of time, and consciousness are offered to it from all sides. They carry the person as if in a stream, and one needs hardly to swim for oneself. On the other hand, however, life is composed more and more of these impersonal contents and offerings which tend to displace the genuine personal colorations and incomparabilities. This results in the individual's summoning the utmost in uniqueness and particularization, in order to preserve his most personal core. He has to exaggerate this personal element in order to remain audible even to himself.

CRITICAL THINKING QUESTIONS

1. In what respects does the metropolis symbolize modern society?

2. What does Simmel mean by suggesting that in modern cities, people experience an "intensification of nervous stimulation"? How do we react "with our heads instead of with our hearts"?

3. What does Simmel see as the achievements of modern urban life? What does he think has been lost in the process?

66

No Place for Home

SEAN CONDON

Because of rampant drug use, the Downtown Eastside of Vancouver has received extensive national and international media attention. But the neighbourhood also houses many of Vancouver's poorest inhabitants. This reading discusses the development pressures this neighbourhood faces as land prices continue to rise in Vancouver, already Canada's most expensive housing market. With the Olympics in 2010, the struggle over housing is becoming even more intensified, as low-income housing is further threatened by tourist accommodation.

One by one, the tenants of the Burns Block hotel pour out of the building and onto the street, their belongings tucked under their arms and their faces carrying looks of shock and anger. It's a warm afternoon in March 2006, and the Vancouver Fire Department has just given the tenants crammed into the 18-unit building in Vancouver's Downtown Eastside an hour's notice to vacate their rooms. The building was condemned as a fire trap because the fire exits were blocked, the escapes screwed shut, sprinklers broken and extinguishers left untested.

Outside, the tenants are greeted by a circus of city officials trying to herd them into a nearby shelter; local news reporters rush to capture their distress; and community activists scream that city officials shut the building down unnecessarily. Some tenants yell at the owner for allowing

the building to fall into disrepair, while the owner deflects blame back onto the city for gentrifying the Downtown Eastside, Vancouver's infamous drug ghetto. As the accusations fly, most of the tenants try to come to grips with the fact that they are now homeless.

"I don't know what I'm going to do," says Alfred Melnychuk, a 53-year-old former heroin addict, with tears in his eyes. Like many of Canada's wandering youth of the early '70s, the Saskatchewan native was drawn to the Downtown Eastside for its drug scene. He was seduced by heroin and spent most of the '80s in jail for possession. Now infected with hepatitis C, he got clean four years ago and had been living in relative stability in the Burns Block for two years. "I already paid my rent yesterday and now I'm out on the street. I got no more money and no place to go."

Stretching roughly a mile along Hastings Avenue, the Downtown Eastside is one of

Source: Sean Condon. 2007. "No Place for Home." *This Magazine*, 40(5) (March–April), pp. 18–22.

Vancouver's oldest neighbourhoods. Here, third-world poverty sits next to the city's main tourist area, just a short distance from the heart of downtown. Central American refugees openly sell crack cocaine, underage prostitutes sell their bodies, homeless dumpster divers sell empty bottles and cans, and crack and heroin addicts drift aimlessly outside North America's only safe-injection site. It is where alleged serial killer Robert Pickton picked up many of the prostitutes he's accused of killing on his suburban pig farm. The median household income in what is commonly referred to as Canada's poorest postal code is $12,000. More than 40 percent of the residents subsist on welfare, and they're lucky to live past 50. One of the most ethnically diverse neighbourhoods in the city, it is also home to Vancouver's largest Aboriginal community.

The Burns Block was one of 125 single room occupancy (SRO) hotels that fill the Downtown Eastside. Like many of the neighbourhood's century-old SROs, the Burns Block was a mess and a home to addicts, dealers, sex workers and mentally ill. Plagued by poverty and addiction, many of the Downtown Eastside's 16,000 residents depend on cheap hotels like the Burns Block, which account for over a third of the area's 13,000 housing units. SROs are hardly comfortable—the rooms are roughly 100 square feet and don't typically have bathrooms or kitchens, though they do often come with mice, cockroaches and bedbugs. With the average one-bedroom apartment in Vancouver going for more than $900 a month, a $325 SRO is often the only alternative for the city's low-income residents.

The century-old hotels were once used to house transient loggers and fishermen, but as drugs have permeated the area over the past two decades, these buildings have been transformed into permanent homes for the city's most desperate. Unintentionally, they have become an important stop-gap against homelessness.

After years of neglect, the Downtown Eastside is now in the middle of a major development boom and city revitalization campaign that threatens to displace thousands of its low-income residents. With the 2010 Winter Olympic Games only three years away, the city is accelerating gentrification of the notorious neighbourhood before thousands of visitors and international media arrive in Vancouver. At the same time, the city's core has run out of land, and the Downtown Eastside is being regarded as its potential new frontier.

In April 2004, Larry Beasley, Vancouver's former co-director of urban planning, gave a speech called "The Shift East" to the city's top urban developers. He announced that, despite its problems, the Downtown Eastside "will become a focus for development—beyond a shadow of a doubt." With a growing economy and relentless real estate drive across the region, suddenly the decrepit SRO hotels have become extremely valuable. The owner of the Burns Block, Nick Bahrami, purchased the hotel in 2003 for $550,000 and is now selling the empty building for a remarkable $2.5 million.

With the dual forces of pressure and potential now in full swing, SRO hotels are going down like dominos. Over the past four years, Vancouver has lost more than 800 units of low-income housing as SROs have been closed, converted, or have raised their rates beyond the $325 allocated to welfare recipients for rent. While the Downtown Eastside is in desperate need of repair, neither the city nor the province has set up a safety net to catch the residents who are being displaced by the development frenzy. As drug hotels and seedy bars give way to swanky lofts and hipster hangouts, many in the Downtown Eastside believe they are seeing the beginning of the end for its residents. Kim Kerr, the executive director of the Downtown Eastside Residents Association (DERA), an advocacy organization, says that if the city doesn't figure out how to stop the slide, the Downtown Eastside will become a neighbourhood for the affluent only.

"You will see the social services move out of the Downtown Eastside, you'll see folks thrown out on the street, and these people won't be tolerated in what will become another wealthy neighbourhood in Vancouver," Kerr says.

According to the City of Vancouver's 2005 Housing Plan for the Downtown Eastside, if SROs aren't replaced with social housing, the consequences could be tragic. "Without a policy of one-for-one replacement and comprehensive housing, health and social services, the already fragile lives of many residents would become more insecure and chaotic," the report states. "This could lead to more neighbourhood impacts through increased homelessness, substance abuse, crime, and erratic street behaviour. If housing stock is lost in this area, many low-income people would literally have no place to live, as there is little housing available elsewhere at social assistance-level rents. SROs are the last tier of housing before homelessness."

Because of major welfare cuts by the British Columbia government five years ago, Vancouver already has a growing homelessness problem that has seen the number of people sleeping on the streets double from just over 600 in 2002 to at least 1,300 in 2005 (2,200 across Greater Vancouver). But despite the city's own blunt admission of the importance in keeping SROs open—unless they are replaced by social housing—it has embarked on an aggressive campaign to clean up the hotels that could see many of them shut down. In late 2005, the police completed a sting operation called Project Haven on three of the area's worst SROs, in which undercover officers discovered numerous cases of drug trafficking, welfare fraud and stolen goods.

The Vancouver Agreement is a seven-year-old, $20 million, multi-level governmental urban project focused on the Downtown Eastside. One of its four main priorities is to "turn problem hotels, particularly those that offer single-room-occupancy housing, into safe, clean places to live."

Former Vancouver police inspector Ken Frail, who led Project Haven, conducted a survey of 51 hotels in the area as part of the initiative. His report highlights the deplorable conditions in many of the buildings. It found that 80 percent have bedbugs, with over 2,200 fire code violations in approximately 2,700 rooms. Because of the disproportionate number of mentally ill in the neighbourhood, the buildings are also the source of hundreds of emergency calls a year. For Frail, it provides the proof that these buildings need to go.

"When I end up looking at the Downtown Eastside, I see an area frozen as an historic zone and I really think that that community is totally out of balance," he says. "It's been allowed to stagnate. A lot of the buildings are past their useful existence and I'm much more supportive of seeing an amount of development in that area,"

While cleaning up SROs and providing better living conditions is a commendable goal, the plan is backfiring. David Eby, a lawyer with the Pivot Legal Society—a non-profit legal advocacy organization in the Downtown Eastside—says that since the province only gives welfare recipients $325 a month for rent (a figure that has remained frozen since 1994), SRO owners don't profit enough to provide decent accommodation. As the city cracks down, it's no longer worth it for owners to keep running the buildings as low-income residences for those who are the hardest to house.

"The Vancouver Agreement's survey of the worst hotels has put a lot of pressure on hotel owners that really aren't making any money anyway because the welfare rates are so low," says Eby, "and the problem is that it makes their business case much more difficult to justify keeping it open and that's why we've seen so many closures."

According to a recent report by Pivot called *Cracks in the Foundation*, the situation is getting desperate. A week before the Burns Block shut down, the 36-unit Pender Hotel, just a block and a half away, closed its doors. The building had fallen into disrepair a few months earlier when the fire department had stormed in looking for a crystal meth lab, knocking down most of the doors. The meth lab was never found, the doors weren't replaced and most tenants fled the dilapidated hotel. Pivot launched a lawsuit against the city, but that didn't stop the building from being sold for $1.25 million to Georgia Laine Developments, which last November also bought the Gastown hotel, of Project Haven notoriety. The company plans to turn the former drug den into a boutique hotel, and to erect a condominium on the vacant site beside it. Such conversions are becoming more frequent: Last September, the owner of the 37-unit American Hotel on Main Street kicked out its tenants and boarded up the building, with plans to turn part of the site into condominiums—despite the fact that both the province and the city deemed the evictions illegal.

In 1970 the entire city's SRO stock was 13,300 units, but the figure now sits at just over 6,000—and the number is shrinking. Pivot could find only one SRO hotel in the entire Downtown Eastside that had vacant rooms at the province's $325 welfare rate. Meanwhile, the city has been unable to keep up with the losses. The 2003 Homeless Action Plan called for the creation of 800 units of social housing, and the purchase of one SRO hotel a year. But last year Vancouver only provided funding for 155 units of social housing, and rising real estate values kept the city from buying an SRO. Pivot predicts that Vancouver's homeless rate will triple by 2010—just in time for the Olympics—unless more housing is built.

While the Olympics are often cited as the reason for the city's stratospheric real estate prices, the development fever sweeping through the Downtown Eastside has more to do with location and timing. As unbelievable as it is now, the neighbourhood was once the city's primary shopping strip. From the early 1900s to the 1980s, East Hastings hosted many of the city's top shops and restaurants. As the city shifted its focus to the western half of downtown, the neighbourhood deteriorated. By the 1980s many of the retail shops and small businesses had packed up, abandoning buildings that still sit empty. The closing of Woodward's, the neighbourhood's retail mecca, in 1993 was the final blow. Around the same time, crack cocaine overtook heroin as the drug of choice and the area descended into chaos and HIV rates in the Downtown Eastside rose faster than anywhere else in North America.

In recent years the abandoned Woodward's building has become a symbol of the conflict between competing interests in the area. In the late 1990s, the provincial NDP government had slated the building for social housing, but when the B.C. Liberals took power in 2001, they froze spending on all new social housing projects and tried to sell Woodward's off to a private developer, prompting activists and residents to move into the building in protest.

The Woodward's squat lasted three months, and helped bring attention to the neighbourhood's housing problems, creating enough public pressure to force the Liberals to sell the building to the city instead, which revived the social housing plan. Once the Woodward's development is completed in 2009, the $280-million project will include 200 social housing units and 536 condominiums, plus Simon Fraser University's School for the Contemporary Arts, retail stores and non-profit offices. Then-mayor Larry Campbell called Woodward's the key to kick-starting the Downtown Eastside's revitalization. Ironically, the development is responsible for kick-starting the neighbourhood's rising real estate values as well.

When the Woodward's condos went on sale last April, a massive advertising campaign told prospective buyers to "Be Bold or Move to the Suburbs." All 536 condos were sold in less than 12 hours, some going for as high as $1 million. The ripple effect has been tremendous. According to city staff, since March 2005, 13 SROs have fetched double the asking price of three years earlier. They attribute the city's inability to purchase an SRO in the neighbourhood to the Woodward's hype. Today there are "for sale" signs up and down East Hastings and the number of development permits the city has issued in the neighbourhood has more than tripled in some areas. Developers and realtors moving into the Downtown Eastside say this is inevitable since there's no more property left downtown.

"Show me a way to have an address that close to the downtown core of a major North American city and keep property values depressed," says Bob Rennie, the realtor responsible for the Woodward's condos. Rennie says the responsibility for disappearing affordable units lies with the city for not ensuring that the neighbourhood's other developments follow the Woodward's model. Instead, the city's vision for the neighbourhood may be causing more harm than good. Last year, the city approved construction of the Carrall Street Greenway, a $5-million project to attract businesses back to the Downtown Eastside. The greenway will connect the city's popular seawall walkway with the Downtown Eastside and once it's completed, tourists will be able to stroll directly from Stanley Park into the heart of the neighbourhood. The Burns Block and the Pender Hotel sit on the Greenway's path.

The fear of eviction is beginning to sweep through the Downtown Eastside. Most of the older residents saw this show play out during Expo '86, when more than 1,000 tenants were kicked out of downtown SROs and pushed into the Downtown Eastside so the owners could fill units with tourists. The evictions were credited with at least 10 deaths from either suicide or illness. Many residents now fear a repeat of that time as the Olympics near. Not surprisingly, the Downtown Eastside has a concentration of social services to serve the drug addicted, mentally ill, or both. There is no way to know what the impact will be if people have to leave the area.

"It gives you severe depression," says Kurt Scott, a 56-year-old tenant at the Astoria Hotel, which was the third of the SROs targeted in Project Haven. "I don't know where I'd go. I can't afford $350 a month and most of the places around here are going for $385. There are a lot of people down here that have nowhere else to go. This is their home."

Down the hall from where Scott makes his coffee, his neighbour, Lori Shaw, a 49-year-old handicapped native woman, watches television while she waits for her meal to be delivered. Having lost her husband a few years ago, she threatens to put a needle to her cat and her own neck if she's forced to move.

Many people in the Downtown Eastside are beginning to get a sickening sense that time is running out on them. The Olympics are just three years away, and it would take at least that long to build a new housing project. The province, the city and VANOC have all said they will make major announcements this spring about social housing, but considering how little they have done so far, there is skepticism. Though both the federal and provincial governments are awash in billion-dollar surpluses, neither has given any indication that the money will go into housing. The next few months are critical for the Downtown Eastside and its poor residents. Without short-term plans for preventing the closure and conversion of SRO hotels and long-term solutions toward building a real Olympic housing legacy, the neighbourhood will be lost to development and many of its residents lost to the streets.

CRITICAL THINKING QUESTIONS

1. Who do you think should be responsible for housing the poor? If land prices rise, should only those who can afford it be granted shelter? Where should those unable to afford housing live? Is homelessness an option? Why or why not?

2. Do you think there is a relationship between the health of a society and how it treats its poor?

3. List some social problems that are likely to result from increased homelessness. What costs, in economic terms, are associated with this (e.g., crime, including drug-taking, takes significant financial resources to fight: police, courts, incarceration)?

67

Africville: The Life and Death of a Canadian Black Community

DONALD H. CLAIRMONT AND DENNIS WILLIAM MAGILL

Clairmont and Magill review the effects of an urban redevelopment program that relocated 80 black families in Halifax during the 1960s. The program was intended to promote humanitarian motives but the experience of Africville demonstrates the many problems associated with forced relocation programs.

To seek social change, without due recognition of the manifest and latent functions performed by the social organization undergoing change, is to indulge in social ritual rather than social engineering.[1]

— Robert K. Merton

Halifax, the foundation city of English-speaking Canada, experienced much change during its first two hundred years of existence. Yet the facelift and redevelopment it has undergone since the late 1950s have effected a change as dramatic as the 1917 explosion that levelled much of the city. Stimulated by the Stephenson Report of 1957,[2] urban renewal and redevelopment have resulted in the relocation of thousands of people, the demolition of hundreds of buildings, and the construction of impressive business

Source: From Donald H. Clairmont and Dennis W. Magill. 1999. *Africville: The Life and Death of a Canadian Black Community*, Third Edition (pp. 1–19). Toronto: Canadian Scholars' Press. Reprinted by permission of Canadian Scholars' Press Inc.

and governmental complexes. The Africville relocation was part of the larger redevelopment pattern; Africville residents constituted some eight to ten percent of the people affected by approved urban renewal schemes in the city of Halifax during the relocation years.

Africville was a black community within the city of Halifax, inhabited by approximately four hundred people, comprising eighty families, many of whom were descended from settlers who had moved there over a century ago. Tucked away in a corner of the city, relatively invisible, and thought of as a "shack town," Africville was a depressed community both in physical and in socioeconomic terms. Its dwellings were located beside the city dump, and railroad tracks cut across the one dirt road leading into the area. Sewerage, lighting, and other public services were conspicuously absent. The people had little education, very low incomes, and many were underemployed. Property claims were in chaos.

Only a handful of families could establish legal title; others claimed squatter rights; and still others rented. Africville, long a black mark against society, had been designated for future industrial and harbour development. Many observers reported that despite these liabilities there was a strong sense of community and that some residents expressed satisfaction with living in Africville.

In 1964 the small black ghetto of Africville began to be phased out of existence. By that time most residents of Halifax, black and white, had come to think of Africville as "the slum by the dump." Most Haligonians, including some Africville residents, did not regard the community as viable and recognized a need for planned social change. The relocation plan announced by the city of Halifax, which purported to be more than simply a real estate operation, appeared to be a response to this need. The plan emphasized humanitarian concern, included employment and education programs, and referred to the creation of new opportunities for the people of Africville. To the general public, the proposed relocation was a progressive step.

In addition to official pronouncements, there were other indications that the Africville program would be more humane and progressive than the typical North American urban relocation. Halifax city council had adopted recommendations contained in a report submitted by a noted Canadian welfare specialist experienced in urban renewal. There was much preliminary discussion of the relocation by city officials among themselves, with Africville residents, and with a "caretaker" group of black and white professionals associated with the Halifax Human Rights Advisory Committee. Relocation plans were not *ad hoc* and haphazard. City officials were required to articulate their policies well and in detail; many implications and alternatives were considered.

There were also indications in the relocation decision-making structure that the Africville program might realize its official rhetoric. A social worker was appointed by the city to take front-line responsibility for the varied aspects of the relocation and to act as liaison between the city administration and the relocatees. The social worker, who was on loan from the Nova Scotia Department of Public Welfare, had a measure of autonomy vis-à-vis the city and an independent contingency fund to meet day-to-day emergencies and opportunities with a minimum of bureaucratic delay. In negotiating the real estate aspects of relocation, the social worker brought proposed agreements before a special advisory committee consisting of aldermen and several members of the Halifax Human Rights Advisory Committee.

In terms of its rationale, public rhetoric, and organizational structure, the Africville relocation seemed worthy of study. The plan was *liberal-oriented* (that is, aimed at ending segregation and providing improved opportunities for the disadvantaged), *welfare-oriented* (that is, it hoped to coordinate employment, educational, and rehabilitative programs with the rehousing of people), and run by experts (that is, the planning, execution, and advise were provided by professionals). An examination of the Africville relocation could be expected to yield greater fundamental insight into planned social change than would a study of typical relocation programs that were accomplished by administrative fiat and stressed primarily the physical removal of persons. It seemed important to study and evaluate the Africville relocation both in its particularity and against the background of general relocation issues.

There were additional reasons for studying the Africville relocation. First, Africville was part of a trend in the 1960s for governmental initiative in relocation programs, and there was reason to expect that other tentative relocations in Nova Scotia and elsewhere would be patterned after the Africville experience. Second, Africville had attracted national and even international notice, and there was broad public interest in the relocation. Third, accounts of pre-relocation social conditions and attitudes were available. Two surveys had been conducted[3] and other material was available in city records. Finally, in 1968 the Africville relocation had already been acclaimed locally as a success. One city alderman noted:

The social significance of the Africville program is already beginning to show positive results as far as individual families are concerned. The children are performing more satisfactorily in school and they seem to take more of an interest in their new surroundings. This report is not intended to indicate that the program has been 100 percent successful; however I believe it can be said that it has been at least 75 percent, judging by the comments of the relocated families.[4]

Private communication with city officials and relocation officials in the United States and Canada brought forth praise for the organization and rhetoric of the Africville relocation.

Was the Africville relocation a success? If so, from whose perspective? To what extent? What accounted for the success or lack of it? It is hoped that answers to these and related questions will contribute to an appreciation of the Africville relocation and of relocation generally.

THE RELOCATION PHENOMENON

Relocation must be seen in the context of a general North American mobility pattern, and certain distinctive features should be noted. The most important distinction is that relocation is part of planned social change carried out, or at least approved, by public agency. The initiation of relocation, as seen by the relocatees, is usually involuntary and an immediate function of the political process. Our present concern is with relocation as it pertains to private residences, involves neighbourhoods or communities, and is a function of comprehensive programs of social change. This kind of relocation accounts for but a small measure of the mobility noted in Canada and the United States, but it was significant because it was distinctive. It was noted earlier that the Africville relocation was itself part of a much larger redevelopment project in the city of Halifax. In terms of the sweep of lifestyle change, even such large urban projects have been dwarfed

by post–Second World War Canadian relocation projects in the Arctic and in Newfoundland. In 1953, Newfoundland, with 6000 miles of coastline and approximately 1150 settlements, undertook a program to move people from the small outposts to larger viable communities which could be serviced efficiently. Between 1965 and 1970 over 3250 households were moved.[5]

As many low-income Americans and Canadians can testify, urban renewal is a prime example of forced relocation. Urban renewal legislation began in the 1940s in both countries. By 1968 approximately forty-five Canadian urban redevelopments had been initiated at a cost of 270 million dollars for 1500 cleared acres.[6] While the scope of urban renewal in Canada was quite small in the light of American experience, the Canadian program was significant enough that one can complain that there were too few Canadian studies looking into the politics, issues, and human consequences of renewal programs. To overcome this lack of knowledge and to place the Africville relocation in perspective, more comprehensive themes will be discussed in this [selection].

From a political-administrative perspective there are four relocation models: the traditional, development, liberal-welfare, and political. The Africville project is the best Canadian example of the liberal-welfare type of relocation. . . . [T]hese models vary along six dimensions: (1) ideological premises; (2) formulation of policy; (3) implementation of policy; (4) intended beneficiaries; (5) central actors and organizational units; and (6) key problems. These models are ideal types to which actual relocation programs correspond to a greater or lesser degree.

THE DEVELOPMENT MODEL

The development model was the most prevalent political-administrative approach to relocation in North America. This type of relocation was usually justified in terms of supposed benefits for the system as a whole, whether the system is society, the city, etc. It was usually initiated by order of political authorities and administered by bureaucrats; it was not anticipated that relocatees would benefit other than indirectly. The underlying ideology of the development model was system-oriented and neo-capitalist; an accurate statement of its premise in urban renewal has been offered by Wallace: "[it considers] renewal, as a public activity, to be intervention in a market and competitive system and to be justified by the need to make up for imperfections in the market mechanism that impede the adjustment process, to eliminate conditions which are economic or social liabilities."[7] In the context of contemporary urban renewal, the development model incorporated the usual city-design approach, focusing on questions of beautification, zoning, and structure,[8] and was usually intended to increase the city tax base and achieve civic pride or attract industry.

The development model can be illustrated by past urban renewal programs in Toronto. Ignoring relocatees as viable interest groups the programs operated implicitly on the basis of certain ideological premises: to correct imperfections in the social system (removal of so-called slums) and overall system development (economic growth), or both. As is the case in many Canadian cities, Toronto's past development policy was closely linked to the businesses and commercial-property industry which provided homes, apartment buildings, shopping centres, and industrial complexes. Thus the elimination of "blight areas" and construction of highrise apartment and office buildings generated an important source of urban revenue. Referring to this policy of "dollar planning," Fraser observed:

As long as Toronto, [in 1972] like all other municipalities in Canada has to depend upon property taxes as its sole source of income, the overwhelming power of development interests in determining the direction and quality of Toronto's growth will remain unchallenged.

... [T]he key to a municipality's prosperity remains its rate of growth; Toronto planners have been consistently ignored by city councils that have been over the years almost exclusively uninterested in any discussions about the quality of that development.[9]

A non-urban example of the development model of relocation has been described by John Matthiasson, in his study of the forced relocation of a band of Cree Indians in Northern Manitoba. The Cree were relocated to make way for a gigantic power project; they were not involved in the project planning and despite their displeasure "they accepted in a fatalistic manner the announcement of the relocation. They believed that the decision had been made by higher authorities, and that they had neither the right nor power to question it."[10]

The development model of relocation had its limitations. In particular, its econocentric and "undemocratic" features were criticized. The assumption that relocatees benefit indirectly from relocation was challenged, as was the premise that the system as a whole somehow redistributed fairly the benefits accruing from forcing people to move and facilitating the development of private industry. Some critics argued that if one included social-psychological factors in one's conception of costs, the relocatees could be seen as subsidizing the rest of the system. The criticism had some effect, and the liberal-welfare model became increasingly common.[11] One official explained:

In the fifteen years since [urban renewal's] inception, we have seen a progressive broadening of the concept and a strengthening of tools. We have seen, increasingly, both the need for, and realization of, rapprochement between physical and social planning, between renewal and social action. But the fully effective liaison of the two approaches has almost everywhere been frustrated by the absence of the tools to deal as effectively with the problems of human beings as with the problems of physical decay and blight.[12]

Another writer has observed,

social welfare can no longer be treated as the responsibility of private and more or less bountiful ladies and gentlemen or as the less respected branch of the social welfare community and the city government. Tied as it is to the concerns as dear to the heart of the country as economic prosperity it merits a place in the inner sanctum, particularly of planning commissions.[13]

THE LIBERAL-WELFARE MODEL

The "rediscovery" of poverty,[14] the war on poverty, the increasing pressure "from below" upon the development model, and the broadening definition of urban renewal led to the widespread emergence of the liberal-welfare-oriented approach. The liberal-welfare model, like the development model, emphasized expertise and technical knowledge in its operation and administration, and invariably was initiated by public authority. The principal difference is that the liberal-welfare model purported to benefit the relocatees primarily and directly. Under this model, welfare officials often saw themselves as "caretakers" for the relocatees; one relocation official has said, "the department of relocation is the tenants' advocate."[15] The liberal-welfare model of relocation was characterized by a host of social welfare programs supplemental to housing policies and was regarded as an opportunity for a multifaceted attack on poverty and other problems. It was this liberal-welfare model and its assumptions that shaped the rhetoric underlying the 1963–64 decision to relocate Africville.

Ideologically, the liberal-welfare model was much like the development model in that it tended to operate with a consensus model of society and posited a basic congruency between the interests of relocatees and those of society as a whole[;] it was "undemocratic" in the same sense as the development model; the low-status relocatees were accorded little attention, either as participants in the implicit political process or as contributions to specific policies or plans of action. There was an effort, however, to persuade rather than to ignore the relocatees. Criticism of the liberal-welfare model of relocation was related primarily to the ideological level. Some writers noted that liberal welfarism had become part of the establishment of contemporary North American society.[16] Its proponents were presumed to be handmaidens of strong vested interests, reconciling the disadvantaged and patching up the symptoms of social malaise. Critics pointed out that the special programs associated with the liberal-welfare model of relocation tended to be short-term and unsuccessful. The welfare rhetoric often diverted attention from the gains and benefits accruing to the middle-income and elite groups in society. The critics attacked the liberal-welfare model on the premise that the social problems to which it is ostensibly directed could be solved only through profound structural change effecting a redistribution of resources, and by providing relocatees with the consciousness and resources to restructure their own lives.

The liberal-welfare model is best illustrated by the Africville relocation. . . . The community of Africville was defined as a social problem, and relocation was regarded as an intervention strategy designed to help solve the "social and economic problems of Africville residents." The central actors in the formation and implementation of relocation policy were politicians, bureaucrats, experts, and middle-class caretakers; there was no meaningful *collective* participation by Africville residents. The relocatees were to be major beneficiaries through compensation, welfare payments, and rehabilitative retraining programs. The major problem with the relocation was that, although rooted in liberal-welfare rhetoric, it failed to achieve its manifest goals.

THE POLITICAL MODEL

The liberal-welfare model of relocation was revised and developed both as a response to criticism at the ideological level and in reaction to its lack of operational success. There was a growing interest in citizen participation in all phases of relocation; in the firmer acceptance, structurally and culturally, of the advocacy function of relocation officials; in the coordination of relocation services; and in the provision of resources. It is difficult to assess how far this interest has been translated into fact. There appeared to be a shift in the 1970s, at least conceptually, to the political model of relocation and a frank recognition that relocation usually entailed a conflict of interest, for example, between the relocatees and the city. There was an attempt to structure the conflict by providing relocatees with resources to develop a parallel structure to that of the government. Although society and the relocatee were considered to benefit equally, this political perspective assumed that relocatees benefited both directly and indirectly; directly in terms of, say, housing and other welfare services, and indirectly by participating in the basic decision-making and the determination of their life situation. The political model of relocation was based on the premise that social problems were political problems and emphasized solutions through political action; relocation was approached primarily as a situation in which problems were solved not by the application of expertise but by the resolution of conflicting interests.

Beyond the considerable costs (the dollar cost is less hidden than in the other relocation model) and administrative difficulties entailed, there were other grounds for criticism of the political model. There was a tendency to overemphasize the solidarity and common interests of relocatees, to exaggerate the multiplying effects of political participation in relocation,[17] and to raise serious questions about how far government could proceed or would proceed in fostering extra-parliamentary political action.

Citizen participation, a core element in the political model, was institutionalized in the United States by the community action programs of the 1964 Economic Opportunity Act. Numerous books and articles, far too many to cite, have discussed the reasons, operations, and failures of "maximum feasible participation" of the poor in the war on poverty.[18] Citizen participation was also part of the United States model city programs, which required that local residents be involved in the planning process and implementation of changes in their neighbourhoods. Contrasted with the United States, Canada has relatively few examples of related social-animation projects. The rise of "militant" citizen

groups was a phenomenon which developed later in Canada. The public outcry against the community work of the Company of Young Canadians and the subsequent governmental intervention to close this organization may be an indication of the limits of this perspective. The only Canadian publication illustrating the political model of a relocation is Fraser's study of Toronto's Trefann Court. Trefann Court residents successfully fought off a development-type relocation project; subsequently, the conflict arising from different interests was recognized as an integral part of the city's social organization. Despite internal community conflict between homeowners and tenants, a number of community residents, leaning heavily on outside "resource people," developed a cohesive organization and set up a working committee (a parallel structure) to establish a conceptual scheme for community change in conjunction with the existing city bureaucracy. The Trefann Court case also pointed to a key problem in the political model, that of assessing the representativeness of any one group of citizens to speak, argue, or vote for an entire community. With the establishment of "parallel structures," many citizens grow frustrated with the tedious detail involved in committee work. In Fraser's words:

The fact that the Working Committee operated under formal rules of order, dominated by minutes, reports, rules of procedure and legislative decorum widened the gap between the committee and the community. As debates became more lengthy, detailed and technical, the meetings became harder to follow for the ordinary Trefann resident who might drop in.[19]

THE TRADITIONAL MODEL

Finally, there is the traditional model of relocation in North American society. This is a limiting type of relocation carried out under governmental auspices, for it is a form of planned social change characterized by self-help and self-direction. It is the neighbourhood or community leaders, often indigenous minority-group leaders working through indigenous social organizations, who plan and carry out the relocation, generally with official support and some resource commitment by government agencies. The traditional model entails a largely laissez-faire strategy whereby the relocatees benefit directly and technical expertise is used to advise rather than to direct. Criticism of this approach contends that, without political action, neither the available resources nor the generation of initiative can be effective in the case of low-status groups.

There are numerous examples of the traditional model of relocation. Group settlement and resettlement in various parts of Canada have been common. The relocation of Beechville, a black community on the outskirts of Halifax, is an example within the Halifax metropolitan area. Community leaders, anticipating a government attempt to relocate the residents, organized themselves into a co-operative housing association, received funds from Central Mortgage and Housing Corporation, and reorganized their community partly on their own terms. The scope available for traditional relocation models lessens as society becomes more technocratic and centralized.

CONCEPTUAL FRAMEWORK

. . . [O]ur emphasis will be on the liberal-welfare model of planned social change and its implementation during the Africville relocation. During the analysis we focus on questions of power and exchange among the various participants of the relocation. Thus, from the perspective of power and exchange,[20] we can examine the power resources and relationships among the individual persons and groups involved in the relocation, the historical evolution of these social facts, the goals held by the different parties, and the strategies and tactics employed in establishing the terms of the relocation "contract." We can also analyse the role of outsiders, experts, and community "leaders" and focus on questions such as the mobilization of advocacy, relocation resistances and

alternatives, and the relation of rhetoric to action. It is vital in the Africville case to have a larger historical view, observing the historical exchange patterns between the city and the Africville people and tracing the implications of these patterns in making Africville "ripe for relocation" and in influencing the relocation decision-making and mechanics.

An aspect of this perspective concerns the context of negotiations and the bargaining strategies developed by the parties involved. Accordingly, attention was devoted to probing the relocatees' knowledge about the relocation; their strategies (use of lawyers, co-operation with fellow relocatees, and development of special arguments in dealing with city officials), and their perceptions of the city's goals, strategies, and resources. The relocation social worker completed a questionnaire concerning each relocated family which paid considerable attention to his negotiations with relocatees and his perception of their goals, strategies, and resources. This perspective included the concepts of rewards, costs, profits, and distributive justice. It would appear, for instance, that relocatees would have been satisfied with the relocation if rewards exceeded costs and if they thought that the city and other relocatees would not "get a better deal." Information concerning rewards, costs, sense of distributive justice, and satisfaction was obtained through the questionnaires, the interviews, and the case studies.

Despite problems in measuring each relocatee's perception of the relative profit accruing to himself or herself, other relocatees, and the city of Halifax, and problems occasioned by differences between long-term and short-term effects, this power and exchange approach is significant for the relocation literature[,] which often appears to keep aloof from the "blood and guts" of relocation transaction. Equally important, by placing the Africville relocation within a typology of relocation models, it is possible to explore the domain consensus (that is, the basic terms of reference held in common and prerequisite to any exchange) associated with the liberal-welfare approach, and especially how such *domain* consensus (for example, "disadvantaged communities or people have few intrinsically valuable resources and need to be guided by sympathetic experts") develops and how it sets the limits and context of bargaining and reciprocity.

RESEARCH STRATEGIES

The methods employed in this study were varied: questionnaires, in-depth interviews, historical documents, newspapers, case studies, and "bull sessions" with relocatees. A useful baseline source of data was the survey of Halifax blacks, including Africville [residents], conducted in 1959 by the Institute of Public Affairs, Dalhousie University. The original questionnaires were available for re-analysis, an important consideration since many of the data were not published and the published material contained several significant inaccuracies.[21] The 1959 survey questionnaire provided basic demographic data as well as information concerning mobility aspirations, employment, education, and social life.

The collection of data for this study began in 1968. The researchers arranged for two students from the Maritime School of Social Work to prepare twenty case studies.[22] A review of the students' case studies and field notes, guided by the perspective developed by the researchers, aided the drafting of a questionnaire. In 1968 current addresses of the relocatees were also traced and brief acquaintance interviews were conducted.

The most intensive data collection period was June to December 1969. One of the researchers (D. W. M.) conducted in-depth, tape-recorded interviews with individual people associated with the relocation decision-making and implementation: politicians, city officials, middle-class caretakers, the relocation social worker, consultants, and Africville relocatees involved in the decision-making. During these interviews an open-ended interview guide[23] was used to explore knowledge of Africville and awareness of

pre-1964 relocation attempts and also the actual relocation decision-making and mechanics. Each of the approximately two-hour interviews was transcribed and analysed for patterns. Many quotations used in this book are taken from these tape-recorded interviews.

Concurrently, the other researcher (D. H. C.), with two assistants, was meeting informally with the relocatees, individually and in "bull sessions." On the basis of these experiences and the case studies, we all drafted and pre-tested an extensive questionnaire. From September to December, 1969, the questionnaire was employed by interviewers hired and trained by the researchers. The lengthy questionnaire[24] asked about the relocatee's background characteristics: life in Africville, personal knowledge of relocation decision-making processes, relocation strategies, negotiations, costs, rewards, and post-relocation conditions. The questionnaire was given to all household heads and spouses who had lived in Africville and had received a relocation settlement of any kind. Approximately 140 persons were interviewed, several in places as far distant as Winnipeg and Toronto.

In June, 1969, the relocation social worker spent eight days answering a questionnaire[25] on the relocatees' background characteristics, his relocation bargaining with each relocatee, and his perception of the latter's rewards, costs, and strategies. Such data enabled us to analyse more precisely the relationships among parties to the relocation, for similar data from the relocatees and their perception of the relocation social worker were obtained from the relocatee questionnaire.

Two other research tactics were employed at the same time as the interviews were conducted. One of our assistants was conducting in-depth, tape-recorded interviews with black leaders in the Halifax area concerning their assessment of Africville and the implications of relocation. Another assistant was gathering historical data and interviewing selected Africville relocatees concerning the historical development of the community. Important sources of historical data were the minutes of Halifax City Council (read from 1852 to 1969), reports of the Board of Halifax School Commissioners, the Nova Scotia Public Archives, files in the Registry of Deeds, the Halifax *Mail-Star* library, and the minutes of the Halifax Human Rights Advisory Committee. In all phases of research, the Africville files in the Social Planning Department, City of Halifax were of especial value.

PHASES OF THE AFRICVILLE STUDY

The Africville Relocation Report, in addition to being an examination of relocation and planned social change and a contribution to the sparse literature on blacks in Nova Scotia, represents a fusion of research and action. The researchers did not begin the study until virtually all the Africville people had been relocated, and the research strategy resulted in the study being more than an evaluation.[26] The process of obtaining collective as well as individual responses, and of establishing a meaningful exchange with relocatees, fostered collective action from former Africville residents. Some local government officials objected to what they have referred to as the researchers' "activist" bias. The researchers maintain, however, that exchanges had to be worked out with the subjects of research as well as with the funding agencies. The liberal ethic posits informed voluntary consent as fundamental to adult social interaction; informed voluntary consent requires, in turn, meaningful exchange among the participants.

The study began in October, 1968 with a meeting of relocated Africville people. This was the first time since relocation that former residents of Africville had met collectively. This stormy meeting, called by the researchers, was a public airing of relocatee grievances and led to relocatee support of the proposed study. Subsequent talk of forming committees to press grievances with the city of Halifax was an important

result of the meeting. The researchers encouraged this tendency, for the expressed grievances appeared legitimate, and the researchers considered that it would be both possible and important to tap a collective or group dimension in the relocation process as well as to study the usual social-psychological considerations.

Later in the same week, at a meeting that the researchers had arranged with city officials, relocation caretakers, and civic leaders, the researchers related the expressed grievances of the relocatees and urged remedial action. General support for the proposed study was obtained at this second meeting, and the pending reconsideration of relocation by the city's newly created Social Planning Department was crystallized.

During the winter and spring of 1969, as the present study was being planned in detail, the action-stimulus of the researchers' early efforts was bearing fruit. Social Planning Department officials were meeting with the relocatees and, as it were, planning the second phase (not initially called for) of the Africville relocation. With provincial and municipal grants totalling seventy thousand dollars, the Seaview Credit Union was organized to assist relocatees experiencing financial crises; in addition, plans were formulated to meet housing and employment needs, and special consideration was to be given to former Africville residents whose needs could be met within the city's existing welfare system. A relocatee was hired to manage the credit union and to assist with other anticipated programs.

During the main data-gathering period, the summer of 1969, and in line with a decision to obtain collective as well as individual responses, the researchers met with informed groups of Africville relocatees to discuss current and future remedial action[;] it became apparent that the so-called second phase of the relocation would be inadequate to meet the people's needs. There was little identification with the credit union and it was floundering, for many relocatees who became members were either unable or unwilling to repay loans. Other anticipated programs and action promised by the city were delayed or forgotten due to bureaucratic entanglements and to lack of organization and pressure on the part of the relocatees.

The relocatees still had legitimate grievances related to unkept promises made at the time of relocation and later. With the formation of the Africville Action Committee, a third phase of the relocation began in the fall of 1969 and winter of 1970. The task of this new committee, developed from group discussions held between the researchers and relocatees, was to effect governmental redress through organized pressure. Several position papers were developed by the Africville Action Committee and negotiations were reopened with the city of Halifax. Although numerous meetings of relocatees were held during the first half of 1970, problems within the Africville Action Committee and the absence of resource people until the fall of 1970 hindered progress. With the committee stumbling along, and the credit union and other city-sponsored projects either ineffectual or nonexistent, the relocation process appeared to have petered out. The action committee was reactivated when one of the authors (D. H. C.) returned to Halifax permanently in the fall of 1970 and groups of relocatees were subsequently reinvolved in reading and criticizing a draft of the present study and in evaluating the relocation and the remedial action taken. Since the fall of 1970, the Africville Action Committee was active. Widespread support for its claims was obtained from community organizations, subcommittees were established to deal with questions of employment, housing, and financial compensation; and city council authorized the establishment of a city negotiating team to meet with representatives of the action committee.

In 1974, at the time of publication of the first edition of this book, the Africville Action Committee, to all intents and purposes, had ceased to function. Although it could claim some credit for a special employment training program through which a number of unemployed Africville

relocatees had found jobs, the action committee fell far short of its goals.

The city's lack of a positive imaginative response and the internal organizational problems of the action committee hindered other proposals. What remained in 1974 was a reorganized credit union, a modest base for further redress and group action. However, by 1999 the Seaview Credit Union was no longer in existence; it had collapsed over two decades ago. However, the community is not dead. . . . Africville still thrives in the hearts and minds of many of the relocatees. In addition, Africville still has rich symbolic value for fostering black consciousness in Nova Scotia.

POSTSCRIPT

Throughout the study, we consciously and deliberately attempted to achieve a viable fusion of research and social responsibility. The research focused on the collective responses of the group as well as on individual responses. At each stage in the study (conception, data gathering, data analysis, and preparation for publication) the collective and individual inputs that gave the study an action potential were obtained from relocatees. Drafts of appropriate chapters were sent for critical comment to officials and others involved in the relocation. The study became a stimulus to action because the normal researcher-subject exchanges could be worked out in concrete, actual terms. This was preferable to the usual research situation where, in effecting exchanges with the people being studied, the researcher typically makes vague references to the possible benefit of the study and does little or nothing to follow up implied promises of action.[27] But of course, our research strategy has its weakness too. It is difficult to feel satisfied that the kind of exchange relations that we established had productive consequences. Despite our involvement (in the early 1970s) with petitions, committee work, and attempts at rational problem solving, little redress of the inadequacies of the relocation program was achieved and the manifest goals of the liberal-welfare rhetoric of the relocation remain, in large measure, unrealized.

CRITICAL THINKING QUESTIONS

1. Review the key characteristics of the *development* and *liberal-welfare* relocation models. What are the strengths and weaknesses of each?

2. Have there been any relocation or revitalization programs in your community? If so, which relocation model appears to have provided the justification for the move? Are the people who were relocated still in the community today?

3. In your opinion, can we effectively revitalize our communities without forcing people to move? How?

NOTES

1. *Social Theory and Social Structure* (Glencoe, IL: The Free Press, 1949), p. 80.

2. Gordon Stephenson, *A Redevelopment Study of Halifax, Nova Scotia* (Halifax, NS: City of Halifax, 1957).

3. *The Condition of the Negroes of Halifax City, Nova Scotia* (Halifax: Institute of Public Affairs, Dalhousie University, 1962); and G. Brand, *Interdepartmental Committee on Human Rights: Survey Reports* (Halifax, NS: Nova Scotia Department of Welfare, Social Development Division, 1963).

4. Minutes of the Halifax City Council, Halifax, NS, September 14, 1967.

5. The Government of Newfoundland initiated the program in 1953. In 1965 a joint federal-provincial program was initiated under a resettlement act. In 1970 the program was placed under the direction of the Federal Department of Regional Economic Expansion. For an overview of the resettlement program, see Noel Iverson and D. Ralph Matthews, *Communities in Decline: An Examination of Household Resettlement in Newfoundland,* Newfoundland Social and Economic Studies, No. 6, (St. John's, NF: Memorial University of Newfoundland, Institute of Social and Economic Research, 1968). For a critical assessment of studies of the resettlement program, see Jim Lotz, "Resettlement and Social Change in Newfoundland," *Canadian Review of Sociology and Anthropology 8* (February, 1971): 48–59.

6. See Table 4, "Completed Redevelopment Projects" in *Urban Renewal* (Toronto: Centre for Urban and Community Studies, University of Toronto, 1968). Reprinted from *University of Toronto Law Journal,* 18. No. 3 (1968): 243.

7. David A. Wallace, "The Conceptualizing of Urban Renewal," *Urban Renewal* (Toronto: Centre for Urban and Community Studies, University of Toronto, 1968), 251.

8. An example of such a project is one reported by Thurz in southwest Washington, DC. Little was done for the relocatees, but the relocation was widely acclaimed for its futuristic redevelopment design. For a critique of this approach, see Daniel Thurz, *Where Are They Now?* Washington, D.C.: Health and Welfare Council of the National Capital Area, 1966). See also, Jane Jacobs, *The Death and Life of Great American Cities* (New York: Random House, 1961).

9. Graham Fraser, *Fighting Back: Urban Renewal in Trefann Court* (Toronto: Hakkert, 1972), p. 55.

10. John Matthiasson, "Forced Relocation: An Evaluative Case Study," paper presented at the annual meeting of the Canadian Sociology and Anthropology Association, Winnipeg, 1970.

11. In recent years some minor progressive modifications have been introduced with reference to the development model; these deal with advance notice and public hearings, relocation compensation, and the availability of housing stock. See, Robert P. Groberg, *Centralized Relocation* (Washington, D.C.: National Association of Housing and Redevelopment Officials, 1969).

12. William L. Slayton, "Poverty and Urban Renewal," quoted in Hans B. C. Spiegel, "Human Considerations in Urban Renewal," *Urban Renewal,* op. cit., 311.

13. Elizabeth Wood, "Social Welfare Planning," quoted in Spiegel, op. cit., 315.

14. For a discussion of this, see Kenneth Craig, "Sociologists and Motivating Strategies," M.A. thesis, University of Guelph, Department of Sociology, 1971.

15. Groberg, op. cit., p. 172.

16. See Alvin W. Gouldner, *The Coming Crisis of Western Sociology* (New York: Basic Books, 1970), pp. 500–02.

17. Relocation is a short-term consideration, for most services brought to bear on relocatee problems rarely extend beyond rehousing. A more general critique of the multiplying effect of citizens' involvement in relocation is given by S. M. Miller and Frank Riessman, *Social Class and Social Policy* (New York: Basic Books Inc., 1968).

18. The historical antecedents and reasons for the legislation are discussed in Daniel Moynihan, *Maximum Feasible Misunderstanding* (New York: Free Press, 1970). For an alternative interpretation, see Francis Fox Piven and Richard A. Cloward, *Regulating the Poor: The Functions of Public Welfare* (New York: Random Vintage Books, 1972), pp. 248–84. The operation of the program is discussed by Ralph M. Kramer, *Participation of the Poor: Comparative Community Case Studies* in *the War on Poverty* (Englewood Cliffs, NJ: Prentice Hall, 1969).

19. Fraser, op. cit., p. 262.

20. For a discussion of this theoretical perspective, see Peter M. Blau, *Exchange and Power in Social Life* (New York: Wiley, 1964); and George Caspar Homans, *Social Behavior: Its Elementary Forms* (New York: Harcourt, Brace and World, 1961).

21. *The Condition of the Negroes of Halifax City,* Nova Scotia, op. cit.

22. Sarah M. Beaton, "Effects of Relocation: A Study of Ten Families Relocated from Africville, Halifax, Nova Scotia," Master of Social Work Thesis, Maritime School of Social Work, Halifax, NS, 1969; and Bernard MacDougall, "Urban Relocation of Africville Residents," Master of Social Work Thesis, Maritime School of Social Work, Halifax, NS, 1969.

23. The interview guide is published in Donald H. Clairmont and Dennis W. Magill, *Africville Relocation Report* (Halifax, NS: Institute of Public Affairs, Dalhousie University, 1971), pp. A131–A135.

24. Ibid., pp. A97–A128.

25. Ibid., pp. A83–A96.

26. Some relocation studies have been carried out as part of the relocation decision-making, see William H. Key, *When People Are Forced to Move* (Topeka, KS: Menninger Foundation, 1967, mimeographed[);] others have been concurrent with the relocating of people, see Herbert J. Gans, *The Urban Villagers: Group and Class in The Life of Italian Americans* (New York: The Free Press, 1962). The present study is unique in that it fostered collective action carried out after the relocation.

27. See Craig, op. cit.

68

Let's *Reduce* Global Population!

J. KENNETH SMAIL

A familiar concern is holding the line on world population increase. But, some people are asking, has population growth already gone too far? In this selection, Ken Smail argues that the long-term "carrying capacity" of the planet may only be half the number of people we have now. And the time left to begin reducing population is running out fast.

The main point of this essay is simply stated. Within the next half-century, it is essential for the human species to have in place a flexible voluntary, equitable, and internationally coordinated plan to dramatically reduce world population by at least two-thirds. This process of voluntary consensus building—local, national, and global—must begin now.

The mathematical inevitability that human numbers will continue their dramatic increase over the next two generations (to perhaps 9 billion or more by the year 2050), the high probability that this numerical increase will worsen the problems that already plague humanity (economic, political, environmental, social, moral, etc.), and the growing realization that the Earth may only be able to support a global human

Source: The revised version of the essay, "Negative Population Growth" (Smail, 1995), revised and expanded in *Population and Environment* (Smail, 1997a) and *Politics and the Life Sciences* (Smail, 1997b). Reprinted with permission.

population in the 2 to 3 billion range at an "adequate to comfortable" standard of living, only reinforce this sense of urgency.

There are, however, hopeful signs. In recent years, we have finally begun to come to terms with the fact that the consequences of the twentieth century's rapid and seemingly uncontrolled population growth will soon place us—if it has not done so already—in the greatest crisis our species has yet encountered.

TEN INESCAPABLE REALITIES

In order better to appreciate the scope and ramifications of this still partly hidden crisis, I shall briefly call attention to ten essential and inescapable realities that must be fully understood and soon confronted.

First, during the present century world population will have grown from somewhere around

1.6 billion in 1900 to slightly more than 6 billion by the year 2000, an almost fourfold increase in but 100 years. This is an unprecedented numerical expansion. Throughout human history, world population growth measured over similar 100-year intervals has been virtually nonexistent or, at most, modestly incremental; it has only become markedly exponential within the last few hundred years. To illustrate this on a more easily comprehensible scale, based on the recent rate of increase of nearly 90 million per year, human population growth during the 1990s alone amounted to nearly 1 billion, an astonishing 20 percent increase in but little more than a single decade. Just by itself, this increase is equivalent to the total global population in the year 1800 and is approximately triple the estimated world population (ca. 300 million) at the height of the Roman Empire. It is a chastening thought that even moderate demographic projections suggest that this billion-per-decade rate of increase will continue well into the century, and that the current global total of 6 billion (late 1999 estimate) could easily reach 9 to 10 billion by mid-twenty-first century.

Second, even if a fully effective program of zero population growth (ZPG) were implemented immediately, by limiting human fertility to what demographers term the *replacement rate* (roughly 2.1 children per female), global population would nevertheless continue its rapid rate of expansion. In fact, demographers estimate that it would take at least two to three generations (fifty to seventy-five years) at ZPG fertility levels just to reach a point of population stability, unfortunately at numbers considerably higher than at present. This powerful *population momentum* results from the fact that an unusually high proportion (nearly one-third) of the current world population is under the age of fifteen and has not yet reproduced. Even more broad-based population profiles may be found throughout the developing world, where the under-fifteen age cohort often exceeds 40 percent and where birth rates have remained high even as mortality rates have fallen. While there are some recent indications

that fertility rates are beginning to decline, the current composite for the less-developed world—excluding China—is still nearly double (ca. 3.8) that needed for ZPG.

Third, in addition to fertility levels, it is essential to understand that population growth is also significantly affected by changes in mortality rates. In fact, demographic transition theory suggests that the earlier stages of rapid population expansion are typically fueled more by significant reductions in death rates (i.e., decreased childhood mortality and/or enhanced adult longevity) than by changes in birth rates. Nor does recent empirical data suggest that average human life expectancy has reached anywhere near its theoretical upper limit, in either the developing or developed worlds. Consequently, unless there appears a deadly pandemic, a devastating world war or a massive breakdown in public health (or a combination of all three), it is obvious that ongoing global gains in human longevity will continue to make a major contribution to world population expansion over the next half-century, regardless of whatever progress might be made in reducing fertility.

Fourth, all previous examples of significant human population expansion—and subsequent (occasionally rapid) decline—have been primarily local or, at most, regional phenomena. At the present time, given the current global rate of increase of some 220,000 people per day (more than 9,000 per hour), it is ludicrous to speak of significant empty spaces left on Earth to colonize, certainly when compared with but a century ago. And it is ridiculous to suggest that "off Earth" (extraterrestrial) migration will somehow be sufficient to siphon away excess human population, in either the near or more distant future.

Fifth, given the data and observations presented thus far, it becomes increasingly apparent that the time span available for implementing an effective program of population "control" may be quite limited, with a window of opportunity—even in the more optimistic scenarios—that may not extend much beyond the middle of the next century. As mentioned previously, most middle-of-the-road demographic projections for the year 2050—two generations from now—are in the 8 to 9 billion range. Several observations might help to bring these demographic estimates and the above-mentioned "limited" time span into somewhat better perspective:

- the year 2050 is closer to the present than the year 1950
- an infant born in 2000 will be only fifty years old in the year 2050
- a young person entering the job market in the early twenty-first century will have reached retirement age in the year 2050

These observations also make it quite clear that *those already born*—ourselves, our children, and our grandchildren—will have to confront the overwhelming impact of an additional 3 to 4 billion people.

Sixth, the Earth's long-term carrying capacity, in terms of resources, is indeed finite, despite the continuing use of economic models predicated on seemingly unlimited growth, and notwithstanding the high probability of continued scientific/technological progress. Some further terminological clarification may be useful. "Long-term" is most reasonably defined on the order of several hundred years, at least; it emphatically does not mean the five-to-fifteen-year horizon typical of much economic forecasting or political prognostication. Over this much longer time span, it thus becomes much more appropriate—perhaps even essential to civilizational survival—to define a sustainable human population size in terms of optimums rather than maximums. Further, *what "could" be supported in the short term is not necessarily what "should" be humanity's goal over the longer term.*

As far as resources are concerned, whether these be characterized as renewable or nonrenewable, it is becoming increasingly apparent that the era of inexpensive energy (derived from fossil fuels), adequate food supplies (whether plant or animal), readily available or easily extractable raw materials (from wood to minerals), plentiful fresh water, and readily accessible "open space" is rapidly coming to a close, almost certainly within the next half-century. And finally, the consequences of future scientific/technological advances—whether in terms of energy production, technological efficiency, agricultural productivity, or creation of alternative materials—are much more likely to be incremental than revolutionary, notwithstanding frequent and grandiose claims for the latter.

Seventh, rhetoric about "sustainable growth" is at best a continuing exercise in economic self-deception and at worst a politically pernicious oxymoron. Almost certainly, working toward some sort of *steady-state sustainability* is much more realistic scientifically, (probably) more attainable economically, and (perhaps) more prudent politically. Assertions that the Earth might be able to support a population of 10, 15, or even 20 billion people for an indefinite period of time at a standard of living superior to the present are not only cruelly misleading but almost certainly false. Rather, extrapolations from the work of a growing number of ecologists, demographers, and numerous others suggest the distinct possibility that *the Earth's true carrying capacity—defined simply as humans in long-term adaptive balance with their ecological setting, resource base, and each other—may already have been exceeded by a factor of two or more.*

To the best of my knowledge, no evidence contradicts this sobering—perhaps even frightening—assessment. Consequently, since at some point in the not-too-distant future the negative consequences and ecological damage stemming from the mutually reinforcing effects of excessive human reproduction and overconsumption of resources could well become irreversible, and because there is only one Earth with which to experiment, it is undoubtedly better for our species to err on the side of prudence, exercising wherever possible a cautious and careful stewardship.

Eighth, only about 20 percent of the current world population (ca. 1.2 billion people) could be said to have a *generally adequate* standard of living, defined here as a level of affluence roughly approximating that of the so-called "developed" world (Western Europe, Japan, and North America). The other 80 percent (ca. 4.8 billion), incorporating most of the inhabitants of what have been termed the "developing nations," live in conditions ranging from mild deprivation to severe deficiency. Despite well-intentioned efforts to the contrary, there is little evidence that this imbalance is going to decrease in any significant way, and a strong likelihood that it may get worse, particularly in view of the fact that more than 90 percent of all future population expansion is projected to occur in these less-developed regions of the world. In fact, there is growing concern that when this burgeoning population growth in the developing world is combined with excessive or wasteful per capita energy and resource consumption in much of the developed world, widespread environmental deterioration (systemic breakdown?) in a number of the Earth's more heavily stressed ecosystems will become increasingly likely. This is especially worrisome in regions already beset by short-sighted or counterproductive economic policies, chronic political instability, and growing social unrest, particularly when one considers that nearly all nations in the less-developed world currently have an understandable desire—not surprisingly expressed as a fundamental right—to increase their standard of living (per capita energy and resource consumption) to something approximating "first world" levels.

Ninth, to follow up on the point just made, the total impact of human numbers on the global environment is often described as the product of three basic multipliers: (1) population size; (2) per capita energy and resource consumption (affluence); and (3) technological efficiency in the production, utilization, and conservation of such energy and resources. This relationship is usually expressed by some variant of the now well-known I = PAT equation: Impact = Population × Affluence × Technology. This simple formula enables one to demonstrate much more clearly the quantitative scope of humanity's dilemma over the next fifty to seventy-five years, particularly if the following projections are anywhere near accurate:

- human population could well *double* by the end of the twenty-first century, from our current 6 billion to perhaps 12 billion or more
- global energy and resource consumption could easily quadruple or more during the same period, particularly if (as just indicated in item 8) the less-developed nations are successful in their current efforts to significantly improve their citizens' standard of living to something approaching developed-world norms
- new technologies applied to current energy and resource inefficiencies might be successful in reducing per capita waste or effluence *by half*, or even *two-thirds*, in both the developed and developing worlds

Given these reasonable estimates, the conclusion seems inescapable that the human species' total impact on the Earth's already stressed ecosystem could easily *triple to quadruple* by the middle of the twenty-first century. This impact could be even greater if current (and future) efforts at energy and resource conservation turn out to be less successful than hoped for, or if (as seems likely) the mathematical relationship between these several multipliers is something more than simply linear. It is therefore very important to keep a close watch—for harbingers of future trends and/or problems—on current events in the growing group of nations now experiencing rapid economic development and modernization, with particular attention being given to ongoing changes in India and China, two states whose combined size represents nearly half the population of the less-developed world.

Tenth, and finally, there are two additional considerations—matters not usually factored into the I = PAT equation—that must also be taken into account in any attempt to coordinate appropriate responses to the rapidly increasing global environmental impact described in points 6 through 9. First, given current and likely ongoing scientific uncertainties about environmental limits and ecosystem resilience, not to mention the potential dangers of irreversible damage if such limits are stretched too far (i.e., a permanently reduced carrying capacity), it is extremely important to design into any future planning an adequate safety factor (or sufficient margin for error). In other words, any attempt at "guided social engineering" on the massive scale that will clearly be necessary over the next century will require at least as much attention to safety margins, internal coordination, and systems redundancy as may be found in other major engineering accomplishments—from designing airplanes to building the Channel Tunnel to landing astronauts on the moon.

In addition, such planning must consider yet another seemingly intractable problem. Because the human species not only shares the Earth—but has also co-evolved—with literally millions of other life forms, the closely related issues of wilderness conservation and biodiversity preservation must also be taken fully into account, on several different levels (pragmatic, aesthetic, and moral). In simplest terms, it has now become a matter of critical importance to ask some very basic questions about what proportion of the Earth's surface the human species has the right to exploit or transform—or, conversely, how much of the Earth's surface should be reserved for the protection and preservation of all other life forms. As many have argued, often in eloquent terms, our species will likely be more successful in confronting and resolving these questions—not to mention the other complex problems that are now crowding in upon us—*if we can collectively come to regard ourselves more as the Earth's long-term stewards than its absolute masters.*

To sum up, if the above "inescapable realities" are indeed valid, it is obvious that rational,

equitable, and attainable population goals will have to be established in the very near future. It is also obvious that these goals will have to address—and in some fashion resolve—a powerful internal conflict: how to create and sustain an adequate standard of living for all the world's peoples, minimizing as much as possible the growing inequities between rich and poor, while simultaneously neither overstressing nor exceeding the Earth's longer-term carrying capacity. *I submit that these goals cannot be reached, or this conflict resolved, unless and until world population is dramatically reduced—to somewhere around 2 to 3 billion people—within the next two centuries.*

CRITICAL THINKING QUESTIONS

1. Why, according to this reading, is simply holding the line on population increase not enough?

2. What about the fact that humans share the Earth with millions of other life forms? In facing up to the problem of population increase, what responsibility do we have for other species?

3. All in all, do you agree with Smail that we must find a way to reduce global population? Why or why not?

REFERENCES

Smail, J. Kenneth. 1995. Confronting the 21st century's hidden crisis: Reducing human numbers by 80%. *NPG Forum.* Teaneck, NJ: Negative Population Growth.

———. 1997a. Averting the 21st century's demographic crisis: Can human numbers be reduced by 75%? *Population and Environment*, 18(6): 565–80.

———. 1997b. Beyond population stabilization: The case for dramatically reducing global human numbers. Roundtable: World Population Policy commentary and responses. *Politics and the Life Sciences*, 16, 2 (September, 1997): 183–236.

69

Why Humanity Faces Ultimate Catastrophe

THOMAS ROBERT MALTHUS

Environment and Society

CLASSIC

CONTEMPORARY

CROSS-CULTURAL

In this selection, from "An Essay on the Principle of Population," Thomas Robert Malthus foretells human calamity. His dire prediction is based on a single assertion: Human beings will overwhelm the earth's capacity to provide for us. Many of today's environmentalists (sometimes termed "neo-Malthusians") accept this principle and echo his early warning.

STATEMENT OF THE SUBJECT: RATIOS OF THE INCREASE OF POPULATION AND FOOD

In an inquiry concerning the improvement of society, the mode of conducting the subject which naturally presents itself is

1. To investigate the causes that have hitherto impeded the progress of mankind towards happiness

2. To examine the probability of the total or partial removal of the causes in [the] future

Source: From *On the Principle of Population*, Vol. I, by T. R. Malthus (New York: E. P. Dutton & Co., Inc., 1914; orig. 1798).

To enter fully into this question, and to enumerate all the causes that have hitherto influenced human improvement, would be much beyond the power of an individual. The principal object of the present essay is to examine the effects of one great cause intimately united with the very nature of man; which, though it has been constantly and powerfully operating since the commencement of society, has been little noticed by the writers who have treated this subject. The facts which establish the existence of this cause have, indeed, been repeatedly stated and acknowledged; but its natural and necessary effects have been almost totally overlooked; though probably among these effects may be reckoned a very considerable portion of that vice and misery, and of that unequal distribution of the bounties of nature, which it has been the unceasing object of the enlightened philanthropist in all ages to correct.

The cause to which I allude is the constant tendency in all animated life to increase beyond the nourishment prepared for it.

It is observed by Dr. Franklin that there is no bound to the prolific nature of plants or animals but what is made by their crowding and interfering with each other's means of subsistence. Were the face of the earth, he says, vacant of other plants, it might be gradually sowed and overspread with one kind only, as for instance with fennel: and were it empty of other inhabitants, it might in a few ages be replenished from one nation only, as for instance with Englishmen.[1]

This is incontrovertibly true. Through the animal and vegetable kingdoms Nature has scattered the seeds of life abroad with the most profuse and liberal hand; but has been comparatively sparing in the room and the nourishment necessary to rear them. The germs of existence contained in this earth, if they could freely develop themselves, would fill millions of worlds in the course of a few thousand years. Necessity, that imperious, all pervading law of nature, restrains them within the prescribed bounds. The race of plants and the race of animals shrink under this great restrictive law; and man cannot by any efforts of reason escape from it.

In plants and irrational animals, the view of the subject is simple. They are all impelled by a powerful instinct to the increase of their species; and this instinct is interrupted by no doubts about providing for their offspring. Wherever therefore there is liberty, the power of increase is exerted; and the super-abundant effects are repressed afterwards by want of room and nourishment.

The effects of this check on man are more complicated. Impelled to the increase of his species by an equally powerful instinct, reason interrupts his career, and asks him whether he may not bring beings into the world for whom he cannot provide the means of support. If he attends to this natural suggestion, the restriction too frequently produces vice. If he hear it not, the human race will be constantly endeavouring to increase beyond the mean of subsistence. But as, by the law of our nature which makes food necessary to the life of man, population can never actually increase beyond the lowest nourishment capable of supporting it, a strong check on population, from the difficulty of acquiring food, must be constantly in operation. This difficulty must fall somewhere, and must necessarily be severely felt in some or other of the various forms of misery, or the fear of misery, by a large portion of mankind.

That population has this constant tendency to increase beyond the means of subsistence, and that it is kept to its necessary level by these causes, will sufficiently appear from a review of the different states of society in which man has existed. But, before we proceed to this review, the subject will, perhaps, be seen in a clearer light if we endeavour to ascertain what would be the natural increase of population if left to exert itself with perfect freedom; and what might be expected to be the rate of increase in the production of the earth under the most favourable circumstances of human industry.

It will be allowed that no country has hitherto been known where the manners were so pure and simple, and the means of subsistence so abundant, that no check whatever has existed to early marriages from the difficulty of providing for a family, and that no waste of the human species has been occasioned by vicious customs, by towns, by unhealthy occupations, or too severe labour. Consequently in no state that we have yet known has the power of population been left to exert itself with perfect freedom.

Whether the law of marriage be instituted, or not, the dictate of nature and virtue seems to be an early attachment to one woman; and where there were no impediments of any kind in the way of a union to which such an attachment would lead, and no causes of depopulation afterwards, the increase of the human species would be evidently much greater than any increase which has been hitherto known. . . .

It may safely be pronounced, . . . that population, when unchecked, goes on doubling itself every twenty-five years, or increases in a geometrical ratio.

The rate according to which the productions of the earth may be supposed to increase, it will not be so easy to determine. Of this, however, we may be perfectly certain, that the ratio of their increase in a limited territory must be of a totally different nature from the ratio of the increase of population. A thousand millions are just as easily doubled every twenty-five years by the power of population as a thousand. But the food to support the increase from the greater number will by no means be obtained with the same facility. Man is necessarily confined in room. When acre has been added to acre till all the fertile land is occupied, the yearly increase of food must depend upon the melioration of the land already in possession. This is a fund, which, from the nature of all soils, instead of increasing, must be gradually diminishing. But population, could it be supplied with food, would go on with unexhausted vigour; and the increase of one period would furnish the power of a greater increase the next, and this without any limit. . . .

Europe is by no means so fully peopled as it might be. In Europe there is the fairest chance that human industry may receive its best direction. The science of agriculture has been much studied in England and Scotland; and there is still a great portion of uncultivated land in these countries. Let us consider at what rate the produce of this island might be supposed to increase under circumstances the most favourable to improvement.

If it be allowed that by the best possible policy, and great encouragements to agriculture, the average produce of the island could be doubled in the first twenty-five years, it will be allowing, probably, a greater increase than could with reason be expected.

In the next twenty-five years, it is impossible to suppose that the produce could be quadrupled. It would be contrary to all our knowledge of the properties of land. The improvement of the barren parts would be a work of time and labour; and it must be evident to those who have the slightest acquaintance with agricultural subjects that, in proportion as cultivation extended, the additions that could yearly be made to the former average produce must be gradually and regularly diminishing. That we may be the better able to compare the increase of population and food, let us make a supposition, which, without pretending to accuracy, is clearly more favourable to the power of production in the earth than any experience we have had of its qualities will warrant.

Let us suppose that the yearly additions which might be made to the former average produce, instead of decreasing, which they certainly would do, were to remain the same; and that the produce of this island might be increased every twenty-five years by a quantity equal to what it at present produces. The most enthusiastic speculator cannot suppose a greater increase than this. In a few centuries it would make every acre of land in the island like a garden.

If this supposition be applied to the whole earth, and if it be allowed that the subsistence for man which the earth affords might be increased every twenty-five years by a quantity equal to what it at present produces, this will be supposing a rate of increase much greater than we can imagine that any possible exertions of mankind could make it.

It may be fairly pronounced, therefore, that, considering the present average state of the earth, the means of subsistence, under circumstances the most favourable to human industry, could not possibly be made to increase faster than in an arithmetical ratio.

The necessary effects of these two different rates of increase, when brought together, will be very striking. Let us call the population of this island 11 millions; and suppose the present produce equal to the easy support of such a number.

In the first twenty-five years the population would be 22 millions, and the food being also doubled, the means of subsistence would be equal to this increase. In the next twenty-five years, the population would be 44 millions, and the means of subsistence only equal to the support of 33 millions. In the next period the population would be 88 millions, and the means of subsistence just equal to the support of half that number. And, at the conclusion of the first century, the population would be 176 millions, and the means of subsistence only equal to the support of 55 millions, leaving a population of 121 millions totally unprovided for.

Taking the whole earth, instead of this island, emigration would of course be excluded; and, supposing the present population equal to a thousand millions, the human species would increase as the numbers, 1, 2, 4, 8, 16, 32, 64, 128, 256, and subsistence as 1, 2, 3, 4, 5, 6, 7, 8, 9. In two centuries the population would be to the means of subsistence as 256 to 9; in three centuries as 4,096 to 13, and in 2,000 years the difference would be almost incalculable. . . .

CRITICAL THINKING QUESTIONS

1. According to Malthus, at what rate does human population increase? At what rate can the earth's food supplies be increased?
2. Malthus published his essay in 1798; in the two centuries since then, has his dire prediction come to pass? Why, or why not?
3. Following Malthus's thinking, what should be the cornerstone of the world's program to protect the environment? Do you agree with his position or not?

NOTE

1. Franklin's Miscell, p. 9.

70

Environment and
Society

Fool's Paradise

CLASSIC

CONTEMPORARY

RONALD WRIGHT

CROSS-CULTURAL

Global warming, deforestation, and the loss of farm land are just a few of the more pressing contemporary environmental problems that the world faces. Will we have the foresight—and more importantly, the political will—to properly address these issues? This chapter highlights an environmental disaster of the past and considers what this might teach us about contemporary problems relating to the over-consumption of resources and the environmental degradation that this entails.

The greatest wonder of the ancient world is how recent it all is. No city or monument is much more than 5,000 years old. Only about seventy lifetimes, of seventy years, have been lived end to end since civilization began. Its entire run occupies a mere 0.2 per cent of the two and a half million years since our first ancestor sharpened a stone.

...I outlined the rise and fall of "man the hunter" in the Old Stone Age. His very progress, his perfection of weapons and techniques, led directly to the end of hunting as a way of life (except in a few places where conditions favoured the prey). Next came the discovery of farming—likely by women—during the New Stone Age, or Neolithic period, in several parts of the world. And from that grew our experiment of civilization, which began as many independent enterprises but,

in the past few centuries, has coalesced (mainly by hostile takeover) into one big system that covers the earth.

There are signs that this experiment, like hunting, is now in danger of falling victim to its own success. I've already mentioned nuclear weapons and greenhouse gases. The big bang in the atom is obviously deadlier than the small bangs in millions of engines; but if we are unlucky or unwise, both could end civilization on its present scale. Much simpler technologies have proved fatal in the past. Sometimes the trouble lies in a particular invention or idea; but it also lies in social structure, in the way people tend to behave when squeezed together in urban civilizations, where power and wealth rise upward and the many are ruled by the few.

As I mentioned earlier, the wrecks of our failed experiments lie in deserts and jungles like fallen airliners whose flight recorders can tell us what went wrong. Archaeology is the best tool we

Source: Ronald Wright. 2004. In *A Short History of Progress,* pp. 55–63. Toronto: House of Anansi Press.

have for looking ahead, because it provides a deep reading of the direction and momentum of our course through time: what we are, where we have come from, and therefore where we are most likely to be going.

Unlike written history, which is often highly edited, archaeology can uncover the deeds we have forgotten, or choose to forget. A realistic understanding of the past is quite a new thing, a late fruit of the Enlightenment, although people of many times have felt the tug of what the Elizabethan antiquarian William Camden called the "back-looking curiousity." Antiquity, he wrote, "hath a certaine resemblance with eternity. [It] is a sweet food of the mind."[1]

Not everyone's mind was so open in his day. A Spanish viceroy of Peru who had just seen the Inca capital high in the Andes, with its walls of giant stones fitted like gems, wrote back to his king: "I have examined the fortress that [the Incas] built . . . which shows clearly the work of the Devil . . . for it does not seem possible that the strength and skill of men could have made it."[2]

Even today, some opt for the comforts of mystification, preferring to believe that the wonders of the ancient world were built by Atlanteans, gods, or space travellers, instead of by thousands toiling in the sun. Such thinking robs our forerunners of their due, and us of their experience. Because then one can believe whatever one likes about the past—without having to confront the bones, potsherds, and inscriptions which tell us that people all over the world, time and again, have made similar advances and mistakes.

About two centuries after the Spanish invasion of Peru, a Dutch fleet in the South Seas, far to the west of Chile and below the Tropic of Capricorn, came upon a sight hardly less awesome, and even more inexplicable, than the megalithic buildings of the Andes. On Easter Day, 1722, the Dutchmen sighted an unknown island so treeless and eroded that they mistook its barren hills for dunes. They were amazed, as they drew near, to see hundreds of stone images, some as tall as an

Amsterdam house. "We could not comprehend how it was possible that these people, who are devoid of heavy thick timber [or] strong ropes, nevertheless had been able to erect such images, which were fully thirty feet high."[3] Captain Cook later confirmed the island's desolation, finding "no wood for fuel; nor any fresh water worth taking on board." He described the islanders' tiny canoes, made from scraps of driftwood stitched together like shoe leather, as the worst in the Pacific. Nature, he concluded, had "been exceedingly sparing of her favours to this spot."[4]

The great mystery of Easter Island that struck all early visitors was not just that these colossal statues stood in such a tiny and remote corner of the world, but that the stones seemed to have been put there without tackle, as if set down from the sky. The Spaniards who had credited the Devil with the splendours of Inca architecture were merely unable to recognize another culture's achievements. But even scientific observers could not, at first, account for the megaliths of Easter Island. The figures stood there mockingly, defying common sense.

We now know the answer to the riddle, and it is a chilling one. With all due respect to Captain Cook, Nature had not been unusually stingy with her favours. Pollen studies of the island's crater lakes have shown that it was once well watered and green, with rich volcanic soil supporting thick woods of the Chilean wine palm, a fine timber that can grow as big as an oak. No natural disaster had changed that: no eruption, drought, or disease. The catastrophe on Easter Island was man.

Rapa Nui, as Polynesians call the place, was settled during the fifth century A.D. by migrants from the Marquesas or the Gambiers who arrived in big catamarans stocked with their usual range of crops and animals: dogs, chickens, edible rats, sugar cane, bananas, sweet potatoes, and mulberry for making bark cloth. (Thor Heyerdahl's theory that the island was peopled from South America has not been supported by recent work, though sporadic contact between Peru and

Oceania probably did take place.) Easter Island proved too cold for breadfruit and coconut palms, but it was rich in seafood: fish, seals, porpoises, turtles, and nesting seabirds. Within five or six centuries, the settlers had multiplied to about 10,000 people—a lot for sixty-four square miles. They built villages with good houses on stone footings and cleared all the best land for fields. Socially they split into clans and ranks—nobles, priests, commoners—and there may have been a paramount chief, or "king." Like Polynesians on some other islands, each clan began to honour its ancestry with impressive stone images. These were hewn from the yielding volcanic tuff of a crater and set up on platforms by the shore. As time went on, the statue cult became increasingly rivalrous and extravagant, reaching its apogee during Europe's high Middle Ages, while the Plantagenet kings ruled England.

Each generation of images grew bigger than the last, demanding more timber, rope, and manpower for hauling to the *ahu,* or altars. Trees were cut faster than they could grow, a problem worsened by the settlers' rats, who ate the seeds and saplings. By A.D. 1400, no more tree pollen is found in the annual layers of the crater lakes: the woods had been utterly destroyed by both the largest and the smallest mammal on the island.

We might think that in such a limited place, where, from the height of Terevaka, islanders could survey their whole world at a glance, steps would have been taken to halt the cutting, to protect the saplings, to replant. We might think that as trees became scarce, the erection of statues would have been curtailed, and timber reserved for essential purposes such as boatbuilding and roofing. But that is not what happened. The people who felled the last tree could see it was the last, could know with complete certainty that there would never be another. And they felled it anyway. All shade vanished from the land except the hard-edged shadows cast by the petrified ancestors, whom the people loved all the more because they made them feel less alone.

For a generation or so, there was enough old lumber to haul the great stones and still keep a few canoes seaworthy for deep water. But the day came when the last good boat was gone. The people then knew there would be little seafood and—worse—no way of escape. The word for wood, *rakau,* became the dearest in their language. Wars broke out over ancient planks and worm-eaten bits of jetsam. They ate all their dogs and nearly all the nesting birds, and the unbearable stillness of the place deepened with animal silences. There was nothing left now but the *moai,* the stone giants who had devoured the land. And still these promised the return of plenty, if only the people would keep faith and honour them with increase. But how will we take you to the altars? asked the carvers, and the *moai* answered that when the time came, they would walk there on their own. So the sound of hammering still rang from the quarries, and the crater walls came alive with hundreds of new giants, growing even bigger now they had no need of human transport. The tallest ever set on an altar is over thirty feet high and weighs eighty tons; the tallest ever *carved* is sixty-five feet long and more than *two hundred* tons, comparable to the greatest stones worked by the Incas or Egyptians. Except, of course, that it never budged an inch.

By the end there were more than a thousand *moai,* one for every ten islanders in their heyday. But the good days were gone—gone with the good earth, which had been carried away on the endless wind and washed by flash floods into the sea. The people had been seduced by a kind of progress that becomes a mania, an "ideological pathology," as some anthropologists call it. When Europeans arrived in the eighteenth century, the worst was over; they found only one or two living souls per statue, a sorry remnant, "small, lean, timid and miserable," in Cook's words.[5] Now without roof beams, many people were dwelling in caves; their only buildings were stone henhouses where they guarded this last non-human protein from one another day and night. The Europeans heard tales of how the warrior class had taken power, how the island had convulsed with burning villages, gory battles, and cannibal feasts. The one innovation of this end-period was to turn the use of obsidian (a razor-keen volcanic glass) from toolmaking to weapons.[6] Daggers and spearheads became the commonest artefacts on the island, hoarded in pits like the grenades and assault rifles kept by modern-day survivalists.

Even this was not quite the nadir. Between the Dutch visit of 1722 and Cook's fifty years later, the people again made war on each other and, for the first time, on the ancestors as well. Cook found *moai* toppled from their platforms, cracked and beheaded, the ruins littered with human bone. There is no reliable account of how or why this happened. Perhaps it started as the ultimate atrocity between enemy clans, like European nations bombing cathedrals in the Second World War. Perhaps it began with the shattering of the island's solitude by strangers in floating castles of unimaginable wealth and menace. These possessors of wood were also bringers of death and disease. Scuffles with sailors often ended with natives gunned down on the beach.

We do not know exactly what promises had been made by the demanding *moai* to the people, but it seems likely that the arrival of an outside world might have exposed certain illusions of the statue cult, replacing compulsive belief with equally compulsive disenchantment. Whatever its animus, the destruction on Rapa Nui raged for at least seventy years. Each foreign ship saw fewer upright statues, until not one giant was left standing on its altar. The work of demolition must have been extremely arduous for the few descendants of the builders. Its thoroughness and deliberation speak of something deeper than clan warfare: of a people angry at their reckless fathers, of a revolt against the dead.

The lesson that Rapa Nui holds for our world has not gone unremarked. In the epilogue to their 1992 book, *Easter Island, Earth Island*, the archaeologists Paul Bahn and John Flenley are explicit. The islanders, they write:

carried out for us the experiment of permitting unrestricted population growth, profligate use of resources, destruction of the environment and boundless confidence in their religion to take care of the future. The result was an ecological disaster leading to a population crash. . . . Do we have to repeat the experiment on [a] grand scale? . . . Is the human personality always the same as that of the person who felled the last tree?[7]

The last tree. The last mammoth. The last dodo. And soon perhaps the last fish and the last gorilla. On the basis of what police call "form," we are serial killers beyond reason. But has this always been, and must it always be, the case? Are all human systems doomed to stagger along under the mounting weight of their internal logic until it crushes them? As I have proposed, the answers—and, I think, the remedies—lie in the fates of past societies.

CRITICAL THINKING QUESTIONS

1. Wright writes that the demise of societies can be structurally determined. What does he mean by that? Can you think of some structures that will have to be changed in order to avert environmental crises in contemporary society?

2. Do you think writers like Malthus (previous reading) and Ronald Wright are too pessimistic in their analysis? History has shown Malthus to be overly negative and his essay is often used to argue against any limitations to growth. Do you think contemporary doomsayers are likewise overly pessimistic? Will they also be proven wrong as human ingenuity will avert any environmental disasters? Why or why not? Give specific examples that support your opinion.

3. Which environmental problems do you think require the most immediate attention? What are some social problems that will likely result from these environmental problems? Are you generally optimistic or pessimistic about the outcome of these problems?

NOTES

1. Quoted in Daniel, *The Idea of Prehistory,* pp. 14–15.
2. Letter of Francisco de Toledo, March 25, 1571, quoted in Luis A. Pardo, ed., *Saqsaywaman* no. 1 (July 1970): 144.
3. From *The Journal of Jacob Roggeveen,* trans. and ed. Andrew Sharp (Oxford: Clarendon Press, 1970). Quoted in Paul Bahn and John Flenley, *Easter Island, Earth Island* (London: Thames and Hudson, 1992), p. 13, and more fully in Catherine and Michel Orliac, *Easter Island,* trans. Paul G. Bahn, (New York: Harry N. Abrams, 1995), pp. 98–99.
4. Orliac, *Easter Island,* p. 17.
5. James Cook, quoted in ibid., p. 170.
6. Ibid., p. 165.
7. Bahn and Flenley, *Easter Island,* pp. 213, 218.

71

Supporting Indigenous Peoples

ALAN THEIN DURNING

A particular concern of many environmentalists (and social scientists) is the steady loss of this planet's cultural diversity as thousands of small societies are pushed aside by the relentless march of economic development. This selection describes the problem and points out that protecting indigenous peoples is not just a matter of justice—the well-being of everyone in the world depends on it.

In July 1992, an aged chief of the Lumad people in the Philippines—a man with a price on his head for his opposition to local energy development—sat at the base of the cloud-covered volcano Mount Apo and made a simple plea.

"Our Christian brothers are enjoying their life here in the plains," said eighty-six-year-old Chief Tulalang Maway, sweeping his arm toward the provincial town of Kidapawan and the agricultural lands beyond, lands his tribe long ago ceded to immigrants from afar. Turning toward the mountain—a Lumad sacred site that he has vowed to defend "to the last drop of blood"—Maway slowly finished his thought, "We only ask them to leave us our last sanctuary."

Source: "Supporting Indigenous Peoples," by Alan Thein Durning, in *State of the World 1993: A Worldwatch Institute Report on Progress Toward a Sustainable Society,* edited by Lester R. Brown et al. Copyright © 1993 by Worldwatch Institute. Reprinted by permission of W. W. Norton & Company, Inc.

Chief Maway's words could have been spoken by almost any tribal Filipino, or, for that matter, any Native American, Australian aborigine, African pygmy, or member of one of the world's thousands of other distinct indigenous cultures. All have ancient ties to the land, water, and wildlife of their ancestral domains, and all are endangered by onrushing forces of the outside world. They have been decimated by violence and plagues. Their cultures have been eroded by missionaries and exploited by wily entrepreneurs. Their subsistence economies have been dismantled in the pursuit of national development. And their homelands have been invaded by commercial resource extractors and overrun by landless peasants.

Chief Maway's entreaty, in its essence, is the call of indigenous peoples everywhere: the plea that their lands be spared further abuse, that their birthright be returned to them. It is a petition that the world's dominant cultures have long ignored, believing the passing of native peoples and their antiquated ways was an inevitable, if lamentable, cost of progress. That view, never morally defensible, is now demonstrably untenable.

Indigenous peoples are the sole guardians of vast, little-disturbed habitats in remote parts of every continent. These territories, which together encompass an area larger than Australia, provide important ecological services: They regulate hydrological cycles, maintain local and global climatic stability, and harbor a wealth of biological and genetic diversity. Indeed, indigenous homelands may provide safe haven for more endangered plant and animal species than all the world's nature reserves. Native peoples, moreover, often hold the key to these vaults of biological diversity. They possess a body of ecological knowledge—encoded in their languages, customs, and subsistence practices—that rivals the libraries of modern science.

The human rights enshrined in international law have long demanded that states shield indigenous cultures, but instead these cultures have been dismembered. A more self-interested appeal appears to be in order: Supporting indigenous survival is an objective necessity, even for those callous to the justice of the cause. As a practical matter, the world's dominant cultures cannot sustain the earth's ecological health—a requisite of human advancement—without the aid of the world's endangered cultures. Biological diversity is inextricably linked to cultural diversity.

Around the globe, indigenous peoples are fighting for their ancestral territories. They are struggling in courts and national parliaments, gaining power through new mass movements and international campaigns, and—as on the slopes of Mount Apo—defending their inheritance with their lives. The question is, Who will stand with them?

STATE OF THE NATIONS

Indigenous peoples (or "native" or "tribal" peoples) are found on every continent and in most countries [see Table 71.1]. The extreme variations in their ways of life and current circumstances defy ready definition. Indeed, many anthropologists insist that indigenous peoples are defined only by the way they define themselves: They think of themselves as members of a distinct people. Still, many indigenous cultures share a number of characteristics that help describe, if not define, them.

They are typically descendants of the original inhabitants of an area taken over by more powerful outsiders. They are distinct from their country's dominant group in language, culture, or religion. Most have a custodial concept of land and other resources, in part defining themselves in relation to the habitat from which they draw their livelihood. They commonly live in or maintain strong ties to a subsistence economy; many are, or are descendants of, hunter-gatherers, fishers, nomadic or seasonal herders, shifting forest farmers, or subsistence peasant cultivators. And their social relations are often tribal, involving collective management of natural resources, thick networks of bonds between individuals, and group decision making, often by consensus among elders.

Measured by spoken languages, the single best indicator of a distinct culture, all the world's people belong to 6,000 cultures; 4,000–5,000 of these are indigenous ones. Of the 5.5 billion humans on the planet, some 190 million to 625 million are indigenous people. (These ranges are wide because of varying definitions of "indigenous." The higher figures include ethnic nations that lack political autonomy, such as Tibetans, Kurds, and Zulus, while the lower figures count only smaller, subnational societies.) In some countries, especially those settled by Europeans in the past five centuries, indigenous populations are fairly easy to count [see Table 71.2]. By contrast, lines between indigenous peoples and ethnic minorities are difficult to draw in Asia and Africa, where cultural diversity remains greatest.

Regardless of where lines are drawn, however, human cultures are disappearing at unprecedented rates. Worldwide, the loss of cultural diversity is keeping pace with the global loss of biological

TABLE 71.1   Indigenous Peoples of the World, 1992

Region	Indigenous Peoples
Africa and Middle East	Great cultural diversity throughout continent; "indigenous" share hotly contested lands. Some 25–30 million nomadic herders or pastoralists in East Africa, Sahel, and Arabian peninsula include Bedouin, Dinka, Masai, Turkana. San (Bushmen) of Namibia and Botswana and pygmies of central African rain forest, both traditionally hunter-gatherers, have occupied present homelands for at least 20,000 years (25–350 million indigenous people overall, depending on definitions; 2,000 languages)
Americas	Native Americans concentrated near centers of ancient civilizations: Aztec in Mexico, Mayan in Central America, and Incan in Andes of Bolivia, Ecuador, and Peru. In Latin America, most Indians farm small plots; in North America, 2 million Indians live in cities and on reservations (42 million; 900 languages)
Arctic	Inuit (Eskimo) and other Arctic peoples of North America, Greenland, and Siberia traditionally fishers, whalers, and hunters. Sami (Lapp) of northern Scandinavia are traditionally reindeer herders (2 million; 50 languages)
East Asia	Chinese indigenous peoples, numbering up to 82 million, mostly subsistence farmers such as Bulang of south China or former pastoralists such as ethnic Mongolians of north and west China. Ainu of Japan and aboriginal Taiwanese now largely industrial laborers (12–84 million; 150 languages)
Oceania	Aborigines of Australia and Maoris of New Zealand, traditionally farmers, fishers, hunters, and gatherers. Many now raise livestock. Islanders of South Pacific continue to fish and harvest marine resources (3 million; 500 languages)
South Asia	Gond, Bhil, and other adivasis, or tribal peoples, inhabit forest belt of central India. In Bangladesh, adivasis concentrated in Chittagong hills on Burmese border, several million tribal farmers and pastoralists in Afghanistan, Pakistan, Nepal, Iran, and central Asian republics of former Soviet Union (74–91 million; 700 languages)
Southeast Asia	Tribal Hmong, Karen, and other forest-farming peoples form Asia ethnic mosaic covering up lands. Indigenous population follows distribution of forest: Laos has more forest and tribal peoples, Myanmar and Vietnam have less forest and fewer people, and Thailand and mainland Malaysia have the least. Tribal peoples are concentrated at the extreme ends of the Philippine and Indonesian archipelagos. Island of New Guinea—split politically between Indonesia and Papua New Guinea—populated by indigenous tribes (32–55 million; 1,950 languages)

Source: Worldwatch Institute.

diversity. Anthropologist Jason Clay of Cultural Survival in Cambridge, Massachusetts, writes, "there have been more . . . extinctions of tribal peoples in this century than in any other in history." Brazil alone lost eighty-seven tribes in the first half of the century. One-third of North American languages and two-thirds of Australian languages have disappeared since 1800—the overwhelming share of them since 1900.

Cultures are dying out even faster than the peoples who belong to them. University of Alaska linguist Michael Krauss projects that half the world's languages—the storehouses of peoples' intellectual heritages—will disappear within a century. These languages, and arguably the cultures they embody, are no longer passed on to sufficient numbers of children to ensure their survival. Krauss likens such cultures to animal

species doomed to extinction because their populations are below the threshold needed for adequate reproduction. Only 5 percent of all languages, moreover, enjoy the relative safety of having at least a half-million speakers.

To trace the history of indigenous peoples' subjugation is simply to recast the story of the rise of the world's dominant cultures: the spread of Han Chinese into Central and Southeast Asia, the ascent of Aryan empires on the Indian subcontinent, the southward advance of Bantu cultures across Africa, and the creation of a world economy first through European colonialism and then through industrial development. Surviving indigenous cultures are often but tattered remnants of their predecessors' societies.

When Christopher Columbus reached the New World in 1492, there were perhaps 54 million

TABLE 71.2 Estimated Populations of Indigenous
Peoples, Selected Countries, 1992

Country	Population[a] (millions)	Share of National Population (percent)
Papua New Guinea	3.0	77
Bolivia	5.6	70
Guatemala	4.6	47
Peru	9.0	40
Ecuador	3.8	38
Myanmar	14.0	33
Laos	1.3	30
Mexico	10.9	12
New Zealand	0.4	12
Chile	1.2	9
Philippines	6.0	9
India	63.0	7
Malaysia	0.8	4
Canada	0.9	4
Australia	0.4	2
Brazil	1.5	1
Bangladesh	1.2	1
Thailand	0.5	1
United States	2.0	1

[a]Generally excludes those of mixed ancestry.

Source: Worldwatch Institute.

people in the Americas, almost as many as in Europe at the time; their numbers plummeted, however, as plagues radiated from the landfalls of the conquistadors. Five centuries later, the indigenous peoples of the Americas, numbering some 42 million, have yet to match their earlier population. Similar contractions followed the arrival of Europeans in Australia, New Zealand, and Siberia.

Worldwide, virtually no indigenous peoples remain entirely isolated from national societies. By indoctrination or brute force, nations have assimilated native groups into the cultural mainstream. As a consequence, few follow the ways of their ancestors unchanged. Just one tenth of the Penan hunter-gatherers continue to hunt in the rain forests of Malaysian Borneo. A similar share of the Sami (Lapp) reindeer-herders of northern Scandinavia accompany their herds on the Arctic ranges. Half of North American Indians and many New Zealand Maori dwell in cities.

Tragically, indigenous peoples whose cultures are besieged frequently end up on the bottom of the national economy. They are often the first sent to war for the state, as in Namibia and the Philippines, and the last to go to work: Unemployment in Canadian Indian communities averages 50 percent. They are overrepresented among migrant laborers in India, beggars in Mexico, and uranium miners in the United States. They are often drawn into the shadow economy: They grow drug crops in northern Thailand, run gambling casinos in the United States, and sell their daughters into prostitution in Taiwan. Everywhere, racism against them is rampant. India's adivasis, or tribal people, endure hardships comparable to the "untouchables," the most downtrodden caste.

Native peoples' inferior social status is sometimes codified in national law and perpetuated by institutionalized abuse. Many members of the hill tribes in Thailand are denied citizenship, and until 1988 the Brazilian constitution legally classified Indians as minors and wards of the state. In the extreme, nation-states are simply genocidal: Burmese soldiers systemically raped, murdered, and enslaved thousands of Arakanese villagers in early 1992. Guatemala has exterminated perhaps 100,000 Mayans in its three-decade counterinsurgency. Similar numbers of indigenous people have died in East Timor and Irian Jaya since 1970 at the hands of Indonesian forces intent on solidifying their power.

In much of the world, the oppression that indigenous peoples suffer has indelibly marked their own psyches, manifesting itself in depression and social disintegration. Says Tamara Gliminova of the Khant people of Siberia, "When they spit into your soul for this long, there is little left."

HOMELANDS

Indigenous peoples not yet engulfed in modern societies live mostly in what Mexican anthropologist Gonzalo Aguirre Beltran called "regions of refuge," places so rugged, desolate, or remote that they have been little disturbed by the industrial economy. They remain in these areas for tragic reasons. Peoples in more fertile lands were eradicated outright to make way for settlers and plantations, or they retreated—sometimes at gun point—into these natural havens. Whereas indigenous peoples exercised de facto control over most of the earth's ecosystems as recently as two centuries ago, the territory they now occupy is reduced to an estimated 12 to 19 percent of the earth's land area—depending, again, on where the line between indigenous peoples and ethnic nations is drawn. And governments recognize their ownership of but a fraction of that area.

Gaining legal protection for the remainder of their subsistence base is most indigenous peoples' highest political priority. If they lose this struggle, their cultures stand little chance of surviving. As the World Council of Indigenous Peoples, a global federation based in Canada, wrote in 1985, "Next to shooting Indigenous Peoples, the surest way to kill us is to separate us from our part of the Earth." Most native peoples are bound to their land through relationships both practical and spiritual, routine and historical. Tribal Filipino Edtami Mansayagan, attempting to communicate the pain he feels at the destruction of the rivers, valleys, meadows, and hillsides of his people's mountain domain, exclaims, "These are the living pages of our un-written history." The question of who shall control resources in the regions of refuge is the crux of indigenous survival.

Indigenous homelands are important not only to endangered cultures; they are also of exceptional ecological value. Intact indigenous communities and little-disturbed ecosystems overlap with singular regularity, from the coastal swamps of South America to the shifting sands of the Sahara, from the ice floes of the circumpolar north to the coral reefs of the South Pacific. When, for example, a National Geographic Society team in Washington, D.C., compiled a map of Indian lands and remaining forest cover in Central America in 1992, they confirmed the personal observation of Geodisio Castillo, a Kuna Indian from Panama: "Where there are forests there are indigenous people, and where there are indigenous people there are forests."

Because populations of both indigenous peoples and unique plant and animal species are numerically concentrated in remnant habitats in the tropics—precisely the regions of refuge that Beltran was referring to—the biosphere's most diverse habitats are usually homes to endangered cultures. The persistence of biological diversity in these regions is no accident. In the Philippines and Thailand, both representative cases, little more than a third of the land officially zoned as forest remains forest-covered; the tracts that do still stand are largely those protected by tribal people.

The relationship between cultural diversity and biological diversity stands out even in global statistics. Just nine countries together account for 60 percent of human languages. Of these nine centers of cultural diversity, six are also on the roster of biological "megadiversity" countries— nations with exceptional numbers of unique plant and animal species. . . . By the same token, two-thirds of all megadiversity countries also rank at the top of the cultural diversity league, with more than 100 languages spoken in each.

Everywhere, the world economy now intrudes on what is left of native lands, as it has for centuries. Writes World Bank anthropologist Shelton Davis: "The creation of a . . . global economy . . . has meant the pillage of native peoples' lands, labor and resources and their enforced acculturation and spiritual conquest. Each cycle of global economic expansion—the search for gold and spices in the sixteenth century, the fur trade and sugar estate economics of the seventeenth and eighteenth centuries, the rise of the great coffee, copra and . . . tropical fruit plantations in the late nineteenth and early twentieth centuries, the modern search for petroleum, strategic minerals, and tropical hardwoods—was based upon the exploitation of natural resources or primary commodities and led to the displacement of indigenous peoples and the undermining of traditional cultures."

The juggernaut of the money economy has not slowed in the late twentieth century; if anything, it has accelerated. Soaring consumer demand among the world's fortunate and bur-geoning populations among the unfortunate fuel the economy's drive into native peoples' territo-ries. Loggers, miners, commercial fishers, small farmers, plantation growers, dam builders, oil drillers—all come to seek their fortunes. Govern-ments that equate progress with export earnings aid them, and military establishments bent on controlling far-flung territories back them.

Logging, in particular, is a menace because so many indigenous peoples dwell in woodlands. Japanese builders, for example, are devouring the ancient hardwood forests of tropical Borneo, home of the Penan and other Dayak peoples[,] for disposable concrete molds. Most mahogany exported from Latin America is now logged ille-gally on Indian reserves and most nonplantation teak cut in Asia currently comes from tribal lands in the war-torn hills of Myanmar.

The consequences of mining on native lands are also ruinous. In the late eighties, for instance, tens of thousands of gold prospectors infiltrated the remote northern Brazilian haven of the Yanomami, the last large, isolated group of in-digenous peoples in the Americas. The miners turned streams into sewers, contaminated the en-vironment with the 1,000 tons of toxic mercury they used to purify gold, and precipitated an epidemic of malaria that killed more than a thousand children and elders. Just in time, the Brazilian government recognized and began defending the Yanomami homeland in early 1992, a rare and hopeful precedent in the annals of indigenous history. Still, in Brazil overall, mining concessions overlap 34 percent of Indian lands. . . .

Other energy projects, especially large dams, also take their toll on native habitats. In the north of Canada, the provincial electric utility Hydro Quebec completed a massive project called James Bay I in 1985, inundating vast areas of Cree Indian hunting grounds and unexpectedly contaminating fisheries with naturally occurring heavy metals that had previously been locked away in the soil. The Cree and neighboring Inuit

tribes have organized against the project's next gigantic phase, James Bay II. The $60-billion project would tame eleven wild rivers, altering a France-sized area to generate 27,000 megawatts of exportable power. As Matthew Coon-Come, Grand Chief of the Cree, says, "The only people who have the right to build dams on our territory are the beavers." . . .

Commercial producers have also taken over indigenous lands for large-scale agriculture. The Barabaig herders of Tanzania have lost more than 400 square kilometers of dry-season range to a mechanized wheat farm. Private ranchers in Botswana have enclosed grazing lands for their own use, and Australian ranchers have usurped aboriginal lands. In peninsular Malaysia, palm and rubber plantations have left the Orang Asli (Original Peoples) with tiny fractions of their ancient tropical forests.

Less dramatic but more pervasive is the ubiq-uitous invasion of small farmers onto indigenous lands. Sometimes sponsored by the state but ulti-mately driven by population growth and maldis-tribution of farmland, poor settlers encroach on native lands everywhere. In Indonesia during the eighties, for example, the government shifted 2 million people from densely populated islands such as Java to 800,000 hectares of newly cleared plots in sparsely populated indigenous provinces such as Irian Jaya, Kalimantan, and Sumatra. Half the area settled was virgin forest—much of it indigenous territory. . . .

Few states recognize indigenous peoples' rights over homelands, and where they do, those rights are often partial, qualified, or of ambiguous legal force. Countries may recognize customary rights in theory, but enforce common or statutory law against those rights whenever there is a con-flict; or they may sanction indigenous rights but refuse to enforce them. Through this cloud of legal contradictions a few countries stand out as exceptional. Papua New Guinea and Ecuador acknowledge indigenous title to large shares of national territory, and Canada and Australia recognize rights over extensive areas. . . . Still, across all the earth's climatic and ecological zones—from the Arctic tundra to the temperate and nontropical forests to the savannahs and deserts—native peoples control slim shares of their ancestral domains. . . .

STEWARDS

Sustainable use of local resources is simple self-preservation for people whose way of life is tied to the fertility and natural abundance of the land. Any community that knows its children and grandchildren will live exactly where it does is more apt to take a longer view than a community without attachments to local places.

Moreover, native peoples frequently aim to preserve not just a standard of living but a way of life rooted in the uniqueness of a local place. Colombian anthropologist Martin von Hildebrand notes, "The Indians often tell me that the difference between a colonist [a non-Indian settler] and an Indian is that the colonist wants to leave money for his children and that the Indians want to leave forests for their children."

Indigenous peoples' unmediated dependence on natural abundance has its parallel in their peerless ecological knowledge. Most forest-dwelling tribes display an utter mastery of botany. One typical group, the Shuar people of Ecuador's Amazonian lowlands, uses 800 species of plants for medicine, food, animal fodder, fuel, construction, fishing, and hunting supplies.

Native peoples commonly know as much about ecological processes that affect the availability of natural resources as they do about those resources' diverse uses. South Pacific islanders can predict to the day and hour the beginning of the annual spawning runs of many fish. Whaling peoples of northern Canada have proved to skeptical western marine biologists that bowhead whales migrate under pack ice. Coastal aborigines in Australia distinguish between eighty different tidal conditions.

Specialists trained in western science often fail to recognize indigenous ecological knowledge because of the cultural and religious ways in which indigenous peoples record and transmit that learning. Ways of life that developed over scores of generations could only thrive by encoding ecological sustainability into the body of practice, myth, and taboo that passes from parent to child. . . .

What are the conditions in which traditional systems of ecological management can persist in the modern world? First, indigenous peoples must have secure rights to their subsistence base—rights that are not only recognized but enforced by the state and, ideally, backed by international law. Latin American tribes such as the Shuar of Ecuador, when threatened with losing their land, have cleared their own forests and taken up cattle ranching, because these actions prove ownership in Latin America. Had Ecuador backed up the Shuar's land rights, the ranching would have been unnecessary.

Second, for indigenous ecological stewardship to survive the onslaught of the outside world, indigenous peoples must be organized politically and the state in which they reside must allow democratic initiatives. The Khant and Mansi peoples of Siberia, just as most indigenous people in the former Soviet Union, were nominally autonomous in their customary territories under Soviet law, but political repression precluded the organized defense of that terrain until the end of the eighties. Since then, the peoples of Siberia have begun organizing themselves to turn paper rights into real local control. In neighboring China, in contrast, indigenous homelands remain pure legal fictions because the state crushes all representative organizations.

Third, indigenous communities must have access to information, support, and advice from friendly sources if they are to surmount the obstacles of the outside world. The tribal people of Papua New Guinea know much about their local environments, for example, but they know little about the impacts of large-scale logging and mining. Foreign and domestic investors have often played on this ignorance, assuring remote groups that no lasting harm would result from leasing parts of their land to resource extractors. If the forest peoples of Papua New Guinea could learn from the experience of indigenous peoples elsewhere—through supportive organizations and indigenous peoples' federations—they might be more careful.

A handful of peoples around the world have succeeded in satisfying all three of these conditions. . . .

RISING FROM THE FRONTIER

From the smallest tribal settlements to the U.N. General Assembly, indigenous peoples' organizations are making themselves felt. Their grassroots movements have spread rapidly since 1970, gaining strength in numbers and through improvement of their political skills. They have pooled their talents in regional, national, and global federations to broaden their influence. This uprising, which like any movement has its share of internal rivalries, may eventually bring fundamental advances in the status of all endangered cultures. . . .

In a world where almost all nations have publicly committed themselves to the goal of sustainable development and most have signed a global treaty for the protection of biological diversity, the questions of cultural survival and indigenous homelands cannot be avoided much longer. As guardians and stewards of remote and fragile ecosystems, indigenous cultures could play a crucial role in safeguarding humanity's planetary home. But they cannot do it alone. They need the support of international law and national policy, and they need the understanding and aid of the world's more numerous peoples.

Giving native peoples power over their own lives raises issues for the world's dominant culture as well—a consumerist and individualist culture born in Europe and bred in the United States. Indeed, indigenous peoples may offer more than a best-bet alternative for preserving the outlying areas where they live. They may offer living examples of cultural patterns that can help revive ancient values within everyone: devotion to future generations, ethical regard for nature, and commitment to community among people. The question may be, then, Are indigenous peoples the past, or are they the future?

CRITICAL THINKING QUESTIONS

1. How many indigenous cultures are there on this planet? What general traits do they have in common?

2. Why are the world's tribal peoples disappearing?

3. The author asserts that sustaining the world's natural environment depends on assuring the future of indigenous peoples. Why is this so?

Collective
Behaviour and
Social Movements

CLASSIC

CONTEMPORARY

CROSS-CULTURAL

72

On the Origins of Social Movements

JO FREEMAN

According to Jo Freeman, a "spark of life" sometimes transforms a group of like-minded people into a social movement. In this excerpt from her work, Freeman analyzes this process, illustrating her ideas with an account of the civil rights movement and the women's movement in the United States.

Most movements have inconspicuous beginnings. The significant elements of their origins are usually forgotten or distorted by the time a trained observer seeks to trace them out. Perhaps this is why the theoretical literature on social movements usually concentrates on causes (Gurr, 1970; Davies, 1962; Oberschall, 1973) and motivations (Toch, 1965; Cantril, 1941; Hoffer, 1951; Adorno et al., 1950), while the "spark of life" by which the "mass is to cross the threshold of organizational life" (Lowi, 1971: 41) has received scant attention. . . .

From where do the people come who make up the initial, organizing cadre of a movement? How do they come together, and how do they come to share a similar view of the world in circumstances that compel them to political action? In what ways does the nature of the original center affect the future development of the movement?

Before answering these questions, let us first look at data on the origins of [two] social movements prominent in the sixties and seventies: civil rights . . . and women's liberation. These data identify recurrent elements involved in movement formation. The ways in which these elements interact, given a sufficient level of strain, would support the following propositions:

Source: From *Social Movements of the Sixties and Seventies*, ed. Jo Freeman, pp. 8–13, 17–30, copyright © 1983 by Jo Freeman. Reprinted by permission.

Proposition 1. The need for a *preexisting communications network* or infrastructure within the social base of a movement is a primary prerequisite for "spontaneous" activity. Masses alone do not form movements, however discontented they may be. Groups of previously unorganized individuals may spontaneously form into small local associations—usually along the lines of informal social networks—in response to a specific strain or crisis. If they are not linked in some manner, however, the protest does not become generalized but remains a local irritant or dissolves completely. If a movement is to spread rapidly, the communications network must already exist. If only the rudiments of a network exist, movement formation requires a high input of "organizing" activity.

Proposition 2. Not just any communications network will do. It must be a network that is co-optable to the new ideas of the incipient movement. To be co-optable, it must be composed of like-minded people whose backgrounds, experiences, or location in the social structure make them receptive to the ideas of a specific new movement.

Proposition 3. Given the existence of a co-optable communications network, or at least the rudimentary development of a potential one, and a situation of strain, one or more precipitants are required. Here, two distinct patterns emerge that often overlap. In one, a crisis galvanizes the network into spontaneous action in a new direction. In the other, one or more persons begin organizing a new organization or disseminating a new idea. For spontaneous action to occur, the communications network must be well formed or the initial protest will not survive the incipient stage. If it is not well formed, organizing efforts must occur; that is, one or more persons must specifically attempt to construct a movement. To be successful, organizers must be skilled and must have a fertile field in which to work. If no communications network already exists, there must at least be emerging spontaneous groups that are acutely attuned to the issue, albeit uncoordinated. To sum up, if a co-optable communications network is already established, a crisis is all that is necessary to galvanize it. If it is rudimentary, an organizing cadre of one or more persons is necessary. Such a cadre is superfluous if the former conditions fully exist, but it is essential if they do not.

THE CIVIL RIGHTS MOVEMENT

The civil rights movement has two origins, although one contributed significantly to the other. The first can be dated from December 7, 1955, when the arrest of Rosa Parks for occupying a "white" seat on a bus stimulated both the Montgomery Bus Boycott and the formation of the Montgomery Improvement Association. The second can be dated either from February 1, 1960, when four freshmen at A & T College in Greensboro, North Carolina, sat in at a white lunch counter, or from April 15 to 17, when a conference at Shaw University in Raleigh, North Carolina, resulted in the formation of the Student Non-Violent Coordinating Committee. To understand why there were two origins one has to understand the social structure of the southern black community, as an incipient generation gap alone is inadequate to explain it.

Within this community the two most important institutions, often the only institutions, were the church and the black college. They provided the primary networks through which most southern blacks interacted and communicated with one another on a regular basis. In turn, the colleges and churches were linked in a regional communications network. These institutions were also the source of black leadership, for being a "preacher or a teacher" were the main status positions in black society. Of the two, the church was by far the more important; it touched on more people's lives and was the largest and oldest institution in the black community. Even during slavery there had been an "invisible church." After emancipation, "organized religious life became the chief means by which a structured or organized social life came into existence among the Negro masses" (Frazier, 1963: 17). Furthermore, preachers were more economically independent of white society than were teachers.

Neither of these institutions represented all the segments of black society, but the segments they did represent eventually formed the main social base for supplying civil rights activists. The church was composed of a male leadership and a largely middle-aged, lower-class female followership. The black colleges were the homes of black intellectuals and middle-class youth, male and female.

Both origins of the civil rights movement resulted in the formation of new organizations, despite the fact that at least three seemingly potential social movement organizations already existed. The wealthiest of these was the Urban League, founded in 1910. It, however, was not only largely restricted to a small portion of the black and white bourgeoisie but, until 1961, felt itself to be "essentially a social service agency" (Clark, 1966: 245).

Founded in 1909, the National Association for the Advancement of Colored People (NAACP) pursued channels of legal change until it finally persuaded the Supreme Court to abolish educational segregation in *Brown v. Board of Education*. More than any other single event, this decision created the atmosphere of rising expectations that helped precipitate the movement. The NAACP suffered from its own success, however. Having organized itself primarily to support court cases and utilize other "respectable" means, it "either was not able or did not desire to modify its program in response to new demands. It believed it should continue its important work by using those techniques it had already perfected" (Blumer, 1951: 199).

The Congress of Racial Equality, like the other two organizations, was founded in the North. It began "in 1942 as the Chicago Committee of Racial Equality, which was composed primarily of students at the University of Chicago.

An offshoot of the pacifist Fellowship of Reconciliation, its leaders were middle-class intellectual reformers, less prominent and more alienated from the mainstream of American society than the founders of the NAACP. They regarded the NAACP's legalism as too gradualist and ineffective, and aimed to apply Gandhian techniques of non-violent direct action to the problem of race relations in the United States. A year later, the Chicago Committee joined with a half dozen other groups that had emerged across the country, mostly under the encouragement of the F. O. R. to form a federation known as the Congress of Racial Equality" (Rudwick & Meier, 1970: 10).

CORE's activities anticipated many of the main forms of protest of the civil rights movement, and its attitudes certainly seemed to fit CORE for the role of a major civil rights organization. But though it became quite influential, at the time the movement actually began, CORE had declined almost to the point of extinction. Its failure reflects the historical reality that organizations are less likely to create social movements than be created by them. More important, CORE was poorly situated to lead a movement of southern blacks. Northern-based and composed primarily of pacifist intellectuals, it had no roots in any of the existing structures of the black community, and in the North these structures were themselves weak. CORE could be a source of ideas, but not of coordination.

The coordination of a new movement required the creation of a new organization. But that was not apparent until after the Montgomery bus boycott began. That boycott was organized through institutions already existing in the black community of Montgomery.

Rosa Parks's refusal to give up her seat on the bus to a white man was not the first time such defiance of segregation laws had occurred. There had been talk of a boycott the previous time, but after local black leaders had a congenial meeting with the city commissioners, nothing happened— on either side (King, 1958: 37–41). When Parks, a former secretary of the local NAACP, was arrested, she immediately called E. D. Nixon, at that time the president of the local chapter. He not only bailed her out but informed a few influential women in the city, most of whom were members of the Women's Political Council. After numerous phone calls between their members, it was the WPC that actually suggested the boycott, and E. D. Nixon who initially organized it (ibid.: 44–5).

The Montgomery Improvement Association (MIA) was formed at a meeting of eighteen ministers and civic leaders the Monday after Parks's conviction and a day of successful boycotting, to provide ongoing coordination. No one then suspected that coordination would be necessary for over a year, with car pools organized to provide alternative transportation for seventeen thousand riders a day. During this time the MIA grew slowly to a staff of ten in order to handle the voluminous correspondence, as well as to provide rides and keep the movement's momentum going. The organization, and the car pools, were financed by $250,000 in donations that poured in from all over the world in response to heavy press publicity about the boycott. But the organizational framework for the boycott and the MIA was the church. Most, although not all, of the officers were ministers, and Sunday meetings with congregations continued to be the main means of communicating with members of the black community and encouraging them to continue the protest.

The boycott did not end until the federal courts ruled Alabama's bus segregation laws unconstitutional late in 1956—at the same time that state courts ruled the boycott illegal. In the meantime, black leaders throughout the South had visited Montgomery, and out of the discussions came agreement to continue antisegregation protests regularly and systematically under the aegis of a new organization, the Southern Christian Leadership Conference. The NAACP could not lead the protests because, according to an SCLC pamphlet, "during the late fifties, the NAACP had been driven out of some Southern

states. Its branches were outlawed as foreign corporations and its lawyers were charged with barratry, that is, persistently inciting litigation."

On January 10, 1957, over one hundred people gathered in Atlanta at a meeting called by four ministers, including Martin Luther King. Bayard Rustin drew up the "working papers." Initially called the Southern Leadership Conference on Transportation and Nonviolent Integration, the SCLC never developed a mass base even when it changed its name. It established numerous "affiliates" but did most of its work through the churches in the communities to which it sent its fieldworkers.

The church was not just the only institution available for a movement to work through; in many ways it was ideal. It performed "the central organizing function in the Negro community" (Holloway, 1969: 22), providing both access to large masses of people on a regular basis and a natural leadership. As Wyatt Tee Walker, former executive director of SCLC, commented, "The Church today is central to the movement. If a Negro's going to have a meeting, where's he going to have it? Mostly he doesn't have a Masonic lodge, and he's not going to get the public schools. And the church is the primary means of communication" (Brink & Harris, 1964: 103). Thus the church eventually came to be the center of the voter registration drives as well as many of the other activities of the civil rights movement.

Even the young men and women of SNCC had to use the church, though they had trouble doing so because, unlike most of the officers of SCLC, they were not themselves ministers and thus did not have a "fraternal" connection. Instead they tended to draw many of their resources and people from outside the particular town in which they were working by utilizing their natural organizational base, the college.

SNCC did not begin the sit-ins, but came out of them. Once begun, the idea of the sit-in spread initially by means of the mass media. But such sit-ins almost always took place in towns where there were Negro colleges, and groups on these campuses essentially organized the sit-in activities of their communities. Nonetheless, "CORE, with its long emphasis of nonviolent direct action, played an important part, once the sit-ins began, as an educational and organizing agent" (Zinn, 1964: 23). CORE had very few staff in the South, but there were enough to at least hold classes and practice sessions in nonviolence.

It was SCLC, however, that was actually responsible for the formation of SNCC; though it might well have organized itself eventually. Ella Baker, then executive secretary of SCLC, thought something should be done to coordinate the rapidly spreading sit-ins in 1960, and many members of SCLC thought it might be appropriate to organize a youth group. With SCLC money, Baker persuaded her alma mater, Shaw University, to provide facilities to contact the groups at centers of sit-in activity. Some two hundred people showed up for the meeting, decided to have no official connection with SCLC beyond a "friendly relationship," and formed the Student Non-Violent Coordinating Committee (Zinn, 1964: 32–34). It had no members, and its field-workers numbered two hundred at their highest point, but it was from the campuses, especially the southern black colleges, that it drew its sustenance and upon which its organizational base rested. . . .

THE WOMEN'S LIBERATION MOVEMENT[1]

Women are not well organized. Historically tied to the family and isolated from their own kind, only in the nineteenth century did women in this country have the opportunity to develop independent associations of their own. These associations took years and years of careful organizational work to build. Eventually they formed the basis for the suffrage movement of the early twentieth century. The associations took less time to die. Today the Women's Trade Union League, the General Federation of Women's Clubs, the

Women's Christian Temperance Union, not to mention the powerful National Women's Suffrage Association, are all either dead or a pale shadow of their former selves.

As of 1960, not one organization of women had the potential to become a social movement organization, nor was there any form of "neutral" structure of interaction to provide the base for such an organization. The closest exception to the former was the National Women's Party, which has remained dedicated to feminist concerns since its inception in 1916. However, the NWP has been essentially a lobbying group for the Equal Rights Amendment since 1923. From the beginning, the NWP believed that a small group of women concentrating their efforts in the right places was more effective than a mass appeal, and so was not appalled by the fact that as late as 1969 even the majority of avowed feminists in this country had never heard of the ERA or the NWP.

The one large women's organization that might have provided a base for a social movement was the 180,000-member Federation of Business and Professional Women's Clubs. Yet, while it has steadily lobbied for legislation of importance to women, as late as "1966 BPW rejected a number of suggestions that it redefine . . . goals and tactics and become a kind of 'NAACP for women' . . . out of fear of being labeled 'feminist'" (Hole & Levine, 1971: 89).

Before any social movement could develop among women, there had to be created a structure to bring potential feminist sympathizers together. To be sure, groups such as the BPW, and institutions such as the women's colleges, might be a good source of adherents for such a movement. But they were determined not to be the source of leadership.

What happened in the 1960s was the development of two new communications networks in which women played prominent roles that allowed, even forced, an awakened interest in the old feminist ideas. As a result, the movement actually has two origins, from two different strata of society, with two different styles, orientations, values, and forms of organization. The first of these will be referred to as the "older branch" of the movement, partially because it began first and partially because it was on the older side of the "generation gap" that pervaded the sixties. Its most prominent organization is the National Organization for Women (NOW), which was also the first to be formed. The style of its organization tended to be traditional with elected officers, boards of directors, bylaws, and the other trappings of democratic procedure. Conversely, the "younger branch" consisted of innumerable small groups engaged in a variety of activities whose contact with one another was always tenuous (Freeman, 1975: 50).

The forces that led to NOW's formation were set in motion in 1961 when President Kennedy established the President's Commission on the Status of Women at the behest of Esther Petersen, then director of the Women's Bureau. Its 1963 report, *American Women*, and subsequent committee publications documented just how thoroughly women were denied many rights and opportunities. The most significant response to the activity of the President's commission was the establishment of some fifty state commissions to do similar research on a state level. The Presidential and State Commission activity laid the groundwork for the future movement in two significant ways: (1) It unearthed ample evidence of women's unequal status and in the process convinced many previously uninterested women that something should be done; (2) It created a climate of expectations that something would be done. The women of the Presidential and State Commissions who were exposed to these influences exchanged visits, correspondence, and staff, and met with one another at an annual commission convention. They were in a position to share and mutually reinforce their growing awareness and concern over women's issues. These commissions thus provided an embryonic communications network.

During this time, two other events of significance occurred. The first was the publication of Betty Friedan's *The Feminine Mystique* in 1963. A quick best seller, the book stimulated many women to question the *status quo* and some women to suggest to Friedan that an organization be formed to do something about it. The second event was the addition of "sex" to the 1964 Civil Rights Act.

Many thought the "sex" provision was a joke, and the Equal Employment Opportunity Commission treated it as one, refusing to enforce it seriously. But a rapidly growing feminist coterie within the EEOC argued that "sex" would be taken more seriously if there were "some sort of NAACP for women" to put pressure on the government.

On June 30, 1966, these three strands of incipient feminism came together, and NOW was tied from the knot. At that time, government officials running the Third National Conference of Commissions on the Status of Women, ironically titled "Targets for Action," forbade the presentation of a suggested resolution calling for the EEOC to treat sex discrimination with the same consideration as race discrimination. The officials said one government agency could not be allowed to pressure another, despite the fact that the state commissions were not federal agencies. The small group of women who desired such a resolution had met the night before in Friedan's hotel room to discuss the possibility of a civil rights organization for women. Not convinced of its need, they chose instead to propose the resolution. When conference officials vetoed it, they held a whispered conversation over lunch and agreed to form an action organization "to bring women into full participation in the mainstream of American society now, assuming all the privileges and responsibilities thereof in truly equal partnership with men." The name NOW was coined by Friedan who was at the conference doing research on a book. When word leaked out, twenty-eight women paid five dollars each to join before the day was over (Friedan, 1967: 4).

By the time the organizing conference was held the following October 29 through 30, over three hundred men and women had become charter members. It is impossible to do a breakdown on the composition of the charter membership, but one of the officers and board is possible. Such a breakdown accurately reflected NOW's origins. Friedan was president, two former EEOC commissioners were vice presidents, a representative of the United Auto Workers Women's Committee was secretary-treasurer, and there were seven past and present members of the State Commissions on the Status of Women on the twenty member board. One hundred twenty-six of the charter members were Wisconsin residents—and Wisconsin had the most active state Commission. Occupationally, the board and officers were primarily from the professions, labor, government, and communications fields. Of these, only those from labor had any experience in organizing, and they resigned a year later in a dispute over support of the Equal Rights Amendment. Instead of organizational experience, what the early NOW members had was experience in working with and in the media, and it was here that their early efforts were aimed.

As a result, NOW often gave the impression of being larger than it was. It was highly successful in getting in the press; much less successful in either bringing about concrete changes or forming an organization. Thus it was not until 1970, when the national press simultaneously did major stories on the women's liberation movement, that NOW's membership increased significantly.

In the meantime, unaware of and unknown to NOW, the EEOC, or the State Commissions, younger women began forming their own movement. Here, too, the groundwork had been laid some years before. The different social action projects of the sixties had attracted many women, who were quickly shunted into traditional roles and faced with the self-evident contradiction of working in a "freedom movement" but not being very free. No single "youth movement" activity or organization is responsible for forming the younger branch of the women's liberation movement, but together they created a "radical community" in which like-minded people continually interacted or were made aware of one another. This community provided the necessary network of communication and its radical ideas the framework of analysis that "explained" the dismal situation in which radical women found themselves.

Papers had been circulated on women and individual temporary women's caucuses had been held as early as 1964 (see Hayden & King, 1966). But it was not until 1967 and 1968 that the groups developed a determined, if cautious, continuity and began to consciously expand themselves. At least five groups in five different cities (Chicago, Toronto, Detroit, Seattle, and Gainesville, Florida) formed spontaneously, independently of one another. They came at an auspicious moment, for 1967 was the year in which the blacks kicked the whites out of the civil rights movement, student power was discredited by SDS, and the New Left was on the wane. Only draft resistance activities were on the increase, and this movement more than any other exemplified the social inequities of the sexes. Men could resist the draft. Women could only counsel resistance.

At this point, there were few opportunities available for political work. Some women fit well into the secondary role of draft counseling. Many didn't. For years their complaints of unfair treatment had been forestalled by movement men with the dictum that those things could wait until after the Revolution. Now these political women found time on their hands, but still the men would not listen.

A typical example was the event that precipitated the formation of the Chicago group, the first independent group in this country. At the August 1967 National Conference for New Politics convention a women's caucus met for days, but was told its resolution wasn't significant enough to merit a floor discussion. By threatening to tie up the convention with procedural motions the women succeeded in having their statement tacked to the end of the agenda. It was never discussed. The chair refused to recognize any of the many women standing by the microphone, their hands straining upwards. When he instead called on someone to speak on "the forgotten American, the American Indian," five women rushed the podium to demand an explanation. But the chairman just patted one of them on the head (literally) and told her, "Cool down, little girl. We have more important things to talk about than women's problems."

The "little girl" was Shulamith Firestone, future author of *The Dialectic of Sex*, and she didn't cool down. Instead she joined with another Chicago woman she met there who had unsuccessfully tried to organize a women's group that summer, to call a meeting of the women who had halfheartedly attended those summer meetings. Telling their stories to those women, they stimulated sufficient rage to carry the group for three months, and by that time it was a permanent institution.

Another somewhat similar event occurred in Seattle the following winter. At the University of Washington, an SDS organizer was explaining to a large meeting how white college youth established rapport with the poor whites with whom they were working. "He noted that sometimes after analyzing societal ills, the men shared leisure time by 'balling a chick together.' He pointed out that such activities did much to enhance the political consciousness of the poor white youth. A woman in the audience asked, 'And what did it do for the consciousness of the chick?'" (Hole & Levine, 1971: 120). After the meeting, a handful of enraged women formed Seattle's first group.

Subsequent groups to the initial five were largely organized rather than formed spontaneously out of recent events. In particular, the Chicago group was responsible for the formation of many new groups in Chicago and in other cities. Unlike NOW, the women in the first groups had had years of experience as trained organizers. They knew how to utilize the infrastructure of the radical community, the underground press, and the free universities to disseminate women's liberation ideas. Chicago, as a center of New Left activity, had the largest number of politically conscious organizers. Many traveled widely to leftist conferences and demonstrations, and most used the opportunity to talk with other women about the new movement. In spite of public derision by radical men, or perhaps because of it, young women steadily formed new groups around the country.

ANALYSIS

From these data there appear to be four essential elements involved in movement formation: (1) the growth of a preexisting communications network that is (2) co-optable to the ideas of the new movement; (3) a series of crises that galvanize into action people involved in a co-optable network, and/or (4) subsequent organizing effort to weld the spontaneous groups together into a movement. Each of these elements needs to be examined in detail.

COMMUNICATIONS NETWORK

. . . The women's liberation movement . . . illustrates the importance of a network precisely because the conditions for a movement existed before a network came into being, but the movement didn't exist until afterward. Analysts of socioeconomic causes have concluded that the movement could have started anytime within a twenty-year period. Strain for women was as great in 1955 as in 1965 (Ferriss, 1971). What changed was the organizational situation. It was not until new networks emerged among women aware of inequities beyond local boundaries that a movement could grow past the point of occasional, spontaneous uprisings. The fact that two distinct movements, with two separate origins, developed from two networks unaware of each other is further evidence of the key role of preexisting communications networks as the fertile soil in which new movements can sprout.

References to the importance of a preexisting communications network appear frequently in case studies of social movements, though the theoretical writers were much slower to recognize their salience. According to Buck (1920: 43–4), the Grange established a degree of organization among American farmers in the nineteenth century that greatly facilitated the spread of future farmers' protests. Lipset has reported that in Saskatchewan, "the rapid acceptance of new ideas and movements . . . can be attributed mainly to the high degree of organization. . . . The role of the social structure of the western wheat belt in facilitating the rise of new movements has never been sufficiently appreciated by historians and sociologists. Repeated challenges and crises forced the western farmers to create many more community institutions (especially cooperatives and economic pressure groups) than are necessary in a more stable area. These groups in turn provided a structural basis for immediate action in critical situations. [Therefore] though it was a new radical party, the C. C. F. did not have to build up an organization from scratch" (1959: 206).

Similarly, Heberle (1951: 232) reports several findings that Nazism was most successful in small, well-integrated communities. As Lipset put it, these findings "sharply challenge the various interpretations of Nazism as the product of the growth of anomie and the general rootlessness of modern urban industrial society" (1959: 146).

Indirect evidence attesting to the essential role of formal and informal communications networks is found in diffusion theory, which emphasizes the importance of personal interaction rather than impersonal media communication in the spread of ideas (Rogers, 1962; Lionberger, 1960). This personal influence occurs through the organizational patterns of a community (Lionberger, 1960: 73). It does not occur through the mass media. The mass media may be a source of information, but they are not a key source of influence.

Their lesser importance in relation to preexisting communications networks was examined in one study on "The Failure of an Incipient Social Movement" (Jackson, Peterson, Bull, Monsen, & Richmond, 1960). In 1957 a potential tax protest movement in Los Angeles generated considerable interest and publicity for a little over a month but was dead within a year. According to the authors, this did not reflect a lack of public notice. They concluded that "mass communication alone is probably insufficient without a network of communication specifically linking those interested in the matter. . . . If a movement is to grow rapidly, it cannot rely upon its own network of communication, but must capitalize on networks already in existence" (p. 37).

A major reason it took social scientists so long to acknowledge the importance of communications networks was because the prevailing theories of the post–World War II era emphasized increasing social dislocation and anomie. Mass society theorists, as they were called, hypothesized that significant community institutions that linked individuals to governing elites were breaking down, that society was becoming a mass of isolated individuals. These individuals were seen as increasingly irresponsible and ungovernable, prone to irrational protests because they had no mediating institutions through which to pursue grievances (Kornhauser, 1959).

In emphasizing disintegrating vertical connections, mass society theorists passed lightly over the role of horizontal ones, only occasionally acknowledging that "the combination of internal contact and external isolation facilitates the work of the mass agitator" (Kornhauser, 1959: 218). This focus changed in the early seventies. Pinard's study of the Social Credit Party of Quebec (1971) severely criticized mass society theory, arguing instead that "when strains are severe and widespread a new movement is more likely to meet its early success among the more strongly integrated citizens" (Pinard, 1971: 192).

This insight was expanded by Oberschall (1973), who created a six-cell table to predict both the occurrence and type of protest. As did the mass society theorists, Oberschall said that even when there are grievances, protest will not occur outside institutional channels by those who are connected, through their own leadership or patron/client relationships, with governing elites. Among those who are segmented from such elites, the type of protest will be determined by whether there is communal, associational, or little organization. In the latter case, discontent is expressed through riots or other short-lived violent uprisings. "It is under conditions of strong . . . ties and segmentation that the possibility of the rapid spread of opposition movements on a continuous basis exists" (p. 123).

The movements we have studied would confirm Oberschall's conclusions, but not as strongly as he makes them. In all these cases a preexisting communications network was a necessary but insufficient condition for movement formation. Yet the newly formed networks among student radicals, welfare recipients, and women can hardly compare with the longstanding ties provided by the southern black churches and colleges. Their ties were tenuous and may not have survived the demise of their movements.

The importance of segmentation, or lack of connection with relevant elites, is less obvious in the sixties' movements. The higher socioeconomic status of incipient feminists and Movement leaders would imply greater access to elites than is true for blacks or welfare recipients. If Oberschall were correct, these closer connections should either have permitted easier and more rapid grievance solutions or more effective social control. They did neither. Indeed, it was the group most closely connected to decision-making elites—women of the Presidential and State Commission—who were among the earliest to see the need of a protest organization. Women of the younger branch of the movement did have their grievances against the men of the New Left effectively suppressed for several years, but even they eventually rejected this kind of elite control, even when it meant rejecting the men.

Conversely, Piven and Cloward show that the establishment of closer ties between leaders of local welfare rights groups and welfare workers through advisory councils and community coordinators led to a curtailment of militance and the institutionalization of grievances (1977: 326–31). They also argue that the development of government-funded community programs effectively co-opted many local black movement leaders in the North and that federal channeling of black protest in the South into voter registration projects focused the movement there into traditional electoral politics (ibid.: 253). In short, the evidence about the role of segmentation in movement formation is ambiguous. The effect may be varied considerably by the nature of the political system.

CO-OPTABILITY

A recurrent theme in our studies is that not just any communications network will do. It must be one that is co-optable to the ideas of the new movement. The Business and Professional Women's (BPW) clubs were a network among women, but having rejected feminism, they could not overcome the ideological barrier to new political action until after feminism became established. . . .

On the other hand, the women on the Presidential and State Commissions and the feminist coterie of the EEOC were co-optable largely because their immersion in the facts of female status and the details of sex discrimination cases made them very conscious of the need for change. Likewise, the young women of the "radical community" lived in an atmosphere of questioning, confrontation, and change. They absorbed an ideology of "freedom" and "liberation" far more potent than any latent "antifeminism" might have been. . . .

Exactly what makes a network co-optable is harder to elucidate. Pinard (1971: 186) noted the necessity for groups to *possess* or *develop* an ideology or simply subjective interests congruent with that of a new movement" for them to "act as mobilizing rather than restraining agents toward that movement," but did not further explore what affected the "primary group climate." More illumination is provided by the diffusion of innovation studies that point out the necessity for new ideas to fit in with already established norms for changes to happen easily. Furthermore, a social system that has as a value "innovativeness" (as the radical community did) will more rapidly adopt ideas than one that looks upon the habitual performance of traditional practices as the ideal (as most organized women's groups did in the fifties). Usually, as Lionberger (1960: 91) points out, "people act in terms of past experience and knowledge." People who have had similar experiences are likely to share similar perceptions of a situation and to mutually reinforce those perceptions as well as their subsequent interpretation. A co-optable network, then, is one whose members have had common experiences that predispose them to be receptive to the particular new ideas of the incipient movement and who are not faced with structural or ideological barriers to action. If the new movement as an "innovation" can interpret these experiences and perceptions in ways that point out channels for social action, then participation in a social movement becomes the logical thing to do.

THE ROLE OF CRISES

As our examples have illustrated, similar perceptions must be translated into action. This is often done by a crisis. For blacks in Montgomery, this was generated by Rosa Parks's refusal to give up her seat on a bus to a white man. For women who formed the older branch of the women's movement, the impetus to organize was the refusal of the EEOC to enforce the sex provision of Title VII, precipitated by the concomitant refusal of federal officials at the conference to allow a supportive resolution. For younger women there were a series of minor crises.

While not all movements are formed by such precipitating events, they are quite common as they serve to crystallize and focus discontent. From their own experiences, directly and concretely, people feel the need for change in a situation that allows for an exchange of feelings with others, mutual validation, and a subsequent reinforcement of innovative interpretation. Perception of an immediate need for change is a major factor in predisposing people to accept new ideas (Rogers, 1962: 280). Nothing makes desire for change more acute than a crisis. Such a crisis need not be a major one; it need only embody collective discontent.

ORGANIZING EFFORTS

A crisis will only catalyze a well-formed communications network. If such networks are embryonically developed or only partially co-optable, the potentially active individuals in them must be linked together by someone. . . . As Jackson et al. (1960: 37) stated, "Some protest may persist where the source of trouble is constantly present. But interest ordinarily cannot be maintained unless there is a welding of spontaneous groups into some stable organization." In other words, people must be organized. Social movements do not simply occur.

The role of the organizer in movement formation is another neglected aspect of the theoretical literature. There has been great concern with leadership, but the two roles are distinct and not always performed by the same individual. In the early stages of a movement, it is the organizer much more than any leader who is important, and such an individual or cadre must often operate behind the scenes. The nature and function of these two roles was most clearly evident in the Townsend old-age movement of the thirties. Townsend was the "charismatic" leader, but the movement was organized by his partner, real estate promoter Robert Clements. Townsend himself acknowledges that without Clements's help, the movement would never have gone beyond the idea stage (Holzman, 1963).

The importance of organizers is pervasive in the sixties' movements. Dr. King may have been the public spokesperson of the Montgomery Bus Boycott who caught the eye of the media, but it was E. D. Nixon who organized it. Certainly the "organizing cadre" that young women in the radical community came to be was key to the growth of that branch of the women's liberation movement, despite the fact that no "leaders" were produced (and were actively discouraged). The existence of many leaders but no organizers in the older branch of the women's liberation movement readily explains its subsequent slow development. . . .

The function of the organizer has been explored indirectly by other analysts. Rogers (1962) devotes many pages to the "change agent" who, while he does not necessarily weld a group together or "construct" a movement, does many of the same things for agricultural innovation that an organizer does for political change. Mass society theory makes frequent reference to the "agitator," though not in a truly informative way. Interest groups are often organized by single individuals and some of them evolve into social movements. Salisbury's study of farmers' organizations finds this a recurrent theme. He also discovered that "a considerable number of farm groups were subsidized by other, older, groups. . . . The Farm Bureau was organized and long sustained by subsidies, some from federal and state governments, and some by local businessmen" (Salisbury, 1969: 13).

These patterns are similar to ones we have found in the formation of social movements. Other organizations, even the government, often serve as training centers for organizers and sources of material support to aid the formation of groups and/or movements. The civil rights movement was the training ground for many an organizer of other movements. . . . The role of the government in the formation of the National Welfare Rights Organization was so significant that it would lead one to wonder if this association should be considered more of an interest group in the traditional sense than a movement "core" organization.

From all this it would appear that training as an organizer or at least as a proselytizer or entrepreneur of some kind is a necessary background for those individuals who act as movement innovators. Even in something as seemingly spontaneous as a social movement, the professional is more valuable than the amateur.

CRITICAL THINKING QUESTIONS

1. Why has the role of communications networks in the formation of social movements only recently received the attention of researchers?

2. How do leadership roles emerge in social movements? Are "leaders" the same as "organizers"?

3. Cite some similarities and differences in the development of the civil rights movement and the women's movement.

NOTE

1. Data for this section are based on my observations while a founder and participant in the younger branch of the Chicago women's liberation movement from 1967 through 1969 and editor of the first (at that time, only) national newsletter. I was able, through extensive correspondence and interviews, to keep a record of how each group around the country started, where the organizers got the idea from, who they had talked to, what conferences were held and who attended, the political affiliations (or lack of them) of the first members, and so forth. Although I was a member of Chicago NOW, information on the origins of it and the other older branch organizations comes entirely through ex post facto interviews of the principals and examination of early papers in preparation for my dissertation on the women's liberation movement. Most of my informants requested that their contribution remain confidential.

REFERENCES

Adorno, L. W., et al. 1950. *The authoritarian personality.* New York: Harper & Row.

Blumer, H. 1951. Social movements. In *New outline of the principles of sociology*, ed. A. M. Lee. New York: Barnes and Noble.

Brink, W., and L. Harris. 1964. *The Negro revolution in America*. New York: Simon & Schuster.

Buck, S. J. 1920. *The agrarian crusade*. New Haven, Conn.: Yale University Press.

Cantril, H. 1941. *The psychology of social movements*. New York: Wiley.

Clark, K. B. 1966. The civil rights movement: Momentum and organization. *Daedalus*, Winter.

Davies, J. C. 1962. Toward a theory of revolution. *American Sociological Review*, 27(1): 5–19.

Ferriss, A. L. 1971. *Indicators of trends in the status of American women*. New York: Russell Sage Foundation.

Firestone, S. 1971. *Dialectics of sex*. New York: Morrow.

Frazier, E. F. 1963. *The Negro church in America*. New York: Schocken.

Freeman, J. 1975. *The politics of women's liberation*. New York: Longman.

Friedan, B. 1963. *The feminine mystique*. New York: Dell.

———. 1967. NOW: How it began. *Women Speaking*, April.

Gurr, T. 1970. *Why men rebel*. Princeton, N.J.: Princeton University Press.

Hayden, C., and M. King. 1966. A kind of memo. *Liberation*, April.

Heberle, R. 1951. *Social movements*. New York: Appleton-Century-Crofts.

Hoffer, E. 1951. *The true believer*. New York: Harper & Row.

Hole, J., and E. Levine. 1971. *Rebirth of feminism*. New York: Quadrangle.

Holloway, H. 1969. *The politics of the Southern Negro*. New York: Random House.

Holzman, A. 1963. *The Townsend movement: A political study*. New York: Bookman.

Jackson, M., et al. 1960. The failure of an incipient social movement. *Pacific Sociological Review*, 3(1): 40.

King, M. L., Jr. 1958. *Stride toward freedom*. New York: Harper & Row.

Kornhauser, W. 1959. *The politics of mass society*. Glencoe, Ill.: Free Press.

Lionberger, H. F. 1960. *Adoption of new ideas and practices*. Ames: Iowa State University Press.

Lipset, S. M. 1959. *Agrarian socialism*. Berkeley: University of California Press.

Lowi, T. J. 1971. *The politics of discord*. New York: Basic Books.

Oberschall, A. 1973. *Social conflict and social movements*. Englewood Cliffs, N.J.: Prentice-Hall.

Pinard, M. 1971. *The rise of a third party: A study in crisis politics*. Englewood Cliffs, N.J.: Prentice-Hall.

Piven, F. F., and R. Cloward. 1977. *Poor people's movements: Why they succeed, how they fail*. New York: Pantheon.

Rogers, E. M. 1962. *Diffusion of innovations*. New York: Free Press.

Rudwick, E., and A. Meier. 1970. Organizational structure and goal succession: A comparative analysis of the NAACP and CORE, 1964–1968. *Social Science Quarterly*, 51 (June).

Salisbury, R. H. 1969. An exchange theory of interest groups. *Midwest Journal of Political Science*, 13(1), (February).

Toch, H. 1965. *The social psychology of social movements*. Indianapolis, IN.: Bobbs-Merrill.

Zinn, H. 1964. SNCC: *The new abolitionists*. Boston: Beacon Press.

73

Collective
Behaviour and
Social Movements

The Animal Rights Movement as a Moral Crusade

CLASSIC

CONTEMPORARY

CROSS-CULTURAL

JAMES M. JASPER AND DOROTHY NELKIN

Although the number of animal rights organizations in the United States is small compared to the membership of other social movements, animal rights activists have enjoyed numerous victories since the 1980s. Why has this small group been so successful? James M. Jasper and Dorothy Nelkin provide some of the answers. They describe the animal rights movement as a "moral crusade" that relies, for example, on sympathetic media coverage, sentimental views about pets, and coalitions with other recent protest movements to achieve their objectives.

On a warm spring day in May, 1980, Henry Spira was on Manhattan's posh Fifth Avenue with a flatbed truck filled with white rabbits. With him were 300 more demonstrators, many of them dressed in bunny suits. On the sidewalk in front of the headquarters of the cosmetics giant Revlon, they were protesting that company's extensive use of white rabbits to test the safety of new products. The demonstrators were angry about procedures in which substances were placed in rabbits' eyes to test if these ingredients caused redness, swelling, or cloudiness. Many demonstrators had been drawn to the protest by full-page advertisements in the *New York Times* and other papers that asked, "How many rabbits does Revlon blind for beauty's sake?"

Source: Reprinted with the permission of The Free Press, a Division of Simon & Schuster Adult Publishing Group, from *The Animal Rights Crusade: The Growth of a Moral Protest* by James M. Jasper and Dorothy Nelkin. Copyright © 1992 by James M. Jasper and Dorothy Nelkin.

After a friend left him a cat in 1973, Spira, a burly man in his early fifties, had become increasingly outraged over humans' treatment of animals, wondering about "the appropriateness of cuddling one animal while sticking a knife and fork into others." He grew more and more critical of such common practices as wearing furs and leather and eating meat. For more than a year he had talked to Revlon officials, hoping to persuade them to contribute several hundred thousand dollars to help develop alternative tests that did not use live animals. When Revlon officials listened politely but then ignored him, he put together a coalition of 400 animal groups, mostly humane societies operating spay clinics and offering cats and dogs for adoption. And he gathered funds for the newspaper ads. He felt public opinion would be on his side: "I think there are very few people on the street who'll say, 'Yeah, go around and blind rabbits to produce another mascara.'"[1]

Following the May rally, public protests continued alongside Spira's private negotiations, and in December 1980 Revlon capitulated, announcing that it would provide Rockefeller University $750,000 for research on alternative tests. Soon other companies followed Revlon's lead; by 1987 many had ended live animal testing; and the cosmetics industry claimed to have contributed about $5 million to alternatives research.

Four years after the Revlon demonstration, another effort to liberate animals unfolded in the laboratories of the University of Pennsylvania Medical School. On Memorial Day weekend in 1984, five members of the Animal Liberation Front (ALF) surreptitiously entered the deserted research lab of Thomas Gennarelli, who headed a team of researchers studying the effects of severe head injuries. Underway for fourteen years, these experiments currently involved severe shocks and injuries—similar to whiplash in car accidents—to the heads of baboons. The intruders destroyed equipment worth $20,000 and removed sixty hours of videotapes made to document the experiments.

The members of the ALF shared Henry Spira's goal of eliminating any use of animals for human needs, but they felt a stronger sense of urgency that compelled them to break the law. In most of their break-ins—Pennsylvania was one of more than 100 entries—the ALF has liberated animals rather than videotapes. Its members value animal lives so highly that they feel a moral obligation to act to save them, even to damage property in doing so. Violence against property, they claim, is justified to stop violence against living beings (the animals they liberate). As one activist put it, "Property laws are artificial constructs. We feel we answer to a higher law."[2]

Perhaps the most important result of the Memorial Day break-in is what then happened to the videotapes. The ALF, an illegal group designated as a "terrorist" organization by the FBI, passed the tapes to another animal rights group, People for the Ethical Treatment of Animals (PETA). PETA edited the tapes into a twenty-minute film called *Unnecessary Fuss*, which portrayed bantering among researchers and joking about the injured animals—"mocking them," as animal activists put it. It also appeared that the animals were not fully anesthetized. Scientists were painted as callous, even sadistic, and so brutal that discussion with them about their methods would be useless: Direct action against such research was the only appropriate response. The film proved a powerful instrument for PETA in its efforts to recruit new and committed members to an emerging protest movement.

The Revlon and University of Pennsylvania incidents are just two among thousands of recent animal rights protests, lawsuits, break-ins, and other actions that have targeted scientific laboratories, cosmetic and pharmaceutical firms, slaughterhouses and butchers, fur ranchers and retailers, rodeos and circuses, hunters and trappers, carriage drivers, and even zoos. Since the late 1970s, new animal "rights" organizations have rejuvenated the older and larger animal welfare movement, and together they are reshaping public awareness of animals. As many as 10 to 15 million Americans send money to animal protection groups, which have proliferated: By 1990, there were several thousand animal welfare and several hundred animal rights organizations in the United States. Some focus on particular animals (The Beaver Defenders, Bat Conservation International); others have a religious bent (Life for God's Stray Animals, Jews for Animal Rights); some are organized around tactics (the Animal Legal Defense Fund); others protest particular uses or abuses of animals (Students United Protesting Research Experiments on Sentient Subjects); still others represent links with related causes (Feminists for Animal Rights). The pull of these groups was evident in June 1990, when 30,000 people participated in a march on Washington for animal rights, with slogans such as "Fur Is Dead," "No Tax Dollars for Torture," and "Blinding Bunnies Is Not Beautiful."

Renewed concerns about animals have generated a powerful social movement driven by a simple moral position: Animals are similar enough to humans to deserve serious moral consideration. They are sentient beings entitled to dignified lives, and they should be treated as ends, not as means. Protectors ask how we can love our pets, yet experiment on identical animals in laboratories; how we can cuddle one animal, yet eat another. They have themselves mostly given up meat, dairy products, and eggs; they refuse to wear leather shoes or belts; they do not patronize the products of certain corporations; and many will not wear wool—let alone fur—garments. While some would allow occasional animal research if subjects are fully sedated and the benefits outweigh the harm, others say this concession violates the inherent right of animals to a full life independent of human goals. Movement leaders often use the morally charged language of good and evil, and their political actions and rhetorical style often display an absolutism that discourages discussion or negotiation with those who disagree.

The new movement has exploded into Americans' awareness. Animal rights has been the cover story of magazines as diverse as *Newsweek*, *U.S. News and World Report*, *New York Magazine*, the *Atlantic Monthly*, the *New Republic*, the *Village Voice*, the *Progressive*, and the lawyers' weekly *National Law Journal*; its issues have been featured in network television series like *L.A. Law*, *MacGyver*, and *Designing Women*; it has been examined in major news programs such as *48 Hours*. Despite a tendency to focus on secretive and sensationalist ALF commandos, most media coverage has been sympathetic to the ideas of the movement. Typically, the activists are portrayed as eccentric, but their positions are treated with respect. Comic strips such as *Doonesbury* and *Bloom County* have favorably portrayed animal activists and their issues. *Saturday Night Live* at least recognized the controversy over fur coats in a skit titled "They're Better Off Dead." Celebrities such as Bob Barker, Doris Day, Casey Kasem, River Phoenix, and several of *The Golden Girls* have given their support to the cause.

Consumer goods have followed suit. One Barbie Doll is an "animal loving" Barbie, marketed as an animal rights volunteer—even as real-life activists attack the mink stole sold by the Spiegel Company for other Barbie Dolls. Vegetarian food is sold for the dogs of those with strict animal rights sensibilities. Public opinion polls show a slippage of support for scientific research using animals, even when it generates information about human health. Activists have delivered a crippling blow to the American fur industry—from which it may never recover. Animal protection is not only one of today's fastest-growing protest movements, it is one of the most effective.

The social roots of this movement lie in the changed relationship between humans and their fellow creatures that resulted from urbanization and industrialization in Western societies, as city dwellers began to encounter animals only as family pets, and less and less as instruments of labor and production. Animals have accompanied men and women throughout their history, some as members of the family to be cherished, others as tools to be used. But in modern times the balance between these attitudes—one sentimental, the other instrumental—has been questioned, as more and more people insist that all animals be treated as though they were partners—"companion animals"—rather than objects.

In the United States, the first societies to prevent cruelty to animals were founded in the 1860s as part of the more general humanitarian impulse of the time. While these societies persisted, further expansion of this animal welfare movement took place in the 1950s, with the founding of such organizations as the Humane Society of the United States. Most of these groups concentrated on problems associated with the growing number of pets: overpopulation and frequent abandonment, the issue of shelters, and the frequency of brutality and cruelty. These humane societies and welfare organizations saw animal cruelty coming from poorly educated or abusive individuals, not from the systematic activities of institutions.

A new ideological agenda for animal protection emerged dramatically in the late 1970s, combining ideas from several sources. It retained the animal welfare tradition's concern for animals as sentient beings that should be protected from unnecessary cruelty. But animal activists added a new language of "rights" as the basis for demanding animal liberation. In the individualist culture of America, "rights talk" is often the only way to express moral values and demands. Rights—whether of patients, women, fetuses, or animals—are accepted as a moral trump card that cannot be disputed. Justified in terms of tradition, nature, or fundamental moral principles, rights are considered nonnegotiable. Protectors compare animal rights to human rights, and the charge of "speciesism" takes its place alongside racism and sexism. Wildlife traffickers are engaged in a "monkey slave trade," laboratories become "torture chambers," and animal testing is a "holocaust."

The moral vision of animal rightists is partly drawn from other movements, especially feminism and environmentalism. At the core of these ideologies is a critique of "instrumentalism," the confusion of ends and means said to prevail in contemporary society. According to this critique, instrumental attitudes reduce nature and women, as well as other humans—all with inherent value as ends in themselves—to the status of things and tools. At the same time, instrumentalism promotes technologies, markets, and bureaucracies—all intended to be the means for attaining the good life—to the status of ends. Uneasiness with instrumental attitudes is widespread: Many people feel that there is something wrong with basing all decisions on economic values; that science lacks a human face; that consumer society creates artificial needs rather than satisfying real ones; that humans are treated like cogs in a machine.

Recent protest movements—ranging from Christian fundamentalists to radical feminists—insist that policies and decisions be guided by moral values and social needs, not by profits, technological feasibility, or bureaucratic inertia.

Just as environmentalists question the exploitation of nature for commercial purposes, so animal rights advocates demand the end of animal exploitation for human gain. Animals, like human beings or nature, should be treated as ends rather than as means. This view grounded the mistreatment of animals in institutions rather than blaming misguided individuals. Rather than searching for individual scientists who inflicted unusual pain on their animal subjects, activists condemned all research using live animals, thereby attacking the heart of biomedical science. Instead of criticizing the occasional circus for its cruelty in training animals, they rejected any use of animals to entertain people as exploitation and humiliation. Here was a new view of the relationship between animals and human institutions, one that often condemned the very essence of those institutions. The appeal of this critique helps explain the transformation of animal protection into a radical animal rights movement.

But a fuller explanation lies in common cultural beliefs and implicit understandings about animals in our society, since the treatment of other species often reflects a culture's moral concerns. Animals were the first subject of painting—on the walls of caves—and the first metaphors in human thought—for example, as symbols of tribes and families. They may have been the first objects to be worshiped, perceived as embodiments of spirits. Animals exhibit enough diversity of behavior and attributes to provide an extensive vocabulary for our own thinking. Throughout recorded history, men and women have found that animals were "good to think with," a rich source of symbols that humans could use to impose order on the world. They are blank slates onto which people have projected their beliefs about the state of nature, about "natural" forms of hierarchy and social organization, about language and rationality, and about moral behavior. Lessons are drawn from the supposed behavior of tortoises and hares, from the social organization of ants and grasshoppers, from the territoriality of lions and wolves.

We also project onto animals the characteristics of humans—sensitivity to pain, emotional bonds such as love and loyalty, the ability to plan and communicate. People have long endowed animals with human characteristics—crafty foxes, greedy pigs, lazy cats. Conversely, they use animals to characterize humans—people chatter like magpies, work like mules, and squirrel things away. We speak of male chauvinist pigs; we complain that Uncle Pete hogs the sports section. We use expressions like rat's nest, rat race, dirty rat, and smelling a rat. The sloth was even unlucky enough to be named after one of the seven deadly sins. But we can also romanticize animals, projecting onto them traits that make them better than people: a goodness, innocence, and purity rarely found in human company. Animals often come to represent the best in human nature, those qualities we cherish and try to protect.

If animals share so many human characteristics, what are the essential differences? The distinction between humans and other animals is the key issue in the growing number of disputes over animal protection. "A life is a life," whether human or nonhuman, is a common refrain in animal rights rhetoric. Ironically, science itself has helped to blur the boundaries between humans and other animals. Evolutionary biology, after all, is controversial among Christian fundamentalists precisely because it violates the long assumed distinction between man and the animal world. While religious movements like creationists struggle to maintain boundaries, believing Man was created in God's image, animal rightists have taken biologists literally, denying moral distinctions between species as the "effluvium of a discredited metaphysics."[3]

For most people, the boundaries between animals and humans are intuitively clear. A human life is simply worth more than a nonhuman life, and while animals deserve some moral consideration, they are not to be exempt from human use. Such distinctions, however, remain matters of belief, not of evidence; they are affected by cultural preferences, personal values, and moral sentiments—traits not entirely open to rational persuasion. Rhetoric that compares animal suffering with the holocaust, that equates speciesism with racism, has emotive power for those who blur the boundaries between humans and other species. For others, these metaphors appear outlandish, threatening, dangerously defying accepted categories. The conflict between animal advocates and animal users is far more than a matter of contrasting tastes or interests. Opposing world views, concepts of identity, ideas of community, are all at stake. The animal rights controversy is about the treatment of animals, but it is also about our definition of ourselves and of a moral society. For this reason, it cannot be easily resolved.

Animal rights is a moral crusade. Its adherents act upon explicit moral beliefs and values to pursue a social order consistent with their principles. Their fervent moral vision crowds out other concerns. Most moral crusades focus on single issues: Some focus on abortion; others on drunken driving; still others on the evils of pornography. Their members—moral missionaries—often insist they have no broader partisan agenda. They are less interested in material benefits for themselves than in correcting perceived injustices. Animals are a perfect cause for such a crusade; seen as innocent victims whose mistreatment demands immediate redress, they are an appealing lightning rod for moral concerns.

The symbolic importance of animals in this crusade underscores the importance of ideas in inspiring social movements, shaping their tactics, and enhancing or limiting their effects. To organize a crusade, movement leaders appeal to the moral sentiments of like-minded citizens, inciting their anger with emotive rhetoric and strategies ranging from colorful public rallies to clandestine break-ins that free animals from laboratories. The language of moral crusades is sometimes shrill, self-righteous, and uncompromising, for bedrock principles are nonnegotiable. In the strident style of Old Testament prophets, scolding and condemning their society, organizers point to evils that surround them and to catastrophes that will befall society in the absence of reform. Extreme and even illegal strategies and tactics are seen as justified in order to stop widespread immoral practices. Their sense of moral urgency encourages believers to ignore laws and conventional political processes, and they organize themselves into groups structured for quick action, not participatory debate. Proselytizing and interventionist in their style, such crusades frequently appear dangerous to those who do not share their judgmental and uncompromising views.

Yet animal protection groups vary widely in their aims and thus in their shrillness. Contrasting goals, tactics, and philosophical positions bring forth different organizations that form a continuum from reformist to radical. However, they tend to cluster into three kinds of groups that we label welfarist, pragmatist, and fundamentalist. In the humane tradition of the ASPCA, animal *welfarists* accept most current uses of animals, but seek to minimize their suffering and pain. They view animals as distinct from humans, but as objects entitled to compassion. Their reformist position, advocated through public education and lobbying for protective legislation, has long enjoyed wide public support and continues to do so. Welfarist groups like the SPCAs and the Humane Society of the United States existed before the animal rights movement appeared, and remain the largest, most powerful organizations.

In the late 1970s, however, more radical groups formed on the fringes of the animal welfare movement, redefining the issue of animal welfare as one of animal rights. Some of these new advocates organized around the well-articulated and widely disseminated utilitarian perspective of philosopher Peter Singer. Because animals could feel pain and pleasure, Singer argued that they deserved moral consideration, and he demanded drastic reduction in their use. The *pragmatist* groups feel that certain species deserve greater consideration than others, and would allow humans to use animals when the benefits deriving from their use outweigh their suffering. They seek to reduce animal use through legal actions, political protest, and negotiation. Henry Spira is a prominent example of a pragmatist.

Some of these new advocates, however, demanded the immediate abolition of all exploitation of animals, on the grounds that animals have inherent, inviolable rights. These more extreme animal rights *fundamentalists* believe that people should never use animals for their own pleasures or interests, regardless of the benefits. Some see even the ownership of pets as a distortion of the animals' natural lives. Insisting that increased understanding of head injuries does not justify harming baboons, the Animal Liberation Front expresses the fundamentalists' position, as well as their compelling sense of urgency. Although far less numerous than pragmatist or welfarist organizations, these groups set the tone of the new animal rights movement. And they are growing in size and wealth.

These distinctions are not absolute or rigid. Some activists, for example, believe in full animal rights, but pursue their goals with pragmatic strategies. Many shift their language and tactics depending on the issue or political arena. And all are tempted to indulge in fundamentalist rhetoric that simplifies the moral issues and demonizes opponents. But these three labels are useful to highlight important differences and tensions within a movement often described in monolithic terms. For the movement itself is divided over many issues: whether the same attention should be given to helping wild animals and domestic ones, whether insects or reptiles should be championed as fervently as furry mammals, and, especially, whether destructive tactics are acceptable.

Nevertheless, welfarists, pragmatists, and fundamentalists cooperate on specific issues, and their interests as well as rhetoric often merge. Together, they form a remarkably powerful animal protection movement, in which the pragmatists and fundamentalists represent the radical wing—the animal rights crusade. These crusaders would like to challenge Americans to rethink their fundamental beliefs about themselves and their connection to the world around them. They wonder if the boundaries we have drawn between ourselves and other animals are as rigid as we suppose. They would force us to extend the rights we promote for humans to other species. They want nothing short of a moral revolution that would change our food and clothing, our science and health care, our entire relationship to the natural world.

CRITICAL THINKING QUESTIONS

1. In the previous reading, Jo Freeman maintains that social movements develop when (1) there is an effective communications network, (2) the communications network is co-optable, (3) a crisis propels like-minded people into action, and (4) people are organized to act. Are these characteristics useful or not in explaining the emergence and success of the animal rights movement?

2. Why do Jasper and Nelkin describe the animal rights movement as a "moral crusade"

rather than, for example, a "lunatic fringe" or a terrorist group that vandalizes and destroys scientific research laboratories?

3. Jasper and Nelkin propose a continuum of animal rights organizations that includes welfarists, pragmatists, and fundamentalists. Prepare a short typology of these three groups in terms of their (a) beliefs, (b) major goals, and (c) primary strategies to accomplish their goals. Using your typology, describe what you think are the strengths and weaknesses of each group in developing acceptable public policies that protect animals.

NOTES

1. Quoted in "Animals in Testing. How the CPI Is Handling a Hot Issue," *Chemical Week* 135, 23 (December 5, 1984), 38.
2. Quoted in Richard J. Brenneman, "Animal 'liberator' promises more raids on labs," *Sacramento Bee* (July 2, 1984), B1.
3. James Rachels, *Created from Animals* (New York: Oxford University Press, 1990).

Collective
Behaviour and
Social Movements

CLASSIC

CONTEMPORARY

CROSS-CULTURAL

74

Abortion Movements in Poland, Great Britain, and the United States

JANET HADLEY

Perhaps one of the best-known feminist slogans during the early 1970s was that "A woman has a right to choose" whether or not to terminate a pregnancy. About 38 percent of the world's population live in countries where abortion has been available on request. Although abortion has been legal in the United States and most of Europe for at least twenty-five years, it remains an explosive issue in many countries and has spawned "for" and "against" social movements and collective behaviour. In this reading, Janet Hadley examines some of the controversies and campaigns of abortion rights movements in Poland, the United States, and Great Britain.

In recent years in the United States, in Poland, and in Ireland, too, national politics has at times been convulsed by the issue of abortion. In Germany the historic reunification of East and West almost foundered amid wrangling about conflicting abortion laws. How can abortion, hardly an issue comparable to the great affairs of state, such as the economy or national security, have an impact such as this?

This is an account, first, of how post-Communist Poland found itself in the grip of the abortion debate and secondly how the issue came to be such a seemingly permanent shadow on the political landscape in the United States, in the wake of the Supreme Court's 1973 landmark decision on abortion in the case of *Roe v. Wade*. It offers some ideas about why.

Source: From "God's Bullies: Attacks on Abortion," by Janet Hadley, *Feminist Review*, Vol. 48 (Fall 1994), pp. 94–113. Reprinted by permission of the author.

The account focuses on abortion, primarily as a method of birth control, which women have always sought out, legally when they can, illegally when they must. The controversies and campaigns recorded and the ideas offered here concentrate on women's access to affordable, safe and legal abortion—an essential part of women's reproductive freedom in a world where 500 women die every day from the complications of unsafe abortion (World Health Organization, 1993).

The way abortion has at times dominated public debate in both Poland and the United States can hardly be exaggerated, but the contexts are very different. At times, during the 1992 American presidential election campaign, it seemed as if the fate of the United States for the next four years hung solely on the thread of the abortion issue. Economic issues, national security, even political scandals were all pushed into the background. But no one was too surprised to encounter this wild card in the United States' electoral politics. It had been thus, on and off, for around twenty years, since the 1973 Supreme Court judgement which had sanctioned abortion as a woman's constitutional right.

It was, however, probably a lot harder for anyone to have predicted events in Poland where, for more than four years, well before the forty-year-old Communist regime was finally sloughed off, abortion took centre stage. The renascent right in Poland selected abortion as the first block of the social welfare system for demolition. The battle over it highlights the new relationship between the Roman Catholic Church—once the main element of opposition alongside Solidarity—and the state. As the democratization of Eastern Europe got under way, abortion was one of the first laws to come under fire (Einhorn, 1993).

In some ways the abortion debate in Poland, which of all the former Soviet bloc countries has undergone by far the most draconian reversal of its abortion law, is quite straightforward: The opponents of abortion are solidly Roman Catholic and perceive their efforts as part of the task of rescuing Poland from its years of godlessness. The debate in Poland harks back to the relatively straightforward arguments which took place in Britain at the time of the passing of the Abortion Act in 1967.

In the United States, on the other hand, the issue has been linked to a much more extensive catalogue of perceived "social degeneracy." Opposition to abortion in the United States involves a curious alliance of religious and secular New Right groupings and much of the driving force has been provided, not by the Roman Catholic Church, but by evangelical Christians. . . .

POLAND: NO PLACE TO BE A WOMAN

. . . What we have been witnessing in Poland since 1989, according to one observer, is the "Church's colossal efforts to replace a totalitarian state with a theocracy" (Kissling, 1992). Weekly Masses from Rome are broadcast on Polish TV these days. Scientific conferences open with High Mass, blessings and so on, and military personnel are sent on pilgrimages. Classes in religion (i.e., Roman Catholicism) are mandatory for children in state schools. There is little doubt that the bishops of Poland, who behave more like leaders of a political party than as simple guardians of moral values, have their sights set not only on banning abortion but also divorce, provision of contraception, and other hallmarks of a secular society. One commentator wrote in 1991:

From the very beginning until its unexpected culmination in June [1991—when a draft anti-abortion bill was rejected by parliament in the face of huge pro-choice demonstrations] the Polish controversy on abortion was a classic example of political conflict. Nobody cared any more about subtle moral or political arguments. It was clear that who wins the abortion debate will control the political situation in Poland. (Szawarski, 1991)

The irony is that not only was June 1991 far from being the "culmination," but also that nobody today could be said to have won. (Women, of course, lost.)

The final law, signed by President Lech Walesa in February 1993, was seen by opponents of abortion as a compromise. It is much weaker than they would have liked. The original anti-abortion bill, first published in 1989, promised three years' imprisonment for a woman who induced her own abortion, as well for any doctor caught performing an illegal operation. Under the new law, two years' imprisonment awaits an abortionist, but a woman inducing her own abortion will not face gaol [jail].

The new law allows abortion when a woman's life or health is in danger, after rape or incest, or if there is suspected fetal abnormality. But prenatal testing is only permissible if there is a family history of genetic disorder. There are token provisions urging local authorities to provide contraceptive services.

The Church's Power and Influence

The religious context of the abortion row in Poland goes a long way to explaining how it came to be such a passionate, extreme and dominating issue. Around 95 percent of its 39 million people consider themselves Catholic and there is a very strong family tradition of Catholicism, which during the Communist era greatly strengthened the Church as a focus of national identity and a shelter for opposition. Having a Polish Pope helps too; when John Paul II visited in 1991, he urged his fellow Poles to free themselves from a law permitting abortion, which he called a tragic inheritance of Communism.

Even when the Communist grip seemed at its most unyielding, the Church consistently harried the authorities on issues of sexual control. In a recent survey, conducted since the fall of the Communists, and reported in the *Guardian* (9/14/93), 95 percent of Polish women said they rely on personal experience for their sex education and 73 percent said they had had an unplanned pregnancy.

The only sex-education manual ever produced in Poland had to be withdrawn because of Church protest. Roman Catholic opposition to contraception has been effective—76 percent of the urban population and 87 percent of the rural population use only Church-approved 'natural' methods of fertility control (Mrugala, 1991). (Priests often determine what is sold in local pharmacies.) Poland's 1956 abortion law contained no conscience clause, but the Church's success in pressuring doctors can be judged from the fact that in some state hospitals, staff refusal made it impossible to get an abortion. As early as 1973, Church protests over the rising abortion rate and the behaviour of "callous young women" forced the government to set up a commission to consider whether the law needed amending (Okolski, 1988).

But the pressures on women to have abortions were very strong. Even for those who wanted it, contraception has never been easily available, and was of notoriously poor quality. Abortion—which was free in state hospitals after 1959, and easy to obtain—was therefore the main method of birth control. Women only had to report that they were "in a difficult life situation." "Poland's hard life finds more and more women choosing abortions," reported *The New York Times* in 1983, citing families in some cities waiting eighteen years to obtain a small apartment. Despite the Church's denunciations, there were an estimated 600,000 abortions a year, compared to just 700,000 live births.

Times may have been hard in 1983, but the economic "shock therapy" of post-Communist Poland has brought unimaginable hardship in its wake. Unemployment is now 2.8 million and will be one-fifth of the workforce in three years' time. The bishops have deplored this, by urging *women* to leave the labour market, to ease unemployment and ensure that men's wages increase. They have made no adverse comment on the virtual shut-down of state-financed child care.

The Bishops, the State, and the Medical Profession

The episcopate first floated the idea of outlawing abortion in 1988, deeming it to be a mortal threat to the "biological substance of the nation." In the spring of 1989 an Unborn Child Protection Bill was published and the Pope hurried to send his congratulations.

In 1990, however, long before the legislative battle had got into its stride, the Ministry of Health took its own initiative, saying that women wanting abortion would now need the permission of three physicians and of a psychologist, whose appointment had been approved by the local bishop, and that an abortion for social reasons must be requested in writing (*The New York Times*, 4/21/92). The psychologist's job is to dissuade women, mainly by putting the frighteners on them. Sterilization and the in-vitro fertilization programme were suspended.

As Poland created its first parliament, abortion became the bellwether for fitness to serve. Anyone supporting abortion rights was traduced as a surreptitious advocate for Communism. Throughout 1990 and 1991 the battle raged, overshadowing the upheavals of the new market economy. Huge demonstrations in favour of abortion took place in Warsaw and women's groups began to get organized to defend abortion rights. Solidarity was split on the issue. Bills were proposed and defeated in dizzying succession. Parish priests threatened to withhold sacraments from anyone who did not sign the petitions against "killing innocent children."

The anti-abortion movement targeted not only abortion but family planning provision, too, blocking the launch of an information campaign in the textile city of Lodz, where there has been an unusually high rate of congenital abnormalities among babies born to women working in the textile factories (Rich, 1991). Their activity was partly financed by pro-life organizations from the United States, such as Human Life International. This evangelical group, fired by a vision of "re-Christianized united Europe stretching from the Atlantic to the Urals," vowed to "flood Eastern Europe" with films, videos (such as *The Silent Scream* which has been shown in Polish schools), fetal models and other propaganda. In 1992, Operation Rescue blockaded a clinic in the Baltic port of Gdynia, with protesters from the United States, Canada and the U.K.

Although one smear in circulation was that "only communists and Jews favor abortion," there is little direct evidence that the anti-abortion campaign was fuelled by a nationalist pro-natalism—a desire to demographically overwhelm Poland's minorities. There was, however, a definite bid to appeal to a repressive notion of proper and traditional Polish "womanhood." The term "emancipation for women" is laden with Communist overtones and has often in reality meant the notorious "double burden" or overloading of women, in Poland and Eastern Europe in general, in which they have been expected to shoulder full-time jobs as well as forty hours a week shopping, cooking, cleaning, laundry, with only the aid of very poor-quality pre-school child care and medical care (Jankowska, 1993). Against such a reality, a misty vision of womanhood may have a definite allure.

May 1992 brought another turn of the screw. A new code of medical ethics made it professionally unethical for doctors to perform abortions except in cases of rape or incest or when the woman's life was in danger. Violations would lead to suspension of the doctor's license. The code effectively ended hospital abortions and prenatal testing: Some institutions put up signs, "No Abortions."

The issue continued to rock the government, which twice postponed a final vote on abortion. By the end of 1992, the conflict was extreme enough to threaten the fragile coalition government, an improbable seven-party affair. A million people signed a petition for a referendum. Meanwhile, 61 percent of Poles said they favoured the provisions of the 1956 law.

Turning the Clock Back

Nevertheless, when the government could postpone a vote no longer, a law was finally passed early in 1993. Under the new law, only 3 percent of the abortions previously performed in Poland are now deemed legal. Two years in gaol awaits an illegal abortionist, but there is no punishment for a woman who obtains an illegal operation. Although it is the most restrictive abortion law in Europe, apart from Ireland's, pro-choice campaigners comforted themselves with the rueful thought that things could easily have been much worse.

The legislation satisfies no one. Both sides have vowed to fight on. Even before President Lech Walesa signed the new law, the 1992 doctors' code—a de facto ban on abortions in Poland—was having its effect. The Warsaw police morgue has begun receiving bodies of women bearing witness to botched abortions. For the last three years, cases of infanticide have steadily increased.

Deaths will be outnumbered by injuries. Romania, where abortion was illegal until the fall of Ceausescu in 1989, shows the way. Staff at a clinic for women in Bucharest, set up by Marie Stopes International, found that 80 percent of patients were suffering from past incompetent abortions.

A helpline set up in Warsaw by pro-abortion campaigners is receiving calls from men seeking advice because their wives are refusing to have sex any more. Women are phoning for help, reporting that even in circumstances which comply with the new law, they are being refused operations. In Poland's deep Catholic south, a pregnant Cracow woman, furnished with a police report confirming that she had been raped, was refused help at the hospital (Hoell, 1993).

All the desolately familiar symptoms of outlawed abortion are there: police raids on clinics, small ads appearing in the newspapers: "Gynaecologist: Interventions." The price is $350 to $1,000: The average monthly wage is $200. For professional women "medical tours" can be arranged—to the Ukraine, to Kaliningrad, even to Holland. (But not to the Czech Republic, which in the wake of Poland's new law, moved swiftly to outlaw abortions for foreign visitors.)

Paradoxically, the last few years have seen a burgeoning of women's organizations, formed to defend abortion and women's rights. It is an irony, comments Hanna Jankowska, "when the word 'feminist' sounds in this country like an insult" (1993). But sustaining the momentum of such organizations is uphill work. People are consumed by the effort to cope with the effects of 38 percent inflation.

There are signs that the Church may have overplayed its hand in its attempt to introduce a legislative version of "absolute morality" as part of a plan to create a theocratic Poland. There was strong public support for a referendum on abortion, which the Church opposed, and its popularity has dropped by half since Communism

collapsed, according to opinion polls (*Catholic Herald*, 9/9/93). The Irish Church found itself in similar trouble after the referendum on abortion in Ireland in 1992, an event which was much reported in the Polish media.

But it is hard to draw sound parallels with Ireland: The Republic is certainly behind the times, but there are signs that slowly things are creeping forward for women in Ireland. Nothing compares with the crudeness with which the clock hands have been wrenched *back* in Poland.

In September 1993, the political coalition which fostered the anti-abortion legislation suffered a crushing defeat in national elections. The pace of reform was thought to be the main culprit, but the unpopularity of the anti-abortion law was also held to blame. Pro-abortion campaigners are preparing a new bill to reverse the law, scarcely before the ink is dry. In January 1994, Polish doctors amended their medical code, somewhat relaxing the abortion guidelines and increasing scope for prenatal diagnosis of fetal abnormalities.

The bishops and their allies intend to press on towards a theocratic state. They have stated: "We must reject the false and harmful belief— which unfortunately is grounded in social consciousness—that a secular state is perceived as the only and fundamental guarantee of freedom and equality of citizens" (Szawarski, 1991). If they succeed in creating a model Roman Catholic state, it will be women who suffer most directly. That is why no one in Poland, on whichever side of the abortion divide, underestimates the importance of the struggle around abortion as a stalking horse for what may yet come.

It is not possible to yoke together the national experience of abortion politics in Poland with that of the United States, only to offer them as two distinct examples of how abortion seemed at times to be the tail that wagged the dog of national politics. It has been quite remarkable to find abortion ricocheting around the political arena in Poland and other Eastern European countries. But the issue has played a crucial part in the politics of the

United States for almost twenty years: in itself an astonishing phenomenon.

USA, 1973—THE SUPREME COURT LIGHTS THE FUSE

Until the historic U.S. Supreme Court judgment of 1973, in the case of *Roe v. Wade* (which I shall call plain *Roe*), abortion was not a major issue in the United States. In the late 1960s, when campaigners for abortion reform in California asked people to sign petitions, it took so long for people to think and talk before deciding where they stood that no more than four or five signatures could be gathered in an afternoon's work (Luker, 1984).

But the spark of *Roe* caught dry tinder at once and is still burning. Today, everyone has an opinion on abortion: After thousands of opinion polls, hours of TV debating, radio phone-ins and miles of newsprint, people know with certainty whether they are "pro-choice" or "pro-life."

In the late nineteenth century it was doctors who pressed for anti-abortion legislation in the United States, partly to strengthen the delineation of medicine as a regulated, elite profession. Making abortion illegal, unless performed by a doctor, was an effective way of cutting the ground from under the "quacks." The laws granted doctors alone the discretion to decide when a woman's life was sufficiently endangered to justify the loss of fetal life.

For almost seventy years legal abortion was a matter for medical judgement. Its prevalence and the criteria used varied enormously. Women who could not get legal abortions resorted to illegal practitioners and practices. But in the 1950s and 1960s exclusive medical control over abortion began to crumble.

Briefly, women's lives were changing as they entered the labour market in increasing numbers—for a married woman an unintended pregnancy became much more of a disaster than in the past; secondly, the improvements of medicine and obstetrics made pregnancy and childbirth much safer and made it harder for doctors to cloak a decision to perform an abortion for a wealthy patient behind the excuse that continuing the pregnancy would gravely endanger her health. Doctors' work became much more hospital-based and could be more easily scrutinized and regulated than when they worked in private consulting rooms.

Thirdly, women began to question the right of doctors and lawyers, or anyone, to decide whether or not they should have to continue an unintended pregnancy. Finally, the effects of the Thalidomide cases and the advent of effective contraception all played a part in dragging decisions and policies on abortion into the harsh public light of politics.

Some states began to permit abortion. Between 1967 and 1973, seventeen states rescinded their restrictions on abortion. Thousands of women crossed state boundaries to obtain abortions (Gold, 1990). Abortion was happening, despite its continuing prohibition under federal law.

Several decades of Supreme Court decisions— for instance, acknowledging it was no business of the state (or states) to seek to outlaw the use and purchase of contraceptives—had smoothed the path towards the *Roe* judgment, but nonetheless, when it eventually came, it was quite dramatic. The court said that a woman's right to obtain an abortion, like her right to use contraception without government interference, is constitutionally protected, as part of her fundamental right to privacy. And that because the right to privacy is fundamental (rights under the American constitution are ranked, and *fundamental* trumps every other kind of right) states must show a "compelling interest" before they can intervene.

The court stressed that, of course, the decision to abort must be made together with a doctor. But it devised a sliding scale of maternal/fetal rights, practically sanctioning "abortion on demand" in the first trimester and gradually increasing the amount of protection afforded to the fetus as the weeks of pregnancy progressed.

No Room for Compromise

The significance of the Supreme Court ruling in 1973 was that it turned abortion into a constitutional issue, declaring it a fundamental right of the female citizen, and sweeping away all the various state restrictions. In doing so it called into question the deeply held beliefs of people accustomed to thinking that *theirs* was the majority opinion and set the state on a collision course with an indefatigable group of its citizens. As long as abortion had been purely a medical issue, as it is in Britain (see below), it had been much more difficult to challenge, and far less in the public domain.

The absolute divide between right-to-life/pro-life/anti-choice/anti-abortion people, and the rest is the embryo or fetus. If you believe that the embryo or later the fetus is a person, a human being in the fullest sense, the moral equivalent of a woman, everything else falls into place. The Supreme Court questioned this notion and opened the door to the years of court challenge, endless legislative pressure and single-issue pressure-group politics. For those who believe that abortion is the equivalent of homicide there can hardly be a compromise.

The impact of the *Roe* judgement was enormous. Overnight literally, the opposition mobilized.[1] Its attack has had two aims: to upset and overturn the judicial applecart and at the same time to erect as many obstacles as possible between a woman and a legal abortion. It's been a busy twenty years: *Roe* has been harried almost to extinction by state regulations, such as imposed waiting periods, demands for "informed consent," such as making the woman look at images of fetal development—at all stages, no matter how early her own pregnancy. As pro-choice campaigner Lawrence Lader said, after *Roe*, "We thought we had won. We were wrong" (*Family Planning World*, Jan/Feb, 1992).

At first, state attempts to regulate abortion after *Roe* received a cool response in the Supreme Court, but as the New Right has gained power and judges appointed to the court became more conservative, so the judgements have hardened against abortion rights.

Wide-Ranging Success for Abortion's Opponents

The cultural and political climate today is of course very different from that surrounding *Roe* in 1973. On the day of the Supreme Court's ruling on *Roe*, newspapers reported an agreement which might bring an end to the war in Vietnam and carried obituaries of former President Lyndon B. Johnson, whose presidency was marked domestically by the civil rights movement, Black Power and the movement against the war in Vietnam. This is not the place to rehearse the cultural "backlash" of the years since then except to highlight how wide-ranging it has been.

Susan Faludi, for instance, recounts the fate of a script for the TV show *Cagney and Lacey*. In "Choices," as the early 1980s' episode was to be called, Cagney—the single woman in the feisty female cop duo—became pregnant. CBS programming executives went berserk at the mere idea of abortion (even as an option to be rejected). They demanded numerous rewrites until in the final version, Cagney only mistakenly thinks she is pregnant. "Lacey . . . tells her that if she had been pregnant she should have got married. Abortion is never offered as a choice" (Faludi, 1992: 186).

The anti-abortion lobby drew comfort not only from *Cagney and Lacey* but also from the White House. As the violence against clinics increased in 1984 after Ronald Reagan's election to a second term as president, he refused to condemn the actions and their perpetrators (Blanchard & Prewitt, 1993).[2]

Opinion polls show that Americans' attitude to abortion was and generally remains "permit but discourage." It was not very hard to convert such ambivalence into support for restrictions on government funding and so on. The most significant curtailment of rights for low-income women was the Hyde Amendment of 1979 which denied Medicaid funding for abortion, except where a woman's life is in danger. There have also been severe and wide-ranging restrictions on the use of public facilities for abortion: It is illegal, for instance, to perform a private abortion in a private building standing on publicly owned land. By 1979 no federal funds could be used to provide abortion or abortion-related services (Petchesky, 1984).

Today, only half the United States' medical schools even offer the option of training in abortion procedures, and fewer and fewer young doctors are willing to perform abortions. Many gynaecologists still performing abortions are reaching retirement, and in a 1985 study, two-thirds of the gynaecologists in the United States stated that they would not terminate pregnancy. Who would choose to conduct their professional working life in a bullet-proof vest, with an armed guard at the clinic door? In 1988, 83 percent of all United States counties lacked any facilities for abortion, and those counties contain 31 percent of U.S. women aged between fifteen and forty-four (Alan Guttmacher Institute, 1993).

A shadowy world of unlicensed, unregulated abortion facilities in private doctors' offices is beginning to emerge. There are estimated to be several dozen in New York City alone, and a doctor there was recently prosecuted for a botched abortion on a twenty-one-year-old immigrant woman, who subsequently gave birth to a severely mutilated infant (*Family Planning World*, May/June, 1993).

And yet, despite all the legislative obstacles and the physical harassment, the anti-abortion movement has made no dent in the number of abortions taking place in the United States. The overall figure has hovered steadily around 1.6 million a year.

Who Opposes Abortion Rights?

The intimidation of anti-abortion activists, such as Operation Rescue, or the Lambs of Christ, and the violence and terrorism against abortion clinics is what immediately comes to mind when thinking about abortion's opponents, but it is not the only face of the opposition.

After the *Roe* judgment, the Catholic Church was the first into action, with plangent denunciation and millions of dollars poured into new anti-abortion organizations. But as the New Right in the Republican party set out deliberately to woo the anti-abortion voters, as part of its efforts to shift the party itself to the right, the anti-abortion alliance became a curious blend—from Catholics to born-again Christian evangelicals, to more secular "New Right" types. It was ultimately to prove a volatile coalition.

Abortion has been and still is the kernel of a protracted campaign against the social trends of the second half of the twentieth century, and for a reinstatement of "traditional family values." The Reagan presidency boosted the legitimacy, power and influence of "God's bullies" as they have been aptly called. Although the specific goal of the anti-abortionists is to outlaw abortions, it is important to see this in a wider context of conservatism, attacks on welfare and so on.

The movement has two faces—first, the lobbyists and court challengers, as well as the image-makers, whose ideological offensive has sought to control the public perception of abortion and the women who seek it (Petchesky, 1984). In 1990 alone there were 465 abortion-related bills presented to state legislatures (McKeegan, 1992). The anti-abortion lobby has used its muscle in the ballot box with considerable effect. Single-issue voting can tip the scales when results are close and election turnouts are low. Packing state legislatures and other elected bodies has been a systematic strategy and for twenty years abortion has wracked the United States, from school boards to Congress.

Secondly, there is the face of direct action, some of it peaceful, but nevertheless extremely intimidating, some of it violent and explicitly women-hating. In 1991 in Wichita, south Kansas, there were more than 2,600 arrests as 30,000 anti-abortion protesters blockaded an abortion clinic. In the last fifteen years around a hundred clinics have been bombed or set on fire. Others have had medical equipment wrecked. Clinic staff and their families have been harassed; doctors have been shot at; in March 1993, one was even killed. Pregnant women arriving at abortion clinics have had to run a gauntlet of screaming demonstrators, some hurling plastic fetal models, some videotaping their faces and noting the numbers on their car license plates for subsequent tracing and personal harassment.

A study of men convicted of anti-abortion violence concluded that they are "clearly acting out of a desire to maintain the dependent status of women." Many also favour policies such as capital and corporal punishment (Blanchard & Prewitt, 1993). Somewhat in a grey area of legality lie the fake abortion clinics which have been set up and are listed in the Yellow Pages, which harangue women who turn up hoping to arrange an abortion, and force them to look at often gruesome pictures of fetuses. . . .

WHY HAS BRITAIN'S ABORTION DEBATE BEEN DIFFERENT?

It seems worth briefly comparing the struggle in the United States with that in Britain, whose political process has never been gripped by the throat as it has in the United States. Pro-choice Republican Senator Robert Packwood explained what the attentions of a single-minded group such as the U.S. anti-abortion lobby mean to his daily political life:

[The pro-lifers] are a frightening force. They are people who are with you 99 percent of the time, but if you vote against them on this issue it doesn't matter what else you stand for. (Tribe, 1992)

That's hard to imagine in Britain. Of course, there have been times when abortion has been a hot issue in the U.K., swelling MPs' mailbags and prompting heated exchanges on *Question Time*, but it has at no time been such dynamite,

compelling British MPs to refer their every political step to its impact on those of their supporters who oppose abortion. Part of the reason is that Britain is relatively indifferent to religion and has no comparably powerful, organized fundamentalist or Roman Catholic population. Also, laws made in the United States Supreme Court positively invite legal challenge and counter-challenge. Laws made by Parliament are more resilient in general.

What's more, part of the reason is in the abortion law itself. It is for doctors, says Britain's 1967 Abortion Act—two doctors—to decide whether a woman needs an abortion, under the terms specified by the law. The rights of women do not remotely enter into it. Many campaigners who have defended the provisions of the 1967 Act, from no less than sixteen parliamentary attempts to curtail its scope, believe that it is the Act's reliance on doctors that has allowed it to escape relatively unscathed after twenty-five years.

When opponents of abortion in Britain have attacked the Act, its defenders have quite legitimately and cogently been able to point out that it is not *women* who make the final decision, but (respectable) professionals. (Funding cuts in the National Health Service and excessive Department of Health regulations have more stealthily debilitated abortion provision in Britain—that is another story.) Although the inherent paternalism in the framing of the Act is not only demeaning but has also led to unfair geographical differences in women's access to a sympathetic, prompt abortion service, the pragmatic, defensive value of investing the responsibility in the medical profession is worth noting.

CRITICAL THINKING QUESTIONS

1. Numerous physicians who provide abortion services have been murdered and Planned Parenthood clinics bombed in the United States. Why, in contrast, has Poland not experienced such violent attacks on the medical profession and on women who seek abortions?

2. Why, in contrast to the United States and Poland, has there been little debate about abortion in Great Britain?

3. Opponents of abortion in Europe and the United States often describe abortion as a breakdown of "social values" and the "traditional family." In contrast, proponents of abortion emphasize a woman's reproductive rights. According to Hadley, how do politics, religion, and economics ultimately shape policy and many women's destiny in abortion debates?

NOTES

1. Kristin Luker (Luker, 1984) describes how would-be activists phoned around frantically in the days after the court decision, trying to find an organization to join. Many of them—women, married, housewives with small children, had never joined anything before—not even the school parent-teacher association.

2. Ronald Reagan not only refused to condemn the violence, in 1984 he wrote a bizarre call-to-arms against abortion, with help from Malcolm Muggeridge (*Abortion and the Conscience of the Nation*. Nashville: Thomas Nelson, 1984).

REFERENCES

Alan Guttmacher Institute. 1993. *Abortion in the United States: Facts in brief.* New York.

Blanchard, D., and T. J. Prewitt. 1993. *Religious violence and abortion.* University Press of Florida.

Einhorn, B. 1993. Polish backlash. *Everywoman*, April.

Faludi, S. 1992. *Backlash.* London: Vintage.

Gold, R. B. 1990. *Abortion and women's health: The turning point for America.* New York: Alan Guttmacher Institute.

Hoell, S. 1993. Strict new law drives abortion underground in Poland. *Reuters*, 14 December.

Jankowska, H. 1993. The reproductive rights campaign in Poland. *Women's Studies International Forum*, 16(3): 291–96.

Kissling, F. 1992. The Church's heavy hand in Poland. *Planned Parenthood in Europe*, 21(2): 18–9.

Luker, K. 1984. *Abortion and the politics of motherhood.* Berkeley: University of California Press.

McKeegan, M. 1992. *Mutiny in the ranks of the right.* New York: The Free Press, Maxwell Macmillan International.

Mrugala, G. 1991. Polish family planning in crisis: The Roman Catholic influence. *Planned Parenthood in Europe*, 20(2): 4–5.

Okolski, M. 1988. Poland. In *International handbook on abortion*, P. Sachdev. New York: Greenwood Press.

Petchesky, R. 1984. *Abortion and woman's choice.* New York: Longman.

Rich, Vera. 1991. Poland: Abortion and contraception. *Lancet*, 338, 875, (13 July): 108–09.

Szawarski, Z. 1991. Abortion in Poland. *British Journal of Obstetrics and Gynaecology*, 98: 1202–04.

Tribe, L. 1992. *Abortion: The clash of absolutes.* New York, Norton.

World Health Organization. 1993. *Progress in human reproductive research*, No. 25. Geneva.

75

The Disenchantment
of Modern Life

MAX WEBER

In this excerpt from a speech, "Science as a Vocation," delivered at Munich University in 1918, Weber claims that the rise of science has changed our way of thinking about the world. Where, in the past, humans confronted a world of mystical forces beyond our comprehension, now we assume that all things yield to human comprehension. Thus, Weber concludes, the world has become "disenchanted." Notice, however, that something is lost in the process—for, unlike the churches of the past, science can provide no answer to questions of ultimate meaning in life.

Scientific progress is a fraction, the most important fraction, of the process of intellectualization which we have been undergoing for thousands of years and which nowadays is usually judged in such an extremely negative way. Let us first clarify what this intellectualist rationalization, created by science and by scientifically oriented technology, means practically.

Does it mean that we, today, for instance, everyone sitting in this hall, have a greater knowledge of the conditions of life under which we exist than has an American Indian or a Hottentot? Hardly. Unless he is a physicist, one who rides on the streetcar has no idea how the car happened to get into motion. And he does not need to know. He is satisfied that he may "count"

on the behavior of the streetcar, and he orients his conduct according to this expectation; but he knows nothing about what it takes to produce such a car so that it can move. The savage knows incomparably more about his tools. When we spend money today I bet that even if there are colleagues of political economy here in the hall, almost every one of them will hold a different answer in readiness to the question: How does it happen that one can buy something for money—sometimes more and sometimes less? The savage knows what he does in order to get his daily food and which institutions serve him in this pursuit. The increasing intellectualization and rationalization do *not,* therefore, indicate an increased and general knowledge of the conditions under which one lives.

It means something else, namely, the knowledge or belief that if one but wished one could learn it at any time. Hence, it means that principally there are no mysterious incalculable forces

Source: Excerpts from *Max Weber: Essays in Sociology* by Max Weber, edited by H. H. Gerth & C. Wright Mills, translated by H. H. Gerth & C. Wright Mills. Translation copyright © 1946, 1958 by H. H. Gerth and C. Wright Mills. Used by permission of Oxford University Press.

that come into play, but rather that one can, in principle, master all things by calculation. This means that the world is disenchanted. One need no longer have recourse to magical means in order to master or implore the spirits, as did the savage, for whom such mysterious powers existed. Technical means and calculations perform the service. This above all is what intellectualization means. . . .

Science today is a "vocation" organized in special disciplines in the service of self-clarification and knowledge of interrelated facts. It is not the gift of grace of seers and prophets dispensing sacred values and revelations, nor does it partake of the contemplation of sages and philosophers about the meaning of the universe. This, to be sure, is the inescapable condition of our historical situation. We cannot evade it so long as we remain true to ourselves. And if Tolstoi's question recurs to you: As science does not, who is to answer the question: "What shall we do, and, how shall we arrange our lives?" or, in the words used here tonight: "Which of the warring gods should we serve? Or should we serve perhaps an entirely different god, and who is he?" then one can say that only a prophet or a savior can give the answers. . . .

To the person who cannot bear the fate of the times like a man, one must say: May he rather return silently, without the usual publicity build-up of renegades, but simply and plainly. The arms of the old churches are opened widely and compassionately for him. After all, they do not make it hard for him. One way or another he has to bring his "intellectual sacrifice"—that is inevitable. If he can really do it, we shall not rebuke him. For such an intellectual sacrifice in favor of an unconditional religious devotion is ethically quite a different matter than the evasion of the plain duty of intellectual integrity, which sets in if one

lacks the courage to clarify one's own ultimate standpoint and rather facilitates this duty by feeble relative judgments. In my eyes, such religious return stands higher than the academic prophecy, which does not clearly realize that in the lecture-rooms of the university no other virtue holds but plain intellectual integrity: Integrity, however, compels us to state that for the many who today tarry for new prophets and saviors, the situation is the same as resounds in the beautiful Edomite watchman's song of the period of exile that has been included among Isaiah's oracles:

He calleth to me out of Seir, Watchman, what of the night? The watchman said, The morning cometh, and also the night: if ye will enquire, enquire ye: return, come.

The people to whom this was said has enquired and tarried for more than two millennia, and we are shaken when we realize its fate. From this we want to draw the lesson that nothing is gained by yearning and tarrying alone, and we shall act differently. We shall set to work and meet the "demands of the day," in human relations as well as in our vocation. This, however, is plain and simple, if each finds and obeys the demon who holds the fibers of his very life.

CRITICAL THINKING QUESTIONS

1. In what sense do members of a traditional society know more about their world than we do? In what sense do we know more?

2. What is "Tolstoi's question"? Why can science not answer it?

3. What does Weber see as the great burden of living in a modern society? In other words, what comforts of the past are less available to modern people?

76

Internet Censorship as "Cybriety": Freud, McLuhan, and Medial Pleasures

TONY TREMBLAY

In this article, Tremblay suggests that our social concern over questionable media content is nothing new. Long before the Internet there were many media expressions that challenged social convention. Tremblay's analysis of Internet censorship draws much insight from a historical review of media content and social change.

In November 1995, the sleepy Canadian town of Sackville, New Brunswick, was witness to what Freud and Foucault might have called an age-old autoerotic drama, one characterized by a predictable latency—a discrepancy between action and reaction, performance and reception. The event to which I am referring took place at Mount Allison University's Owens Art Gallery, where performance art and theater are regularly staged. Student Chris Yorke and a female actor, clad only in smashed eggs and silver tree tinsel, performed simulated oral sex on one another in front of an audience of almost fifty people. Although no one in the audience complained, and no one walked out, the viewers' acceptance, even appreciation, of the performance did little to sanction it. Very little. When the performance was subsequently reviewed in the local newspaper, the public's moral outrage was silently and decisively marshaled. A few days later, Chris Yorke was charged with public indecency. In finding Yorke guilty of indecency in the performance of his art, New Brunswick Judge Irwin Lampert declared that "community standards are the best measure of what is obscene and what is not." Yorke's only comment was as historically encoded as the judge's: "Human sexuality has been the subject of art for centuries; I feel violated by this decision" (*Telegraph Journal* E5). Indeed, Yorke had been subject to the same social forces that violated the turn-of-the-century performance artists of *Serpentine Dance* (1895) and *Pull Down the Curtains, Suzie* (1904), two early peepshows made for Edison's Kinet[o]scope. If the Mount Allison situation teaches us anything, it is how fundamentally sexuality is inscribed with cultural sanction, and how that sanction recurs as regular historical performance.

Source: The complete contents of this article originally appeared in *Mosaic, a journal for the interdisciplinary study of literature*, Vol. 32.1, Spring 1999, pp. 167–82. Reprinted with permission of the publisher.

With increasing frequency over the last few years, the Internet has become a flash point for the debate between free speech and censorship. Various Netscape sites have been removed from the Web, and others have been blackened by Internet Providers to protest social sanction. Two years ago in the United States, Congress hurriedly passed the Communication Decency Act, only to see it ruled unconstitutional a short time later. In Canada, a January 1999 British Columbia judgment challenged the legality of restricting access to child pornography on the Web. Since that ruling, public opinion has been galvanized for censure: the call for Internet censorship—what I am terming "cybriety" (cyber-sobriety)—has been mobilized. The Internet, that vast mystical panacea that holds, we are told, so much of our hope for the future, is under threat. What are we to make of this, we non-cybrarians, occasional-surfers of the virtual world? In the early days of this debate, we can be certain of only one thing: left to the pundits, censorship becomes obscured. As Sallie Tisdale writes, "Censorship . . . makes it impossible not only to talk about the censored object, but about censorship" (Tisdale, p. 13). "Pornography," concurs Walter Kendrick, "names an argument, not a thing" (Kendrick, p. 31). And so censorship debates, regardless of what is being censored, are ideologically laden. These debates therefore require some historio-cultural archaeology to make sense of them.

The novel, photography/film, and now the Internet are good sites with which to ground an exploration of the social psychology of censorship, as these are not only our most popular media, but those which perhaps best illustrate the action of all new media in the self-satisfying ("autoerotic") and unregulated ("offensive") stage of infancy. I do not mean to suggest any kind of structural evolution across these media, but to point simply to a historical recurrence that is observable in each medium's infancy, the time when each thrives in the unreflexive rapture of its own autoeroticism, independent of the sanction of the censor. Hybridizing

McLuhan and Freud, I will argue that because all media are extensions of the body—speech extends the ear, print extends the eye—any new medium is inherently pleasurable; and, being pleasurable, any new medium invites the infantile game of daring, a pushing of the limits of what is "socially" acceptable in order to fulfill desire. Just as Freud's infant, outside social sanction, fetishizes its own body, fondling itself in the most embarrassing of public/ (*private*) places, so will I show that the human body is fetishized vicariously through all new media. Being bodily, all new media are therefore dangerous, as are all *new* technologies, a condition that further invites embargo. In "outering" the Central Nervous System, the Internet, as McLuhan predicted, is likewise bodily, given to an age-old autoerotic drama that is rife with the inevitability of social sanction. My essay will illustrate how a recourse to literary history and to diegetic (or narrative) pattern is particularly instructive in the exploration of censorship as a cultural phenomenon.

Sixteenth-century readers of the novel, the new narrative form of the time, were much less prudish than we are today, their openness reflected in a heady engagement with the lower-class anthropomorphism of sin, sex, the grotesque, and other bodily subversions. That a Benedictine monk was one of the most accomplished at presenting this orgiastic carnival of delights is simply a condition of pre-Reformation Christianity. Rabelais knew, as did the Roman Church fathers, that the otherwise respectable citizens of court and abbey were spectators, and, as spectators, they were voyeurs, always seeking an uncensored vista from which to watch the lower classes in the frenzy of their physicality. Rabelais's advance was to use the new narrative medium, the novel, to create a space and conditions (privacy and anonymity) within which learned spectators could discreetly exercise their fetish.

The significance of the new medium of the novel in this consideration of media lies in its formal and thematic generosity in meeting and satisfying an audience, as all new forms do. In extending us outward, all new media and technology *inevitably* satisfy, holding us, at least in their infancy, in the spell of Freud's autoerotic "mirror stage." The provenance of the new medium of the novel was significant too, for not only was it populist in terms of autoerotic content, but in structural ancestry as well. Rising from "the rich soil" of verse narratives (Church, p. 19), those oral forms that could *not* be sanctioned, the new genre paralleled the unlegislated folktale, which was "full of blunt, amused, and salacious stories . . . of castration and masturbation and incest, necrophilia and zoophilia, the mysterious power of the vagina and the clitoris" (Tisdale, p. 13).

In his work on scribal culture, McLuhan referred to this "becoming" as a spontaneous "outering" of the full sensibility of the people. So rare was this full flowering, McLuhan wrote, that it has found expression only in medieval, Restoration, and modern renewals. If McLuhan and Walter Ong are correct in suggesting that the Gutenberg press changed the medieval psyche from an ear to an eye reliance, then 16th-century readers were also "seeing" the world vicariously (and phenomenologically) for the first time, much as we are experiencing the world today for the first time through virtual and in some cases synchronous multi-media. In the span of less than one hundred years, then, the body was celebrated both in "becoming" (the late-Medieval carnivalesque) and in sensory recombination (the early-Renaissance carnality that swapped an ear for an eye). The sensory stimulus must have been unimaginably emancipating, wildly titillating, and, therefore, terribly threatening.

The autoeroticism of the new medium of the novel, when considered in the light of the onanistic eroticism of silent reading, suggests a medieval psyche that was fully invested in its own program of channeling desire. In its infancy, the novel was a representation of the body that lay below the surface of a coercive culture; reading was therefore a sensual delight, evident in Alberto Manguel's playful evocation of Colette's early reading fantasies:

It is summer. Sunk deep in the soft bed among feather pillows, with the inconstant rumble of carts on the cobble-stones outside the window in the Rue de l'Hospice in the grey village of Saint-Sauveur-en-Puisaye, an eight-year-old girl is silently reading Victor Hugo's *Les Misérables*. She doesn't read many books; she reads the same ones over and over again. She loves *Les Misérables* with what she'll later call "a reasoning passion"; she feels she can nestle in its pages "like a dog in its kennel." Every night she longs to follow Jean Valjean on his agonizing peregrinations, meet Cosette again, meet Marius, even the dreaded Javert. . . . Her mother does not believe in fiction: "so many complications, so much passionate love in those novels." (Manguel, p. 140)

The emergence and coercion of the 16th-century novel reveals that the "producerly" delight that Manguel attributes to Colette must exist covertly, otherwise risk being sanctioned in the "Name of the Father."

With the advent of photography at the height of the Victorian era, the diegetic cycle of corporeal form and censorship was repeated yet again, this time in response to the "zoögyroscopes" and wet-plate photographs of "the human figure in motion" (Muybridge, p. viii). Knowing that the body, as opposed to the word, is defined in movement, photography pioneers Eadweard Muybridge and Thomas Eakins produced stills of nude bodies in motion—women washing clothes, men jumping, etc. By the time of the "kinematograph" at the turn of the century (*kinema* from the Greek, meaning "motion"), early film opportunists began producing "loops," known today as "skinflicks," which presented versions of porn and erotica to both male and female viewers alike, many of whom gathered to watch these celluloid vaudevilles in polite company and respectable surroundings (Czitrom, p. 46). The more recent history of film also reveals that film producers not only understood, but were willing to monopolize on, the autoerotic tactility of their medium. Anthony Crabbe's research found that it was almost solely producers and corporate shareholders who challenged censors when the "traditional film industry [of the early 1970s] was in sharp decline" (Crabbe, p. 48). The resulting "decensorship of the time" not only produced our modern culture's classic *blue nuits* (*Au Pair Girls, Behind the Green Door, Deep Throat*, and *Emmanuelle*), but more fundamentally brought people back to the theater, renewing again the people's desire for a marketplace carnality, and renewing again the cycle of prudish outcry and embargo. That film chose vaudeville as its first "popular" spectacle and rescue, just as the 16th-century novel chose the carnivalesque, is a curious and instructive recurrence indeed, establishing populist precedents for the inundation of "Adult" Cyber Malls on the Internet.

This short analysis of our most popular narrative media illustrates that, in terms of the evolution of their forms, the novel and photography/film are similar in fundamental ways: they begin, in infancy, in an unreflexive drama of autoeroticism; they suffer through the mediating and coercive ideologies of corporate sanction; and they emerge as mature forms when they begin to foreground and problematize their own discursives, as if their greatest fears were their own "base" tendencies. To maintain corporeal sovereignty (the authority of the body), both forms then go underground, where "'specialist' sex" and other expressions of the body, regardless of whether in film or book form, are available to those who want them.

Today, cyber theorists reiterate the by now familiar insights of Rabelais, Muybridge, and Mulvey. Cameron Bailey's work is one such reiteration, suggesting that with the Internet "the suburban ideal of postwar North America returns in virtual form: communication at a safe distance, community without contact. Is it any wonder that when movies visualize the Net's matrix of communication, it so often resembles the cool, aerial patterns of a suburb at night?" (Bailey, p. 22). Claudia Springer concurs with Bailey, noting that "at a time when paranoia over human contact in response to the AIDS virus is common, human interaction should occur through computerized communication, with the participants far apart and unable to touch each other" (Springer, p. 71). Much of the efficacy and the enticement

of the Internet, then, is that it is so anonymous; "browsers," "lurkers," "hyperqueens," and those in "MUDs" and "cyberdrag" can be whomever or whatever they choose without anyone ever knowing who they really are—or can they? This is the key question that always attends the constructed private spaces of autoeroticism. Are those spaces secure enough? In the case of the computer, the electronic footprints left in cyberspace in secret files like "NETSCAPE.HST" are often enough, when discovered, to wrest the subject from his illusory symbiosis with the imaginary.

Once again, a reversion to narrative dreamwork is instructive. In Irwin Winkler's 1995 cyber-thriller *The Net*, Sandra Bullock's computer wizardry complements her reclusiveness, affording her a rich, anonymous identity. So vivifying is this private-world onanism that one of her computer's screen-saver messages reads, "The computer is the ultimate condom." Wrapped in cyber-shield, her psyche lives in abandon, pleasuring itself at will. She exists as a kind of etherized libido without any incarnate identity. When her scant "real" identity is stolen, she is hard-pressed to locate another fleshy being who can corroborate the materiality of her existence. The film's sexual metaphor was wisely chosen, as this historio-diegetic exploration of media has demonstrated; for, while condoms protect the innocent in the high-risk application of their primal business, they also sometimes don't, a breaking that foregrounds identity as nothing else does, with paternity being the ultimate exposure. So, yes, condoms and the Net do license risky behavior—both mask identity to free the libido—but both can also rupture, an imprimatur of risk that is the exact opposite of what the reclusive identity, Mulvey's already "alienated subject," seeks.

This paradox, evident also in De Palma's *Body Double*, is a result of our historical mind/body schizophrenia, which in the late 20th century is manifest as our culture's simultaneous technofetish and technophobia. We seek vicarious gratification through our extended sensoria, of which virtual technologies and the Internet are the newest extensions, but at the same time fear that bodily abandon is either dangerous or unworthy of our high rationalism—hence the censure. In fear of reprisal, sanction, or worse, fulfillment, we construct taboos, like the contemporary cybermyth that computers will themselves become sensate and, like a teacher, parent, or omniscient God, will exact great revenge for our masturbatory inclinations. The Internet may very well be our most advanced technology today, but the deep grammar of its formal apparatus is not new. In opening private spaces within which humans can cross dress, don multiple personalities, and explore their repressed sexualities, the Internet is but the latest anthropomorphic envelope. Its targeting by censors should not be read as specific to its own nature, but as specific to the nature of all new media. The furor over Internet censorship is tantamount to a recurrence of the psychoanalytic morality play that has gone on since the Church fathers censored the Bacchanalia and since social forces mollified, sanitized, and "coerced" the autoeroticism of various other extensions of the body.

It should be no surprise that another censorship movement is forming in Germany today, this time in response to the Internet. And while, at least on the surface, a good deal of Germany's lead in the Internet censorship area appears to be rooted in the suppression of hate, the definition of hate is easily expandable beyond race and religion to include other ideological texts, such as the body. This malleability of application lends itself to what Tzvetan Todorov referred to as a "contagion" of ideology. And while it is foolish to argue against the suppression of hate, it should not follow that the body is part of that which is suppressed, for, as this essay illustrates, hate is not part of the spontaneous action of new media in vivifying the body. Actually, just the opposite. As Todorov understood, hate, like sexuality, has become discourse; and so it is left to the critic, finally, to perform the delicate surgery that separates one ideology from another—in the case of this essay, the body and its

technological extensions (the book, photography/film, and the Internet).

As McLuhan counseled, "The essence of education" should provide "civil defense against media fallout (i.e., against 'the subliminal operation of our own technologies')" (*Gutenberg Galaxy*, p. 246). Will we forever ignore history, will we be led in deference again, looking to television and other politically motivated interests to form our opinions? If we allow ourselves to become embroiled in a cleverly orchestrated debate that speaks to gender and other ideologically charged "blind spots," as Walter Kendrick calls them, then the answer is surely YES. The lesson offered by McLuhan lies in his own reversion to history and narrative to seek that which recurs in human behavior when humans embrace new media and technologies. That lesson imparts a simple but demanding humanism: that we must not release anyone from the responsibility of clear statement, historical precedent, and vital particulars. The Internet can be as complex as its current industrial "discourse," or as simple as a recurring historical moment, one which again extends human desire into the expressive realms of the autoerotic. Given the evidence thus far, I hold for the latter. Internet censorship, or cybriety, is not new; it is a re-run of our favorite drama, the psychoanalytic morality play that teeters between our desires and our fear of their fulfillment.

CRITICAL THINKING QUESTIONS

1. Do you agree with Tremblay's assertion that efforts to censor the Internet are a reflection of nothing new but rather represent a continuation of social responses that have occurred in the past? Discuss.

2. With reference to the article, discuss the pros and cons of censoring content on the Internet.

3. Which medium, the Internet or television, do you see as having a greater influence on social change? Do you think your answer might be different in ten years? Why?

REFERENCES

Bailey, Cameron. 1995. Virtual skin: Articulating race in cyberspace: *Border/Lines.* No. 38/39 (December): 19–24.

Church, Richard. 1957. *The growth of the English novel.* London: Methuen.

Crabbe, Anthony. 1988. Feature-length sex films. *Perspectives on pornography: Sexuality in film and literature,* ed. Gary Day and Clive Bloom, 44–66. New York: St. Martin's.

Czitrom, Daniel. 1982. *Media and the American mind: From Morse to McLuhan.* Chapel Hill: University of North Carolina Press.

Kendrick, Walter. 1987. *The secret museum: Pornography in modern culture.* New York: Penguin.

Manguel, Alberto. 1996. *A history of reading.* Toronto: Knopf.

McLuhan, Marshall. 1962. *The Gutenberg galaxy: The making of typographic man.* Toronto: University of Toronto Press.

——. 1964. *Understanding media: The extensions of man.* New York: McGraw-Hill.

Mulvey, Laura. 1989. Visual pleasure and narrative cinema and Afterthoughts on "visual pleasure and narrative cinema" inspired by King Vidor's *Duel in the Sun* (1946). *Visual and other pleasures.* 14–26; 29–38. Bloomington: Indiana University Press.

Muybridge, Eadweard. 1955. *The human figure in motion.* New York: Dover.

The Net. Dir. Irwin Winkler. Written by John Brancato and Michael Ferris. With Sandra Bullock, Jeremy Northam, and Dennis Miller. Columbia Pictures. 1995.

Springer, Claudia. 1996. *Electronic eros: Bodies and desire in the postindustrial age.* Austin: University of Texas Press.

Telegraph Journal. [Saint John, NB]. 1997. Community shouldn't define obscenity. 22 February: E5.

Tisdale, Sallie. 1994. *Talk dirty to me: An intimate philosophy of sex.* New York: Anchor.

Todorov, Tzvetan. 1977. *The poetics of prose,* trans. Richard Howard. Ithaca: Cornell University Press.

77

The Price of Modernization: The Case of Brazil's Kaiapo Indians

MARLISE SIMONS

Among the billions of poor people throughout the Third World, few will have a chance for a better life. But this is exactly what has happened to the Kaiapo, people who live deep in Brazil's rain forest. Has affluence been the blessing that the Kaiapo imagined it would be? To at least some of their number, the modernization of the Kaiapo amounts to little more than the systematic destruction of their traditional way of life.

It is getting dark when Chief Kanhonk sits down in the yard outside his home, ready for a long evening of conversation. Night birds are calling from the bush that sparkles with fireflies. Whooping frogs make a racket by the river. No one seems worried by the squadron of bats sweeping low overhead.

It is that important moment of the day when Indians of the Amazon, who use no written language, meet to talk, pass on information, and tell stories. The night is when they recall ancestral customs, interpret dreams, and comment on changes in nature and other events of the day. But from a nearby home come the sounds of a powerful rival: A television set is screeching cartoons at a group of children. I understand now why, that morning, by way of saying hello, these naked

Source: "The Amazon's Savvy Indians," by Marlise Simons, *The New York Times Magazine*, February 26, 1989, pp. 36–37, 48–52. Copyright © 1989 by The New York Times Company. Reprinted by permission of The New York Times.

children of the rain forest had shouted things like "He-Man" and "Flintstones."

Three years ago, when money from the sale of gold nuggets and mahogany trees was pouring into Gorotire, Chief Kanhonk agreed to bring in television, or the "big ghost," as it is called here. A shiny satellite dish now stands on the earthen plaza like an alien sculpture, signaling that Gorotire—a small settlement of some 800 people on the Fresco River, a tributary of the Amazon—has become one of the wealthiest Indian villages in Brazil.

Yet Chief Kanhonk appears to regret his decision. "I have been saying that people must buy useful things like knives or fishing hooks," he says darkly. "Television does not fill the stomach. It only shows our children and grandchildren white people's things."

The "big ghost" is just one of the changes that have been sweeping over Gorotire, but it seems to be worrying the elders the most. Some believe it is powerful enough to rob them of their culture. Bebtopup, the oldest medicine man in the village, explains his misgivings: "The night is the time the old people teach the young people. Television has stolen the night."

When I discuss this with Eduardo Viveiros, a Brazilian anthropologist who works with a more isolated Amazonian tribe, he seems less worried. "At least they quickly understood the consequences of watching television," he says. "Many people never discover. Now Gorotire can make a choice."

It was the issue of choice that first drew me to the Kaiapo Indians of the lower Amazon Basin. They seemed to be challenging the widely held notion that forest Indians are defenseless in face of the pressures of the competitive and predatory Western world around them. Unlike most of Brazil's 230,000 Indians, they go out into the white world to defend their interests, and it is no longer unusual to see Kaiapo men—in their stunning body paint and feathered headdresses—showing up in Congress in Brasilia, the nation's capital, or lobbying by doing a war dance outside a government office. They have even bought Western gadgets to record and film their festivals.

Once the masters of immense stretches of forest and savannas, the Kaiapo were for hundreds of years among the most skillful farmers and hunters and fiercest warriors of central Brazil. They terrified other tribes with their raids. From the seventeenth to the nineteenth centuries, they not only resisted the slaving raids of the Portuguese invaders but they also attacked white traders and gold prospectors with such a vengeance that royal orders came from Portugal to destroy the Kaiapo. The white man's wrath and his diseases killed many, yet there are still close to 3,600 Kaiapo in more than a dozen different villages near the Xingu River. They have quarreled and regrouped, but their lands, several vast reservations, are more secure than those of many other tribes.

After many years of isolation in the forest, the Kaiapo now have to deal with the growing encroachments of white society. "They are going through a great transition," says Darrell Posey, an American anthropologist who has worked in Gorotire for more than a decade. "Their survival is a miracle in itself. But I worry whether they can go on making the changes on their own terms."

Colombia, Ecuador, Peru, and Venezuela—four of nine nations in the Amazon Basin, which harbors some 800,000 Indians—each have large numbers of tropical-forest Indians. But nowhere are pressures on Indian land as great as they are in Brazil. As the Amazon is opened up, developers bring in highways, settlers, cattle ranchers, mines, and hydroelectric dams. In Brazil alone, more than ninety tribes have disappeared since the beginning of this century.

The clearing of large areas of the rain forest and the fate of the Indians are also rapidly becoming an issue of international concern. Interest in the region has risen as ecological concerns, such as ozone depletion, the greenhouse effect, and other changes in the global environment become political issues. More attention is paid to scientists who are alarmed at the destruction of the rain forest—a vital flywheel in the world's climate and the nursery of at least half of the world's plant and animal species.

This has also prompted an increasing interest in the highly structured world of the forest Indians and their ancient and intricate knowledge of nature that permits them to survive in the tropical jungle without destroying it. (The Hall of South American Peoples, which includes a life-size model of a Kaiapo warrior, recently opened at the Museum of Natural History in New York City.)

As Indians find greater support among environmentalists, they also get more organized in their fight to protect their habitat. The Kaiapo held their first international congress last week in Altamira, in central Brazil, protesting government plans to build several massive dams that would flood Indian land.

In Brazil, Indian tribes occupy 10 percent of the nation's territory, although much of their land has not been demarcated. Brazil's past military regimes elevated Indian affairs to a national-security issue, because many tribes live in large areas of border land. It is official policy to integrate Indians into the larger society, and the National Indian Foundation, with its 4,900 employees, is in charge of implementing this.

In my eighteen years in Latin America, I have heard many politicians and anthropologists discuss what is usually called "the Indian problem," what to "do" about cultures that have changed little in thousands of years. One school of thought holds that the remote tribes should be kept isolated and protected until they can slowly make their own choices. Another school accepts that the Indian world is on the wane, and talks about "guiding" the Indians toward inevitable change—a process that should take several generations.

But some anthropologists and politicians, including the Brazilian government, believe in still more rapid integration. When Romeo Jucá was head of the Indian Foundation, he said that it was only right for Indians to exploit their wealth, even if it meant acculturation. "We have to be careful how fast we go," he said, "but being Indian does not mean you have to be poor."

Gerardo Reichel-Dolmatoff is one of Latin America's most respected anthropologists. He insists that the Indians are their own best guides into Western society. An Austrian-born Colombian, Reichel-Dolmatoff has worked in Colombia's forests, at the Amazon's headwaters, for almost fifty years. "We cannot choose for them," he insists. "And we cannot put them into reserves, ghettos, ashokas. They are not museum exhibits. . . . If Indians choose the negative aspects of our civilization, we cannot control that. If there is one basic truth in anthropology, it is that cultures change. Static cultures do not exist."

The Indians themselves are pleading for more protection and respect for their cultures. Conrad Gorinsky, son of a Guyana Indian mother and himself a chemist in London, recently said: "We don't want the Indians to change because we have them comfortably in the back of our mind like a kind of Shangri-La, something we can turn to even if we work ourselves to death in New York. But we are hounding and maligning them instead of recognizing them as the guardians of the forests, of the world's genetic banks, of our germ plasm and lifelines."

The aboriginal peoples we call Indians are as different from one another as, say, Europeans are. Even the most isolated groups remain separate fiefdoms with widely varying experiences, beliefs, and histories. The degree of contact they have with the outside world is just as varied.

I first met Kaiapo tribesmen three years ago in Belém, a large city at the mouth of the Amazon. I saw them again in Brasilia, the capital. In both places, they demonstrated their political skills and capacity to mobilize, showing up in large numbers to protest measures by the government. They seemed particularly adept at commanding the attention of the press. Their body paint, feathers, and other paraphernalia made them appear warlike, exotic, and photogenic.

Back in Gorotire, as it turns out, they are more "ordinary." Wearing feathers and beads, explains Kubei, a chief's son, is for special occasions. "It's our suit and tie." Besides the satellite dish, the Kaiapo also have their own small airplane. Their new wealth has also given them the luxury of hiring non-Indians to help plant new fields. But they remain ready to attack white intruders; some of the adult men have markings on their chests that record the number of outsiders they have killed.

Two roads fan out from the center of Gorotire. A new sand track leads east on a five-hour drive to the town of Redenção. The other road goes south and, in a sense, it leads into the past. Dipping into the forest, it becomes a path that meanders through open patches where the Kaiapo women grow corn, sweet potatoes, bananas, manioc. On the plain ahead, it joins an ancient trail system that once reached for hundreds of miles into northern and western Brazil.

One morning, Beptopup (medicine man, shaman, connoisseur of nature), the anthropologist

Darrell Posey (who speaks the Kaiapo language), and I wander into the bush. Beptopup walks past the plants the way you go down a street where you know everyone. Stopping, nodding, his face lighting up with happy recognition, he sometimes goes into a song—a soft, high-pitch chant for a particular plant.

He picks leaves, each one familiar, each one useful. One serves to remove body hair. Another, he says, can prevent pregnancy. The underside of one leaf is so rough it is used to sandpaper wood and file fingernails. Beptopup collects his plants in the morning, he says, because "that is when they have the most strength."

Stopping at a shrub, we look at the large circle around its stem, where nothing grows. "This and other plants have been sent to a laboratory for analysis," says Posey. "We think this one has a natural weedkiller."

Beptopup holds up a branch of what he calls the "eye of the jaguar." "This was our flashlight," he says, showing how to set it afire and swing it gently so its strong glow will light one's path.

One afternoon, when the heat has crept into everything, the women and children come back from the fields to their village. They stop and sit in a creek to escape the swirling gnats and buzzing bees. Others sit outside their homes, going about their age-old business. One woman plucks the radiant feathers of a dead macaw. Another removes her eyebrows and eyelashes, because the Kaiapo women think they are ugly. (A nurse once told me that this custom might have a hygienic origin—to ward off parasites, for instance.) Kaiapo women also deepen their foreheads by shaving the top of their head in a triangle that reaches the crown—a fearsome sight to the unaccustomed eye.

I envy a mother who is clearly enjoying herself fingerpainting her three children. She draws black designs with genipap juice. On the face and the feet she puts red dye from the "urucu," or annatto, plant; Indians say it keeps away chiggers and ticks.

Change has come to Gorotire along the other road, the one leading east to Redenção. Recent

Kaiapo history is full of "firsts," but a notable turning point came when prospectors struck gold on Gorotire land in 1980. The Kaiapo raided the camp, twenty miles from the village, but failed to drive away the trespassers. Then they made a deal.

Last fall, when I was visiting Gorotire, about 2,000 gold diggers were stripping the land to the bone farther upstream, and the River Fresco passed the village the color of mud, its water contaminated with oil and mercury. I heard no one complain about that. Gorotire gets 7 percent of the mine's profits—several pounds of gold a week.

In 1984, a lumber company completed the first road. It signed a contract with the Indian Foundation for Gorotire's mahogany (the Indians are wards of the Brazilian government). Most of the mahogany is gone now, and the government agency split the profits with the Kaiapo. Gorotire chose to spend its gold and timber profits on new water and electricity lines and rows of brick houses. Only about half of the inhabitants now live in traditional palm-frond huts.

The young Kaiapo who earn a salary as supervisors at the gold camp have bought their own gas stoves, radios, sofas, and mattresses. For the community, the four tribal chiefs ordered several boats, trucks, and a small plane that ferries people and goods among nearby Kaiapo villages.

One evening, a truck arriving from Redenção—bringing rice, sugar, bottled gas, oil for the generator—is another reminder of how fast Gorotire is adapting to a Western economy. From being a largely self-sufficient community of hunters and farmers, it is now increasingly dependent on outside goods. In Gorotire, it is clearly money, no longer disease or violence, that has become the greatest catalyst for change. Money has given the Kaiapo the means and the confidence to travel and lobby for their rights. At the same time, it is making them more vulnerable.

I have seen other villages where Indians have received large sums of money—for the passage of a railroad or a powerline, or from a mining company. Such money is usually released in installments, through banks, but its arrival has put new strains on the role of the chiefs. Money and goods have introduced a new, materialistic expression of power in societies that have been egalitarian. Among most Indians, a man's prestige has always depended not on what he acquires but on what he gives away.

In Gorotire, some of the young men complain that the chiefs are not distributing community money and goods equally, that the chiefs' relatives and favorites are getting a bigger share and more privileges.

Darrell Posey, the anthropologist, believes the greatest political change came with the road. With it, he says, "the Kaiapo chiefs lost control of which people and what goods would come in." Previously, the chiefs had been the sole distributors. They had also played the vital roles of keeping the peace and leading the ceremonies. Now, the chiefs hardly know the liturgy of the ceremonies; their main task seems to be to deal with the outside world.

The transition is also changing the role of the medicine man. Bebtopup, for example, has an arsenal of remedies for the common ailments—fevers, diarrheas, snake bites, wounds. But he and his colleagues have lost prestige because they do not know how to deal with the diseases brought to Gorotire by white men, such as the pneumonia that strikes the children and the malaria spreading from the gold miners' camp.

Anthropologists sometimes say that when outsiders visit the Indian world, they often focus on themes central not to Indians but to themselves. This might explain why I was so bothered by the garbage, the flotsam of Western civilization.

Gorotire's setting is Arcadian. It lies on a bluff overlooking the River Fresco, with views of the forests across and the mountains behind. Spring rains bring waterfalls and blossoms. But these days the village is awash with rusting cans, plastic wrappers, tapes sprung from their cassettes, discarded mattresses, and clothes. New domestic animals such as dogs, pigs, and ducks have left a carpet of droppings. And giant rats, which suddenly appeared some years ago, seem to be everywhere; some have bitten small children.

"Indians have never had garbage that was not biodegradable," says Sandra Machado, a Brazilian researching Kaiapo farming techniques here. "No one wants to take care of it."

It is a mild moonlit evening, and in the men's house many Kaiapo are watching soccer on television. The bank of the river is a quieter place to talk.

"If you look beyond the garbage and the stone houses, this is still a strong and coherent indigenous culture," says Darrell Posey, speaking of the mixed feelings he has about a decade of developments in Gorotire. "Despite everything, the language is alive, the festivals and initiation rights are observed."

Posey says that the Kaiapo in Gorotire and in other villages continue with their age-old natural farming techniques, using plants to fix nitrogen in the soil, chunks of termite nests instead of chemical fertilizers, plant infusions to kill pests, the nests of ferocious ants to protect fruit trees from other ant predators.

Biologists often complain that there have been many studies of exotic rituals, paraphernalia, and kinships of Indians, but that Western science has paid scant attention to the Indians' use of animals and plants.

Like others working in the Amazon region, Posey worries about the gap between the old and the young. "The old chiefs are turning over decisions to the young because they can drive a truck or operate a video machine or go to the bank," he says. "But the young people don't see the relevance of learning the tribal knowledge and it's being lost."

"You can afford to lose one generation," he adds, "because grandparents do the teaching of their grandchildren. But you cannot afford to lose two generations."

Gorotire has a small Government school, designed to help Indians integrate into the national society. The teacher, who speaks only Portuguese, has started organizing annual Independence Day parades. On the blackboard is a list of patriotic holidays, including Independence Day and the Day of the Soldier. I ask the children later what a soldier is. "Something of white people," one of them says.

Chief Poropot agrees that everyone must learn Portuguese. "The language of the Kaiapo is very ancient and it will never end," he says. "But the women and the children need to learn Portuguese to defend themselves."

Defend themselves?

"If they go to shop in Redenção, they have to talk," he says. "If they get sick, they cannot tell the doctor what they have."

Thirty miles from Gorotire, in the village of Aukre, another Kaiapo tribe is choosing a different strategy for change. Its best-known member is Paiakan, thirty-seven years old, the son of Chief Tikiri.

Calm and articulate, Paiakan has been named to "keep an eye on the whites" in the state capital of Belém. He acts as a kind of roving ambassador for the Kaiapo, even though each village is autonomous. When Kaiapo interests are threatened, he sends out warnings to the communities.

Paiakan's contacts with the outside world and the many pitfalls it holds for Indians have made him more conservative, he says, more so than in the early days, in the 1970s, when he first left home to work on the Trans-Amazonian Highway. As his father's main adviser, he has insisted that Aukre remain a traditional village.

It is built in the age-old circle of mud-and-thatch huts. There is no television, running water, pigs, or piles of garbage. Paiakan and his father have also banned logging and gold digging. This appears to have saved Aukre from the consumerism—and widespread influenza and malaria—of Gorotire.

"The lumber men have come to us with their bags of money," he says. "And we know we have a lot of gold. But we do not want to bring a lot of money in. The Indian still does not know the value of white man's objects or how to treat them." Paiakan cites clothing as an example. "The Indian wears something until it is stiff with dirt, then he throws it out."

But people now want things from the "world of the whites," he continues. "Pressure from the white society is so strong, there is no wall that can stop it." It is the task of the chief to measure the change, provide explanations, he says. "If someone wants to get a radio or a tape recorder, the chiefs cannot stop it."

In Aukre, where two aging chiefs are still in charge of buying goods for the community, they say that they will not buy gadgets. "We explain we cannot buy this thing for you because we do not have the batteries you need and we cannot repair it," Paiakan says.

Of late, Paiakan has been invited abroad to campaign for the protection of the rain forest. He knows the problem only too well. Ranchers have moved almost to the reservation's doorstep, felled trees, and set massive forest fires. Because of deforestation, there have been unusual changes in the water level of the Fresco River.

"Our people are getting very disoriented," says Paiakan. "It would be as if people from another planet came to your cities and started to tear down your houses. The forest is our home." With all the destruction going on, he continues, "the breath of life is drifting up and away from us."

At the age of seventy-eight and retired from teaching at the University of California at Los Angeles, the anthropologist Gerardo Reichel-Dolmatoff lives in Bogotá, Colombia, and is still writing. After studying changes in the Amazon for five decades, he is not optimistic about the prospects for the Indians.

"In Colombia, I don't know of a single case where an aboriginal culture has found a strong adaptive mechanism," he says. "Physical survival is possible. But I have not seen the ancient values replaced by a workable value system. I wish I could be more positive. But in fifty years I have seen too many traditions being lost, too many tribes disappear.

"For 500 years we have witnessed the destruction of the Indians. Now we are witnessing the destruction of the habitat. I suggest more field work, and immediate field work, because soon it will be too late."

At a conference on ethnobiology last fall, Reichel-Dolmatoff urged scientists to insist on spreading the message that Western science has much to learn from Indians, from their well-adapted lives and deeply felt beliefs, their view that whatever man subtracts he must restore by other means.

What suggestions has he made to Indians?

"Indians have to stay in touch with their language—that is absolutely essential," he says. "It embodies their thought patterns, their values, their philosophy." Moreover, he says, talented young Indians should be given a modern academic education, but also the chance to keep in touch with their people. "They come from cultures based on extraordinary realism and imagery. They should not be forced to enter at the lowest level of our society."

One night, I ask the chiefs in Gorotire: What happens if the gold runs out? After all, most of the mahogany is already gone. Young tribesmen have wanted to invest some of the income, and the chiefs have accepted the idea. Gorotire has bought a home in Belém for Kaiapo who travel there, as well as three houses in Redenção. There is talk of buying a farm, a curious thought, perhaps, for a community that lives on 8 million acres of land. But the Kaiapo, so they say, want it so that white farmers can grow rice for them.

And there is talk of planting new mahogany trees. Soon the conversation turns to a bird that a tribesman explains is very important. It is the bird, he says, that spreads the mahogany seeds.

CRITICAL THINKING QUESTIONS

1. What have been the short-term consequences of the Kaiapo's new wealth? What are their long-term prospects?

2. What arguments can be made in support of continued effort by the Kaiapo to economically develop their resources? What arguments can be made against doing so?

3. In what ways are other countries involved in the changes taking place in the Amazon Basin?